Contents

10 *Argument*   539

Contents by Theme

Preface

Although composition is a course about writing, we also think it must be a course about reading—good, challenging, smart reading that stimulates student thinking. It hardly matters what the reading is about: international politics, gardening, basketball, fashion design, architecture, the ecology of the great ape, the history of igneous rocks, Harry Potter, or Jane Austen. The important thing is that the reading lights up the minds of students enrolled in this composition course, keeps them turning pages, invites them to think, react, discuss, and—most importantly—to write. We hope the readings in this book have that effect on your students. Frankly, there is no other reason to publish *Rhetorical Choices*. It is the prime directive of textbooks: Do something that will make a difference.

This book was created to fulfill that purpose. We chose these readings because we are convinced they are invigorating in ways that will engage students and encourage them to write. Although we believe that student writing should lie at the heart of any composition class, most of us use readings to stimulate discussion, introduce students to potential topics for their own essays, and provide models of fine prose for them to emulate. In preparing this book, we tried to remain mindful of all three of these goals.

Our intention was to offer you, the instructor, ways to help your students analyze language and language users, language and culture, and language and politics. We believe that a reading text designed to foster writing should foreground the political and cultural contexts behind the readings and challenge students to respond to these texts in ways that enable their growth as writers. Typically, textbooks that stress instruction in writing methods fail to accentuate how personal, cultural, and political factors are connected to rhetorical decisionmaking. Our goal was to bring together an array of multicultural and multigenre selections that reflect a wide range of linguistic, cultural, and political concerns. Linked to those readings are questions designed to solicit active responses about rhetorical choices and the linguistic, cultural, and political factors that writers often consider as they make those choices.

The traditional modes of discourse that organize this volume are useful strategies for analyzing, developing, and organizing writing. We decided to organize this book according to nine major modes of discourse: narration, description, definition, exemplification, classification, process analysis, comparison and contrast, cause and effect, and argument. We believe these time-honored rhetorical categories will enable students to learn how sophisticated writers write—so that they can master, in their own writing, sophisticated strategies that will serve them well as they progress through college and beyond. We also had a number of other principles to which we tried to remain true:

Modeling the Modes: When we first began this project, a veteran of the textbook wars recommended that first and foremost we should choose selections that best illustrate the modes. This we have tried to do. Our hope is that you can open this book at random, read a selection, and state with a strong degree of certainty which mode is being illustrated. Clearly, some of the modes represent strategies more than genres; we are thinking here of modes like process or exemplification, where the focus is more on methods of development than on an entire formal structure. Such methods, however, have become time-honored ways to teach the modes because of their usefulness within the classroom.

Familiar and Original Readings: Most of us who teach composition regularly rely on certain assignments that have proven successful time and again. In putting together the selections for this book—a process that involved many visions and revisions—we sought to provide a rich mix of classic and contemporary titles, familiar and less familiar authors. No anthology can include everyone's favorite author or title, but we think we have brought together a feast of some useful proportions. Many of the writers represented in this collection are quite familiar and distinguished. Others, although less known, are worthy of wider exposure. We hope all the selections spur your students on to do additional reading by these authors and others.

Linked Themes: Whenever possible, we sought to create links among the selections. Many of them are focused on similar concerns about language use and dialect; others treat similar themes or subjects. We have tried to highlight those linkages by their placement within the chapters or by making explicit references to them in our apparatus. When selections resonate with each other, they promote more sustained discussion and often lead to richer, more deeply contextualized writing assignments.

Straight Talk: *Rhetorical Choices* is a modal reader with an edge, and that edge grows out of our commitment to develop a book that is intellectually challenging, socially aware, and sensitive to the changing nature of language and culture in this country. We have provided the kinds of teaching aids that we think will be helpful, but we did not want to patronize instructors or condescend to students. This is a college reader. The selections, for the most part, are demanding and require not just reading but re-reading. We think that is what most college instructors—and college students, for that matter—want out of their experience.

Questions for Responding and Writing: Following each selection, we offer instructors two sets of questions. The first, entitled "Analyzing Rhetorical Choices," asks students to examine the styles, structures, and modes, focusing particularly on the craft of writing. The second, "Writing About Issues and Contexts," invites students to think more speculatively about the topics and to relate the essays to other works and the world outside the text.

Strategies and Essay Assignments: At the end of every chapter we include two additional teaching tools. The first one is entitled "Strategies for Writers," and it offers a set of very explicit guides to writing each mode, referencing each suggestion to specific selections. Following that, we offer a final section in each chapter called "Research and Writing Assignments." In this section, we provide multiple essay assignments that call upon students to engage in further research while extending the themes and issues raised in the readings.

Ease of Use: Finally, we have put together a book that we think will work in multiple ways in multiple classrooms, without over-encumbering instructors—and students—with peripheral and extraneous supplementary materials. The focus in this text is on reading critically and then helping students to incorporate the meanings and modes into their own essays. The most important question we kept asking ourselves was "What kind of book would we want to teach in our own writing classes?" *Rhetorical Choices* is that book.

Instructor's Manual

This guide offers the features that you would expect in an instructor's manual, and some that you might not, all of them condensed into a short, easy-to-navigate text that allows you to begin planning and teaching your own course quickly. You will find chapter overviews that provide notes on each of the modes presented in the textbook, sample responses to the readings, suggested writing exercises, and syllabi and sample grading rubrics you can use or amend as you see fit. In addition, this manual presents several short statements on the big questions that all writing teachers must struggle with, no matter how much expertise they have in the field. These statements, "An Overview of Writing and Writing Instruction" and "Making Access Real: Thoughts on Integrating Communication Technologies in the Writing Classroom," lay out the ideas and commitments that undergird this textbook and manual, but also trace those big questions in ways that we hope will lead you to push the commitments you already have or even help you enter those conversations if you happen to be a new instructor.

Acknowledgments

Many people deserve to be thanked for their help, support, understanding, and forbearance in helping us bring *Rhetorical Choices* into the light of day. For first suggesting this project to us, we want to acknowledge Anne Smith and Tisha Rossi. For her constancy and support even in the darkest days of author fatigue, Lynn Huddon deserves the Nobel Prize for editorship. Katharine Glynn made an immense difference in helping us discover and strengthen what was best in our own work. And we are also deeply indebted to the entire team at Longman, from editorial assistants (thanks, Esther!) to marketing, and to the production group. It takes a village to raise a book . . .

For our editorial summits, we typically met in Chicago—Oak Park to be specific. Surrounded by some of the finest examples of Frank Lloyd Wright architecture, we spent long days and nights collaborating, our days almost always beginning with breakfast at the Onion Roll. Holley Court gave us room to work, as did Oak Park Temple, and we thank them both. Deborah's family—David Gilman, Roger Gilman, her dad Reinhard Holdstein, and especially daughter Emily Gilman (our muse!)—cheered us on and we are appreciative of their interest and support. Keith's daughter, Amina, and his and Charles's wives, Sharyn Gilyard and Patricia Ellis, also sacrificed many nights and weekends so that the three of us could read, write, think, and assemble our work. Thank you all from the bottom of our collective hearts. Indeed, there were some days—and months, for that matter—when we spent more time with each other, both physically and virtually, than we did with our own families.

We also owe a great debt to our students. They often tested these readings and assignments, helping us to refine, reshape, revise. And they always reminded us of the goal: to do a book that makes a difference in their daily intellectual lives. Finally, we want to thank our many professional colleagues who teach at community colleges, four-year schools, and comprehensive universities across the country. We have profited from your enthusiasm for teaching, your enlightened criticisms, your passion for the printed word, your devotion to learning, your friendship and your support.

To the many reviewers who provided valuable feedback at many stages, our thanks to: Christopher Baker, Armstrong Atlantic State University; Dan Baldwin, Muscatine Community College; Mark Bernier, Blinn College; Alexander M. Bruce, Florida Southern College; Lisa L. Colman, Southeastern Oklahoma State University; Kathleen Dorantes, Imperial Valley College; Thomas E. Fish, Cumberland College; Raymond Foster, Scottsdale Community College; Frederic Giacobazzi, Kirtland Community College; Mary Hurst, Cuyahoga Community College; Kimmarie Lewis, Lord Fairfax Community College; Joseph F. McCadden, Burlington County College; Jamie Molitoris, Monmouth University; Kevin Nebergall, Kirkwood Community College; and Victor Uszerowicz, Miami Dade Community College.

KEITH GILYARD
DEBORAH H. HOLDSTEIN
CHARLES I. SCHUSTER

1

Writers, Readers, and Rhetorical Choices

Why is it that college graduates are generally more satisfied with their lives, have greater interest in the arts and culture, engage more often in civic affairs, vote in greater numbers, and travel abroad more often than those who attain only a high school degree? Why is it that they earn, on average, about $1,000,000 more throughout their careers than their high school–educated peers? Part of the answer is that they have been taught to engage rigorously in analysis, inquiry, and argument. That is, they have learned how to read challenging material, analyze it, develop their own perspectives and positions in writing, and engage in thoughtful, ongoing oral and written debates about significant issues: affirmative action, sports and morality, gender equity, individual rights versus the collective good of society. These kinds of activities, of course, typically occur in most first-year composition courses, and their importance explains why such courses are required in most universities: They enable students to succeed within their majors and to become capable citizens within society. To say this another way, learning how to read, write, analyze, argue, and engage in this kind of intellectual activity depends on knowing how to make meaningful and effective rhetorical choices. Hence the title of this book.

We understand that the word *rhetoric* often carries a pejorative implication in the popular media, but for the three of us and for many of our colleagues around the country who teach composition and literature, the word is a positive one. To learn about rhetoric is to learn about argument and persuasion. Rhetoric is the study of language in all its various uses. To be an accomplished rhetorician means knowing a subject well and being able to engage in meaningful discussion with others about it. It also means having the ability to persuade others, not through deceit or distortion but through logical analysis, presentation of facts and data, and the crafting of effective, powerful, and—yes—beautiful language. That is why the phrase "rhetorical choices" means so much to us: To be able to make such choices intelligently lies at the heart of what it means to be part of an educated citizenry.

With respect to writing—the particular concern that motivated us to create this book—the phrase "rhetorical choices" means that successful student writers learn how to pay close attention to the ways in which their language use affects others. They will become more conscious about how to craft appropriate structures and phrasing, more able to find the kinds of factual and knowledgeable support that can persuade readers to change their minds. Through making meaningful rhetorical choices, writers can make effective arguments. This kind of mastery involves speculation by students about their roles and development as student-citizens in the context of conversations swirling around them, both on campus and in the larger culture. This is the reason that this text is a *reader* or *sourcebook*—and why its focus is on the rhetorical choices that writers make to bring readers into a thoughtful and informed conversation about issues and arguments, visions and values. It is our attempt to outline a rich discussion about a range of compelling issues for students in a college writing classroom.

This book is also a *rhetoric* in the sense that it offers selections by various writers as models of admirable writing, models that can be imitated. We do not contend that these are the only admirable models available or that imitating such models is the only way to become a successful writer. Neither proposition is true, but writers often use the writings of others to strengthen themselves as writers. They draw inspiration by experiencing the skill and genius of other accomplished authors. Often they learn how to solve problems in their own writing by seeing how published authors use perspective, structure, tone, organization, and evidence or the ways they establish mood or tone. To do this requires that a reader learn how to read as a writer, a concept that we will develop later in this chapter. All these uses of reading work best when applied to outstanding examples of written work, the kinds of examples that we have included in this book. Reading and analyzing models is thus an important activity for writers and at the very least serves as a means to illustrate problems, solutions, and possibilities.

Anthologies such as this tend to be organized in one of two ways: by rhetorical modes (such as this one), or by theme (see our alternative table of contents). We find that modes-oriented readers are very instructive and even liberating. We are convinced that reading essays and other texts within a modal framework can help you become a more sophisticated reader and writer. For one thing, reading in this way provides clear examples centered on techniques, such as using narration to tell a story or employing comparison and contrast when examining two related subjects. Such discussions of technique are greatly enhanced when they can be anchored to specific modes of discourse, to the forms that emerge when writers engage topics passionately.

We recognize that placing essays in a particular category or mode is often arbitrary. We have organized the selections in this book according to modes primarily to highlight certain structural aspects of a particular work, not to limit or neglect its other and various strengths. In fact many, if not all, of these selections could be placed in several categories. This is part of our point. The readings selected for this book illustrate that these modes and essays are flexible, not the categorized, inviolate texts or, in the case of the modes, the impenetrable boundaries they may seem to represent. Indeed, you might well move a certain essay that is in the Argument section to Definition (or vice versa). For instance, Malcolm X's "My First Conk" describes a process but is also part of his autobiography, a narrative; Norman Cousins's essay, "Who Killed Benny Paret?" is both argument and an example of cause and effect. Alice Walker's "Am I Blue?" represents narration as well as description, cause, and effect, and to some extent, comparison and contrast. Julia Alvarez's "Snow" can be called both description and narration. How could there be narration without description? How could there be effective arguments without exemplification? Nonetheless, using categories, or modes, provides a vehicle for you to begin to look at the texts carefully and to consider how and why a writer shaped an essay in a certain way. To think about essays, stories, and poems this way lies at the heart of rhetorical understanding, at making informed rhetorical choices as both a writer and a reader.

In addition to their rhetorical value, the modes have real-world, practical implications. Physicians must compare and contrast the relative value of different medications or sets of symptoms; travel agents describe cruise ships and define the terms of various cruise packages; attorneys must argue effectively to prosecute or defend; teachers define and explain; businesspeople must also argue, define, and compare costs; consumers' guides classify and rate products and services; and so on. Using modes can also help each of us understand that we, as readers, must be constantly teaching ourselves how to read as we undertake more and more difficult material.

Finally, this is a book based on notions of how to learn writing, on what it means to be a reader and writer both within the composition classroom and beyond. Sourcebooks and rhetorics are not objective or neutral objects that show up in classrooms on their own; they don't spring from the head of Zeus. They get there because people in various situations—authors, editors, publishers, writing program administrators, instructors—make decisions based on their notions of what ought to happen in a writing classroom. Our approach, explicit in this chapter and implied throughout this book, is that learning to write is best facilitated through a *critical perspective about language*—that is, one that suggests the subjective nature of writing and the teaching of writing. Such an approach stresses the political nature of language and instruction and welcomes the attempts of students from various literacy backgrounds to negotiate successfully the language demands of academic institutions. In addition, our approach emphasizes the importance of reading with both pleasure and understanding. If the reading and writing you do in this course are to be meaningful, it is essential to read for enjoyment and to be able to appreciate the craft of writing—that is, the kinds of rhetorical choices that these authors made as they wrote.

Further, you need to approach the readings in this book with the perspective that writing is done in various ways by different writers—that there is no one way to write, just as there is no one way to read. Thus we do not engage in talk about *the* writing process or even *the* reading process. Because there are multiple ways to read and write, we offer no one recipe for how to bake good essays. Nor do we offer any formulas for instant improvement. Our aim is to provide a rich array of possibilities, to keep things flexible, and to provide a tempting and nutritious banquet of readings that can sustain you over the entire term. What we hope you will provide is energy, commitment, a willingness to engage thoughtfully and critically with the readings and your own writing. In other words, we think rhetorical models are important, but they need to be integrated into a curricular approach that takes advantage of the interest, artistry, and imagination of students and teachers. In the end, this book is not so much about reading within the modes as it is about gaining rhetorical power and intellectual acumen through broadened knowledge and understanding.

Ways of Learning to Write

Every classroom is driven by theories. Instructors who lecture exclusively have a theory, which they may or may not articulate, that knowledge is best created and communicated through the monologic presentation of material. Conversely, instructors who favor more student-teacher exchange believe that knowledge is best fashioned in dialogue. We feel that you, as a student, should be informed about the theories that drive instruction in your writing classes and that there should be ongoing discussions about the learning process throughout the semester. In this section, we outline some notions that we think should infuse writing classrooms, and we provide the reasons we think so. We are not saying that these are the only concepts around which courses should revolve, but our experiences tell us that these are crucial principles deserving of explicit scrutiny. By reading our thoughts about classroom instruction, you will, we hope, become absorbed in and reflective about your own learning, just as we ask you to absorb and reflect on the readings in this volume.

Thinking as a Writer

It is a truth almost universally acknowledged that the more you write, the better writer you will become. More specifically, such practice will make you not only a better writer—because you will become increasingly adept at making informed rhetorical choices—but also a better thinker. The complexities of the writing process—however you demonstrate these in whatever ways of composing work for you—are exactly the qualities that foster your ability to think well. And the ability to think in complex ways demonstrates exactly what is meant by the often overused term *critical thinking.*

Although many of us wish there were a simple plan, a formula, for writing, there is not. Writing is rarely easy, and perceptions of what it means to be a good writer are complicated by a kind of writing folklore: "If I were a good writer, this wouldn't be so hard." "If I were a good writer, I wouldn't have to go back and edit and revise." "If I were a good writer, this would come out right the first time." Nothing could be further from the truth. As evidenced by the revised and edited manuscripts of poet-critic John Keats, on display in the British Museum, even highly skilled and experienced writers do not expect to "get it right the first time." We have selected essays and devised questions to prompt your own critical sensibilities and help you develop your own ways of analyzing, responding, and writing.

Writing is not only a means of learning, but it is also a form of exploration—a means of taking chances and risks, both intellectual and practical. Suppose you have just read a particularly complex selection in this book. Your instructor asks you to write a paper. As you begin the paper—perhaps by jotting notes on the article—you are seized by a sense of chaos. How on earth will you write this? Yet this sense of intellectual chaos might be for you a fully appropriate, inevitable stage of the writing process—that exploratory time when you will begin to think through the article, formulate your own response to it, argue effectively using evidence from the text, and so forth. If this is a paper to be written outside class, you might clear the kitchen table, find your favorite beverage, pace a bit, and write longhand on a yellow legal pad before turning to your computer.

Whatever the rituals of your writing process, you ultimately must commit to paper or to the cyber world your rhetorical choices, well—and responsibly—articulated. Indeed, although your writing in its various guises might well entertain, inform, describe, define—and suit any of the modes we use as starting points for thinking and writing in this book—writing is most significantly a way of building trust with your readers as you analyze and argue. Yet however you get to the point at which you have your final (or as Ann Berthoff called it, your "best-yet") draft, the writing process rarely moves in a neat linear fashion from prewriting to writing to revising to editing. Instead, it's a messy, recursive set of acts. For instance, let's go back to that paper your instructor assigned as a response to a complex selection in this book. As you write, you might create a few draft paragraphs, and then turn back and add to them, redo a paragraph ot two completely, and then decide that you'd better keep them and see if they will work well toward the end of your paper rather than the beginning. Or you might decide that you need additional evidence from the article to make your points; once you reread the article, you discover that you want to re-work the paragraphs you've written yet again. In fact, if you could see the number of drafts this chapter went through before being printed, you would be either heartened or discouraged—the former because even professional writers revise, the latter because, frankly, even for professional writers, the processes of revising and editing never quite seem to end. The risk? That your point will be far more complex than you had imagined, taking more concentration, time, and revision than you had thought; that your readers might not agree with your viewpoint, however well argued. But these are exactly the types of risks that are worth taking. The clearly articulated path, the path with direction, is far more useful than the path of least resistance.

Writing for Multiple Purposes and Audiences

Although we have implicitly encouraged you to adopt a writing process that might seem very time-consuming—with time spent just sitting at your kitchen table, sipping your favorite beverage, gathering your thoughts—there will always be different occasions for writing that encourage and challenge your flexibility as a writer. This is a *good* thing. In the necessarily bumpy process that ultimately shaped this chapter, we found each of us primarily drafting sections of it on our own and, on rare occasions, together (when we could be in the same room). After extensive conversations among the three of us about a particular section, one of us would immediately begin to draft a portion of the chapter just to "get it down." Sometimes a section seemed to fall into place immediately, while other parts took much longer. Then one of us would put everything together and see how, or if, the pieces fit.

As we've already noted, the writing process is more often than not anything but linear. You may find yourself adding new information as you revise; you may find yourself moving one section from the end of your paper to the middle; you may find yourself at the editing stage (often a final stage) with the first section of a paper before you even draft the next. While you may always wish for the opportunity to draft and redraft and edit and revise (in other words, for the opportunity to honor your own, inevitably idiosyncratic, writing process), this will be impossible during any number of writing situations—for instance, an hour-long, in-class essay exam. In that case, your audience is clearly the teacher, and it's your responsibility to marshal evidence from classroom discussions, readings in the textbook, and so forth to make concise, well-developed, and well-argued points in a relatively short period.

Similarly, on the job, you may not have what appears to be the luxury of working alone, drafting in a leisurely fashion. Indeed, reports in the corporate world are increasingly collaborative, requiring members of a particular working team to strike a balance among different voices, ways of writing, and ways of contributing. It is useful, therefore, for you to work with your colleagues in class to talk through your responses to particularly controversial ideas you may find in these essays. Further, despite the extensive use of e-mail on the job, employers will not accept reports that reflect the rhetorical choices popular among teenagers using Instant Messenger. Using shorthand like "CU later" or the number 4 instead of the word *for* will not impress the corporate community, where sending even brief posts with feedback on important issues must be highly literate in the conventional sense. In this way, out-of-class, on-line discussion groups with your writer-colleagues and your instructor in response to discussion questions for the essays in this volume (or to brainstorm and create your own and then respond to them) will give you the opportunity to do the best you can when you must organize your thoughts, compose, and send out for feedback some writing that will become public more quickly than you'd usually prefer. It will also help you determine, as a writer, ways to meet the expectations of the often complex audiences for whom you write. Remember that a document can have a life beyond your intended audience. The same is true for e-mail. What seems to be an ephemeral, nearly invisible message sent off with the click of a mouse not only has a life of its own but is considered a form of durable communication—so much so that e-mail has long been "discoverable" as evidence in court.

Given all this, it is not surprising that instructors often emphasize the importance of analyzing the audience for your writing, often suggesting that you reach for readership beyond the teacher, beyond the classroom. For whom do we write, especially if it is not just for the instructor? It is true that assessing your readers, your possible audience, can help you anticipate potential objections to your argument and at the same time reinforce the deeply social dimension of writing.

Using Your Native Linguistic Abilities

In any given classroom, you'll find a broad spectrum of linguistic ability among students. Although it's impossible to be aware of every nuance in this regard, we encourage classrooms that nurture, rather than penalize, every writer who has a relatively wide gap to negotiate between native discourse and Standard Written English. Not only do we view this action as a socially just intervention into the use of dominant discourses to disable writers, but we also feel that building on already existing linguistic strengths is the most viable way to encourage you and your classmates to develop into lifelong writers *and* achieve the writing standards set by colleges and universities.

Focusing on Mechanics in Context

Part of your obligation and ultimate authority as a writer depends, as we have noted, on your communicating clearly, concisely, and responsibly. While acknowledging the power relationships in the classroom and beyond that create a dominant discourse, we believe part of that obligation involves what is often dismissed or criticized as "correctness" in punctuation and mechanics. Writers are often stymied, even blocked from writing, when they pressure themselves to try to be "correct" as they draft. Most writers will agree that even in the most expeditious forms of communication—for instance, that important e-mail response to your supervisor regarding a departmental project for which you have primary responsibility—it is wise, if not essential, to save concern for mechanics and punctuation for last, just before you print out a report or click "send" to dispatch that important e-mail.

Like it or not, we often move among "communities," and each community requires us to speak and write differently and to make different rhetorical choices. Just as there are different occasions for writing (the out-of-class essay versus, say, the quick memo to the supervisor), so too are there different contexts for ways of speaking and different levels of what might be seen as "acceptable" in those contexts.

Just as one context can be more appropriate for neighborhood or family ways of speaking than another, such instances of context can be equally crucial for punctuation and mechanics. Like style, tone, word choice, and other aspects of a writer's concerns, too many punctuation and mechanical errors can get in the way of your readers being able to appreciate what you've done and what you hope to accomplish. To some readers, your level of correctness can, for good or ill, be an indication of your level of "conventional" education, whether or not their assessment is accurate.

The context in which you practice your sensitivity to mechanical and other forms of correctness can make a difference as well. One of us recalls being quite the achiever regarding commas in the sixth grade—as long as it was in the very limited context of workbook exercises. Because it's difficult to transfer the isolated examples in a workbook to "real" writing, use an English handbook as you review your own writing. Don't assume that you're an expert in mechanics because you've scored well in an on-line workbook.

Considering Language, Power, and Citizenship

The philosopher and theorist Mikhail Bakhtin determined that there is no language that is not connected to specific social relationships; these are, in turn, connected to larger, very powerful economic, political, and ideological systems. While we might affirm the importance of writing "appropriately" for different occasions, encourage and expect mechanical correctness that matches the demands of a dominant discourse, and hold other teacherly—sometimes restrictive—views of what it means to write and to be a "good" writer, we also encourage you to question issues of language and power within your classroom and within the essays that you read and analyze from this collection (this introductory chapter included). We encourage you to determine what it means to be a writer in your class—relationships between and among your colleague-writers and the instructor, say— and what it means to be a writer in relation to these questions of language and power within your college or university and beyond.

To close out this section while continuing to stress the need for all of us to stay attuned to questions of language and power, we ask you to consider the following text about the Arctic National Wildlife Refuge that was displayed on the Web site of the U.S. Fish and Wildlife Service during the week after George W. Bush's inauguration:

> One hundred thirty-five species of birds are known to use the area, including numerous shorebirds, waterfowl, loons, songbirds, and raptors.
>
> One notable example is the snow goose. Large numbers of snow geese, varying each year from 15,000 to more than 300,000 birds, feed on the Arctic Refuge coastal tundra for three to four weeks each fall. They feed on cottongrass and other plants to build up fat reserves in preparation for their journey south, eating as much as a third of their body weight each day. The rich vegetation of the coastal tundra enables them to increase fat reserves by 400 percent in only two to three weeks.
>
> Snow geese feed on small patches of vegetation that are widely distributed across the Refuge's coastal tundra, so a large area is necessary to meet their needs. They are extremely sensitive to disturbance, often flying away from their feeding sites when human activities occur several miles distant.

Compare this with the text that appeared on the Web site before its post-inauguration revision. The parts of the previous version that were revised or deleted are italicized:

> One hundred thirty-five species of birds are known to use the area, including numerous shorebirds, waterfowl, loons, songbirds, and rap-

tors. *Oil development in the Arctic Refuge would result in habitat loss, disturbance, and displacement or abandonment of important nesting, feeding, molting, and staging areas.*

One species of bird that could be greatly impacted by oil development is the snow goose. Large numbers of snow geese, varying each year from 15,000 to more than 300,000 birds, feed on the Arctic Refuge coastal tundra for three to four weeks each fall. They feed on cottongrass and other plants to build up fat reserves in preparation for their journey south, eating as much as a third of their body weight each day. The rich vegetation of the coastal tundra enables them to increase fat reserves by 400 percent in only two to three weeks.

Snow geese feed on small patches of vegetation that are widely distributed across the Refuge's coastal tundra, so a large area is necessary to meet their needs. They are extremely sensitive to disturbance, often flying away from their feeding sites when human activities occur several miles distant. *Oil exploration and development would displace snow geese from areas that are critically important to them.*

How does the deleted text change the meaning? How do these changes affect your notions of language, power, and citizenship?

Readers and Rhetorical Choices

Because readings are the centerpiece of this book and fundamental to the courses in which they are used, we want to share our general views about reading to point classroom discussion in directions we think are most profitable. First, we view reading to be a constructive activity rather than one in which readers "receive" messages from texts. Language is *indexical*; that is, it suggests a range of meanings and offers a wide spectrum of rhetorical choices. Sure, sometimes the meaning of language seems both clear and unambiguous, as when E. Annie Proulx writes in *The Gourmet Gardener*:

> Older authorities believed the radish originated in China, but it was extensively grown in ancient Egypt, Greece, and Rome. The Greeks thought the radish so fine that in offerings to Apollo radishes made of gold were laid before the god, while beets rated only silver, and turnips, lead.

Even language this clear, however, cannot guarantee all readers equal access to its range of meanings in exactly the same way. For example, who are these "older authorities"? How old are they, and what kind of authority do they have? Who is Apollo, and what does Proulx mean by saying that gold radishes were "laid before" him? What is the context for these two statements about the radish? What are Proulx's purposes in writing about it?

Even a single word can carry multiple meanings. Consider the word *sunset*. We could probably all agree on a technical definition that would incorporate some insight about the rotation of the earth on its axis as it orbits the sun and the sun's slow decline in the west each evening. In other words, we could pretty much agree on what the word denotes. However, if we were all asked to envision a sunset or express the associations we have with the word *sunset*, which is another way of asking what *sunset* connotes or means, we would inevitably describe different visions. We might include scenes from apartment windows, front porches, beaches, parks, cities, trains, buses, airplanes, movies, and other locations. The visions we recall would also be attached to memories, ranging from very vague to sharply specific, and might be connected to emotions—joy, defeat, sadness, renewal. The word might even trigger other associations: the strong bond of friendship or love with a specific individual or the smell of an ocean breeze off the Pacific. Some of us might simply speak of the sun setting behind the trees, while others of us might be as elaborate as novelist John Oliver Killens in *The Cotillion*:

> She felt that if her father did materialize in the deep glow of the Harlem sunset she would break into a run like in the old days when she was six and seven and eight and believed in a jolly, old, fat white man by the name of Santa Claus, and thought the whole wide world was right there on her block in Harlem, and God was great and God was good and everything was for the best, because He worked mysteriously, the Grand Magician of them all. Cars honking, racing motors, fumes belching, children screaming, cursing, squealing, laughing. She stared past the busy intersection clear across Seventh Avenue all the way west to the river where the sun was a blazing disk of fire and washing the streets with a million colors and descending slowly down between the buildings at the very end of the street, down down it was sinking slowly sinking to set afire the Hudson River. Her eyes filled up and almost overflowed at the beauty of the Harlem sunset. The tenements bathed in soft sweet tender shadows now. She took one long last look down toward the other end of her block. Come around the corner, Daddy! Come around the corner! And I will run again to meet you. She turned toward the house. Maybe he was already home. Silently she prayed he was already in the house.

To understand all that *sunset* means in this passage, you would have to consider, at the very least, the theme of innocence and its loss, the idea of reflection amid commotion, the love of place, and the mixed emotions about faith and belief (the loss of belief in Santa Claus and the commitment to prayer). And if this passage is doing its work, it will trigger certain kinds of identification with the young girl's feelings of hope and loss, identification and understanding, shaped and colored by your own experiences. It is this range of possible meanings that makes language indexical, that makes it in a very real sense always much more than the sum of its parts.

Clearly, language conveys meaning, but at the same time, readers give shape to that meaning based on their level of attention, personal experience, reading background, ability to analyze and interpret the text, and multiple other factors. Reading is, therefore, a social act, one that is much more similar to writing than many people assume. Both emerge from interactions between self and others, self and words, self and experiences. If you understand how complicated the question of meaning can become when we are dealing with a single word or a short passage, you can appreciate how active and engaged your mental faculties must be to interpret and build knowledge from the complex texts encountered in academics and beyond. Generally, you are not merely "decoding information" from something that is fixed and stable; rather, you are negotiating an understanding that must variously take into account the writer's intentions, the meaning of words on the page, and your own perspectives.

Reading for Pleasure

Although we have offered a complex analysis of reading and the nature of interpretation, we do not want to obscure one simple and fundamental truth: the importance of reading for pleasure, which is essential for anyone who wants to improve as both a reader and a writer. It hardly matters what a person reads—mysteries, magazines, historical novels, science fiction, romance novels—they all can be useful. Of primary importance is to read with enjoyment and understanding.

We stress this because good writers are always good readers. A good reader brings a special attention to reading along with the appropriate skills. By special attention, we mean that good readers choose readings that stretch their understanding and enrich their abilities, readings that have to be read with full attention, not while watching TV. And by appropriate skills, we mean that good readers are constantly learning how to improve their reading abilities because they pay attention to the structures of reading: forms, patterns, meanings, rhythms, tones, suggestions, nuances—those various elements that make up the craft of writing.

As an example, let's return once again to E. Annie Proulx's *The Gourmet Gardener*, a practical guide that provides information to people who want to grow their own fruits, vegetables, and herbs. Dozens of such books can be found in the bookstore offering information, illustrations, and specific how-to advice. What sets Proulx's work apart from the mainstream, however, is her ability to present information in a way that sparks the imagination with words and phrasing that lift the subject off the page. Here, for example, is the opening of her section on that most prosaic of vegetables, cauliflower:

> Cauliflower, with its pure and saintly white florets, is really a thick, malformed flower cluster packed into a dense corymb. The undulating surface of the whole head looks like a miniature hilly landscape under snow. Few vegetables are so beautiful, and so amusing to arrange.
>
> Botanically cauliflower is classed with broccoli, though it is more tender to frost, more delicate in flavor, and a greater challenge to the gardener who wants to grow perfect heads.
>
> Cauliflower has seniority; it was known long before the more pedestrian broccoli.

Proulx offers a short lyrical description of cauliflower, including the simile of a snowy landscape to describe its appearance and then briefly contrasting it with broccoli. Her use of the phrase "pure and saintly" suggests that this vegetable possesses a holy quality, but she provides a stylistic counterpoint to that interpretation by using the words *thick* and *malformed*, which imply that the cauliflower is coarse and even somewhat unnatural. That she includes the unfamiliar word *corymb* should drive us toward the dictionary, and it reminds us that we are reading the work of an expert, someone familiar with the technical botanical terms. The short second paragraph (just one sentence) provides useful information by contrasting cauliflower with its cousin, broccoli. The opening sentence of her third paragraph makes us think of cauliflower as part of an aristocratic class or as a member of a governmental body (like the House or Senate) because of the word *seniority*. Following this sentence are several pages of text that are part scientific, part historical, part descriptive, part process, and part pure gardening information all bound together in a style that constantly surprises and, Proulx hopes, delights the reader.

Reading and Relating

It should be clear by now that becoming a better reader is integral to improving as a writer. Reading teaches us to attend to words; to learn the ways language is shaped into meaning; to become more sensitive to the tone, mood, and nuance of language; to concentrate on complex thoughts and issues. That is, it instructs us in how to make sound and sensitive rhetorical choices that we can apply to our own speaking and writing. It builds our intuitions, especially if we learn to read as writers, to read not only for content and pleasure but also with an awareness of what writers do to create richness and eloquence in their prose. Writing grows out of reading and, of course, good writing becomes something intended to be read.

But there is another important dimension to reading and writing that needs to be considered because it is fundamental to success: relationship. Because relationship is invisible to the eye, most textbooks and many instructors have a difficult time talking about it, but it is fundamental in many ways. Enrolling in a composition class is, after all, not usually the choice of the student; most often it is a required class or at the very least strongly recommended. Most students take it because they need it or are placed into it or can't avoid it. Those of us who teach this class start with a disadvantage that few other instructors share: Because many of our students feel they would rather be just about anywhere than in a writing class, we spend the first few weeks of the term striving to reorient our students to the pleasures and satisfactions inherent to the course. Thus many composition courses start students off with community-building activities, pleasurable readings, small-group discussions, and other forms of confidence-building activities. These are important because they help reorient students, taking away some of the sting of being in a "required" class.

This is one aspect of the "relationship" we are describing here: To succeed as a reader and writer, you must find ways to create a meaningful, productive, personal relationship with your work. You must find a way to care about a critical connection with required readings and assigned essay topics. In fact, creating this kind of relationship is intrinsic to performing any work at a high level.

All the authors included in this anthology found some way to stand in meaningful relationship with their writing, subject, language, and audience. They discovered something intrinsically satisfying in doing their research, structuring and organizing their thoughts, and putting the words down on paper. Let's examine sections of two essays to illustrate how this can be done, how reading in terms of relationship can help students discover models to form this kind of stance on their own. For starters, here is the opening to Barbara Ehrenreich's "What I've Learned from Men":

> For many years I believed that women had only one thing to learn from men: how to get the attention of a waiter by some means short of

kicking over the table and shrieking. Never in my life have I gotten the attention of a waiter, unless it was an off-duty waiter whose car I'd accidentally scraped in a parking lot somewhere. Men, however, can summon a maître d' just by thinking the word "coffee," and this is a power women would be well-advised to study. What else would we possibly want to learn from them? How to interrupt someone in mid-sentence as if you were performing an act of conversational euthanasia? How to drop a pair of socks three feet from an open hamper and keep right on walking? How to make those weird guttural gargling sounds in the bathroom?

But now, at mid-life, I am willing to admit that there are some real and useful things to learn from men. Not from all men—in fact, we may have the most to learn from some of the men we like the least. This realization does not mean that my feminist principles have gone soft with age: what I think women could learn from men is how to get *tough*. After more than a decade of consciousness-raising, assertiveness training, and hand-to-hand combat in the battle of the sexes, we're still too ladylike. Let me try that again—we're just too *damn* ladylike.

Ehrenreich signals her dislike of certain forms of arrogant male behavior, but she does so with a gesture of irony in which she praises overly assertive male actions. By keeping her sense of humor, Ehrenreich maintains a relationship with her subject (particularly, the male subject) that is both admiring and despising, critical and appreciative. It is a relationship that keeps her in tension with her subject. Men who act in this way are not just insensitive louts; they are insensitive louts who have a firm sense of their own power and place in the world, something women often do not have, or do not have in sufficient quantity. Women who learn this lesson may lose some of their "femininity," but they will gain increased sovereignty and will be less victimized in their everyday encounters with men (or the occasional assertive woman). It might be said that part of the pleasure of reading (and rereading) this essay is experiencing the ways Ehrenreich applies this ironic stance toward her subject.

Here is a paragraph from Michael Davitt Bell's "Magic Time," in which he discusses the importance of politeness and manners when interacting with friends and strangers who speak to him about his cancer:

> To speak of manners in the context of cancer and dying may seem jarring, even insincere, but it shouldn't. For as the great novelists of manners, the Jane Austens and the Henry Jameses, all knew, the etiquette of communication and miscommunication, the comedy of understanding and misunderstanding, is not only deeply fascinating and entertaining but also profoundly significant. These novelists knew that once the

misunderstandings have been cleared up, just before the ending, the possibility of love and of true communication has come to exist. And much more love, more interesting love, is possible than if no difficulties and misunderstandings had occurred in the first place. After all, you can't have the satisfying resolution of the ending if you don't start with conflict and crisis.

For Bell, cancer is certainly a disease he wishes he did not have, but he also recognizes that it has offered him a gift, the ability to discover what is most real and most important in his life. He finds a way to stand in relationship to his subject, cancer, so that he not only lives with it fully but also reflects on it philosophically. As does Ehrenreich, and all the authors in this book, Bell offers a complex view of his subject, one that cannot easily be characterized by a single phrase or 10-word summary. Moreover, both Bell and Ehrenreich reveal a singular truth about writing—namely, that significant subjects often lie directly before us, concealed by their seeming obviousness. Part of what it means to be a writer is to discover the extraordinary in the ordinary, the insights that can arise when we look hard at the world around us.

Getting Started

If there is one principle we would like to emphasize, it is that every composition course should be challenging, both for you the student and for your instructor. We realize that many composition courses are viewed, at least initially, as courses that students take because they have to, and that instructors sometimes teach because of need rather than desire. We feel differently. When the teaching of composition is centered on the ideas of language as a medium for expression, on argument in all its complexities, and on what it means to make intelligent rhetorical choices about readers and writers, texts and contexts, then it becomes a complex and exciting course, both to teach and to take.

This anthology, we hope, promotes this view. The selections we have chosen offer a range of possibilities, but we hope they always prove provocative and require more than one reading. The discussion questions are intended to promote active class discussion about topics of importance. The suggestions for writing are designed to extend those discussions through the written word, through draft after draft, which is really the only way most of us have to refine our thinking and build some precision into our composing processes.

Most of all, we hope that this book, combined with your experience in this course, makes you a more knowledgeable rhetorician, able to make the best possible choices about your writing. Writing is a primary form of expression, but it is also a primary means for reflection, the consolidation of meaning, the exploration of ideas. Writing extends thought. When done well, it produces immense satisfaction and real effects in the world.

Part and parcel of our concern with reading and instructional theory is our belief that critical reading and the accompanying discussion in a classroom community are essential preparation for citizenship in a democracy. Many of our social problems have not been resolved, and emerging perspectives, including some of yours, need to be brought to bear on these issues. Your ability to provide new insights is a function of how independently you learn to think. In an essay titled "Democratic Vistas," the poet Walt Whitman writes that "Not the book needs so much to be the complete thing, but the reader of the book does. That were to make a nation of supple and athletic minds, well-train'd, intuitive, used to depend on themselves, and not on a few coteries of writers." Like Whitman, we see criticism as an indispensable habit of mind. We have attempted, with respect to the readings in this book, to pose questions that spur you to consider aspects of language and culture that you might otherwise have ignored. But we have tried not to be overly directive, as we know your individual responses are important matters. We hope that your engagement with these texts, both in and out of class, will help you become more analytically inclusive, less reductive—and more creative—in your deliberations.

We wish you a productive academic experience, one that will help you make the best rhetorical choices possible, in school and beyond.

2
Narration

"*I couldn't believe that . . .*" "*When that happened, I was think-ing . . .*" "*What I didn't understand was . . .*" Such comments are often part of conversations that follow memorable social events. Some peo-ple spend more time talking about a previous night's party, for exam-ple, than they actually spent at the affair. To truly comprehend what transpired, they need to confirm, order, or come to grips with their ex-periences and perceptions at a more leisurely pace. They need to con-struct stories, or *narratives.* As noted short story writer and University of Alabama professor Michael Martone phrases it, "In the stories we tell ourselves, we tell ourselves."

To *narrate*, then, is to structure a select group of past events or im-pressions into a coherent and presumably interesting story for listeners and readers. Narratives are often used to develop and support a formal argument. A prospective law student might be required to submit a statement of personal experience to support her application. A student might recall instances of hate crimes on campus to advance his claim that strong measures need to be taken by the administration to curb or eliminate such acts. In other instances, narratives or anecdotes may be considered entertainment, just tales to provoke wonderment or laugh-ter, to evoke fear or even sadness. Whatever the case, it is important to remember that all storytellers are *narrating subjects*. That is, all nar-rators operate out of particular histories and social contexts, and they all convey particular viewpoints. To refer to a group of people as *clients* as opposed to *students*, to all of us as *mankind* as opposed to *humankind,* or to a set of political relations as *slavery* as opposed to *enslavement* is to reflect a particular perspective. Labeling an entire language variety a *nonstandard dialect* instead of regarding it as an appropriate alternative is another example of the narrator's viewpoint. Writer Amy Tan reflects on this perspective in her essay (included in this chapter) on the language of her mother, who emigrated from China to the United States: "Like others, I have described it to people as 'broken' or 'fractured' English. But I wince when I say that. It has always bothered me that I can think of no way to describe it other than 'broken,' as if it were damaged and needed to be fixed, as if it lacked a certain wholeness and soundness."

Being keenly aware of linguistic choice is an exciting and fruitful way for you to examine texts. However, it is more than a simple exercise. Practicing such awareness helps you pay fuller attention to all elements of language use and helps you make more informed decisions about your own language choices. Tan remarks that in her writing, "I use them all—all the Englishes I grew up with." Good storytellers like Tan tend to be proficient at envisioning the audience they want to affect and are mindful of the ways in which their words may be understood. Therefore, it is important that, to the extent you can, you remain aware of all the messages your words convey. It is also important, even crucial, that you practice identifying the viewpoints in the narratives you hear and read. Becoming critical readers of narratives will help you to devote critical attention to those you produce.

The most pertinent questions about any narrative or anecdote you write will be, "What happened?" and "So what?" You will be expected to identify a situation, set the scene, unfold a worthy plot, and resolve the story in a compelling and logical way. You always tell something by what you choose to report or omit. But obviously you cannot include every single aspect related to your narrative. Therefore, select anecdotes that best contribute to making your point. You would not want to slow the pace too much by including extraneous material. If you are recounting an automobile accident, for example, mentioning the color of the traffic signals is probably more useful than dwelling on the colors of the drivers' socks.

A primary goal of all writers is to have the readers keep turning the page. It is the only way to convey the controlling idea thoroughly. If readers lose interest in your story, they will not finish it unless they are required to do so, and in those circumstances, their final impression is not likely to be favorable. A principal means of holding the attention of readers is the use of evaluation, a term employed by distinguished linguist and professor William Labov in his study of narrative. This is the way narrators embed in their stories commentary designed to elicit concern from readers (keep them from asking, so what?) and influence readers to empathize or sympathize with them. Narrators are always trying to get people to be on their side. For example, in telling a story of how you became terribly ill, reasonably requested an extension of a paper deadline, and then were denied by an inflexible instructor, the citing of the illness along with the descriptors *reasonably* and *inflexible* serve as evaluative commentary. This story is different from one in which you merely state, "I was going to miss the deadline. I asked for an extension. The instructor said no." While it is true that someone might respond compassionately toward the latter story, and toward you in any event, most readers would need evaluative commentary before they could share your perspective, care about your predicament, or see you as a victim. Although excessive moralizing can ruin your story, by supplying evaluation you create the sympathetic figure you want to project.

To create the coherent framework that is fundamental to narratives or anecdotes, you need to bear in mind several other specific techniques. Chronology is the strongest structural feature of stories, and you need to portray a clear sense of a beginning, a middle, and an end. However, it is often dramatically effective to begin a story in the middle—what is known as *in media res*. You can imagine many stories written about the controversial presidential election of 2000 commencing with an anecdote about the close and contested outcome in Florida. A writer could then shift to describing earlier events during the election that made the vote in Florida a crucial issue. In other words, the writer could use a *flashback*. Another technique is a *flashforward*. The topic of a story could be negotiations about election procedures that did not go as well as they might have in, say, the 1990s. A writer could then flash-forward—"Look what ended up happening in 2000 as a result"—before shifting back to a narrative about the earlier events. In any case, the writer must use clear transitional markers to keep the sense of order straight for readers. Such guides include words like *then*, *next*, and *subsequently* or phrases like *but let me not get ahead of myself* or *let me backtrack a minute*. In addition to transitional devices, verb tense can help maintain a sense of sequence. The writer should use verbs in a manner that is logically consistent and promotes the overall clarity of the writing.

Although your narratives always suggest something about your own position, they do not have to be about your actions or be told in *first person*, which can be called the *I* or *we* perspective. Third-person viewpoint—*he, she, it, they*—is a common alternative. Some stories are even written in the second-person or *you* mode. Consider novelist William Styron's depiction in *Lie Down in Darkness* of a passenger who has journeyed by train from Richmond to Port Warwick:

> You get up and say good-by to the novelty salesman, who is going on across the bay by ferry, and you pull your bag from the rack and climb down off the train onto the station dock where the smell of the water is clean and refreshing after the flatulent warmth of the car and where, thirty yards away, your girl or your friends are waiting with expectant grins—"Oh there he is!"—and as you walk toward them you've already forgotten the novelty salesman forever, and the ride down. It's going to be a hot day.

Dialogue is also a key device for dramatizing narratives. To hold readers' interest, it should probably be used sparingly. To be convincing, it should be as realistic as possible, which means it captures as much as possible the rhythm, vocabulary, and syntax of the speakers represented.

Ronald Kellogg, author of *The Psychology of Writing*, reminds us that narratives are such a fundamental aspect of human consciousness, even to logico-deductive thought, that we often are blind to their importance. Practically all of us, in fact, do much storytelling all the time. Conscious awareness of narration and the skill to use its structural elements well are, as we have been trying to show, important abilities for writers to develop.

Annie Dillard (1945–   ) essayist, memoirist, poet, and novelist, is a professor of English and writer in residence at Wesleyan University. Dillard, a native of Pittsburgh, Pennsylvania, and the recipient of awards from the Guggenheim Foundation and the National Endowment for the Arts, has published widely, with works appearing in such journals and magazines as The Atlantic, Harper's Magazine, Cosmopolitan, *and* The Christian Science Monitor. *She is the author of numerous books, including* Pilgrim at Tinker Creek *(1974), for which she received the Pulitzer Prize for general nonfiction;* Teaching a Stone to Talk *(1982);* The Living *(1992);* Mornings Like This *(1996); and* For the Time Being *(1999). The selection below has been excerpted from her celebrated autobiography,* An American Childhood *(1987).*

Annie Dillard

The Chase

Some boys taught me to play football. This was fine sport. You thought up a new strategy for every play and whispered it to the others. You went out for a pass, fooling everyone. Best, you got to throw yourself mightily at someone's running legs. Either you brought him down or you hit the ground flat out on your chin, with your arms empty before you. It was all or nothing. If you hesitated in fear, you would miss and get hurt: you would take a hard fall while the kid got away, or you would get kicked in the face while the kid got away. But if you flung yourself wholeheartedly at the back of his knees—if you gathered and joined body and soul and pointed them diving fearlessly—then you likely wouldn't get hurt, and you'd stop the ball. Your fate, and your team's score, depended on your concentration and courage. Nothing girls did could compare with it.

Boys welcomed me at baseball, too, for I had, through enthusiastic practice, what was weirdly known as a boy's arm. In winter, in the snow, there was neither baseball nor football, so the boys and I threw snowballs at passing cars. I got in trouble throwing snowballs, and have seldom been happier since.

On one weekday morning after Christmas, six inches of new snow had just fallen. We were standing up to our boot tops in snow on a front yard on trafficked Reynolds Street, waiting for cars. The cars traveled Reynolds Street slowly and evenly; they were targets all but wrapped in red ribbons, cream puffs. We couldn't miss.

I was seven; the boys were eight, nine, and ten. The oldest two Fahey boys were there—Mikey and Peter—polite blond boys who lived near me on Lloyd Street, and who already had four brothers and sisters. My parents approved Mikey and Peter Fahey. Chickie McBride was there, a tough kid, and Billy Paul and Mackie Kean too, from across Reynolds, where the boys grew up dark and furious, grew up skinny, knowing, and skilled. We had all drifted from our houses that morning looking for action, and had found it here on Reynolds Street.

5   It was cloudy but cold. The cars' tires laid behind them on the snowy street a complex trail of beige chunks like crenellated castle walls. I had stepped on some earlier; they squeaked. We could have wished for more traffic. When a car came, we all popped it one. In the intervals between cars we reverted to the natural solitude of children.

I started making an iceball—a perfect iceball, from perfectly white snow, perfectly spherical, and squeezed perfectly translucent so no snow remained all the way through. (The Fahey boys and I considered it unfair actually to throw an iceball at somebody, but it had been known to happen.)

I had just embarked on the iceball project when we heard tire chains come clanking from afar. A black Buick was moving toward us down the street. We all spread out, banged together some regular snowballs, took aim, and, when the Buick drew nigh, fired.

A soft snowball hit the driver's windshield right before the driver's face. It made a smashed star with a hump in the middle.

Often, of course, we hit our target, but this time, the only time in all of life, the car pulled over and stopped. Its wide black door opened; a man got out of it, running. He didn't even close the car door.

10   He ran after us, and we ran away from him, up the snowy Reynolds sidewalk. At the corner, I looked back; incredibly, he was still after us. He was in city clothes: a suit and tie, street shoes. Any normal adult would have quit, having sprung us into flight and made his point. This man was gaining on us. He was a thin man, all action. All of a sudden, we were running for our lives.

Wordless, we split up. We were on our turf; we could lose ourselves in the neighborhood backyards, everyone for himself. I paused and considered. Everyone had vanished except Mikey Fahey, who was just rounding the corner of a yellow brick house. Poor Mikey, I trailed him.

The driver of the Buick sensibly picked the two of us to follow. The man apparently had all day.

He chased Mikey and me around the yellow house and up a backyard path we knew by heart: under a low tree, up a bank, through a hedge, down some snowy steps, and across the grocery store's delivery driveway. We smashed through a gap in another hedge, entered a scruffy backyard and ran around its back porch and tight between houses to Edgerton Avenue; we ran across Edgerton to an alley and up our own sliding woodpile to the Halls' front yard; he kept coming. We ran up Lloyd Street and wound through mazy backyards toward the steep hilltop at Willard and Lang.

He chased us silently, block after block. He chased us silently over picket fences, through thorny hedges, between houses, around garbage cans, and across streets. Every time I glanced back, choking for breath, I expected he would have quit. He must have been as breathless as we were. His jacket strained over his body. It was an immense discovery, pounding into my hot head with every sliding, joyous step, that this ordinary adult evidently knew what I thought only children who trained at football knew: that you have to fling yourself at what you're doing, you have to point yourself, forget yourself, aim, dive.

Mikey and I had nowhere to go, in our own neighborhood or out of it, but away from this man who was chasing us. He impelled us forward; we compelled him to follow our route. The air was cold; every breath tore my throat. We kept running, block after block; we kept improvising, backyard after backyard, running a frantic course and choosing it simultaneously, failing always to find small places or hard places to slow him down, and discovering always, exhilarated, dismayed, that only bare speed could save us—for he would never give up, this man—and we were losing speed.

15   He chased us through the backyard labyrinths of ten blocks before he caught us by our jackets. He caught us and we all stopped.

We three stood staggering, half blinded, coughing, in an obscure hilltop backyard: a man in his twenties, a boy, a girl. He had released our jackets, our pursuer, our captor, our hero: he knew we weren't going anywhere. We all played by the rules. Mikey and I unzipped our jackets. I pulled off my sopping mittens. Our tracks multiplied in the backyard's new snow. We had been breaking new snow all morning. We didn't look at each other. I was cherishing my excitement. The man's lower pants legs were wet; his cuffs were full of snow, and there was a prow of snow beneath them on his shoes and socks. Some trees bordered the little flat backyard, some messy winter trees. There was no one around: a clearing in a grove, and we the only players.

It was a long time before he could speak. I had some difficulty at first recalling why we were there. My lips felt swollen; I couldn't see out of the sides of my eyes; I kept coughing.

"You stupid kids," he began perfunctorily.

We listened perfunctorily indeed, if we listened at all, for the chewing out was redundant, a mere formality, and beside the point. The point was that he had chased us passionately without giving up, and so he had caught us. Now he came down to earth. I wanted the glory to last forever.

20   But how could the glory have lasted forever? We could have run through every backyard in North America until we got to Panama. But when he trapped us at the lip of the Panama Canal, what precisely could he have done to prolong the drama of the chase and cap its glory? I brooded about this for the next few years. He could only have fried Mikey Fahey and me in boiling oil, say, or dismembered us piecemeal, or staked us to anthills. None of which I really wanted, and none of which any adult was likely to do, even in the spirit of fun. He could only chew us out there in the Panamanian jungle, after months or years of exalting pursuit. He could only begin, "You stupid kids," and continue in his ordinary Pittsburgh accent with his normal righteous anger and the usual common sense.

If in that snowy backyard the driver of the black Buick had cut off our heads, Mikey's and mine, I would have died happy, for nothing has required so much of me since as being chased all over Pittsburgh in the middle of winter—running terrified, exhausted—by this sainted, skinny, furious red-headed man who wished to have a word with us. I don't know how he found his way back to his car.

Analyzing Rhetorical Choices

1.   Dillard provides a lot of details: the names of the boys, the color and make of the car the children hit with their snowballs, the names of the streets down which the man chases them. On the other hand, other details are withheld. For example, she does not talk about her successes or failures in actually playing football. Nor do she, Mikey, and their pursuer encounter a single person during a chase that lasted, based on her description, some half a mile and at least ten minutes. Which details in Dillard's narrative are particularly convincing to you, and which additional details

would you like to see provided? What overall impression does she make on you?

2. Dillard writes, "I got in trouble throwing snowballs, and have seldom been happier since." She also describes her pursuer as "our hero." What makes her happy and the chaser heroic? How are these ideas developed in the essay? How are they related to the description of playing football?

3. In your view, how does Dillard's style capture the thoughts of a seven-year-old? How does the language used make her viewpoint convincing—or not?

4. Relative to the conclusion of the chase, Dillard suggests that words were anticlimactic and contributed nothing to the adventure. Actions had said it all. Yet the paradox for her is that for the experience to inform others she must use words. Who does Dillard imagine to be her audience?

Writing About Issues and Contexts

1. An autobiography is a challenging form to write: The author must find a way to write about his or her life without being self-indulgent and in a way that interests readers. Given this selection, how well do you think Dillard succeeds?

2. Dillard writes about the effort involved in playing football: "Nothing girls did could compare with it." How do you feel about this statement? Is it a plausible statement to make about 1950s Pittsburgh? Or about now? Why?

3. "The Chase" describes a classic conflict that arises because of the acts of children and the response of one adult. In what ways, if any, are the children's actions representative of most children? In what ways are they not? In what ways, if any, are the adult's actions representative of most adults? In what ways are they not? Does the man here represent anything—other than a man whose windshield got pounded by some snowballs?

4. What impact is Dillard hoping to make with this anecdote?

Born in Roxie, Mississippi, **Richard Wright** *(1908–1960) became one of the most important writers in American history. After childhood and adolescence in the South, Wright moved with his family to Chicago where he became serious about a writing career. In Chicago, he wrote fiction, nonfiction, and poetry as a member of the John Reed Club and an employee of the Works Progress Administration. Wright moved to New York in 1937; he settled in Paris in 1947. Known for his powerful descriptions of environments and their effects on people, he is best known for the story collection* Uncle Tom's Children *(1938); the novels* Native Son *(1940) and* The Outsider *(1953); as well as his memoir* Black Boy *(1945). This selection is chapter 13 of* Black Boy.

Richard Wright
The Library Card

One morning I arrived early at work and went into the bank lobby where the Negro porter was mopping. I stood at a counter and picked up the Memphis *Commercial Appeal* and began my free reading of the press. I came finally to the editorial page and saw an article dealing with one H. L. Mencken. I knew by hearsay that he was the editor of the *American Mercury*, but aside from that I knew nothing about him. The article was a furious denunciation of Mencken, concluding with one, hot, short sentence: Mencken is a fool.

I wondered what on earth this Mencken had done to call down upon him the scorn of the South. The only people I had ever heard denounced in the South were Negroes, and this man was not a Negro. Then what ideas did Mencken hold that made a newspaper like the *Commercial Appeal* castigate him publicly? Undoubtedly he must be advocating ideas that the South did not like. Were there, then, people other then Negroes who criticized the South? I knew that during the Civil War the South had hated northern whites, but I had not encountered such hate during my life. Knowing no more of Mencken than I did at that moment, I felt a vague sympathy for him. Had not the South, which had assigned me the role of a non-man, cast at him its hardest words?

Now, how could I find out about this Mencken? There was a huge library near the riverfront, but I knew that Negroes were not allowed to patronize its shelves any more than they were the parks and play-

grounds of the city. I had gone into the library several times to get
books for the white men on the job. Which of them would now help me
to get books? And how could I read them without causing concern to
the white men with whom I worked? I had so far been successful in
hiding my thoughts and feelings from them, but I knew that I would
create hostility if I went about this business of reading in a clumsy
way.

I weighed the personalities of the men on the job. There was Don,
a Jew; but I distrusted him. His position was not much better than
mine and I knew that he was uneasy and insecure; he had always
treated me in an offhand, bantering way that barely concealed his
contempt. I was afraid to ask him to help me to get books; his frantic
desire to demonstrate a racial solidarity with the whites against
Negroes might make him betray me.

5   Then how about the boss? No, he was a Baptist and I had the suspicion that he would not be quite able to comprehend why a black boy
would want to read Mencken. There were other white men on the job
whose attitudes showed clearly that they were Kluxers or sympathiz-
ers, and they were out of the question.

There remained only one man whose attitude did not fit into an
anti-Negro category, for I had heard the white men refer to him as a
"Pope lover." He was an Irish Catholic and was hated by the white
Southerners. I knew that he read books, because I had got him volumes from the library several times. Since he, too, was an object of
hatred, I felt that he might refuse me but would hardly betray me. I
hesitated, weighing and balancing the imponderable realities.

One morning I paused before the Catholic fellow's desk.

"I want to ask you a favor," I whispered to him.

"What is it?"

10   "I want to read. I can't get books from the library. I wonder if
you'd let me use your card?"

He looked at me suspiciously.

"My card is full most of the time," he said.

"I see," I said and waited, posing my question silently.

"You're not trying to get me into trouble, are you, boy?" he asked,
staring at me.

15   "Oh, no, sir."

"What book do you want?"

"A book by H. L. Mencken."

"Which one?"

"I don't know. Has he written more than one?"

20   "He has written several."

"I didn't know that."

"What makes you want to read Mencken?"

"Oh, I just saw his name in the newspaper," I said.

"It's good of you to want to read," he said. "But you ought to read the right things."

25   I said nothing. Would he want to supervise my reading?

"Let me think," he said. "I'll figure out something."

I turned from him and he called me back. He stared at me quizzically.

"Richard, don't mention this to the other white men," he said.

"I understand," I said. "I won't say a word."

30   A few days later he called me to him.

"I've got a card in my wife's name," he said. "Here's mine."

"Thank you, sir."

"Do you think you can manage it?"

"I'll manage fine," I said.

35   "If they suspect you, you'll get in trouble," he said.

"I'll write the same kind of notes to the library that you wrote when you sent me for books," I told him. "I'll sign your name."

He laughed.

"Go ahead. Let me see what you get," he said.

That afternoon I addressed myself to forging a note. Now, what were the names of books written by H. L. Mencken? I did not know any of them. I finally wrote what I thought would be a foolproof note: *Dear Madam: Will you please let this nigger boy*—I used the word "nigger" to make the librarian feel that I could not possibly be the author of the note—*have some books by H. L. Mencken?* I forged the white man's name.

40   I entered the library as I had always done when on errands for whites, but I felt that I would somehow slip up and betray myself. I doffed my hat, stood a respectful distance from the desk, looked as unbookish as possible, and waited for the white patrons to be taken care of. When the desk was clear of people, I still waited. The white librarian looked at me.

"What do you want, boy?"

As though I did not possess the power of speech, I stepped forward and simply handed her the forged note, not parting my lips.

"What books by Mencken does he want?" she asked.

"I don't know, ma'am," I said, avoiding her eyes.

45   "Who gave you this card?"

"Mr. Falk," I said.

"Where is he?"

"He's at work, at the M—Optical Company," I said. "I've been in here for him before."

"I remember," the woman said. "But he never wrote notes like this."

50   Oh, God, she's suspicious. Perhaps she would not let me have the books? If she had turned her back at that moment, I would have ducked out the door and never gone back. Then I thought of a bold idea.

"You can call him up, ma'am," I said, my heart pounding.

"You're not using these books, are you?" she asked pointedly.

"Oh, no, ma'am. I can't read."

"I don't know what he wants by Mencken," she said under her breath.

55   I knew now that I had won; she was thinking of other things and the race question had gone out of her mind. She went to the shelves. Once or twice she looked over her shoulder at me, as though she was still doubtful. Finally she came forward with two books in her hand.

"I'm sending him two books," she said. "But tell Mr. Falk to come in next time, or send me the names of the books he wants. I don't know what he wants to read."

I said nothing. She stamped the card and handed me the books. Not daring to glance at them, I went out of the library, fearing that the woman would call me back for further questioning. A block away from the library I opened one of the books and read a title: *A Book of Prefaces*. I was nearing my nineteenth birthday and I did not know how to pronounce the word "preface." I thumbed the pages and saw strange words and strange names. I shook my head, disappointed. I looked at the other book; it was called *Prejudices*. I knew what that word meant; I had heard it all my life. And right off I was on guard against Mencken's books. Why would a man want to call a book *Prejudices*? The word was so stained with all my memories of racial hate that I could not conceive of anybody using it for a title. Perhaps I had made a mistake about Mencken? A man who had prejudices must be wrong.

When I showed the books to Mr. Falk, he looked at me and frowned.

"That librarian might telephone you," I warned him.

60   "That's all right," he said. "But when you're through reading those books, I want you to tell me what you get out of them."

That night in my rented room, while letting the hot water run over my can of pork and beans in the sink, I opened *A Book of Prefaces* and began to read. I was jarred and shocked by the style, the clear, clean, sweeping sentences. Why did he write like that? And how did one write like that? I pictured the man as a raging demon, slashing with his pen, consumed with hate, denouncing everything American, extolling everything European or German, laughing at the weaknesses of people, mocking God, authority. What was this? I stood up, trying to realize what reality lay behind the meaning of the words . . . Yes, this man was fighting, fighting with words. He was using words as a weapon, using them as one would use a club. Could words be weapons? Well, yes, for here they were. Then, maybe, perhaps, I could use them as a weapon? No. It frightened me. I read on and what amazed me was not what he said, but how on earth anybody had the courage to say it.

Occasionally I glanced up to reassure myself that I was alone in the room. Who were these men about whom Mencken was talking so passionately? Who was Anatole France? Joseph Conrad? Sinclair Lewis, Sherwood Anderson, Dostoevski, George Moore, Gustave Flaubert, Maupassant, Tolstoy, Frank Harris, Mark Twain, Thomas Hardy, Arnold Bennett, Stephen Crane, Zola, Norris, Gorky, Bergson, Ibsen, Balzac, Bernard Shaw, Dumas, Poe, Thomas Mann, O. Henry, Dreiser, H. G. Wells, Gogol, T. S. Eliot, Gide, Baudelaire, Edgar Lee Masters, Stendhal, Turgenev, Huneker, Nietzsche, and scores of others? Were these men real? Did they exist or had they existed? And how did one pronounce their names?

I ran across many words whose meanings I did not know, and I either looked them up in a dictionary or, before I had a chance to do that, encountered the word in a context that made its meaning clear. But what strange world was this? I concluded the book with the conviction that I had somehow overlooked something terribly important in life. I had once tried to write, had once reveled in feeling, had let my crude imagination roam, but the impulse to dream had been slowly beaten out of me by experience. Now it surged up again and I hungered for books, new ways of looking and seeing. It was not a matter of believing or disbelieving what I read, but of feeling something new, of being affected by something that made the look of the world different.

As dawn broke I ate my pork and beans, feeling dopey, sleepy. I went to work, but the mood of the book would not die; it lingered, coloring everything I saw, heard, did. I now felt that I knew what the white men were feeling. Merely because I had read a book that had spoken of how they lived and thought, I identified myself with that book. I felt vaguely guilty. Would I, filled with bookish notions, act in a manner that would make the whites dislike me?

65   I forged more notes and my trips to the library became frequent. Reading grew into a passion. My first serious novel was Sinclair Lewis's *Main Street*. It made me see my boss, Mr. Gerald, and identify him as an American type. I would smile when I saw him lugging his golf bags into the office. I had always felt a vast distance separating me from the boss, and now I felt closer to him, though still distant. I felt now that I knew him, that I could feel the very limits of his narrow life. And this had happened because I had read a novel about a mythical man called George F. Babbitt.

    The plots and stories in the novels did not interest me so much as the point of view revealed. I gave myself over to each novel without reserve, without trying to criticize it; it was enough for me to see and feel something different. And for me, everything was something different. Reading was like a drug, a dope. The novels created moods in which I lived for days. But I could not conquer my sense of guilt, my feeling that the white men around me knew that I was changing, that I had begun to regard them differently.

    Whenever I brought a book to the job, I wrapped it in newspaper—a habit that was to persist for years in other cities and under other circumstances. But some of the white men pried into my packages when I was absent and they questioned me.

    "Boy, what are you reading those books for?"

    "Oh, I don't know, sir."

70   "That's deep stuff you're reading, boy."

    "I'm just killing time, sir."

    "You'll addle your brains if you don't watch out."

    I read Dreiser's *Jennie Gerhardt* and *Sister Carrie* and they revived in me a vivid sense of my mother's suffering; I was overwhelmed. I grew silent, wondering about the life around me. It would have been impossible for me to have told anyone what I derived from these novels, for it was nothing less than a sense of life itself. All my life had shaped me for the realism, the naturalism of the modern novel, and I could not read enough of them.

    Steeped in new moods and ideas, I bought a ream of paper and tried to write; but nothing would come, or what did come was flat beyond telling. I discovered that more than desire and feeling were necessary to write and I dropped the idea. Yet I still wondered how it was possible to know people sufficiently to write about them? Could I ever learn about life and people? To me, with my vast ignorance, my Jim Crow station in life, it seemed a task impossible of achievement. I now knew what being a Negro meant: I could endure the hunger. I had learned to live with hate. But to feel that there were feelings denied me, that the very breath of life itself was beyond my reach, that more than anything else hurt, wounded me. I had a new hunger.

75 In buoying me up, reading also cast me down, made me see what was possible, what I had missed. My tension returned, new, terrible, bitter, surging, almost too great to be contained. I no longer *felt* that the world about me was hostile, killing; I *knew* it. A million times I asked myself what I could do to save myself, and there were no answers. I seemed forever condemned, ringed by walls.

I did not discuss my reading with Mr. Falk, who had lent me his library card; it would have meant talking about myself and that would have been too painful. I smiled each day, fighting desperately to maintain my old behavior, to keep my disposition seemingly sunny. But some of the white men discerned that I had begun to brood.

"Wake up there, boy!" Mr. Olin said one day.

"Sir!" I answered for the lack of a better word.

"You act like you've stolen something," he said.

80 I laughed in the way I knew he expected me to laugh, but I resolved to be more conscious of myself, to watch my every act, to guard and hide the new knowledge that was dawning within me.

If I went north, would it be possible for me to build a new life then? But how could a man build a life upon vague, unformed yearnings? I wanted to write and I did not even know the English language: I bought English grammars and found them dull. I felt that I was getting a better sense of the language from novels than from grammars. I read hard, discarding a writer as soon as I felt that I had grasped his point of view. At night the printed page stood before my eyes in sleep.

Mrs. Moss, my landlady, asked me one Sunday morning:

"Son, what is this you keep on reading?"

"Oh, nothing. Just novels."

85 "What you get out of 'em?"

"I'm just killing time," I said.

"I hope you know your own mind," she said in a tone which implied that she doubted if I had a mind.

I knew of no Negroes who read the books I liked and I wondered if any Negroes ever thought of them. I knew that there were Negro doctors, lawyers, newspapermen, but I never saw any of them. When I read a Negro newspaper I never caught the faintest echo of my preoccupation in its pages. I felt trapped and occasionally, for a few days, I would stop reading. But a vague hunger would come over me for books, books that opened up new avenues of feeling and seeing, and again I would forge another note to the white librarian. Again I would read and wonder as only the naïve and unlettered can read and wonder, feeling that I carried a secret, criminal burden about with me each day.

That winter my mother and brother came and we set up housekeeping, buying furniture on the installment plan, being cheated and yet knowing no way to avoid it. I began to eat warm food and to my surprise found that regular meals enabled me to read faster. I may have lived through many illnesses and survived them, never suspecting that I was ill. My brother obtained a job and we began to save toward the trip north, plotting our time, setting tentative dates for departure. I told none of the white men on the job that I was planning to go north; I knew that the moment they felt I was thinking of the North they would change toward me. It would have made them feel that I did not like the life I was living, and because my life was completely conditioned by what they said or did, it would have been tantamount to challenging them.

90 I could calculate my chances for life in the South as a Negro fairly clearly now.

I could fight the southern whites by organizing with other Negroes, as my grandfather had done. But I knew that I could never win that way; there were many whites and there were but few blacks. They were strong and we were weak. Outright black rebellion could never win. If I fought openly I would die and I did not want to die. News of lynchings were frequent.

I could submit and live the life of a genial slave, but that was impossible. All of my life had shaped me to live by my own feelings and thoughts. I could make up to Bess and marry her and inherit the house. But that, too, would be the life of a slave; if I did that, I would crush to death something within me, and I would hate myself as much as I knew the whites already hated those who had submitted. Neither could I ever willingly present myself to be kicked, as Shorty had done. I would rather have died than do that.

I could drain off my restlessness by fighting with Shorty and Harrison. I had seen many Negroes solve the problem of being black by transferring their hatred of themselves to others with a black skin and fighting them. I would have to be cold to do that, and I was not cold and I could never be.

I could, of course, forget what I had read, thrust the whites out of my mind, forget them; and find release from anxiety and longing in sex and alcohol. But the memory of how my father had conducted himself made that course repugnant. If I did not want others to violate my life, how could I voluntarily violate it myself?

95   I had no hope whatever of being a professional man. Not only had I been so conditioned that I did not desire it, but the fulfillment of such an ambition was beyond my capabilities. Well-to-do Negroes lived in a world that was almost as alien to me as the world inhabited by whites.

What, then, was there? I held my life in my mind, in my consciousness each day, feeling at times that I would stumble and drop it, spill it forever. My reading had created a vast sense of distance between me and the world in which I lived and tried to make a living, and that sense of distance was increasing each day. My days and nights were one long, quiet, continuously contained dream of terror, tension, and anxiety. I wondered how long I could bear it.

Analyzing Rhetorical Choices

1. Wright ends his first paragraph with this sentence: "The article was a furious denunciation of Mencken, concluding with one, hot, short sentence: Mencken is a fool." After reading the quiet, reportorial description that precedes this sentence, how does this sentence affect you? What is the effect of the phrase "concluding with one, hot, short sentence"?

2. Why do you think Wright includes two fairly extended dialogues: one between him and Mr. Falk and the other between him and the librarian? What do we learn from these encounters? What is the main point Wright is trying to dramatize?

3. The author seems to claim complete ignorance of the fact that people other than Negroes criticized the South. How credible a claim do you think this is, and why is his assertion important in his narrative?

Writing About Issues and Contexts

1. Wright includes several anecdotes about literacy: forging notes to the librarian, faking the inability to read, borrowing a library card, disguising book covers. What is the relevance of these anecdotes to ideas of your own about the role of literacy in education and in the larger society?

2. Wright feels that he has, in some explicit sense, been conditioned to a specific kind of life as a Negro in the South—and that the program of reading that he undertakes changes him. Do you agree? How are most of us similarly conditioned? Do you think that the

views we have of others and of ourselves are frequently determined
by our culture? How so?

3. Wright makes a racial distinction between Jews and whites, criti-
    cizing Don because he identifies more with whites than with
    Negroes. Mr. Falk, on the other hand, is an Irish Catholic hated by
    white Southerners and thus a potential ally. Are the author's classi-
    fications and analysis still as relevant as they were in 1927?
    Explain your response, being careful to examine your assumptions
    closely.

4. Regarding the merit of grammar books versus novels, Wright asserts
    "I felt that I was getting a better sense of the language from novels than
    from grammars." What is your opinion of his assessment?

*James Thurber (1894–1961) was born in Columbus, Ohio, and gradu-
ated from Ohio State University, where he was editor of the campus humor magazine. A prominent American humorist and satirist, in 1927 he
began a long career on the staff of* The New Yorker *as a writer and car-
toonist. Much of his work first appeared in the magazine. Thurber is best
known for his story "The Secret Life of Walter Mitty." Among his many
books are* My Life and Hard Times *(1933), from which this selection is
taken.* My World and Welcome to It *(1942), and* Thurber Country *(1953).*

James Thurber
University Days

I passed all the other courses that I took at my university, but I
could never pass botany. This was because all botany students had to
spend several hours a week in a laboratory looking through a microscope at plant cells, and I could never see through a microscope. I
never once saw a cell through a microscope. This used to enrage my
instructor. He would wander around the laboratory pleased with the
progress all the students were making in drawing the involved and, so
I am told, interesting structure of flower cells, until he came to me. I
would just be standing there. "I can't see anything," I would say. He
would begin patiently enough, explaining how anybody can see
through a microscope, but he would always end up in a fury, claiming
that I could *too* see through the microscope but just pretended that I
couldn't. "It takes away from the beauty of flowers anyway," I used to
tell him. "We are not concerned with beauty in this course," he would
say. "We are concerned solely with what I may call the *mechanics* of
flars." "Well," I'd say, "I can't see anything." "Try it just once again,"
he'd say, and I would put my eye to the microscope and see nothing at
all, except now and again a nebulous milky substance—a phenomenon
of maladjustment. You were supposed to see a vivid, restless clockwork
of sharply defined plant cells. "I see what looks like a lot of milk," I
would tell him. This, he claimed, was the result of my not having adjusted the microscope properly, so he would readjust it for me, or
rather, for himself. And I would look again and see milk.

I finally took a deferred pass, as they called it, and waited a year
and tried again. (You had to pass one of the biological sciences or you
couldn't graduate.) The professor had come back from vacation brown

as a berry, bright-eyed, and eager to explain cell-structure again to his classes. "Well," he said to me, cheerily, when we met in the first laboratory hour of the semester, "we're going to see cells this time, aren't we?" "Yes, sir," I said. Students to right of me and to left of me and in front of me were seeing cells; what's more, they were quietly drawing pictures of them in their notebooks. Of course, I didn't see anything.

"We'll try it," the professor said to me, grimly, "with every adjustment of the microscope known to man. As God is my witness, I'll arrange this glass so that you see cells through it or I'll give up teaching. In twenty-two years of botany, I—" He cut off abruptly for he was beginning to quiver all over, like Lionel Barrymore, and he genuinely wished to hold onto his temper; his scenes with me had taken a great deal out of him.

So we tried it with every adjustment of the microscope known to man. With only one of them did I see anything but blackness or the familiar lacteal opacity, and that time I saw, to my pleasure and amazement, a variegated constellation of flecks, specks, and dots. These I hastily drew. The instructor, noting my activity, came back from an adjoining desk, a smile on his lips and his eyebrows high in hope. He looked at my cell drawing. "What's that?" he demanded, with a hint of a squeal in his voice. "That's what I saw," I said. "You didn't, you didn't, you *didn't!*" he screamed, losing control of his temper instantly, and he bent over and squinted into the microscope. His head snapped up. "That's your eye!" he shouted. "You've fixed the lens so that it reflects! You've drawn your eye!"

5   Another course that I didn't like, but somehow managed to pass, was economics. I went to that class straight from the botany class, which didn't help me any in understanding either subject. I used to get them mixed up. But not as mixed up as another student in my economics class who came there direct from a physics laboratory. He was a tackle on the football team, named Bolenciecwcz. At that time Ohio State University had one of the best football teams in the country, and Bolenciecwcz was one of its outstanding stars. In order to be eligible to play it was necessary for him to keep up in his studies, a very difficult matter, for while he was not dumber than an ox he was not any smarter. Most of his professors were lenient and helped him along. None gave him more hints in answering questions or asked him simpler ones than the economics professor, a thin, timid man named Bassum. One day when we were on the subject of transportation and distribution, it came Bolenciecwcz's turn to answer a question. "Name one means of transportation," the professor said to him. No light came

into the big tackle's eyes. "Just any means of transportation," said the professor. Bolenciecwcz sat staring at him. "That is," pursued the professor, "any medium, agency, or method of going from one place to another." Bolenciecwcz had the look of a man who is being led into a trap. "You may choose among steam, horse-drawn, or electrically propelled vehicles," said the instructor. "I might suggest the one which we commonly take in making long journeys across land." There was a profound silence in which everybody stirred uneasily, including Bolenciecwcz and Mr. Bassum. Mr. Bassum abruptly broke this silence in an amazing manner. "Choo-choo-choo," he said, in a low voice, and turned instantly scarlet. He glanced appealingly around the room. All of us, of course, shared Mr. Bassum's desire that Bolenciecwcz should stay abreast of the class in economics, for the Illinois game, one of the hardest and most important of the season, was only a week off. "Toot, too, too-toooooooot!" some student with a deep voice moaned, and we all looked encouragingly at Bolenciecwcz. Somebody else gave a fine imitation of a locomotive letting off steam. Mr. Bassum himself rounded off the little show. "Ding, dong, ding, dong," he said, hopefully. Bolenciecwcz was staring at the floor now, trying to think, his great brow furrowed, his huge hands rubbing together, his face red.

"How did you come to college this year, Mr. Bolenciecwcz?" asked the professor. "*Chuffa* chuffa, *chuffa* chuffa."

"M'father sent me," said the football player.

"What on?" asked Bassum.

"I git an 'lowance," said the tackle, in a low, husky voice, obviously embarrassed.

10   "No, no," said Bassum. "Name a means of transportation. What did you *ride* here on?"

"Train," said Bolenciecwcz.

"Quite right," said the professor. "Now, Mr. Nugent, will you tell us—"

If I went through anguish in botany and economics—for different reasons—gymnasium work was even worse. I don't even like to think about it. They wouldn't let you play games or join the exercises with your glasses on and I couldn't see with mine off. I bumped into professors, horizontal bars, agricultural students, and swinging iron rings. Not being able to see, I could take it but I couldn't dish it out. Also, in order to pass gymnasium (and you had to pass it to graduate) you had to learn to swim if you didn't know how. I didn't like the swimming pool, I didn't like swimming, and I didn't like the swimming instructor, and after all these years I still don't. I never swam but I passed my gym work anyway, by having another student give my gymnasium number (978) and swim across the pool in my place. He was a quiet, amiable blond youth, number 473, and he would have seen through a microscope for me if we could have got away with it, but we couldn't get away with it. Another thing I didn't like about gymnasium work was that they made you strip the day you registered. It is impossible for me to be happy when I am stripped and being asked a lot of questions. Still, I did better than a lanky agricultural student who was cross-examined just before I was. They asked each student what college he was in—that is, whether Arts, Engineering, Commerce, or Agriculture. "What college are you in?" the instructor snapped at the youth in front of me. "Ohio State University," he said promptly.

It wasn't that agricultural student but it was another a whole lot like him who decided to take up journalism, possibly on the ground that when farming went to hell he could fall back on newspaper work. He didn't realize, of course, that that would be very much like falling back full-length on a kit of carpenter's tools. Haskins didn't seem cut out for journalism, being too embarrassed to talk to anybody and unable to use a typewriter, but the editor of the college paper assigned him to the cow barns, the sheep house, the horse pavilion, and the animal husbandry department generally. This was a genuinely big "beat," for it took up five times as much ground and got ten times as great a legislative appropriation as the College of Liberal Arts. The agricultural student knew animals, but nevertheless his stories were dull and colorlessly written. He took all afternoon on each of them, on account of having to hunt for each letter on the typewriter. Once in a while he had to ask somebody to help him hunt. *C* and *L*, in particular, were hard letters for him to find. His editor finally got pretty much annoyed at the farmer-journalist because his pieces were so uninteresting. "See here, Haskins," he snapped at him one day, "why is it we never have anything hot from you on the horse pavilion? Here we have two hundred head of horses on this campus—more than any other university in the Western Conference except Purdue—and yet you never get any real lowdown on them. Now shoot over to the horse barns and dig up something lively." Haskins shambled out and came back in about an hour; he said he had something. "Well, start it off snappily," said the editor. "Something people will read." Haskins set to work and in a couple of hours brought a sheet of typewritten paper to the desk; it was a two-hundred-word story about some disease that had broken out among the horses. Its opening sentence was simple but arresting. It read: "Who has noticed the sores on the tops of the horses in the animal husbandry building?"

15   Ohio State was a land grant university and therefore two years of military drill was compulsory. We drilled with old Springfield rifles and studied the tactics of the Civil War even though the World War was going on at the time. At 11 o'clock each morning thousands of freshmen and sophomores used to deploy over the campus, moodily creeping up on the old chemistry building. It was good training for the kind of warfare that was waged at Shiloh but it had no connection with what was going on in Europe. Some people used to think there was German money behind it, but they didn't say so or they would have been thrown in jail as German spies. It was a period of muddy thought and marked, I believe, the decline of higher education in the Middle West.

As a soldier I was never any good at all. Most of the cadets were glumly indifferent soldiers, but I was no good at all. Once General Littlefield, who was commandant of the cadet corps, popped up in front of me during regimental drill and snapped, "You are the main trouble with this university!" I think he meant that my type was the main trouble with the university but he may have meant me individually. I was mediocre at drill, certainly—that is, until my senior year. By that time I had drilled longer than anybody else in the Western Conference, having failed at military at the end of each preceding year so that I had to do it all over again. I was the only senior still in uniform. The uniform which, when new, had made me look like an interurban railway conductor, now that it had become faded and too tight made me look like Bert Williams in his bellboy act. This had a definitely bad effect on my morale. Even so, I had become by sheer practice little short of wonderful at squad maneuvers.

One day General Littlefield picked our company out of the whole regiment and tried to get it mixed up by putting it through one movement after another as fast as we could execute them: squads right, squads left, squads on right into line, squads right about, squads left front into line, etc. In about three minutes one hundred and nine men were marching in one direction and I was marching away from them at an angle of forty degrees all alone. "Company, halt!" shouted General Littlefield. "That man is the only man who has it right!" I was made a corporal for my achievement.

The next day General Littlefield summoned me to his office. He was swatting flies when I went in. I was silent and he was silent too, for a long time. I don't think he remembered me or why he had sent for me, but he didn't want to admit it. He swatted some more flies, keeping his eyes on them narrowly before he let go with the swatter. "Button up your coat!" he snapped. Looking back on it now I can see that he meant me although he was looking at a fly, but I just stood there. Another fly came to rest on a paper in front of the general and began rubbing its hind legs together. The General lifted the swatter cautiously. I moved restlessly and the fly flew away. "You startled him!" barked General Littlefield, looking at me severely. I said I was sorry. "That won't help the situation!" snapped the General, with cold military logic. I didn't see what I could do except offer to chase some more flies toward his desk, but I didn't say anything. He stared out the window at the far-away figures of co-eds crossing the campus toward the library. Finally, he told me I could go. So I went. He either didn't know which cadet I was or else he forgot what he wanted to see me about. It may have been that he wished to apologize for having called me the main trouble with the university; or maybe he had decided to compliment me on my brilliant drilling of the day before and then at the last minute decided not to. I don't know. I don't think about it much any more.

Analyzing Rhetorical Choices

1. Thurber does not make his point explicit. Why do you think this strategy is used? What do you think is his thesis or main idea?
2. In Thurber's narrative, there is more focus on humorous anecdotes and dramatic buildup than on reflection and analysis. What do you think of his approach to his topic?
3. How do you respond to Thurber's use of stereotyping? What is the relationship between stereotyping and humor?

Writing About Issues and Contexts

1. Given your own "university days" many years after Thurber's, do you see connections between Thurber's experiences and your own, and could or would you write about your experiences in similar fashion? Why or why not? How would your narrative differ? For what reasons?
2. Thurber is recalling events during his college life while World War I is unfolding, as he mentions briefly in his narrative. What might be the connection between his choice of humor and world events?

Of course, you would have to know much more about Thurber to give an expansive answer specific to him, but what would you speculate about the relationship between his method of rendering a story and current political events?

3. What other aspects of life at Ohio State University during World War I would you be interested in or have questions about?

Elizabeth Alexander (1962–) was born in New York City and raised in Washington, D.C. She gives numerous poetry readings and lectures widely on literature. She has taught at the University of Chicago and currently teaches at the Cave Canem Poetry Workshop and at Yale University. Volumes of her poetry include The Venus Hottentot *(1990) and* Body of Life *(1996). "Narrative: Ali" first appeared in 1994 and is included in her latest collection,* Antebellum Dream Book *(2001).*

Elizabeth Alexander

Narrative: Ali

A poem in twelve rounds

1.

My head so big
they had to pry
me out. I'm sorry
Bird (is what I call
5 my mother). Cassius
Marcellus Clay,
Muhammad Ali;
you can say
my name in any
10 language, any
continent: Ali.

2.

Two photographs
of Emmett Till,
born my year,
15 on my birthday.
One, he's smiling,
happy, and the other one
is after. His mother
did the bold thing,
20 kept the casket open,
made the thousands look upon

his bulging eyes,
his twisted neck,
her lynched black boy.
25 I couldn't sleep
for thinking,
Emmett Till.

One day I went
down to the train tracks,
30 found some iron
shoe shine rests
and planted them
between the ties
and waited
35 for a train to come,
and watched the train
derail, and ran,
and after that
I slept at night.

3.

40 I need to train
around people,
hear them talk,
talk back. I need
to hear the traffic,
45 see people in
the barbershop,
people getting
shoeshines, talking,
hear them talk,
50 talk back.

4.

Bottom line: Olympic gold
can't buy a black man
a Louisville hamburger
in nineteen-sixty.

55 Wasn't even real gold.
I watched the river
drag the ribbon down,
red, white, and blue.

        5.

Laying on the bed
60 praying for a wife,
in walk Sonji Roi.

Pretty little shape.
Do you like
chop suey?

65 Can I wash your hair
underneath
that wig?

Lay on the bed,
Girl. Lie
70 with me.

Shake to the east,
to the north,
south, west—

but remember,
75 remember, I need
a Muslim wife. So

Quit using lipstick.
Quit your boogaloo.
Cover up your knees

80 like a Muslim
wife, religion,
religion, a Muslim

wife. Eleven
months with Sonji,
85 first woman I loved.

6.

There's not
too many days
that pass that I
don't think
90 of how it started,
but I know
no Great White Hope
can beat
a true black champ.
95 Jerry Quarry
could have been
a movie star,
a millionaire,
a Senator,
100 a President—
he only had
to do one thing,
is whip me,
but he can't.

7. Dressing Room Visitor

105 He opened
up his shirt:
"KKK" cut
in his chest.
He dropped
110 his trousers:
latticed scars
where testicles
should be. His face
bewildered, frozen,
115 in the Alabama woods
that night in 1966
when they left him
for dead, his testicles
in a Dixie cup.
120 You a warning,
they told him,
to smart-mouth,

sassy-acting niggers,
meaning niggers
125 still alive,
meaning any nigger,
meaning niggers
like me.

8. Training

Unsweetened grapefruit juice
130 will melt my stomach down.
Don't drive if you can walk,
don't walk if you can run.
I add a mile each day
and run in eight-pound boots.

135 My knuckles sometimes burst
the glove. I let dead skin
build up, and then I peel it,
let it scar, so I don't bleed
as much. My bones
140 absorb the shock.

I train in three-minute
spurts, like rounds: three
rounds big bag, three speed
bag, three jump rope, one
145 minute breaks,
no more, no less.

Am I too old? Eat only
kosher meat. Eat cabbage,
carrots, beets, and watch
150 the weight come down:
two-thirty, two-twenty,
two-ten, two-oh-nine.

9.

Will I go
like Kid Paret,

155 a fractured
skull, a ten-day
sleep, dreaming
alligators, pork-
chops, saxophones,
160 slow grinds, funk,
fishbowls, lightbulbs,
bats, typewriters,
tuning forks, funk,
clocks, red rubber
165 ball, what you see
in that lifetime
knockout minute
on the cusp?
You could be
170 let go,
you could be
snatched back.

10. Rumble in the Jungle

Ali boma ye,
Ali boma ye,
175 means kill him, Ali,
which is different
from a whupping
which is what I give,
but I lead them chanting
180 anyway, *Ali*
boma ye, because
here in Africa
black people fly
planes and run countries.

185 I'm still making up
for the foolishness
I said when I was
Clay from Louisville,
where I learned Africans
190 lived naked in straw
huts eating tiger meat,

grunting and grinning,
swinging from vines,
pounding their chests—

195 I pound my chest but of my own accord.

    11.

I said to Joe Frazier,
first thing, get a good house
in case you get crippled
so you and your family
200 can sleep somewhere. Always
keep one good Cadillac.
And watch how you dress
with that cowboy hat,
pink suits, white shoes—
205 that's how pimps dress,
or kids, and you a champ,
or wish you were, 'cause
I can whip you in the ring
or whip you in the street.
210 Now back to clothes,
wear dark clothes, suits,
black suits, like you the best
at what you do, like you
President of the World.
215 Dress like that.
Put them yellow pants away.

We dinosaurs gotta
look good, gotta sound
good, gotta be good,
220 the greatest, that's what
I told Joe Frazier,
and he said to me,
we both bad niggers.
We don't do no crawlin'.

    12.

225 They called me "the fistic pariah."

They said I didn't love my country,
called me a race-hater, called me out
of my name, waited for me
to come out on a streetcar, shot at me,
230 hexed me, cursed me, wished me
all manner of ill-will,
told me I was finished.

Here I am,
like the song says,
235 *come and take me,*

"The People's Champ,"

myself,
Muhammad.

Analyzing Rhetorical Choices

1. The poet is employing the first-person point of view to tell a story about Muhammad Ali. In what ways is this an effective strategy? What might the effect have been if Alexander had given the same basic information in a third-person poem or in an essay about Ali?

2. "Rounds" three and seven feature repetition. What special effect, if any, does this have? Do you see it as an effective rhetorical device? Why or why not?

3. In round five, the poet writes "in walk Sonji Roi." In round seven, she writes, "You a warning." These are both examples of African American Vernacular English. In the first instance, the poet is adhering to a rule that allows no distinction for third-person-singular use of the verb, as required in Standard English ("in walk*s* Sonji Roi"). The second construction is an example of *zero copula*, or the absence of a form of the helping verb *to be* (not the standard "you *are* a warning") when the action is not reoccurring or the assertion is one of all-time truth not related to reoccurring events. Do these vernacular uses of language add anything to the poem, in your view? Explain your response. What would you say about the vernacular use of language in general?

4. What is Alexander's argument about Ali? What impression is she trying to make?

Writing About Issues and Contexts

1. We get a sense of Ali's career unfolding against the backdrop of the Civil Rights movement. What is the relationship of his career to the movement? What does Alexander do to make this aspect of the narrative interesting? What do you think of Ali's advice to Joe Frazier?

2. Why is keeping the casket open, as Emmett Till's mother did, the "bold thing" and seemingly the right thing?

The daughter of Chinese immigrants, **Amy Tan** *(1952–) was born in Oakland, California. She grew up mainly in Northern California but finished high school in Switzerland. Once back in the United States, she studied English and linguistics, eventually earning a master's degree in linguistics from San Jose State University and taking doctoral courses at Berkeley. She worked with children with disabilities and ran her own communications business before turning to a writing career in the mid-1980s. Her novels include* The Joy Luck Club *(1989), for which she received the National Book Award;* The Kitchen God's Wife *(1991);* The Hundred Secret Senses *(1995); and* The Bonesetter's Daughter *(2001). The essay in this chapter was first published in 1990.*

Amy Tan

Mother Tongue

I am not a scholar of English or literature. I cannot give you much more than personal opinions on the English language and its variations in this country or others.

I am a writer. And by that definition, I am someone who has always loved language. I am fascinated by language in daily life. I spend a great deal of my time thinking about the power of language—the way it can evoke an emotion, a visual image, a complex idea, or a simple truth. Language is the tool of my trade. And I use them all—all the Englishes I grew up with.

Recently, I was made keenly aware of the different Englishes I do use. I was giving a talk to a large group of people, the same talk I had already given to half a dozen other groups. The nature of the talk was about my writing, my life, and my book, *The Joy Luck Club.* The talk was going along well enough, until I remembered one major difference that made the whole talk sound wrong. My mother was in the room. And it was perhaps the first time she had heard me give a lengthy speech, using the kind of English I have never used with her. I was saying things like, "The intersection of memory upon imagination" and "There is an aspect of my fiction that relates to thus-and-thus"—a speech filled with carefully wrought grammatical phrases, burdened, it suddenly seemed to me, with nominalized forms, past perfect tenses, conditional phrases, all the forms of standard English that I had learned in school and through books, the forms of English I did not use at home with my mother.

Just last week, I was walking down the street with my mother, and I again found myself conscious of the English I was using, the English I do use with her. We were talking about the price of new and used furniture and I heard myself saying this: "Not waste money that way." My husband was with us as well, and he didn't notice any switch in my English. And then I realized why. It's because over the twenty years we've been together I've often used that same kind of English with him, and sometimes he even uses it with me. It has become our language of intimacy, a different sort of English that relates to family talk, the language I grew up with.

5   So you'll have some idea of what this family talk I heard sounds like, I'll quote what my mother said during a recent conversation which I videotaped and then transcribed. During this conversation, my mother was talking about a political gangster in Shanghai who had the same last name as her family's, Du, and how the gangster in his early years wanted to be adopted by her family, which was rich by comparison. Later, the gangster became more powerful, far richer than my mother's family, and one day showed up at my mother's wedding to pay his respects. Here's what she said in part: "Du Yusong having business like fruit stand. Like off the street kind. He is Du like Du Zong—but not Tsung-ming Island people. The local people call pu-tong, the river east side, he belong to that side local people. That man want to ask Du Zong father take him in like become own family. Du Zong father wasn't look down on him, but didn't take seriously, until that man big like become a mafia. Now important person, very hard to inviting him. Chinese way, came only to show respect, don't stay for dinner. Respect for making big celebration, he shows up. Mean gives lots of respect Chinese custom. Chinese social life that way. If too important won't have to stay too long. He come to my wedding. I didn't see, I heard it. I gone to boy's side, they have YMCA dinner. Chinese age I was nineteen."

You should know that my mother's expressive command of English belies how much she actually understands. She reads the *Forbes* report, listens to *Wall Street Week*, converses daily with her stockbroker, reads all of Shirley MacLaine's books with ease—all kinds of things I can't begin to understand. Yet some of my friends tell me they understand 50 percent of what my mother says. Some say they understand 80 to 90 percent. Some say they understand none of it, as if she were speaking pure Chinese. But to me, my mother's

English is perfectly clear, perfectly natural. It's my mother tongue. Her language, as I hear it, is vivid, direct, full of observation and imagery. That was the language that helped shape the way I saw things, expressed things, made sense of the world.

Lately, I've been giving more thought to the kind of English my mother speaks. Like others, I have described it to people as "broken" or "fractured" English. But I wince when I say that. It has always bothered me that I can think of no way to describe it other than "broken," as if it were damaged and needed to be fixed, as if it lacked a certain wholeness and soundness. I've heard other terms used, "limited English," for example. But they seem just as bad, as if everything is limited, including people's perceptions of the limited English speaker.

I know this for a fact, because when I was growing up, my mother's "limited" English limited *my* perception of her. I was ashamed of her English. I believed that her English reflected the quality of what she had to say. That is, because she expressed them imperfectly her thoughts were imperfect. And I had plenty of empirical evidence to support me: the fact that people in department stores, at banks, and at restaurants did not take her seriously, did not give her good service, pretended not to understand her, or even acted as if they did not hear her.

My mother has long realized the limitations of her English as well. When I was fifteen, she used to have me call people on the phone to pretend I was she. In this guise, I was forced to ask for information or even to complain and yell at people who had been rude to her. One time it was a call to her stockbroker in New York. She had cashed out her small portfolio and it just so happened we were going to go to New York the next week, our very first trip outside California. I had to get on the phone and say in an adolescent voice that was not very convincing, "This is Mrs. Tan."

10   And my mother was standing in the back whispering loudly, "Why he don't send me check, already two weeks late. So mad he lie to me, losing me money."

And then I said in perfect English, "Yes, I'm getting rather concerned. You had agreed to send the check two weeks ago, but it hasn't arrived."

Then she began to talk more loudly. "What he want, I come to New York tell him front of his boss, you cheating me?" And I was trying to calm her down, make her be quiet, while telling the stockbroker, "I can't tolerate any more excuses. If I don't receive the check immediately, I am going to have to speak to your manager when I'm in New York next week." And sure enough, the following week there we were in front of this astonished stockbroker, and I was sitting there red-faced and quiet, and my mother, the real Mrs. Tan, was shouting at his boss in her impeccable broken English.

We used a similar routine just five days ago, for a situation that was far less humorous. My mother had gone to the hospital for an appointment, to find out about a benign brain tumor a CAT scan had revealed a month ago. She said she had spoken very good English, her best English, no mistakes. Still, she said, the hospital did not apologize when they said they had lost the CAT scan and she had come for nothing. She said they did not seem to have any sympathy when she told them she was anxious to know the exact diagnosis, since her husband and son had both died of brain tumors. She said they would not give her any more information until the next time and she would have to make another appointment for that. So she said she would not leave until the doctor called her daughter. She wouldn't budge. And when the doctor finally called her daughter, me, who spoke in perfect English—lo and behold—we had assurances the CAT scan would be found, promises that a conference call on Monday would be held, and apologies for any suffering my mother had gone through for a most regrettable mistake.

I think my mother's English almost had an effect on limiting my possibilities in life as well. Sociologists and linguists probably will tell you that a person's developing language skills are more influenced by peers. But I do think that the language spoken in the family, especially in immigrant families which are more insular, plays a large role in shaping the language of the child. And I believe that it affected my results on achievement tests, IQ tests, and the SAT. While my English skills were never judged as poor, compared to math, English could not be considered my strong suit. In grade school I did moderately well, getting perhaps B's, sometimes B-pluses, in English and scoring perhaps in the sixtieth or seventieth percentile on achievement tests. But those scores were not good enough to override the opinion that my true abilities lay in math and science, because in those areas I achieved A's and scored in the ninetieth percentile or higher.

15   This was understandable. Math is precise; there is only one correct answer. Whereas, for me at least, the answers on English tests were always a judgment call, a matter of opinion and personal experience. Those tests were constructed around items like fill-in-the-blank sentence completion, such as, "Even though Tom was ___, Mary thought he was ___." And the correct answer always seemed to be the most

bland combinations of thoughts, for example, "Even though Tom was shy, Mary thought he was charming," with the grammatical structure "even though" limiting the correct answer to some sort of semantic opposites, so you wouldn't get answers like, "Even though Tom was foolish, Mary thought he was ridiculous." Well, according to my mother, there were very few limitations as to what Tom could have been and what Mary might have thought of him. So I never did well on tests like that.

The same was true with word analogies, pairs of words in which you were supposed to find some sort of logical, semantic relationship—for example, "*Sunset* is to *nightfall* as ____ is to ____." And here you would be presented with a list of four possible pairs, one of which showed the same kind of relationship: *red* is to *stoplight, bus* is to *arrival, chills* is to *fever, yawn* is to *boring.* Well, I could never think that way. I knew what the tests were asking, but I could not block out of my mind the images already created by the first pair, "*sunset* is to *nightfall*"—and I would see a burst of colors against a darkening sky, the moon rising, the lowering of a curtain of stars. And all the other pairs of words—red, bus, stoplight, boring—just threw up a mass of confusing images, making it impossible for me to sort out something as logical as saying: "A sunset precedes nightfall" is the same as "a chill precedes a fever." The only way I would have gotten that answer right would have been to imagine an associative situation, for example, my being disobedient and staying out past sunset, catching a chill at night, which turns into feverish pneumonia as punishment, which indeed did happen to me.

I have been thinking about all this lately, about my mother's English, about achievement tests. Because lately I've been asked, as a writer, why there are not more Asian Americans represented in American literature. Why are there few Asian Americans enrolled in creative writing programs? Why do so many Chinese students go into engineering? Well, these are broad sociological questions I can't begin to answer. But I have noticed in surveys—in fact, just last week—that Asian students, as a whole, always do significantly better on math achievement tests than in English. And this makes me think that there are other Asian-American students whose English spoken in the home might also be described as "broken" or "limited." And perhaps they also have teachers who are steering them away from writing and into math and science, which is what happened to me.

Fortunately, I happened to be rebellious in nature and enjoy the challenge of disproving assumptions made about me. I became an

English major my first year in college, after being enrolled as premed. I started writing nonfiction as a freelancer the week after I was told by my former boss that writing was my worst skill and I should hone my talents toward account management.

But it wasn't until 1985 that I finally began to write fiction. And at first I wrote using what I thought to be wittily crafted sentences, sentences that would finally prove I had mastery over the English language. Here's an example from the first draft of a story that later made its way into *The Joy Luck Club*, but without this line: "That was my mental quandary in its nascent state." A terrible line, which I can barely pronounce.

20   Fortunately, for reasons I won't get into today, I later decided I should envision a reader for the stories I would write. And the reader I decided upon was my mother, because these were stories about mothers. So with this reader in mind—and in fact she did read my early drafts—I began to write stories using all the Englishes I grew up with: the English I spoke to my mother, which for lack of a better term might be described as "simple"; the English she used with me, which for lack of a better term might be described as "broken"; my translation of her Chinese, which could certainly be described as "watered down"; and what I imagined to be her translation of her Chinese if she could speak in perfect English, her internal language, and for that I sought to preserve the essence, but neither an English nor a Chinese structure. I wanted to capture what language ability tests can never reveal: her intent, her passion, her imagery, the rhythms of her speech and the nature of her thoughts.

Apart from what any critic had to say about my writing, I knew I had succeeded where it counted when my mother finished reading my book and gave me her verdict: "So easy to read."

Analyzing Rhetorical Choices

1.   As noted previously, Tan declares that in her writing she uses all the Englishes she grew up with. In this essay, she uses her mother's language as dialogue, which makes the dialogue realistic. Her mother's language is in a frame, however, separate from the words that are outside of quotation marks. How might Tan have used her mother tongue in the rest of the piece? Comment on whether or not this would have been effective.

2.   Tan uses anecdotes to illustrate how language prejudice operates in hospitals, education, and the business world. How persuasive do you find Tan's anecdotes?

3. Concerning English and literature, Tan writes that, because she is not a scholar, she "cannot give you much more than personal opinions." We know that Tan holds a graduate degree in language study. What is the effect, then, of her claiming not to be a scholar?

Writing About Issues and Contexts

1. Tan writes of her mother's language, "That was the language that helped shape the way I saw things, expressed things, made sense of the world." Can you give examples of how and why your native language variety influences your view of the world?
2. Tan uses her Englishes to write professionally. In your estimation, can her approach be applied in the classroom? Explain your response.
3. Tan mentions that large numbers of Chinese students go into engineering. Have you been aware of or had any personal experience with particular groups of students being steered in a specific academic direction? Why do you think this occurs?

George Orwell (1903–1950) was the pen name of Eric Arthur Blair. He was born in India, where his father served as a British civil servant while India was under British rule. Orwell was raised and educated in England before joining the Indian Imperial Police and serving in Burma (now Myanmar), a land in Southeast Asia also under British control. As opposition to British colonialism stirred within him, he left the police and returned to Europe. He wrote prolifically and was also active politically, fighting in the Spanish Civil War against fascism. Orwell is best known for his novels Animal Farm *(1946) and* 1984 *(1949), both warnings about the dangers of totalitarian regimes. His nonfiction has been gathered in* Collected Essays, Journalism, and Letters *(1968). The following essay was written in 1936.*

George Orwell
Shooting an Elephant

In Moulmein, in Lower Burma, I was hated by large numbers of people—the only time in my life that I have been important enough for this to happen to me. I was sub-divisional police officer of the town, and in an aimless, petty kind of way anti-European feeling was very bitter. No one had the guts to raise a riot, but if a European woman went through the bazaars alone somebody would probably spit betel juice over her dress. As a police officer I was an obvious target and was baited whenever it seemed safe to do so. When a nimble Burman tripped me up on the football field and the referee (another Burman) looked the other way, the crowd yelled with hideous laughter. This happened more than once. In the end the sneering yellow faces of young men that met me everywhere, the insults hooted after me when I was at a safe distance, got badly on my nerves. The young Buddhist priests were the worst of all. There were several thousands of them in the town and none of them seemed to have anything to do except stand on street corners and jeer at Europeans.

All this was perplexing and upsetting. For at the time I had already made up my mind that imperialism was an evil thing and the sooner I chucked up my job and got out of it the better. Theoretically—and secretly, of course—I was all for the Burmese and all against their oppressors, the British. As for the job I was doing, I hated it more bitterly than I can perhaps make clear. In a job like that you see the dirty work of Empire at close quarters. The wretched prisoners huddling in the stinking cages of the lockups, the grey, cowed faces of the long-term convicts, the scarred buttocks of the men who had been flogged with bamboos—all these oppressed me with an intolerable sense of guilt. But I could get nothing into perspective. I was young and ill-educated and I had had to think out my problems in the utter silence that is imposed on every Englishman in the East. I did not even know that the British Empire is dying, still less did I know that it is a great deal better than the younger empires that are going to supplant it. All I knew was that I was stuck between my hatred of the empire I served and my rage against the evil-spirited little beasts who tried to make my job impossible. With one part of my mind I thought of the British Raj as an unbreakable tyranny, as something clamped down, in *saecula saeculorum*,* upon the will of prostrate peoples; with another part I thought that the greatest joy in the world would be to drive a bayonet into a Buddhist priest's guts. Feelings like these are the normal by-products of imperialism; ask any Anglo-Indian official, if you can catch him off duty.

One day something happened which in a roundabout way was enlightening. It was a tiny incident in itself, but it gave me a better glimpse than I had had before of the real nature of imperialism—the real motives for which despotic governments act. Early one morning the sub-inspector at a police station the other end of the town rang me up on the phone and said that an elephant was ravaging the bazaar. Would I please come and do something about it? I did not know what I could do, but I wanted to see what was happening and I got on to a pony and started out. I took my rifle, an old .44 Winchester and much too small to kill an elephant, but I thought the noise might be useful *in terrorem*. Various Burmans stopped me on the way and told me about the elephant's doings. It was not, of course, a wild elephant, but a tame one which had gone "must."† It had been chained up, as tame elephants always are when their attack of "must" is due, but on the previous night it had broken its chain and escaped. Its mahout,‡ the only person who could manage it when it was in that state, had set out in pursuit, but had taken the wrong direction and was now twelve hours' journey away, and in the morning the elephant had suddenly

---

*From the beginning of time.
†Gone beserk.
‡Elephant handler.

reappeared in the town. The Burmese population had no weapons and were quite helpless against it. It had already destroyed somebody's bamboo hut, killed a cow, and raided some fruit-stalls and devoured the stock; also it had met the municipal rubbish van and, when the driver jumped out and took to his heels, had turned the van over and inflicted violences upon it.

The Burmese sub-inspector and some Indian constables were waiting for me in the quarter where the elephant had been seen. It was a very poor quarter, a labyrinth of squalid bamboo huts, thatched with palm-leaf, winding all over a steep hillside. I remember that it was a cloudy, stuffy morning at the beginning of the rains. We began questioning people as to where the elephant had gone, and, as usual, failed to get any definite information. That is invariably the case in the East; a story always sounds clear enough at a distance, but the nearer you get to the scene of events the vaguer it becomes. Some of the people said that the elephant had gone in one direction, some said that he had gone in another, some professed not even to have heard of an elephant. I had almost made up my mind that the whole story was a pack of lies, when we heard yells a little distance away. There was a loud, scandalized cry of "Go away, child! Go away this instant!" and an old woman with a switch in her hand came round the corner of a hut, violently shooing away a crowd of naked children. Some more women followed, clicking their tongues and exclaiming; evidently there was something that the children ought not to have seen. I rounded the hut and saw a man's dead body sprawling in the mud. He was an Indian, a black Dravidian coolie, almost naked, and he could not have been dead many minutes. The people said that the elephant had come suddenly upon him round the corner of the hut, caught him with its trunk, put its foot on his back, and ground him into the earth. This was the rainy season and the ground was soft, and his face had scored a trench a foot deep and a couple of yards long. He was lying on his belly with arms crucified and head sharply twisted to one side. His face was coated with mud, the eyes wide open, the teeth bared and grinning with an expression of unendurable agony. (Never tell me, by the way, that the dead look peaceful. Most of the corpses I have seen looked devilish.) The friction of the great beast's foot had stripped the skin from his back as neatly as one skins a rabbit. As soon as I saw the dead man I sent an orderly to a friend's house nearby to borrow an elephant rifle. I had already sent back the pony, not wanting it to go mad with fright and throw me if it smelled the elephant.

5   The orderly came back in a few minutes with a rifle and five cartridges, and meanwhile some Burmans had arrived and told us that

the elephant was in the paddy fields below, only a few hundred yards away. As I started forward practically the whole population of the quarter flocked out of the houses and followed me. They had seen the rifle and were all shouting excitedly that I was going to shoot the elephant. They had not shown much interest in the elephant when he was merely ravaging their homes, but it was different now that he was going to be shot. It was a bit of fun to them, as it would be to an English crowd; besides they wanted the meat. It made me vaguely uneasy. I had no intention of shooting the elephant—I had merely sent for the rifle to defend myself if necessary—and it is always unnerving to have a crowd following you. I marched down the hill, looking and feeling a fool, with the rifle over my shoulder and an ever-growing army of people jostling at my heels. At the bottom, when you got away from the huts, there was a metalled road and beyond that a miry waste of paddy fields a thousand yards across, not yet ploughed but soggy from the first rains and dotted with coarse grass. The elephant was standing eight yards from the road, his left side towards us. He took not the slightest notice of the crowd's approach. He was tearing up bunches of grass, beating them against his knees to clean them and stuffing them into his mouth.

I had halted on the road. As soon as I saw the elephant I knew with perfect certainty that I ought not to shoot him. It is a serious matter to shoot a working elephant—it is comparable to destroying a huge and costly piece of machinery—and obviously one ought not to do it if it can possibly be avoided. And at that distance, peacefully eating, the elephant looked no more dangerous than a cow. I thought then and I think now that his attack of "must" was already passing off; in which case he would merely wander harmlessly about until the mahout came back and caught him. Moreover, I did not in the least want to shoot him. I decided that I would watch him for a little while to make sure that he did not turn savage again, and then go home.

But at that moment I glanced around at the crowd that had followed me. It was an immense crowd, two thousand at the least and growing every minute. It blocked the road for a long distance on either side. I looked at the sea of yellow faces above the garish clothes—faces all happy and excited over this bit of fun, all certain that the elephant was going to be shot. They were watching me as they would watch a conjurer about to perform a trick. They did not like me, but with the magical rifle in my hands I was momentarily worth watching. And suddenly I realized that I should have to shoot the elephant after all. The people expected it of me and I had got to do it; I could feel their two thousand wills pressing me forward, irresistibly. And it was at this moment, as I stood there with the rifle in my hands, that I first grasped the hollowness, the futility of the white man's dominion in the East. Here was I, the white man with his gun, standing in front of the unarmed native crowd—seemingly the leading actor of the piece; but in reality I was only an absurd puppet pushed to and fro by the will of those yellow faces behind. I perceived in this moment that when the white man turns tyrant it is his own freedom that he destroys. He becomes a sort of hollow, posing dummy, the conventionalized figure of a sahib.* For it is the condition of his rule that he shall spend his life in trying to impress the "natives," and so in every crisis he has got to do what the "natives" expect of him. He wears a mask, and his face grows to fit it. I had got to shoot the elephant. I had committed myself to doing it when I sent for the rifle. A sahib has got to act like a sahib; he has got to appear resolute, to know his own mind and do definite things. To come all that way, rifle in hand, with two thousand people marching at my heels, and then to trail feebly away, having done nothing—no, that was impossible. The crowd would laugh at me. And my whole life, every white man's life in the East, was one long struggle not to be laughed at.

But I did not want to shoot the elephant. I watched him beating his bunch of grass against his knees, with the preoccupied grandmotherly air that elephants have. It seemed to me that it would be murder to shoot him. At that age I was not squeamish about killing animals, but I had never shot an elephant and never wanted to. (Somehow it always seems worse to kill a *large* animal.) Besides, there was the beast's owner to be considered. Alive, the elephant was worth at least a hundred pounds; dead, he would only be worth the value of his tusks, five pounds, possibly. But I had got to act quickly. I turned to some experienced-looking Burmans who had been there when we arrived, and asked them how the elephant had been behaving. They all said the same thing: he took no notice of you if you left him alone, but he might charge if you went too close to him.

It was perfectly clear to me what I ought to do. I ought to walk up to within, say, twenty-five yards of the elephant and test his behavior. If he charged I could shoot, if he took no notice of me it would be safe to leave him until the mahout came back. But also I knew that I was going to do no such thing. I was a poor shot with a rifle and the

---

*An official.

ground was soft mud into which one would sink at every step. If the elephant charged and I missed him, I should have about as much chance as a toad under a steamroller. But even then I was not thinking particularly of my own skin, only of the watchful yellow faces behind. For at that moment, with the crowd watching me, I was not afraid in the ordinary sense, as I would have been if I had been alone. A white man mustn't be frightened in front of "natives"; and so, in general, he isn't frightened. The sole thought in my mind was that if anything went wrong those two thousand Burmans would see me pursued, caught, trampled on, and reduced to a grinning corpse like that Indian up the hill. And if that happened it was quite probable that some of them would laugh. That would never do. There was only one alternative. I shoved the cartridges into the magazine and lay down on the road to get a better aim.

10   The crowd drew very still, and a deep, low, happy sigh, as of people who see the theatre curtain go up at last, breathed from innumerable throats. They were going to have their bit of fun after all. The rifle was a beautiful German thing with cross-hair sights. I did not then know that in shooting an elephant one would shoot to cut an imaginary bar running from ear-hole to ear-hole. I ought, therefore, as the elephant was sideways on, to have aimed straight at his ear-hole; actually I aimed several inches in front of this, thinking the brain would be further forward.

When I pulled the trigger I did not hear the bang or feel the kick—one never does when a shot goes home—but I heard the devilish roar of glee that went up from the crowd. In that instant, in too short a time, one would have thought, even for the bullet to get there, a mysterious, terrible change had come over the elephant. He neither stirred nor fell, but every line on his body had altered. He looked suddenly stricken, shrunken, immensely old, as though the frightful impact of the bullet had paralyzed him without knocking him down. At last, after what seemed a long time—it might have been five seconds, I dare say—he sagged flabbily to his knees. His mouth slobbered. An enormous senility seemed to have settled upon him. One could have imagined him thousands of years old. I fired again into the same spot. At the second shot he did not collapse but climbed with desperate slowness to his feet and stood weakly upright, with legs sagging and head drooping. I fired a third time. That was the shot that did for him. You could see the agony of it jolt his whole body and knock the last remnant of strength from his legs. But in falling he seemed for a moment to rise, for as his hind legs collapsed beneath him he seemed to tower upwards like a huge rock toppling, his trunk reaching skywards like a tree. He trumpeted, for the first and only time. And then down he came, his belly towards me, with a crash that seemed to shake the ground even where I lay.

I got up. The Burmans were already racing past me across the mud. It was obvious that the elephant would never rise again, but he was not dead. He was breathing very rhythmically with long rattling gasps, his great mound of a side painfully rising and falling. His mouth was wide open—I could see far down into the caverns of pale pink throat. I waited a long time for him to die, but his breathing did not weaken. Finally, I fired my two remaining shots into the spot where I thought his heart must be. The thick blood welled out of him like red velvet, but still he did not die. His body did not even jerk when the shots hit him, the tortured breathing continued without a pause. He was dying, very slowly and in great agony, but in some world remote from me where not even a bullet could damage him further. I felt that I had got to put an end to that dreadful noise. It seemed dreadful to see the great beast lying there, powerless to move and yet powerless to die, and not even to be able to finish him. I sent back for my small rifle and poured shot after shot into his heart and down his throat. They seemed to make no impression. The tortured gasps continued as steadily as the ticking of a clock.

In the end I could not stand it any longer and went away. I heard later that it took him half an hour to die. Burmans were bringing dahs* and baskets even before I left, and I was told they had stripped his body almost to the bones by the afternoon.

Afterwards, of course, there were endless discussions about the shooting of the elephant. The owner was furious, but he was only an Indian and could do nothing. Besides, legally I had done the right thing, for a mad elephant has to be killed, like a mad dog, if its owner fails to control it. Among the Europeans opinion was divided. The older men said I was right, the younger men said it was a damn shame to shoot an elephant for killing a coolie, because an elephant was worth more than any damn Coringhee coolie. And afterwards I was very glad that the coolie had been killed; it put me legally in the right and it gave me a sufficient pretext for shooting the elephant. I often wondered whether any of the others grasped that I had done it solely to avoid looking a fool.

---

*Knives.

Analyzing Rhetorical Choices

1. The point of Orwell's narrative is to provide insight into the "real nature of imperialism." How does Orwell do this? Consider language use, organization, and selection of details. What might a Burmese perspective be?
2. The Burmese man who was killed by the elephant is described as both crucified and devilish, terms that don't normally go together in our culture. What point do you think Orwell is making with this description?

Writing About Issues and Contexts

1. Orwell seems to be arguing, in part, that imperialism has severe effects on the imperialists themselves. What are these effects? Is it proper to speak of the rulers as victims? Why or why not? In what other situations can the power structure be said to suffer?
2. Although sympathetic to the political plight of the natives, Orwell still thinks of deriving pleasure from stabbing a Buddhist priest. How is his impulse connected to language deprivation, that is, a situation where, as Orwell describes it, there was "silence imposed on every Englishman in the East"?

A native of San Francisco, California, **Shirley Jackson** *(1919–1965) attended the University of Rochester and Syracuse University. At Syracuse, she became the fiction editor of* The Syracusan, *a campus magazine. With her future husband, critic Stanley Edgar Hyman, she cofounded a second campus publication,* The Spectre. *Jackson is widely known for her suspenseful short stories and novels. Her most famous story is "The Lottery." Her novels include* The Haunting of Hill House *(1959), which was the basis for a successful movie titled* The Haunting. *A mother of four, she also wrote memoirs about her domestic life,* Life Among the Savages *(1953) and* Raising Demons *(1957).*

Shirley Jackson

Seven Types of Ambiguity

The basement room of the bookstore seemed to be enormous; it stretched in long rows of books off into dimness at either end, with books lined in tall bookcases along the walls, and books standing in piles on the floor. At the foot of the spiral staircase winding down from the neat small store upstairs, Mr. Harris, owner and sales-clerk of the bookstore, had a small desk, cluttered with catalogues, lighted by one dirty overhead lamp. The same lamp served to light the shelves which crowded heavily around Mr. Harris' desk; farther away, along the lines of book tables, there were other dirty overhead lamps, to be lighted by pulling a string and turned off by the customer when he was ready to grope his way back to Mr. Harris' desk, pay for his purchases and have them wrapped. Mr. Harris, who knew the position of any author or any title in all the heavy shelves, had one customer at the moment, a boy of about eighteen, who was standing far down the long room directly under one of the lamps, leafing through a book he had selected from the shelves. It was cold in the big basement room; both Mr. Harris and the boy had their coats on. Occasionally Mr. Harris got up from his desk to put a meagre shovelful of coal on a small iron stove which stood in the curve of the staircase. Except when Mr. Harris got up, or the boy turned to put a book back into the shelves and take out another, the room was quiet, the books standing silent in the dim light.

Then the silence was broken by the sound of the door opening in the little upstairs bookshop where Mr. Harris kept his best-sellers and art books on display. There was the sound of voices, while both Mr. Harris and the boy listened, and then the girl who took care of the up-stairs bookshop said, "Right on down the stairs. Mr. Harris will help you."

Mr. Harris got up and walked around to the foot of the stairs, turning on another of the overhead lamps so that his new customer would be able to see his way down. The boy put his book back in the shelves and stood with his hand on the back of it, still listening.

When Mr. Harris saw that it was a woman coming down the stairs he stood back politely and said, "Watch the bottom step. There's one more than people think." The woman stepped carefully down and stood looking around. While she stood there a man came carefully around the turn in the staircase, ducking his head so his hat would clear the low ceiling. "Watch the bottom step," the woman said in a soft clear voice. The man came down beside her and raised his head to look around as she had.

5   "Quite a lot of books you have here," he said.

Mr. Harris smiled his professional smile. "Can I help you?"

The woman looked at the man, and he hesitated a minute and then said, "We want to get some books. Quite a few of them." He waved his hand inclusively. "Sets of books."

"Well, if it's books you want," Mr. Harris said, and smiled again. "Maybe the lady would like to come over and sit down?" He led the way around to his desk, the woman following him and the man walk-ing uneasily between the tables of books, his hands close to his sides as though he were afraid of breaking something. Mr. Harris gave the lady his desk chair and then sat down on the edge of his desk, shoving aside a pile of catalogues.

"This is a very interesting place," the lady said, in the same soft voice she had used when she spoke before. She was middle-aged and nicely dressed; all her clothes were fairly new, but quiet and well planned for her age and air of shyness. The man was big and hearty-looking, his face reddened by the cold air and his big hands holding a pair of wool gloves uneasily.

10   "We'd like to buy some of your books," the man said. "Some good books."

"Anything in particular?" Mr. Harris asked.

The man laughed loudly, but with embarrassment. "Tell the truth," he said, "I sound sort of foolish, now. But I don't know much about these things, like books." In the large quiet store his voice seemed to echo, after his wife's soft voice and Mr. Harris'. "We were sort of hoping you'd be able to tell us," he said. "None of this trash they turn out nowadays." He cleared this throat. "Something like Dickens," he said.

"Dickens," Mr. Harris said.

"I used to read Dickens when I was a kid," the man said. "Books like that, now, good books." He looked up as the boy who had been standing off among the books came over to them. "I'd like to read Dickens again," the big man said.

15 "Mr. Harris," the boy asked quietly.

Mr. Harris looked up. "Yes, Mr. Clark?" he said.

The boy came closer to the desk, as though unwilling to interrupt Mr. Harris with his customers. "I'd like to take another look at the Empson," he said.

Mr. Harris turned to the glass-doored bookcase immediately behind his desk and selected a book. "Here it is," he said, "You'll have it read through before you buy it at this rate." He smiled at the big man and his wife. "Some day he's going to come in and buy that book," he said, "and I'm going to go out of business from shock."

The boy turned away, holding the book, and the big man leaned forward to Mr. Harris. "I figure I'd like two good sets, big, like Dickens," he said, "and then a couple of smaller sets."

20 "And a copy of *Jane Eyre*," his wife said, in her soft voice. "I used to love that book," she said to Mr. Harris.

"I can let you have a very nice set of the Brontës," Mr. Harris said. "Beautiful binding."

"I want them to look nice," the man said, "but solid, for reading. I'm going to read through all of Dickens again."

The boy came back to the desk, holding the book out to Mr. Harris. "It still looks good," he said.

"It's right here when you want it," Mr. Harris said, turning back to the bookcase with the book. "It's pretty scarce, that book."

25 "I guess it'll be here a while longer," the boy said.

"What's the name of this book?" the big man asked curiously.

"*Seven Types of Ambiguity*," the boy said. "It's quite a good book."

"There's a fine name for a book," the big man said to Mr. Harris. "Pretty smart young fellow, reading books with names like that."

"It's a good book," the boy repeated.

30 "I'm trying to buy some books myself," the big man said to the boy. "I want to catch up on a few I've missed. Dickens, I've always liked his books."

"Meredith is good," the boy said. "You ever try reading Meredith?"

"Meredith," the big man said. "Let's see a few of your books," he said to Mr. Harris. "I'd sort of like to pick out a few I want."

"Can I take the gentleman down there?" the boy said to Mr. Harris. "I've got to go back anyway to get my hat."

"I'll go with the young man and look at the books, Mother," the big man said to his wife. "You stay here and keep warm."

35   "Fine," Mr. Harris said. "He knows where the books are as well as I do," he said to the big man.

The boy started off down the aisle between the book tables, and the big man followed, still walking carefully, trying not to touch anything. They went down past the lamp still burning where the boy had left his hat and gloves, and the boy turned on another lamp further down. "Mr. Harris keeps most of his sets around here," the boy said. "Let's see what we can find." He squatted down in front of the bookcases, touching the backs of the rows of books lightly with his fingers. "How do you feel about the prices?" he asked.

"I'm willing to pay a reasonable amount for the books I have in mind," the big man said. He touched the book in front of him experimentally, with one finger. "A hundred and fifty, two hundred dollars altogether."

The boy looked up at him and laughed. "That ought to get you some nice books," he said.

"Never saw so many books in my life," the big man said. "I never thought I'd see the day when I'd just walk into a bookstore and buy up all the books I always wanted to read."

40   "It's a good feeling."

"I never got a chance to read much," the man said. "Went right into the machine-shop where my father worked when I was much younger than you, and worked ever since. Now all of a sudden I find I have a little more money than I used to, and Mother and I decided we'd like to get ourselves a few things we always wanted."

"Your wife was interested in the Brontës," the boy said. "Here's a very good set."

The man leaned down to look at the books the boy pointed out. "I don't know much about these things," he said. "They look nice, all alike. What's the next set?"

"Carlyle," the boy said. "You can skip him. He's not quite what you're looking for. Meredith is good. And Thackeray. I think you'd want Thackeray; he's a great writer."

45   The man took one of the books the boy handed him and opened it carefully, using only two fingers from each of his big hands. "This looks fine," he said.

"I'll write them down," the boy said. He took a pencil and a pocket memorandum from his coat pocket. "Brontës," he said, "Dickens, Meredith, Thackeray." He ran his hand along each of the sets as he read them off.

The big man narrowed his eyes. "I ought to take one more," he said. "These won't quite fill up the bookcase I got for them."

"Jane Austen," the boy said. "Your wife would be pleased with that."

"You read all these books?" the man asked.

50   "Most of them," the boy said.

The man was quiet for a minute and then he went on, "I never got much of a chance to read anything, going to work so early. I've got a lot to catch up on."

"You're going to have a fine time," the boy said.

"That book you had a while back," the man said. "What was that book?"

"It's aesthetics," the boy said. "About literature. It's very scarce. I've been trying to buy it for quite a while and haven't had the money."

55   "You go to college?" the man asked.

"Yes."

"Here's one I ought to read again," the man said. "Mark Twain. I read a couple of his books when I was a kid. But I guess I have enough to start on." He stood up.

The boy rose too, smiling. "You're going to have to do a lot of reading."

"I like to read," the man said. "I really like to read."

60   He started back down the aisles, going straight for Mr. Harris' desk. The boy turned off the lamps and followed, stopping to get his hat and gloves. When the big man reached Mr. Harris' desk he said to his wife, "That's sure a smart kid. He knows those books right and left."

"Did you pick out what you want?" his wife asked.

"The kid has a fine list for me." He turned to Mr. Harris and went on, "It's quite an experience seeing a kid like that liking books the way he does. When I was his age I was working for four or five years."

The boy came up with the slip of paper in his hand. "These ought to hold him for a while," he said to Mr. Harris.

Mr. Harris glanced at the list and nodded. "That Thackeray's a nice set of books," he said.

65   The boy had put his hat on and was standing at the foot of the stairs. "Hope you enjoy them," he said. "I'll be back for another look at that Empson, Mr. Harris."

"I'll try to keep it around for you," Mr. Harris said. "I can't promise to hold it, you know."

"I'll just count on it's being here," the boy said.

"Thanks, son," the big man called out as the boy started up the stairs. "Appreciate your helping me."

"That's all right," the boy said.

70   "He's sure a smart kid," the man said to Mr. Harris. "He's got a great chance, with an education like that."

"He's a nice young fellow," Mr. Harris said, "and he sure wants that book."

"You think he'll ever buy it?" the big man asked.

"I doubt it," Mr. Harris said. "If you'll just write down your name and address, I'll add these prices."

Mr. Harris began to note down the prices of the books, copying from the boy's neat list. After the big man had written his name and address, he stood for a minute drumming his fingers on the desk, and then he said, "Can I have another look at that book?"

75   "The Empson?" Mr. Harris said, looking up.

"The one the boy was so interested in." Mr. Harris reached around to the bookcase in back of him and took out the book. The big man held it delicately, as he had held the others, and he frowned as he turned the pages. Then he put the book down on Mr. Harris' desk.

"If he isn't going to buy it, will it be all right if I put this in with the rest?" he asked.

Mr. Harris looked up from his figures for a minute, and then he made the entry on his list. He added quickly, wrote down the total, and then pushed the paper across the desk to the big man. While the man checked over the figures Mr. Harris turned to the woman and said, "Your husband has bought a lot of very pleasant reading."

"I'm glad to hear it," she said. "We've been looking forward to it for a long time."

80   The big man counted out the money carefully, handing the bills to Mr. Harris. Mr. Harris put the money in the top drawer of his desk and said, "We can have these delivered to you by the end of the week, if that will be all right."

"Fine," the big man said. "Ready, Mother?"

The woman rose, and the big man stood back to let her go ahead of him. Mr. Harris followed, stopping near the stairs to say to the woman, "Watch the bottom step."

They started up the stairs and Mr. Harris stood watching them until they got to the turn. Then he switched off the dirty overhead lamp and went back to his desk.

Analyzing Rhetorical Choices

1. How is this story informed by the contrasts between the middle-aged man, the circumstances of his own youth, and the life of Mr. Clark, who is the youth in the story? How do these connections develop the plot?

2. The basement room is filled with "books standing silent in dim light"—Dickens, the Brontës, Meredith, Thackeray. The "loudest" book, or the one Mr. Clark is most interested in, becomes the symbol that attracts the customer. Why does the symbol become as important as the books by Dickens and the others?

3. Jackson seems to be making a point about the need for readers to participate in the meaning-making process. They must be active in order to resolve matters that could be considered ambiguous. What do you imagine happens after the purchase of the books? What details in the story lead you to this conclusion? Why does Jackson title the story, "Seven Types of Ambiguity"?

Writing About Issues and Contexts

1. The customer equates contemporary writing with "trash." He suggests that traditional works are superior. What current debates in the arts about the new versus the old interest you? If so, what are your opinions?

2. What does literacy mean to the middle-aged couple? How does their view reflect what they think about the culture they live in? What is the nature of the woman's involvement in this anecdote?

Strategies for Writers: Narration

1. Draft a narrative or an essay in which the use of anecdotes is the dominant approach. Your instructor is part of your audience, but try to set up as wide an audience as possible. You can exchange papers with your classmates. You can also find friends, family members, and other people outside the class who may agree to read your work. Perhaps you, your classmates, and instructor can develop a class magazine. Or maybe you can make a contribution to a school or community publication. Shirley Jackson published about fifteen stories in campus magazines while she was in college. Remember that people love good tales.

2. As you prepare your draft, think of your audience and the point you want to make. Consider the readers you envision reaching, and ask yourself which types of anecdotes would appeal to them and be appropriate for your purpose. You don't necessarily have to start with a consciously forceful argument. You may aim to be fairly subtle like Thurber or Jackson. Or you may declare your intention like Dillard, who writes, explaining the chase, that, *"The point was* that he had chased us passionately without giving up, and so he had caught us"* (emphasis added). Wright and Orwell provide detailed analysis of the anecdotes they use. Whichever way you proceed, remember that your writing will reflect some perspective and leave some impression on readers in any case.

3. Decide which viewpoint you favor—first, second, or third person—and whether you will employ singular or plural. Choose whether you want to use dialogue, and consider what purpose it would serve. Select the anecdotes you want to present and their sequence. It could be helpful to make an outline of events to guide you in writing your draft. You may even want to get feedback from others about your list of anecdotes before you begin writing.

4. Read and reread your draft. Share it with your instructor, classmates, and anyone else who is willing to assist. Ask readers to interpret your piece and comment on your tone, choice of language, and selection of incidents. Evaluate how closely their interpretations match your intentions, and then consider how, if necessary, you can make your point more clear. Do you need a more direct approach? Do you need more or fewer anecdotes? Do you need different kinds of anecdotes? Have you chosen the best sequence?

5. Pay particular attention to dialogue and linguistic diversity if they are features of your text. Are you using too much dialogue? Are certain speech varieties framed, as in Amy Tan's essay? Or are language varieties mixed throughout the narrative, a technique Orwell uses? Solicit reactions related to these matters from your instructor, classmates, and others.

6. As you revise, remind yourself of the point you are trying to make or the impression you wish the reader to form. Does your work reflect your experiences and the influence of the wider culture in the ways you wish? Does it represent your best effort to leave a mark on the thinking of others?

Research and Writing Assignments

1. In "The Chase," Annie Dillard recounts childhood rituals as well as eventful moments related to childhood patterns of behavior. Write a narrative that traces your own involvement in community rituals as a child or even at present. In the course of your narrative, explain the reasons for your participation. As does Dillard, point out significant moments of self-awareness and what they have revealed to you about yourself and others.

2. Write a narrative that relates your own discovery of H. L. Mencken. Perhaps your story will begin with your response to Richard Wright's "The Library Card." Detail your own process of consulting the Internet, the library, or other sources of information. Record your own reactions to some of Mencken's work as well as to what critics have written about him.

3. The essays by James Thurber, Amy Tan, and George Orwell are largely about the difficulties—but also the possibilities—of negotiating a world that extends beyond the environment in which one is raised. For Thurber, it is college life; for Tan and her mother, it is the literary world and U.S. culture in general; and for Orwell, it is colonial Burma. Write a narrative about your experiences in an unfamiliar cultural situation. Comment on whether your experiences were positive or negative and on what strategies for negotiating this unfamiliarity, if any, you found beneficial.

4. Using Elizabeth Alexander's "Narrative: Ali" as a model, compose a short biography of someone you value, and do so in first-person narrative verse. Be sure to research your subject thoroughly, but choose the most interesting and salient details

to hold your audience's interest. Further, as Alexander does, try your best to capture the voice of your subject.

5. Write a short piece of fiction that illustrates a point or issue about which you are concerned. As Shirley Jackson does in "Seven Types of Ambiguity," try to dramatize your point as much as possible by using characters and dialogue.

3

Description

Part of your job as a writer involves getting your readers to focus on the scenes or portrayals you value the most. This helps you convey your impressions of objects, people, and situations. One way of achieving your goal is to provide information that appeals to readers' sensory apparatus—their abilities to see, hear, touch, taste, and smell. When you are pursuing conscious, calculated writing of this sort, you are engaged in *description*. Consider the first sentence of Richard Wright's depiction in *12 Million Black Voices* of a certain landscape:

> The land we till is beautiful, with red and black and brown clay, with fresh and hungry smells, with pine trees and palm trees, with rolling hills and swampy delta—an unbelievably fertile land, bounded on the north by the states of Pennsylvania, Ohio, Illinois, and Indiana, on the south by the Gulf of Mexico, on the west by the Mississippi River, and on the east by the Atlantic Ocean.

This is a more vivid and compelling opening than "We farm beautiful land that is hilly with a lot of trees in the South."

Wright continues to make strong appeals to our senses as he describes the yearly cycle:

> Our southern springs are filled with quiet noises and scenes of growth. Apple buds laugh into blossom. Honeysuckles creep up the sides of houses. Sunflowers nod in the hot fields. From mossy tree to mossy tree—oak, elm, willow, aspen, sycamore, dogwood, cedar, walnut, ash, and hickory—bright green leaves jut from a million branches to form an awning that tries to shield and shade the earth. Blue and pink kites of small boys sail in the windy air.

In the summer the magnolia trees fill the countryside with sweet scent for long miles. Days are slumberous, and the skies are high and thronged with clouds that ride fast. At midday the sun blazes and bleaches the soil. Butterflies flit through the heat; wasps sing their sharp, straight lines; birds fluff and flounce, piping in querulous joy. Nights are covered with canopies sometimes blue and sometimes black, canopies that sag low with ripe and nervous stars. The throaty boast of frogs momentarily drowns out the call and counter-call of crickets.

In autumn the land is afire with color. Red and brown leaves lift and flutter dryly, becoming entangled in the stiff grass and cornstalks. Cotton is picked and ginned; cane is crushed and its juice is simmered down into molasses; yams are grubbed out of the clay; hogs are slaughtered and cured in lingering smoke; corn is husked and ground into meal. At twilight the sky is full of wild geese winging ever southward, and bats jerk through the air. At night the winds blow free.

In winter the forests resound with the bite of steel axes eating into tall trees as men gather wood for the leaden days of cold. The guns of hunters snap and crack. Long days of rain come, and our swollen creeks rush to join a hundred rivers that wash across the land and make great harbors where they feed the gulf or the sea. Occasionally the rivers leap their banks and leave new thick layers of silt to enrich the earth, and then the look of the land is garish, bleak, suffused with a first-day stillness, strangeness, and awe.

Description can be an essential element in all writing. Wright's descriptive passage, for example, serves as prelude to an explanation about exploitative economic practices. Consider, too, Annie Dillard's comment in "The Chase" about the perils of making a tackle in football: "Either you brought him down or you hit the ground flat out on your chin, with your arms empty before you." And James Thurber's observation of his botany professor in "University Days": "The professor had come back from vacation brown as a berry, bright-eyed, and eager to explain cell-structure again to his classes." Although description can be powerful when employed in parts of an essay, it can also be the dominant pattern, as in some of the essays in this chapter, including Yusef Komunyakaa's "Blue," Gordon Parks's "Flavio's Home," and Barry Lopez's "The Stone Horse."

Whether description is the primary or secondary focus in an essay, the key to using it effectively is the appropriate selection of details to convey a *dominant impression*. Such an impression deepens your persuasive effort and helps you obtain identification with your perspective, something you are always seeking from your audience. If description is the primary method of your work, you should establish the dominant impression early and develop it consistently with well-chosen details. If the details are too numerous and minuscule, your audience is likely to view the writing as dull, perhaps irrelevant, and may not even read it. If you are describing the joys of using a computer, for instance, you would not want to get overly technical for a general audience, though providing a plethora of technical details might be perfect for other readers.

Description is frequently categorized as *objective* or *subjective*, but these classifications can be problematic. The first term is meant to signify that the writer is dispassionately describing the characteristics of an object, person, or situation without manifesting any personal bias. A laboratory report based on a chemistry experiment might serve as an example of objective writing. In subjective writing, authors deliberately attempt to make their feelings evident; an example might be an editorializing description of a river polluted by industrial waste. Most people, however, will not be restricted to writing technical reports or totally subjective statements. In fact, the distinction is often hard to maintain. Nearly all scientific reports omit some details, an act that reveals a viewpoint, and every now and then some scientist is caught falsifying data, an offense that certainly makes an objective-sounding document subjective. Likewise, even a ranting, one-sided, negative portrayal of someone could seem totally objective to a person who happens to share that author's perspective.

To organize your descriptive essay or passage, you might brainstorm a list of sensory details and then choose those that best make your point. Your thesis might be implied, as it often is in descriptive essays, or you might state it explicitly and then develop or illustrate it with your chosen details. You could present your material chronologically, as in a narrative. Alice Walker's "Am I Blue?" is an example of this. You could even organize a particular descriptive passage into a time sequence. Consider Barry Lopez's recollection of a series of sounds coming from a nearby village:

> The first sounds from this collection of ramshackle houses in a grove of cottonwoods were the distracted dawn voices of dogs. I heard them intermingled with the cries of a rooster. Later, the high-pitched voices of children calling out to each other came disembodied through the dry desert air. Now, a little after seven. I could hear someone practicing on the trumpet, the same rough phrases over and over. I suddenly remembered how as children we had tried to get the rhythm of a galloping horse with hands against our thighs, or by fluttering our tongues against the roofs of our mouths.

After the trumpet, the impatient calls of adults summoning children. Sunday morning. Wood smoke hung like a lens in the trees. The first car starts—a cold eight-cylinder engine, of Chrysler extraction perhaps, goosed to life, then throttled back to murmur through dual mufflers, the obligato music of a shade-tree mechanic. The rote bark of mongrel dogs at dawn, the jagged outcries of men and women, an engine coming to life. Like a thousand villages from West Virginia to Guadalajara.

Another aspect of descriptive writing involves the use of a spatial principle—bottom to top, left to right, foreground and background. Walker does this, for instance, in her opening paragraph, as she describes a meadow "that appeared to run from the end of our deck [foreground] straight into the mountains [background]." Notice how Gordon Parks uses the words *between, beneath, below, under,* and *down* in his description of a shack in Brazil:

> The shack was about six by ten feet. Its grimy walls were a patchwork of misshapen boards with large gaps between them, revealing other shacks below silted against the slopes. The floor, rotting under layers of grease and dirt, caught shafts of light slanting down through spaces in the roof. A large hole in the far corner served as a toilet. Beneath that hole was the sloping mountainside.

Regardless of the organizational scheme, you would do well to use orienting language, as Parks does, to keep your readers clear about the point you are developing. Richard Wright, as we have seen, chooses the seasons as an organizing device.

Good description often relies heavily on special figures of speech such as *personification, simile,* and *metaphor.* Personification is the attributing of human qualities to nonhuman entities—apple buds laughing into blossom, sunflowers nodding, rivers leaping their banks. Simile and metaphor are comparisons of two objects that are apparently dissimilar. A simile uses *like* or *as* to make the comparison. Commenting on outboard motors, E. B. White writes that "they whined about one's ears like mosquitoes." A metaphor makes the comparison directly, as does Harriet Tubman in her description of a Civil War battle she witnessed: "And then we saw the lightning, and that was the guns. And then we heard the thunder and that was the big guns. And then we heard the rain falling and that was the drops of blood falling. And when we came to get in the crops, it was dead men that we reaped."

Successful description entails the general use of vivid imagery, stretching for lively verbs, strong adjectives, and expressive adverbs.

Alice Walker does not depict Blue as merely "eating stalks." She writes that he was "munching the dried stalks half-heartedly." Julia Alvarez uses the phrase "ominous bell" in relation to the signal for an air-raid drill.

Description is a powerful tool for relating ideas and shaping perceptions—two of your primary goals as a writer. These are also goals that you, as a human, are abundantly equipped to perform. You are more sophisticated in capturing detail than any camera invented. Barring disability, you can see and hear from any angle—and touch, taste, smell, and think.

A native of Bogalusa, Louisiana, **Yusef Komunyakaa** *(1947–   ) won the Pulitzer Prize for poetry in 1994 for* Magic City. *Komunyakaa is on the faculty of Princeton University. His other volumes include* Dien Cai Dau *(1988),* Neon Vernacular *(1993),* Thieves of Paradise *(1998), and* Talking Dirty to the Gods *(2001). "Blue," the selection included in this chapter, is from* Blue Notes: Essays, Interviews, and Commentaries *(2000).*

Yusef Komunyakaa

Blue

I have always loved blue. One of my first memories is my teenaged mother standing in the bedroom doorway in a silk slip pale as the shine inside an abalone. From grub worm to midday sky on the plains, blue is the insides of something mysterious and lonely. I'd look at fish and birds, thinking the sky and water colored them. The first abyss is blue. An artist must go beyond the mercy of satin or water— from a gutty hue to that which is close to royal purple. All the seasons and blossoms in between. Lavender. Theatrical and outrageous electric. Almost gray. True and false blue. Water and oil. The gas jet breathing in oblivion. The unstruck match. The blue of absence. The blue of deep presence. The insides of something perfect. Primary: we can only subtract what it is from what it is, and what's left is almost what it is. A feather on a bed of pine needles. My father's work clothes at the end of two seasons of blood, sweat, and tears. The blackened iron wash pot filled with white things and Red Devil Lye—the glow of pine knots under a winter sky in Bogalusa. The 1950s. Bluing in a #3 galvanized tub of whites, and the sheets and pillowcases and Sunday shirts pinned to the clothesline like a painter's daytime. The future. The red Kissing Camels against a Colorado sky in the Garden of the Gods. The South China Sea. Skin beneath the palest blue in Saigon. Mosaic tiles on walls and floors. I lingered for hours at a window in Urbino, gazing at poppies on low hills against the sky. A hue precious as lapis lazuli crushed into ultramarine, as Perugino washed his brushes one hundred times to steal the only color that brightened his nightmares.

Analyzing Rhetorical Choices

1. Komunyakaa associates the color blue both with abstractions—absence, presence—and concrete objects—sky, water. Identify all the author's descriptions associated with blue, and divide them into abstract and concrete categories.
2. How do the descriptions of concrete objects and abstractions create different impacts on you as a reader?
3. How do the various elements within this vignette create a whole?

Writing About Issues and Contexts

1. With phrases like "one of my first memories" and "the future," Komunyakaa signals that he has organized his piece chronologically. What is his reason for referring to the South China Sea, Saigon, and Urbino?
2. The writer describes his lingering for hours in front of an art gallery window. How do you think this relates to the earlier descriptions of his parents?

*Fiction writer, poet, and essayist **Alice Walker** (1944–   ) was born in Eatonton, Georgia. A graduate of Sarah Lawrence College, she currently resides in Mendocino, California. She has received several awards for her writing. Her books include the novels* The Third Life of Grange Copeland *(1970);* Meridian *(1976);* The Color Purple *(1982), which won the Pulitzer Prize; and* By the Light of My Father's Smile *(1998). Her poetry collections include* Her Blue Body Everything We Know: Earthling Poems *(1990). Among her essay volumes are* In Search of Our Mother's Gardens *(1983) and* Living by the Word *(1988), from which the following essay is taken.*

Alice Walker
Am I Blue?

"Ain't these tears in these eyes tellin' you?"

For about three years my companion and I rented a small house in the country that stood on the edge of a large meadow that appeared to run from the end of our deck straight into the mountains. The mountains, however, were quite far away, and between us and them there was, in fact, a town. It was one of the many pleasant aspects of the house that you never really were aware of this.

It was a house of many windows, low, wide, nearly floor to ceiling in the living room, which faced the meadow, and it was from one of these that I first saw our closest neighbor, a large white horse, cropping grass, flipping its mane, and ambling about—not over the entire meadow, which stretched well out of sight of the house, but over the five or so fenced-in acres that were next to the twenty-odd that we had rented. I soon learned that the horse, whose name was Blue, belonged to a man who lived in another town, but was boarded by our neighbors next door. Occasionally, one of the children, usually a stocky teen-ager, but sometimes a much younger girl or boy, could be seen riding Blue. They would appear in the meadow, climb up on his back, ride furiously for ten or fifteen minutes, then get off, slap Blue on the flanks, and not be seen again for a month or more.

There were many apple trees in our yard, and one by the fence that Blue could almost reach. We were soon in the habit of feeding him apples, which he relished, especially because by the middle of summer the meadow grasses—so green and succulent since January—had dried out from lack of rain, and Blue stumbled about munching the dried stalks half-heartedly. Sometimes he would stand very still just by the apple tree, and when one of us came out he would whinny, snort loudly, or stamp the ground. This meant, of course: I want an apple.

It was quite wonderful to pick a few apples, or collect those that had fallen to the ground overnight, and patiently hold them, one by one, up to his large, toothy mouth. I remained as thrilled as a child by his flexible dark lips, huge, cubelike teeth that crunched the apples, core and all, with such finality, and his high, broad-breasted *enormity*; beside which, I felt small indeed. When I was a child, I used to ride horses, and was especially friendly with one named Nan until the day I was riding and my brother deliberately spooked her and I was thrown, head first, against the trunk of a tree. When I came to, I was in bed and my mother was bending worriedly over me; we silently agreed that perhaps horseback riding was not the safest sport for me. Since then I have walked, and prefer walking to horseback riding—but I had forgotten the depth of feeling one could see in horses' eyes.

5 I was therefore unprepared for the expression in Blue's. Blue was lonely. Blue was horribly lonely and bored. I was not shocked that this should be the case; five acres to tramp by yourself, endlessly, even in the most beautiful of meadows—and his was—cannot provide many interesting events, and once rainy season turned to dry that was about it. No, I was shocked that I had forgotten that human animals and nonhuman animals can communicate quite well; if we are brought up around animals as children we take this for granted. By the time we are adults we no longer remember. However, the animals have not changed. They are in fact *completed* creations (at least they seem to be, so much more than we) who are not likely *to* change; it is their nature to express themselves. What else are they going to express? And they do. And, generally speaking, they are ignored.

After giving Blue the apples, I would wander back to the house, aware that he was observing me. Were more apples not forthcoming then? Was that to be his sole entertainment for the day? My partner's small son had decided he wanted to learn how to piece a quilt; we worked in silence on our respective squares as I thought . . .

Well, about slavery: about white children, who were raised by black people, who knew their first all-accepting love from black women, and then, when they were twelve or so, were told they must "forget" the deep levels of communication between themselves and "mammy" that they knew. Later they would be able to relate quite calmly, "My old mammy was sold to another good family." "My old mammy was ____ ____." Fill in the blank. Many more years later a white woman would say: "I can't understand these Negroes, these blacks. What do they want? They're so different from us."

And about the Indians, considered to be "like animals" by the "settlers" (a very benign euphemism for what they actually were), who did not understand their description as a compliment.

And about the thousands of American men who marry Japanese, Korean, Filipina, and other non-English-speaking women and of how happy they report they are, "*blissfully*," until their brides learn to speak English, at which point the marriages tend to fall apart. What then did the men see, when they looked into the eyes of the women they married, before they could speak English? Apparently only their own reflections.

10   I thought of society's impatience with the young. "Why are they playing the music so loud?" Perhaps the children have listened to much of the music of oppressed people their parents danced to before they were born, with its passionate but soft cries for acceptance and love, and they have wondered why their parents failed to hear.

I do not know how long Blue had inhabited his five beautiful, boring acres before we moved into our house; a year after we had arrived—and had also traveled to other valleys, other cities, other worlds—he was still there.

But then, in our second year at the house, something happened in Blue's life. One morning, looking out the window at the fog that lay like a ribbon over the meadow, I saw another horse, a brown one, at the other end of Blue's field. Blue appeared to be afraid of it, and for several days made no attempt to go near. We went away for a week. When we returned, Blue had decided to make friends and the two horses ambled or galloped along together, and Blue did not come nearly as often to the fence underneath the apple tree.

When he did, bringing his new friend with him, there was a different look in his eyes. A look of independence, of self-possession, of inalienable *horse*ness. His friend eventually became pregnant. For months and months there was, it seemed to me, a mutual feeling between me and the horses of justice, of peace. I fed apples to them both. The look in Blue's eyes was one of unabashed "this is *it*ness."

It did not, however, last forever. One day, after a visit to the city, I went out to give Blue some apples. He stood waiting, or so I thought, though not beneath the tree. When I shook the tree and jumped back from the shower of apples, he made no move. I carried some over to him. He managed to half-crunch one. The rest he let fall to the ground. I dreaded looking into his eyes—because I had of course noticed that Brown, his partner, had gone—but I did look. If I had been born into slavery, and my partner had been sold or killed, my eyes would have looked like that. The children next door explained that Blue's partner had been "put with him" (the same expression that old people used, I had noticed, when speaking of an ancestor during slavery who had been impregnated by her owner) so that they could mate and she conceive. Since that was accomplished, she had been taken back by her owner, who lived somewhere else.

15   Will she be back? I asked.

They didn't know.

Blue was like a crazed person. Blue *was*, to me, a crazed person. He galloped furiously, as if he were being ridden, around and around his five beautiful acres. He whinnied until he couldn't. He tore at the ground with his hooves. He butted himself against his single shade tree. He looked always and always toward the road down which his partner had gone. And then, occasionally, when he came up for apples, or I took apples to him, he looked at me. It was a look so piercing, so full of grief, a look so *human*, I almost laughed (I felt too sad to cry) to think there are people who do not know that animals suffer. People like me who have forgotten, and daily forget, all that animals try to tell us. "Everything you do to us will happen to you; we are your teachers, as you are ours. We are one lesson" is essentially it, I think. There are those who never once have even considered animals' rights: those who have been taught that animals actually want to be used and abused by us, as small children "love" to be frightened, or women "love" to be mutilated and raped. . . . They are the great-grandchildren of those who honestly thought, because someone taught them this: "Women can't think," and "niggers can't faint." But most disturbing of all, in Blue's large brown eyes was a new look, more painful than the look of despair: the look of disgust with human beings, with life; the look of hatred. And it was odd what the look of hatred did. It gave him, for the first time, the look of a beast. And what that meant was that he had put up a barrier within to protect himself from further violence; all the apples in the world wouldn't change that fact.

And so Blue remained, a beautiful part of our landscape, very peaceful to look at from the window, white against the grass. Once a friend came to visit and said, looking out on the soothing view: "And it *would* have to be a *white* horse; the very image of freedom." And I thought, yes, the animals are forced to become for us merely "images" of what they once so beautifully expressed. And we are used to drinking milk from containers showing "contented" cows, whose real lives we want to hear nothing about, eating eggs and drumsticks form "happy" hens, and munching hamburgers advertised by bulls of integrity who seem to command their fate.

As we talked of freedom and justice one day for all, we sat down to steaks. I am eating misery, I thought, as I took the first bite. And spit it out.

Analyzing Rhetorical Choices

1. Which details or phrases allow you to picture Blue's physical appearance and activities in your mind's eye?
2. Which details or phrases reveal the horse's "inner state"?
3. Is Blue a symbol, and if so, of what?

Writing About Issues and Contexts

1. How do you respond to Walker's suggestion that nonhuman animals are more *completed* than we are?
2. What do you think of Walker's references to the other social issues she mentions? Are her observations and analyses persuasive?
3. What is your stance on animal rights and your response to Walker's reaction at the end of the essay?

Born in New York City, **Julia Alvarez** *(1950–   ) was moved to the Dominican Republic shortly thereafter. She returned in 1960. She attended boarding schools and high school, going on to earn a bachelor's degree from Middlebury College and a master's degree from Syracuse University. She is currently a professor of English at Middlebury College. Her titles include* How the Garcia Girls Lost Their Accents *(1990),* In the Time of Butterflies *(1994),* Yo! *(1997), and the poetry volumes* Homecoming *(1984) and* The Other Side/El Otro Lado *(1995). The following story is from* How the Garcia Girls Lost Their Accents.

Julia Alvarez

Snow

Yolanda

Our first year in New York we rented a small apartment with a Catholic school nearby, taught by the Sisters of Charity, hefty women in long black gowns and bonnets that made them look peculiar, like dolls in mourning. I liked them a lot, especially my grandmotherly fourth grade teacher, Sister Zoe. I had a lovely name, she said, and she had me teach the whole class how to pronounce it. *Yo-lan-da.* As the only immigrant in my class, I was put in a special seat in the first row by the window, apart from the other children so that Sister Zoe could tutor me without disturbing them. Slowly, she enunciated the new words I was to repeat: *laundromat, corn flakes, subway, snow.*

Soon I picked up enough English to understand holocaust was in the air. Sister Zoe explained to a wide-eyed classroom what was happening in Cuba. Russian missiles were being assembled, trained supposedly on New York City. President Kennedy, looking worried too, was on the television at home, explaining we might have to go to war against the Communists. At school, we had air-raid drills: an ominous bell would go off and we'd file into the hall, fall to the floor, cover our heads with our coats, and imagine our hair falling out, the bones in our arms going soft. At home, Mami and my sisters and I said a rosary for world peace. I heard new vocabulary: *nuclear bomb, radioactive fallout, bomb shelter.* Sister Zoe explained how it would happen. She drew a picture of a mushroom on the blackboard and dotted a flurry of chalkmarks for the dusty fallout that would kill us all.

The months grew cold, November, December. It was dark when I got up in the morning, frosty when I followed my breath to school. One morning as I sat at my desk daydreaming out the window, I saw dots in the air like the ones Sister Zoe had drawn—random at first, then lots and lots. I shrieked, "Bomb! Bomb!" Sister Zoe jerked around, her full black skirt ballooning as she hurried to my side. A few girls began to cry.

But then Sister Zoe's shocked look faded. "Why, Yolanda dear, that's snow!" She laughed. "Snow."

5   "Snow," I repeated. I looked out the window warily. All my life I had heard about the white crystals that fell out of American skies in the winter. From my desk I watched the fine powder dust the sidewalk and parked cars below. Each flake was different, Sister Zoe had said, like a person, irreplaceable and beautiful.

Analyzing Rhetorical Choices

1. Locate phrases in addition to "like dolls in mourning" and "wide-eyed classroom" that help you imagine the setting that Alvarez portrays. How do they contribute to your understanding?

2. Alvarez closes by comparing snowflakes to individual people. What do you feel is the major point of her piece?

Writing About Issues and Contexts

1. What do you think of the classroom arrangement whereby the narrator sat apart to receive individual tutoring?

2. How does the Cold War climate of the early 1960s, as depicted by the author, compare and contrast to your sense of the international political arena today?

*Born in Mount Vernon, New York, **Elwyn Brooks White** (1899–1983)
graduated from Cornell University in 1921. He enjoyed longtime associations with both* The New Yorker *and* Harper's Magazine. *A prolific essayist, his works have been collected in* One Man's Meat *(1942), where the
following selection appeared,* The Points of My Compass *(1962), the* E. B.
White Reader *(1966), and* Writings from the New Yorker, 1925–1976
(1990). White also authored the children's classics Stuart Little *(1945)
and* Charlotte's Web *(1952).*

E. B. White
Once More to the Lake

One summer, along about 1904, my father rented a camp on a
lake in Maine and took us all there for the month of August. We all got
ringworm from some kittens and had to rub Pond's Extract on our
arms and legs night and morning, and my father rolled over in a canoe
with all his clothes on; but outside of that the vacation was a success
and from then on none of us ever thought there was any place in the
world like that lake in Maine. We returned summer after summer—always on August 1st for one month. I have since become a salt-water
man, but sometimes in summer there are days when the restlessness of
the tides and the fearful cold of the sea water and the incessant wind
which blows across the afternoon and into the evening make me wish
for the placidity of a lake in the woods. A few weeks ago this feeling
got so strong I bought myself a couple of bass hooks and a spinner and
returned to the lake where we used to go, for a week's fishing and to
revisit old haunts.

I took along my son, who had never had any fresh water up his
nose and who had seen lily pads only from train windows. On the journey over to the lake I began to wonder what it would be like. I wondered how time would have marred this unique, this holy spot—the
coves and streams, the hills that the sun set behind, the camps and the
paths behind the camps. I was sure that the tarred road would have
found it out and I wondered in what other ways it would be desolated.
It is strange how much you can remember about places like that once
you allow your mind to return into the grooves which lead back. You
remember one thing, and that suddenly reminds you of another thing.
I guess I remembered clearest of all the early mornings, when the lake

was cool and motionless, remembered how the bedroom smelled of the lumber it was made of and the wet woods whose scent entered through the screen. The partitions in the camp were thin and did not extend clear to the top of the rooms, and as I was always the first up I would dress softly so as not to wake the others, and sneak out into the sweet outdoors and start out in the canoe, keeping close along the shore in the long shadows of the pines. I remembered being very careful never to rub my paddle against the gunwale for fear of disturbing the stillness of the cathedral.

The lake had never been what you would call a wild lake. There were cottages sprinkled around the shores, and it was in farming country although the shores of the lake were quite heavily wooded. Some of the cottages were owned by nearby farmers, and you would live at the shore and eat your meals at the farmhouse. That's what our family did. But although it wasn't wild, it was a fairly large and undisturbed lake and there were places in it which, to a child at least, seemed infinitely remote and primeval.

I was right about the tar: it led to within half a mile of the shore. But when I got back there, with my boy, and we settled into a camp near a farmhouse and into the kind of summertime I had known, I could tell that it was going to be pretty much the same as it had been before—I knew it, lying in bed the first morning, smelling the bedroom, and hearing the boy sneak quietly out and go off along the shore in a boat. I began to sustain the illusion that he was I, and therefore, by simple transposition, that I was my father. This sensation persisted, kept cropping up all the time we were there. It was not an entirely new feeling, but in this setting it grew much stronger. I seemed to be living a dual existence. I would be in the middle of some simple act, I would be picking up a bait box or laying down a table fork, or I would be saying something, and suddenly it would be not I but my father who was saying the words or making the gesture. It gave me a creepy sensation.

5   We went fishing the first morning. I felt the same damp moss covering the worms in the bait can, and saw the dragonfly alight on the tip of my rod as it hovered a few inches from the surface of the water. It was the arrival of this fly that convinced me beyond any doubt that everything was as it always had been, that the years were a mirage and there had been no years. The small waves were the same, chucking the rowboat under the chin as we fished at anchor, and the boat was the same boat, the same color green and the ribs broken in the same places, and under the floor-boards the same freshwater leavings and débris—the dead helgramite, the wisps of moss, the rusty discarded

fishhook, the dried blood from yesterday's catch. We stared silently at the tips of our rods, at the dragonflies that came and went. I lowered the tip of mine into the water, tentatively, pensively dislodging the fly, which darted two feet away, poised, darted two feet back, and came to rest again a little farther up the rod. There had been no years between the ducking of this dragonfly and the other one—the one that was part of memory. I looked at the boy, who was silently watching his fly, and it was my hands that held his rod, my eyes watching. I felt dizzy and didn't know which rod I was at the end of.

We caught two bass, hauling them in briskly as though they were mackerel, pulling them over the side of the boat in a businesslike manner without any landing net, and stunning them with a blow on the back of the head. When we got back for a swim before lunch, the lake was exactly where we had left it, the same number of inches from the dock, and there was only the merest suggestion of a breeze. This seemed an utterly enchanted sea, this lake you could leave to its own devices for a few hours and come back to, and find that it had not stirred, this constant and trustworthy body of water. In the shallows, the dark, water-soaked sticks and twigs, smooth and old, were undulating in clusters on the bottom against the clean ribbed sand, and the track of the mussel was plain. A school of minnows swam by, each minnow with its small individual shadow, doubling the attendance, so clear and sharp in the sunlight. Some of the other campers were in swimming, along the shore, one of them with a cake of soap, and the water felt thin and clear and unsubstantial. Over the years there had been this person with the cake of soap, this cultist, and here he was. There had been no years.

Up to the farmhouse to dinner through the teeming, dusty field, the road under our sneakers was only a two-track road. The middle track was missing, the one with the marks of the hooves and the splotches of dried, flaky manure. There had always been three tracks to choose from in choosing which track to walk in; now the choice was narrowed down to two. For a moment I missed terribly the middle alternative. But the way led past the tennis court, and something about the way it lay there in the sun reassured me; the tape had loosened along the backline, the alleys were green with plantains and other weeds, and the net (installed in June and removed in September) sagged in the dry noon, and the whole place steamed with midday heat and hunger and emptiness. There was a choice of pie for dessert, and one was blueberry and one was apple, and the waitresses were the same country girls, there having been no passage of time, only the illusion of it as in a dropped curtain—the waitresses were still fifteen;

their hair had been washed, that was the only difference—they had been to the movies and seen the pretty girls with the clean hair.

Summertime, oh summertime, pattern of life indelible, the fade-proof lake, the woods unshatterable, the pasture with the sweetfern and the juniper forever and ever, summer without end; this was the background, and the life along the shore was the design, the cottages with their innocent and tranquil design, their tiny docks with the flagpole and the American flag floating against the white clouds in the blue sky, the little paths over the roots of the trees leading from camp to camp and the paths leading back to the outhouses and the can of lime for sprinkling, and at the souvenir counters at the store the miniature birch-bark canoes and the post cards that showed things looking a little better than they looked. This was the American family at play, escaping the city heat, wondering whether the newcomers in the camp at the head of the cove were "common" or "nice," wondering whether it was true that the people who drove up for Sunday dinner at the farmhouse were turned away because there wasn't enough chicken.

It seemed to me, as I keep remembering all this, that those times and those summers had been infinitely precious and worth saving. There had been jollity and peace and goodness. The arriving (at the beginning of August) had been so big a business in itself, at the railway station the farm wagon drawn up, the first smell of the pineladen air, the first glimpse of the smiling farmer, and the great importance of the trunks and your father's enormous authority in such matters, and the feel of the wagon under you for the long ten-mile haul, and at the top of the last long hill catching the first view of the lake after eleven months of not seeing this cherished body of water. The shouts and cries of the other campers when they saw you, and the trunks to be unpacked, to give up their rich burden. (Arriving was less exciting nowadays, when you sneaked up in your car and parked it under a tree near the camp and took out the bags and in five minutes it was all over, no fuss, no loud wonderful fuss about trunks.)

10   Peace and goodness and jollity. The only thing that was wrong now, really, was the sound of the place, an unfamiliar nervous sound of the outboard motors. This was the note that jarred, the one thing that would sometimes break the illusion and set the years moving. In those other summertimes all motors were inboard; and when they were at a little distance, the noise they made was a sedative, an ingredient of summer sleep. They were one-cylinder and two-cylinder engines, and some were make-and-break and some were jump-spark, but they all made a sleepy sound across the lake. The one-lungers throbbed and fluttered, and the twin-cylinder ones purred and purred, and that was

a quiet sound too. But now the campers all had outboards. In the day-time, in the hot mornings, these motors made a petulant, irritable sound; at night, in the still evening when the afterglow lit the water, they whined about one's ears like mosquitoes. My boy loved our rented outboard, and his great desire was to achieve single-handed mastery over it, and authority, and he soon learned the trick of choking it a lit-tle (but not too much), and the adjustment of the needle valve. Watching him I would remember the things you could do with the old one-cylinder engine with the heavy flywheel, how you could have it eating out of your hand if you got really close to it spiritually. Motor boats in those days didn't have clutches, and you would make a land-ing by shutting off the motor at the proper time and coasting in with a dead rudder. But there was a way of reversing them, if you learned the trick, by cutting the switch and putting it on again exactly on the final dying revolution of the flywheel, so that it would kick back against compression and begin reversing. Approaching a dock in a strong fol-lowing breeze, it was difficult to slow up sufficiently by the ordinary coasting method, and if a boy felt he had complete mastery over his motor, he was tempted to keep it running beyond its time and then re-verse it a few feet from the dock. It took a cool nerve, because if you threw the switch a twentieth of a second too soon you could catch the flywheel when it still had speed enough to go up past center, and the boat would leap ahead, charging bull-fashion at the dock.

We had a good week at the camp. The bass were biting well and the sun shone endlessly, day after day. We would be tired at night and lie down in the accumulated heat of the little bedrooms after the long hot day and the breeze would stir almost imperceptibly outside and the smell of the swamp drift in through the rusty screens. Sleep would come easily and in the morning the red squirrel would be on the roof, tapping out his gay routine. I kept remembering everything, lying in bed in the mornings—the small steamboat that had a long rounded stern like the lip of a Ubangi, how quietly she ran on the moonlight sails, when the older boys played their mandolins and the girls sang and we ate doughnuts dipped in sugar, and how sweet the music was on the water in the shining night, and what it had felt like to think about girls then. After breakfast we would go up to the store and the things were in the same place—the minnows in a bottle, the plugs and spinners disarranged and pawed over by the youngsters from the boys' camp, the fig newtons and the Beeman's gum. Outside, the road was tarred and cars stood in front of the store. Inside, all was just as it had always been, except there was more Coca-Cola and not so much Moxie and root beer and birch beer and sarsaparilla. We would walk out with a bottle of pop apiece and sometimes the pop would backfire up our noses and hurt. We explored the streams, quietly, where the turtles slid off the sunny logs and dug their way into the soft bottom; and we lay on the town wharf and fed worms to the tame bass. Everywhere we went I had trouble making out which was I, the one walking at my side, the one walking in my pants.

One afternoon while we were there at that lake a thunderstorm came up. It was like the revival of an old melodrama that I had seen long ago with childish awe. The second-act climax of the drama of the electrical disturbance over a lake in America had not changed in any important respect. This was the big scene, still the big scene. The whole thing was so familiar, the first feeling of oppression and heat and a general air around camp of not wanting to go very far away. In midafternoon (it was all the same) a curious darkening of the sky, and a lull in everything that had made life tick; and then the way the boats suddenly swung the other way at their moorings with the coming of a breeze out of the new quarter, and the premonitory rumble. Then the kettle drum, then the snare, then the bass drum and cymbals, then crackling light against the dark, and the gods grinning and licking their chops in the hills. Afterward the calm, the rain steadily rustling in the calm lake, the return of light and hope and spirits, and the campers running out in joy and relief to go swimming in the rain, their bright cries perpetuating the deathless joke about how they were getting simply drenched, and the children screaming with delight at the new sensation of bathing in the rain, and the joke about getting drenched linking the generations in a strong indestructible chain. And the comedian who waded in carrying an umbrella.

When the others went swimming my son said he was going in too. He pulled his dripping trunks from the line where they had hung all through the shower, and wrung them out. Languidly, and with no thought of going in, I watched him, his hard little body, skinny and bare, saw him wince slightly as he pulled up around his vitals the small, soggy, icy garment. As he buckled the swollen belt suddenly my groin felt the chill of death.

Analyzing Rhetorical Choices

1. In your view, which instances of descriptive language or sensory details best convey the sense of setting?
2. What do you think about the absence in the essay of dialogue or commentary from White's son? How is this essay weaker or stronger for this absence?

3. How convincing is White's concluding line? Explain whether you read it literally or as a literary invention.

Writing About Issues and Contexts

1. How does White use the past to reflect on the present and the present to reflect on the past? Are there any ways that you can successfully relive the past or resist modernization? Explain your response.
2. Does White's essay remind you of anyone you know? Envision yourself having an experience similar to the one described by the author, and write about it in several paragraphs.

***Sherman J. Alexie Jr.** (1966–   ) grew up on the Spokane Indian Reservation in Wellpinit, Washington. He attended Washington State University and soon after graduating published* The Business of Fancydancing: Stories and Poems *(1992), from which this selection comes. His subsequent books include a volume of poetry,* Walter Flowing Home: Poems *(1996); a collection of stories and poems,* One Stick Song *(2000); two story collections,* The Lone Ranger and Tonto Fistfight in Heaven *(1994) and* Ten Little Indians *(2003); and a novel,* Indian Killer *(1998).*

Sherman Alexie

Father Coming Home

THEN   Father coming home from work. Me, waiting on the front steps, watching him walk slowly and carefully, like half of a real Indian. The other half stumbling, carrying the black metal lunch box with maybe half a sandwich, maybe the last drink of good coffee out of the thermos, maybe the last bite of a dream.

SPOKANE   Father coming home from work five days a week. Me, waiting every day until the day he doesn't come walking home, because he cut his knee in half with a chainsaw. Me, visiting my father laying in bed in the hospital in Spokane. Both of us, watching the color television until my mother comes from shopping at Goodwill or Salvation Army, until the nurses come in telling us we have to go.

CEREMONIES   Father coming home from the hospital in a wheelchair. Me, waiting for him to stand up and teach me how to shoot free throws. Me, running up to him one day and jumping hard into his lap, forgetting about his knee. Father holding me tight against his chest, dark and muddy, squeezing his pain into my thin ribs, his eyes staying clear.

AFTER   Father coming home from the mailbox, exercising his knee again and again. Me, looking up from the floor as he's shaking his head because there is no check, no tiny miracles coming in the mail. Father bouncing the basketball, shooting lay-in after lay-in, working the knee until it bleeds along the scars. Father crying from the pain late at night, watching television. Me, pretending to be asleep. All of us listening to canned laughter.

INSOMNIA   Father coming home from another job interview,
5   limping only a little but more than enough to keep
                    hearing no, no, no. Me, eating potatoes again in the
kitchen, my mother's face growing darker and darker by halves. One
half still mostly beautiful, still mostly Indian, the other half something
all-crazy and all-hungry. Me, waking her up in the middle of the night,
telling her my stomach is empty. Her throwing me outside in my underwear and locking the door. Me, trying anything to get back in.

HOMECOMING   Father coming home from drinking, after being
                    gone for weeks. Me, following him around all the
                    time. Him, never leaving my sight, going into the
bathroom. Me, sitting outside the door, waiting, knocking on the wood
every few seconds, asking him *Are you there? Are you still there?*

NOW   Father coming home finally from a part-time job.
                    Driving a water truck for the BIA. Me, waiting on
                    the front steps, watching him come home early
every day. Him, telling my mother when they think I can't hear, he
doesn't know if he's strong enough. Father telling mother he was driving the truck down Little Falls Hill, trying to downshift but his knee
not strong enough to keep holding the clutch in. Me, holding my
breath. Him, driving around the corner on two wheels, tons and tons of
water, half-insane. Me, closing my eyes. Him, balancing, always ready
to fall. Me, holding onto father with all my strength.

Analyzing Rhetorical Choices

1. How effective is the structure of "Father Coming Home"? In particular, what is your response to the flush-left subtitles and the
   repetition of "Father coming home. . . . Me . . . "?
2. What would you guess the narrator's age to be? In what ways, if
   any, is the narrator's voice appropriate?
3. How long a period do you think is represented in the piece?

Writing About Issues and Contexts

1. Do you think that the father should have taken the job with the
   Bureau of Indian Affairs (BIA), given his injury? Explain.
2. What conclusions or assumptions do you make about compensation, the economics, and the part-time job with the BIA?

Rachel Guido deVries (1947–) is a novelist and poet. Her works include the novel Tender Warriors *(1986) and the poetry volume* How to Sing to a Dago *(1997), from which this selection is taken.*

Rachel Guido deVries

On Alabama Ave., Paterson, NJ, 1954

At seven I dreamed again and again
of plummeting down the narrow stairs
into the arms of Mario the greenhorn
with his curly black hair. Old
5 Mrs. Pepe cleaned scungilli outside
on the porch. I watched her big hands
go in and out of the pot and thought
about her son Mario wishing he were
my pop. In the tiny flat on the third
10 floor. Pop was already bald and bellowing
rage. Mamma bit her tongue into silence
she never stopped wishing on me.

When Mamma's five sisters came over
she was happy. They talked dirty
15 in Calabrian and laughed loud. They
smacked each other on the back or
grabbed hands, smoked cigarettes and
ate the whole time, coffee cake, macaroni,
meatballs, biscotti, and fruit. Little
20 apricots sweet and delicate and yellow,
and tossed the smooth brown pits
on a blue plate, where they clattered
like dice.

Analyzing Rhetorical Choices

1. Why do you think deVries breaks the two stanzas where she does?
2. What kinds of assumptions does deVries make about her readers, given her word choices in this poem?

3. The poet closes with the imagery of apricot pits clattering like dice. Do you think that she intends the word *dice* to have social relevance as well? If so, what is she implying?

Writing About Issues and Contexts

1. Describe at least one comparable memory concerning childhood that you wish you could have changed.
2. How would you compare the domestic roles portrayed in 1954 to those of today?

An award-winning photographer, writer, composer, and filmmaker,
Gordon Parks *(1912–   ) was born in Fort Scott, Kansas. He grew up in
Kansas and Minnesota, and he was the first African American photographer to serve on the staffs of* Life *and* Vogue. *His famous* Life *photo-essay
about Flavio, a print version of which is included here, was published
in 1961. His books include the novel* The Learning Tree *(1963); his first
autobiography,* A Choice of Weapons *(1966);* Flavio *(1978); and his third
autobiography,* Voices in the Mirror *(1990). He also directed the classic
film* Shaft *(1971).*

Gordon Parks

Flavio's Home

I've never lost my fierce grudge against poverty. It is the most savage of all human afflictions, claiming victims who can't mobilize their
efforts against it, who often lack strength to digest what little food they
scrounge up to survive. It keeps growing, multiplying, spreading like a
cancer. In my wanderings I attack it wherever I can—in barrios, slums
and favelas.

Catacumba was the name of the favela where I found Flavio da
Silva. It was wickedly hot. The noon sun baked the mud-rot of the wet
mountainside. Garbage and human excrement clogged the open sew-
ers snaking down the slopes. José Gallo, a *Life* reporter, and I rested in
the shade of a jacaranda tree halfway up Rio de Janeiro's most infamous deathtrap. Below and above us were a maze of shacks, but in the
distance alongside the beach stood the gleaming white homes of the
rich.

Breathing hard, balancing a tin of water on his head, a small boy
climbed toward us. He was miserably thin, naked but for filthy denim
shorts. His legs resembled sticks covered with skin and screwed into
his feet. Death was all over him, in his sunken eyes, cheeks and jaun-
diced coloring. He stopped for breath, coughing, his chest heaving as
water slopped over his bony shoulders. Then jerking sideways like a
mechanical toy, he smiled a smile I will never forget. Turning, he went
on up the mountainside.

The detailed *Life* assignment in my back pocket was to find an
impoverished father with a family, to examine his earnings, political
leanings, religion, friends, dreams and frustrations. I had been sent to

do an essay on poverty. This frail boy bent under his load said more to me about poverty than a dozen poor fathers. I touched Gallo, and we got up and followed the boy to where he entered a shack near the top of the mountainside. It was a leaning crumpled place of old plankings with a rusted tin roof. From inside we heard the babblings of several children. José knocked. The door opened and the boy stood smiling with a bawling naked baby in his arms.

5   Still smiling, he whacked the baby's rump, invited us in and offered us a box to sit on. The only other recognizable furniture was a sagging bed and a broken baby's crib. Flavio was twelve, and with Gallo acting as interpreter, he introduced his younger brothers and sisters: "Mario, the bad one; Baptista, the good one; Albia, Isabel and the baby Zacarias." Two other girls burst into the shack, screaming and pounding on one another. Flavio jumped in and parted them. "Shut up, you two." He pointed at the older girl. "That's Maria, the nasty one." She spit in his face. He smacked her and pointed to the smaller sister. "That's Luzia. She thinks she's pretty."

Having finished the introductions, he went to build a fire under the stove—a rusted, bent top of an old gas range resting on several bricks. Beneath it was a piece of tin that caught the hot coals. The shack was about six by ten feet. Its grimy walls were a patchwork of misshapen boards with large gaps between them, revealing other shacks below stilted against the slopes. The floor, rotting under layers of grease and dirt, caught shafts of light slanting down through spaces in the roof. A large hole in the far corner served as a toilet. Beneath that hole was the sloping mountainside. Pockets of poverty in New York's Harlem, on Chicago's south side, in Puerto Rico's infamous El Fungito seemed pale by comparison. None of them had prepared me for this one in the favela of Catacumba.

Flavio washed rice in a large dishpan, then washed Zacarias's feet in the same water. But even that dirty water wasn't to be wasted. He tossed in a chunk of lye soap and ordered each child to wash up. When they were finished he splashed the water over the dirty floor, and, dropping to his knees, he scrubbed the planks until the black suds sank in. Just before sundown he put beans on the stove to warm, then left, saying he would be back shortly. "Don't let them burn," he cautioned Maria. "If they do and Poppa beats me, you'll get it later." Maria, happy to get at the licking spoon, switched over and began to stir the beans. Then slyly she dipped out a spoonful and swallowed them. Luzia eyed her. "I see you. I'm going to tell on you for stealing our supper."

Maria's eyes flashed anger. "You do and I'll beat you, you little bitch." Luzia threw a stick at Maria and fled out the door. Zacarias dropped off to sleep. Mario, the bad one, slouched in a corner and sucked his thumb. Isabel and Albia sat on the floor clinging to each other with a strange tenderness. Isabel held onto Albia's hair and Albia clutched at Isabel's neck. They appeared frozen in an act of quiet violence.

Flavio returned with wood, dumped it beside the stove and sat down to rest for a few minutes, then went down the mountain for more water. It was dark when he finally came back, his body sagging from exhaustion. No longer smiling, he suddenly had the look of an old man and by now we could see that he kept the family going. In the closed torment of that pitiful shack, he was waging a hopeless battle against starvation. The da Silva children were living in a coffin.

10   When at last the parents came in, Gallo and I seemed to be part of the family. Flavio had already told them we were there. "Gordunn Americano!" Luzia said, pointing at me. José, the father, viewed us with skepticism. Nair, his pregnant wife, seemed tired beyond speaking. Hardly acknowledging our presence, she picked up Zacarias, placed him on her shoulder and gently patted his behind. Flavio scurried about like a frightened rat, his silence plainly expressing the fear he held of his father. Impatiently, José da Silva waited for Flavio to serve dinner. He sat in the center of the bed with his legs crossed beneath him, frowning, waiting. There were only three tin plates. Flavio filled them with black beans and rice, then placed them before his father. José da Silva tasted them, chewed for several moments, then nodded his approval for the others to start. Only he and Nair had spoons; the children ate with their fingers. Flavio ate off the top of a coffee can. Afraid to offer us food, he edged his rice and beans toward us, gesturing for us to take some. We refused. He smiled, knowing we understood.

Later, when we got down to the difficult business of obtaining permission from José da Silva to photograph his family, he hemmed and hawed, wallowing in the pleasant authority of the decision maker. He finally gave in, but his manner told us that he expected something in return. As we were saying good night Flavio began to cough violently. For a few moments his lungs seemed to be tearing apart. I wanted to get away as quickly as possible. It was cowardly of me, but the bluish cast of his skin beneath the sweat, the choking and spitting were suddenly unbearable.

Gallo and I moved cautiously down through the darkness trying not to appear as strangers. The Catacumba was no place for strangers after sundown. Desperate criminals hid out there. To hunt them out, the police came in packs, but only in daylight. Gallo cautioned me. "If you get caught up here after dark it's best to stay at the da Silvas' until morning." As we drove toward the city the large white buildings of the rich loomed up. The world behind us seemed like a bad dream. I had already decided to get the boy Flavio to a doctor, and as quickly as possible.

The plush lobby of my hotel on the Copacabana waterfront was crammed with people in formal attire. With the stink of the favela in my clothes, I hurried to the elevator hoping no passengers would be aboard. But as the door was closing a beautiful girl in a white lace gown stepped in. I moved as far away as possible. Her escort entered behind her, swept her into his arms and they indulged in a kiss that lasted until they exited on the next floor. Neither of them seemed to realize that I was there. The room I returned to seemed to be oversized; the da Silva shack would have fitted into one corner of it. The steak dinner I had would have fed the da Silvas for three days.

Billowing clouds blanketed Mount Corcovado as we approached the favela the following morning. Suddenly the sun burst through, silhouetting Cristo Redentor, the towering sculpture of Christ with arms extended, its back turned against the slopes of Catacumba. The square at the entrance to the favela bustled with hundreds of favelados. Long lines waited at the sole water spigot. Others waited at the only toilet on the entire mountainside. Women, unable to pay for soap, beat dirt from their wash at laundry tubs. Men, burdened with lumber, picks and shovels and tools important to their existence threaded their way through the noisy throngs. Dogs snarled, barked and fought. Woodsmoke mixed with the stench of rotting things. In the mist curling over the higher paths, columns of favelados climbed like ants with wood and water cans on their heads.

15   We came upon Nair bent over her tub of wash. She wiped away sweat with her apron and managed a smile. We asked for her husband and she pointed to a tiny shack off to her right. This was José's store, where he sold kerosene and bleach. He was sitting on a box, dozing. Sensing our presence, he awoke and commenced complaining about his back. "It kills me. The doctors don't help because I have no money. Always talk and a little pink pill that does no good. Ah, what is to become of me?" A woman came to buy bleach. He filled her bottle. She dropped a few coins and as she walked away his eyes stayed on her backside until she was out of sight. Then he was complaining about his back again.

"How much do you earn a day?" Gallo asked.

"Seventy-five cents. On a good day maybe a dollar."

"Why aren't the kids in school?"

"I don't have money for the clothes they need to go to school."

20 "Has Flavio seen a doctor?"

He pointed to a one-story wooden building. "That's the clinic right there. They're mad because I built my store in front of their place. I won't tear it down so they won't help my kids. Talk, talk, talk and pink pills." We bid him good-bye and started climbing, following mud trails, jutting rock, slime-filled holes and shack after shack propped against the slopes on shaky pilings. We sidestepped a dead cat covered with maggots. I held my breath for an instant, only to inhale the stench of human excrement and garbage. Bare feet and legs with open sores climbed above us—evils of the terrible soil they trod every day, and there were seven hundred thousand or more afflicted people in favelas around Rio alone. Touching me, Gallo pointed to Flavio climbing ahead of us carrying firewood. He stopped to glance at a man descending with a small coffin on his shoulder. A woman and a small child followed him. When I lifted my camera, grumbling erupted from a group of men sharing beer beneath a tree.

"They're threatening," Gallo said. "Keep moving. They fear cameras. Think they're evil eyes bringing bad luck." Turning to watch the funeral procession, Flavio caught sight of us and waited. When we took the wood from him he protested, saying he was used to carrying it. He gave in when I hung my camera around his neck. Then, beaming, he climbed on ahead of us.

The fog had lifted and in the crisp morning light the shack looked more squalid. Inside the kids seemed even noisier. Flavio smiled and spoke above their racket. "Someday I want to live in a real house on a real street with good pots and pans and a bed with sheets." He lit the fire to warm leftovers from the night before. Stale rice and beans—for breakfast and supper. No lunch; midday eating was out of the question. Smoke rose and curled up through the ceiling's cracks. An air current forced it back, filling the place and Flavio's lungs with fumes. A coughing spasm doubled him up, turned his skin blue under viscous sweat. I handed him a cup of water, but he waved it away. His stomach tightened as he dropped to his knees. His veins throbbed as if they would burst. Frustrated, we could only watch; there was nothing we could do to help. Strangely, none of his brothers or sisters appeared to notice. None of them stopped doing whatever they were doing. Perhaps they had seen it too often. After five interminable minutes it was over, and he got to his feet, smiling as though it had all been a joke. "Maria, it's time for Zacarias to be washed!"

"But there's rice in the pan!"

25   "Dump it in another pan—and don't spill water!"

Maria picked up Zacarias, who screamed, not wanting to be washed. Irritated, Maria gave him a solid smack on his bare bottom. Flavio stepped over and gave her the same, then a free-for-all started with Flavio, Maria and Mario slinging fists at one another. Mario got one in the eye and fled the shack calling Flavio a dirty son-of-a-bitch. Zacarias wound up on the floor sucking his thumb and escaping his washing. The black bean and rice breakfast helped to get things back to normal. Now it was time to get Flavio to the doctor.

The clinic was crowded with patients—mothers and children covered with open sores, a paralytic teenager, a man with an ear in a state of decay, an aged blind couple holding hands in doubled darkness. Throughout the place came wailings of hunger and hurt. Flavio sat nervously between Gallo and me. "What will the doctor do to me?" he kept asking.

"We'll see. We'll wait and see."

In all, there were over fifty people. Finally, after two hours, it was Flavio's turn and he broke out in a sweat, though he smiled at the nurse as he passed through the door to the doctor's office. The nurse ignored it; in this place of misery, smiles were unexpected.

30   The doctor, a large, beady-eyed man with a crew cut, had an air of impatience. Hardly acknowledging our presence, he began to examine the frightened Flavio. "Open your mouth. Say 'Ah.' Jump up and down. Breathe out. Take off those pants. Bend over. Stand up. Cough. Cough louder. Louder." He did it all with such cold efficiency. Then he spoke to us in English so Flavio wouldn't understand. "This little chap has just about had it." My heart sank. Flavio was smiling, happy to be over with the examination. He was handed a bottle of cough medicine and a small box of pink pills, then asked to step outside and wait.

"This the da Silva kid?"

"Yes."

"What's your interest in him?"

"We want to help in some way."

35   "I'm afraid you're too late. He's wasted with bronchial asthma, malnutrition and, I suspect, tuberculosis. His heart, lungs and teeth are all bad." He paused and wearily rubbed his forehead. "All that at the ripe old age of twelve. And these hills are packed with other kids

just as bad off. Last year ten thousand died from dysentery alone. But what can we do? You saw what's waiting outside. It's like this every day. There's hardly enough money to buy aspirin. A few wealthy people who care help keep us going." He was quiet for a moment. "Maybe the right climate, the right diet, and constant medical care might. . . ." He stopped and shook his head. "Naw. That poor lad's finished. He might last another year—maybe not." We thanked him and left.

"What did he say?" Flavio asked as we scaled the hill.

"Everything's going to be all right, Flav. there's nothing to worry about."

It had clouded over again by the time we reached the top. The rain swept in, clearing the mountain of Corcovado. The huge Christ figure loomed up again with clouds swirling around it. And to it I said a quick prayer for the boy walking beside us. He smiled as if he had read my thoughts. "Papa says 'El Christo' has turned his back on the favela."

"You're going to be all right, Flavio."

40 "I'm not scared of death. It's my brothers and sisters I worry about. What would they do?"

"You'll be all right, Flavio."

Analyzing Rhetorical Choices

1. What are the most stark descriptions in the essay? How do they serve the author's purpose in terms of creating a dominant impression?
2. What does Parks mean in stating that Isabel and Albia "appeared frozen in an act of quiet violence"?
3. At the end of the essay, why doesn't Parks answer Flavio's question?

Writing About Issues and Contexts

1. Parks eventually brought Flavio to the United States where he was successfully treated for his illnesses. Support from *Life* magazine readers enabled the da Silva family to move away from Caracumba. What else might be done to offer systemic relief to the residents of the *favela*?
2. What kind of impact would a photo-essay on poverty like that of Parks have today if it appeared in a national publication?
3. What are the arguments for or against population control in areas like Caracumba?

Formerly a landscape photographer, **Barry Lopez** *(1945–   ) is currently regarded as one of the nation's premier nature writers. He has numerous awards, including the National Book Award in 1986 for* Arctic Dreams. *His other books include* Of Wolves and Men *(1979),* The Rediscovery of North America *(1990),* Field Notes *(1994), and* Light Action in the Caribbean *(2001). "The Stone Horse" first appeared in the writing periodical* Antaeus *in 1986.*

Barry Lopez

The Stone Horse

I

The deserts of southern California, the high, relatively cooler and wetter Mojave and the hotter, dryer Sonoran to the south of it, carry the signatures of many cultures. Prehistoric rock drawings in the Mojave's Coso Range, probably the greatest concentration of petroglyphs in North America, are at least three thousand years old. Big-game-hunting cultures that flourished six or seven thousand years before that are known from broken spear tips, choppers, and burins left scattered along the shores of great Pleistocene lakes, long since evaporated. Weapons and tools discovered at China Lake may be thirty thousand years old; and worked stone from a quarry in the Calico Mountains is, some argue, evidence that human beings were here more than 200,000 years ago.

Because of the long-term stability of such arid environments, much of this prehistoric stone evidence still lies exposed on the ground, accessible to anyone who passes by—the studious, the acquisitive, the indifferent, the merely curious. Archaeologists do not agree on the sequence of cultural history beyond about twelve thousand years ago, but it is clear that these broken bits of chalcedony, chert, and obsidian, like the animal drawings and geometric designs etched on walls of basalt throughout the desert, anchor the earliest threads of human history, the first record of human endeavor here.

Western man did not enter the California desert until the end of the eighteenth century, 250 years after Coronado brought his soldiers into the Zuni pueblos in a bewildered search for the cities of Cibola.

The earliest appraisals of the land were cursory, hurried. People traveled *through* it, en route to Santa Fe or the California coastal settlements. Only miners tarried. In 1823 what had been Spain's became Mexico's, and in 1848 what had been Mexico's became America's; but the bare, jagged mountains and dry lake beds, the vast and uniform plains of creosote bush and yucca plants, remained as obscure as the northern Sudan until the end of the nineteenth century.

Before 1940 the tangible evidence of twentieth-century man's passage here consisted of very little—the hard tracery of travel corridors; the widely scattered, relatively insignificant evidence of mining operations; and the fair expanse of irrigated fields at the desert's periphery. In the space of a hundred years or so the wagon roads were paved, railroads were laid down, and canals and high-tension lines were built to bring water and electricity across the desert to Los Angeles from the Colorado River. The dark mouths of gold, talc, and tin mines yawned from the bony flanks of desert ranges. Dust-encrusted chemical plants stood at work on the lonely edges of dry lake beds. And crops of grapes, lettuce, dates, alfalfa, and cotton covered the Coachella and Imperial valleys, north and south of the Salton Sea, and the Palo Verde Valley along the Colorado.

5   These developments proceeded with little or no awareness of earlier human occupations by cultures that preceded those of the historic Indians—the Mojave, the Chemehuevi, the Quechan. (Extensive irrigation began actually to change the climate of the Sonoran Desert, and human settlements, the railroads, and farming introduced many new, successful plants into the region.)

During World War II, the American military moved into the desert in great force, to train troops and to test equipment. They found the clear weather conducive to year-round flying, the dry air and isolation very attractive. After the war, a complex of training grounds, storage facilities, and gunnery and test ranges was permanently settled on more than three million acres of military reservations. Few perceived the extent or significance of the destruction of the aboriginal sites that took place during tank maneuvers and bombing runs or in the laying out of highways, railroads, mining districts, and irrigated fields. The few who intuited that something like an American Dordogne Valley lay exposed here were (only) amateur archaeologists; even they reasoned that the desert was too vast for any of this to matter.

After World War II, people began moving out of the crowded Los Angeles basin into homes in Lucerne, Apple, and Antelope valleys in the western Mojave. They emigrated as well to a stretch of resort land at the foot of the San Jacinto Mountains that included Palm Springs, and farther out to old railroad and military towns like Twentynine Palms and Barstow. People also began exploring the desert, at first in military-surplus jeeps and then with a variety of all-terrain and off-road vehicles that became available in the 1960s. By the mid-1970s, the number of people using such vehicles for desert recreation had increased exponentially. Most came and went in innocent curiosity; the few who didn't wreaked a havoc all out of proportion to their numbers. The disturbance of previously isolated archaeological sites increased by an order of magnitude. Many sites were vandalized before archaeologists, themselves late to the desert, had any firm grasp of the bounds of human history in the desert. It was as though in the same moment an Aztec library had been discovered intact various lacunae had begun to appear.

The vandalism was of three sorts: the general disturbance usually caused by souvenir hunters and by the curious and the oblivious; the wholesale stripping of a place by professional thieves for black-market sale and trade; and outright destruction, in which vehicles were actually used to ram and trench an area. By 1980, the Bureau of Land Management estimated that probably 35 percent of the archaeological sites in the desert had been vandalized. The destruction at some places by rifles and shotguns, or by power winches mounted on vehicles, was, if one cared for history, demoralizing to behold.

In spite of public education, land closures, and stricter law enforcement in recent years, the BLM estimates that, annually, about 1 percent of the archaeological record in the desert continues to be destroyed or stolen.

II

10   A BLM archaeologist told me, with understandable reluctance, where to find the intaglio. I spread my Automobile Club of Southern California map of Imperial County out on his desk, and he traced the route with a pink felt-tip pen. The line crossed Interstate 8 and then turned west along the Mexican border.

"You can't drive any farther than about here," he said, marking a small X. "There's boulders in the wash. You walk up past them."

On a separate piece of paper he drew a route in a smaller scale that would take me up the arroyo to a certain point where I was to cross back east, to another arroyo. At its head, on higher ground just to the north, I would find the horse.

"It's tough to spot unless you know it's there. Once you pick it up . . ." He shook his head slowly, in a gesture of wonder at its existence.

I waited until I held his eye. I assured him I would not tell anyone else how to get there. He looked at me with stoical despair, like a man who had been robbed twice, whose belief in human beings was offered without conviction.

15   I did not go until the following day because I wanted to see it at dawn. I ate breakfast at four A.M. in El Centro and then drove south. The route was easy to follow, though the last section of road proved difficult, broken and drifted over with sand in some spots. I came to the barricade of boulders and parked. It was light enough by then to find my way over the ground with little trouble. The contours of the landscape were stark, without any masking vegetation. I worried only about rattlesnakes.

I traversed the stone plain as directed, but, in spite of the frankness of the land, I came on the horse unawares. In the first moment of recognition I was without feeling. I recalled later being startled, and that I held my breath. It was laid out on the ground with its head to the east, three times life size. As I took in its outline I felt a growing concentration of all my senses, as though my attentiveness to the pale rose color of the morning sky and other peripheral images had now ceased to be important. I was aware that I was straining for sound in the windless air, and I felt the uneven pressure of the earth hard against my feet. The horse, outlined in a standing profile of the dark ground, was as vivid before me as a bed of tulips.

I've come upon animals suddenly before, and felt a similar tension, a precipitate heightening of the senses. And I have felt the inexplicable but sharply boosted intensity of a wild moment in the bush, where it is not until some minutes later that you discover the source of electricity—the warm remains of a grizzly bear kill, or the still moist tracks of a wolverine.

But this was slightly different. I felt I had stepped into an unoccupied corridor. I had no familiar sense of history, the temporal structure in which to think: this horse was made by Quechan people three hundred years ago. I felt instead a headlong rush of images: people hunting wild horses with spears on the Pleistocene veld of southern California; Cortés riding across the causeway into Montezuma's Tenochtitlán; a short-legged Comanche, astride his horse like some sort of ferret, slashing through cavalry lines of young men who rode like farmers; a hoof exploding past my face one morning in a corral in Wyoming. These images had the weight and silence of stone.

When I released my breath, the images softened. My initial feeling, of facing a wild animal in a remote region, was replaced with a calm sense of antiquity. It was then that I became conscious, like an ordinary tourist, of what was before me, and thought: this horse was probably laid out by Quechan people. But when? I wondered. The first horses they saw, I knew, might have been those that came north from Mexico in 1692 with Father Eusebio Kino. But Cocopa people, I recalled, also came this far north on occasion, to fight with their neighbors, the Quechan. And *they* could have seen horses with Melchior Díaz, at the mouth of the Colorado River in the fall of 1540. So, it could be four hundred years old. (No one in fact knows.)

20   I still had not moved. I took my eyes off the horse for a moment to look south over the desert plain into Mexico, to look east past its head at the brightening sunrise, to situate myself. Then, finally, I brought my trailing foot slowly forward and stood erect. Sunlight was running like a thin sheet of water over the stony ground and it threw the horse into relief. It looked as though no hand had ever disturbed the stones that gave it its form.

The horse had been brought to life on ground called desert pavement, a tight, flat matrix of small cobbles blasted smooth by sand-laden winds. The uniform, monochromatic blackness of the stones, a patina of iron and magnesium oxides called desert varnish, is caused by long-term exposure to the sun. To make this type of low-relief ground glyph, or intaglio, the artist either selectively turns individual stones over to their lighter side or removes areas of stone to expose the lighter soil underneath, creating a negative image. This horse, about eighteen feet from brow to rump and eight feet from withers to hoof, had been made in the latter way, and its outline was bermed at certain points with low ridges of stone a few inches high to enhance its three-dimensional qualities. (The left side of the horse was in full profile; each leg was extended at 90 degrees to the body and fully visible, as though seen in three-quarter profile.)

I was not eager to move. The moment I did I would be back in the flow of time, the horse no longer quivering in the same way before me. I did not want to feel again the sequence of quotidian events—to be drawn off into deliberation and analysis. A human being, a four-footed animal, the open land. That was all that was present—and a "thoughtless" understanding of the very old desires bearing on this particular animal: to hunt it, to render it, to fathom it, to subjugate it, to honor it, to take it as a companion.

What finally made me move was the light. The sun now filled the shallow basin of the horse's body. The weighted line of the stone berm created the illusion of a mane and the distinctive roundness of an equine belly. The change in definition impelled me. I moved to the left, circling past its rump, to see how the light might flesh the horse out from various points of view. I circled it completely before squatting on my haunches. Ten or fifteen minutes later I chose another view. The third time I moved, to a point near the rear hooves, I spotted a stone tool at my feet. I stared at it a long while, more in awe than disbelief, before reaching out to pick it up. I turned it over in my left palm and took it between my fingers to feel its cutting edge. It is always difficult, especially with something so portable, to rechannel the desire to steal.

I spent several hours with the horse. As I changed positions and as the angle of the light continued to change I noticed a number of things. The angle at which the pastern carried the hoof away from the ankle was perfect. Also, stones had been placed within the image to suggest at precisely the right spot the left shoulder above the foreleg. The line that joined thigh and hock was similarly accurate. The muzzle alone seemed distorted—but perhaps these stones had been moved by a later hand. It was an admirably accurate representation, but not what a breeder would call perfect conformation. There was the suggestion of a bowed neck and an undershot jaw, and the tail, as full as a winter coyote's, did not appear to be precisely to scale.

25   The more I thought about it, the more I felt I was looking at an individual horse, a unique combination of generic and specific detail. It was easy to imagine one of Kino's horses as a model, or a horse that ran off from one of Coronado's columns. What kind of horses would these have been? I wondered. In the sixteenth century the most sought-after horses in Europe were Spanish, the offspring of Arabian stock and Barbary horses that the Moors brought to Iberia and bred to the older, eastern European strains brought in by the Romans. The model for this horse, I speculated, could easily have been a palomino, or a descendant of horses trained for lion hunting in North Africa.

A few generations ago, cowboys, cavalry quartermasters, and draymen would have taken this horse before me under consideration and not let up their scrutiny until they had its heritage fixed to their satisfaction. Today, the distinction between draft and harness horses is arcane knowledge, and no image may come to mind for a blue roan or a claybank horse. The loss of such refinement in everyday conversation leaves me unsettled. People praise the Eskimo's ability to distinguish among forty types of snow but forget the skill of others who routinely differentiate between overo and tobiano pintos. Such distinctions are made for the same reason. You have to do it to be able to talk clearly about the world.

For parts of two years I worked as a horse wrangler and packer in Wyoming. It is dim knowledge now; I would have to think to remember if a buckskin was a kind of dun horse. And I couldn't throw a double-diamond hitch over a set of panniers—the packer's basic tiedown—without guidance. As I squatted there in the desert, however, these more personal memories seemed tenuous in comparison with the sweep of this animal in human time. My memories had no depth. I thought of the Hittite cavalry riding against the Syrians 3,500 years ago. And the first of the Chinese emperors, Ch'in Shih Huang, buried in Shensi Province in 210 B.C. with thousands of life-size horses and soldiers, a terra-cotta guardian army. What could I know of what was in the mind of whoever made this horse? Was there some racial memory of it as an animal that had once fed the artist's ancestors and then disappeared from North America? And then returned in this strange alliance with another race of men?

Certainly, whoever it was, the artist had observed the animal very closely. Certainly the animal's speed had impressed him. Among the first things the Quechan would have learned from an encounter with Kino's horses was that their own long-distance runners—men who could run down mule deer—were no match for this animal.

From where I squatted I could look far out over the Mexican plain. Juan Bautista de Anza passed this way in 1774, extending El Camino Real into Alta California from Sinaloa. He was followed by others, all of them astride the magical horse; *gente de razón*, the people of reason, coming into the country of *los primitivos*. The horse, like the stone animals of Egypt, urged these memories upon me. And as I drew them up from some forgotten corner of my mind—huge horses carved in the white chalk downs of southern England by an Iron Age people; Spanish horses rearing and wheeling in fear before alligators in Florida—the images seemed tethered before me. With this sense of proportion, a memory of my own—the morning I almost lost my face to a horse's hoof—now had somewhere to fit.

30   I rose up and began to walk slowly around the horse again. I had taken the first long measure of it and was now looking for a way to depart, a new angle of light, a fading of the image itself before the rising sun, that would break its hold on me. As I circled, feeling both heady and serene at the encounter, I realized again how strangely vivid it was. It had been created on a barren bajada between two arroyos, as

nondescript a place as one could imagine. The only plant life here was a few wands of ocotillo cactus. The ground beneath my shoes was so hard it wouldn't take the print of a heavy animal even after a rain. The only sounds I heard here were the voices of quail.

The archaeologist had been correct. For all its forcefulness, the horse is inconspicuous. If you don't care to see it you can walk right past it. That pleases him, I think. Unmarked on this bleak shoulder of the plain, the site signals to no one; so he wants no protective fences here, no informative plaque, to act as beacons. He would rather take a chance that no motorcyclist, no aimless wanderer with a flair for violence and a depth of ignorance, will ever find his way here.

The archaeologist had given me something before I left his office that now seemed peculiar—an aerial photograph of the horse. It is widely believed that an aerial view of an intaglio provides a fair and accurate depiction. It does not. In the photograph the horse looks somewhat crudely constructed; from the ground it appears far more deftly rendered. The photograph is of a single moment, and in that split second the horse seems vaguely impotent. I watched light pool in the intaglio at dawn; I imagine you could watch it withdraw at dusk and sense the same animation I did. In those prolonged moments its shape and so, too, its general character changed—noticeably. The living quality of the image, its immediacy to the eye, was brought out by the light-in-time, not, at least here, in the camera's frozen instant.

Intaglios, I thought, were never meant to be seen by gods in the sky above. They were meant to be seen by people on the ground, over a long period of shifting light. This could even be true of the huge figures on the Plain of Nazca in Peru, where people could walk for the length of a day beside them. It is our own impatience that leads us to think otherwise.

This process of abstraction, almost unintentional, drew me gradually away from the horse. I came to a position of attention at the edge of the sphere of its influence. With a slight bow I paid my respects to the horse, its maker, and the history of us all, and departed.

III

35 A short distance away I stopped the car in the middle of the road to make a few notes. I could not write down what I was thinking when I was with the horse. It would have seemed disrespectful, and it would have required another kind of attention. So now I patiently drained my memory of the details it had fastened itself upon. The road I'd

stopped on was adjacent to the All American Canal, the major source of water for the Imperial and Coachella valleys. The water flowed west placidly. A disjointed flock of coots, small, dark birds with white bills, was paddling against the current, foraging in the rushes.

I was peripherally aware of the birds as I wrote, the only movement in the desert, and of a series of sounds from a village a half-mile away. The first sounds from this collection of ramshackle houses in a grove of cottonwoods were the distracted dawn voices of dogs. I heard them intermingled with the cries of a rooster. Later, the high-pitched voices of children calling out to each other came disembodied through the dry desert air. Now, a little after seven, I could hear someone practicing on the trumpet, the same rough phrases played over and over. I suddenly remembered how as children we had tried to get the rhythm of a galloping horse with hands against our thighs, or by fluttering our tongues against the roofs of our mouths.

After the trumpet, the impatient calls of adults summoning children. Sunday morning. Wood smoke hung like a lens in the trees. The first car starts—a cold eight-cylinder engine, of Chrysler extraction perhaps, goosed to life, then throttled back to murmur through dual mufflers, the obligato music of a shade-tree mechanic. The rote bark of mongrel dogs at dawn, the jagged outcries of men and women, an engine coming to life. Like a thousand villages from West Virginia to Guadalajara.

I finished my notes—where was I going to find a description of the horses that came north with the conquistadors? Did their manes come forward prominently over the brow, like this one's, like the forelocks of Blackfeet and Assiniboin men in nineteenth-century paintings? I set the notes on the seat beside me.

The road followed the canal for a while and then arced north, toward Interstate 8. It was slow driving and I fell to thinking how the desert had changed since Anza had come through. New plants and animals—the MacDougall cottonwood, the English house sparrow, the chukar from India—have about them now the air of the native-born. Of the native species, some—no one knows how many—are extinct. The populations of many others, especially the animals, have been sharply reduced. The idea of a desert impoverished by agricultural poisons and varmint hunters, by off-road vehicles and military operations, did not seem as disturbing to me, however, as this other horror, now that I had been those hours with the horse. The vandals, the few who crowbar rock art off the desert's walls, who dig up graves, who punish the ground that holds intaglios, are people who devour history.

Their self-centered scorn, their disrespect for ideas and images beyond their ken, create the awful atmosphere of loose ends in which totalitarianism thrives, in which the past is merely curious or wrong.

40   I thought about the horse sitting out there on the unprotected plain. I enumerated its qualities in my mind until a sense of its vulnerability receded and it became an anchor for something else. I remembered that history, a history like this one, which ran deeper than Mexico, deeper than the Spanish, was a kind of medicine. It permitted the great breadth of human expression to reverberate, and it did not urge you to locate its apotheosis in the present.

Each of us, individuals and civilizations, has been held upside down like Achilles in the River Styx. The artist mixing his colors in the dim light of Altamira; an Egyptian ruler living still now, wrapped in his byssus, stored against time in a pyramid; the faded Dorset culture of the Arctic; the Hmong and Samburu and Walbiri of historic time; the modern nations. This great, imperfect stretch of human expression is the clarification and encouragement, the urging and the reminder, we call history. And it is inscribed everywhere in the face of the land, from the mountain passes of the Himalayas to a nameless bajada in the California desert.

Small birds rose up in the road ahead, startled, and flew off. I prayed no infidel would ever find that horse.

Analyzing Rhetorical Choices

1. How would you describe Lopez's tone in this essay, and what is your reaction to it?
2. How effective are the rather lengthy sections about history, especially in the first section of the essay?
3. Lopez includes a number of key metaphors and descriptions of setting. Which ones seem to work particularly well?

Writing About Issues and Contexts

1. How, in your view, could we strike the best balance between the preservation of historical artifacts and modern demands for space to build, for example, military facilities?
2. Are there sites/sights that you would leave home at four o'clock in the morning to visit? Describe at least one or two, and connect these to the essay.
3. What similarities, if any, do you see between Lopez's essay and those by Alice Walker and E. B. White?

Strategies for Writers: Description

1. Practice writing essays, vignettes, or poems in which you focus on description. Challenge yourself to find highly expressive verbs and modifiers. Strive to come up with metaphors that convey your ideas most vividly.

2. Share your efforts with students, instructors, family, and friends. Ask specifically about their reactions to your images. Note other feedback as well. Consider all responses as you revise.

3. Reread Gordon Parks's portrayal of the *favela* he visited for a second day, as "billowing clouds blanketed Mount Corcovado." Use this passage as a model to create a description of a scene.

4. Similarly, study James Thurber's extended simile comparing a thunderstorm to an old melodrama. Write an extended simile on a subject of interest to you.

5. Try to give an animal, perhaps your pet, a personality the way Alice Walker does Blue.

6. Like Lopez in the presence of the stone horse, contemplate an object or place and try to record a "headlong rush of images."

7. Reread some of the selections in this chapter, concentrating on identifying the sensory details. Add descriptions involving senses not referred to in specific passages. For example, deVries does not include details about taste. What might such details be?

8. Prepare your work for additional sharing or publication. Proofread with attention to elements such as word omissions, spelling, punctuation, and grammar. If necessary, solicit help from a style manual and people willing to help in this process.

Research and Writing Assignments

1. Following the example of Yusef Komunyakaa's "Blue" and Alice Walker's "Am I Blue?" consider a color or other characteristic—red, yellow, hunger, thirst, ambition—and write a descriptive passage that illustrates a specific point, perspective, or personality by exploring the characteristic in detail. Push yourself to produce as many relevant appeals to the senses as you can.

2. As you have read, Julia Alvarez, Rachel Guido deVries, and Sherman Alexie provide descriptive sketches that also function as tales about coming of age amid social and political tensions. Write a descriptive essay that reflects your own childhood un-

derstanding of family or wider social issues. Emphasize any dramatic learning episodes that you recall, such as Yolanda's introduction to snow.

3. In "Once More to the Lake," the author returns to an important scene of his youth and has a revelation. If possible, return to a significant scene of your childhood and describe it in detail. In any event, write about a site you once frequented and reveal any new insights you may now have that are associated with the place.

4. Description can be an important device in highlighting an issue of concern to the writer. In "Flavio's Home," Gordon Parks employs descriptive writing to portray the effects of poverty. Draw attention to a major social issue or condition and use descriptive writing to help state your case.

5. Research or visit a location that is unfamiliar to you and write an essay about it. As Barry Lopez does in "The Stone Horse," incorporate descriptive details to give readers a full sense of the geography.

4
Definition

Definition is one of the most basic ways that we learn, especially when encountering a new or specialized language or confronting unfamiliar words and concepts. This is true when we are children but is just as important for college students confronted with unfamiliar words and concepts. An instructor or textbook might state, "At that stage, Metterlink's ideas were still inchoate," or "Let's hope that the United States is able to resile from its current position on global warming." If we lack definitions for key words, these sentences are confusing. Likewise, without consulting a bound or on-line dictionary, it is probably difficult for many readers to understand the following, admittedly pretentious, sentence: "Her indefatigable desire to resort to eponymous references produced holophrastic results that left me intellectually enervated and downright morose." To make sense of this statement requires an understanding of word definitions as well as the ability to put those definitions together to create coherent understanding.

At its most basic level, definition is about understanding words and being able to infuse spoken and written sentences with meaning. It is a transaction between writer and reader that is accomplished through words and text. We would add that most of us have been guilty at one time or another of reading complex passages of prose and guessing wrongly at the meanings of words, or misusing words and concepts in our own writing and speaking—because we were unwilling to consult a dictionary or reference book. Anyone who makes this kind of mistake might well be considered . . . gormless. (Note: if you are interested in the play of word definitions, we encourage you to subscribe to a free online service known as Wordsmith, located at *http://www.wordsmith.org* or check out Says You! at *http://www.wgbh.org/radio/saysyou/*.)

Important though word definition is—and it is fundamental to reading and writing—our focus here is on a mode of writing called *extended definition*. Extended definition occurs when a writer chooses to define a complex subject, usually because it is significant to a general readership and also interests the writer. Perhaps a better way to think about extended definition is to label it as a specific kind of explanation, one that takes on difficult and abstract concepts and offers an improved understanding of them. Thus definition as a mode of writing is essential to improving understanding and communication because it almost always establishes the meaning of a term, concept, or idea by connecting it to a larger context.

Typically the most successful extended definition essays result when the writer chooses to explore one subject from a variety of possibilities and then shares the result with an audience. For example, a class focusing on protest movements in political history might engage in an extended discussion about the concept of free speech. One of the group's first questions is likely to be: "What is free speech?" In order to answer this question, which obviously entails a definition essay of some kind, students will probably need to trace this concept right back to its origin, namely the First Amendment, which guarantees free speech to all Americans. Defining free speech in terms of the First Amendment leads to a further challenge, however, because its short, succinct statement leaves ample room for interpretation:

The First Amendment

> Congress shall make no law respecting an establishment of religion, or prohibiting the free exercise thereof; or abridging the freedom of speech, or of the press; or the right of the people peaceably to assemble, and to petition the government for a redress of grievances.

Is advocating violent revolution protected by the First Amendment? How about hate speech? Or racist expressions? Or detailed explanations of how to make homemade incendiary devices? Debates about the meaning of the First Amendment—in essence, about its extended definition—continue to this day. According to Kenneth Paulson of the Freedom Forum, the First Amendment is fundamental to our democratic government and is little understood or appreciated by most Americans who would like to see it narrowed. His June 2000 essay, published on *www.freedomforum.org*, follows.

Where Americans Stand on Freedom

There was a time in this country's history when free speech was truly dangerous.

Consider the courage of the original signers of the Declaration of Independence. By subscribing to such a revolutionary document, they knew they were putting their lives and their honor at risk. And in fact, five were captured and tortured by the British as traitors; nine died in the War of Independence; and at least 12 of the 56 had their homes destroyed.

They knew the risks. Congress didn't distribute signed copies of the Declaration until January 18, 1777, giving the signers some cover until after Continental army victories at Trenton and Princeton.

Americans today rarely see free speech in a heroic light. In fact, the First Amendment Center's new State of the First Amendment Survey suggests we are a nation that sometimes loses sight of its most fundamental freedoms.

Respondents to the survey, which was conducted this spring by the University of Connecticut's Center for Survey Research & Analysis, embrace the ideals of the First Amendment but have reservations about the reality.

- Fifty-one percent said the press has too much freedom to do what it wants. A year ago, a similar number, 53%, also said the news media had excessive freedom.
- Fifty-one percent said art should not be placed in public places if it may offend some members of the community.
- Forty percent said musicians should not be allowed to sing offensive songs in public.
- Sixty-seven percent said that public remarks offensive to racial groups should not be allowed; 36% would support a law that banned such speech.
- Fifty-three percent said that public speech that offends members of a religious group should not be allowed.
- Fifty-four percent think the government should be involved in rating entertainment programs that are shown on television.
- Three-quarters of the respondents believe that violence on television and in video games and music lyrics contributes to violence in real life. Eighty-three percent think violence on television contributes to violence in real life; 74% think violent video games do the same, and 72% think violent music lyrics are to blame.

One of the striking things about the survey is the significant percentage of Americans who are ready to ban expression that currently is protected by the Constitution.

- For example, 84% said that people should not be allowed to burn the American flag in an act of political protest. In 1989, the

Supreme Court upheld flag-burning as a Constitutionally protected exercise in free speech.

- The survey also suggests that a sizable number of Americans believe there's a threshold for freedom of religion. One respondent in five said that freedom to worship "was never meant to apply to religious groups that the majority of people consider extreme or fringe."

- Thirty-one percent said a group should not be allowed to hold a rally for a cause or an issue if it offends others in the community.

Most surprising is the finding that Americans are apparently becoming reluctant to offend. The issue stretches far beyond being a simple matter of political correctness. It's about embracing civility at the cost of freedom.

Thomas Jefferson and the rest of the co-signers of the Declaration of Independence probably never would have envisioned the likes of today's popular culture.

But while the appeal of Marilyn Manson, Quentin Tarantino and *South Park* probably would have escaped them, those original American rebels clearly understood what freedom means.

They recognized that the right to express unpopular opinions and provocative ideas is the very cornerstone of our democracy.

As we again celebrate our nation's birth, there is no better time to remember the founders' mission—or their message.

For Paulson, freedom of speech is a right that must be protected, even at the cost of one's own life. Yet others disagree with his extended definition, or at least offer differing interpretations. Many U.S. courts, for example, have struggled with defining what the authors of the Constitution and the Bill of Rights specifically intended by the First Amendment, reminding us that a great many attempts at definition are ongoing and successive. One of the most famous judicial formulations concerning free speech, for example, occurred as a result of a specific antiwar protest directed at American troops during World War I. In the 1919 decision *Schenck* v. *the United States,*

Justice Oliver Wendell Holmes stated . . . his famous aphorism about "falsely shouting fire in a theatre" and set forth a "clear and present danger test" to judge whether speech is protected by the First Amendment. "The question," he wrote, "is whether the words are used in such circumstances and are of such a nature as to create a clear and present danger that they will bring about the substantive evils that Congress has the right to prevent. It is a question of proximity and degree." The Supreme Court affirmed the convictions of the defendants for conspiring to violate certain federal statutes by attempting to incite subordination in the armed forces and interfere with recruitment and enlistment. During wartime, the defendants mailed to new recruits and enlisted men leaflets that compared military conscription to involuntary servitude and urged them to assert constitutional rights.

For Holmes and the Supreme Court, the right to free speech as stated in the First Amendment does not extend to every expression. It has its limits and can be abridged if it imposes a clear and present danger to specific audiences. In essence, the U.S. Supreme Court redefined the concept of free speech in this decision, and it continues to redefine it today in terms of antiabortion protests, Internet communication, antigovernment expression, music lyrics, and so forth. As individuals offer new views of traditional concepts and challenge commonplace social/political assumptions, they are continuously redefining fundamental concepts while refining their meanings in order to make them fit within contemporary circumstances.

For the mode of definition to succeed, writers must contribute something new, something more than just "publicly shared meaning." Publicly shared meaning refers to that body of knowledge most people already know. For example, most people already know that the First Amendment guarantees "freedom of speech," and that this freedom is basic to our democracy. To write an essay that extends the definition only this far would not educate readers. But if this concept is applied to a complex subject, such as patriotism and political protest, an extended definition essay about free speech becomes much more worthwhile, in large part because it becomes more informative and complex. The World Wide Web features many commentaries on censorship, patriotism, and political protest; two are featured below:

> ***Broadside Policy Institute*** (We are a non-profit 501(c)3 organization that is dedicated to preserving and giving voice to the principle of the Declaration of Independence.)

> ### The True Meaning of Patriotism
> by Mark Hofer, *Broadside Magazine*, and Matt Hofer, *Carolina Review*
>
> Events on and since September 11th have caused many to respond. Some have responded by placing American flags in front of their homes or on their cars. Others have protested until they got sore throats. Some have been called unpatriotic in their actions. However, this accusation is often used too loosely and degrades the potency of the accusation to those who deserve it. To be fair to those accusing and those accused of being unpatriotic it is essential to know what patriotism actually is.

The base of the word *patriotism* comes from the Latin word *patria*, meaning fatherland or homeland. The suffix *-ism* is Greek meaning belief in, practice of, or condition of. The literal definition is then belief in one's country. But patriotism goes beyond that definition. We all believe in France as a country, but are not necessarily French patriots. A better definition, and the one offered by Merriam-Webster Online, is "one who loves his or her country and supports its authority and interests."

Those who are saying that something is unpatriotic because it goes against government are simplistic. As everyone well knows, the government is not always correct in its decisions. Japanese internment camps, for example, were one of the American government's mistakes during World War II. 120,000 people of Japanese ancestry were forcefully and indiscriminately placed in these camps to cut down on the number of Japanese spies in the United States. Although upheld by the Supreme Court and considered an issue of national security, history has proven any form of concentration camps atrocious.

Conversely, radicals who declare that democracy demands dissent are merely trying to justify their own senseless actions. Democracy demands dialogue and debate, not dissent, to encourage both sides of any issue to work toward the best, most developed conclusions. When we as a nation break into purely contradictory factions, then the constructive nature of the debate crumbles.

Many have declared themselves patriotic for simply expressing rights reaffirmed by the United States Constitution. However, expressing rights is not necessarily patriotic or constructive. For example, burning the U.S. flag is certainly unpatriotic, though the right to do so is guaranteed by the First Amendment.

President Ronald Reagan made his views on what patriotism is clear in his Farewell Address on January 20, 1989:

> An informed patriotism is what we want. And are we doing a good enough job teaching our children what America is and what she represents in the long history of the world? Those of us who are over 35 or so years of age grew up in a different America. We were taught, very directly, what it means to be an American. And we absorbed, almost in the air, a love of country and an appreciation of its institutions. If you didn't get these things from your family you got them from the neighborhood, from the father down the street who fought in Korea or the family who lost someone at Anzio. Or you could get a sense of patriotism from school. And if all else failed you could get a sense of patriotism from the popular culture. The movies celebrated democratic values and implicitly reinforced the idea that America was special. TV was like that, too, through the mid-sixties.

Patriotism to him meant "a love of country and an appreciation of its institutions." This love and appreciation came from learning the history of our country, learning the democratic values for which so many have fought and died here and around the world. This was not the blind faith in the government or blind opposition to the government. This patriotism was the *informed* love and appreciation for the government. Fighting to change the country is patriotic, but you must know why you are changing it and why the new way is better.

What a shame it is that some have come to believe that patriotism is blind, unhealthy, or even vile. It is also shameful how patriotism has been oversimplified by some to mean unquestioning support for the government, which then allows radicals to rail patriots for any and all government institutions with which they disagree. Patriots Alexander Hamilton and Thomas Jefferson found themselves on opposing sides on almost all the big issues of their time, but today neither is more a patriot than the other. In the light of September 11th, patriotism should still be viewed through the seasoned lens of history.

The Observer (serving Notre Dame and Saint Mary's Universities)

Patriotism Entails Criticizing the Government
by Michael Collins, *Daily Kent Stater*

During the past year there has been a lot of talk about patriotism. As we all display our American flags (often incorrectly) and cheer America on in the fight against terrorism, there has been a lot of debate about what patriotism really means.

Notice that the definition does not include words like government or flag. It only refers to the country. It also does not include the word hate, only love and devotion.

Yet of late all these other words seem to have been added to the definition of patriotism in the minds of citizens. One cannot be patriotic if one disagrees with the government. One cannot be patriotic if one burns the flag or flies it upside down.

In order to be patriotic, you must hate those who do not agree with our government, or those who aren't in our country.

These definitions are not true patriotism. Our government is not our country and neither is our flag. Our country stands alone, independent of these other things. Our flag is only a symbol. Granted it is a very powerful symbol, but it is still a symbol nonetheless. Although the government runs our country, it cannot stand alone. It relies on the consent of the governed. If there is one object or organization that can be defined as our country, it is our Constitution.

Our Constitution creates and defines our country. It gives the values that we as Americans should hold closest to our hearts. Our government can change, our flag can change, but only the entire country working together can change the Constitution. Our Constitution creates our most sacred values like freedom, freedom of expression, freedom of religion. These are the ideas that give birth to "love for or devotion to" my country. These are the things that make me feel patriotic.

Our flag is a symbol of our freedom. That freedom includes the right to fly the flag upside down or even to burn it. The code for displaying the flag states that the flag should only be flown upside down "as a signal of dire distress in instances of extreme danger to life or property." Many people feel that our freedoms are in a state of "dire distress," not by planes flying into buildings, but by our own government. When they burn the flag, they are not saying that they hate our country. They are saying that they believe our own government is destroying the freedoms that our country holds most dear. They believe that our freedom itself is indeed burning.

Our freedom of expression gives us the right to question our government's actions. Citizens who blindly accept the battles we are fighting are not exercising that right. Many seem perfectly happy to take that right away from us. This is not patriotism. To not exercise the rights that make our country great is to risk losing them. The patriots are the ones fighting for the ideals for which our country stands, not those mindlessly bobbing their heads in agreement.

Whether you agree with the government's actions or not isn't what is important. It is the questioning itself. I do agree with some of the government's actions, and I disagree with others. But it is the fact that I am actually forming my own opinion that makes me patriotic.

The next time someone talks about patriotism, take a moment to stop and think about what the word really means. You may find patriots in places you did not expect.

This column first appeared in the September 19 edition of the Daily Kent Stater, *the campus newspaper of Kent State University. It is reprinted here courtesy of U-WIRE. The views expressed in this column are those of the author and not necessarily those of* The Observer.

Mark and Matt Hofer and Michael Collins disagree about the definitions of central terms, especially *patriotism* and *protest*—and the relation between them. Both perspectives have value and need to be considered, and a definitional essay might well incorporate assertions of meaning from both columns. When is it appropriate to protest against government actions? Is flying the American flag upside down an act of desecration or patriotic concern? Is there a point at which protest undermines pride in country? Is dialogue and debate preferable to dissent in a meaningful definition of patriotism? Such questions reside at the heart of a definition essay that explores this subject.

When writing a definition essay, writers usually focus immediate attention directly on the word or concept being defined, making a declaration early on that they will be "defining X" or "explaining the meaning of X." Thus most extended definition essays do not keep the reader in suspense regarding their primary purpose. In "The Holocaust," for example, Bruno Bettelheim makes clear from the outset that he will define the word *Holocaust*, just as Gretel Ehrlich signals her interest in defining *men* by the very choice of her title. This makes sense, since we usually read extended definition essays because we are intrigued by the word or concept being defined. Because we can look up the word or concept in a reference book, what we are looking for in a definition essay is something more. That "more" is the unique perspective that a writer can bring to the act of writing. Successful definition essays give readers the meaning of a term—but in ways that reflect the particular and personal point of view of the writer. That is the reason writers attempt a definition essay: to give their own personal shape and flavor to the meaning of a word, a concept, a thing, or a place. We see this in all the essays in this section, from Lisa Kanae's definition of *pidgin*, which she ties to the concrete example of her brother, to Judy Brady's "I Want a Wife" and Gloria Naylor's "The Meanings of a Word."

As a general rule, readers need details and examples. Few of us can understand generalities and abstractions, even once we know a great deal about a field or discipline. One of the dangers of writing in the definition mode is that the writer can veer off into generalities or use an overly technical or pretentious vocabulary in an attempt to impress readers or simply to express vague truths. Either approach is a mistake. One of the great challenges of writing a definition essay is to blend general and specific, abstract and concrete. In some of the other modes (narration, comparison/contrast, description, to name just three) the mode itself steers a writer toward the use of details. But definition essays push writers toward generalizing, and this is dangerous. Writers must constantly remain vigilant to the need for examples and the use of specifics.

Readers want to know what a word or concept means, and they especially want a definition essay to have relevance to their own lives and experiences. Successful definition essays place their definitions within a larger framework, contextualizing them within a specific and knowable setting. Readers best understand words and concepts when they are defined in terms of local culture, history, neighborhood, school, disciplines, or politics. A writer might try to define the word *creativity* in general terms, but the essay will best succeed if the author considers creativity in light of writing a particular poem, developing a new software application, or discovering a new concept about social conformity and individual choice. Grounding a definition in a specific context can provide the relevance readers crave and allow the writer to make use of specific examples and particulars that hold a definition essay within everyday reality.

Judy Brady (1937–   ) was born in San Francisco, California, where she currently lives. She earned a bachelor of fine arts degree in painting from the University of Iowa in 1962 and resists calling herself a writer. Although she refers to herself as "a disenfranchised (and fired) housewife, now secretary," Brady writes a regular column for the Women's Cancer Research Center and in 1991 published the anthology 1 in 3 Women with Cancer Confront an Epidemic. *Her most popular essay, "I Want a Wife," first appeared in the spring 1972 issue of* Ms. *magazine.*

Judy Brady
I Want a Wife

I belong to that classification of people known as wives. I am A Wife. And, not altogether incidentally, I am a mother.

Not too long ago a male friend of mine appeared on the scene fresh from a recent divorce. He had one child, who is, of course, with his ex-wife. He is looking for another wife. As I thought about him while I was ironing one evening, it suddenly occurred to me that I, too, would like to have a wife. Why do I want a wife?

I would like to go back to school so that I can become economically independent, support myself, and, if need be, support those dependent upon me. I want a wife who will work and send me to school. And while I am going to school I want a wife to take care of my children. I want a wife to keep track of the children's doctor and dentist appointments. And to keep track of mine, too. I want a wife to make sure my children eat properly and are kept clean. I want a wife who will wash the children's clothes and keep them mended. I want a wife who is a good nurturant attendant to my children, who arranges for their schooling, makes sure that they have an adequate social life with their peers, takes them to the park, the zoo, etc. I want a wife who takes care of the children when they are sick, a wife who arranges to be around when the children need special care, because, of course, I cannot miss classes at school. My wife must arrange to lose time at work and not lose the job. It may mean a small cut in my wife's income from time to time, but I guess I can tolerate that. Needless to say, my wife will arrange and pay for the care of the children while my wife is working.

I want a wife who will take care of *my* physical needs. I want a wife who will keep my house clean. A wife who will pick up after my children, a wife who will pick up after me. I want a wife who will keep my clothes clean, ironed, mended, replaced when need be, and who will see to it that my personal things are kept in their proper place so that I can find what I need the minute I need it. I want a wife who cooks the meals, a wife who is a *good* cook. I want a wife who will plan the menus, do the necessary grocery shopping, prepare the meals, serve them pleasantly, and then do the cleaning up while I do my studying. I want a wife who will care for me when I am sick and sympathize with my pain and loss of time from school. I want a wife to go along when our family takes a vacation so that someone can continue to care for me and my children when I need a rest and change of scene.

5   I want a wife who will not bother me with rambling complaints about a wife's duties. But I want a wife who will listen to me when I feel the need to explain a rather difficult point I have come across in my course of studies. And I want a wife who will type my papers for me when I have written them.

I want a wife who will take care of the details of my social life. When my wife and I are invited out by my friends, I want a wife who will take care of the babysitting arrangements. When I meet people at school that I like and want to entertain, I want a wife who will have the house clean, will prepare a special meal, serve it to me and my friends, and not interrupt when I talk about things that interest me and my friends. I want a wife who will have arranged that the children are fed and ready for bed before my guests arrive so that the children do not bother us. I want a wife who takes care of the needs of my guests so that they feel comfortable, who makes sure that they have an ashtray, that they are passed the hors d'oeuvres, that they are offered a second helping of the food, that their wine glasses are replenished when necessary, that their coffee is served to them as they like it. And I want a wife who knows that sometimes I need a night out by myself.

I want a wife who is sensitive to my sexual needs, a wife who makes love passionately and eagerly when I feel like it, a wife who makes sure that I am satisfied. And, of course, I want a wife who will not demand sexual attention when I am not in the mood for it. I want a wife who assumes the complete responsibility for birth control, because I do not want more children. I want a wife who will remain sexually faithful to me so that I do not have to clutter up my intellectual life with jealousies. And I want a wife who understands that *my* sexual needs may entail more than strict adherence to monogamy. I must, after all, be able to relate to people as fully as possible.

If, by chance, I find another person more suitable as a wife than the wife I already have, I want the liberty to replace my present wife with another one. Naturally, I will expect a fresh new life; my wife will take the children and be solely responsible for them so that I am left free.

When I am through with school and have a job, I want my wife to quit working and remain at home so that my wife can more fully and completely take care of a wife's duties.

10   My God, who *wouldn't* want a wife?

Analyzing Rhetorical Choices

1. What is the effect of Brady's opening sentence, "I belong to that classification of people known as wives." Why do you think she uses the phrase "classification of people"?
2. Why does Brady keep repeating "I want a wife"? What effect(s) does this phrase have as a consequence of its being continually repeated?
3. Comment on Brady's use of italics in this essay. In what ways is it effective, distracting, or overly dramatic?

Writing About Issues and Contexts

1. In what ways, if any, is Brady's essay an accurate definition of a wife? In what ways, if any, is it a distortion?
2. If Brady is accurate in describing a wife, what is a husband? Define one in several paragraphs, imitating Brady's style or any other that you deem appropriate.

*Elaine Potter Richardson (1949–   ) was born in St. John's, Antigua,
which was then a British colony in the Caribbean. She came to the United
States in 1966 at the age of 17; a fictional account of her experience
growing up and leaving home can be found in her novel,* Annie John
*(1985). After working in a variety of jobs, including as a nanny, she began
writing for the "Talk of the Town" section of* The New Yorker *magazine
and assumed the literary name of **Jamaica Kincaid**, by which she is best
known today. Kincaid has published many books, primarily focused on her
family experiences, including* Lucy *(1990) and* Autobiography of My
Mother *(1994). She has also published an angry account of colonization,*
A Small Place *(1988). She lives in Vermont with her husband, son, and
daughter.*

Jamaica Kincaid

Girl

Wash the white clothes on Monday and put them on the stone heap;
wash the color clothes on Tuesday and put them on the clothesline to
dry; don't walk barehead in the hot sun; cook pumpkin fritters in very
hot sweet oil; soak your little clothes right after you take them off; when
buying cotton to make yourself a nice blouse, be sure that it doesn't have
gum on it, because that way it won't hold up well after a wash; soak salt
fish overnight before you cook it; is it true that you sing benna in
Sunday school?; always eat your food in such a way that it won't turn
someone else's stomach; on Sundays try to walk like a lady and not like
the slut you are so bent on becoming; don't sing benna in Sunday school;
you mustn't speak to wharf-rat boys, not even to give directions; don't
eat fruits on the street—flies will follow you; *but I don't sing benna on
Sundays at all and never in Sunday school;* this is how to sew on a button; this is how to make a button-hole for the button you have just
sewed on; this is how to hem a dress when you see the hem coming down
and so to prevent yourself from looking like the slut I know you are so
bent on becoming; this is how you iron your father's khaki shirt so that it
doesn't have a crease; this is how you iron your father's khaki pants so
that they don't have a crease; this is how you grow okra—far from the
house, because okra tree harbors red ants; when you are growing
dasheen, make sure it gets plenty of water or else it makes your throat
itch when you are eating it; this is how you sweep a corner; this is how
you sweep a whole house; this is how you sweep a yard; this is how you

smile to someone you don't like too much; this is how you smile to someone you don't like at all; this is how you smile to someone you like completely; this is how you set a table for tea; this is how you set a table for dinner; this is how you set a table for dinner with an important guest; this is how you set a table for lunch; this is how you set a table for breakfast; this is how to behave in the presence of men who don't know you very well, and this way they won't recognize immediately the slut I have warned you against becoming; be sure to wash every day, even if it is with your own spit; don't squat down to play marbles—you are not a boy, you know; don't pick people's flowers—you might catch something; don't throw stones at blackbirds, because it might not be a blackbird at all; this is how to make a bread pudding; this is how to make doukona; this is how to make pepper pot; this is how to make a good medicine for a cold; this is how to make a good medicine to throw away a child before it even becomes a child; this is how to catch a fish; this is how to throw back a fish you don't like, and that way something bad won't fall on you; this is how to bully a man; this is how a man bullies you; this is how to love a man, and if this doesn't work there are other ways, and if they don't work don't feel too bad about giving up; this is how to spit up in the air if you feel like it, and this is how to move quick so that it doesn't fall on you; this is how to make ends meet; always squeeze bread to make sure it's fresh; *but what if the baker won't let me feel the bread?*; you mean to say that after all you are really going to be the kind of woman who the baker won't let near the bread?

Analyzing Rhetorical Choices

1. Who is the speaker of this essay? Who is speaking in italics? How would you characterize the interaction, however slight, of these two speakers?
2. Why do you think Kincaid wrote this essay all as one sentence? What effect does this form have on you, as reader? Evaluate its effectiveness (or ineffectiveness).

Writing About Issues and Contexts

1. Who is this "girl"? Who does the speaker want her to be?
2. According to this essay, how would you define the ideal girl? What kinds of traits and values does she have?
3. Evaluate the advice being given here, in terms of how valuable it is to a girl, especially one growing up within a very hierarchical and traditional island society such as Antigua's.

Jesse Ventura (1949–   ) served as governor of Minnesota from 1998 to 2002. Formerly, he gained fame as a wrestler and was featured in several films, including Predator. *Dennis Anderson is the "Outdoors" columnist for the* Minneapolis–St. Paul Star Tribune, *and Allen Garber was the commissioner of the Minnesota Department of Natural Resources. This interview appeared on the* Star Tribune's *Web site, and soon afterward, Governor Ventura apologized for his comments to hunters and to the general public.*

Jesse Ventura

Hunting and Conservation

Jesse Ventura: Instead of you interviewing me, I'm going to interview you.

Dennis Anderson: You're going to interview me?

Ventura: Yeah. I took great offense to your article on Sunday, very big offense, insinuating that Commissioner Garber and I somehow aren't reputable people and that we can't be trusted with DNR money. And also the insinuation that somehow I don't know about wildlife, hunting, and fishing. On what do you base your opinions and your knowledge of me on?

Anderson: I didn't say you didn't know anything about hunting.

5 *Ventura:* You insinuate it all the time. I read it in your articles all the time. Well, first of all, let me tell you something. My family and I have owned a lake cabin for forty-four years in the state of Minnesota. That's a lot more than Bud Grant [the former coach of the Minnesota Vikings]. To my knowledge, he's in Wisconsin.

Anderson: How'd he get into this?

Ventura: I just threw him out there for practical purposes. 'Cause he testified against me once and said I didn't know anything about hunting or fishing. All right, I've owned a lake cabin for forty-four years. My parents, and now I, own it; they're gone. Second of all, when it comes to hunting—I got your résumé. You ever done military service?

Anderson: You have my résumé?

Ventura: Yeah, I got your file. You ever done military service?

10 *Anderson:* No.

Ventura: You haven't? Well, Commissioner Garber and I
have. He has two tours to Vietnam and I have one as a
Navy SEAL and then seventeen months in Southeast
Asia, and I'll just tell you this: Until you hunted man, you
haven't hunted yet. Because you need to hunt something
that can shoot back at you to really classify yourself as a
hunter. You need to understand the feeling of what it's
like to go into the field and know that your opposition can
take you out. Not just go out there and shoot Bambi.

Anderson: This doesn't have anything to do with conservation.

Ventura: No, but it has to do with being a sportsman, in my
opinion.

Anderson: The military has something to do with conservation?

15 *Ventura:* Yeah, yeah, 'cause it's called hunting.

Anderson: I miss the connection.

Ventura: What I don't like is this insinuation that Commissioner Garber doesn't understand how to hunt. He's been
protecting the public for twenty-six years as an FBI agent.
He did two tours of Vietnam. Again, that's hunting. Going
out and shooting Bambi, to me, isn't hunting. Because you
walk out there, and you're going to shoot some poor little
animal that can't shoot back, that offers no defense. And
that's being a sportsman and a hunter?

Anderson [Gesturing at Allen Garber]: He doesn't hunt.
That's the deal. He doesn't hunt.

Allen Garber: I went deer hunting this year by the way,
Dennis. I went pheasant hunting last year. You don't
know everything.

20 *Ventura:* That's right. And you don't consider war hunting?

Anderson: Not in the context that we're discussing.

Ventura: Really. I do.

Anderson: Well, you do. I don't.

Ventura: Well, that's 'cause you have no experience at it.

25 *Anderson:* Have you hunted deer?

Ventura: No.

Anderson: That's my point then, I guess.

Ventura: My point is, the deer can't shoot back. Have you
hunted man?

Anderson: No.

30 *Ventura:* Then you have no basis to talk from, pal. Because
hunting a deer, big deal. Big deal.

Anderson: I'm not saying it is a big deal.

Ventura: So don't tell me I'm not a hunter. The training is to
hunt, to hunt something and be successful. I find that it's

far more challenging to hunt something that can potentially do harm back to you than to go out and hunt something that sits around and eats twigs and leaves in the middle of the woods, and then you've got the gall to tell me I'm
not a hunter? You better talk to Commander Marsinko
about that too, what the definition of being a hunter is.

Anderson: As I was saying, my issue is conservation. It's not
being effected in this state, and needs to be if we want to
continue our heritage.

Ventura: And let me say from a personal note, all the
friends that I grew up with are all avid hunters and fishermen. And they do it with their own money. I mean,
they're not paid by a newspaper to go out and hire a
guide for them and go out and write a story.

35 *Anderson:* Don't insult me.

Ventura: You insult me all the time.

Anderson: I don't need a guide to take me out to hunt and
fish. I'm not a newspaper guy—

Ventura: You're not?

Anderson: —who needs help to go out and hunt and fish.

40 *Ventura:* The only thing I see here on your résumé is you've
been a newspaper guy your whole life.

Anderson: I was a truck driver for thirty years, coast to
coast, Canada to Mexico.

Ventura: Okay, well, that's not in there. So I guess you don't
brag about that. Just please don't insinuate to me that I
don't care. And I don't understand the state's woods, waters, and fields. I've only had a lake cabin for forty-four
years, but I don't understand it. All my friends are
hunters and fishermen. You know who I consult when I
want to know about it? Not you. Them.

Anderson: Do you understand the status of the state's water-
sheds? They're in dismal shape. Do you understand up-
lands? Wetlands? It's not your fault. I'm just saying . . .

Ventura: Do I understand it? Yeah. I watch what goes on.
And please don't insinuate that I don't care. I do care. And
don't ever think I'm not a hunter just because my job now
doesn't allow me to do it every weekend. And just because
I choose, having man, that there's no thrill for me to go out
and shoot Bambi. You have to understand that many people, like Mr. Garber and I, when you go through and
you're trained in combat, and you hunt the ultimate foe,
well, it becomes very difficult, and I can't speak for Al, but
for me, I can't draw down on Bambi. I can't shoot him.

45 *Anderson:* I don't care whether you hunt or not.

Ventura: You miss my point. That still doesn't mean I'm not a hunter. And it's wrong for you to insinuate that I don't know how to hunt. Because when you hunt the ultimate foe, which is man, who can shoot back, you're the best hunter on the planet.

Anderson: I don't care whether someone hunts. I care about conservation.

Ventura: Let me put it to you this way, Dennis. You've alienated me so bad, I rarely read you.

Anderson: Do you read the Sports section?

50   *Ventura:* Yes.

Anderson: Well, more people read Outdoors than Sports Sunday, so you're in the minority.

Ventura: That's true. But why am I not reading you? Because you're negative to me every time I pick up the paper. You sit and portray to the public I don't know a damn thing about the outdoors: I don't know how to hunt; I don't know how to fish; I don't know nothing. You know. So after a while, I quit reading it. Because you can't read stuff like that and maintain your sanity at this job.

Analyzing Rhetorical Choices

1. Describe the relationship between the men and how their personal attacks short-circuit any possibility of achieving consensus.
2. This transcript includes language that would be considered colloquial and informal, such as "He doesn't hunt. That's the deal." How does this language influence your reading and your view of Ventura, Anderson, and Garber?

Writing About Issues and Contexts

1. In what ways is it more or less effective to publish this as a transcript rather than as an essay?
2. What is Governor Ventura's definition of hunting? Is his definition a good one? Why or why not?
3. Why can't Dennis Anderson and Jesse Ventura communicate with each other? What are they really disagreeing about?

Born in Vienna, Austria, **Bruno Bettelheim** (1903–1990) eventually went on to earn a Ph.D. in psychology from the University of Vienna in 1938. He survived the Holocaust and came to the United States in 1939, becoming a naturalized citizen in 1944. From 1944–1973 he served as a professor of psychology at the University of Chicago. Drawing on his own experiences in the concentration camps and the horrific experiences of the children he witnessed there, Bettelheim became one of the world's leading authorities on childhood emotional disorders. His groundbreaking books on this subject include Treatment of Emotionally Disturbed Children (1950), Dialogues with Mothers (1962), and The Uses of Enchantment: The Meaning and Importance of Fairy Tales (1976). Bettelheim died in 1990, committing suicide after a long illness. His New York Times obituary described him as "a gifted writer . . . with a great literary and moral sensibility," qualities that are evident in this selection from a much longer essay in the book Surviving and Other Essays (1979).

Bruno Bettelheim

The Holocaust

To begin with, it was not the hapless victims of the Nazis who named their incomprehensible and totally unmasterable fate the "holocaust." It was the Americans who applied this artificial and highly technical term to the Nazi extermination of the European Jews. But while the event when named as mass murder most foul evokes the most immediate, most powerful revulsion, when it is designated by a rare technical term, we must first in our minds translate it back into emotionally meaningful language. Using technical or specially created terms instead of words from our common vocabulary is one of the best-known and most widely used distancing devices, separating the intellectual from the emotional experience. Talking about "the holocaust" permits us to manage it intellectually where the raw facts, when given their ordinary names, would overwhelm us emotionally—because it was catastrophe beyond comprehension, beyond the limits of our imagination, unless we force ourselves against our desire to extend it to encompass these terrible events.

This linguistic circumlocution began while it all was only in the planning stage. Even the Nazis—usually given to grossness in language and action—shied away from facing openly what they were up to and called this vile mass murder "the final solution of the Jewish problem." After all, solving a problem can be made to appear like an honorable enterprise, as long as we are not forced to recognize that the solution we are about to embark on consists of the completely unprovoked, vicious murder of millions of helpless men, women, and children. The Nuremberg judges of these Nazi criminals followed their example of circumlocution by coining a neologism out of one Greek and one Latin root: genocide. These artificially created technical terms fail to connect with our strongest feelings. The horror of murder is part of our most common human heritage. From earliest infancy on, it arouses violent abhorrence in us. Therefore in whatever form it appears we should give such an act its true designation and not hide it behind polite, erudite terms created out of classical words.

To call this vile mass murder "the holocaust" is not to give it a special name emphasizing its uniqueness which would permit, over time, the word becoming invested with feelings germane to the event it refers to. The correct definition of *holocaust* is "burnt offering." As such, it is part of the language of the psalmist, a meaningful word to all who have some acquaintance with the Bible, full of the richest emotional connotations. By using the term "holocaust," entirely false associations are established through conscious and unconscious connotations between the most vicious of mass murders and ancient rituals of a deeply religious nature.

Using a word with such strong unconscious religious connotations when speaking of the murder of millions of Jews robs the victims of this abominable mass murder of the only thing left to them: their uniqueness. Calling the most callous, most brutal, most horrid, most heinous mass murder a burnt offering is a sacrilege, a profanation of God and man.

5   Martyrdom is part of our religious heritage. A martyr, burned at the stake, is a burnt offering to his god. And it is true that after the Jews were asphyxiated, the victims' corpses were burned. But I believe we fool ourselves if we think we are honoring the victims of systematic murder by using this term, which has the highest moral connotations. By doing so, we connect for our own psychological reasons what happened in the extermination camps with historical events we deeply regret, but also greatly admire. We do so because this makes it easier for us to cope; only in doing so we cope with our distorted image of what happened, not with the events the way they did happen.

By calling the victims of the Nazis martyrs, we falsify their fate. The true meaning of *martyr* is: "One who voluntarily undergoes the penalty of death for refusing to renounce his faith" (*Oxford English Dictionary*).The Nazis made sure that nobody could mistakenly think that their victims were murdered for their religious beliefs. Renouncing their faith would have saved none of them. Those who had converted to Christianity were gassed, as were those who were atheists, and those who were deeply religious Jews. They did not die for any conviction, and certainly not out of choice.

Millions of Jews were systematically slaughtered, as were untold other "undesirables," not for any convictions of theirs, but only because they stood in the way of the realization of an illusion. They neither died for their convictions, nor were they slaughtered because of their convictions, but only in consequence of the Nazis' delusional belief about what was required to protect the purity of their assumed superior racial endowment, and what they thought necessary to guarantee them the living space they believed they needed and were entitled to. Thus while these millions were slaughtered for an idea, they did not die for one.

Millions—men, women, and children—were processed after they had been utterly brutalized, their humanity destroyed, their clothes torn from their bodies. Naked, they were sorted into those who were destined to be murdered immediately, and those others who had a short-term usefulness as slave labor. But after a brief interval they, too, were to be herded into the same gas chambers into which the others were immediately piled, there to be asphyxiated so that, in their last moments, they could not prevent themselves from fighting each other in vain for a last breath of air.

To call these most wretched victims of a murderous delusion, of destructive drives run rampant, martyrs or a burnt offering is a distortion invented for our comfort, small as it may be. It pretends that this most vicious of mass murders had some deeper meaning; that in some fashion the victims either offered themselves or at least became sacrifices to a higher cause. It robs them of the last recognition which could be theirs, denies them the last dignity we could accord them: to face and accept what their death was all about, not embellishing it for the small psychological relief this may give us.

10   We could feel so much better if the victims had acted out of choice. For our emotional relief, therefore, we dwell on the tiny minority who did exercise some choice: the resistance fighters of the Warsaw ghetto, for example, and others like them. We are ready to overlook the fact that these people fought back only at a time when everything was lost, when the overwhelming majority of those who had been

forced into the ghettos had already been exterminated without resisting. Certainly those few who finally fought for their survival and their convictions, risking and losing their lives in doing so, deserve our admiration; their deeds give us a moral lift. But the more we dwell on these few, the more unfair are we to the memory of the millions who were slaughtered—who gave in, did not fight back—because we deny them the only thing which up to the very end remained uniquely their own: their fate.

Analyzing Rhetorical Choices

1. How would you describe the diction and sentence structure in this selection? Choose some specific words and sentences that you find challenging and offer definitions and paraphrases.

2. What etymological information does Bettelheim provide in this selection? Why does he do this?

3. How does Bettelheim express his outrage at the different terms used to describe the victims of the Nazis? What alternative description would you suggest to describe these victims that would be true to the spirit of Bettelheim's essay?

Writing About Issues and Contexts

1. Does this essay define? If so, what exactly does it define and what are the essential terms of its central definition?

2. What is wrong with using the word *holocaust* to describe the destruction of the Nazis' victims? What are the potential political effects of "linguistic circumlocution"? What is wrong with the word *martyr*?

3. Bettelheim writes, "Millions of Jews were systematically slaughtered, as were untold other 'undesirables,' not for any convictions of theirs, but only because they stood in the way of the realization of an illusion." What does he mean by this? What does he mean by the word *illusion* here?

Lisa Kanae *(1960–   ) was born in Honolulu, Hawai'i. At the age of 30, she decided to return to college and completing a bachelor's degree and then earning a master's in English from the University of Hawai'i at Manoa where she was the recipient of the 1999 Patricia Sumei Saiki Creative Writing Award; 1998 Academy of American Poets Harold Taylor Prize; 1997–1998 Red Mandarin and Lady Yi-suen Shen Scholarship Award; and the 1996–1997 Hemingway Award for Creative Nonfiction. Kanae's prose and poetry is published in `Oiwi: A Native Hawaiian Journal, Bamboo Ridge Press publications, Hybolics, and Tinfish. She currently teaches English composition and literature courses at Kapi`olani Community College on the island of O`ahu. "Pidgin" is an excerpt from Kanae's memoir essay,* Sista Tongue *(2001), which weaves the social history of Hawai'i Creole English with personal experience and general attitudes toward dialect and language.*

Lisa Kanae

Pidgin

Editor's Note: The unusual typographic features of this essay in the pages that follow are not a mistake. Lisa Linn Kanae expresses her meaning in Sista Tongue *both in terms of the explicit meanings of words and the implicit meanings of graphic design. As closely as possible, we have tried to remain true to the appearance of the pages as they were originally printed; thus the pages that follow approximate the format of the book as it was originally printed. Cover and book design are by Kristin Kaleinani Gonzales, a native Hawai'ian, who earned her bachelor's in fine arts degree from the University of Hawai'i at Manoa and much of whose artwork examines the complex meanings of identity and culture.*

Wendell Johnson, Professor of Speech Pathology and Psychology, University of Iowa and editor of Speech Handicapped School Children, writes that self-expression, self-communication, and communication between the speaker and other persons are the fundamental purposes of speech. According to Professor Johnson,

 a speech disorder occurs when all of the basic functions of speech are affected to some degree and, in certain cases, one function may be more seriously disturbed than another (6).

148 •

My little bradda not mento, so you betta
stop teasing him all da time jus cuz you
tink you can talk more betta dan him.
Jus cuz you can go one regula-kine
school—not da special-kine school
whea da teacha clamp one rula-looking
kine ting on your tongue.

Wot? You no believe me?

I saw yum fo real kine. I promise! I dunno why da
teacha did dat to him. Jus cuz my litto bradda get
hard time fo talk no mean he stupid. He no can—
was dat word again—arteekcolate? My fadda tea
him all da time. Call him "short tongue." Sometime
Popo Lum, da landlady downstairs, talk to Harold-
Boy like he deaf and dumb or something.

Sheeze.

He only four years old, try.

Articulation: when tongue, jaw, teeth, lips, and palate alter the air stream coming from the vocal cords creating sounds, which make up syllables, which make up words. The most important structure of articulation is the tongue, which is responsible for effecting the changes in the mouth basic to the production of all but a few sounds. The tongue is so essential to human speech, languages are often referred to as "tongues" (Hanson 1–9).

I hold my madda's hand everytime da school bus from da special school come fo take Harold-Boy away. Insai dat bus get funny-kine looking childrens. E, I bet dey hate for talk too. One boy look like he stay wearing one bird cage ova his head. Only his eyes move. Get one girl wit magnifying glasses—da kine for kill ants—strap to her head. She get metal sticks stuck to her legs too. Get one nodda girl who no can stay still. She use to pull out her hair beefo da bus driva wen force her for wear white seat belts across her chest and her legs. And get one supa skinny boy, he just stare at my bradda.

"Wot you looking at?" I yell

"Badda you?"

Da skinny boy no say nutting. Gala gala drips from his crooked lip. His collar stay all wet.

"Be good now," I tell my little bradda. "Bum-bye wen you come home we go watch cartoon, kay?"

The body of the tongue is shaped like a broad-based anvil;
the body is what we see when we look into the mouth. The
body of the tongue is divided into four parts: the tip, the
blade, the front, and the back. What we cannot see when we
look into the mouth is the tongue's root. (Hanson 1–9)

Creole languages are primarily born out of necessity. In his 1936 article, "The Competition of Languages in Hawaii," Dr. John E. Reinecke, whose scholarly work has contributed to the scientific study of Creole languages, defines a Creole dialect by describing its function in plantation communities:

> **A Creole dialect is a greatly simplified, makeshift form of a European language which has arisen in master-servant situations on a large scale between European employers and (usually) non-European laborers. It is especially common in plantation regions, and is necessary where the laborers are drawn from several linguistic groups.** *(7)*

Reinecke points out that the formation of a Creole language met the need for a "medium of communication between members of non-English speaking groups" (Reinecke 105).

In many cases, plantation labor populations were so ethnically diverse that a Creole language became the only feasible means of communication between the different ethnic groups—

—a common tongue of the working class.

This lingua franca was not only used between groups of multi-ethnic laborers, it was also used between the laborers and the plantation "masters." Reinecke writes that it would be impossible for the plantation "master" to become proficient in every language of the ethnically diverse labor groups; therefore Creole was also used as a "language of command" (18) because "masters rarely deign to learn the speech of the servile population" (18).

Plantation "masters" used Creole languages to create class stratification between "master" and "servant" laborer. Creole languages were also used to enforce and maintain that class stratification by keeping the laborer ignorant of the "master's" ruling class language. Joseph Vendryes, author of <u>Language: A Linguistic Introduction to History</u>, writes Creoles were once considered the speech of "inferior beings . . . a subordinate class whose superiors have never troubled nor desired to make them speak any language correctly " (Vendryes qtd. in Reinecke 18).

At firs my madda was supa worried dat Harold-Boy neva start talking da same time as me and my cousin dem. Now she stay mo worried, because he no can talk like everybody else. But, not like everybody in dis house talk good English. My madda, she every time tell me,

"you not going get one good job if you no can talk good English. People going tink you stupid."

Stupid?

Gee, no wonda she stay all
hu-hu about Harold-Boy.
Me, at leese I can talk. But
Harold-Boy . . . das one
different story. He get
one—watchoo call—one
speech impedment. Das why
dey treat him like he mento.
Piss me off.

My litto bradda no belong on dat bus wit all dose handicap freaks.

There is a general understanding among listeners of a language that identifies whether a sound comes within what is considered normal limits or whether we sense something is wrong or misarticulated. This impression of misarticulation may be generally referred to as baby talk, lazy tongue movement, or any other variety of descriptive terms that imply the listener has some trouble understanding what is being said (Rousey 34).

Only me can undahstand wot Harold-Boy trying fo say.

Itah, itah: sister.

Wuh-yol: world.

Too-too-, too-too: Popeye da Sailor Man.

Harold-Boy smile up wen Popeye squeeze da
can, eat da spinach, beat up Brutus. Harold-Boy,
he make oojee kine face wen Olive Oil like kiss
Popeye all ova, and he love to sing along wit da
Popeye song.

You like <u>undahstand</u> my bradda or wot?

Try let him sing.

What kind of social implications does a "language of command" created for "master-servant" environments have upon the descendants of that "servile population," especially when those descendants continue to use an evolved form of that Creole generations later—after the plantation has closed down, and the laborer is revered as an ancestor? Today, half of the State of Hawai'i's population of approximately one million people speaks Hawai'i Creole English (HCE) (Romaine 527).

<u>I am one voice out of that</u> one million.

Analyzing Rhetorical Choices

1. How do you respond to the structure of the two opening paragraphs? What is your response to the radical shift in tone and formality, and to the lack of transition between the first two paragraphs?
2. How does the speaker choose to characterize herself and her brother, Harold-Boy? How do you respond to her statement that "My litto bradda no belong on dat bus wit all dose handicap freaks"?
3. Kanae writes in two different versions of English, Pidgin and Standard. Which is more effective? Why? How does the creative spelling of Pidgin affect you as a reader?
4. Why do you think Kanae uses the various kinds of spacing and typefaces? How do they affect you as a reader?

Writing About Issues and Contexts

1. According to Kanae, what is Pidgin? How does it function socially among the populations that speak it?
2. At one point in *Sista Tongue*, Kanae exemplifies what she means by Pidgin by writing, "Go bus out da pidgin wen trying fo get one ka-ma'aina discount from da local guy or gal behind da rent-a-car counta. Garrans da haole tourist at da same counta going pay mo money fo rent one car." What does this passage mean? How would you interpret it socially in terms of what it says about relations among Pidgin speakers and between Pidgin and non-Pidgin speakers?
3. Is the narrator's mother correct when she says, "you not going get one good job if you no can talk good English. People going tink you stupid." Analyze this statement in terms of your own insights and experiences, writing a balanced assessment of its accuracy.
4. Interpret the title, *Sista Tongue*. What are the implications of this title in relation to the author? The subject? You the reader?

Gloria Naylor (1950–   ) was born in New York City, graduated from Brooklyn College in 1981, and went on to receive her master's in African American literature at Yale. Naylor has written numerous works, including five interconnected novels: The Women of Brewster Place *(1982), for which she received an American Book Award for best new novel;* Linden Hills *(1985);* Mama Day *(1988);* Bailey's Café *(1992); and* The Men of Brewster Place *(1998). In 1989,* The Women of Brewster Place *was adapted as a television miniseries starring Oprah Winfrey.*

Gloria Naylor

The Meanings of a Word

Language is the subject. It is the written form with which I've managed to keep the wolf away from the door and, in diaries, to keep my sanity. In spite of this, I consider the written word inferior to the spoken, and much of the frustration experienced by novelists is the awareness that whatever we manage to capture in even the most transcendent passages falls far short of the richness of life. Dialogue achieves its power in the dynamics of a fleeting moment of sight, sound, smell, and touch.

I'm not going to enter the debate here about whether it is language that shapes reality or vice versa. That battle is doomed to be waged whenever we seek intermittent reprieve from the chicken and egg dispute. I will simply take the position that the spoken word, like the written word, amounts to a nonsensical arrangement of sounds or letters without a consensus that assigns "meaning." And building from the meanings of what we hear, we order reality. Words themselves are innocuous; it is the consensus that gives them true power.

I remember the first time I heard the word *nigger*. In my third-grade class, our math tests were being passed down the rows, and as I handed the papers to a little boy in back of me, I remarked that once again he had received a much lower mark than I did. He snatched his test from me and spit out that word. Had he called me a nymphomaniac or a necrophiliac, I couldn't have been more puzzled. I didn't know what a nigger was, but I knew that whatever it meant, it was something he shouldn't have called me. This was verified when I raised my hand, and in a loud voice repeated what he had said and watched the teacher scold him for using a "bad" word. I was later to go home and ask the inevitable question that every black parent must face—"Mommy, what does 'nigger' mean?"

And what exactly did it mean? Thinking back, I realize that this could not have been the first time the word was used in my presence. I was part of a large extended family that had migrated from the rural South after World War II and formed a close-knit network that gravitated around my maternal grandparents. Their ground-floor apartment in one of the buildings they owned in Harlem was a weekend mecca for my immediate family, along with countless aunts, uncles, and cousins who brought along assorted friends. It was a bustling and open house with assorted neighbors and tenants popping in and out to exchange bits of gossip, pick up an old quarrel, or referee the ongoing checkers game in which my grandmother cheated shamelessly. They were all there to let down their hair and put up their feet after a week of labor in the factories, laundries, and shipyards of New York.

5   Amid the clamor, which could reach deafening proportions—two or three conversations going on simultaneously, punctuated by the sound of a baby's crying somewhere in the back rooms or out on the street—there was still a rigid set of rules about what was said and how. Older children were sent out of the living room when it was time to get into the juicy details about "you-know-who" up on the third floor who had gone and gotten herself "p·r·e·g·n·a·n·t!" But my parents, knowing that I could spell well beyond my years, always demanded that I follow the others out to play. Beyond sexual misconduct and death, everything else was considered harmless for our young ears. And so among the anecdotes of the triumphs and disappointments in the various workings of their lives, the word *nigger* was used in my presence, but it was set within contexts and inflections that caused it to register in my mind as something else.

In the singular, the word was always applied to a man who had distinguished himself in some situation that brought their approval for his strength, intelligence, or drive:

"Did Johnny really do that?"

"I'm telling you, that nigger pulled in $6,000 of overtime last year. Said he got enough for a down payment on a house."

When used with a possessive adjective by a woman—"my nigger"— it became a term of endearment for husband or boyfriend. But it could be more than just a term applied to a man. In their mouths it became the pure essence of manhood—a disembodied force that channeled their past history of struggle and present survival against the odds into a victorious statement of being: "Yeah, that old foreman found out quick enough—you don't mess with a nigger."

10   In the plural, it became a description of some group within the community that had overstepped the bounds of decency as my family defined it: Parents who neglected their children, a drunken couple who fought in public, people who simply refused to look for work, those with excessively dirty mouths or unkempt households were all "trifling niggers." This particular circle could forgive hard times, unemployment, the occasional bout of depression—they had gone through all of that themselves—but the unforgivable sin was lack of self-respect.

A woman could never be a *nigger* in the singular, with its connotation of confirming worth. The noun *girl* was its closest equivalent in that sense, but only when used in direct address and regardless of the gender doing the addressing. *Girl* was a token of respect for a woman. The one-syllable word was drawn out to sound like three in recognition of the extra ounce of wit, nerve or daring that the woman had shown in the situation under discussion.

"G·i·r·l, stop. You mean you said that to his face?"

But if the word was used in a third-person reference or shortened so that it almost snapped out of the mouth, it always involved some element of communal disapproval. And age became an important factor in these exchanges. It was only between individuals of the same generation, or from an older person to a younger (but never the other way around), that "girl" would be considered a compliment.

I don't agree with the argument that use of the word *nigger* at this social stratum of the black community was an internalization of racism. The dynamics were the exact opposite: the people in my grandmother's living room took a word that whites used to signify worthlessness or degradation and rendered it impotent. Gathering there together, they transformed *nigger* to signify the varied and complex human beings they knew themselves to be. If the word was to disappear totally from the mouths of even the most liberal of white society, no one in that room was naive enough to believe it would disappear from white minds. Meeting the word head-on, they proved it had absolutely nothing to do with the way they were determined to live their lives.

15   So there must have been dozens of times that the word *nigger* was spoken in front of me before I reached the third grade. But I didn't "hear" it until it was said by a small pair of lips that had already learned it could be a way to humiliate me. That was the word I went home and asked my mother about. And since she knew that I had to grow up in America, she took me in her lap and explained.

Analyzing Rhetorical Choices

1. Analyze Naylor's opening paragraph in terms of formality, shifts in tone, parallel structure, alliteration, and other stylistic uses of language.
2. Naylor seems intent on shocking the reader with her opening sentence of the third paragraph. In what ways is this sentence an effective opening to the rest of the essay?
3. Why does Naylor additionally define the term *girl*? How does this contribute to the essay? Are there affectionate terms like *girl* in your everyday language that are specific to your cultural experience? If so, list several of them and use them in sentences that express this affection.

Writing About Issues and Contexts

1. How does Naylor's opening paragraph relate to the topic she analyzes? Offer your own view whether "Words themselves are innocuous; it is the consensus that gives them true power."
2. Naylor writes that "the word *nigger* was used in my presence, but it was set within contexts and inflections that caused it to register in my mind as something else." What does she mean by this? What is registered in her mind when the word *nigger* is used within her family setting?
3. Is the use of this word by blacks themselves "an internalization of racism"? Are similar derogatory terms used by other ethnic groups? Why or why not?

   How can we make sense of the "negative" terms that members of a particular ethnicity or subculture may use when referring to themselves?

Born in Santa Barbara, California, **Gretel Ehrlich** *(1946–) attended Bennington College, UCLA Film School, and the New School for Social Research. She has written numerous books, including* Heart Mountain *(1988),* Islands, the Universe, Home *(1991),* A Match to the Heart *(1994), and most recently,* Any Clear Thing That Blinds Us with Surprise: Seven Seasons in Greenland *(2001). In addition to her career as a writer, Ehrlich has worked as a ranch hand, sheepherder, and documentary film-maker for the Public Broadcasting System. Her essays about being a sheepherder in Wyoming came together to form the book* The Solace of Open Spaces *(1985), which was five years in the making. The collection of 12 essays, which includes "About Men," won awards from the American Academy of Arts and Letters and the Whiting Foundation.*

Gretel Ehrlich
About Men

When I'm in New York but feeling lonely for Wyoming I look for the Marlboro ads in the subway. What I'm aching to see is horseflesh, the glint of a spur, a line of distant mountains, brimming creeks, and a reminder of the ranchers and cowboys I've ridden with for the last eight years. But the men I see in those posters with their stern, humorless looks remind me of no one I know here. In our hellbent earnestness to romanticize the cowboy we've ironically disesteemed his true character. If he's "strong and silent" it's because there's probably no one to talk to. If he "rides away into the sunset" it's because he's been on horseback since four in the morning moving cattle and he's trying, fifteen hours later, to get home to his family. If he's "a rugged individualist" he's also part of a team: ranch work is teamwork and even the glorified open-range cowboys of the 1880s rode up and down the Chisholm Trail in the company of twenty or thirty other riders. Instead of the macho, trigger-happy man our culture has perversely wanted him to be, the cowboy is more apt to be convivial, quirky, and softhearted. To be "tough" on a ranch has nothing to do with conquests and displays of power. More often than not, circumstances—like the colt he's riding or an unexpected blizzard—are overpowering him. It's not toughness but "toughing it out" that counts. In other words, this macho, cultural artifact the cowboy has become is simply a man who possesses resilience, patience, and an instinct for survival. "Cowboys are just like a pile of rocks—everything happens to them. They get climbed on, kicked, rained and snowed on, scuffed up by wind. Their job is 'just to take it,'" one old-timer told me.

A cowboy is someone who loves his work. Since the hours are long—ten to fifteen hours a day—and the pay is $30 he has to. What's required of him is an odd mixture of physical vigor and maternalism. His part of the beef-raising industry is to birth and nurture calves and take care of their mothers. For the most part his work is done on horseback and in a lifetime he sees and comes to know more animals than people. The iconic myth surrounding him is built on American notions of heroism: the index of a man's value as measured in physical courage. Such ideas have perverted manliness into a self-absorbed race for cheap thrills. In a rancher's world, courage has less to do with facing danger than with acting spontaneously—usually on behalf of an animal or another rider. If a cow is stuck in a boghole he throws a loop around her neck, takes his dally (a half hitch around the saddle horn), and pulls her out with horsepower. If a calf is born sick, he may take her home, warm her in front of the kitchen fire, and massage her legs until dawn. One friend, whose favorite horse was trying to swim a lake with hobbles on, dove under water and cut her legs loose with a knife, then swam her to shore, his arm around her neck lifeguard-style, and saved her from drowning. Because these incidents are usually linked to someone or something outside himself, the westerner's courage is self-less, a form of compassion.

The physical punishment that goes with cowboying is greatly underplayed. Once fear is dispensed with, the threshold of pain rises to meet the demands of the job. When Jane Fonda asked Robert Redford (in the film *Electric Horseman*) if he was sick as he struggled to his feet one morning, he replied, "No, just bent." For once the movies had it right. The cowboys I was sitting with laughed in agreement. Cowboys are rarely complainers; they show their stoicism by laughing at themselves.

If a rancher or cowboy has been thought of as a "man's man"—laconic, hard-drinking, inscrutable—there's almost no place in which the balancing act between male and female, manliness and femininity, can be more natural. If he's gruff, handsome, and physically fit on the outside, he's androgynous at the core. Ranchers are midwives, hunters, nurturers, providers, and conservationists all at once. What we've interpreted as toughness—weathered skin, calloused hands, a squint in the eye and a growl in the voice—only masks the tenderness inside. "Now don't go telling me these lambs are cute," one rancher warned me the first day I walked into the football-field-sized lambing sheds. The next thing I knew he was holding a black lamb. "Ain't this little rat good-lookin'?"

5 So many of the men who came to the West were southerners—men looking for work and a new life after the Civil War—that chivalrousness and strict codes of honor were soon thought of as western traits. There were very few women in Wyoming during territorial days, so when they did arrive (some as mail-order brides from places like Philadelphia) there was a stand-offishness between the sexes and a formality that persists now. Ranchers still tip their hats and say, "Howdy, ma'am" instead of shaking hands with me.

Even young cowboys are often evasive with women. It's not that they're Jekyll and Hyde creatures—gentle with animals and rough on women—but rather, that they don't know how to bring their tenderness into the house and lack the vocabulary to express the complexity of what they feel. Dancing wildly all night becomes a metaphor for the explosive emotions pent up inside, and when these are, on occasion, released, they're so battery-charged and potent that one caress of the face or one "I love you" will peal for a long while.

The geographical vastness and the social isolation here make emotional evolution seem impossible. Those contradictions of the heart between respectability, logic, and convention on the one hand, and impulse, passion, and intuition on the other, played out wordlessly against the paradisical beauty of the West, give cowboys a wide-eyed but drawn look. Their lips pucker up, not with kisses but with immutability. They may want to break out, staying up all night with a lover just to talk, but they don't know how and can't imagine what the consequences will be. Those rare occasions when they do bare themselves result in confusion. "I feel as if I'd sprained my heart," one friend told me a month after such a meeting.

My friend Ted Hoagland wrote, "No one is as fragile as a woman but no one is as fragile as a man." For all the women here who use "fragileness" to avoid work or as a sexual ploy, there are men who try to hide theirs, all the while clinging to an adolescent dependency on women to cook their meals, wash their clothes, and keep the ranch house warm in winter. But there is true vulnerability in evidence here. Because these men work with animals, not machines or numbers, because they live outside in landscapes of torrential beauty, because they are confined to a place and a routine embellished with awesome variables, because calves die in the arms that pulled others into life, because they go to the mountains as if on a pilgrimage to find out what makes a herd of elk tick, their strength is also a softness, their toughness, a rare delicacy.

Analyzing Rhetorical Choices

1. Why do you think Ehrlich begins her essay by describing the Marlboro man? Why do you think she focuses exclusively on the cowboy?
2. What does Ehrlich accomplish with her series of "if" sentences in the opening paragraph? How is this contrastive pattern continued through the rest of the paragraph and generally through the essay?
3. Explain the meaning and rhetorical power of Ehrlich's statement, "If he's gruff, handsome, and physically fit on the outside, he's androgynous at the core."
4. Write an analysis of Ehrlich's last paragraph. What stylistic devices does she use, and how effective are they?

Writing About Issues and Contexts

1. What qualities are associated with the cowboy? How has the popular image of the cowboy "disesteemed his truest character"?
2. Ehrlich attempts to redefine the cowboy in order to reclaim him from the romantic image that can be found in most popular media. Describe the ways this essay deals with cowboys. In what ways is it realistic? Romantic? Honest? Idealistic?
3. Ehrlich writes, "Their lips pucker up, not with kisses but with immutability." What does she mean by this? How is this statement central to her definition of the cowboy?

*An eloquent spokesperson for compassionate understanding and human rights, **Elie Wiesel** (1928–   ) was born in Sighet, Romania, and grew up in a world that centered on family, religious study, community, and God. All this came crashing down when, at the age of 16, his village was destroyed and he was deported to Auschwitz along with his father. Wiesel survived internment and was liberated in April 1945, four months after his father perished. An account of his experiences can be found in his extremely powerful book* Night *(1958), in which he states, "Never shall I forget those moments which murdered my God and my soul and turned my dreams to dust. Never shall I forget these things, even if I am condemned to live as long as God Himself. Never." Wiesel was appointed chair of the Presidential Commission on the Holocaust and in 1985 was awarded the Congressional Medal of Achievement. In 1986, he was awarded the Nobel Peace Prize for his life's work speaking and writing about the catastrophic effects of hatred and prejudice.*

Elie Wiesel

How Can We Understand Their Hatred?

Fanaticism today is not a nice word; it carries an unpleasant connotation. But in ancient times, fanatics enjoyed a more favorable reaction from the public. They were linked to religion and, more specifically, to religious experience. In the Bible, Pinhas was praised for slaying a sinner. The Prophet Elijah was admired as an extreme opponent of the wicked Queen Jezebel. Later, in Islam, *fana* (meaning the annihilation of the will) described the Sufi's desire to attain ecstasy in his union with the divine.

Today, in our modern language, fanaticism refers to excessive behavior, uncritical political opinions, ethnic zeal and religious bigotry. How did this come to be?

Previous centuries suffered from tribal and religious wars and from national extremism, but our last century was ravaged mainly by ideological and secular hatred. Nazism and communism moved fanaticism to unprecedented dimensions—dimensions future historians may term as absolute. Stalin used Terror just as Hitler used Death to oppress tens of millions of people: Never have man-made ideologies introduced so much evil into society; never have they given Death so much power.

Early in my own life, I experienced the consequences of fanaticism. On Sept. 11, like so many others throughout the world, I saw its terrible consequences again. Glued for days to the television, I witnessed unthinkable acts of terror. How, I asked myself, after the last century's horrors, could fanaticism still hold sway?

5   On reflection, I believe that fanaticism appeals to people for a variety of reasons. But on the deepest level, fanaticism is seductive because it makes the fanatic feel less alone.

The fanatic fails to understand that the tragedy of man is that, in essential matters, we are each condemned to be alone—we can never break out of the "self." How does one cease being one's own jailer? By becoming each other's prisoner. The fanatic thinks he can tear down the walls of his cell by joining other fanatics. No need to think—the Party does the thinking for him, and the deciding for him.

The fanatic is stubborn, obstinate, dogmatic: Everything for him is black or white, curse or blessing, friend or foe—and nothing in between. He has no taste for or interest in nuances. Does he seek clarity? Driven by irrational impulses, he wants everything to be visible and necessarily clear.

The fanatic simplifies matters: He is immune to doubt and to hesitation. Intellectual exercise is distasteful, and the art and beauty of dialogue alien to him. Other people's ideas or theories are of no use to him. He is never bothered by difficult problems: A decree or a bullet solves them . . . immediately. The fanatic feels nothing but disdain toward intellectuals who spend precious time analyzing, dissecting, debating philosophical notions and hypotheses. What matters to the fanatic is the outcome—not the way leading there.

And more: The fanatic derides and hates tolerance, which he perceives as weakness, resignation or submission. That is why he despises women: Their tenderness is to him a sign of passivity. The fanatic's only interest is domination by fear and terror. Violence is his favorite language—a vulgar language filled with obscenities: He doesn't speak, he shouts; he doesn't listen, he is too busy yelling; he doesn't think, he doesn't want *anyone* to think.

10   In other words, the fanatic, intoxicated with hatred, tries to reduce everybody to his own size.

He has a goal and is ready to pay any price to achieve it. Or more precisely: He is ready to make *others* pay any price in order to achieve it.

The fanatic feels important, for he presumes being capable of altering—and dominating—the course of history. Using the obscure power of hatred, he feels he can—and must—take charge of man's fate. Working in the dark, forever involved in plots and counterplots, he thinks his mission is to abolish the present state of affairs and replace it with his own system. No wonder that he, the human failure, now feels proud and superior.

The fanatic who kills in God's name makes his God a murderer.

Let me conclude with this thought:

15 Of all the "isms" produced by the past centuries, fanaticism alone survives. We have witnessed the downfall of Nazism, the defeat of fascism and the abdication of communism. But fanaticism is still alive. And it is spreading fast. As horrible as it may sound, racial hatred, anti-Semitism and bin Laden terrorism are popular and still glorified in certain communities.

How can the fanatics be brought back to moral sanity? How can the killers and suicide warriors be disarmed?

If there is a simple answer, I do not know it. All I know is that, as we embark on this newest century, we cannot continue to live with fanaticism—and only we ourselves can stem it.

How are we to do this?

We must first fight indifference.

20 Indifference to evil is the enemy of good, for indifference is the enemy of everything that exalts the honor of man. We fight indifference through education; we diminish it through compassion. The most efficient remedy? Memory.

To remember means to recognize a time other than the present; to remember means to acknowledge the possibility of a dialogue. In recalling an event, I provoke its rebirth in me. In evoking a face, I place myself in relationship to it. In remembering a landscape, I oppose it to the walls that imprison me. The memory of an ancient joy or defeat is proof that nothing is definitive, nor is it irrevocable. To live through a catastrophe is bad; to forget it is worse.

And so, as we move forward from Sept. 11, let us continue to remember. For memory may be our most powerful weapon against fanaticism.

Analyzing Rhetorical Choices

1. Why does Wiesel turn to the Bible for his early account of fanaticism? How does that strengthen his rhetorical position?

2. Analyze the following sentence of Wiesel's in terms of its stylistic effectiveness: "Stalin used Terror just as Hitler used Death to oppress tens of millions of people: Never have man-made ideologies introduced so much evil into society; never have they given Death so much power."
3. Wiesel divides his essay into three parts. What does each part do? How well do they relate to each other?

Writing About Issues and Contexts

1. According to Wiesel, what is fanaticism? How has the meaning of the word, in terms of social acceptance, changed over time?
2. What is the appeal of fanaticism? Are you fanatical about something, and if so, what? Is fanaticism always bad? What connotations does it convey?
3. What argument is Wiesel attempting to make about remembrance and relationship? Why does he argue that memory "may be our most powerful weapon against fanaticism"? Offer your response.

*English born and educated, **Jonathan Raban** (1942–   ) now resides in Seattle, where he writes on numerous topics in a wide variety of modes and genres. Perhaps best known for his travel books—including* Arabia: A Journey through the Labyrinth *(1979),* Old Glory: An American Voyage *(1981), and* Bad Land: An American Romance *(1996), he is also the author of* Passage to Juneau: A Sea and Its Meanings *(1999),* Foreign Land *(1985), and editor of* The Oxford Book of the Sea *(1992), an anthology of literary works in both prose and poetry. His works have won awards from the Royal Society of Literature and the National Book Critics' Circle.*

Jonathan Raban

My Holy War

When I was growing up in England, churches were still by far the tallest buildings in the landscape. With their towers and battlements, these domestic fortresses of Christendom, built as much to intimidate as to inspire, were close cousins and coevals of the Crusader castles in Turkey and the Middle East, like Birecik, Markab, and Crac des Chevaliers, whose lordly ruins I later saw, always from a distance and always with an unwelcome pang of déjà vu. My boarding school was attached to Worcester Cathedral, a magnificent crenellated pile, from the top of whose two-hundred-foot tower you could, so it was said, see clear across six counties. It was also said that a threepenny bit flipped out from the tower onto the head of an unwary passerby would cause instant death. This maneuver wasn't as easy as it may sound, and the cathedral roof below the tower was spattered with coins that had failed to reach their target, several of them mine.

The cathedral was full of emblems of Christianity's violent past. In the choir was King John's tomb, topped with a marble effigy of the King, brother of Richard the Lionheart, who taxed England dry to pay for his bloody Third Crusade against Saladin. In the south aisle, a museum case held a number of small treasures under dusty glass. I particularly relished a curled, yellowish-brown object that looked like a half-eaten cannoli shell. A faded label, inscribed in sepia ink, proclaimed it to be the skin of a flayed Dane. I never quite believed in children's hymns like "Gentle Jesus, meek and mild"; one had only to look around Christian buildings to see that this was a religion of the sword, of imperial conquest, of torture and coercion—a great, antique war machine, disguised as an engine of sweetness and light.

My father was a clergyman who came to ordination late, after a successful wartime career as an artillery officer followed by a spell as the regional secretary of a Christian voluntary organization. I was, from age twelve, a sullen atheist. Pimple-faced, voice treacherously skidding from baritone to falsetto, I tried to explain to my father that religion had always done more bad in the world than it had done good: What about the Spanish Inquisition? What about the Salem witch trials? What about the Thirty Years' War? What about the Bishops and the Bomb? It was obvious: religion was over—finished, a long disease for which the cure had been found in the form of mass education and a taste of modest material well-being. My father, in the yellowed dog collar that had seen service around my grandfather's neck and the ancient black cassock that had been passed on to him by my great-uncle Cyril, was an egregious (fast becoming my favorite word) anachronism, and might just as well have gone strolling around the village in codpiece and tights.

It was a lot easier to be a budding atheist in the mid-nineteen-fifties than it was to be a budding vicar. The churches of England, grand as they appeared from a distance, were riddled with worm and rot. Beside each church stood a giant plywood thermometer, precariously rigged with guy ropes, recording the progress of the restoration fund for the tower or the roof. The thermometers often perished in the weather before the red paint began to climb the scale. Sunday congregations were thin and growing thinner—lost to TV, the home-improvement craze, and weekend jaunts in the new family car.

5   After his curacy, my father's first full parish was a sprawling village, Pennington, on the outskirts of Lymington, in Hampshire. Luckily for him, the church was Victorian and not in a state of imminent physical collapse, and a fair sprinkling of parishioners still showed up at services. The local gentry came to Matins, to set an example to the villagers, and because the church porch was their gathering point before they climbed into their Jaguars and Rovers and swept off for pre-luncheon sherry. The farmers came. So did the retired Army types, who addressed my father as Padre, along with a dutiful remnant of shopkeepers and agricultural laborers.

Like most sixteen-year-olds, as I was then, I could see inside people's heads. None of the churchgoers actually believed. They might go through the motions, singing the hymns, crossing their hands to accept the Communion wafer, covering their eyes in the performance of public prayer, but they didn't really think that the world had been created by a Palestinian peasant, or that a personal paradise of harps and angels awaited them on the far side of their last visit to the Lymington

hospital. These dark-suited hypocrites no more subscribed to my father's ritualist, Anglo-Catholic theology, with its transformational
magic, than I did. I could tell, for I was an angry fundamentalist with
a lock on truth, and as militant in my own way as any fanatic with a
holy book. I could understand the idea of a Church Militant, but a
church without passion, without conviction, without the steel of the
true believer was beyond my adolescent comprehension.

It would be nearly twenty years before Philip Larkin wrote the
lines that I wanted to quote to my father in 1958: "Religion . . . / That
vast moth-eaten musical brocade / Created to pretend we never die."
Even in rural Pennington, even on Sundays, we were on the brink of a
new and saner world of secular realism. God would join the rest of our
discarded toys up in the attic; the pretense of belief would be gone
soon; and no one would ever again go into battle high on the hallu-
cinogen of religious superstition. The idea that any religion would
have sufficient power left in it to fuel a twenty-first-century war would
have struck me as grotesque.

My father's second parish, to which he moved in the mid-nineteen-
sixties, was the kind of place that bishops describe as "a challenge"—a
vast, shabby council estate, Millbrook, built by the city of Southampton
to house its poorest citizens. The ugly purpose-built brick church was
dwarfed by twenty-five-story tower blocks with vandalized elevators
and urinous concrete stairwells, into which were packed new immigrants, single mothers, recidivists temporarily at liberty from their prisons, the unlucky, the feckless, the jobless, the chronically dependent.
The windy shopping plaza at the center of the estate was largely un-
tenanted. For some twenty thousand people, there was a ladies' hair-
dresser, a liquor store, and a grocery smaller than the average American
7-Eleven.

The experience of ministering to this impossible parish radicalized
my father. A lifelong reflex Conservative voter, he joined the Labour
Party. His High Church theology became ever more attenuated and
symbolic. He climbed his way through the tower blocks less as a priest
than as a psychiatric social worker. He grew a beard that made him
look like Karl Marx, left his dog collar in the drawer, and went about
in an open-necked plaid flannel shirt. Although his church congregations were now tiny, he worked around the clock, negotiating with the
authorities on behalf of his parishioners, succoring the needy, coun-
selling the desperate, befriending the friendless.

10   In Millbrook, the Anglicans, the Catholics, and the Methodists
were all in the same boat—down to the same dwindling, elderly band

of congregants. My father's vicarage became an ecumenical center for the local clergy, fellow-pilgrims in the stony landscape of twentieth-century unbelief. My mother served tea to the Methodists while my father shared his Haig whiskey with the Irish Catholic priest. Left out of these cheerful conferences were the proprietors of what my father called "tin tabernacles"—sectarians of unorthodox hue, like Spiritualists, Seventh-Day Adventists, charismatics, Pentecostals. I was now teaching the literature of the American Puritans, at a Welsh university college, and was getting professionally involved with serious theocrats, like Cotton and Increase Mather, whose take-no-prisoners style of religious practice struck a strangely warming chord in my atheistic, Marxist heart.

The despised tin tabernacles didn't appear to find Millbrook stony ground at all. There was always a good crowd on the balding grass outside the Pentecostal chapel on Sunday mornings, and many of the people there looked disconcertingly young. I had been taught to think of the wilder reaches of English nonconformity as marginal and eccentric, if not certifiably insane, and wrote off the Pentecostals as an irrelevant blip on the smooth graph of rising skepticism and declining superstition. The coming age of reason wouldn't be forestalled by ninety or so suburban enthusiasts, in puffy nylon golf jackets and raspberry-pink twinsets, talking in tongues. But I should have paid more attention. Millbrook was an issue, and so were tin tabernacles—small, disestablished powerhouses of vehemence and zeal. I made no connection then between the modern English illuminists and their American cousins and ancestors. Had I actually visited a tin tabernacle, I might have heard an echo of Jonathan Edwards preaching on "Sinners in the Hands of an Angry God," and realized that something was up—a new era of religious ferocity.

The leading players in the September 11th attacks found their vocations as fanatical holy warriors not in the God-fearing Middle East but in the most profane quarters of big cities in the West. Back home in Egypt, Lebanon, Saudi Arabia, their fathers, brothers, uncles have formed an incredulous chorus. "He was a donkey when it came to politics." "He was a normal person. . . . He drank alcohol, he had girlfriends." "His personality and his life bore no relation to the kind of things that happened." "We are in shock. . . . We thought he liked the U.S.A." In Europe and the United States, each of these ordinary, insecure, unprepossessing men learned to think of himself as someone who might yet have a spectacular career, as a martyr. This peculiar strain of religious belief, with its equal measures of rage and passion for death, was hatched in Egypt more than fifty years ago, and seems to have found an ideal growing climate in exile, in the most secular-looking landscape yet devised: the low-rent, rootless, multilingual suburbs.

The essential charter of the jihad movement—its "Mein Kampf"—is Sayyid Qutb's "Milestones" (1964). Before Qutb toured the United States, between 1948 and 1950, he was best known as an Egyptian novelist, poet, and critic. After his time here, he became famous as an Islamic ideologue and a member of the Muslim Brotherhood, the Cairo-based think tank and home of theocratic revolution. He achieved martyrdom in 1966, when he was executed by Gamal Abdel Nasser. His book lives on. It can be found, in whole or in part, on many of the Internet sites created by Muslim students.

The heart of Qutb's argument rests on a rhetorical flourish: the modern world exactly reflects the state of things at the beginning of the seventh century, before the Koran was revealed to the Prophet Muhammad. The richest parts of Arabia were then occupied by foreign imperialists—Romans and Persians. Drinking, fornication, shopping, and vulgar entertainment were the chief pursuits of a morally bankrupt society sunk in *jahiliyyah*, the condition of ignorance, barbarism, and chaos from which the Arabs were providentially rescued by the gift of the Koran. They toppled their foreign oppressors and established the *khilafah*, or caliphate; that is, the nation (*ummah*) of Islam, which existed, though in steadily deteriorating form, until 1924, when the last caliph was deposed. The Sykes-Picot Agreement, of 1916, in which the British and the French carved up Arabia into colonial spheres of influence, lent symmetry to the argument: history was on rewind, with the Romans and Persians walking backward onto the screen. The twentieth century was a new *jahiliyyah*, and the great project of the Islamic revival was the restoration of the rule of Allah by force of arms. The coming jihad must be global in scale. Qutb wrote, "This religion is really a universal declaration of the freedom of man from servitude to other men and from servitude to his own desires. It is a declaration that sovereignty belongs to God alone and that He is the Lord of all the worlds."

15   Qutb didn't join the Muslim Brotherhood until 1952—three years after the assassination of the movement's founder, Hassan al-Banna, and two years after Qutb's spell of expatriation in the United States. Firsthand experience of Western *jahiliyyah* seems to have transformed Qutb from a devout but orthodox believer into the architect of worldwide jihad. His American writing (fragments of it were translated and published by John Calvert last year in the journal *Islam and Christian-Muslim Relations*) shows him as a lonely naïf, adrift in a

world of lewd temptations. Although Qutb was forty-two when he sailed from Alexandria for New York in 1948 (the Farouk regime was paying him to study American education methods), his voice sounds painfully young. On the voyage out, a "drunken, semi-naked" woman showed up at the door to his cabin, an American government agent, dispatched by Langley expressly to corrupt him—or so he told his Egyptian biographer years later. Qutb's sense of extreme moral precariousness comes to the fore in every encounter. Few men past the age of forty can ever have felt their immortal souls to be in such danger at a church hop as Qutb did when he attended one in Greeley, Colorado. The pastor, doubling as disk jockey, lowered the lights to impart "a romantic, dreamy effect," and put on a record of "Baby, It's Cold Outside" (presumably the Esther Williams and Ricardo Montalban version, from the soundtrack of the 1949 hit movie "Neptune's Daughter"). "The dancing intensified. . . . The hall swarmed with legs. . . . Arms circled arms, lips met lips, chests met chests, and the atmosphere was full of love." We're in the psychodrama of temptation here—the language tumescent with arousal, even as it affects a tone of detachment and disdain.

In his Koranic commentary, "In the Shade of the Qur'an," Qutb suggested that the believer's brief sojourn on earth should be spent "purifying the filthy marsh of this world." Rich, sexy, Truman-era America gave him a taste of this world at its filthiest and marshiest. His American letters show him wading fastidiously, a lone pilgrim, through "the life of *jahiliyyah,* hollow and full of contradictions, defects and evils." American jazz, football, wrestling, movies (though he confessed to enjoying "Gone with the Wind" and "Wuthering Heights"), the talk of cars and money supplied Qutb with ammunition for his great theological assault on "this rubbish heap of the West"; and so did the dedication of his Greeley neighbors to weekend lawn maintenance. America, with its natural disposition to clamor and excess, has always been a happy hunting ground for puritans of every denomination; Qutb scored a notable first when he hit on lawn mowing as a target for a spiritual critique of the West. But sex, not lawns—shameless, American, *jahili* sex—was clearly uppermost on the mind of this lifelong bachelor. The word "desire" ripples through "Milestones," and always, it seems, meaning the same thing—the drunken temptress on the ship, a tattooed boy in a Washington, D.C., coffee shop, the terrible peril of the church hop.

The Muslim Brotherhood's Hassan al-Banna, who attempted to liberate Egypt form its corrupt "apostate" monarchy, had told his followers to "prepare for jihad and be lovers of death." It is easy to see death's erotic allure for a man of Qutb's temperament, raised on the Koran's worldly and sensual depiction of the hereafter. The Gardens of Bliss resemble nothing so much as the great Playboy Mansion in the sky, watered by underground springs (all sorts of delightful wetness abound in Paradise), and furnished with cushions and carpets designed for life on the horizontal. Male entrants are greeted by "companions"—"maidens, chaste, restraining their glances, whom no man or jinn before them has touched." Qutb insisted that the descriptions of Heaven in the Koran were symbolic, not literal. The pomegranates wouldn't really be pomegranates, nor the maidens really maidens. These "luxuries . . . similar to luxuries enjoyed in this life" were there to "help us to imagine the ultimate of sweetness and joy." Yet the Koranic Paradise remains obdurately earthbound, full of nubile girls unzipping plantains. It reads like the dream of a repressed and awkward man who might be a young soldier on a foreign posting, or Sayyid Qutb in Greeley, Colorado, or Mohamed Atta in Harburg, Germany.

Like many homesick people, living outside their language in an abrasive foreign culture, Qutb aggrandized his loneliness into heroic solitude. Walking the streets of Greeley, he was the secret, lone agent of God's will. In "Milestones," there's a passage that is unmistakably a portrait of Qutb in America: "The Believer from his height looks down at the people drowning in dirt and mud. He may be the only one; yet he is not dejected or grieved, nor does his heart desire that he take off his neat and immaculate garments and join the crowd." Being able to look down on people drowning in dirt and mud makes you feel taller, the better to "enjoy" your faith as you survey the obscene couplings of the little folk who roll in the ordure below.

This is exactly the posture that hard-line Islamists who live in the West today are advised to adopt. Web sites and magazines of the radical Muslim diaspora are preoccupied to the point of obsession with the issue of "living with *Kufr*." *Kufr*—a simpler notion than *jahiliyyah*—is disbelief; *kuffar* are unbelievers or infidels. "It is a fact of life that we must, to some extent, keep close company with the *kuffar*. This is almost unavoidable given that we work, study, and unfortunately play with them," Amir Abdullah wrote in an article entitled "Preserving the Islamic Identity in the West: Threats and Solutions," published in the magazine *Nida'ul Islam*, in the spring of 1997. "The likeness of Islam and *kuffar* is like that of fresh clear spring water and water brought up from the bottom of a suburban sewer. If even a drop of the filthy water enters the clean water, the clarity diminishes. Likewise it takes only a drop of the filth of disbelief to contaminate Islam in the West."

20   *Kufr* leaks through the TV set into Muslim homes, bringing "moral bankruptcy" to the living room, turning children against parents, wives against husbands: "The news provides us with an insight into the world around us. A world where mujahideen are called 'terrorists,' where the Straight Path is called 'Islamic Fundamentalism,' and where all Muslims are misogynistic wife-bashers." The *kuffar* lie in wait for tender innocents: "Muslim families, having lost much of their Islamic values, have sold out to the West. By sending our children to kindergarten and child care centers, we are sending our children to be suckled by the Shaytan." Or, as the title of an article on One Ummah (a mainstream Muslim Web site, and no great friend to radical Islamism) puts it, "Do You Know What Shaytan Is Feeding Your Baby?"

Nida'ul Islam, which I take to be the *New Left Review* of the Islamist revolution, is published in Lakemba, a nondescript low-rise suburb nine miles southwest of downtown Sydney, and aims to reflect "the Jihad stream amongst the Islamic movements." Long, admiring interviews with Sheikh Omar Abdel Rahman and Osama bin Laden run alongside political analyses of "apostate" regimes in Muslim countries (the Sauds, Mubarak, Qaddafi, Hussein, Musharraf), extracts from "Milestones," and advice columns on topics like adjusting to college, shaving the beard, what to do about Christmas, and choosing a wife. The magazine consistently represents the life of the Muslim in the West as a hazardous survival exercise in enemy-occupied territory. *Kufr* is an oppression as real as any Middle Eastern tyranny. In some ways, it's even more dangerous to live among the *kuffar* than in, say, Fahd's Arabia or Mubarak's Egypt, because the forces of *kufr* are more insidious and omnipresent. The Shaytan stalks the suburbs, trying to catch believers off guard. A Christmas card arrives in the mail. Someone from the office invites you to have a drink with him after work. Your daughter begs to be allowed to go to the prom. You find your own eyes straying to the window of the adult-lingerie store. You had better remember your Sayyid Qutb:

> There is only one place on earth which can be called the house of Islam, and it is that place where an Islamic state is established and the Shari'ah is the authority and God's laws are observed. . . . The rest of the world is the house of war.

Collaboration with the enemy will result in punishment in the hereafter. If, for instance, you cast your vote in a *kufr* election, you commit the mortal sin of *shirk*—which is to associate other gods or rulers with Allah. Last June, when the rest of the British press were busy endorsing Tony Blair or William Hague, the monthly *Khilafah Magazine* published a special election issue in which it endorsed God. As Qutb said, "A Muslim has no nationality except his belief."

What is loosely called the Muslim world has given its inhabitants ample experience of oppression; of constant surveillance by the secret police and their informers; of jail, torture, summary execution performed as a fête champêtre in the market square. (In 1978, I saw—or, rather, heard—two men shot like this in front of a large and eager crowd in Sanaa, Yemen; Polaroid pictures of their exploding heads were hawked, minutes later, as valuable souvenirs.) Many of the key texts of Islamic revolution were written in exile, in hiding, or in a prison cell. A consciousness forged in conditions of tyranny is often liable to find tyranny wherever in the world it settles—in Haldon Street, Lakemba, or in Gloucester Road, London S.W.7. Islamism—which by no means signifies Islam at large—needs oppression. A powerful sense of *kufr* helps the believer to live in Western exile in the necessary state of chronic persecution, from which his theology was born, and on which its survival depends.

It also confers a heroic glamour on the everyday alienation felt by the immigrant—especially the male immigrant—who struggles to keep his head up in a foreign culture. The American who condescends to you because she doesn't understand your funny accent is not simply being bad-mannered; she's evil—an agent of the Shaytan. Your corrosive solitude is the measure of your invincible superiority to the *kuffar*, in their hell-bound ignorance and corruption. You are not as they are. You make a point of not shaking hands with the female examiner of your thesis. When the next-door neighbors toss a ball that happens to roll across your path, you walk on without looking up. At Shuckum's Raw Bar and Grill, you loudly put down the barmaid in a row over the forty-eight-dollar tab. At Huffman Aviation, you grab the seat cushion belonging to another student, and refuse to give it back. These are not displays of sullen adolescent aggression; they're moral gestures, designed to put the *kuffar* in their rightful place. It's what certain angry, frustrated young men have always secretly dreamed of—a theology of rebellion, rooted in hostility and contempt.

25   Since the deposition of the last caliph, in 1924, Islam has had no one to speak with authority on its behalf. It relies instead on a quarrelsome army of jurists and scholars, each of whom interprets the Koran, the Sunna (stories of the Prophet's exemplary life), and the Hadith (the Prophet's sayings) according to his own lights, which leads to a

marvellous profusion of schisms, sects, and heresies. We've had a taste of this in recent months, as various scholars (a generously inclusive term) have construed the meaning of the word "jihad" for a Western audience.

There is greater jihad (Jihad al-Akbar) and lesser jihad (Jihad al-Asghar), and total impassioned disagreement as to which is which. Is greater jihad an internal struggle against one's own desires? Or is it war, on a literal battlefield, against the *kuffar*? For every moderate imam who categorically states that it is the first, there's a radical Islamist who argues, with equal plausibility, that it's the second. The best you can discover about the "true" meaning of "jihad" is that you were a fool to ask the question in the first place.

We know to our cost what the word means to "the jihad stream," though we seem to be hopelessly ignorant of the width and depth of that sectarian branch of the Islamic river. American Muslims of the kind who agree to be interviewed by reporters invariably say that it's a piddling and heretical rivulet, while Osama bin Laden and his claque boast that it's more on the scale of the Amazon or the Nile. It has found its way into virtually every major Western city. It is taught by charismatic mullahs in hundreds of suburban Islamic tin tabernacles, like Sheikh Omar Abdel Rahman's community mosque in Jersey City and Abu Hamza al-Mazri's mosque in Finsbury Park, London. Several of the suspects in the September 11th attacks were said to have plugged into it on the Internet from their lodgings in Florida and San Diego. Marwan al-Shehhi and Mohamed Atta found it in a tiny improvised mosque in Harburg, across from Hamburg on the wrong side of the Elbe.

One thing I have in common with Mohamed Atta is a long-standing affection for the Aleppo souk, about which he wrote his thesis at Hamburg-Harburg Technical University. I spent seventeen days in Aleppo in the nineteen-seventies, with no other commission than to lose myself in that maze of ripe-smelling underground streets and limestone tunnels, each one dedicated to a single commodity—gold, hides, soap, transistor radios, rugs, spices, plastic toys, ouds (the Arabic ancestors of the lute), canned vegetables, silks, rope, copperware, shoes. Walk far enough in the Aleppo souk, navigating with your nose, and you'd eventually find any object you could name. I checked with Google to see just how long the souk actually is, if all its streets were laid end to end, and found it to be, variously, seven, eight, ten, twelve, thirteen, sixteen, and "about 30" kilometres. That haziness corresponds exactly with my memory of the place, which is geometrically contained and yet has a labyrinthine infinitude. It can be walked through in a few minutes, or it can go on forever. Lit with strings of flyspecked low-wattage bulbs, it is—or was—an Arabia in miniature; a lovely, complex urban organism that had, when I was there, in 1978, collapsed gracefully into the fifteenth century. Tourism in Syria then amounted to little more than the occasional coachload of Soviet factory workers, though Aleppo outside the souk was becoming an untidy mess of concrete and cinder block, its narrow streets choked with drivers who kept their thumbs permanently on their horns.

Twenty years later, Mohamed Atta saw the souk as being under siege by tourists and their architecture of fast-food restaurants and multistory hotels. One glance at a picture of the two-hundred-and-fifty-room Chahba Cham Palace, a memorably ugly brute that now towers over Aleppo, is enough to make me warm to Atta's thesis that the souk is dying, fatally polluted by the Western-style developments that surround it.

30   In Harburg, as Atta meditated on the poisoning of Aleppo, he found his way to the Al-Tauhid mosque, where the anti-American Islamist theology of the imam made a snug fit with Atta's academic pursuits. The particular object of Atta's abomination was the American skyscraper—the global symbol of the insolent power of the *kuffar*. His thesis topic couldn't have been better chosen to illustrate the dark preoccupations of the jihad stream: in the Aleppo souk, Atta had found an age-old, smelly world of half-lit arched passages, violated by shameless and greedy *kufr* intruders—an image that might spring straight from the pages of Sayyid Qutb, where sex and jihad are intimately entwined.

Atta's architectural ideas, his displacement in the wilderness of outer Hamburg, and his growing fury at the apostate regime in his native Egypt, combined with an acute sexual squeamishness, all coalesced with the paranoid Koranic scholarship of the Al-Tauhid mosque, and he resolved to contribute his life to the cause of Allah. It's the business of religion to put two and two together and make five. The dialectic of purity and pollution led him to the "noble obligation" of martyrdom. He let his beard grow. He took to scraping the frosting off cakes, lest it contain lard. His manner changed from smiling and polite to the frigid altitude of the believer, stepping fastidiously through the filth of *kufr*. He went missing for the duration of 1998, a period most likely spent in an Al Qaeda training camp in Afghanistan.

Ministering to the alienated and the displaced, my father wore his beliefs thin to the point of transparency. The idea that alienation and displacement might themselves constitute the basis of a religious awakening would have been repellent to him. Broad Church Anglicanism was about reaching out to the margins to reclaim people for the center: born in political compromise, the Church of England had little appetite for protest and none for rage.

"Woe to the bloody city of Lichfield!" George Fox, the first Quaker, shouted as he walked barefoot through the town in 1651. You'd never catch a member of the Anglican clergy doing that. Fox wrote proudly of the "mighty dread" that his preaching inspired, and of the fear of the citizens when they learned that "the man in leathern britches has come." Like his hat, which remained defiantly stuck to his head when he was indoors, the leather gear was an outward sign of Fox's spiritual estrangement from the depraved world of seventeenth-century England. Fox and his original Quakers (the "new fanatic sect, of dangerous principles," as John Evelyn described them in his diary in 1656) might have created a real stir in Millbrook; but my father, going about the parish in plain clothes, with his increasingly plain-clothes theology, had little to offer to the angry, the excluded, the exploited, the male young.

As I see now, my own atheism—my ultimate weapon in the Oedipal war—was really a dissident religious creed, full of furious conviction and an inchoate, adolescent hunger for the battlefield. It went hand in hand with membership in the Campaign for Nuclear Disarmament. The first time I entered my father's Pennington vicarage wearing the three-legged runic peace symbol on my lapel, it met with an immensely satisfactory response: "I will not have your wearing that badge in this house." From then on, I was a nuclear fundamentalist.

35   I waylaid girls and frightened them with the deadly poetry of kilotons, neutrons, gamma rays, fallout, and radiation sickness. At one mile . . . at two . . . at five. As my father had the Gospels, so I had the bomb. I used it daily, to make mushroom clouds all over Hampshire, and to gain converts to my brand of millennialism. The box of badges that I kept in my bedroom rapidly emptied. I secretly indoctrinated my younger brothers, aged nine and ten, telling them that God was finished, and that we were at world's end, unless I and my kind won out against the deaf, blind, stupid old men of the establishment, like the Vicar of Pennington, who were leading us down the path to certain annihilation.

C.N.D. was then led by John Collins, the "Red Canon," a renegade Anglican priest of whom my father richly disapproved, and the ancient, spry, pixieish Bertrand Russell, atheism's own philosopher-king. The organization must have been embarrassed by its militant-extremist faction—the young men of warrior age for whom the peace symbol was a regimental badge and C.N.D. their rampaging army.

Each Easter, we marched—out of step and out of uniform, but marched—in loose platoons, under rippling banners, from Aldermaston, site of the Atomic Weapons Research Establishment, to Trafalgar Square, sleeping rough and living off the land like guerrillas. For mile after rainy mile, we sang "The Red Flag":

> The people's flag is deepest red
> It shrouded oft our martyred dead;
> And ere their limbs grew stiff and cold
> Their hearts' blood dyed its every fold.

I can still feel the intense warming glow of unearned righteousness that accompanied the singing of these words. Midway between Bracknell and Windsor, standing shoulder to shoulder with the world's oppressed, voicing our hatred of the belligerent power of the United States and its puppet nations in the NATO alliance, we were bathed in personal glory:

> Then raise the scarlet standard high!
> Beneath its shade we'll live and die.
> Though cowards flinch and traitors sneer
> We'll keep the red flag flying high!

Back at the vicarage, my father blew a gust of St. Bruno pipe smoke over the remains of breakfast, and said, "So you think Mr. Macmillan needs to take moral guidance from a bunch of spotty teenagers, do you?" Nothing like a traitor's sneer to harden belief into the steel of true zealotry: I finished him off with a single round from my thought-murder gun.

40   Lately, I've been keeping that angry boy on hand, to read the literature of jihad on my behalf. As skeptical as I am, he nevertheless reports with a scowl that he can connect with it pretty well. And, perhaps, he should. He was an unwitting participant in the fervor. It was his father who was the less deceived. The Vicar of Pennington, later Rural Dean of Southampton, went to his grave a rationalist, a stoic, a rueful humanist in a world ablaze with passionate supernatural convictions.

The running cliché about the Afghan war is that it is a conflict between a "modern" and a "medieval" world view. The reassuring implication is that its outcome is a foregone conclusion. Although Mullah Omar and his immediate colleagues did look as if they'd escaped from the cast of a production of "Ali Baba and the Forty Thieves" (their retro fashion itself a telegenic political statement), the wider jihad movement is not a benighted relic of the Middle Ages but a modern construct, built and operated by thoroughly modern young men.

The first reported British casualties in this war were amateur soldiers from Luton, Crawley, Leicester, and London who had enlisted with the Taliban and were promptly claimed as martyrs by the Tottenham-based Islamist organization Al-Muhajiroun (the Emigrants). The suburban mujahideen were second-generation Englishmen, several of them university educated, who sacrificed the prospect of well-paid secular careers for their shot at paradise. In Lahore, Abdul Momin, a twenty-five-year-old civil engineer from east London, bound for Kabul, told a reporter from the *Observer*, "I did not like London because it is spiritually rotten. I want to live a proper Muslim life." In Luton, a young Muslim told the *Guardian*, "Lots of us believe that it is right to fight against the Americans and the British, even if we have grown up in Britain."

Trooping off to find their corner of a foreign field, in much the same spirit as an earlier generation went to Spain with the International Brigade, the volunteers were Web designers, engineers, students, delivery drivers. They came across as cool, wired types, as comfortable in their modernity as any of their fellow-surfers in the Internet cafés. So did Mohamed Atta, Hani Hanjour, Ziad Jarrah, and the other hijack suspects, who left a forensic spoor of brand names across the length and breadth of the United States. We know them best as efficient modern consumers—of Parrot-Ice, Tommy Hilfiger, Econo Lodge, AAA discounts, Starbucks, Cyber Zone, Golden Tee '97 golf at Shuckum's Raw Bar and Grill, Salem cigarettes, Heineken and Budweiser, Chinese takeout from Wo Hop III, lap-dancing at Nardone's Sports Go-Go Bar and the Olympic Garden Topless Cabaret.

There's nothing unmodern about a world view that recoils from the spiritual emptiness of the urban-industrial West. Sayyid Qutb began "Milestones" with the observation that Marxism and capitalism were in a state of terminal moral exhaustion:

> The leadership of mankind by Western man is now on the decline,
> not because Western culture has become poor materially or because
> its economic and military power has become weak. The period of the
> Western system has come to an end primarily because it is deprived of
> those life-giving values which enabled it to be the leader of mankind.
> . . . At this crucial and bewildering juncture, the turn of Islam and the
> Muslim community has arrived.

45   Spengler and Toynbee stand conveniently at Qutb's elbow, to aid
and abet the coming revolution. The bankrupt West has failed
mankind. The present cycle is coming to its inevitable end. Now it's
Islam's "turn."

If "Milestones" exhibits an intense, prurient disgust at the fallen
morals of the modern city, berates the present with allusions to the
splendors of the ancient past, prophesies the end of Western civilization, and holds up religion as the purifying force in a contaminated
world, it's in distinguished company, for these are also the essential
themes of "The Waste Land," the archtext of literary modernism. At
least one radical Islamist is on record as having been a T. S. Eliot
fan—Fathi Shiqaqi, the leader of the Palestinian Islamic Jihad, who
was assassinated in 1995—and it's not hard to see how Eliot's characteristic preoccupations could chime with those of the decline-of-the-
West jihadis. It would appall Eliot, the Anglo-Catholic churchwarden,
to hear it, but his vision of a society collapsing into spiritual ruin is
very close to what Qutb tries to conjure in his depiction of *jahiliyyah*.
The moral indictment of the West, central to the Islamist case, has impeccable Western credentials.

Far from being antiquated or alien, most of the intellectual baggage of the jihad movement, like the life style of its guerrillas, is disconcertingly familiar. It's like seeing a stranger sitting at the wheel of
what you always thought was your car. A photograph of one of the
British volunteers for service with the Taliban showed him in a T-shirt
blazoned with the slogan "The Final Revelation, the Final Message,
the Final System, the Final Conquest: Islam"—a message as modern
in its way as the medium that carried it.

Recently, much solemn incredulity has been expended on the case
of John Walker, the "American Talib." Closely echoing the male relatives of the hijack suspects, Walker's father, a lawyer, said, "I can't
connect the dots between where John was and where John is." Yet,
given the twin American traditions of experimental religiosity and tireless self-reinvention, the dots don't seem all that far apart. On one

level, at least, Walker appears to have led an almost mythical American life in its seemingly frictionless transformations: earning his high-school diploma at sixteen, converting to Islam (via hip-hop and the Internet) after reading "The Autobiography of Malcolm X," becoming a fluent Arabist in Yemen, then a devout jihadi at a Pakistani madrasah—before he then became a guerrilla in Kashmir and Afghanistan. His evolving identity required a succession of new names—Suleyman al-Lindh, Suleyman al-Faris, Abdul Hamid. With family money, an appetite for travel, a pious idealism, a quickness of mind, and extraordinary cultural adaptability, this son of Marin County is a dark and extreme version of a classic American type, of the kind who might have been found on the road to Marrakech or Ladakh, or hanging out with Peruvian revolutionaries—and never more so than when, interviewed on his stretcher by CNN, he was found to speak English with a distinct Arabic accent. "My heart became attached to them," he said of the Taliban, as if translating from a finer, more eloquent language than the one to which he was born. Seeing Walker, and his commonsensical Catholic father, I was sent into a spin of uncomfortable recollection.

As well as prosecuting Walker for conspiring to kill Americans, the United States authorities might also usefully install him in a university somewhere and turn him into a research project. Psychologists, theologians, political scientists, and cultural historians could then sit at his feet and draw him out on the subject of why the call to jihad answers so resonantly the yearnings of clever, unhappy, well-heeled young men, from Mill Valley and Luton as well as from Cairo and Jidda. What he says might be merely as alarming as anything to be found in the caves of Tora Bora, and a lot more difficult to defeat.

Analyzing Rhetorical Choices

1. How would you describe Raban's tone toward the English church, his father, and Sayyid Qutb's form of fundamentalism? How can you distinguish between what Raban is saying and what he really means in those passages?

2. In writing about Qutb, Muslim fundamentalism, and terrorists, Raban runs the risk of demonizing them, of making them into irrational, evil, one-dimensional beasts. How does he try to make his analysis complex in terms of the rhetorical choices that he makes? In what ways does he succeed, or fail?

3. Raban occasionally shifts into the second person. Where does he do this? What effects does this shift have on the reader? Why do you think he do this?

4. Critique Raban's final paragraph, including his word choice and his final sentence. How do his diction and language reinforce his conclusion that the jihad will not be easy to defeat?

Writing About Issues and Contexts

1. Raban states that when he was growing up, he was convinced that "The idea that any religion would have sufficient power left in it to fuel a twenty-first century war would have struck me as grotesque." How do you interpret this statement in light of the essay? Is the idea grotesque? Should it be? Given this statement, how do you interpret Raban's own commitment to the causes of nuclear disarmament?

2. Based on Raban's analysis, what principles and beliefs reside at the heart of Sayyid Qutb's *Milestones*? In what ways, if any, do Qutb's conclusions reflect the thinking of many Americans?

3. Raban writes that it is "easy to see death's erotic allure for a man of Qutb's temperament." What does he mean by this? What is the "erotic allure" of death that attracts men and women who have fundamentalist views similar to those held by Qutb?

4. Raban attempts to dispel the notion that the war in Afghanistan is "between a 'modern' and a 'medieval' world view." Agree or disagree with this thesis, and offer your own reasoning, based on Raban's essay and articles you have read in the press.

Born in England but raised in Canada, **Malcolm Gladwell** *(1963–   )*
graduated with a degree in history from the University of Toronto in 1984.
For nine years, from 1987 to 1996, he worked for The Washington Post,
first as a science writer and then as New York City bureau chief. Currently
a staff writer for The New Yorker, *Gladwell is well known as someone who*
can take on a wide variety of subjects, from "failure" to "French fries." His
book, The Tipping Point *(2000), which examines why major changes in*
our society often happen suddenly and unexpectedly, was a New York
Times *bestseller. The following essay first appeared in* The New Yorker.

Malcolm Gladwell

The Art of Failure

Why Some People Choke and Others Panic

There was a moment, in the third and deciding set of the 1993
Wimbledon final, when Jana Novotna seemed invincible. She was
leading 4–1 and serving at 40–30, meaning that she was one point
from winning the game, and just five points from the most coveted
championship in tennis. She had just hit a backhand to her opponent,
Steffi Graf, that skimmed the net and landed so abruptly on the far
side of the court that Graf could only watch, in flat-footed frustration.
The stands at Center Court were packed. The Duke and Duchess of
Kent were in their customary place in the royal box. Novotna was in
white, poised and confident, her blond hair held back with a head-
band—and then something happened. She served the ball straight into
the net. She stopped and steadied herself for the second serve—the
toss, the arch of the back—but this time it was worse. Her swing
seemed halfhearted, all arm and no legs and torso. Double fault. On
the next point, she was slow to react to a high shot by Graf, and badly
missed on a forehand volley. At game point, she hit an overhead
straight into the net. Instead of 5–1, it was now 4–2. Graf to serve: an
easy victory, 4–3. Novotna to serve. She wasn't tossing the ball high
enough. Her head was down. Her movements had slowed markedly.
She double-faulted once, twice, three times. Pulled wide by a Graf
forehand, Novotna inexplicably hit a low, flat shot directly at Graf, instead of a high crosscourt forehand that would have given her time to
get back into position: 4–4. Did she suddenly realize how terrifyingly

close she was to victory? Did she remember that she had never won a major tournament before? Did she look across the net and see Steffi Graf—Steffi Graf!—the greatest player of her generation?

On the baseline, awaiting Graf's serve, Novotna was now visibly agitated, rocking back and forth, jumping up and down. She talked to herself under her breath. Her eyes darted around the court. Graf took the game at love; Novotna, moving as if in slow motion, did not win a single point: 5–4, Graf. On the sidelines, Novotna wiped her racquet and her face with a towel, and then each finger individually. It was her turn to serve. She missed a routine volley wide, shook her head, talked to herself. She missed her first serve, made the second, then, in the resulting rally, mis-hit a backhand so badly that it sailed off her racquet as if launched into flight. Novotna was unrecognizable, not an élite tennis player but a beginner again. She was crumbling under pressure, but exactly why was as baffling to her as it was to all those looking on. Isn't pressure supposed to bring out the best in us? We try harder. We concentrate harder. We get a boost of adrenaline. We care more about how well we perform. So what was happening to her?

At championship point, Novotna hit a low, cautious, and shallow lob to Graf. Graf answered with an unreturnable overhead smash, and, mercifully, it was over. Stunned, Novotna moved to the net. Graf kissed her twice. At the awards ceremony, the Duchess of Kent handed Novotna the runner-up's trophy, a small silver plate, and whispered something in her ear, and what Novotna had done finally caught up with her. There she was, sweaty and exhausted, looming over the delicate white-haired Duchess in her pearl necklace. The Duchess reached up and pulled her head down onto her shoulder, and Novotna started to sob.

Human beings sometimes falter under pressure. Pilots crash and divers drown. Under the glare of competition, basketball players cannot find the basket and golfers cannot find the pin. When that happens, we say variously that people have "panicked" or, to use the sports colloquialism, "choked." But what do those words mean? Both are pejoratives. To choke or panic is considered to be as bad as to quit. But are all forms of failure equal? And what do the forms in which we fail say about who we are and how we think? We live in an age obsessed with success, with documenting the myriad ways by which talented people overcome challenges and obstacles. There is as much to be learned, though, from documenting the myriad ways in which talented people sometimes fail.

5   "Choking" sounds like a vague and all-encompassing term, yet it describes a very specific kind of failure. For example, psychologists of-

ten use a primitive video game to test motor skills. They'll sit you in front of a computer with a screen that shows four boxes in a row, and a keyboard that has four corresponding buttons in a row. One at a time, x's start to appear in the boxes on the screen, and you are told that every time this happens you are to push the key corresponding to the box. According to Daniel Willingham, a psychologist at the University of Virginia, if you're told ahead of time about the pattern in which those x's will appear, your reaction time in hitting the right key will improve dramatically. You'll play the game very carefully for a few rounds, until you've learned the sequence, and then you'll get faster and faster. Willingham calls this "explicit learning." But suppose you're not told that the x's appear in a regular sequence, and even after playing the game for a while you're not aware that there is a pattern. You'll still get faster: you'll learn the sequence unconsciously. Willingham calls that "implicit learning"—learning that takes place outside of awareness. These two learning systems are quite separate, based in different parts of the brain. Willingham says that when you are first taught something—say, how to hit a backhand or an overhead forehand—you think it through in a very deliberate, mechanical manner. But as you get better the implicit system takes over: you start to hit a backhand fluidly, without thinking. The basal ganglia, where implicit learning partially resides, are concerned with force and timing, and when that system kicks in you begin to develop touch and accuracy, the ability to hit a drop shot or place a serve at a hundred miles per hour. "This is something that is going to happen gradually," Willingham says. "You hit several thousand forehands, after a while you may still be attending to it. But not very much. In the end, you don't really notice what your hand is doing at all."

Under conditions of stress, however, the explicit system sometimes takes over. That's what it means to choke. When Jana Novotna faltered at Wimbledon, it was because she began thinking about her shots again. She lost her fluidity, her touch. She double-faulted on her serves and mis-hit her overheads, the shots that demand the greatest sensitivity in force and timing. She seemed like a different person—playing with the slow, cautious deliberation of a beginner—because, in a sense, she was a beginner again: she was relying on a learning system that she hadn't used to hit serves and overhead forehands and volleys since she was first taught tennis, as a child. The same thing has happened to Chuck Knoblauch, the New York Yankees' second baseman, who inexplicably has had trouble throwing the ball to first base. Under the stress of playing in front of forty thousand fans at Yankee Stadium,

Knoblauch finds himself reverting to explicit mode, throwing like a Little Leaguer again.

Panic is something else altogether. Consider the following account of a scuba-diving accident, recounted to me by Ephimia Morphew, a human-factors specialist at NASA: "It was an open-water certification dive, Monterey Bay, California, about ten years ago. I was nineteen. I'd been diving for two weeks. This was my first time in the open ocean without the instructor. Just my buddy and I. We had to go about forty feet down, to the bottom of the ocean, and do an exercise where we took our regulators out of our mouth, picked up a spare one that we had on our vest, and practiced breathing out of the spare. My buddy did hers. Then it was my turn. I removed my regulator. I lifted up my secondary regulator. I put it in my mouth, exhaled, to clear the lines, and then I inhaled, and, to my surprise, it was water. I inhaled water. Then the hose that connected that mouthpiece to my tank, my air source, came unlatched and air from the hose came exploding into my face.

"Right away, my hand reached out for my partner's air supply, as if I was going to rip it out. It was without thought. It was a physiological response. My eyes are seeing my hand do something irresponsible. I'm fighting with myself. Don't do it. Then I searched my mind for what I could do. And nothing came to mind. All I could remember was one thing: If you can't take care of yourself, let your buddy take care of you. I let my hand fall back to my side, and I just stood there."

This is a textbook example of panic. In that moment, Morphew stopped thinking. She forgot that she had another source of air, one that worked perfectly well and that, moments before, she had taken out of her mouth. She forgot that her partner had a working air supply as well, which could easily be shared, and she forgot that grabbing her partner's regulator would imperil both of them. All she had was her most basic instinct: get air. Stress wipes out short-term memory. People with lots of experience tend not to panic, because when the stress suppresses their short-term memory they still have some residue of experience to draw on. But what did a novice like Morphew have? "I searched my mind for what I could do. And nothing came to mind."

10   Panic also causes what psychologists call perceptual narrowing. In one study, from the early seventies, a group of subjects were asked to perform a visual acuity task while undergoing what they thought was a sixty-foot dive in a pressure chamber. At the same time, they were asked to push a button whenever they saw a small light flash on and off in their peripheral vision. The subjects in the pressure chamber

had much higher heart rates than the control group, indicating that they were under stress. That stress didn't affect their accuracy at the visual-acuity task, but they were only half as good as the control group at picking up the peripheral light. "You tend to focus or obsess on one thing," Morphew says. "There's a famous airplane example, where the landing light went off, and the pilots had no way of knowing if the landing gear was down. The pilots were so focussed on that light that no one noticed the autopilot had been disengaged, and they crashed the plane." Morphew reached for her buddy's air supply because it was the only air supply she could see.

Panic, in this sense, is the opposite of choking. Choking is about thinking too much. Panic is about thinking too little. Choking is about loss of instinct. Panic is reversion to instinct. They may look the same, but they are worlds apart.

Why does this distinction matter? In some instances, it doesn't much. If you lose a close tennis match, it's of little moment whether you choked or panicked; either way, you lost. But there are clearly cases when how failure happens is central to understanding why failure happens.

Take the plane crash in which John F. Kennedy, Jr., was killed last summer. The details of the flight are well known. On a Friday evening last July, Kennedy took off with his wife and sister-in-law for Martha's Vineyard. The night was hazy, and Kennedy flew along the Connecticut coastline, using the trail of lights below him as a guide. At Westerly, Rhode Island, he left the shoreline, heading straight out over Rhode Island Sound, and at that point, apparently disoriented by the darkness and haze, he began a series of curious maneuvers: He banked his plane to the right, farther out into the ocean, and then to the left. He climbed and descended. He sped up and slowed down. Just a few miles from his destination, Kennedy lost control of the plane, and it crashed into the ocean.

Kennedy's mistake, in technical terms, was that he failed to keep his wings level. That was critical, because when a plane banks to one side it begins to turn and its wings lose some of their vertical lift. Left unchecked, this process accelerates. The angle of the bank increases, the turn gets sharper and sharper, and the plane starts to dive toward the ground in an ever-narrowing corkscrew. Pilots call this the graveyard spiral. And why didn't Kennedy stop the dive? Because, in times of low visibility and high stress, keeping your wings level—indeed, even knowing whether you are in a graveyard spiral—turns out to be surprisingly difficult. Kennedy failed under pressure.

15   Had Kennedy been flying during the day or with a clear moon, he would have been fine. If you are the pilot, looking straight ahead from the cockpit, the angle of your wings will be obvious from the straight line of the horizon in front of you. But when it's dark outside the horizon disappears. There is no external measure of the plane's bank. On the ground, we know whether we are level even when it's dark, because of the motion-sensing mechanisms in the inner ear. In a spiral dive, though, the effect of the plane's G-force on the inner ear means that the pilot feels perfectly level even if his plane is not. Similarly, when you are in a jetliner that is banking at thirty degrees after takeoff, the book on your neighbor's lap does not slide into your lap, nor will a pen on the floor roll toward the "down" side of the plane. The physics of flying is such that an airplane in the midst of a turn always feels perfectly level to someone inside the cabin.

      This is a difficult notion, and to understand it I went flying with William Langewiesche, the author of a superb book on flying, "Inside the Sky." We met at San Jose Airport, in the jet center where the Silicon Valley billionaires keep their private planes. Langewiesche is a rugged man in his forties, deeply tanned, and handsome in the way that pilots (at least since the movie "The Right Stuff") are supposed to be. We took off at dusk, heading out toward Monterey Bay, until we had left the lights of the coast behind and night had erased the horizon. Langewiesche let the plane bank gently to the left. He took his hands off the stick. The sky told me nothing now, so I concentrated on the instruments. The nose of the plane was dropping. The gyroscope told me that we were banking, first fifteen, then thirty, then forty-five degrees. "We're in a spiral dive," Langewiesche said calmly. Our airspeed was steadily accelerating, from a hundred and eighty to a hundred and ninety to two hundred knots. The needle on the altimeter was moving down. The plane was dropping like a stone, at three thousand feet per minute. I could hear, faintly, a slight increase in the hum of the engine, and the wind noise as we picked up speed. But if Langewiesche and I had been talking I would have caught none of that. Had the cabin been unpressurized, my ears might have popped, particularly as we went into the steep part of the dive. But beyond that? Nothing at all. In a spiral dive, the G-load—the force of inertia— is normal. As Langewiesche puts it, the plane likes to spiral-dive. The total time elapsed since we started diving was no more than six or seven seconds. Suddenly, Langewiesche straightened the wings and pulled back on the stick to get the nose of the plane up, breaking out of the dive. Only now did I feel the full force of the G-load, pushing me back in my seat. "You feel no G-load in a bank," Langewiesche said. "There's nothing more confusing for the uninitiated."

I asked Langewiesche how much longer we could have fallen. "Within five seconds, we would have exceeded the limits of the airplane," he replied, by which he meant that the force of trying to pull out of the dive would have broken the plane into pieces. I looked away from the instruments and asked Langewiesche to spiral-dive again, this time without telling me. I sat and waited. I was about to tell Langewiesche that he could start diving anytime, when, suddenly, I was thrown back in my chair. "We just lost a thousand feet," he said.

This inability to sense, experientially, what your plane is doing is what makes night flying so stressful. And this was the stress that Kennedy must have felt when he turned out across the water at Westerly, leaving the guiding lights of the Connecticut coastline behind him. A pilot who flew into Nantucket that night told the National Transportation Safety Board that when he descended over Martha's Vineyard he looked down and there was "nothing to see. There was no horizon and no light. . . . I thought the island might [have] suffered a power failure." Kennedy was now blind, in every sense, and he must have known the danger he was in. He had very little experience in flying strictly by instruments. Most of the time when he had flown up to the Vineyard the horizon or lights had still been visible. That strange, final sequence of maneuvers was Kennedy's frantic search for a clearing in the haze. He was trying to pick up the lights of Martha's Vineyard, to restore the lost horizon. Between the lines of the National Transportation Safety Board's report on the crash, you can almost feel his desperation:

> About 2138 the target began a right turn in a southerly direction. About 30 seconds later, the target stopped its descent at 2200 feet and began a climb that lasted another 30 seconds. During this period of time, the target stopped the turn, and the airspeed decreased to about 153 KIAS. About 2139, the target leveled off at 2500 feet and flew in a southeasterly direction. About 50 seconds later, the target entered a left turn and climbed to 2600 feet. As the target continued in the left turn, it began a descent that reached a rate of about 900 fpm.

But was he choking or panicking? Here the distinction between those two states is critical. Had he choked, he would have reverted to the mode of explicit learning. His movements in the cockpit would have become markedly slower and less fluid. He would have gone back to the mechanical, self-conscious application of the lessons he had first received as a pilot—and that might have been a good thing. Kennedy needed to think, to concentrate on his instruments, to break away from the instinctive flying that served him when he had a visible horizon.

20   But instead, from all appearances, he panicked. At the moment when he needed to remember the lessons he had been taught about instrument flying, his mind—like Morphew's when she was underwater—must have gone blank. Instead of reviewing the instruments, he seems to have been focussed on one question: Where are the lights of Martha's Vineyard? His gyroscope and his other instruments may well have become as invisible as the peripheral lights in the underwater-panic experiments. He had fallen back on his instincts—on the way the plane felt—and in the dark, of course, instinct can tell you nothing. The N.T.S.B. report says that the last time the Piper's wings were level was seven seconds past 9:40, and the plane hit the water at about 9:41, so the critical period here was less than sixty seconds. At twenty-five seconds past the minute, the plane was tilted at an angle greater than forty-five degrees. Inside the cockpit it would have felt normal. At some point, Kennedy must have heard the rising wind outside, or the roar of the engine as it picked up speed. Again, relying on instinct, he might have pulled back on the stick, trying to raise the nose of the plane. But pulling back on the stick without first levelling the wings only makes the spiral tighter and the problem worse. It's also possible that Kennedy did nothing at all, and that he was frozen at the controls, still frantically searching for the lights of the Vineyard, when his plane hit the water. Sometimes pilots don't even try to make it out of a spiral dive. Langewiesche calls that "one G all the way down."

What happened to Kennedy that night illustrates a second major difference between panicking and choking. Panicking is conventional failure, of the sort we tacitly understand. Kennedy panicked because he didn't know enough about instrument flying. If he'd had another year in the air, he might not have panicked, and that fits with what we believe—that performance ought to improve with experience, and that pressure is an obstacle that the diligent can overcome. But choking makes little intuitive sense. Novotna's problem wasn't lack of diligence; she was as superbly conditioned and schooled as anyone on the tennis tour. And what did experience do for her? In 1995, in the third round of the French Open, Novotna choked even more spectacularly than she had against Graf, losing to Chanda Rubin after surrendering a 5–0 lead in the third set. There seems little doubt that part of the reason for her collapse against Rubin was her collapse against Graf—that the second failure built on the first, making it possible for her to be up 5–0 in the third set and yet entertain the thought I can still lose. If panicking is conventional failure, choking is paradoxical failure.

Claude Steele, a psychologist at Stanford University, and his colleagues have done a number of experiments in recent years looking at how certain groups perform under pressure, and their findings go to the heart of what is so strange about choking. Steele and Joshua Aronson found that when they gave a group of Stanford undergraduates a standardized test and told them that it was a measure of their intellectual ability, the white students did much better than their black counterparts. But when the same test was presented simply as an abstract laboratory tool, with no relevance to ability, the scores of blacks and whites were virtually identical. Steele and Aronson attribute this disparity to what they call "stereotype threat": when black students are put into a situation where they are directly confronted with a stereotype about their group—in this case, one having to do with intelligence—the resulting pressure causes their performance to suffer.

Steele and others have found stereotype threat at work in any situation where groups are depicted in negative ways. Give a group of qualified women a math test and tell them it will measure their quantitative ability and they'll do much worse than equally skilled men will; present the same test simply as a research tool and they'll do just as well as the men. Or consider a handful of experiments conducted by one of Steele's former graduate students, Julio Garcia, a professor at Tufts University. Garcia gathered together a group of white, athletic students and had a white instructor lead them through a series of physical tests: to jump as high as they could, to do a standing broad jump, and to see how many pushups they could do in twenty seconds. The instructor then asked them to do the tests a second time, and, as you'd expect, Garcia found that the students did a little better on each of the tasks the second time around. Then Garcia ran a second group of students through the tests, this time replacing the instructor between the first and second trials with an African-American. Now the white students ceased to improve on their vertical leaps. He did the experiment again, only this time he replaced the white instructor with a black instructor who was much taller and heavier than the previous black instructor. In this trial, the white students actually jumped less high than they had the first time around. Their performance on the pushups, though, was unchanged in each of the conditions. There is no stereotype, after all, that suggests that whites can't do as many pushups as blacks. The task that was affected was the vertical leap, because of what our culture says: white men can't jump.

It doesn't come as news, of course, that black students aren't as good at test-taking as white students, or that white students aren't as good at jumping as black students. The problem is that we've always assumed that this kind of failure under pressure is panic. What is it we tell underperforming athletes and students? The same thing we tell novice pilots or scuba divers: to work harder, to buckle down, to take the tests of their ability more seriously. But Steele says that when you look at the way black or female students perform under stereotype threat you don't see the wild guessing of a panicked test taker. "What you tend to see is carefulness and second-guessing," he explains. "When you go and interview them, you have the sense that when they are in the stereotype-threat condition they say to themselves, 'Look, I'm going to be careful here. I'm not going to mess things up.' Then, after having decided to take that strategy, they calm down and go through the test. But that's not the way to succeed on a standardized test. The more you do that, the more you will get away from the intuitions that help you, the quick processing. They think they did well, and they are trying to do well. But they are not." This is choking, not panicking. Garcia's athletes and Steele's students are like Novotna, not Kennedy. They failed because they were good at what they did: only those who care about how well they perform ever feel the pressure of stereotype threat. The usual prescription for failure—to work harder and take the test more seriously—would only make their problems worse.

25   That is a hard lesson to grasp, but harder still is the fact that choking requires us to concern ourselves less with the performer and more with the situation in which the performance occurs. Novotna herself could do nothing to prevent her collapse against Graf. The only thing that could have saved her is if—at that critical moment in the third set—the television cameras had been turned off, the Duke and Duchess had gone home, and the spectators had been told to wait outside. In sports, of course, you can't do that. Choking is a central part of the drama of athletic competition, because the spectators have to be there—and the ability to overcome the pressure of the spectators is part of what it means to be a champion. But the same ruthless inflexibility need not govern the rest of our lives. We have to learn that sometimes a poor performance reflects not the innate ability of the performer but the complexion of the audience; and that sometimes a poor test score is the sign not of a poor student but of a good one.

Through the first three rounds of the 1996 Masters golf tournament, Greg Norman held a seemingly insurmountable lead over his nearest rival, the Englishman Nick Faldo. He was the best player in the world. His nickname was the Shark. He didn't saunter down the fairways; he stalked the course, blond and broad-shouldered, his caddy behind him, struggling to keep up. But then came the ninth hole on the tournament's final day. Norman was paired with Faldo, and the two hit their first shots well. They were now facing the green. In front of the pin, there was a steep slope, so that any ball hit short would come rolling back down the hill into oblivion. Faldo shot first, and the ball landed safely long, well past the cup.

Norman was next. He stood over the ball. "The one thing you guard against here is short," the announcer said, stating the obvious. Norman swung and then froze, his club in midair, following the ball in flight. It was short. Norman watched, stone-faced, as the ball rolled thirty yards back down the hill, and with that error something inside of him broke.

At the tenth hole, he hooked the ball to the left, hit his third shot well past the cup, and missed a makable putt. At eleven, Norman had a three-and-a-half-foot putt for par—the kind he had been making all week. He shook out his hands and legs before grasping the club, trying to relax. He missed: his third straight bogey. At twelve, Norman hit the ball straight into the water. At thirteen, he hit it into a patch of pine needles. At sixteen, his movements were so mechanical and out of synch that, when he swung, his hips spun out ahead of his body and the ball sailed into another pond. At that, he took his club and made a frustrated scythelike motion through the grass, because what had been obvious for twenty minutes was now official: he had fumbled away the chance of a lifetime.

Faldo had begun the day six strokes behind Norman. By the time the two started their slow walk to the eighteenth hole, through the throng of spectators, Faldo had a four-stroke lead. But he took those final steps quietly, giving only the smallest of nods, keeping his head low. He understood what had happened on the greens and fairways that day. And he was bound by the particular etiquette of choking, the understanding that what he had earned was something less than a victory and what Norman had suffered was something less than a defeat.

30   When it was all over, Faldo wrapped his arms around Norman. "I don't know what to say—I just want to give you a hug," he whispered, and then he said the only thing you can say to a choker: "I feel horrible about what happened. I'm so sorry." With that, the two men began to cry.

Analyzing Rhetorical Choices

1. Gladwell opens this essay with a representative anecdote. How effective is it, and why? Explain how Gladwell structures this anecdote to increase its dramatic effects.

2. At one point, Gladwell quotes Ephimia Morphew, who cites "a textbook example of panic." Why do you think Gladwell includes that quotation, and why does he use it here? How does it help structure this essay?

3. Locate examples of rhetorical question, anaphora (using the same word to open successive phrases or sentences), and direct address (a shift to the use of *you*) in this essay. In what ways are these rhetorical devices effective?

Writing About Issues and Contexts

1. Gladwell is attempting here to define *failure*. What is failure, according to Gladwell? Why and how do people fail?

2. What is the difference between explicit and implicit learning, according to Gladwell? In your explanation, provide examples of each from your own experience.

3. What kinds of research does Gladwell do to write this essay? How does his research contribute to his understanding, his credibility as an author, and the persuasiveness of the essay?

4. Why do you think Gladwell focuses on the death of John F. Kennedy Jr.? Based on Gladwell's interpretation of this incident and additional research that you do, offer your analysis of what led to the plane crash.

Strategies for Writers: Definition

1. Jamaica Kincaid takes a very simple word, *girl*, and redefines it, as does Judy Brady with the word *wife* and, in a more empirical way, as Gladwell does with the words *choke* and *panic*. What they have done is to choose a term for which there is no universally agreed-on meaning and write an extended definition. What problems do you anticipate if you attempt similarly to define a simple term? What level of specificity does this type of definition require?

2. A related assignment is to define a word that carries with it great potential for controversy. Gloria Naylor's essay, for example, is called "The Meanings of a Word," and she talks about the racially sensitive word *nigger*. Would a white person be able to write an essay defining *nigger*? Can a male define the word *woman* or a woman define the word *man* without invoking controversy? How can you best develop a definition for potentially controversial words like these that carry such problematic meanings in many contexts? What kinds of assurances can you provide your reader that you are proceeding with intelligence and sensitivity?

3. When does defining become stereotyping or dangerous? When is it liberating?

4. Extended definition can embrace other modes and be used in the service of argument. For instance, Lisa Kanae extends her definition of *pidgin* by using forms of narration and ultimately arguing a distinct point of view. While her essay is purportedly a definition of *pidgin*, its purpose is ultimately to change people's minds about language. Good definition is always argument. How will you shape your essay to ostensibly define yet ultimately argue? For what purpose?

5. Definition can be used to extend our understanding and sympathy towards a particular group or class, as Ehrlich does in "About Men" and as Wiesel does in "How Can We Understand Their Hatred?" Will your essay extend sympathy, understanding, enlightenment—in other words, how will you go beyond mere definition toward compelling your readers to re-vision the term or concept you define?

Research and Writing Assignments

1. In their essays, Judy Brady, Jamaica Kincaid, and Gretel Ehrlich choose to consider some aspect of what it means to be defined in terms of gender—that is, the various constructions of maleness or femaleness that get created within cultural life. Thus Brady defines what it means to be a traditional wife, Kincaid a traditional girl within Antiguan society, and Ehrlich redefines the traditional understanding of a cowboy. In an essay that makes explicit use of some of the strategies exhibited in these three essays, define a significant aspect of gendered identity. Some possible topics include scientist, husband, friend, baby, grandparent, boy, athlete.

2. The transcript of "Hunting and Conservation" dramatizes what happens when speakers talk to each other at cross-purposes without having any common definition of key terms. In this case, the conversation has unintended comic effects, largely because of the personalities of the two primary participants: Ventura is blustery and bull-headed, and Anderson is incredulous and at times utterly befuddled by Ventura's "logic." Making use of the kinds of gender differences that Judy Brady, Barbara Ehrenreich, Deborah Tannen, and others write about and using "Hunting and Conservation" as a model, create a transcript of a conversation between a male and a female about some significant idea or concept about which they have little or no agreement. For example, you might choose to write about dating, politeness, feelings, or communication. The transcript should be realistic, and if possible, it should create a comic effect.

3. The kinds of language that people use in everyday interactions can have devastating effects, as the essays by Lisa Kanae and Gloria Naylor (and the poems by Countee Cullen) make clear. As the mother in "Pidgin" says with unintended irony, "You not going get one good job if you no can talk good English. People going tink you stupid." In an essay that incorporates library research by at least two sociolinguists, such as William Labov and John Reinecke Jr., offer your informed perspective on dialect, language use, and social interaction. Your essay can explore your own personal (neighborhood) dialect, analyze words or phrases specific to your culture or community, or consider the principle of "correctness" in speaking and writing.

Whatever approach you take, your essay needs to consider the idea that the inability to use "good English" makes people "tink you stupid."

4. Bruno Bettelheim, Elie Wiesel, and Jonathan Raban focus on the importance of memory as a way to understand the present as well as the past. Their essays put us in mind of the aphorism, "To ignore history is to be doomed to repeat it." Choose a term such as *patriotism, heroism,* or *leadership* and define it, using some U.S. historical accounts to support your definition. How do we understand the term now? How was it understood previously? What kinds of tensions and conflicts exist in our understanding of this word as it is used in public debates following September 11, 2001.

5. Autobiography can be a powerful form, especially when it centers on trying to discover an insight or uncover an individual "truth" that is of real significance to the author—and the audience. We see this principle made clear in essays by Jonathan Raban, Lisa Kanae, and a number of other authors in this book, including Annie Dillard, Richard Wright, Richard Rodriguez, and Frank McCourt. Write an autobiographical essay that centers on a complex issue, problem, or experience that has meaning not only to you but to a more general audience as well. Use Raban's or Kanae's essay as a model, and in a postscript to your essay, explain how it influenced your writing.

6. In "The Art of Failure," Malcolm Gladwell uses the strategy of comparison and contrast to illustrate failure. His analysis of the difference between choking and panicking helps us understand the different ways someone can fail. Raban follows a similar strategy when he writes about the fanaticism of the jihad movement, which he states "is disconcertingly familiar. It's like seeing a stranger sitting at the wheel of what you always thought was your car." Picking up on the strengths in these two essays, write an extended definition of "The Art of Success." Your essay should incorporate at least three outside sources that derive from library or Internet research.

5
Exemplification

What exactly is exemplification? It is the use of details and examples within writing: specific facts, anecdotes, scenes, statistics, research, and information that illustrate, or exemplify, the subject. Writers use it constantly to inject appropriate details into their writing so that their subjects and arguments are anchored in reality. Exemplifying often allows writers to make their subjects vivid, to encourage readers to see, smell, and experience the subject. As a strategy, it often becomes almost intuitive for writers: They offer a generalization and follow it with examples; they put forward a thesis and then offer specific support for it; they make an observation and support it with citations and information. Thus the pattern is a general statement followed by details and examples. The details and examples might be as short as a sentence or as long as several pages, depending on what the writer feels is necessary to explain the subject or make it appear vividly on the page.

One of the most important aspects of exemplifying is selection: determining what kinds of details and examples are needed, where and how they will be used within the writing. There is no magic formula for deciding which examples to include or how many there should be. You are undoubtedly familiar with people who are so laconic that they provide virtually no exemplification, so little in fact that it is almost impossible to understand what they are talking about. On the other end of the spectrum are people who give so many details and facts that you are overwhelmed with minutiae and often so bored that you stop listening. Either extreme has negative consequences, and as a writer, you depend on your readers (instructors, students, peers, supervisors, colleagues) to help you find the middle path: including details that enrich the writing, inform your readers, and keep them turning pages.

Exemplification is especially important when introducing an unfamiliar word, subject, or concept, which is the primary purpose that leads most writers to exemplify their subjects. Larry Good, a composer and humor columnist, describes the annoying problem of having an "ear worm," a problem that has nothing to do with worms at all. To clarify what he means and to add some sizzle to his prose, Good illustrates his short essay with a variety of song lyrics and other forms of exemplification that add to the humor he uses in describing a problem that most people have experienced at one time or another.

I am one of those people who has an internal tape of music that plays constantly in my head. It is a condition that strikes millions of Americans . . . who were subjected to a lot of television in the sixties. It can cause disorientation, an inability to concentrate, and absolute ridicule.

I have approached perfect strangers from behind, in the frozen foods section at City Market, unwittingly humming the Bee Gees "If I can't have you, I don't want nobody, baby, if I can't have you, woh-oo-oh . . . oh." Out loud!

That is why I don't appreciate the constant barrage of low-grade musical "entertainment" that we are all subjected to in nearly all public places now. I am entirely too susceptible to it. Whatever is playing on my internal tape machine starts fighting with the DMX in the room, and invariably the stupidest of the two musics wins. I may enter the shop with a safe and pleasant orchestral arrangement of Beethoven's Waldstein Sonata pulsing in my brain, but I leave the store five minutes later with an internal shriek of "She-ree, Sher-ar-ar-eee, bay-yay-bee (Sherry ba-bee)" which I can expect to repeat hundreds, or even thousands, of times.

What causes this? How can I make it stop? Can I harness this freakish talent so that I can play back music that I would like to hear, instead of music I don't ever want to hear again? These are just a few obvious questions that come to mind with regard to this freakish malady. There is a German word for this—*ohrwarm*—literally translated it means "ear worm."

The ear worm is like a radio station that plays a skipping record, but you can't turn it off, and you can't change the station. I used to wonder why I so often found myself humming "America, the Beautiful" until I realized that every time I turn on my computer printer, it begins a rough version of the melody, and so the ear worm attempts to finish the song. All day. There are plenty of causes, but there are no cures.

The most damnable of ear worms are the one-liners, where you don't know what the next phrase is, or what the words are. Something like the theme from "Happy Days" once you get past "1 o'clock, 2 o'clock, 3 o'clock rock." See what I mean? Sometimes, if you can figure out how it ends, the ear worm will go away. For example, if afflicted with "Sherry Baby" by Frankie Valli and the Four Seasons, you have to know that the falsetto shrieking will resolve with "Sher-ree, won't you come out tonight." It takes a special kind of doctor to treat this sort of affliction.

My wife thinks it is funny to deliberately sneak up on me and sing mellifluous snippets like "Here's a story . . . of a man named Brady. . . ." She has no idea of the mental cruelty involved in such an act. Before I can stop her the damage is done, and the whole Brady Bunch song circles my brain, complete with the Hollywood Squares style television graphic and the wrap-up horn line at the end. "Ba-dum, pa-dum, bum." These are obvious causes, but sometimes secondary suggestions are rewarded with a full-fledged ear worm. The mail cart pulls away from my curb, and suddenly my internal radio is playing "Hey, just a minute, wait a minute, Mister Postman (look at me—Oh, Yeah) is there a package, or a letter for me?" and on and on.

The ear worm can switch from the Beatles' version to the Carpenters' version without pausing. The ear worm doesn't require that I know the lyrics of a piece of music. The ear worm is satisfied with amorphous syllabic onomatopoeia. But I'm not. Is it a package? A letter? A card? Is it "Just-a-minute, wait-a-minute"? or two "wait-a-minutes"? Augh. The thing is driving me crazy. This must be what my brain does when I'm not using it. But I know others suffer just as I do.

There has been a dirge-like tune parading through my head for about two years now, one I can't identify or kill, and though as a musician, I could take this as divine inspiration, it's just not. As a musician, I recognize a lifeless pedantic melody when I hear one, and this melodic blurb doesn't deserve any further musical setting to unleash it on the world.

There are certain melodies that are built from natural elements. Songs like the theme from "Close Encounters" which, in four notes defines the tonal system we use in Western music, are somehow linked to the natural order of things, to physics and acoustics and harmony and melody. So, I could see running around with a bad case of "Close Encounters of the Third Kind" or even a "Pachelbel Canon," and understand that this was just nature at work on my inner muse.

But this doesn't explain today's ear worm "well, twiddle-dee-dee, and twiddle-dee-dum, look out Baby, 'cause here I come." It's crazy. Help.

Larry Good finds a way to make his ear worm concept both familiar and highly individual by carefully selecting precise details, musical
groups, and lyrics to exemplify the ear worm. Incorporating specifics
such as the sound of "Sherry Baby," his wife's cruelly inflicting an ear
worm on him, and the illuminating explanation of the significance of
the theme from the film "Close Encounters of the Third Kind" light up
this essay and help secure it in our memories.

Ear worms aside, certain academic disciplines and scholarly subjects
create expectations about the level of detail that a piece of writing needs.
Historians, for example, mainly focus on facts and details; exemplification is their primary method of establishing historical perspective and
persuading readers that their accounts have genuine validity.
Philosophers, on the other hand, usually focus on abstract principles that
defy exemplification; thus philosophical writing, by its very nature, must
use less exemplification than do the writings of other academic disciplines. A philosophy essay that has the same amount of exemplification
as a history essay is not likely to succeed as well. Different disciplines,
purposes, audiences, and expectations shape the ways exemplification is
used by various writers, including the writers represented in this chapter.

Examine, for a moment, the opening paragraph of the John
McPhee selection. McPhee informs the reader that a "small cabin"
stands in the "Glacier Park Wilderness," that the cabin is about "a
hundred yards off a trail that crosses the Cascade Range," that it
"looked strange" in "midsummer" because it "rose fully two stories"
and "had a high and steeply peaked roof" from which "a ten-foot pole
stuck straight up," to the top of which was tied "a shovel." Three sentences into his essay, McPhee provides a wealth of information about
where he is, what he is seeing, and why it is unusual. Moreover, by the
end of the paragraph, he informs the reader why the cabin is significant: Its height, including the shovel thrusting up above the roof, reveals the huge amount of snow that falls in the Cascade Mountain
Range—snow that ultimately becomes water, which is "a vital matter
to the people below and even far beyond the mountains."

What McPhee does is submerge the reader in a setting, a context,
even the beginnings of an argument about the uses of wilderness versus the uses of natural resources—in this case, copper. He does so by
incorporating a wealth of specific details, every one contributing to the
reader's understanding of the scene and the conflict to come between
David Brower and Charles Park. The details he chooses to include
about Brower and Park further develop their specific characters, val-

ues, and ideological differences. This wealth of detail is characteristic of McPhee's writing: He strives always to render every scene and every individual as fully and completely as he can.

One of the most overlooked reasons a writer uses exemplification is to discover more information about the subject and to gauge when to begin writing. No matter what you are writing about, you must be in command of your subject; you must always know more about your subject than your reader does and more than you include in your essay. The extra, unused material serves as the foundation on which you stand so that your treatment of your subject is just beyond the reach of your readers. If you sit down to write without having this wealth of details, statistics, and particulars at your command, you are not likely to write a successful essay that informs and intrigues your readers. To possess that wealth of knowledge, you must build up your factual resources, as Diane Ackerman does so she can write with authority about the vagaries of taste and appetite.

Years ago, the famous comic duo of Bob and Ray created a radio skit in which Bob interviewed Ray, with Ray assuming the persona of an amateur historian who had just published a massive history of the United States. Their interview went something like the following:

> *Bob:* This is a long history that you have written here. It must be about 1,300 pages long.
>
> *Ray:* Yes, I have tried to be comprehensive and include every possible subject so that I could tell the complete history of this great country.
>
> *Bob:* I certainly appreciate that, but I notice that a few mistakes have crept into your book.
>
> *Ray:* Really?
>
> *Bob:* Yes. For example, you state that the first President of the United States and the Father of Our Country was Lyndon Johnson.
>
> *Ray:* Oh, is that a mistake?
>
> *Bob:* Yes, it is. The person you are referring to is George Washington. A little later in the book you state that the American Civil War began in 1973.
>
> *Ray:* I thought it did begin somewhere around then.
>
> *Bob:* No, it began in 1860.
>
> *Ray:* Well, in a book this size, you can expect a few errors to creep in now and again.
>
> *Bob:* But don't you agree that these are major errors? For example, you also state that the country directly to the south of us is France. But the country located south of us is Mexico.
>
> *Ray:* Well, aren't you doing a bit of nitpicking now? Anybody can make a mistake like that!

One of the aspects of this humorous interview is how unperturbed Ray's character is about all the errors he has committed. And he is wholly unaware of how these errors completely undermine his authority and credibility as an author. Anyone who thinks that Lyndon Johnson is the Father of Our Country or that the Civil War began in 1973 cannot be trusted as a historian. Any writer who exemplifies, carefully checking sources and facts, goes a long way toward writing effectively.

An author in command of his or her facts can establish a great deal of credibility with readers. Diane Ackerman does exactly this in her account of human tastes and culinary preferences. Few readers are likely to know, for example, the extraordinary range of foods that humans eat—from cow's blood and deep-fried songbirds to rats and decaying cucumbers (commonly called pickles). Ackerman's mastery of facts and details—the way she uses exemplification to surprise and amaze—persuades readers that she is in complete control of her subject and thus an authority whom they can confidently trust.

Writers must find ways to prove their expertise to their readers, and one of the best ways to accomplish this goal is through exemplification. By including important details, significant facts and statistics, appropriate quotations from knowledgeable authorities and the like, you can establish meaningful credibility and put yourself in a position to enlarge the perspective of all your readers. No matter what mode of writing you employ—narration, process, comparison/contrast, argumentation—exemplification is a critical and constitutive element of your success as a writer.

The son of a family doctor, **Richard Selzer** *(1928–   ) is a native of Troy, New York, and attended Union College and Yale Medical School. He began writing while still working full time as a general surgeon and a clinical assistant professor of medicine at Yale. Selzer started by publishing stories with a strong element of horror in venues like* Ellery Queen Mystery Magazine, *many of which were subsequently collected in* Rituals of Surgery *(1973). He then turned to relating accounts of his medical experiences. His works have appeared in magazines such as* Esquire, Redbook, *and* Harper's. *His many books include* Mortal Lessons *(1977),* Confessions of a Knife *(1979),* Letters to a Young Doctor *(1982), and* Raising the Dead *(1993), an account of his near-death experience after contracting Legionnaires' disease. This essay is from* Confessions of a Knife.

Richard Selzer

Four Appointments with the Discus Thrower

One

I spy on my patients. Ought not a doctor to observe his patients by any means and from any stance, that he might the more fully assemble the evidence? So I stand in the doorways of hospital rooms and gaze. Oh, it is not all that furtive an act. Those in bed need only look up in order to discover me. But they never do.

From the doorway of Room 542, the man in the bed seems deeply tanned. Blue eyes and close-cropped white hair give him the appearance of vigor and good health. But I know that his skin in not brown from the sun. It is rusted, rather, in the last stage of containing the vile repose within. And the blue eyes are frosted, looking inward like the windows of a snowbound cottage. This man is blind. This man is also legless—the right leg missing from midthigh down, the left from just below the knee. It gives him the look of an ornamental tree, roots and branches pruned to the purpose that the thing should suggest a great tree but be the dwarfed facsimile thereof.

Propped on pillows, he cups his right thigh in both hands. Now and then, he shakes his head as though acknowledging the intensity of his suffering. In all of this, he makes no sound. Is he mute as well as blind?

If he is in pain, why do I not see it in his face? Why is the mouth not opened for shrieking? The eyes not spun skyward? Where are tears? He appears to be waiting for something, something that a blind man cannot watch for, but for which he is no less alert. He is listening.

5 The room in which he dwells is empty of all possessions—the get-well cards, the small private caches of food, the day-old flowers, the slippers—all the usual kickshaws of the sickroom. There is only a bed, a chair, a nightstand, and a tray on wheels that can be swung across his lap for meals. It is a wild island upon which he has been cast. It is Room 542.

Two

"What time is it?" he asks.

"Three o'clock."

"Morning or afternoon?"

"Afternoon."

10 He is silent. There is nothing else he wants to know. Only that another block of time has passed.

"How are you?" I say.

"Who is it?" he asks.

"It's the doctor. How do you feel?"

He does not answer right away.

15 "Feel?" he says.

"I hope you feel better," I say.

I press the button at the side of the bed.

"Down you go," I say.

"Yes, down," he says.

20 He falls back upon the bed awkwardly. His stumps, unweighted by legs and feet, rise in the air, presenting themselves. I unwrap the bandages from the stumps, and begin to cut away the black scabs and the dead glazed fat with scissors and forceps. A shard of white bone comes loose. I pick it away. I wash the wounds with disinfectant and redress the stumps. All this while, he does not speak. What is he thinking behind those lids that do not blink? Is he remembering the burry prickle of love? A time when he was whole? Does he dream of feet? Of when his body was not a rotting log?

He lies solid and inert. In spite of everything, he remains beautiful, as though he were a sailor standing athwart a slanting deck.

"Anything more I can do for you?" I ask.

For a long moment he is silent.

"Yes," he says at last and without the least irony, "you can bring me a pair of shoes."

25 In the corridor, the head nurse is waiting for me.

"We have to do something about him," she says. "Every morning he orders scrambled eggs for breakfast, and instead of eating them, he picks up the plate and throws it against the wall."

"Throws his plate?"

"Nasty. That's what he is. No wonder his family doesn't come to visit. They probably can't stand him any more than we can."

She is waiting for me to do something.

30 "Well?"

"We'll see," I say.

Three

The next morning, I am waiting in the corridor when the kitchen delivers his breakfast. I watch the aide place the tray on the stand and swing it across his lap. She presses the button to raise the head of the bed. Then she leaves.

In this time, which he has somehow identified as morning, the man reaches to find the rim of the tray, then on to find the dome of the covered dish. He lifts off the cover and places it on the stand. He fingers across the plate until he probes the eggs. He lifts the plate in both of his hands, sets it on the palm of his right hand, centers it, balances it. He hefts it up and down slightly, getting the feel of it. Abruptly, he draws back his right arm as far as he can.

There is the crack of the plate breaking against the wall at the foot of his bed and the small wet sound of the scrambled eggs dropping to the floor. Just so does this man break his fast.

35 And then he laughs. It is a sound you have never heard. It is something new under the sun.

Out in the corridor the eyes of the head nurse narrow.

"Laughed, did he?"

She writes something down on her clipboard.

A second aide arrives, brings a second breakfast tray, puts it on the nightstand out of his reach. She looks over at me, shaking her head and making her mouth go. I see that we are to be accomplices.

40 "I've got to feed you," she says to the man.

"Oh, no you don't," the man says.

"Oh, yes I do," the aide says, "after what you just did. Nurse says so."

"Get me my shoes," the man says.

"Here's oatmeal," the aide says. "Open." And she touches the spoon to his lower lip.

45   "I ordered scrambled eggs," says the man.

"That's right," the aide says.

I step forward.

"Is there anything I can do?" I say.

"Who are you?" the man asks.

Four

50   In the evening, I go once more to that ward to make my rounds. The head nurse reports to me that Room 542 is deceased. She has discovered this quite by accident, she says. No, there had been no sound. Nothing. It's a blessing, she says.

I go into his room, a spy looking for secrets. He is still there in his bed. His face is relaxed, grave, dignified, as the faces of the newly dead are. After a while, I turn to leave. My gaze sweeps the wall at the foot of the bed, and I see the place where it has been repeatedly washed, where the wall looks very clean and very white in contrast to the rest, which is dirty and gray.

Analyzing Rhetorical Choices

1. What effect is Selzer after by opening his essay in this way? How do you react to his opening sentence?

2. Why isn't the patient named, other than being called "the discus thrower"?

3. Why do you think Selzer presents his account in four very short parts? How does this presentation affect your response to the essay?

Writing About Issues and Contexts

1. What do the various details that Selzer includes about the patient's room signify about the patient, his views, his emotional state, his psychological well-being?

2. How would you characterize the nurse's response to this patient? How does her response contrast with Selzer's? What accounts for this difference?

3. Is it "a blessing" that this patient dies? Why does Selzer paraphrase this sentiment by ascribing it to the nurse rather than stating this sentiment himself?

By many critical accounts, **John McPhee** (1931–   ) is one of the finest
nonfiction writers in the United States. A native of Princeton, New Jersey,
McPhee is a graduate of Princeton University. He began his career writing scripts for the Robert Montgomery Presents *television show and then*
worked as a writer and editor at Time *from 1957 to 1964. His greatest
ambition was to write for* The New Yorker *magazine, and he was rejected
many times until he finally had his first profile piece accepted. It centered
on New York Knicks basketball player Bill Bradley, who later became a
U.S. Senator representing New Jersey. McPhee is a versatile writer whose
subjects include geology, oranges, tennis, basketball, bark canoes, the
wilderness, the merchant marine, mud slides in California, and the par-
ticularities of life in Alaska. The following selection is the opening of*
Encounters with the Archdruid *(1971), which depicts encounters that en-
vironmentalist David Brower (the archdruid) has with three protagonists.*

John McPhee

Encounters with the Archdruid

A small cabin stands in the Glacier Peak Wilderness, about a hundred yards off a trail that crosses the Cascade Range. In midsummer,
the cabin looked strange in the forest. It was only twelve feet square,
but it rose fully two stories and then had a high and steeply peaked
roof. From the ridge of the roof, moreover, a ten-foot pole stuck
straight up. Tied to the top of the pole was a shovel. To hikers shedding their backpacks at the door of the cabin on a cold summer
evening—as five of us did—it was somewhat unnerving to look up and
think of people walking around in snow perhaps thirty-five feet above,
hunting for that shovel, then digging their way down to the threshold.
Men from the Chelan County Snow Survey use the cabin in winter
while they measure snow depths and snow densities, and figure how
much runoff to expect at the time of thaw. Because of the almost unbelievable amount of snow that can accumulate in that part of the State
of Washington, what they do there is a vital matter to the people below
and even far beyond the mountains.

What we were doing there was something else again. We were
tired. We had walked seven and a half miles uphill since three that af-

ternoon. One of us was in his sixties, another in his fifties, and all of us saw the cabin as a haven from what obviously would have been very cold ground. Until midsummer, the trails had been impassable, and to make the trip we had had to wait for the winter snows to melt. An entry in the register in the cabin said that snow had fallen one week earlier, August 5th. But we had been drawn to the Cascades in part because a great many people believed that they were the most beautiful mountains in the United States. A somewhat smaller and, on the whole, more parochial group felt that these huge, conical peaks, raised in volcanic fire and later carved by moving ice, were the most beautiful mountains in the world. In 1964, the United States Congress set aside this region and others as permanent wilderness, not to receive even the use given a national park; not to be entered by a machine of any kind except in extreme emergency, not to be developed or altered or lumbered—forevermore. Within the structure of this so-called Wilderness Act, however, was a provision known as "the mining exception": all established claims would remain open to mining, and new claims could be made in any wilderness until 1984. At the foot of Glacier Peak, in the center of this particular wilderness, is a copper lode that is half a mile from side to side. The Kennecott Copper Corporation has a patented claim on this deposit and could work it any time. We wanted to have a look at the region while it was still pristine. The others left it to me to add their names to the register in the cabin: Charles Park, geologist, mineral engineer, who believes that if copper were to be found under the White House, the White House should be moved; David Brower, who has been described by Stewart Udall as "the most effective single person on the cutting edge of conservation in this country," leader of a conservation organization called Friends of the Earth; and Larry Snow and Lance Brigham, medical students from the University of Washington, who were along to help with the logistics of the trip and perhaps incidentally to give first aid.

A mouse ran out from under the cabin, made a fast move among the packs, and went back under the cabin. We collected firewood and water. There was a cascade, white and plummeting, beyond the cabin. We changed into warmer clothes and lighter shoes. Brower, who hiked in twill shorts and a T-shirt and soft gray Italian boots, put on a long plaid shirt, trousers, and a pair of basketball shoes. Although he was out of shape, Brower was a prepossessing figure. He was a tall man. He had heavy bones, thick wrists, strong ankles. And he had a delicate, handsome, ruddy face, its features all finely proportioned but slightly too small, too refined, for the size of his frame, suggesting delicacy. His voice was quiet and persuasively mellifluous. He had an engaging smile and flashing white teeth. He was in his late fifties, and he had a windy shock of white hair. Brower had dropped out of college when he was nineteen, and disappeared into the Sierra Nevada. He had spent his life defending mountain ranges and what, by extension, they symbolized to him, and one of the ironies of his life was that his love of the mountains had long since drawn him away from them and into buildings impertinently called skyscrapers, into congressional corridors, into temporary offices in hotel rooms, into battle after battle, and out of shape. (In the idiom of conservation, "battle" is the foremost term for what conservationists do, and conservationist publications are "battle tracts.") Brower's skin was pink from the work of the climb, and when he was taking off his soaked T-shirt he had revealed a fold across his middle. The mouse ran out again from under the cabin, looked around, its nose vibrating, and retreated.

Lance Brigham said, "Stick your head out once more, mouse, and it's curtains for you."

5   Brower said softly, "It's we who are the intruders."

Park had been taking off his boots—made in Canada, of heavy leather—and was putting on a pair of sandals. He grinned cryptically. He, too, had a shock of white hair. He was in his sixties, and he was as trim and hard as a college athlete, which he had once been, and nothing about him suggested that he had ever been out of breath. From his youth to the present, he had spent a high proportion of his life in the out-of-doors, and a high proportion of that in wilderness. Going up the trail that afternoon, with his geologist's pick in his hand, he whacked or chipped at half the boulders and rock faces we passed, and every once in a while, apparently for the sheer hell of it, he rapped the pick's hammer end on the stump of a tree that had been taken to clear the trail.

"That's a habit I developed long ago—banging on rocks and stumps," he said.

"Why?"

"Kodiak bears. I never wanted to take one by surprise. The same is true in Africa of leopards and gorillas. In other words, never take an animal by surprise."

10   Park spoke slowly, not because he was hesitant but simply in a measure that seemed compatible with geologic time. He had an almond face, alert gray eyes, and a mobile smile that tended to concentrate in one or the other corner of his mouth. He was even taller than

Brower, and he wore khaki from head to foot. He had a visored khaki cap.

Not far into the mountains from their eastern extremity, at Lake Chelan, we had come to an oddly formal landmark. It was a sign that said, "You Are Now Entering the Glacier Peak Wilderness Area." In other words, "Take one more step and, by decree, you will enter a pre-served and separate world, you will pass from civilization into wilder-ness." Wilderness was now that definable, that demonstrable, and could be entered in the sense that one enters a room.

Park said, "Will they let me carry my pick in there?"

"Until 1984," said Brower.

We stepped across the line. I said, "If we get lost in here with that pick, we may discover a new copper deposit."

15   Brower said, "If you make a new discovery, I'm here to see that you don't get out."

We moved on into the wilderness. The trail was dusty. It was cov-ered with a light-brown powder too fine to be called sand. Park said it was glacial flour—finely ground rock coming out of the ice, ice of the past and ice of the present. Far above us in the high cirques were gla-ciers—the Lyman Glacier, Isella Glacier, Mary Green Glacier, and, per-haps prophetically, the Company Glacier on Bonanza Peak. The sky was blue and cloudless, a day to remember in the Cascades. Brower said he was disappointed that it was not raining. He explained that he did not like dry duff but preferred the feel and the beauty of a wet and glistening forest, vaporous and dripping. He said that he hoped we would be fortunate enough to have a good rain before the trip was over. He labored slowly up the trail, taking it conservatively, eating thimbleberries and huckleberries as he moved along.

"There are no really old rocks in the Cascades," Park said, nicking a rock in passing. He picked up and admiringly turned in his hand a piece of pistachio-green epidote. Two hundred yards up the trail, he rapped at an outcropping with his pick and said, "That is volcanic." Minutes later, he swung again, sent chips flying, and said, "That is contact rock." This in some way entertained Brower, who laughed and shook his head. I remembered once driving through the Black Hills with Park, and how he would stop his car from time to time and just sit there looking at rocks. As a boy in Delaware, Park used to collect rocks and think about the West. While he was still in Wilmington High School, he had fifty ore minerals in his collection—hematite, mala-chite, galena, chromite. "I wanted to study mining, not particularly geology—mining," he said. "I just wanted to get into rocks. Mining has always appealed to me. It's in the out-of-the-way places."

A serrated ridge several miles from the trail had a reddish glow in the late-afternoon light. "See that color? That's pyrite," Park said, pointing. "Copper often comes with it. If I were in here looking for copper, that's where I'd head." The copper terrain we wanted to see was still more than ten miles away, however, and we stayed on the trail.

We passed a big Douglas fir, at least six feet in diameter, that had crashed to earth in the recent past, and Brower said how nice it was to see it there, to know that some lumber company had never had a chance at it, to see the decay stage of a natural cycle—the forest reclaiming its own. If dead trees are not left to rot, he said, the ecology of the wilderness is disturbed. Park kept his reactions to himself. His eye wandered to a square hole in a cedar stump. He waved his pick in the direction of the stump and said, "Pileated woodpecker." We moved on.

20   After a series of switchbacks had lifted us seven hundred feet in less than a quarter of a mile, we stopped to rest by a stream that was alternately falling through the air and racing down the mountainside. Everywhere, from every slope, the Cascades cascade. Water shoots out of cracks in the rock, it falls over the edges of cliffs, it foams, sprays, runs, and plunges pure and cold. Enough snow and rain fall up there to irrigate Libya, and when water is not actually falling from the sky the sun is melting it from alpine ice. Down the dark-green mountainsides go streamers of white water, and above the timber-line water shines against the rock. In every depression is a tarn, and we had passed a particularly beautiful one a little earlier and, from the escarpment, were looking back at it now. It was called Hart Lake and was fed by a stream that, in turn, fell away from a high and deafening cataract. The stream was interrupted by a series of beaver ponds. All around these free-form pools were stands of alder, aspen, Engelmann's spruce; and in the surrounding mountains, just under the summits, were glaciers and fields of snow. Brower, who is an aesthetician by trade and likes to point to beautiful things, had nothing to say at that moment. Neither did Park. I was remembering the words of a friend of mine in the National Park Service, who had once said to me, "The Glacier Peak Wilderness is probably the most beautiful piece of country we've got. Mining copper there would be like hitting a pretty girl in the face with a shovel. It would be like strip-mining the Garden of Eden."

Park wiped his forehead with his hat. I dipped a cup into the stream and offered him a drink. He hesitated. "Well, why not?" he said, at last. He took the cup and he drank, put the cup down with a smile, wiped his lips, and said, "That's good stuff."

"It's melted glacier ice, isn't it?"

Park nodded, and swallowed a little more.

Brower drank from a cup that was almost identical to mine—stainless steel, with low, sloping sides, a wide flat bottom, a looped wire handle—with the difference that in raised letters on the bottom of Brower's cup were the words "Sierra Club." Brower for seventeen years had been the executive director of the Sierra Club—its leader, its principal strategist, its preeminent fang. In the mountains, a Sierra Club mountaineer eats and drinks everything out of his Sierra Club cup, and in various wildernesses with Brower I had never seen him eat or drink from anything else. In the past, in the High Sierra, he had on occasion rubbed penny-royal-mint leaves over the embossed letters in the bottom of his cup and added snow and whiskey for a kind of high-altitude julep, but he rarely drinks much in the mountains and there was no whiskey at all on this trip. That night at the snow cabin, we ate our dinner from our cups—noodles, beef, chocolate pudding—and hung our packs on high rafters and were asleep before nine. We slept on bunks that had been tiered in the improbable cabin. At two in the morning, we were all awake, with flashlight beams crisscrossing from various heights in the compact blackness.

25

"What the hell is going on?"

"What is it?"

"What's there?"

"Four very beautiful little tan-and-white meadow mice," Brower said.

"Aw, for heaven's sake," Park said, and he went back to sleep.

Analyzing Rhetorical Choices

1. How does McPhee establish the characters of David Brower and Charles Park and dramatize the tension between them? What does each of them stand for in terms of preservation, wilderness, and resources? Are they polar opposites, and if not, explain their similarities. Analyze at least two specific examples of dialogue or dramatic action that illustrate their different views about wilderness.

2. One hallmark of McPhee's style is his use of detail to establish context and meaning. Select five specific instances of exemplification in the opening two paragraphs and explain why you think each is significant and what it contributes to McPhee's overall purpose in writing about Brower and Park.

3. Why do you think McPhee opens his book with the particular scene he does? After all, he could have started it at the beginning of the trip when they enter into the wilderness at Lake Chelan, which would have somewhat simplified the narrative sequence of this account. What purposes are served by starting where he does?

4. How does McPhee keep the reader interested? This is, after all, an account of a hike into the wilderness by two men espousing different points of view, but it is not about a great dramatic event, such as confronting a grizzly or saving the life of a climber stranded on an icy ledge on the mountain peak. Given that this is the opening section of a 250-page book, how does McPhee try to keep the reader turning the pages?

Writing About Issues and Contexts

1. Why do you think McPhee includes the mouse incidents? What do they tell us about general attitudes about wilderness in contrast with Brower's and Park's attitudes?

2. What does McPhee mean when he calls David Brower the Sierra Club's "preeminent fang"?

3. Why does McPhee draw so much attention to Brower's cup? And why does McPhee mention that his is "almost identical"? How does McPhee use these kinds of details to illustrate larger themes and issues?

A reporter for the major newspaper in Portland, the Oregonian, **Emily Tsao** *(1973–) is a journalist and chapter president of the Asian American Journalists Association. Educated at Yale University, Tsao is active in the leadership development of journalists and is a staunch advocate for human rights and equal opportunity. She has written, "Stereotypes affect us all. It is only when we work to change perceptions that true progress can begin." Originally published in* The Washington Post, *the following essay has been widely reprinted.*

Emily Tsao

Thoughts of an Oriental Girl

I am an Oriental girl. Excuse me, I forgot to use my politically correct dictionary. Let me rephrase that. I am an Asian-American woman. Yes, that sounds about right. Excuse me again; I mean politically correct.

When I first stepped onto the campus scene last year, I, like many other anxious freshmen, wanted to fit in. I wanted to wear the right clothes, carry the right bookbag and, most important, say the right things. Speaking to upperclassmen, however, I realized that I had no command of the proper "PC" language.

Girls, it became clear, were to be called women. Freshmen who were girls were to be called freshwomen. Mixed groups of both sexes were to be labeled freshpeople, and upperclassmen were to be referred to as upperclasspeople. Orientals were to be called Asian Americans, blacks were to be called African Americans and Hispanics Latinos.

To me, most of this seemed pointless. Being called a girl doesn't bother me. I'm 18 years old. My mom is a woman. I'm her kid. I don't expect her to refer to me as a woman.

5   I have always referred to my female friends as girls, and still do. I want my boyfriend to call me his girlfriend, not his woman friend.

My friends and I refer to the male students at college as boys or guys. Never men. Kevin Costner and Robert Redford are men. Men don't drink themselves sick at keg parties every weekend, ask Dad for money, or take laundry home to Mom.

For 12 years in high school and grade school, the female students were always girls and the males were boys. Why does going to college with these same peers suddenly make me a woman and the boys men? I certainly don't feel much older or wiser than I did last year. When people refer to me as a woman, I turn around to see who might be standing behind me.

Another fad now is for people to spell women with a "y" in place of the "e"—"womyn." These people want to take the "men" out of "women." Next perhaps they'll invent "femyle."

I've always been gender conscious with my language when it seemed logical. In third grade I referred to the mailman as a mailperson because our mail was sometimes delivered by a woman. I don't think I ever said mailwoman, though, because it just didn't sound right.

10   From elementary through high school, I told people I was Chinese, and if I wanted to refer to all Asians, I used the word "Orientals." I guess I was young and foolish and didn't know any better.

At college I was told that the proper label for me was Asian American, that "Oriental" was a word to describe furniture, not people. But what is the difference? All Asians are still being clumped together, even though each group—Chinese, Korean, Japanese, Indians, Vietnamese and Filipinos, to name just a few—comes from a different country with a different language and culture.

The new "PC" term to describe Asian Americans and all other minorities is "people of color." The reason, I am told, is that the "minority" population has grown to be the majority. But even if that's true, the phrase seems contradictory. Since many African Americans no longer want to be referred to as blacks, why should the term for minorities once again refer to skin color? The same is true for Asians, most of whom find the label "yellow" more offensive than Oriental. And isn't white also a color?

As long as we're throwing out all the old labels, why not replace "white" with "European American." Wasps could be EAASPS (European-American Anglo Saxon Protestants). Well, maybe not. Minority groups want new labels to give themselves a more positive image, but unless the stereotypes disappear as well, is it really going to help very much?

Look at the word "sophomore," which comes from Greek roots meaning "wise fool." PC-conscious sophomores ought to revolt against this offensive phrase. I, however, will not be among them. Changing the word won't make me any smarter, humbler or wiser.

Analyzing Rhetorical Choices

1. How does Tsao establish a conversational tone? Why do you think she does this, and how does it affect you as a reader?

2. What kinds of details and examples does Tsao include to reinforce her irritation at the PC (politically correct) nature of the "campus scene"?

Writing About Issues and Contexts

1. In what ways does Tsao attempt to counteract stereotypical views of Asian Americans, or should we say Oriental men and women? Explain whether you think she succeeds in this effort.

2. Is Tsao correct in writing that "Minority groups want new labels to give themselves a more positive image, but unless the stereotypes disappear as well, is it really going to help very much?" Offer your own response to this statement.

3. Is the kind of language use that Tsao critiques a form of falsification? Why does the college culture create this new vocabulary? Do you consider it a form of PC behavior that overcompensates for the implicit racist, sexist, and classist opinions that can be found among many Americans, even those on college campuses?

*Born in Waukegan, Illinois, **Diane Ackerman** (1948–   ) graduated from*
Pennsylvania State University in 1970 and earned her MFA, MA, and
Ph.D. from Cornell University. In addition to having worked as a social
worker in New York City and as a government researcher at Pennsylvania
State University, Ackerman has taught at many universities, including the
University of Pittsburgh, Washington University, Ohio University, and
New York University. She is a staff writer for The New Yorker *and has*
participated in many readings, residencies, and workshops. A published
poet as well as an accomplished nonfiction writer, Ackerman's books in-
clude The Moon by Whale Light, and Other Adventures among Bats,
Penguins, Crocodilians, and Whales *(1991),* A Natural History of Love
(1994), and The Rarest of the Rare: Vanishing Animals, Timeless Worlds
(1995). The following excerpt is from A Natural History of the Senses,
published in 1990.

Diane Ackerman
The Vagaries of Taste

The Omnivore's Picnic

You have been invited to dinner at the home of extraterrestrials,
and asked to bring friends. Being considerate hosts, they first inquire
if you have any dietary allergies or prohibitions, and then what sort
of food would taste good to you. What do humans eat? they ask.
Images cascade through your mind, a cornucopia of plants, animals,
minerals, liquids, and solids, in a vast array of cuisines. The Masai
enjoy drinking cow's blood. Orientals eat stir-fried puppy. Germans
eat rancid cabbage (sauerkraut), Americans eat decaying cucumbers
(pickles), Italians eat whole deep-fried songbirds, Vietnamese eat
fermented fish dosed with chili peppers, Japanese and others eat
fungus (mushrooms), French eat garlic-soaked snails. Upper-class
Aztecs ate roasted dog (a hairless variety named *xquintli*, which is
still bred in Mexico). Chinese of the Chou dynasty liked rats, which
they called "household deer," and many people still do eat rodents,
as well as grasshoppers, snakes, flightless birds, kangaroos, lobsters,
snails, and bats. Unlike most other animals, which fill a small yet
ample niche in the large web of life on earth, humans are omni-

vorous. The Earth offers perhaps 20,000 edible plants alone. A poor season for eucalyptus will wipe out a population of koala bears, which have no other food source. But human beings are Nature's great ad libbers and revisers. Diversity is our delight. In time of drought, we can ankle off to a new locale, or break open a cactus, or dig a well. When plagues of locusts destroy our crops, we can forage on wild plants and roots. If our herds die, we find protein in insects, beans, and nuts. Not that being an omnivore is easy. A koala bear doesn't have to worry about whether or not its next mouthful will be toxic. In fact, eucalyptus is highly poisonous, but a koala has an elaborately protective gut, so it just eats eucalyptus, exactly as its parents did. Cows graze without fear on grass and grain. But omnivores are anxious eaters. They must continually test new foods to see if they're palatable and nutritious, running the risk of inadvertently poisoning themselves. They must take chances on new flavors, and, doing so, they frequently acquire a taste for something offbeat that, though nutritious, isn't the sort of thing that might normally appeal to them—chili peppers (which Columbus introduced to Europe), tobacco, alcohol, coffee, artichokes, or mustard, for instance. When we were hunter-gatherers, we ate a great variety of foods. Some of us still do, but more often we add spices to what we know, or find at hand, *for variety*, as we like to say. Monotony isn't our code. It's safe, in some ways, but in others it's more dangerous. Most of us prefer our foods cooked to the steaminess of freshly killed prey. We don't have ultrasharp carnivore's teeth, but we don't need them. We've created sharp tools. We do have incisor teeth for slicing fruits, and molars for crushing seeds and nuts, as well as canines for ripping flesh. At times, we eat nasturtiums and pea pods and even the effluvia from the mammary glands of cows, churned until it curdles, or frozen into a solid and attached to pieces of wood.

Our hosts propose a picnic, since their backyard is a meadow lit by two suns, and they welcome us and our friends. Our Japanese friend chooses the appetizer: sushi, including shrimp still alive and wriggling. Our French friend suggests a baguette, or better still croissants, which have an unlikely history, which he insists on telling everyone: To celebrate Austria's victory against the invading Ottoman Turks, bakers created pastry in the shape of the crescent on the Turkish flag, so that the Viennese could devour their enemies at table as they had on the battlefield. Croissants soon spread to France and, during the 1920s, traveled with other French ways to the United States. Our Amazonian friend chooses the main course—nuptial kings and queens of leaf-cutter ants, which taste like walnut butter, followed by roasted turtle and sweet-fleshed piranha. Our German friend insists that we include some spaetzle and a loaf of darkest pumpernickel bread, which gets its name from the verb *pumpern,* "to break wind," and *Nickel,* "the devil," because it was thought to be so hard to digest that even the devil would fart if he ate it. Our Tasaday friend wants some natek, a starchy paste his people make from the insides of caryota palm trees. The English cousin asks for a small platter of potted ox tongues, very aged blue cheese, and, for dessert, trifle—whipped cream and slivered almonds on top of a jam-and-custard pudding thick with sherry-soaked ladyfingers.

To finish our picnic lunch, our Turkish friend proposes coffee in the Turkish style—using a mortar and pestle to break up the beans, rather than milling them. To be helpful, he prepares it for us all, pouring boiling water over coffee grounds through a silver sieve into a pot. He brings this to a light boil, pours it through the sieve again, and offers us some of the clearest, brightest coffee we've ever tasted. According to legend, he explains, coffee was discovered by a ninth-century shepherd, who one day realized that his goats were becoming agitated whenever they browsed on the berries of certain bushes. For four hundred years, people thought only to chew the berries. Raw coffee doesn't brew into anything special, but in the thirteenth century someone decided to roast the berries, which releases a pungent oil and the mossy-bitter aroma now so familiar to us. Our Indian friend passes round cubes of sugar, which we are instructed to let melt on the tongue as we sip our coffee, and our minds roam back to the first recorded instance of sugar, in the Atharvaveda, a sacred Hindu text from 800 B.C., which describes a royal crown made of glittering sugar crystals. Then he circulates a small dish of coriander seeds, and we pinch a few in our fingers, set them on our tongues, and feel our mouths freshen from the aromatic tang. A perfect picnic. We thank our hosts for laying on such a splendid feast, and invite them to our house for dinner next. "What do jujubarians eat?" we ask.

· · ·

The Bloom of a Taste Bud

Seen by scanning electron microscope, our taste buds look as huge as volcanoes on Mars, while those of a shark are beautiful mounds of pastel-colored tissue paper—until we remember what they're used for.

In reality, taste buds are exceedingly small. Adults have about 10,000, grouped by theme (salt, sour, sweet, bitter), at various sites in the mouth. Inside each one, about fifty taste cells busily relay information to a neuron, which will alert the brain. Not much tasting happens in the center of the tongue, but there are also incidental taste buds on the palate, pharynx, and tonsils, which cling like bats to the damp, slimy limestone walls of a cave. Rabbits have 17,000 taste buds, parrots only about 400, cows 25,000. What are they tasting? Maybe a cow needs that many to enjoy a relentless diet of grass.

5   At the tip of the tongue, we taste sweet things; bitter things at the back; sour things at the sides; and salty things spread over the surface, but mainly up front. The tongue is like a kingdom divided into principalities according to sensory talent. It would be as if all those who could see lived to the east, those who could hear lived to the west, those who could taste lived to the south, and those who could touch lived to the north. A flavor traveling through this kingdom is not recognized in the same way in any two places. If we lick an ice cream cone, a lollipop, or a cake-batter-covered finger, we touch the food with the tip of the tongue, where the taste buds for sweetness are, and it gives us an extra jolt of pleasure. A cube of sugar under the tongue won't taste as sweet as one placed *on* the tongue. Our threshold for bitter is the lowest. Because the taste buds for bitter lie at the back of the tongue; as a final defense against danger they can make us gag to keep a substance from sliding down the throat. Some people do, in fact, gag when they take quinine, or drink coffee for the first time, or try olives. Our taste buds can detect sweetness in something even if only one part in two hundred is sweet. Butterflies and blowflies, which have most of their taste organs on their front feet, need only step in a sweet solution to taste it. Dogs, horses, and many other animals have a sweet tooth, as we do. We can detect saltiness in one part in 400, sourness in one part in 130,000, but bitterness in as little as one part in 2,000,000. Nor is it necessary for us to recognize poisonous things as tasting different from one another; they just taste bitter. Distinguishing between bitter and sweet substances is so essential to our lives that it has burst through our language. Children, joy, a trusted friend, a lover all are referred to as "sweet." Regret, an enemy, pain, disappointment, a nasty argument all are referred to as "bitter." The "bitter pill" we metaphorically dread is likely to be poison.

Taste buds got their name from the nineteenth-century German scientists Georg Meissner and Rudolf Wagner, who discovered mounds made up of taste cells that overlap like petals. Taste buds wear out

every week to ten days, and we replace them, although not as frequently over the age of forty-five—our palates really do become jaded
as we get older. It takes a more intense taste to produce the same level
of sensation, and children have the keenest sense of taste. A baby's
mouth has many more taste buds than an adult's, with some even dot-
ting the cheeks. Children adore sweets partly because the tips of their
tongues, more sensitive to sugar, haven't yet been blunted by years of
gourmandizing or trying to eat hot soup before it cools. A person born
without a tongue, or who has had his tongue cut out, still can taste.
Brillat-Savarin tells of a Frenchman in Algeria who was punished for
an attempted prison escape by having "the forepart of his tongue . . .
cut off clear to the ligament." Swallowing was difficult and tiring for
him, although he could still taste fairly well, "but very sour or bitter
things caused him unbearable pain."

Just as we can smell something only when it begins to evaporate,
we can taste something only when it begins to dissolve, and we cannot
do that without saliva. Every taste we can imagine—from mangoes to
hundred-year-old eggs—comes from a combination of the four primary tastes plus one or two others. And yet we can distinguish between tastes with finesse, as wine-, tea-, cheese- and other professional
tasters do. The Greeks and Romans, who were sophisticated about
fish, could tell just by tasting one what waters it came from. As precise
as our sense of taste is, illusions can still surprise us. For example,
MSG doesn't taste saltier than table salt, but it really contains much
more sodium. One of its ingredients, glutamate, blocks our ability to
taste it as salty. A neurologist at the Albert Einstein College of
Medicine once tested the amount of MSG in a bowl of wonton soup in
a Chinese restaurant in Manhattan, and he found 7.5 grams of MSG,
as much sodium as one should limit oneself to in an entire day.

After brushing our teeth in the morning, orange juice tastes bitter.
Why? Because our taste buds have membranes that contain fatlike
phospholipids, and toothpastes contain a detergent that breaks down
fat and grease. So the toothpaste first assaults the membranes with its
detergent, leaving them raw; then chemicals in the toothpaste, such as
formaldehyde, chalk, and saccharin, cause a sour taste when they mix
with the citric and ascorbic acids of orange juice. Chewing the leaves
of the asclepiad (a relative of the milkweed) makes one's ability to
taste sweetness vanish. Sugar would taste bland and gritty. When
Africans chew a berry they call "miraculous fruit," it becomes impossible to taste anything sour: lemons taste sweet, sour wine tastes sweet,
rhubarb tastes sweet. Anything off-puttingly sour suddenly becomes

delicious. A weak enough solution of salt tastes sweet to us, and some people salt melons to enhance the sweet flavor. Lead and beryllium salts can taste treacherously sweet, even though they're poisonous and we ought to be tasting them as bitter.

No two of us taste the same plum. Heredity allows some people to eat asparagus and pee fragrantly afterward (as Proust describes in *Remembrance of Things Past*), or eat artichokes and then taste any drink, even water, as sweet. Some people are more sensitive to bitter tastes than others and find saccharin appalling, while others guzzle diet sodas. Salt cravers have saltier saliva. Their mouths are accustomed to a higher sodium level, and foods must be saltier before they register as salty. Of course, everyone's saliva is different and distinctive, flavored by diet, whether or not they smoke, heredity, perhaps even mood.

10   How strange that we acquire tastes as we grow. Babies don't like olives, mustard, hot pepper, beer, fruits that make one pucker, or coffee. After all, coffee is bitter, a flavor from the forbidden and dangerous realm. To eat a pickle, one risks one's common sense, overrides the body's warning with sheer reason. *Calm down, it's not dangerous,* the brain says, it's novel and interesting, a change, an exhilaration.

Smell contributes grandly to taste. Without smell, wine would still dizzy and lull us, but much of its captivation would be gone. We often smell something before we taste it, and that's enough to make us salivate. Smell and taste share a common airshaft, like residents in a high rise who know which is curry, lasagna, or Cajun night for their neighbors. When something lingers in the mouth, we can smell it, and when we inhale a bitter substance—a nasal decongestant, for example—we often taste it as a brassiness at the back of the throat. Smell hits us faster: It takes 25,000 times more molecules of cherry pie to taste it than to smell it. A head cold, by inhibiting smell, smothers taste.

We normally chew about a hundred times a minute. But, if we let something linger in our mouth, feel its texture, smell its bouquet, roll it around on the tongue, then chew it slowly so that we can hear its echoes, what we're really doing is savoring it, using several senses in a gustatory free-for-all. A food's flavor includes its texture, smell, temperature, color, and painfulness (as in spices), among many other features. Creatures of sound, we like some foods to titillate our hearing more than others. There's a gratifying crunch to a fresh carrot stick, a seductive sizzle to a broiling steak, a rumbling frenzy to soup coming to a boil, an arousing bunching and snapping to a bowl of breakfast cereal. "Food engineers," wizards of subtle persuasion, create products to assault as many of our senses as possible. Committees put a lot of thought into the design of fast foods. As David Bodanis points out with such good humor in *The Secret House*, potato chips are:

> an example of total destruction foods. The wild attack on the plastic wrap, the slashing and tearing you have to go through is exactly what the manufacturers wish. For the thing about crisp foods is that they're louder than non-crisp ones. . . . Destructo-packaging sets a favorable mood. . . . Crisp foods have to be loud in the upper register. They have to produce a high-frequency shattering; foods which generate low-frequency rumblings are crunchy, or slurpy but not crisp. . . .

Companies design potato chips to be too large to fit into the mouth, because in order to hear the high-frequency crackling you need to keep your mouth open. Chips are 80 percent air, and each time we bite one we break open the air-packed cells of the chip, making that noise we call "crispy." Bodanis asks:

> How to get sufficiently rigid cell walls to twang at these squeaking harmonics? Starch them. The starch granules in potatoes are identical to the starch in stiff shirt collars . . . whitewash . . . is . . . near identical in chemical composition. . . . All chips are soaked in fat. . . . So it's a shrapnel of flying starch and fat that produces the conical air-pressure wave when our determined chip-muncher finally gets to finish her chomp.

These are high-tech potato chips, of course, The original potato chip was invented in 1853 by George Crum, a chef at Moon Lake Lodge in Saratoga Springs, New York, who became so angry when a guest demanded thinner and thinner French fries that he sliced them laughably thin (he thought) and fried them until they were varnish-brown. The guest loved them, envious fellow guests requested them, word spread, and ultimately Crum started up his own restaurant, which specialized in potato chips.

The mouth is what keeps the prison of our bodies sealed up tight. Nothing enters for help or harm without passing through the mouth, which is why it was such an early development in evolution. Every slug, insect, and higher animal has a mouth. Even one-celled animals like paramecia have mouths, and the mouth appears immediately in human embryos. The mouth is more than just the beginning of the long pipeline to the anus: It's the door to the body, the place where we greet the world, the parlor of great risk. We use our mouths for other things—language, if we're human; drilling tree bark if we're a woodpecker; sucking blood if we're a mosquito—but the mouth mainly holds the tongue, a thick mucous slab of muscle, wearing minute cleats as if it were an athlete.

Analyzing Rhetorical Choices

1. What is the effect of Ackerman's use of the second-person and third-person plural in this reading? What kinds of relationships do these usages create between reader and text and between reader and author?

2. One characteristic of Ackerman's style is her tendency to elaborate on meanings and terms. She tells us about the different culinary habits of Jews, Malays, Catholics, Anglicans, and Egyptians. She informs us about the number of taste buds on a human tongue and then the number on the tongue of a rabbit, a parrot, and a cow. She writes that the mouth "is more than just the beginning of the long pipeline to the anus: It's the door to the body, the place where we greet the world, the parlor of great risk." Is this technique effective? Why or why not? How does it affect you as a reader?

3. Select at least five uses of metaphors or similes in this selection and discuss them in terms of their originality, descriptive qualities, and rhetorical effectiveness.

4. Evaluate Ackerman's use of exemplification. How well is it integrated into the text? What kinds of sources does she draw upon? Consider as well whether she includes the appropriate amount of information for you as reader, and state your reasoning.

Writing About Issues and Contexts

1. Do you agree that "taste is largely social"? How does Ackerman support this understanding of "taste"? Provide at least one example from your own experience that either validates or undercuts this concept.

2. What is the significance of taste for human beings? What kinds of meanings and values does it have for us, according to Ackerman?

3. How has taste influenced our use of language? Cite specific instances that Ackerman describes along with several examples of your own in which concepts of taste have entered into everyday speaking.

A native of Louisville, Kentucky, **Countee** *(pronounced "Count-ay")*
Cullen *(1903–1946) was born Countee LeRoy Porter but took the name
of Frederick Cullen, the Harlem reverend who adopted the 15-year-old
boy. Cullen earned academic honors at his high school where he was also
elected vice-president of his class and served as editor of the school newspaper. Subsequently, he won poetry prizes as an undergraduate at New
York University and earned a master's degree from Harvard in 1926. A
poet, playwright, essayist, columnist, and children's writer, his published
works include* Color *(1925) and* Copper Sun *(1927). A key figure in the
Harlem Renaissance, Cullen received an award from the National
Association for the Advancement of Colored People (NAACP) for "distinguished achievement in literature by a Negro" in 1927 and was awarded
a prestigious Guggenheim Fellowship to write poetry in France from 1928
to 1930.*

Countee Cullen

For a Lady I Know

She even thinks that up in heaven
Her class lies late and snores,
While poor black cherubs rise at seven
To do celestial chores.

Incident

Once riding in old Baltimore,
Heart-filled, head-filled with glee,
I saw a Baltimorean
Keep looking straight at me.

5 Now I was eight and very small,
And he was no whit bigger,
And so I smiled, but he poked out
His tongue, and called me, "Nigger."

I saw the whole of Baltimore
10 From May until December;

Of all the things that happened there
That's all that I remember.

Analyzing Rhetorical Choices

1. How does the formal simplicity of these two poems contribute to their emotional power? Consider the meter, the rhyme, and the four-line stanzas in your response.

2. Why does Cullen mention the phrase "her class" in "For a Lady I Know"? What effect does the word *celestial* have on the reader, in terms of its placement and complexity, compared with the other words in this poem?

3. Explain the implication of each title. How do they contribute to the overall effect of each poem?

Writing About Issues and Contexts

1. How do these poems reflect different aspects of racial discrimination?

2. How do these two poems relate to the essays later in this section by Henry Louis Gates, Jr., and Amy Wang? How do they relate to Gloria Naylor's essay in Chapter 4?

3. Why is it significant that the Baltimorean in "Incident" is so small and young?

Toni Cade Bambara (1939–1995) was a distinguished writer, lecturer, and civil rights activist. Born in New York City, Bambara attended Queens College and City College in New York City, and she also studied theater, mime, dance, film, and linguistics at eight other institutions in Europe and America. Committed to social change through political action, she worked as a welfare investigator, a community organizer, a literacy instructor, a college professor, and a director of plays and films. She is perhaps best known for her collections of short stories including Gorilla, My Love *(1972, and source of this selection) and* The Sea Birds Are Still Alive *(1977). Her novel* The Salt-Eaters *(1980) is still read and taught widely; it has been described as "an incantation, poem-drunk, myth-happy, mud-caked, jazz-ridden, prodigal in meanings."*

Toni Cade Bambara

The Lesson

Back in the days when everyone was old and stupid or young and foolish and me and Sugar were the only ones just right, this lady moved on our block with nappy hair and proper speech and no makeup. And quite naturally we laughed at her, laughed the way we did at the junk man who went about his business like he was some big-time president and his sorry-ass horse his secretary. And we kinda hated her too, hated the way we did the winos who cluttered up our parks and pissed on our handball walls and stank up our hallways and stairs so you couldn't halfway play hide-and-seek without a goddamn gas mask. Miss Moore was her name. The only woman on the block with no first name. And she was black as hell, cept for her feet, which were fish-white and spooky. And she was always planning these boring-ass things for us to do, us being my cousin, mostly, who lived on the block cause we all moved North the same time and to the same apartment then spread out gradual to breathe. And our parents would yank our heads into some kinda shape and crisp up our clothes so we'd be presentable for travel with Miss Moore, who always looked like she was going to church, though she never did. Which is just one of the things the grownups talked about when they talked behind her back like a dog. But when she came calling with some sachet she'd sewed up or some gingerbread she'd made or some book, why then they'd all be too embarrassed to turn her down and we'd get handed over all spruced up. She'd been to college and said it was only right that she should take responsibility for the young ones' education, and she not even related by marriage or blood. So they'd go for it. Specially Aunt Gretchen. She was the main gofer in the family. You got some ole dumb shit foolishness you want somebody to go for, you send for Aunt Gretchen. She been screwed into the go-along for so long, it's a blood-deep natural thing with her. Which is how she got saddled with me and Sugar and Junior in the first place while our mothers were in a la-de-da apartment up the block having a good ole time.

So this one day, Miss Moore rounds us all up at the mailbox and it's puredee hot and she's knockin herself out about arithmetic. And school suppose to let up in summer I heard, but she don't never let up. And the starch in my pinafore scratching the shit outta me and I'm really hating this nappy-head bitch and her goddamn college degree. I'd much rather go to the pool or to the show where it's cool. So me and Sugar leaning on the mailbox being surly, which is a Miss Moore word. And Flyboy checking out what everybody brought for lunch. And Fat Butt already wasting his peanut-butter-and-jelly sandwich like the pig he is. And Junebug punchin on Q.T.'s arm for potato chips. And Rosie Giraffe shifting from one hip to the other waiting for somebody to step on her foot or ask her if she from Georgia so she can kick ass, preferably Mercedes'. And Miss Moore asking us do we know what money is, like we a bunch of retards. I mean real money, she say, like it's only poker chips or monopoly papers we lay on the grocer. So right away I'm tired of this and say so. And would much rather snatch Sugar and go to the Sunset and terrorize the West Indian kids and take their hair ribbons and their money too. And Miss Moore files that remark away for next week's lesson on brotherhood, I can tell. And finally I say we oughta get to the subway cause it's cooler and besides we might meet some cute boys. Sugar done swiped her mama's lipstick, so we ready.

So we heading down the street and she's boring us silly about what things cost and what our parents make and how much goes for rent and how money ain't divided up right in this country. And then she gets to the part about we all poor and live in the slums, which I don't feature. And I'm ready to speak on that, but she steps out in the street and hails two cabs just like that. Then she hustles half the crew in with her and hands me a five-dollar bill and tells me to calculate 10 percent tip for the driver. And we're off. Me and Sugar and Junebug and Flyboy hangin out the window and hollering to everybody, putting lipstick on each other cause Flyboy a faggot anyway, and making farts with our sweaty armpits. But I'm mostly trying to figure how to spend this money. But they all fascinated with the meter ticking and Junebug starts laying bets to how much it'll read when Flyboy can't hold his breath no more. Then Sugar lays bets as to how much it'll be when we get there. So I'm stuck. Don't nobody want to go for my plan, which is to jump out at the next light and run off to the first bar-b-que we can find. Then the driver tells us to get the hell out cause we there already. And the meter reads eighty-five cents. And I'm stalling to figure out the tip and Sugar say give him a dime. And I decide he don't need it as bad as I do, so later for him. But then he tries to take off with Junebug's foot still in the door so we talk about his mama something ferocious. Then we check out that we on Fifth Avenue and everybody dressed up in stockings. One lady in a fur coat, hot as it is. White folks crazy.

"This is the place," Miss Moore say, presenting it to us in the voice she uses at the museum. "Let's look in the windows before we go in."

5   "Can we steal?" Sugar asks very serious like she's getting the ground rules squared away before she plays. "I beg your pardon," say Miss Moore, and we fall out. So she leads us around the windows of the toy store and me and Sugar screamin, "This is mine, that's mine, I gotta have that, that was made for me, I was born for that," till Big Butt drowns us out.

"Hey, I'm going to buy that there."

"That there? You don't even know what it is, stupid."

"I do so," he say punchin on Rosie Giraffe. "It's a microscope."

"Whatcha gonna do with a microscope, fool?"

10   "Look at things."

"Like what, Ronald?" ask Miss Moore. And Big Butt ain't got the first notion. So here go Miss Moore gabbing about the thousands of bacteria in a drop of water and the somethinorother in a speck of blood and the million and one living things in the air around us is invisible to the naked eye. And what she say that for? Junebug go to town on that "naked" and we rolling. Then Miss Moore ask what it cost. So we all jam into the window smudgin it up and the price tag say $300. So then she ask how long'd take for Big Butt and Junebug to save up their allowances. "Too long," I say. "Yeh," adds Sugar, "outgrown it by that time." And Miss Moore say no, you never outgrow learning instruments. "Why, even medical students and interns and," blah, blah, blah. And we ready to choke Big Butt for bringing it up in the first damn place.

"This here costs four hundred eighty dollars," say Rosie Giraffe. So we pile up all over her to see what she pointin out. My eyes tell me it's a chunk of glass cracked with something heavy, and different-color inks dripped into the splits, then the whole thing put into a oven or something. But for $480 it don't make sense.

"That's a paperweight made of semi-precious stones fused together under tremendous pressure," she explains slowly, with her hands doing the mining and all the factory work.

"So what's a paperweight?" ask Rosie Giraffe.

15   "To weigh paper with, dumbbell," say Flyboy, the wise man from the East.

"Not exactly," say Miss Moore, which is what she say when you warm or way off too. "It's to weigh paper down so it won't scatter and make your desk untidy." So right away me and Sugar curtsy to each other and then to Mercedes who is more the tidy type.

"We don't keep paper on top of the desk in my class," say Junebug, figuring Miss Moore crazy or lyin one.

"At home, then," she say. "Don't you have a calendar and a pencil case and a blotter and a letter-opener on your desk at home where you do your homework?" And she know damn well what our homes look like cause she nosys around in them every chance she gets.

"I don't even have a desk," say Junebug. "Do we?"

20   "No. And I don't get no homework neither," says Big Butt.

"And I don't even have a home," say Flyboy like he do at school to keep the white folks off his back and sorry for him. Send this poor kid to camp posters, is his specialty.

"I do," says Mercedes. "I have a box of stationery on my desk and a picture of my cat. My godmother bought the stationery and the desk. There's a big rose on each sheet and the envelopes smell like roses."

"Who wants to know about your smelly-ass stationery," say Rosie Giraffe fore I can get my two cents in.

"It's important to have a work area all your own so that . . ."

25   "Will you look at this sailboat, please," say Flyboy, cuttin her off and pointin to the thing like it was his. So once again we tumble all over each other to gaze at this magnificent thing in the toy store which is just big enough to maybe sail two kittens across the pond if you strap them to the posts tight. We all start reciting the price tag like we in assembly. "Hand-crafted sailboat of fiberglass at one thousand one hundred ninety-five dollars."

"Unbelievable," I hear myself say and am really stunned. I read it again for myself just in case the group recitation put me in a trance. Same thing. For some reason this pisses me off. We look at Miss Moore and she lookin at us, waiting for I dunno what.

"Who'd pay all that when you can buy a sailboat set for a quarter at Pop's, a tube of glue for a dime, and a ball of string for eight cents? It must have a motor and a whole lot else besides," I say. "My sailboat cost me about fifty cents."

"But will it take water?" say Mercedes with her smart ass.

"Took mine to Alley Pond Park once," say Flyboy. "String broke. Lost it. Pity."

30   "Sailed mine in Central Park and it keeled over and sank. Had to ask my father for another dollar."

"And you got the strap," laugh Big Butt. "The jerk didn't even have a string on it. My old man wailed on his behind."

Little Q.T. was staring hard at the sailboat and you could see he wanted it bad. But he too little and somebody'd just take it from him. So what the hell. "This boat for kids, Miss Moore?"

"Parents silly to buy something like that just to get all broke up," say Rosie Giraffe.

"That much money it should last forever," I figure.

35   "My father'd buy it for me if I wanted it."

"Your father, my ass," say Rosie Giraffe getting a chance to finally push Mercedes.

"Must be rich people shop here," say Q.T.

"You are a very bright boy," say Flyboy. "What was your first clue?" And he rap him on the head with the back of his knuckles, since Q.T. the only one he could get away with. Though Q.T. liable to come up behind you years later and get his licks in when you half expect it.

"What I want to know is," I says to Miss Moore though I never talk to her, I wouldn't give the bitch that satisfaction, "is how much a real boat costs? I figure a thousand'd get you a yacht any day."

40   "Why don't you check that out," she says, "and report back to the group?" Which really pains my ass. If you gonna mess up a perfectly good swim day least you could do is have some answers. "Let's go in," she say like she got something up her sleeve. Only she don't lead the way. So me and Sugar turn the corner to where the entrance is, but when we get there I kinda hang back. Not that I'm scared, what's there to be afraid of, just a toy store. But I feel funny, shame. But what I got to be shamed about? Got as much right to go in as anybody. But somehow I can't seem to get hold of the door, so I step away for Sugar to lead. But she hangs back too. And I look at her and she looks at me and this is ridiculous. I mean, damn, I have never ever been shy about doing nothing or going nowhere. But then

Mercedes steps up and then Rosie Giraffe and Big Butt crowd in behind and shove, and next thing we all stuffed into the doorway with only Mercedes squeezing past us, smoothing out her jumper and walking right down the aisle. Then the rest of us tumble in like a glued-together jigsaw done all wrong. And people lookin at us. And it's like the time me and Sugar crashed into the Catholic church on a dare. But once we got in there and everything so hushed and holy and the candles and the bowin and the handkerchiefs on all the drooping heads, I just couldn't go through with the plan. Which was for me to run up to the altar and do a tap dance while Sugar played the nose flute and messed around in the holy water. And Sugar kept givin me the elbow. Then later teased me so bad I tied her up in the shower and turned it on and locked her in. And she'd be there till this day if Aunt Gretchen hadn't finally figured I was lyin about the boarder takin a shower.

Same thing in the store. We all walkin on tiptoe and hardly touchin the games and puzzles and things. And I watched Miss Moore who is steady watchin us like she waitin for a sign. Like Mama Drewery watches the sky and sniffs the air and takes note of just how much slant is in the bird formation. Then me and Sugar bump smack into each other, so busy gazing at the toys, 'specially the sailboat. But we don't laugh and go into our fat-lady bump-stomach routine. We just stare at that price tag. Then Sugar run a finger over the whole boat. And I'm jealous and want to hit her. Maybe not her, but I sure want to punch somebody in the mouth.

"Whatcha bring us here for, Miss Moore?"

"You sound angry, Sylvia. Are you mad about something?" Givin me one of them grins like she tellin a grown-up joke that never turns out to be funny. And she's lookin very closely at me like maybe she plannin to do my portrait from memory. I'm mad, but I won't give her that satisfaction. So I slouch around the store being very bored and say, "Let's go."

Me and Sugar at the back of the train watchin the tracks whizzin by large then small then gettin gobbled up in the dark. I'm thinkin about this tricky toy I saw in the store. A clown that somersaults on a bar then does chin-ups just cause you yank lightly at his leg. Cost $35. I could see me askin my mother for a $35 birthday clown. "You wanna who that costs what?" she'd say, cocking her head to the side to get a better view of the hole in my head. Thirty-five dollars and the whole household could go visit Granddaddy Nelson in the country. Thirty-five dollars would pay for the rent and the piano bill too. Who are these people that spend that much for performing clowns and $1000 for toy sailboats? What kinda work they do and how they live and how come we ain't in on it? Where we are is who we are, Miss Moore always pointin out. But it don't necessarily have to be that way, she always adds then waits for somebody to say that poor people have to wake up and demand their share of the pie and don't none of us know what kind of pie she talkin about in the first damn place. But she ain't so smart cause I still got her four dollars from the taxi and she sure ain't gettin it. Messin up my day with this shit. Sugar nudges me in my pocket and winks.

45   Miss Moore lines us up in front of the mailbox where we started from, seem like years ago, and I got a headache for thinkin so hard. And we lean all over each other so we can hold up under the draggy-ass lecture she always finishes us off with at the end before we thank her for borin us to tears. But she just looks at us like she readin tea leaves. Finally she say, "Well, what do you think of F. A. O. Schwarz?"

Rosie Giraffe mumbles, "White folks crazy."

"I'd like to go there again when I get my birthday money," says Mercedes, and we shove her out the pack so she has to lean on the mailbox by herself.

"I'd like a shower. Tiring day," say Flyboy.

Then Sugar surprises me by sayin, "You know, Miss Moore, I don't think all of us here put together eat in a year what that sailboat costs." And Miss Moore lights up like somebody goosed her. "And?" she say, urging Sugar on. Only I'm standin on her foot so she don't continue.

50   "Imagine for a minute what kind of society it is in which some people can spend on a toy what it would cost to feed a family of six or seven. What do you think?"

"I think," say Sugar pushing me off her feet like she never done before, cause I whip her ass in a minute, "that this is not much of a democracy if you ask me. Equal chance to pursue happiness means an equal crack at the dough, don't it?" Miss Moore is besides herself and I am disgusted with Sugar's treachery. So I stand on her foot one more time to see if she'll shove me. She shuts up, and Miss Moore looks at me, sorrowfully I'm thinkin. And somethin weird is goin on, I can feel it in my chest.

"Anybody else learn anything today?" lookin dead at me. I walk away and Sugar has to run to catch up and don't even seem to notice when I shrug her arm off my shoulder.

"Well, we got four dollars anyway," she says.

"Uh hunh."

55 "We could go to Hascombs and get half a chocolate layer and then go to the Sunset and still have plenty money for potato chips and ice cream sodas."

"Uh hunh."

"Race you to Hascombs," she say.

We start down the block and she gets ahead which is O.K. by me cause I'm going to the West End and then over to the Drive to think this day through. She can run if she want to and even run faster. But ain't nobody gonna beat me at nuthin.

Analyzing Rhetorical Choices

1. Why do you think Bambara chose to write this story in African American Vernacular English (AAVE)? How is its effectiveness enhanced by the language used to narrate this event?

2. Although Sylvia speaks and narrates in AAVE, Miss Moore does not: she speaks in what many call Standard English. What contrast gets established between the way Sylvia talks and the way Miss Moore talks? What points are driven home by this contrast?

3. Describe how Bambara uses details and specific descriptions to establish the grounds of her argument, and how the story itself is an example of exemplification.

Writing About Issues and Contexts

1. This story is told by Sylvia in a form known as a dramatic monologue. How would you describe Sylvia as she reveals herself in telling this story? How would you describe her values, her neighborhood, and her expectations about herself and her friends?

2. Why does Miss Moore take the kids to F. A. O. Schwarz on Fifth Avenue in New York City, perhaps the most expensive toy store in America? What "lesson" does she have in mind?

3. After seeing the sailboat and its $1,195 price tag, Sylvia and Miss Moore have an exchange in which Miss Moore says, "You sound angry, Sylvia. Are you mad about something?" Is Sylvia mad, and if so, what is she mad about? Why would Miss Moore wish to make her angry?

4. What is the relationship between Miss Moore and the kids on the block, and between Miss Moore and the other adults in the

neighborhood? Does her relationship with Sylvia alter during their visit to F. A. O. Schwarz, and if so how?

5. What is the significance of the last two lines of the story? Do they refer only to a race between Sugar and Sylvia, or to some kind of life lesson? Given Sylvia's final comment in this story, what kind of future would you envision for her?

A well-known academic in African American studies, **Henry Louis Gates, Jr.** *(1950–   ) was born in Keyser, West Virginia, and earned his bachelor's degree from Yale University and his Ph.D. from the University of Cambridge in England. From 1970 to 1971, he served as a general anesthetist at Anglican Mission Hospital in Kilimatinde, Tanzania; in the early 1970s, he also served as a staff reporter and correspondent for the* Times *(London). Gates went on to become director of undergraduate Afro-American studies at Yale and now serves as the head of the African American department at Harvard University. Gates is the general editor of* The Norton Anthology of African-American Literature *and* The Encyclopedia Africana. *His works include* The Signifying Monkey: Towards a Theory of Afro-American Literary Criticism *(1988),* Colored People: A Memoir *(1994),* Thirteen Ways of Looking at a Black Man *(1994), and* Wonders of the African World *(1999). This essay first appeared in* Sports Illustrated.

Henry Louis Gates, Jr.
Delusions of Grandeur

Standing at the bar of an all-black VFW post in my hometown of Piedmont, W.Va., I offered five dollars to anyone who could tell me how many African-American professional athletes were at work today. There are 35 million African-Americans, I said.

"Ten million!" yelled one intrepid soul, too far into his cups.

"No way . . . more than 500,000," said another.

"You mean *all* professional sports," someone interjected, "including golf and tennis, but not counting the brothers from Puerto Rico?"
5 Everyone laughed.

"Fifty thousand, minimum," was another guess.

Here are the facts:

There are 1,200 black professional athletes in the U.S.

There are 12 times more black lawyers than black athletes.
10 There are 2-1/2 times more black dentists than black athletes.

There are 15 times more black doctors than black athletes.

Nobody in my local VFW believed these statistics; in fact, few people would believe them if they weren't reading them in the pages of *Sports Illustrated.* In spite of these statistics, too many African-American youngsters still believe that they have a much better chance of becoming another Magic Johnson or Michael Jordan than they do of matching the achievements of Baltimore Mayor Kurt Schmoke or neurosurgeon Dr. Benjamin Carson, both of whom, like Johnson and Jordan, are black.

In reality, an African-American youngster has about as much chance of becoming a professional athlete as he or she does of winning the lottery. The tragedy for our people, however, is that few of us accept that truth.

Let me confess that I love sports. Like most black people of my generation—I'm 40—I was raised to revere the great black athletic heroes and I never tired of listening to the stories of triumph and defeat that, for blacks, amount to a collective epic much like those of the ancient Greeks: Joe Louis's demolition of Max Schmeling; Satchel Paige's dazzling repertoire of pitches; Jesse Owens's in-your-face performance in Hitler's 1936 Olympics; Willie Mays's over-the-shoulder basket catch; Jackie Robinson's quiet strength when assaulted by racist taunts; and a thousand other grand tales.

Nevertheless, the blind pursuit of attainment in sports is having a devastating effect on our people. Imbued with a belief that our principal avenue to fame and profit is through sport, and seduced by a win-at-any-cost system that corrupts even elementary school students, far too many black kids treat basketball courts and football fields as if they were classrooms in an alternative school system. "O.K., I flunked English," a young athlete will say. "But I got an A plus in slam-dunking."

15   The failure of our public schools to educate athletes is part and parcel of the schools' failure to educate almost everyone. A recent survey of the Philadelphia school system, for example, stated that "more than half of all students in the third, fifth and eighth grades cannot perform minimum math and language tasks." One in four middle school students in that city fails to pass to the next grade each year. It is a sad truth that such statistics are repeated in cities throughout the nation. Young athletes—particularly young black athletes—are especially ill-served. Many of them are functionally illiterate, yet they are passed along from year to year for the greater glory of good old Hometown High. We should not be surprised to learn, then, that only 26.6% of black athletes at the collegiate level earn their degrees. For every successful educated black professional athlete, there are thousands of dead and wounded. Yet young blacks continue to aspire to careers as athletes, and it's no wonder why; when the University of North Carolina recently commissioned a sculptor to create archetypes of its student body, guess which ethnic group was selected to represent athletes?

Those relatively few black athletes who do make it in the professional ranks must be prevailed upon to play a significant role in the education of all of our young people, athlete and nonathlete alike. While some have done so, many others have shirked their social obligations: to earmark small percentages of their incomes for the United Negro College Fund; to appear on television for educational purposes rather than merely to sell sneakers; to let children know the message that becoming a lawyer, a teacher or a doctor does more good for our people than winning the Super Bowl; and to form productive liaisons with educators to help forge solutions to the many ills that beset the black community. These are merely a few modest proposals.

A similar burden falls upon successful blacks in all walks of life. Each of us must strive to make our young people understand the realities. Tell them to cheer Bo Jackson but to emulate novelist Toni Morrison or businessman Reginald Lewis or historian John Hope Franklin or Spelman College president Johnetta Cole—the list is long.

Of course, society as a whole bears responsibility as well. Until colleges stop using young blacks as cannon fodder in the big-business wars of so-called nonprofessional sports, until training a young black's mind becomes as important as training his or her body, we will continue to perpetuate a system akin to that of the Roman gladiators, sacrificing a class of people for the entertainment of the mob.

Analyzing Rhetorical Choices

1. What kinds of proof does Gates offer to support his argument about the importance of education for black youth? How would you describe the effectiveness of the exemplification Gates uses to build his case?

2. Why does Gates open with the scene in the bar? Evaluate its effectiveness.

3. Why was it important to Gates to publish this article in *Sports Illustrated*?

4. Evaluate the rhetorical devices that Gates uses in his final two paragraphs. How do those devices help him end the article with emphasis?

Writing About Issues and Contexts

1. Gates argues that in addition to African Americans themselves, "society as a whole bears responsibility" for black youth's focus on sports rather than education. Evaluate this argument in at least two paragraphs of reasoned analysis that offers a thoughtful perspective on individual choice and societal values.

2. How can we change the way schools educate youth, especially black youth, regarding sports and success? Use evidence from the essay as well as from your own experience.

3. Gates mentions famous blacks—both athletes and nonathletes. Are all these names equally familiar? How does their familiarity among the general public (or lack of it) support his argument?

A native of Pittsburgh, **Amy Wang** (1969–   ) is the daughter of parents who immigrated to the United States two years before her birth. A graduate of Cornell University in 1990, she earned a Master's degree in journalism from the well-known Columbia University School of Journalism. Formerly a copy editor for the Philadelphia Inquirer, Wang published this personal account in that paper's Sunday magazine in 1993. Wang left the Inquirer in 1997, and she is now an assignment editor for The Oregonian in Portland.

Amy Wang

The Same Difference

It was on my way home that the moment of truth swept by—again.

There we were, a friend and I, heading north on the Pennsylvania Turnpike to central New York to visit my parents. Somehow our conversation had parted the curtains before my childhood memories, and before I knew it, I was telling him about an incident I have never quite forgotten.

As I spoke, it was almost as if my adult self were back in Pittsburgh, watching; strange how in my memory the sun is always glinting through a bright haze on that day. The trees are bare, or nearly so, with dark branches that reach out to splinter the sun's rays. I am walking alone, down a white concrete sidewalk littered with leaves, twigs, buckeyes. School is out for the day, and everyone is going home.

From behind come shouts, and I turn to see a group of children from school. A moment passes, and I realize they are shouting at me. I listen for several seconds before the words whip into clarity:

5   Chink! Hey, chink! Chinky chinky chink!

They are running. I am frozen, my heart the only part of me moving, and it is pounding. Then one of them stoops, picks up a twig and hurls it at me. It lands short, a foot away on the sidewalk. Then I turn, still blocks from home, and run. The twigs keep coming, clattering close behind as the others shout and follow. As I run, I think of the steep steps to the front door and despair.

But when I reach the steps and turn around, only silence follows. And when my mother answers the doorbell's ring, she sees only her daughter, cheeks a little flushed, waiting to be let in. Almost instinctively, I know I must not tell her. It would only hurt her, and there is nothing she can do. Besides, it is nothing I want to discuss.

"Wow," he said. "And you were in sixth grade when this happened?"

"Six," I said. "I was 6 when this happened. I was in first grade."

10   He was clearly appalled, his eyes in far focus as he tried to understand how such a thing could happen to a small child. I was concentrating on the road, but even a sidelong glance showed he did not, could not, quite understand. And it was then that I felt the familiar stab of disappointment: the realization that no matter how long we traveled together, we would always be on parallel roads, moving on either side of a great divide. I would never know his assurance as he made his way through a world where his skin color was an assumption, and he would never know my anxiety as I made my way through a world where my skin color was an anguish.

We were silent, and after a while he fell asleep. "Wake me up when we get to Allentown," he had said as he drifted off, and we both smiled, remembering a classmate who had once padded an expense account for profit by driving from New York to Allentown and back twice in two days.

The thought of the old mill town triggered memories of another old mill town, where I had gotten my first job out of college. It was at the local newspaper, working nights on the copy desk. Our shifts ended at 1 A.M., and I often drove home through deserted streets, the hush broken only by the whir of an occasional street-cleaning machine or the clanking of a distant garbage truck. The other drivers on the streets at that hour seemed just as weary, just as intent on getting to bed.

In such an atmosphere I often dream, and so to this day a shadowy, slowed-down quality suffuses the memory of turning my head and looking out the side window one night just in time to see an old red Dodge draw up in the next lane at a traffic light. Inside, four young white crewcut men dressed in denim and flannel strain toward me, their faces distorted with hate, their mouths twisted with invective. Our windows are closed, so I am spared their actual words, but their frenzied pantomime leaves little to be imagined.

When the light turns green I pull away hastily, but they cruise alongside for the next few blocks. By the time they tire of me and swing into a left turn, I am seething with fear and rage. I wait until they are committed to the turn, then raise my middle finger. One of them looks back for a final insult, sees my gesture, and gapes—but only for a moment. He turns, and I know he is screaming at the driver to turn back. I gun it.

15   They never come after me, and I make it home alive. Numb, I crawl into bed. It is only after I lie down that I realize how they might have hurt me, the four of them with their huge Dodge against my tiny Nissan, and I begin to shake. As my mind tumbles, the phone rings. For a moment I think it is them, and then logic returns. I answer, and it is my boyfriend, calling from Boston. I tell him what happened, melting into tears. He is sympathetic, but then he asks: "How do you know they weren't yelling at you because you were a woman?"

   I don't, of course, but that is not the point. His whiteness rushes through the line with the very question. "It doesn't matter," I tell him, and suddenly I can't stand to hear his voice. I tell him I don't want to discuss it anymore, and hang up.

   Somewhere along Route 79 in New York he said, "This is beautiful." I smiled, remembering the years I spent in Finger Lakes country: middle school, high school, college. Here were trees I had climbed, hills I had sledded down, malls I knew by heart; here were roads that led to memories and people who knew my history.

   And it was because I had to come back here that another He was able to betray me. It was during the first summer I spent away from home, working at a magazine in New York. Picture now a pavilion on the grounds of a quiet country club where the staff is enjoying the annual company picnic, and there I am by the jukebox, hovering over the glassed-in 45s as a light mist dampens the grass. As The Contours wail "Do You Love Me," I sway to the beat, attracting a stranger's eyes. In a moment he is introducing himself; in an hour he is sitting by me in the bus taking us back to the city; in a week he is asking me out to dinner.

   I am no longer thinking clearly. On my last day at the magazine, he watches as I clean out my desk, then asks me, in a low but urgent tone, not to forget him. He tells me he wants my address, and a sudden foreboding chill nearly stuns me with its iciness, sending shivers through my hand as I write out the address and phone number. Then I ask for his address and phone number. I do not think to ask him not to forget me.

20   Weeks go by without a word, and then one night, I know. The chill comes back: For days I hate white men, all of them, they all bear the blame for his misdeed. But I have known too many good ones for my fury to last, and finally I am forced to admit that I have been a fool, and that this time, at least, it had nothing to do with race.

"It could have happened to anyone," a (white male) friend tells me. "It happens to everyone."

I am not immediately consoled. But time goes on, and finally, so do I.

By the time we pulled into my parents' driveway, it was nearly dinnertime. I sprang out, glad to stretch, and bounded into the house, but he was slow to follow, and I had discarded my shoulder bag and greeted everyone by the time he finally appeared in the doorway. I went to introduce him, wondering why he was hanging back. Then he raised his eyes to mine as he came up the stairs, and I realized he was nervous: He was in my world now, and he was finally getting an inkling of what I went through every day.

Payback time. At last.

25   Then my mother was there, smiling and shaking his hand, and my father was right behind her, also smiling.

"Welcome," he said.

For a moment, I could see the horizon, where parallel lines sometimes seem to meet.

Analyzing Rhetorical Choices

1. Wang exemplifies her essay by using three examples. How effective are they? Do you end up being persuaded to her point of view about racial hatred? Explain in an extended paragraph.

2. How effective is the device of the car trip? How does it help Wang to write this essay? Is the trip believable? Persuasive?

Writing About Issues and Contexts

1. After the first incident that Wang describes, she is tempted to inform her mother about being harassed by the children but she writes that "instinctively, I know I must not tell her. It would only hurt her, and there is nothing she can do. Besides, it is nothing I want to discuss." Why do you think she feels this way? Offer an analysis of whether she should have spoken to her mother or not, and why.

2. Wang reports that the four young men "never come after me, and I make it home alive." Is she overreacting? How do you read this statement?

3. What is the effect of Wang's statement after being chased home that "when I reach the steps and turn around, only silence follows?"

4. Why does Wang include her friend's misstatement in which he remarks that she was in sixth grade? What does this say about him and about general perceptions that some Americans have about racial discrimination?

*Born in Butte, Montana, **Barbara Ehrenreich** (1941–   ) was educated at Reed College and went on to earn a Ph.D. from Rockefeller University. A self-described socialist and feminist, Ehrenreich has written about student unrest on campus, health care, and most recently, the working poor, particularly women. Her work has been selected for the National Magazine Award, the Ford Foundation Award for Humanistic Perspectives on Contemporary Issues, and the* Los Angeles Times *Book Award, among others. Ehrenreich was also awarded a prestigious Guggenheim Fellowship in 1987. She has published many books, including* Fear of Falling: The Inner Life of the Middle Class *(1989),* The Snarling Citizen: Essays *(1995), and* Nickel and Dimed: On (Not) Getting By in America *(2001). Her essays have been published in many magazines including* Radical America, Nation, Esquire, Vogue, The New Republic, The New York Times Magazine, Mother Jones, *and* Ms., *where this essay first appeared.*

Barbara Ehrenreich

What I've Learned from Men

For many years I believed that women had only one thing to learn from men: how to get the attention of a waiter by some means short of kicking over the table and shrieking. Never in my life have I gotten the attention of a waiter, unless it was an off-duty waiter whose car I'd accidentally scraped in a parking lot somewhere. Men, however, can summon a maître d' just by thinking the word "coffee," and this is a power women would be well-advised to study. What else would we possibly want to learn from them? How to interrupt someone in mid-sentence as if you were performing an act of conversational euthanasia? How to drop a pair of socks three feet from an open hamper and keep right on walking? How to make those weird guttural gargling sounds in the bathroom?

But now, at mid-life, I am willing to admit that there are some real and useful things to learn from men. Not from all men—in fact, we may have the most to learn from some of the men we like the least. This realization does not mean that my feminist principles have gone soft with age: what I think women could learn from men is how to get *tough*. After more than a decade of consciousness-raising, assertiveness training, and hand-to-hand combat in the battle of the sexes, we're still too ladylike. Let me try that again—we're just too *damn* ladylike.

Here is an example from my own experience, a story that I blush to recount. A few years ago, at an international conference held in an exotic and luxurious setting, a prestigious professor invited me to his room for what he said would be an intellectual discussion on matters of theoretical importance. So far, so good. I showed up promptly. But only minutes into the conversation—held in all-too-adjacent chairs—it emerged that he was interested in something more substantial than a meeting of minds. I was disgusted, but not enough to overcome 30-odd years of programming in ladylikeness. Every time his comments took a lecherous turn, I chattered distractingly; every time his hand found its way to my knee, I returned it as if it were something he had misplaced. This went on for an unconscionable period (as much as 20 minutes); then there was a minor scuffle, a dash for the door, and I was out—with nothing violated but my self-esteem. I, a full-grown feminist, conversant with such matters as rape crisis counseling and sexual harassment at the workplace, had behaved like a ninny—or, as I now understand it, like a lady.

The essence of ladylikeness is a persistent servility masked as "niceness." For example, we (women) tend to assume that it is our responsibility to keep everything "nice" even when the person we are with is rude, aggressive, or emotionally AWOL. (In the above example, I was so busy taking responsibility for preserving the veneer of "niceness" that I almost forgot to take responsibility for myself.) In conversations with men, we do almost all the work: sociologists have observed that in male-female social interactions it's the woman who throws out leading questions and verbal encouragements ("So how did you *feel* about that?" and so on) while the man, typically, says "Hmmmm." Wherever we go, we're perpetually smiling—the on-cue smile, like the now-outmoded curtsy, being one of our culture's little rituals of submission. We're trained to feel embarrassed if we're praised, but if we see a criticism coming at us from miles down the road, we rush to acknowledge it. And when we're feeling aggressive or angry or resentful, we just tighten up our smiles or turn them into rueful little moues. In short, we spend a great deal of time acting like wimps.

5   For contrast, think of the macho stars we love to watch. Think, for example, of Mel Gibson facing down punk marauders in "The Road Warrior" . . . John Travolta swaggering his way through the early scenes of "Saturday Night Fever" . . . or Marlon Brando shrugging off the local law in "The Wild One." Would they simper their way through tight spots? Chatter aimlessly to keep the conversation going? Get all clutched up whenever they think they might—just might—have hurt

someone's feelings? No, of course not, and therein, I think, lies their fascination for us.

The attraction of the "tough guy" is that he has—or at least seems to have—what most of us lack, and that is an aura of power and control. In an article, feminist psychiatrist Jean Baker Miller writes that "a woman's using self-determined power for herself is equivalent to selfishness [and] destructiveness"—an equation that makes us want to avoid even the appearance of power. Miller cites cases of women who get depressed just when they're on the verge of success—and of women who do succeed and then bury their achievement in self-deprecation. As an example, she describes one company's periodic meetings to recognize outstanding salespeople: when a woman is asked to say a few words about her achievement, she tends to say something like, "Well, I really don't know how it happened. I guess I was just lucky this time." In contrast, the men will cheerfully own up to the hard work, intelligence, and so on, to which they owe their success. By putting herself down, a woman avoids feeling brazenly powerful and potentially "selfish"; she also does the traditional lady's work of trying to make everyone else feel better ("She's not really so smart, after all, just lucky").

So we might as well get a little tougher. And a good place to start is by cutting back on the small acts of deference that we've been programmed to perform since girlhood. Like unnecessary smiling. For many women—waitresses, flight attendants, receptionists—smiling is an occupational requirement, but there's no reason for anyone to go around grinning when she's not being paid for it. I'd suggest that we save our off-duty smiles for when we truly feel like sharing them, and if you're not sure what to do with your face in the meantime, study Clint Eastwood's expressions—both of them.

Along the same lines, I think women should stop taking responsibility for every human interaction we engage in. In a social encounter with a woman, the average man can go 25 minutes saying nothing more than "You don't say?" "Izzat so?" and, of course, "Hmmmm." Why should we do all the work? By taking so much responsibility for making conversations go well, we act as if we had much more at stake in the encounter than the other party—and that gives him (or her) the power advantage. Every now and then, we deserve to get more out of a conversation than we put into it: I'd suggest not offering information you'd rather not share ("I'm really terrified that my sales plan won't work") and not, out of sheer politeness, soliciting information you don't really want ("Wherever did you get that lovely tie?"). There will be pauses, but they don't have to be awkward for *you*.

It is true that some, perhaps most, men will interpret any decrease in female deference as a deliberate act of hostility. Omit the free smiles and perky conversation-boosters and someone is bound to ask, "Well, what's come over *you* today?" For most of us, the first impulse is to stare at our feet and make vague references to a terminally ill aunt in Atlanta, but we should have as much right to be taciturn as the average (male) taxi driver. If you're taking a vacation from smiles and small talk and some fellow is moved to inquire about what's "bothering" you, just stare back levelly and say, the international debt crisis, the arms race, or the death of God.

10   There are all kinds of ways to toughen up—and potentially move up—at work, and I leave the details to the purveyors of assertiveness training. But Jean Baker Miller's study underscores a fundamental principle that anyone can master on her own. We can stop acting less capable than we actually are. For example, in the matter of taking credit when credit is due, there's a key difference between saying "I was just lucky" and saying "I had a plan and it worked." If you take the credit you deserve, you're letting people know that you were confident you'd succeed all along, and that you fully intend to do so again.

Finally, we may be able to learn something from men about what to do with anger. As a general rule, women get irritated; men get *mad*. We make tight little smiles of ladylike exasperation; they pound on desks and roar. I wouldn't recommend emulating the full basso profundo male tantrum, but women do need ways of expressing justified anger clearly, colorfully, and, when necessary, crudely. If you're not just irritated, but *pissed off*, it might help to say so.

I, for example, have rerun the scene with the prestigious professor many times in my mind. And in my mind, I play it like Bogart. I start by moving my chair over to where I can look the professor full in the face. I let him do the chattering, and when it becomes evident that he has nothing serious to say, I lean back and cross my arms, just to let him know that he's wasting my time. I do not smile, neither do I nod encouragement. Nor, of course, do I respond to his blandishments with apologetic shrugs and blushes. Then, at the first flicker of lechery, I stand up and announce coolly, "All right, I've had enough of this crap." Then I walk out—slowly, deliberately, confidently. Just like a man.

Or—now that I think of it—just like a woman.

Analyzing Rhetorical Choices

1. Is the title of this essay ironic? If so, in what ways? How does the title prepare us for what Ehrenreich is going to say, both on a first reading and on subsequent readings?

2. Ehrenreich closes her first paragraph with a series of rhetorical questions. Extend that paragraph by developing four more rhetorical questions that satirize male behavior and build toward a final, climactic question that completes the paragraph with a crescendo.

3. Describe Ehrenreich's tone, and cite at least three examples from the essay that reinforce that tone. How does the tone, and the perspective that underlies it, keep you interested in the essay?

4. Ehrenreich uses the first-person plural in this essay. How effective is this? Is she in danger of alienating male readers who might pick up *Ms.* magazine and read her essay? Explain whether you think this is a risk worth taking.

Writing About Issues and Contexts

1. Ehrenreich identifies her principles as "feminist." What does she mean by that? What are "feminist principles"?

2. According to Ehrenreich, what is the "essence of ladylikeness"? What examples does she offer to help her describe ladylike behavior? Comment on whether you think her definition is appropriate today and explain your reasoning.

3. Ehrenreich's prime example, the one that is the departure point for this essay, describes her interaction with a prestigious professor who engages in overtly lecherous behavior. How does this example establish a framework for the entire essay?

Strategies for Writers: Exemplification

1. Exemplifying is a way of making your essay richer and more particular; it also can help you create structure and provide a way to develop your essay, as you can see in Richard Selzer's "Four Appointments with the Discus Thrower." It is also a way of making appropriate choices that are rhetorically embedded— that is, choices about data and other specifics that serve your purposes as a writer and are strategically chosen and placed. Look over the draft of your most current essay. Are your examples well chosen? Well developed? Well placed?

2. How is exemplification a part of argument? It certainly involves the choice of appropriate examples to make your case, and it can be called a "type" of argument, a strategy for developing it. Like description, the choice of appropriate details associated with exemplification is crucial to the success of your writing. Exchange your drafts with your classmates; discover whether or not your readers find your details appropriate and useful for your purpose. Reread John McPhee's "Encounters with the Archdruid," respond to the questions at the end of the selection, and review your own draft to see if you immerse your reader in details as does McPhee. Compare your work to Diane Ackerman's "The Vagaries of Taste," and revise to elaborate on any details that need enhancement. Remember, however, that you are the final judge of whether or not the examples you use are appropriate and adequate for your writing.

3. Richard Selzer and Emily Tsao provide details that are unusual and sometimes startling. Exchange drafts with your classmates. Are there ways in which you can take generally good, acceptable examples and make them unusual—even startling—and yet appropriate for your purpose?

4. Countee Cullen has centered each of his two poems on one, specific detail. Select one of these details and make it the subject of an essay. With your classmates, brainstorm lists that help you extend your example. At the same time, notice how definition, narration, and other ways of organizing your writing that we discuss in this volume might be appropriate for your work in this instance.

5. Another way to use examples is through research. If you decide to use secondary materials, your credibility depends on your citing your sources carefully and appropriately. This is often

done by means of footnotes in academic essays, but notice the ways that Ackerman acknowledges her sources in "The Vagaries of Taste."

6. Exemplification places a high value on directness. Some cultures, however, not only value being indirect more than they do being direct but also consider indirectness a virtue. Discuss and debate this issue with your classmates. To what extent are we obliged to take on the styles of the dominant culture? Why or why not?

Research and Writing Assignments

1. Richard Selzer's "Four Appointments with the Discus Thrower" offers four short narrative scenes, each of which exemplifies an important aspect of "the discus thrower." Following Selzer's model, write an essay about an intriguing person you once knew, using at least three dramatic scenes to exemplify his or her character.

2. The debate between David Brower and Charles Park in John McPhee's "Encounters with the Archdruid" is a crucial one that is frequently debated in the American media. In an essay that draws on library research, develop a position paper on resource use, the conservation and preservation of our natural heritage, which is often viewed to be in tension with individual choices about lifestyle and the well-being of the overall economy (and along with it, political stability). Your essay might take the form of a dramatic narrative, like McPhee's or Emily Tsao's, or it might be a more traditional analysis that incorporates a thesis and argument. Because this is a large subject, focus on a specific issue, such as the use of artificial fertilizers, water purity, recycling, or maintaining an appropriate standard of living.

3. Diane Ackerman writes about taste with a strong sense of wonder and pleasure. Using her essay as a model, write an essay that uses the same kind of detail and specificity to explain one of the following everyday activities: sighing, hiccuping, laughing, or yawning. Whatever subject you choose, you will have to do some extensive research (as Ackerman did) to write an essay that conveys new and interesting information.

4. A common theme of several selections in this chapter is explicit expressions of racial discrimination. Countee Cullen, Toni Cade Bambara, and Amy Wang offer various perspectives drawn pri-

marily from childhood, from Cullen's memory of childhood hatred to Wang's memories of anti-Chinese and anti-Asian prejudice. In an essay, examine the complex roots of childhood prejudice. How do children of different ethnicities, who grow up in different neighborhoods, or who practice different customs and religions learn to hate each other? What sociological or tribal purposes does such prejudice serve? What is the relation between childhood prejudice and education, and between childhood prejudice and social class? Since few of us wish to remain "prejudiced," how can we realistically overcome it? This is a subject that is best suited to library research so you can include informed perspectives from respected researchers and scholars in your essay. For instance, you might want to investigate a 2002 study of children in Northern Ireland, which was designed to trace the roots of Catholic/Protestant prejudice.

5. Both Toni Cade Bambara and Barbara Ehrenreich center their essays on the notion of lessons and learning, and both feature narrative. Write your own nonfictional narrative account of an experience you had that taught you something valuable or significant. Be sure to include specific details so the experience can come alive in the reader's imagination. For added effect, try to leave the "lesson" implicit. That is, don't end your narrative essay with a "moral," but tell about something in such a way that your readers can draw their own conclusions about why this event was something that made a significant impact on you.

6. In his essay, Henry Louis Gates, Jr., offers an assessment of the false promise that professional athletics holds out to black youth and the destructive consequences of this false promise. Does athletics offer many students (of most any ethnicity or gender) the hope of a rich and glorious livelihood? Choose a high school or college athlete and interview that individual to see what his or her personal aspirations are in relation to a professional sports career. Then present that information in the form of an essay that features direct quotations from your interview. Your essay can be in the form of either a profile of the student you interview or an essay that analyzes this complex issue and uses your interview as a source for exemplification.

6
Classification

In many ways, our first analytic understanding of the world comes to us through classification. We learn how to identify specific traits and characteristics and from them form general categories of understanding. For example, through intuitive observation, we identify one of our parents as Mom and the other as Dad. Soon after, based on these individual definitions, we make a greater intellectual leap and classify adults in similar roles as mothers or fathers. Ultimately, we meet and interact with other individuals, classifying them as siblings, aunts and uncles, friends, teachers, strangers, and so on. Classifying becomes a way of organizing the world, of putting people, places, and things into meaningful categories so that we can understand them better, relate them to one another, distinguish them more clearly.

This is not a simple or simplistic process. To classify demands keen observational powers, the ability to compare and contrast, strong cognitive skills, and a great deal of judgment. Hurried and unsophisticated attempts at classifying can betray us. If we are hasty or uninformed, we put things into incorrect categories and make judgments that can lead to false generalizations, stereotyping, and reductive thinking. By classifying without doing sufficient research and analysis, we may well overlook key qualities and force subjects into categories in which they do not belong. "That song has a West Coast feel to it," someone might say without realizing that the song comes out of the Austin country music scene. Or in a vain attempt to display vast knowledge, someone might tell everyone, incorrectly, that a scallop is not a mollusk, a telling mistake in classification for those familiar with the movie *Barbershop*.

When done well, classification gives us a powerful way to understand the world. It compels us to look at objects both microscopically (details, specifics, individual traits) and macroscopically (common qualities, general similarities, overarching frameworks). To illustrate how important and how complex classification can be, here is an example from science, a discipline deeply dependent on classification. Chemistry, physics, geology, and biology classify information in ways that allow scientists to understand basic principles and practices. The study of insects is a prime example. At the elementary school level, most kids are interested in insects, or what they call "bugs," fascinated, and sometimes repelled, by beetles, wasps, ants, butterflies, and spiders. But are these all insects? What is the best method for explaining what an insect is, and isn't. The answer, according to elementary school teacher Nancy Goslin—who has put her lesson plan on a Web site, *http://www.successlink.org/great/g9992.html*—is to understand how insects get classified. According to Goslin, who paraphrases good science to simplify the process a bit for elementary students, insects have five characteristics:

1. An exoskeleton
2. Three pairs of legs
3. One pair of antennae
4. Compound eyes
5. Many adults have wings

If every insect has an external skeleton, six legs, one pair of antennae, compound eyes, and (frequently) wings, then yes, beetles, wasps, ants, and butterflies are all insects. But a spider, which has eight legs and no wings, is not. In fact, spiders have other characteristics that place them within the class known as Arachnida, which includes scorpions, mites, and ticks. Making these kinds of classifications helps us better understand the world around us.

At a much more advanced level, scientists make more refined distinctions within this class known as Insecta. It includes more than 25 orders—for instance, Coleoptera (beetles) and Lepidoptera (moths and butterflies)—and within these orders, it is possible to make further refinements and classify an insect according to its family, genus, or species. For elementary school students, a basic understanding of insect classification is sufficient, but those who specialize in the field of entomology (the study of the class Insecta) have to know much more to analyze insects according to their proper classification. They are more likely to use the following complex classificatory scheme:

Insect Classification

Apterygota (wingless insects)
- Thysanura—bristletails
- Diplura—two-tailed bristletails
- Protura—proturans
- Collembola—springtails

Pterygota (winged insects)

Exopterygota (insects with partial metamorphosis)
- Ephemeroptera—mayflies
- Odonata—dragonflies
- Plecoptera—stoneflies
- Orthoptera—crickets and grasshoppers
- Dermaptera—earwigs
- Dictyoptera—cockroaches
- Psocoptera—booklice and barklice
- Mallophaga—biting lice
- Anoplura—sucking lice
- Hemiptera—true bugs
- Thysanoptera—thrips

Endopterygota (insects with complete metamorphosis)
- Neuroptera—lacewings, alderflies, and snakeflies
- Mecoptera—scorpion flies
- Lepidoptera—butterflies and moths
- Trichoptera—caddis flies
- Diptera—true flies
- Siphonaptera—fleas
- Hymenoptera—ants, bees, wasps
- Coleoptera—beetles

What this much more sophisticated and exacting classificatory scheme tells us is that some insects have wings and others do not, and that one of the major distinctions among insects is differentiating those that completely metamorphose (change radically from a larva to an adult, such as from a caterpillar to a moth), and those that metamorphose partially, like aphids and dragonflies. It also tells us that there is a great variety of insects and invites us to study them based on their differences and similarities, according to which they are placed within classifications. Moreover, refined as this taxonomy is, it still leaves scientists room for debate and disagreement. As the author of these particular categories states on his Web site (*http://www.bombaus.freeserve.co.uk/classification.htm*), "Some classifications now place Diplura, Protura, and Collembola outside the class Insecta." Are springtails insects? It looks like the scientific jury is still out.

Like entomologists, everyone engages in sophisticated forms of classification: when deciding how to organize a music collection or when categorizing friends according to their most obvious personality traits. When you read a short piece of writing, you classify it by deciding whether it is a short story, journalistic narrative, magazine article, or scholarly essay. To classify in these ways requires two kinds of knowledge: knowledge of the specific features of the subject and knowledge about the general kinds of categories into which individual subjects might be placed. Thus classifying requires both inductive and deductive kinds of thinking (see Chapter 10 for a brief definition of these terms).

One danger of classifying is binary thinking—the natural tendency to classify things into opposites: right/left, up/down, good/bad, smart/dumb, moral/immoral. Our physical orientation in the world often encourages us toward binary thinking, since we have two eyes, two arms, a front and a back. Much of the time, however, binaries are reductive and false, especially when it comes to complex analysis. Most individuals are neither smart nor dumb but exhibit a range of intellectual abilities. Most people, like most countries in the world, are neither moral nor immoral, neither good nor evil; they behave morally in some respects and less morally in others. Meaningful classification requires sophisticated analysis and the creation of thoughtful categories that reflect the complexity of the subject.

Done well, classification is an extremely useful organizational strategy. For instance, you might consider the various kinds of learning that you have experienced and which are most effective, or the types of activities that best contribute to charitable work in your particular community and the outcomes of these activities. Classification can also be a useful strategy for explaining complex legal and emotional relationships. You might, for example, analyze the various classifications about race according to current (and past) U.S. census practices. Or how cities and geographic regions get classified in terms of whether they are most or least segregated. Or how gemstones are categorized and what those categories mean, both within the jewelry industry and to you personally. Depending on your purpose and audience, you will decide on the most informative and insightful ways to classify so as to best serve your readers.

As you read and analyze the essays in this section, you will notice that some are explicit classification essays, while others reveal their dependence on classification more subtly. Compare, for instance, the ironies and complexities of the lists of categories from *Harper's Magazine* with the William Zinsser essay, "College Pressures," and Malcolm Gladwell's "The Trouble with Fries." As a strategy for organizing an essay, classification—as is the case with all the modes in this book—does not follow lockstep patterns. Rather, it is a way of thinking about a subject that gets expressed in purpose, form, and evidence. The key to successful classification is logical consistency combined with subtle and supple analysis. Classification is never appropriate if it results in easy and formulaic categories and reductive thinking. Both the writer and the reader need to apply classification so that they both discover new insights or a fresh way of looking at the familiar.

Although there are no formulas for writing a classification essay, there are useful strategies. The first is to look for a subject that offers meaningful relationships among its various components. The subject can be as mundane as grading cuts of beef or as arcane as valuing antique dolls. Ideally, the subject should offer you the ability to place different objects along a spectrum or range (of age, quality, density, complexity, etc.). Once you have discovered a subject, you will need to understand it well enough to be able to offer illustrative examples. Exemplification is often the key to a successful classification essay because it anchors your insights with specific illustrations. Finally, you will have to be sure that your essay offers information and insights beyond the obvious. After all, if the reader already knows what you will write, there is no reason to read it.

Selections from *Harper's Magazine*

[Nomenclature]
Begun This Clone War Has

From Flybase, a database of fruit-fly genes maintained by a consortium of research institutions. The genes were named by the researchers who discovered them. Convention suggests that if the genes' human counterparts are discovered, they will be given the same names.

aloof
always early
amontillado
bang senseless
bang sensitive
bride of sevenless
brother of odd with entrails limited
bumper-to-bumper
clootie dumpling
couch potato
crack
crossbronx
currant bun
Daughter killer
daughter of sevenless
Deadpan
deathknell
Dinty
disco-related
dog of glass
effete
eggroll
enoki mushroom
escargot
ether a go-go
faint sausage
fear-of-intimacy

fuzzy onions
genghis khan
glass bottom boat
Godzilla
Grunge
gut feeling
helter-skelter
he's not interested
hoi-polloi
I'm not dead yet
In dunce
inebriated
jekyll and hyde
just odd knobs
ken and barbie
king tubby
klingon
ladybird early
ladybird late
lemming
Lesbian
long island expressway
maelstrom
Malvolio
members only
mozzarella
naked cuticle

nanking
okra
out at first
oxen
pacman
papillote
pentagon
pugilist
quagmire
quick-to-court
redtape
Revolute
roadkill
rolling stone
sawtooth
scab

scott of the antarctic
scruin like at the midline
sevenless
Sex lethal
shank
similar to Deadpan
singles bar
slamdance
spotted dick
stranded at second
super sex combs
Thor
thousand points of light
Trailer hitch
vibrator
viking

Bill Gates Is . . .

The following descriptions of Microsoft chairman Bill Gates are taken from the 33,867 public comments received by the U.S. Justice Department concerning its proposed settlement with Microsoft. The department is required by law to solicit and publish public comments, and to respond to each one, before reaching a final settlement.

a brave boy and son of his parents
a brilliant man
a businessman's role model
a cash cow
a champion
a character
a Communist
a crook and a liar
a Dem
a deserving man
a driven man
a fair and honest man
a fine example of what a person can achieve with determination and
    hard work

a genius
a genius just like Edison or Ford
a genius nerd
a great inventor
a guy who made good and has been punished for his success
a lawyer's son
a man with a vision and the fortitude to make it happen
a patriot
a perfect example of folks who make a difference in our lives, and
    how to improve ourselves!!
a pioneer
a prince of a person
a SELF-MADE person
a shrewd businessman if nothing else
a smart man
a terrorist that doesn't use bullets
a tough competitor
a true American
a true American hero
a true businessman
a very successful man
a wolf in sheep fur
aggressive
an absolute genius
an American
an American patriot
an angel compared to Ken Lay
an excellent businessman
an icon of the American dream
constantly coming up with better ideas for working-class people
essentially amoral
EVIL
generous
involved in some world-domination scheme
just a genius
laughing at the Justice Department
living the American dream
making a mockery of the Court
my hero!
no angel
no better than a criminal

no crook
no genius but a fantastic POKER PLAYER!
no idiot
not a criminal
not a terrorist
not being nominated for Sainthood
not for freedom and innovation
not interested in quality product
not John Galt
not one of my personally favorite people
not Osama bin Laden
not the bad guy
not to be trusted
now more powerful than George Bush
obviously more powerful than the government!
one of the greatest leaders in the history of our capitalist country
one of the major contributors to our economy
one of the true heroes of this country
really afraid of face-to-face or shoulder-to-shoulder competition
reminiscent of earlier American giants like Thomas Edison
right again
sneering inwardly
someone who this country should be very proud of
subject to the provisions of U.S.C. Title 18 Section 96
telling YOU what YOU are going to do
the "Alexander the Great" of product development and marketing
THE ANTICHRIST!!!!
the best businessman ever to walk the Earth
the best of the best!
the computer world's version of a Bin Laden
the J. P. Morgan of his generation
the most respected nonpolitical world leader
the Patron Saint of Computers
the richest man in the world
the smartest (excluding myself of course) man in the U.S.A.
the ultimate capitalist pig
the why we are here from the beginning
Tony Blair's friend
too arrogant by far
totally unacceptable
truly a giver

truly a unique individual
very generous with his money
what America is about
wonderful for giving people such great software
wrong, wrong, wrong, wrong, wrong!!!!!!!!!!

[Roster]
Have a Huang and a Smile

From a list of brands owned by Coca-Cola, published on the Coca-Cola Web site.

Alive
American
Beverly
Bimbo
Bimbo Break
BonAqua
Bori Bori
Bright and Early
Burn
Chippewa
Chivalry
Chotto Kaoru
Chuhai
Cocoteen
Cresta-Ko
DESCA
diet Kia Ora-Ko
Emblem
Eva
Fruktime
Georgia
Gold Spot
Hachimittu
Huang
Inca Kola
Jesus

Jolly Juice
Juggy
Kuli
Lilt
Love Body
Miami
Nevada
New Vegitabeta
Ok
Old Colony-Ko
Pulp
Pump
Qoo
Riwa
Seiryusabo
Shock
Simba
Smart
Squirt-Ko
Supa
Tian Yu Di
Tiky-Ko
Thums Up
Urge
Vegitabeta
Wannabe

Water Salad	Woorijip
Wilkins	Youki

Analyzing Rhetorical Choices

1. These various selections from *Harper's Magazine* reveal different types of naming and classifying. Why did the editors of *Harper's* title each section as they do?

2. In the first piece, "Nomenclature" is placed in brackets. What effect does this have? Why is the title of the piece "Begun This Clone War Has"? What about the piece called "Have a Huang and a Smile" and its bracketed label, "Roster"? How do the lists of names become categories as well? To what effect?

Writing About Issues and Contexts

1. How does the first piece, "Nomenclature," suggest various attitudes toward cloning, the ostensible subject of the section? Select several of the categories or names that you think are the most interesting. What connotative or political effects do these various categories for fruit flies have? What implications might there be for the human genes that will be similarly named?

2. Similarly, "Bill Gates Is . . ." refers to its list of names as "descriptions." How, too, are they categories? To what effect? What seem to be the varieties of ways to describe or categorize the various aspects of Bill Gates as a person and businessman?

3. How does the larger category of "brand names" change depending on cultural contexts, and how might they reflect culture? See if you can, through research, find out which names of soft drinks have been developed into actual products. Why, for instance, does "water salad" as a type or category of beverage seem inappropriate for sale in the United States?

***Judith Viorst** (1936–   ) has written in a wide variety of forms. Her style is marked not only by depth of emotion but also humor. She is well-known for her several books for children, including* Alexander and the Terrible, Horrible, No Good, Very Bad Day *(1982) and* Sad Underwear and Other Complications *(1995). For many years, she has written a column in* Redbook. *She has published books of humorous verse, including* How Did I Get to Be Forty and Other Little Atrocities *(1984), as well as novels, such as* Murdering Mr. Monti: A Merry Little Tale of Sex and Violence *(1994). The following essay appeared in* Redbook *in 1977.*

Judith Viorst

Friends, Good Friends— and Such Good Friends

Women are friends, I once would have said, when they totally love and support and trust each other, and bare to each other the secrets of their souls, and run—no questions asked—to help each other, and tell harsh truths to each other (no, you can't wear that dress unless you lose ten pounds first) when harsh truths must be told.

Women are friends, I once would have said, when they share the same affection for Ingmar Bergman, plus train rides, cats, warm rain, charades, Camus, and hate with equal ardor Newark and Brussels sprouts and Lawrence Welk and camping.

In other words, I once would have said that a friend is a friend all the way, but now I believe that's a narrow point of view. For the friendships I have and the friendships I see are conducted at many levels of intensity, serve many different functions, meet different needs and range from those as all-the-way as the friendship of the soul sisters mentioned above to that of the most nonchalant and casual playmates.

Consider these varieties of friendship:

5   1.   Convenience friends. These are women with whom, if our paths weren't crossing all the time, we'd have no particular reason to be friends: a next-door neighbor, a woman in our car pool, the mother of one of our children's closest friends or maybe some mommy with whom we serve juice and cookies each week at the Glenwood Co-op Nursery.

Convenience friends are convenient indeed. They'll lend us their cups and silverware for a party. They'll drive our kids to soccer when we're sick. They'll take us to pick up our car when we need a lift to the garage. They'll even take our cats when we go on vacation. As we will for them.

But we don't, with convenience friends, ever come too close or tell too much; we maintain our public face and emotional distance. "Which means," says Elaine, "that I'll talk about being overweight but not about being depressed. Which means I'll admit being mad but not blind with rage. Which means that I might say that we're pinched this month but never that I'm worried sick over money."

But which doesn't mean that there isn't sufficient value to be found in these friendships of mutual aid, in convenience friends.

2. Special-interest friends. These friendships aren't intimate, and they needn't involve kids or silverware or cats. Their value lies in some interest jointly shared. And so we may have an office friend or a yoga friend or a tennis friend or a friend from the Women's Democratic Club.

10 "I've got one woman friend," says Joyce, "who likes, as I do, to take psychology courses. Which makes it nice for me—and nice for her. It's fun to go with someone you know and it's fun to discuss what you've learned, driving back from the classes." And for the most part, she says, that's all they discuss.

"I'd say that what we're doing is *doing* together, not being together," Suzanne says of her Tuesday-doubles friends. "It's mainly a tennis relationship, but we play together well. And I guess we all need to have a couple of playmates."

I agree.

My playmate is a shopping friend, a woman of marvelous taste, a woman who knows exactly *where* to buy *what*, and furthermore is a woman who always knows beyond a doubt what one ought to be buying. I don't have the time to keep up with what's new in eyeshadow, hemlines and shoes and whether the smock look is in or finished already. But since (oh, shame!) I care a lot about eyeshadow, hemlines and shoes, and since I don't *want* to wear smocks if the smock look is finished, I'm very glad to have a shopping friend.

3. Historical friends. We all have a friend who knew us when . . . maybe way back in Miss Meltzer's second grade, when our family lived in that three-room flat in Brooklyn, when our dad was out of work for seven months, when our brother Allie got in that fight where they had to call the police, when our sister married the endodontist from

Yonkers and when, the morning after we lost our virginity, she was the first, the only, friend we told.

15   The years have gone by and we've gone separate ways and we've little in common now, but we're still an intimate part of each other's past. And so whenever we go to Detroit we always go to visit this friend of our girlhood. Who knows how we looked before our teeth were straightened. Who knows how we talked before our voice got un-Brooklyned. Who knows what we ate before we learned about artichokes. And who, by her presence, puts us in touch with an earlier part of ourself, a part of ourself it's important never to lose.

"What this friend means to me and what I mean to her," says Grace, "is having a sister without sibling rivalry. We know the texture of each other's lives. She remembers my grandmother's cabbage soup. I remember the way her uncle played the piano. There's simply no other friend who remembers those things."

4. Crossroads friends. Like historical friends, our crossroads friends are important for *what was*—for the friendship we shared at a crucial, now past, time of life. A time, perhaps, when we roomed in college together; or worked as eager young singles in the Big City together; or went together, as my friend Elizabeth and I did, through pregnancy, birth and that scary first year of new motherhood.

Crossroads friends forge powerful links, links strong enough to endure with not much more contact than once-a-year letters at Christmas. And out of respect for those crossroads years, for those dramas and dreams we once shared, we will always be friends.

5. Cross-generational friends. Historical friends and cross-generational friends seem to maintain a special kind of intimacy—dormant but always ready to be revived—and though we may rarely meet, whenever we do connect, it's personal and intense. Another kind of intimacy exists in the friendships that form across generations in what one woman calls her daughter-mother and her mother-daughter relationships.

20   Evelyn's friend is her mother's age—"but I share so much more than I ever could with my mother"—a woman she talks to of music, of books and of life. "What I get from her is the benefit of her experience. What she gets—and enjoys—from me is a youthful perspective. It's a pleasure for both of us."

I have in my own life a precious friend, a woman of 65 who has lived very hard, who is wise, who listens well; who has been where I am and can help me understand it; and who represents not only an ultimate ideal mother to me but also the person I'd like to be when I grow up.

In our daughter role we tend to do more than our share of self-revelation; in our mother role we tend to receive what's revealed. It's another kind of pleasure—playing wise mother to a questing younger person. It's another very lovely kind of friendship.

6. Part-of-a-couple friends. Some of the women we call our friends we never see alone—we see them as part of a couple at couples' parties. And though we share interests in many things and respect each other's views, we aren't moved to deepen the relationship. Whatever the reason, a lack of time or—and this is more likely—a lack of chemistry, our friendship remains in the context of a group. But the fact that our feeling on seeing each other is always, "I'm *so* glad she's here" and the fact that we spend half the evening talking together says that this too, in its own way, counts as a friendship.

(Other part-of-a-couple friends are the friends that came with the marriage, and some of these are friends we could live without. But sometimes, alas, she married our husband's best friend; and sometimes, alas, she *is* our husband's best friend. And so we find ourself dealing with her, somewhat against our will, in a spirit of what I'll call *reluctant* friendship.)

25 7. Men who are friends. I wanted to write just of women friends, but the women I've talked to won't let me—they say I must mention man-woman friendships too. For these friendships can be just as close and as dear as those that we form with women. Listen to Lucy's description of one such friendship:

"We've found we have things to talk about that are different from what he talks about with my husband and different from what I talk about with his wife. So sometimes we call on the phone or meet for lunch. There are similar intellectual interests—we always pass on to each other the books that we love—but there's also something tender and caring too."

In a couple of crises, Lucy says, "he offered himself for talking and for helping. And when someone died in his family he wanted me there. The sexual, flirty part of our friendship is very small, but *some*—just enough to make it fun and different." She thinks—and I agree—that the sexual part, though small, is always *some*, is always there when a man and a woman are friends.

It's only in the past few years that I've made friends with men, in the sense of a friendship that's *mine*, not just part of two couples. And achieving with them the ease and the trust I've found with women friends has value indeed. Under the dryer at home last week, putting on mascara and rouge, I comfortably sat and talked with a fellow named Peter. Peter, I finally decided, could handle the shock of me minus mascara under the dryer. Because we care for each other. Because we're friends.

8.   There are medium friends, and pretty good friends, and very good friends indeed, and these friendships are defined by their level of intimacy. And what we'll reveal at each of these levels of intimacy is calibrated with care. We might tell a medium friend, for example, that yesterday we had a fight with our husband. And we might tell a pretty good friend that this fight with our husband made us so mad that we slept on the couch. And we might tell a very good friend that the reason we got so mad in that fight that we slept on the couch had something to do with that girl who works in his office. But it's only to our very best friends that we're willing to tell all, to tell what's going on with that girl in his office.

30   The best of friends, I still believe, totally love and support and trust each other, and bare to each other the secrets of their souls, and run—no questions asked—to help each other, and tell harsh truths to each other when they must be told.

But we needn't agree about everything (only 12-year-old girl friends agree about *everything*) to tolerate each other's point of view. To accept without judgment. To give and to take without ever keeping score. And to *be* there, as I am for them and as they are for me, to comfort our sorrows, to celebrate our joys.

Analyzing Rhetorical Choices

1.   How does Viorst delineate her categories of friendship? What appears to be her purpose in this essay?
2.   Are there other modes besides classification at work in this essay? What are they? What purpose might they serve?
3.   What is Viorst's tone in this essay? What effect does it have on the reader? What words or phrases create this particular tone?

Writing About Issues and Contexts

1.   Discuss the differences in friendships between and among men and women based on Viorst's essay. Using her essay as a starting point, discuss these issues in terms of your experience, possibly comparing and contrasting her views with yours.
2.   What does it mean to "calibrate with care" the level of intimacy in friendships and other relationships? Do you find the description applicable to your experience?

*Canadian writer **Margaret Atwood** (1939–   ) has written numerous volumes of poetry, including her first,* Double Persephone *(1961), and novels, including* The Edible Woman *(1967),* Cat's Eye *(1988),* The Robber Bride *(1993), and her most celebrated,* The Handmaid's Tale *(1986). Atwood graduated from the University of Toronto in 1961 and earned her master's degree at Radcliffe College in 1962. Also a critic and teacher, Atwood's work focuses on feminist issues.* The Handmaid's Tale *is a futuristic satire, which, like her other work, features intelligent, strong women. The essay "Pornography" grew, in part, from Atwood's research for her 1981 novel,* Bodily Harm.

Margaret Atwood

Pornography

When I was in Finland a few years ago for an international writers' conference, I had occasion to say a few paragraphs in public on the subject of pornography. The context was a discussion of political repression, and I was suggesting the possibility of a link between the two. The immediate result was that a male journalist took several large bites out of me. Prudery and pornography are two halves of the same coin, said he, and I was clearly a prude. What could you expect from an Anglo-Canadian? Afterward, a couple of pleasant Scandinavian men asked me what I had been so worked up about. All "pornography" means, they said, is graphic depictions of whores, and what was the harm in that?

Not until then did it strike me that the male journalist and I had two entirely different things in mind. By "pornography," he meant naked bodies and sex. I, on the other hand, had recently been doing the research for my novel *Bodily Harm*, and was still in a state of shock from some of the material I had seen, including the Ontario Board of Film Censors' "outtakes." By "pornography," I meant women getting their nipples snipped off with garden shears, having meat hooks stuck into their vaginas, being disemboweled; little girls being raped; men (yes, there are some men) being smashed to a pulp and forcibly sodomized. The cutting edge of pornography, as far as I could see, was no longer simple old copulation, hanging from the chandelier or otherwise: it was death, messy, explicit and highly sadistic. I explained this to the nice Scandinavian men. "Oh, but that's just the

United States," they said. "Everyone knows they're sick." In their country, they said, violent "pornography" of that kind was not permitted on television or in movies; indeed, excessive violence of any kind was not permitted. They had drawn a clear line between erotica, which earlier studies had shown did not incite men to more aggressive and brutal behavior toward women, and violence, which later studies indicated did.

Some time after that I was in Saskatchewan, where, because of the scenes in *Bodily Harm*, I found myself on an open-line radio show answering questions about "pornography." Almost no one who phoned in was in favor of it, but again they weren't talking about the same stuff I was, because they hadn't seen it. Some of them were all set to stamp out bathing suits and negligees, and, if possible, any depictions of the female body whatsoever. God, it was implied, did not approve of female bodies, and sex of any kind, including that practiced by bumblebees, should be shoved back into the dark, where it belonged. I had more than a suspicion that *Lady Chatterley's Lover*, Margaret Laurence's *The Diviners*, and indeed most books by most serious modern authors would have ended up as confetti if left in the hands of these callers.

For me, these two experiences illustrate the two poles of the emotionally heated debate that is now thundering around this issue. They also underline the desirability and even the necessity of defining the terms. "Pornography" is now one of those catchalls, like "Marxism" and "feminism," that have become so broad they can mean almost anything, ranging from certain verses in the Bible, ads for skin lotion and sex texts for children to the contents of Penthouse, Naughty '90s postcards and films with titles containing the word *Nazi* that show vicious scenes of torture and killing. It's easy to say that sensible people can tell the difference. Unfortunately, opinions on what constitutes a sensible person vary.

5   But even sensible people tend to lose their cool when they start talking about this subject. They soon stop talking and start yelling, and the name-calling begins. Those in favor of censorship (which may include groups not noticeably in agreement on other issues, such as some feminists and religious fundamentalists) accuse the others of exploiting women through the use of degrading images, contributing to the corruption of children, and adding to the general climate of violence and threat in which both women and children live in this society; or, though they may not give much of a hoot about actual women and

children, they invoke moral standards and God's supposed aversion to "filth," "smut" and deviated *perversion*, which may mean ankles.

The camp in favor of total "freedom of expression" often comes out howling as loud as the Romans would have if told they could no longer have innocent fun watching the lions eat up Christians. It too may include segments of the population who are not natural bedfellows: those who proclaim their God-given right to freedom, including the freedom to tote guns, drive when drunk, drool over chicken porn and get off on videotapes of women being raped and beaten, may be waving the same anticensorship banner as responsible liberals who fear the return of Mrs. Grundy, or gay groups for whom sexual emancipation involves the concept of "sexual theatre." *Whatever turns you on* is a handy motto, as is *A man's home is his castle* (and if it includes a dungeon with beautiful maidens strung up in chains and bleeding from every pore, that's his business).

Meanwhile, theoreticians theorize and speculators speculate. Is today's pornography yet another indication of the hatred of the body, the deep mind-body split, which is supposed to pervade Western Christian society? Is it a backlash against the women's movement by men who are threatened by uppity female behavior in real life, so like to fantasize about women done up like outsize parcels, being turned into hamburger, kneeling at their feet in slavelike adoration or sucking off guns? Is it a sign of collective impotence, of a generation of men who can't relate to real women at all but have to make do with bits of celluloid and paper? Is the current flood just a result of smart marketing and aggressive promotion by the money men in what has now become a multibillion-dollar industry? If they were selling movies about men getting their testicles stuck full of knitting needles by women with swastikas on their sleeves, would they do as well, or is this penchant somehow peculiarly male? If so, why? Is pornography a power trip rather than a sex one? Some say that those ropes, chains, muzzles and other restraining devices are an argument for the immense power female sexuality still wields in the male imagination: you don't put these things on dogs unless you're afraid of them. Others, more literary, wonder about the shift from the 19th-century Magic Women or Femme Fatale image to the lollipop-licker, airhead or turkey-carcass treatment of women in porn today. The proporners don't care much about theory: they merely demand product. The anti-porners don't care about it in the final analysis either: there's dirt on the street, and they want it cleaned up, now.

It seems to me that this conversation, with its *You're-a-prude/You're-a-pervert* dialectic, will never get anywhere as long as we continue to think of this material as just "entertainment." Possibly we're deluded by the packaging, the format: magazine, book, movie, theatrical presentation. We're used to thinking of these things as part of the "entertainment industry," and we're used to thinking of ourselves as free adult people who ought to be able to see any kind of "entertainment" we want to. That was what the First Choice pay-TV debate was all about. After all, it's only entertainment, right? Entertainment means fun, and only a killjoy would be antifun. What's the harm?

This is obviously the central question: *What's the harm?* If there isn't any real harm to any real people, then the antiporners can tsk-tsk and/or throw up as much as they like, but they can't rightfully expect more legal controls or sanctions. However, the no-harm position is far from being proven.

10 (For instance, there's a clear-cut case for banning—as the federal government has proposed—movies, photos and videos that depict children engaging in sex with adults: real children are used to make the movies, and hardly anybody thinks this is ethical. The possibilities for coercion are too great.)

To shift the viewpoint, I'd like to suggest three other models for looking at "pornography"—and here I mean the violent kind.

Those who find the idea of regulating pornographic materials repugnant because they think it's Fascist or Communist or otherwise not in accordance with the principles of an open democratic society should consider that Canada has made it illegal to disseminate material that may lead to hatred toward any group because of race or religion. I suggest that if pornography of the violent kind depicted these acts being done predominantly to Chinese, to blacks, to Catholics, it would be off the market immediately, under the present laws. Why is hate literature illegal? Because whoever made the law thought that such material might incite real people to do real awful things to other real people. The human brain is to a certain extent a computer: garbage in, garbage out. We only hear about the extreme cases (like that of American multimurderer Ted Bundy) in which pornography has contributed to the death and/or mutilation of women and/or men. Although pornography is not the only factor involved in the creation of such deviance, it certainly has upped the ante by suggesting both a variety of techniques and the social acceptability of such actions. Nobody knows yet what effect this stuff is having on the less psychotic.

Studies have shown that a large part of the market for all kinds of porn, soft and hard, is drawn from the 16-to-21-year-old population of young men. Boys used to learn about sex on the street, or (in Italy, according to Fellini movies) from friendly whores, or, in more genteel surroundings, from girls, their parents, or, once upon a time, in school, more or less. Now porn has been added, and sex education in the schools is rapidly being phased out. The buck has been passed, and boys are being taught that all women secretly like to be raped and that real men get high on scooping out women's digestive tracts.

Boys learn their concept of masculinity from other men: is this what most men want them to be learning? If word gets around that rapists are "normal" and even admirable men, will boys feel that in order to be normal, admirable and masculine they will have to be rapists? Human beings are enormously flexible, and how they turn out depends a lot on how they're educated, by the society in which they're immersed as well as by their teachers. In a society that advertises and glorifies rape or even implicitly condones it, more women get raped. It becomes socially acceptable. And at a time when men and the traditional male role have taken a lot of flak and men are confused and casting around for an acceptable way of being male (and, in some cases, not getting much comfort from women on that score), this must be at times a pleasing thought.

15   It would be naïve to think of violent pornography as just harmless entertainment. It's also an educational tool and a powerful propaganda device. What happens when boy educated on porn meets girl brought up on Harlequin romances? The clash of expectations can be heard around the block. She wants him to get down on his knees with a ring, he wants her to get down on all fours with a ring in her nose. Can this marriage be saved?

Pornography has certain things in common with such addictive substances as alcohol and drugs: for some, though by no means for all, it induces chemical changes in the body, which the user finds exciting and pleasurable. It also appears to attract a "hard core" of habitual users and a penumbra of those who use it occasionally but aren't dependent on it in any way. There are also significant numbers of men who aren't much interested in it, not because they're undersexed but because real life is satisfying their needs, which may not require as many appliances as those of users.

For the "hard core," pornography may function as alcohol does for the alcoholic: tolerance develops, and a little is no longer enough.

This may account for the short viewing time and fast turnover in porn theatres. Mary Brown, chairwoman of the Ontario Board of Film Censors, estimates that for every one mainstream movie requesting entrance to Ontario, there is one porno flick. Not only the quantity consumed but the quality of explicitness must escalate, which may account for the growing violence: once the big deal was breasts, then it was genitals, then copulation, then that was no longer enough and the hard users had to have more. The ultimate kick is death, and after that, as the Marquis de Sade so boringly demonstrated, multiple death.

The existence of alcoholism has not led us to ban social drinking. On the other hand, we do have laws about drinking and driving, excessive drunkenness and other abuses of alcohol that may result in injury or death to others.

This leads us back to the key question: what's the harm? Nobody knows, but this society should find out fast, before the saturation point is reached. The Scandinavian studies that showed a connection between depictions of sexual violence and increased impulse toward it on the part of male viewers would be a starting point, but many more questions remain to be raised as well as answered. What, for instance, is the crucial difference between men who are users and men who are not? Does using affect a man's relationship with actual women, and, if so, adversely? Is there a clear line between erotica and violent pornography, or are they on an escalating continuum? Is this a "men versus women" issue, with all men secretly siding with the proporners and all women secretly siding against? (I think not; there *are* lots of men who don't think that running their true love through the Cuisinart is the best way they can think of to spend a Saturday night, and they're just as nauseated by films of someone else doing it as women are.) Is pornography merely an expression of the sexual confusion of this age or an active contributor to it?

20   Nobody wants to go back to the age of official repression, when even piano legs were referred to as "limbs" and had to wear pantaloons to be decent. Neither do we want to end up in George Orwell's *1984*, in which pornography is turned out by the State to keep the proles in a state of torpor, sex itself is considered dirty and the approved practise is only for reproduction. But Rome under the emperors isn't such a good model either.

If all men and women respected each other, if sex were considered joyful and life-enhancing instead of a wallow in germ-filled glop, if everyone were in love all the time, if, in other words, many people's lives were more satisfactory for them than they appear to be now, pornography might just go away on its own. But since this is obviously not happening, we as a society are going to have to make some informed and responsible decisions about how to deal with it.

Analyzing Rhetorical Choices

1. Might there be any particular purpose for Atwood's beginning the essay with a personal story? What effect does this have?
2. What are Atwood's "models" for categorizing pornography? Are they effective? Explain. How do the classifications advance Atwood's argument?

Writing About Issues and Contexts

1. Analyze whether Atwood, in her central argument, seems to value one type of solution over another. Discuss why this might be so.
2. What are the distinctions between acceptable and unacceptable pornography that Atwood describes? Given your reading, observations, and experience, do you agree or disagree? Be sure to back up your points of view.
3. Is Atwood's essay unfair to men? Is the essay realistic? Unduly pessimistic? Read her essay closely to back up your points, and find appropriate evidence—or categories—of your own to either substantiate Atwood or to refute her.

William Zinsser (1922–) was born in New York City and graduated in 1944 from Princeton University. He is particularly well known for his books on writing, including On Writing Well: An Informal Guide to Writing Nonfiction *(in its sixth edition in 1998). He has also worked at the now-defunct New York* Herald Tribune *and was a writer for* Life *magazine and the* New York Times. *Zinsser has also written works on baseball and other aspects of life in the United States. "College Pressures" appeared in 1979 and was written for* Country Journal *magazine. Interestingly, the difficult economic times affecting college students when this essay was published are similar to those affecting college students as this volume goes to press.*

William Zinsser
College Pressures

Dear Carlos: I desperately need a dean's excuse for my chem midterm which will begin in about 1 hour. All I can say is that I totally blew it this week. I've fallen incredibly, inconceivably behind.

Carlos: Help! I'm anxious to hear from you. I'll be in my room and won't leave it until I hear from you. Tomorrow is the last day for. . . .

Carlos: I left town because I started bugging out again. I stayed up all night to finish a take home make-up exam and am typing it to hand in on the 10th. It was due on the 5th. P.S. I'm going to the dentist. Pain is pretty bad.

Carlos: Probably by Friday I'll be able to get back to my studies. Right now I'm going to take a long walk. This whole thing has taken a lot out of me.

5   Carlos: I'm really up the proverbial creek. The problem is I really *bombed* the history final. Since I need that course for my major. . . .

Carlos: Here follows a tale of woe. I went home this weekend, had to help my Mom, & caught a fever so didn't have much time to study. My professor. . . .

Carlos: Aargh! Nothing original but everything's piling up at once. To be brief, my job interview. . . .

Hey Carlos, good news! I've got mononucleosis.

Who are these wretched supplicants, scribbling notes so laden with anxiety, seeking such miracles of postponement and balm? They are men and women who belong to Bradford College, one of the twelve residential colleges at Yale University, and the messages are just a few of the hundreds that they left for their dean, Carlos Hortas—often slipped under his door at 4 A.M.—last year.

10   But students like the ones who wrote those notes can also be found on campuses from coast to coast—especially in New England and at many other private colleges across the country that have high academic standards and highly motivated students. Nobody could doubt that the notes are real. In their urgency and their gallows humor they are authentic voices of a generation that is panicky to succeed.

My own connection with the message writers is that I am master of Bradford College. I live in its Gothic quadrangle and know the students well. (We have 485 of them.) I am privy to their hopes and fears—and also to their stereo music and their piercing cries in the dead of night ("Does anybody *ca-a-are?*"). If they went to Carlos to ask how to get through tomorrow, they come to me to ask how to get through the rest of their lives.

Mainly I try to remind them that the road ahead is a long one and that it will have more unexpected turns than they think. There will be plenty of time to change jobs, change careers, change whole attitudes and approaches. They don't want to hear such liberating news. They want a map—right now—that they can follow unswervingly to career security, financial security, Social Security, and, presumably, a prepaid grave.

What I wish for all students is some release from the clammy grip of the future. I wish them a chance to savor each segment of their education as an experience in itself and not as a grim preparation for the next step. I wish them the right to experiment, to trip and fall, to learn that defeat is as instructive as victory and is not the end of the world.

My wish, of course, is naive. One of the few rights that America does not proclaim is the right to fail. Achievement is the national god, venerated in our media—the million-dollar athlete, the wealthy executive—and glorified in our praise of possessions. In the presence of such a potent state religion, the young are growing up old.

15   I see four kinds of pressure working on college students today: economic pressure, parental pressure, peer pressure, and self-induced pressure. It is easy to look around for villains—to blame the colleges for charging too much money, the professors for assigning too much work, the parents for pushing their children too far, the students for driving themselves too hard. But there are no villains, only victims.

"In the late 1960s," one dean told me, "the typical question that I got from students was 'Why is there so much suffering in the world?' or 'How can I make a contribution?' Today it's 'Do you think it would look better for getting into law school if I did a double major in history and political science, or just majored in one of them?'" Many other deans confirmed this pattern. One said: "They're trying to find an edge—the intangible something that will look better on paper if two students are about equal."

Note the emphasis on looking better. The transcript has become a sacred document, the passport to security. How one appears on paper is more important than how one appears in person. *A* is for Admirable and *B* is for Borderline, even though, in Yale's official system of grading, *A* means "excellent" and *B* means "very good." Today, looking very good is no longer good enough, especially for students who hope to go on to law school or medical school. They know that entrance into the better schools will be an entrance into the better law firms and better medical practices where they will make a lot of money. They also know that the odds are harsh. Yale Law School, for instance, matriculates 170 students from an applicant pool of 3,700; Harvard enrolls 550 from a pool of 7,000.

It's all very well for those of us who write letters of recommendation for our students to stress the qualities of humanity that will make them good lawyers or doctors. And it's nice to think that admission officers are really reading our letters and looking for the extra dimension of commitment or concern. Still, it would be hard for a student not to visualize these officers shuffling so many transcripts studded with *A*s that they regard a *B* as positively shameful.

The pressure is almost as heavy on students who just want to graduate and get a job. Long gone are the days of the "gentleman's C," when students journeyed through college with a certain relaxation, sampling a wide variety of courses—music, art, philosophy, classics, anthropology, poetry, religion—that would send them out as liberally educated men and women. If I were an employer I would rather employ graduates who have this range and curiosity than those who narrowly pursued safe subjects and high grades. I know countless students whose inquiring minds exhilarate me. I like to hear the play of their ideas. I don't know if they're getting *A*s or *C*s, and I don't care. I also like them as people. The country needs them, and they will find satisfying jobs. I tell them to relax. They can't.

20   Nor can I blame them. They live in a brutal economy. Tuition, room, and board at most private colleges now comes to at least

$7,000, not counting books and fees. This might seem to suggest that the colleges are getting rich. But they are equally battered by inflation. Tuition covers only 60 percent of what it costs to educate a student, and ordinarily the remainder comes from what colleges receive in endowments, grants, and gifts. Now the remainder keeps being swallowed by cruel costs—higher every year—of just opening the doors. Heating oil is up. Insurance is up. Postage is up. Health-premium costs are up. Everything is up. Deficits are up. We are witnessing in America the creation of a brotherhood of paupers—colleges, parents, and students, joined by the common bond of debt.

Today it is not unusual for a student, even if he works part time at college and full time during the summer, to accrue $5,000 in loans after four years—loans that he must start to repay within one year after graduation. Exhorted at commencement to go forth into the world, he is already behind as he goes forth. How could he not feel under pressure throughout college to prepare for this day of reckoning? I have used "he" incidentally, only for brevity. Women at Yale are under no less pressure to justify their expensive education to themselves, their parents, and society. In fact, they are probably under more pressure. For although they leave college superbly equipped to bring fresh leadership to traditionally male jobs, society hasn't yet caught up with this fact.

Along with economic pressure goes parental pressure. Inevitably, the two are deeply intertwined.

I see many students taking pre-medical courses with joyless tenacity. They go off to their labs as if they were going to the dentist. It saddens me because I know them in other corners of their life as cheerful people.

"Do you want to go to medical school?" I ask them.

"I guess so," they say, without conviction, or "Not really."

"Then why are you going?"

"Well, my parents want me to be a doctor. They're paying all this money and . . ."

Poor students, poor parents. They are caught in one of the oldest webs of love and duty and guilt. The parents mean well; they are trying to steer their sons and daughters toward a secure future. But the sons and daughters want to major in history or classics or philosophy—subjects with no "practical" value. Where's the payoff on the humanities? It's not easy to persuade such loving parents that the humanities do indeed pay off. The intellectual faculties developed by studying subjects like history and classics—an ability to synthesize and relate, to weigh cause and effect, to see events in perspective—are just the faculties that make creative leaders in business or almost any general field. Still, many fathers would rather put their money on courses that point toward a specific profession—courses that are pre-law, pre-medical, pre-business, or, as I sometimes heard it put, "pre-rich."

But the pressure on students is severe. They are truly torn. One part of them feels obliged to fulfill their parents' expectations; after all, their parents are older and presumably wiser. Another part tells them that the expectations that are right for their parents are not right for them.

30   I know a student who wants to be an artist. She is very obviously an artist and will be a good one—she has already had several modest exhibits. Meanwhile she is growing as a well-rounded person and taking humanistic subjects that will enrich the inner resources out of which her art will grow. But her father is strongly opposed. He thinks that an artist is a "dumb" thing to be. The student vacillates and tries to please everybody. She keeps up with her art somewhat furtively and takes some of the "dumb" courses her father wants her to take—at least they are dumb courses for her. She is a free spirit on a campus of tense students—no small achievement in itself—and she deserves to follow her muse.

Peer pressure and self-induced pressure are also intertwined, and they begin almost at the beginning of freshman year.

"I had a freshman student I'll call Linda," one dean told me, "who came in and said she was under terrible pressure because her roommate, Barbara, was much brighter and studied all the time. I couldn't tell her that Barbara had come in two hours earlier to say the same thing about Linda."

The story is almost funny—except that it's not. It's symptomatic of all the pressures put together. When every student thinks every other student is working harder and doing better, the only solution is to study harder still. I see students going off to the library every night after dinner and coming back when it closes at midnight. I wish they could sometimes forget about their peers and go to a movie. I hear the clacking of typewriters in the hours before dawn. I see the tension in their eyes when exams are approaching and papers are due: *"Will I get everything done?"*

Probably they won't. They will get sick. They will get "blocked." They will sleep. They will oversleep. They will bug out. *Hey Carlos, help!*

35   Part of the problem is that they do more than they are expected to do. A professor will assign five-page papers. Several students will start writing ten-page papers to impress him. Then more students will write ten-page papers, and a few will raise the ante to fifteen. Pity the poor student who is still just doing the assignment.

"Once you have twenty or thirty percent of the student population deliberating overexerting," one dean points out, "it's bad for everybody. When a teacher gets more and more effort from his class, the student who is doing normal work can be perceived as not doing well. The tactic works, psychologically."

Why can't the professor just cut back and not accept longer papers? He can, and he probably will. But by then the term will be half over and the damage done. Grade fever is highly contagious and not easily reversed. Besides, the professor's main concern is with his course. He knows his students only in relation to the course and doesn't know that they are also overexerting in their other courses. Nor is it really his business. He didn't sign up for dealing with the student as a whole person and with all the emotional baggage the student brought along from home. That's what deans, masters, chaplains, and psychiatrists are for.

To some extent this is nothing new: a certain number of professors have always been self-contained islands of scholarship and shyness, more comfortable with books than with people. But the new pauperism has widened the gap still further, for professors who actually like to spend time with students don't have as much time to spend. They also are overexerting. If they are young, they are busy trying to publish in order not to perish, hanging by their fingernails onto a shrinking profession. If they are old and tenured, they are buried under the duties of administering departments—as departmental chairmen or members of committees—that have been thinned out by the budgetary axe.

Ultimately it will be the students' own business to break the circles in which they are trapped. They are too young to be prisoners of their parents' dreams and their classmates' fears. They must be jolted into believing in themselves as unique men and women who have the power to shape their own future.

40   "Violence is being done to the undergraduate experience," says Carlos Hortas. "College should be open-ended: at the end it should open many, many roads. Instead, students are choosing their goal in advance, and their choices narrow as they go along. It's almost as if

they think that the country has been codified in the type of jobs that exist—that they've got to fit into certain slots. Therefore, fit into the best-paying slot.

"They ought to take chances. Not taking chances will lead to a life of colorless mediocrity. They'll be comfortable. But something in the spirit will be missing."

I have painted too drab a portrait of today's students, making them seem a solemn lot. That is only half of their story; if they were so dreary I wouldn't so thoroughly enjoy their company. The other half is that they are easy to like. They are quick to laugh and to offer friendship. They are not introverts. They are usually kind and are more considerate of one another than any student generation I have known.

Nor are they so obsessed with their studies that they avoid sports and extracurricular activities. On the contrary, they juggle their crowded hours to play on a variety of teams, perform with musical and dramatic groups, and write for campus publications. But this in turn is one more cause of anxiety. There are too many choices. Academically, they have 1,300 courses to select from; outside class they have to decide how much spare time they can spare and how to spend it.

This means that they engage in fewer extracurricular pursuits than their predecessors did. If they want to row on the crew and play in the symphony they will eliminate one; in the '60s they would have done both. They also tend to choose activities that are self-limiting. Drama, for instance, is flourishing in all twelve of Yale's residential colleges as it never has before. Students hurl themselves into these productions—as actors, directors, carpenters, and technicians—with a dedication to create the best possible play, knowing that the day will come when the run will end and they can get back to their studies.

45   They also can't afford to be the willing slave of organizations like the *Yale Daily News*. Last spring at the one-hundredth anniversary banquet of that paper—whose past chairmen include such once and future kings as Potter Stewart, Kingman Brewster, and William F. Buckley, Jr.—much was made of the fact that the editorial staff used to be small and totally committed and that "newsies" routinely worked fifty hours a week. In effect they belonged to a club; Newsies is how they defined themselves at Yale. Today's student will write one or two articles a week, when he can, and he defines himself as a student. I've never heard the word Newsie except at the banquet.

If I have described the modern undergraduate primarily as a driven creature who is largely ignoring the blithe spirit inside who keeps trying to come out and play, it's because that's where the crunch is, not only at Yale but throughout American education. It's why I think we should all be worried about the values that are nurturing a generation so fearful of risk and so goal-obsessed at such an early age.

I tell students that there is no one "right" way to get ahead—that each of them is a different person, starting from a different point and bound for a different destination. I tell them that change is a tonic and that all the slots are not codified nor the frontiers closed. One of my ways of telling them is to invite men and women who have achieved success outside the academic world to come and talk informally with my students during the year. They are heads of companies or ad agencies, editors of magazines, politicians, public officials, television magnates, labor leaders, business executives, Broadway producers, artists, writers, economists, photographers, scientists, historians—a mixed bag of achievers.

I ask them to say a few words about how they got started. The students assume that they started in their present profession and knew all along that it was what they wanted to do. Luckily for me, most of them got into their field by a circuitous route, to their surprise, after many detours. The students are startled. They can hardly conceive of a career that was not pre-planned. They can hardly imagine allowing the hand of God or chance to nudge them down some unforeseen trail.

Analyzing Rhetorical Choices

1. Analyze Zinsser's ways of classifying and creating his categories and their effectiveness. How are the categories, as Zinsser says, "intertwined"? How does that help or hinder the essay?

2. Zinsser's writing often reveals his journalistic background. Where, in particular, is this evident? Read the essay closely, looking at paragraphs, word choices, and the like. What function, for instance, do his one-sentence paragraphs serve?

3. Analyze the effectiveness of the introduction, the "notes to Carlos." What is your response as you read these notes?

4. What assumptions does Zinsser seem to make about his audience? On what type of readership would this essay have the greatest impact?

Writing About Issues and Contexts

1. Is there too much pressure on today's college students? Compare your views with Zinsser's.
2. Zinsser outlines the various forms of anxiety that plague students. Why does Zinsser suggest that women might feel greater pressure than do men?
3. Zinsser's essay was published in 1979. To what extent is it still relevant today? Explain your point of view.
4. "[Students] ought to take chances. Not taking chances will lead to a life of colorless mediocrity." How do you respond to this statement?

A winner of numerous awards, including the prestigious National Endowment for the Arts Fiction Award, **Gloria Anzaldúa** *(1942–   ) is described as a "Chicana dyke-feminist, tejana patlache poet, writer, and cultural theorist" from the Rio Grande Valley of south Texas. She has taught at a variety of colleges and universities. Her best-known book,* Borderlands/La Frontera: The New Mestiza *(1987), from which this piece is taken, combines several genres—poetry (in both Spanish and English), memoir, and nonfiction prose. Anzaldúa has also written a children's book,* Friends from the Other Side/Amigos del otro lado *(1993). In addition, she has edited* Making Face, Making Soul/Haciendo Caras: Creative and Critical Perspectives by Women of Color *(1990), which features essays on identity, feminism, racism, and multiple literacies.*

Gloria Anzaldúa

How to Tame a Wild Tongue

"We're going to have to control your tongue," the dentist says, pulling out all the metal from my mouth. Silver bits plop and tinkle into the basin. My mouth is a motherlode.

The dentist is cleaning out my roots. I get a whiff of the stench when I gasp. "I can't cap that tooth yet, you're still draining," he says.

"We're going to have to do something about your tongue," I hear the anger rising in his voice. My tongue keeps pushing out the wads of cotton, pushing back the drills, the long thin needles. "I've never seen anything as strong or as stubborn," he says. And I think, how do you tame a wild tongue, train it to be quiet, how do you bridle and saddle it? How do you make it lie down?

> Who is to say that robbing a people of its language is less violent than war?
>
> —*Ray Gwyn Smith*

I remember being caught speaking Spanish at recess—that was good for three licks on the knuckles with a sharp ruler. I remember being sent to the corner of the classroom for "talking back" to the Anglo teacher when all I was trying to do was tell her how to pronounce my name. "If you want to be American, speak 'American.' If you don't like it, go back to Mexico where you belong."

5   "I want you to speak English. *Pa' hallar buen trabajo tienes que vaber hablar el inglés bien. Qué vale toda tu educación si todavía hablas inglés con un* 'accent,'"[1] my mother would say, mortified that I spoke English like a Mexican. At Pan American University, I, and all Chicano students were required to take two speech classes. Their purpose: to get rid of our accents.

Attacks on one's form of expression with the intent to censor are a violation of the First Amendment. *El Anglo con cara de inocente nos arrancó la lengua.*[2] Wild tongues can't be tamed, they can only be cut out.

Overcoming the Tradition of Silence

> *Abogadas, escupimos el oscuro.*
> *Peleando con nuestra propia sombra*
> *el silencio nos sepulta.*[3]

En boca cerrada no entran moscas. "Flies don't enter a closed mouth" is a saying I kept hearing when I was a child. *Ser habladora* was to be a gossip and a liar, to talk too much. *Muchachitas bien criadas,*[4] well-bred girls don't answer back. *Es una falta de respeto*[5] to talk back to one's mother or father. I remember one of the sins I'd recite to the priest in the confession box the few times I went to confession: talking back to my mother, *hablar pa' 'tras, repelar.*[6] *Hocicona, repelona, chismosa,*[7] having a big mouth, questioning, carrying tales are all signs of being *mal criada.*[8] In my culture they are all words that are derogatory if applied to women—I've never heard them applied to men.

---

[1]"In order to find a good job, you have to know how to speak English well. Of what value is your education if you still speak English with an 'accent.'"
[2]The Anglo with an innocent face tore our tongue out.
[3]"Choked, we spit out darkness / Fighting with our own shadow / The silence buries us."
[4]Well-bred little girls.
[5]It is not respectful.
[6]To talk back, to argue.
[7]Chatterer, arguer, gossip.
[8]Ill-bred girl.

The first time I heard two women, a Puerto Rican and a Cuban, say the word *"nosotras,"*[9] I was shocked. I had not known the word existed. Chicanas use *nosotros*[10] whether we're male or female. We are robbed of our female being by the masculine plural. Language is a male discourse.

> And our tongues have become
> dry   the wilderness has
> dried out our tongues   and
> we have forgotten speech.
>
> —*Irena Klepfisz*

Even our own people, other Spanish speakers *nos quieren poner candados en la boca.*[11] They would hold us back with their bag of *reglas de academia.*[12]

> *Oyé como ladra: el lenguaje de la frontera*[13]
>
> *Quien tiene boca se equivoca.*[14]
>
> —*Mexican saying*

10   *"Pocho,* cultural traitor, you're speaking the oppressor's language by speaking English, you're ruining the Spanish language," I have been accused by various Latinos and Latinas. Chicano Spanish is considered by the purist and by most Latinos deficient, a mutilation of Spanish.

But Chicano Spanish is a border tongue which developed naturally. Change, *evolución, enriquecimiento de palabras nuevas por invención o adopción* have created variants of Chicano Spanish, *un nuevo lenguaje. Un lenguaje que corresponde a un modo de vivir.*[15] Chicano Spanish is not incorrect, it is a living language.

For a people who are neither Spanish nor live in a country in which Spanish is the first language; for a people who live in a country in which English is the reigning tongue but who are not Anglo; for a people who cannot entirely identify with either standard (formal,

---

[9]We (fem.).

[10]We (masc.).

[11]Want to put locks on our mouths.

[12]Academic rules.

[13]Hear how the dog barks: language of the frontier.

[14]"He who has a mouth makes mistakes."

[15]Evolution, enrichment of new words through invention and adoption . . . a new language. A language that corresponds to a way of life.

Castillian) Spanish nor standard English, what recourse is left to them but to create their own language? A language which they can connect their identity to, one capable of communicating the realities and values true to themselves—a language with terms that are neither *español ni inglés*,[16] but both. We speak a patois, a forked tongue, a variation of two languages.

Chicano Spanish sprang out of the Chicanos' need to identify ourselves as a distinct people. We needed a language with which we could communicate with ourselves, a secret language. For some of us, language is a homeland closer than the Southwest—for many Chicanos today live in the Midwest and the East. And because we are a complex, heterogeneous people, we speak many languages. Some of the languages we speak are:

1. Standard English
2. Working class and slang English
3. Standard Spanish
4. Standard Mexican Spanish
5. North Mexican Spanish dialect
6. Chicano Spanish (Texas, New Mexico, Arizona and California have regional variations)
7. Tex-Mex
8. *Pachuco* (called *caló*)

My "home" tongues are the languages I speak with my sister and brothers, with my friends. They are the last five listed, with 6 and 7 being closest to my heart. From school, the media and job situations, I've picked up standard and working class English. From Mamagrande Locha and from reading Spanish and Mexican literature, I've picked up Standard Spanish and Standard Mexican Spanish. From *los recién llegados*, Mexican immigrants, and *braceros*,[17] I learned the North Mexican dialect. With Mexicans I'll try to speak either Standard Mexican Spanish or the North Mexican dialect. From my parents and Chicanos living in the Valley, I picked up Chicano Texas Spanish, and I speak it with my mom, younger brother (who married a Mexican and who rarely mixes Spanish with English), aunts and older relatives.

---

[16]Spanish nor English.
[17]*Los recién llegados:* recent arrivals; *braceros:* laborers.

15   With Chicanas from *Nuevo México* or *Arizona* I will speak Chicano Spanish a little, but often they don't understand what I'm saying. With most California Chicanas I speak entirely in English (unless I forget). When I first moved to San Francisco, I'd rattle off something in Spanish, unintentionally embarrassing them. Often it is only with another Chicana *tejana*[18] that I can talk freely.

Words distorted by English are known as anglicisms or *pochismos*. The *pocho* is an anglicized Mexican or American of Mexican origin who speaks Spanish with an accent characteristic of North Americans and who distorts and reconstructs the language according to the influence of English. Tex-Mex, or Spanglish, comes most naturally to me. I may switch back and forth from English to Spanish in the same sentence or in the same word. With my sister and my brother Nune and with Chicano *tejano* contemporaries I speak in Tex-Mex.

From kids and people my own age I picked up *Pachuco*. *Pachuco* (the language of the zoot suiters) is a language of rebellion, both against Standard Spanish and Standard English. It is a secret language. Adults of the culture and outsiders cannot understand it. It is made up of slang words from both English and Spanish. *Ruca* means girl or woman, *vato* means guy or dude, *chale* means no, *simón* means yes, *churro* is sure, talk is *periquiar*, *pigionear* means petting, *que gacho* means how nerdy, *ponte águila* means watch out, death is called *la pelona*. Through lack of practice and not having others who can speak it, I've lost most of the *Pachuco* tongue.

Chicano Spanish

Chicanos, after 250 years of Spanish/Anglo colonization have developed significant differences in the Spanish we speak. We collapse two adjacent vowels into a single syllable and sometimes shift the stress in certain words such as *maíz/maiz, cohete/cuete*.[19] We leave out certain consonants when they appear between vowels: *lado/lao, mojado/mojao*.[20] Chicanos from South Texas pronounce *f* as *j* as in *jue* (*fue*).[21] Chicanos use "archaisms," words that are no longer in the

---

[18]Texan (fem.).
[19]*Maiz:* corn; *cohete:* rocket.
[20]*Lado:* side; *mojado:* wet.
[21]Went.

Spanish language, words that have been evolved out. We say *semos,
truje, haiga, ansina,* and *naiden.*[22] We retain the "archaic" *j,* as in
jalar,[23] that derives from an earlier *h,* (the French *halar* or the
Germanic *halon* which was lost to standard Spanish in the 16th century), but which is still found in several regional dialects such as the
one spoken in South Texas. (Due to geography, Chicanos from the
Valley of South Texas were cut off linguistically from other Spanish
speakers. We tend to use words that the Spaniards brought over from
Medieval Spain. The majority of the Spanish colonizers in Mexico and
the Southwest came from Extremadura—Hernán Cortés was one of
them—and Andalucía. Andalucians pronounce *ll* like a *y,* and their *d*'s
tend to be absorbed by adjacent vowels: *tirado*[24] becomes *tirao.* They
brought *el lenguaje popular, dialectos y regionalismos.*)[25]

Chicanos and other Spanish speakers also shift *ll* to *y* and *z* to *s.* We
leave out initial syllables, saying *tar* for *estar, toy* for *estoy, hora* for
ahora (*cubanos* and *puertorriqueños*[26] also leave out initial letters of
some words). We also leave out the final syllable such as *pa* for *para.*
The intervocalic *y,* the *ll* as in *tortilla, ella, botella,* gets replaced by
tortia or *tortiya, ea, botea.* We add an additional syllable at the beginning of certain words: *atocar* for *tocar, agastar* for *gastar.* Sometimes
we'll say *lavaste las vacijas,* other times *lavates* (substituting the *ates*
verb endings for the *aste*).[27]

20   We use anglicisms, words borrowed from English: *bola* from ball,
carpeta from carpet, *máchina de lavar* (instead of *lavadora*) from
washing machine. Tex-Mex argot, created by adding a Spanish sound
at the beginning or end of an English word such as *cookiar* for cook,
watchar for watch, *parkiar* for park, and *rapiar* for rape, is the result
of the pressures on Spanish speakers to adapt to English.

We don't use the word *vosotros/as* or its accompanying verb form.
We don't say *claro* (to mean yes), *imagínate,* or *me emociona,*[28] unless

---

[22]*Semos:* we are; *truje:* brought; *haiga:* there is; *ansina:* that (adj.); *naiden:*
nobody.
[23]To pull.
[24]Thrown.
[25]Popular language, dialects, and regionalism.
[26]*Estar:* to be; *estoy:* I am; *ahora:* now; *cubanos, puertorriqueños:* Cubans,
Puerto Ricans.
[27]*Para:* for; *trotilla, ella, botella:* tortilla, she, bottle; *tocar:* to touch; *gastar:*
to spend; *lavaste las vacijas:* did you wash the dishes (*vacijas* is Texan).
[28]*Vosotros/as:* you (plural, formal); *imagínate:* imagine; *me emociona:* I am
moved.

we picked up Spanish from Latinas, out of a book, or in a classroom. Other Spanish-speaking groups are going through the same, or similar, development in their Spanish.

Linguistic Terrorism

Deslenguadas. Somos los del español deficiente.[29] We are your lingistic nightmare, your linguistic aberration, your linguistic *mestisaje*, the subject of your *burla*. Because we speak with tongues of fire we are culturally crucified. Racially, culturally and linguistically *somos huérfanos*[30]—we speak an orphan tongue.

Chicanas who grew up speaking Chicano Spanish have internalized the belief that we speak poor Spanish. It is illegitimate, a bastard language. And because we internalize how our language has been used against us by the dominant culture, we use our language differences against each other.

Chicana feminists often skirt around each other with suspicion and hesitation. For the longest time I couldn't figure it out. Then it dawned on me. To be close to another Chicana is like looking into the mirror. We are afraid of what we'll see there. *Pena.* Shame. Low estimation of self. In childhood we are told that our language is wrong. Repeated attacks on our native tongue diminish our sense of self. The attacks continue throughout our lives.

Chicanas feel uncomfortable talking in Spanish to Latinas, afraid of their censure. Their language was not outlawed in their countries. They had a whole lifetime of being immersed in their native tongue; generations, centuries in which Spanish was a first language, taught in school, heard on radio and TV, and read in the newspaper.

25   If a person, Chicana or Latina, has a low estimation of my native tongue, she also has a low estimation of me. Often with *mexicanas y latinas* we'll speak English as a neutral language. Even among Chicanas we tend to speak English at parties or conferences. Yet, at the same time, we're afraid the other will think we're *agringadas*[31] because we don't speak Chicano Spanish. We oppress each other trying to out-Chicano each other, vying to be the "real" Chicanas, to speak like Chicanos. There is no one Chicano language just as there is no one Chicano experience. A monolingual Chicana whose first language is

---

[29]Loose tongues. We are those with deficient Spanish.
[30]*Mestisaje:* hybrid; *burla:* joke; *somos huérfanos:* we are orphans.
[31]Foreigners, like "gringos."

English or Spanish is just as much a Chicana as one who speaks several variants of Spanish. A Chicana from Michigan or Chicago or Detroit is just as much a Chicana as one from the southwest. Chicano Spanish is as diverse linguistically as it is regionally.

By the end of this century, Spanish speakers will comprise the biggest minority group in the U.S., a country where students in high schools and colleges are encouraged to take French classes because French is considered more "cultured." But for a language to remain alive it must be used. By the end of this century English, and not Spanish, will be the mother tongue of most Chicanos and Latinos.

So, if you want to really hurt me, talk badly about my language. Ethnic identity is twin skin to linguistic identity—I am my language. Until I can take pride in my language, I cannot take pride in myself. Until I can accept as legitimate Chicano Texas Spanish, Tex-Mex and all the other languages I speak, I cannot accept the legitimacy of myself. Until I am free to write bilingually and to switch codes without having always to translate, while I still have to speak English or Spanish when I would rather speak Spanglish, and as long as I have to accommodate the English speakers rather than having them accommodate me, my tongue will be illegitimate.

I will no longer be made to feel ashamed of existing. I will have my voice: Indian, Spanish, white. I will have my serpent's tongue—my woman's voice, my sexual voice, my poet's voice. I will overcome the tradition of silence.

> My fingers
> move sly against your palm
> Like women everywhere, we speak in code . . .
> —*Melanie Kaye/Kantrowitz*

Analyzing Rhetorical Choices

1. Reread the opening of the essay. What are the various metaphorical ways in which Anzaldúa speaks of her tongue, or specifically, of her "wild tongue"? What purpose does this serve in the essay?
2. Why would this essay be included in a section on classification or perhaps, as implied by the title, process? What are the various categories that Anzaldúa sets up, not only to explain the various languages spoken by her people but also to argue her essay?
3. What is Anzaldúa's rhetorical purpose in using Spanish that she translates—and, more importantly, sometimes does not translate?

Should editors provide translations of the Spanish words? What are the consequences of these choices?

4. Who are the audiences for this essay? What is the basis for your analysis and conclusion?

Writing About Issues and Contexts

1. In your view, what are the tensions that exist between the desire to be a "distinct people," as Anzaldúa claims for Chicanos and Chicanas, and the larger pull toward various types of assimilation? Consider whether there are some immigrant groups for whom distinction is often a stigma. If you believe such groups exist, why do you think they feel stigmatized?

2. As Anzaldúa has written, "So if you want to really hurt me, talk badly about my language." Why does speaking against someone's use of language create such a negative effect? How would you characterize the relationship between language and personal identity?

Born in England in 1963, **Malcolm Gladwell** *(1963–   ) grew up in Canada. In 1984, he graduated with a degree in history from the University of Toronto. Gladwell was a reporter for the* Washington Post, *first as a science writer and then as New York City bureau chief, serving the newspaper from 1987 to 1996. Gladwell's most recent book is* The Tipping Point: How Little Things Can Make a Big Difference *(2000)—in his words, "a book about change" and "the social epidemics that surround us." Since leaving the* Post, *he has been a staff writer for* The New Yorker, *in which this article was published in 2001.*

Malcolm Gladwell

The Trouble with Fries

In 1954, a man named Ray Kroc, who made his living selling the five-spindle Multimixer milkshake machine, began hearing about a hamburger stand in San Bernardino, California. This particular restaurant, he was told, had no fewer than eight of his machines in operation, meaning that it could make forty shakes simultaneously. Kroc was astounded. He flew from Chicago to Los Angeles, and drove to San Bernardino, sixty miles away, where he found a small octagonal building on a corner lot. He sat in his car and watched as the workers showed up for the morning shift. They were in starched white shirts and paper hats, and moved with a purposeful discipline. As lunchtime approached, customers began streaming into the parking lot, lining up for bags of hamburgers. Kroc approached a strawberry blonde in a yellow convertible.

"How often do you come here?" he asked.

"Anytime I am in the neighborhood," she replied, and, Kroc would say later, "it was not her sex appeal but the obvious relish with which she devoured the hamburger that made my pulse begin to hammer with excitement." He came back the next morning, and this time set up inside the kitchen, watching the griddle man, the food preparers, and, above all, the French-fry operation, because it was the French fries that truly captured his imagination. They were made from top-quality oblong Idaho russets, eight ounces apiece, deep-fried to a golden brown, and salted with a shaker that, as he put it, kept going like a Salvation Army girl's tambourine. They were crispy on the outside and buttery soft on the inside, and that day Kroc had a vision of a chain of restaurants, just like the one in San Bernardino, selling golden fries from one end of the country to the other. He asked the two brothers who owned the hamburger stand if he could buy their franchise rights. They said yes. Their names were Mac and Dick McDonald.

Ray Kroc was the great visionary of American fast food, the one who brought the lessons of the manufacturing world to the restaurant business. Before the fifties, it was impossible, in most American towns, to buy fries of consistent quality. Ray Kroc was the man who changed that. "The french fry," he once wrote, "would become almost sacrosanct for me, its preparation a ritual to be followed religiously." A potato that has too great a percentage of water—and potatoes, even the standard Idaho russet burbank, vary widely in their water content—will come out soggy at the end of the frying process. It was Kroc, back in the fifties, who sent out field men, armed with hydrometers, to make sure that all his suppliers were producing potatoes in the optimal solids range of twenty to twenty-three per cent. Freshly harvested potatoes, furthermore, are rich in sugars, and if you slice them up and deep-fry them the sugars will caramelize and brown the outside of the fry long before the inside is cooked. To make a crisp French fry, a potato has to be stored at a warm temperature for several weeks in order to convert those sugars to starch. Here Kroc led the way as well, mastering the art of "curing" potatoes by storing them under a giant fan in the basement of his first restaurant, outside Chicago.

5   Perhaps his most enduring achievement, though, was the so-called potato computer—developed for McDonald's by a former electrical engineer for Motorola named Louis Martino—which precisely calibrated the optimal cooking time for a batch of fries. (The key: when a batch of cold raw potatoes is dumped into a vat of cooking oil, the temperature of the fat will drop and then slowly rise. Once the oil has risen three degrees, the fries are ready.) Previously, making high-quality French fries had been an art. The potato computer, the hydrometer, and the curing bins made it a science. By the time Kroc was finished, he had figured out how to turn potatoes into an inexpensive snack that would always be hot, salty, flavorful, and crisp, no matter where or when you bought it.

This was the first fast-food revolution—the mass production of food that had reliable mass appeal. But today, as the McDonald's franchise approaches its fiftieth anniversary, it is clear that fast food needs a second revolution. As many Americans now die every year from obesity-related illnesses—heart disease and complications of diabetes—

as from smoking, and the fast-food toll grows heavier every year. In the fine new book "Fast Food Nation," the journalist Eric Schlosser writes of McDonald's and Burger King in the tone usually reserved for chemical companies, sweatshops, and arms dealers, and, as shocking as that seems at first, it is perfectly appropriate. Ray Kroc's French fries are killing us. Can fast food be fixed?

Fast-food French fries are made from a baking potato like an Idaho russet, or any other variety that is mealy, or starchy, rather than waxy. The potatoes are harvested, cured, washed, peeled, sliced, and then blanched—cooked enough so that the insides have a fluffy texture but not so much that the fry gets soft and breaks. Blanching is followed by drying, and drying by a thirty-second deep fry, to give the potatoes a crisp shell. Then the fries are frozen until the moment of service, when they are deep-fried again, this time for somewhere around three minutes. Depending on the fast-food chain involved, there are other steps interspersed in this process. McDonald's fries, for example, are briefly dipped in a sugar solution, which gives them their golden-brown color; Burger King fries are dipped in a starch batter, which is what gives those fries their distinctive hard shell and audible crunch. But the result is similar. The potato that is first harvested in the field is roughly eighty per cent water. The process of creating a French fry consists, essentially, of removing as much of that water as possible—through blanching, drying, and deep-frying—and replacing it with fat.

Elisabeth Rozin, in her book "The Primal Cheeseburger," points out that the idea of enriching carbohydrates with fat is nothing new. It's a standard part of the cuisine of almost every culture. Bread is buttered; macaroni comes with cheese; dumplings are fried; potatoes are scalloped, baked with milk and cheese, cooked in the dripping of roasting meat, mixed with mayonnaise in a salad, or pan-fried in butterfat as latkes. But, as Rozin argues, deep-frying is in many ways the ideal method of adding fat to carbohydrates. If you put butter on a mashed potato, for instance, the result is texturally unexciting: it simply creates a mush. Pan-frying results in uneven browning and crispness. But when a potato is deep-fried the heat of the oil turns the water inside the potato into steam, which causes the hard granules of starch inside the potato to swell and soften: that's why the inside of the fry is fluffy and light. At the same time, the outward migration of the steam limits the amount of oil that seeps into the interior, preventing the fry from getting greasy and concentrating the oil on the surface, where it turns the outer layer of the potato brown and crisp. "What we have with the french fry," Rozin writes, "is a near perfect enactment of the enriching of a starch food with oil or fat."

This is the trouble with the French fry. The fact that it is cooked in fat makes it unhealthy. But the contrast that deep-frying creates between its interior and its exterior—between the golden shell and the pillowy whiteness beneath—is what makes it so irresistible. The average American now eats a staggering thirty pounds of French fries a year, up from four pounds when Ray Kroc was first figuring out how to mass-produce a crisp fry. Meanwhile, fries themselves have become less healthful. Ray Kroc, in the early days of McDonald's, was a fan of a hot-dog stand on the North Side of Chicago called Sam's, which used what was then called the Chicago method of cooking fries. Sam's cooked its fries in animal fat, and Kroc followed suit, prescribing for his franchises a specially formulated beef tallow called Formula 47 (in reference to the forty-seven-cent McDonald's "All-American meal" of the era: fifteen-cent hamburger, twelve-cent fries, twenty-cent shake). Among aficionados, there is general agreement that those early McDonald's fries were the finest mass-market fries ever made: the beef tallow gave them an unsurpassed rich, buttery taste. But in 1990, in the face of public concern about the health risks of cholesterol in animal-based cooking oil, McDonald's and the other major fast-food houses switched to vegetable oil. That wasn't an improvement, however. In the course of making vegetable oil suitable for deep frying, it is subjected to a chemical process called hydrogenation, which creates a new substance called a trans unsaturated fat. In the hierarchy of fats, polyunsaturated fats—the kind found in regular vegetable oils—are the good kind; they lower your cholesterol. Saturated fats are the bad kind. But trans fats are worse: they wreak havoc with the body's ability to regulate cholesterol. According to a recent study involving some eighty thousand women, for every five-per-cent increase in the amount of saturated fats that a woman consumes, her risk of heart disease increases by seventeen per cent. But only a two-per-cent increase in trans fats will increase her heart-disease risk by ninety-three per cent. Walter Willett, an epidemiologist at Harvard—who helped design the study—estimates that the consumption of trans fats in the United States probably causes about thirty thousand premature deaths a year.

10   McDonald's and the other fast-food houses aren't the only purveyors of trans fats, of course; trans fats are in crackers and potato chips and cookies and any number of other processed foods. Still, a lot of us get a great deal of our trans fats from French fries, and to read the medical evidence on trans fats is to wonder at the odd selectivity of the

outrage that consumers and the legal profession direct at corporate behavior. McDonald's and Burger King and Wendy's have switched to a
product, without disclosing its risks, that may cost human lives. What
is the difference between this and the kind of thing over which consumers sue companies every day?

The French-fry problem ought to have a simple solution: cook
fries in oil that isn't so dangerous. Oils that are rich in monounsatu-
rated fats, like canola oil, aren't nearly as bad for you as saturated
fats, and are generally stable enough for deep-frying. It's also possible
to "fix" animal fats so that they aren' t so problematic. For example,
K. C. Hayes, a nutritionist at Brandeis University, has helped develop
an oil called Appetize. It's largely beef tallow, which gives it a big taste
advantage over vegetable shortening, and makes it stable enough for
deep-frying. But it has been processed to remove the cholesterol, and
has been blended with pure corn oil, in a combination that Hayes says
removes much of the heart-disease risk.

Perhaps the most elegant solution would be for McDonald's and
the other chains to cook their fries in something like Olestra, a fat substitute developed by Procter & Gamble. Ordinary fats are built out of a
molecular structure known as a triglyceride: it's a microscopic tree,
with a trunk made of glycerol and three branches made of fatty acids.
Our bodies can't absorb triglycerides, so in the digestive process each
of the branches is broken off by enzymes and absorbed separately. In
the production of Olestra, the glycerol trunk of a fat is replaced with a
sugar, which has room for not three but eight fatty acids. And our enzymes are unable to break down a fat tree with eight branches—so the
Olestra molecule can't be absorbed by the body at all. "Olestra" is as
much a process as a compound: you can create an "Olestra" version of
any given fat. Potato chips, for instance, tend to be fried in cottonseed
oil, because of its distinctively clean taste. Frito-Lay's no-fat Wow!
chips are made with an Olestra version of cottonseed oil, which be-
haves just like regular cottonseed oil except that it's never digested. A
regular serving of potato chips has a hundred and fifty calories, ninety
of which are fat calories from the cooking oil. A serving of Wow! chips
has seventy-five calories and no fat. If Procter & Gamble were to seek
F.D.A. approval for the use of Olestra in commercial deep-frying
(which it has not yet done), it could make an Olestra version of the old
McDonald's Formula 47, which would deliver every nuance of the old
buttery, meaty tallow at a fraction of the calories.

Olestra, it must be said, does have some drawbacks—in particular, a reputation for what is delicately called "gastrointestinal distress." The F.D.A. has required all Olestra products to carry a somewhat daunting label saying that they may cause "cramping and loose stools." Not surprisingly, sales have been disappointing, and Olestra has never won the full acceptance of the nutrition community. Most of this concern, however, appears to be overstated. Procter & Gamble has done randomized, double-blind studies—one of which involved more than three thousand people over six weeks—and found that people eating typical amounts of Olestra-based chips don't have significantly more gastrointestinal problems than people eating normal chips. Diarrhea is such a common problem in America—nearly a third of adults have at least one episode each month—that even F.D.A. regulators now appear to be convinced that in many of the complaints they received Olestra was unfairly blamed for a problem that was probably caused by something else. The agency has promised Procter & Gamble that the warning label will be reviewed.

Perhaps the best way to put the Olestra controversy into perspective is to compare it to fibre. Fibre is vegetable matter that goes right through you: it's not absorbed by the gastrointestinal tract. Nutritionists tell us to eat it because it helps us lose weight and it lowers cholesterol—even though if you eat too many baked beans or too many bowls of oat bran you will suffer the consequences. Do we put warning labels on boxes of oat bran? No, because the benefits of fibre clearly outweigh its drawbacks. Research has suggested that Olestra, like fibre, helps people lose weight and lowers cholesterol; too much Olestra, like too much fibre, may cause problems. (Actually, too much Olestra may not be as troublesome as too much bran. According to Procter & Gamble, eating a large amount of Olestra—forty grams—causes no more problems than eating a small bowl—twenty grams—of wheat bran.) If we had Olestra fries, then, they shouldn't be eaten for breakfast, lunch, and dinner. In fact, fast-food houses probably shouldn't use hundred-per-cent Olestra; they should cook their fries in a blend, using the Olestra to displace the most dangerous trans and saturated fats. But these are minor details. The point is that it is entirely possible, right now, to make a delicious French fry that does not carry with it a death sentence. A French fry can be much more than a delivery vehicle for fat.

15   Is it really that simple, though? Consider the cautionary tale of the efforts of a group of food scientists at Auburn University, in Alabama,

more than a decade ago to come up with a better hamburger. The Auburn team wanted to create a leaner beef that tasted as good as regular ground beef. They couldn't just remove the fat, because that would leave the meat dry and mealy. They wanted to replace the fat. "If you look at ground beef, it contains moisture, fat, and protein," says Dale Huffman, one of the scientists who spearheaded the Auburn project. "Protein is relatively constant in all beef, at about twenty per cent. The traditional McDonald's ground beef is around twenty per cent fat. The remainder is water. So you have an inverse ratio of water and fat. If you reduce fat, you need to increase water." The goal of the Auburn scientists was to cut about two-thirds of the fat from normal ground beef, which meant that they needed to find something to add to the beef that would hold an equivalent amount of water—and continue to retain that water even as the beef was being grilled. Their choice? Seaweed, or, more precisely, carrageenan. "It's been in use for centuries," Huffman explains. "It's the stuff that keeps the suspension in chocolate milk—otherwise the chocolate would settle at the bottom. It has tremendous water-holding ability. There's a loose bond between the carrageenan and the moisture." They also selected some basic flavor enhancers, designed to make up for the lost fat "taste." The result was a beef patty that was roughly three-quarters water, twenty per cent protein, five per cent or so fat, and a quarter of a per cent seaweed. They called it AU Lean.

It didn't take the Auburn scientists long to realize that they had created something special. They installed a test kitchen in their laboratory, got hold of a McDonald's grill, and began doing blind taste comparisons of AU Lean burgers and traditional twenty-per-cent-fat burgers. Time after time, the AU Lean burgers won. Next, they took their invention into the field. They recruited a hundred families and supplied them with three kinds of ground beef for home cooking over consecutive three-week intervals—regular "market" ground beef with twenty per cent fat, ground beef with five percent fat, and AU Lean. The families were asked to rate the different kinds of beef, without knowing which was which. Again, the AU Lean won hands down—trumping the other two on "likability," "tenderness," "flavorfulness," and "juiciness."

What the Auburn team showed was that, even though people love the taste and feel of fat—and naturally gravitate toward high-fat food—they can be fooled into thinking that there is a lot of fat in something when there isn't. Adam Drewnowski, a nutritionist at the University of Washington, has found a similar effect with cookies. He did blind taste tests of normal and reduced-calorie brownies, biscotti, and chocolate-chip, oatmeal, and peanut-butter cookies. If you cut the sugar content of any of those cookies by twenty-five per cent, he found, people like the cookies much less. But if you cut the fat by twenty-five per cent they barely notice. "People are very finely attuned to how much sugar there is in a liquid or a solid," Drewnowski says. "For fat, there's no sensory break point. Fat comes in so many guises and so many textures it is very difficult to perceive how much is there." This doesn't mean we are oblivious of fat levels, of course. Huffman says that when his group tried to lower the fat in AU Lean below five per cent, people didn't like it anymore. But, within the relatively broad range of between five and twenty-five per cent, you can add water and some flavoring and most people can't tell the difference.

What's more, people appear to be more sensitive to the volume of food they consume than to its calorie content. Barbara Rolls, a nutritionist at Penn State, has demonstrated this principle with satiety studies. She feeds one group of people a high-volume snack and another group a low-volume snack. Even though the two snacks have the same calorie count, she finds that people who eat the high-volume snack feel more satisfied. "People tend to eat a constant weight or volume of food in a given day, not a constant portion of calories," she says. Eating AU Lean, in short, isn't going to leave you with a craving for more calories; you'll feel just as full.

For anyone looking to improve the quality of fast food, all this is heartening news. It means that you should be able to put low-fat cheese and low-fat mayonnaise in a Big Mac without anyone's complaining. It also means that there's no particular reason to use twenty-per-cent-fat ground beef in a fast-food burger. In 1990, using just this argument, the Auburn team suggested to McDonald's that it make a Big Mac out of AU Lean. Shortly thereafter, McDonald's came out with the McLean Deluxe. Other fast-food houses scrambled to follow suit. Nutritionists were delighted. And fast food appeared on the verge of a revolution.

20   Only, it wasn't. The McLean was a flop, and four years later it was off the market. What happened? Part of the problem appears to have been that McDonald's rushed the burger to market before many of the production kinks had been worked out. More important, though, was the psychological handicap the burger faced. People liked AU Lean in blind taste tests because they didn't know it was AU Lean; they were fooled into thinking it was regular ground beef. But nobody was fooled when it came to the McLean Deluxe. It was sold as the healthy choice—and who goes to McDonald's for health food?

Leann Birch, a developmental psychologist at Penn State, has looked at the impact of these sorts of expectations on children. In one experiment, she took a large group of kids and fed them a big lunch. Then she turned them loose in a room with lots of junk food. "What we see is that some kids eat almost nothing," she says. "But other kids really chow down, and one of the things that predicts how much they eat is the extent to which parents have restricted their access to high-fat, high-sugar food in the past: the more the kids have been restricted, the more they eat." Birch explains the results two ways. First, restricting food makes kids think not in terms of their own hunger but in terms of the presence and absence of food. As she puts it, "The kid is essentially saying, 'If the food's here I better get it while I can, whether or not I'm hungry.' We see these five-year-old kids eating as much as four hundred calories." Birch's second finding, though, is more important. Because the children on restricted diets had been told that junk food was bad for them, they clearly thought that it had to taste good. When it comes to junk food, we seem to follow an implicit script that powerfully biases the way we feel about food. We like fries not in spite of the fact that they're unhealthy but because of it.

That is sobering news for those interested in improving the American diet. For years, the nutrition movement in this country has made transparency one of its principal goals: it has assumed that the best way to help people improve their diets is to tell them precisely what's in their food, to label certain foods good and certain foods bad. But transparency can backfire, because sometimes nothing is more deadly for our taste buds than the knowledge that what we are eating is good for us. McDonald's should never have called its new offering the McLean Deluxe, in other words. They should have called it the Burger Supreme or the Monster Burger, and then buried the news about reduced calories and fat in the tiniest type on the remotest corner of their Web site. And if we were to cook fries in some high-tech, healthful cooking oil—whether Olestrized beef tallow or something else with a minimum of trans and saturated fats—the worst thing we could do would be to market them as healthy fries. They will not taste nearly as good if we do. They have to be marketed as better fries, as Classic Fries, as fries that bring back the rich tallowy taste of the original McDonald's.

What, after all, was Ray Kroc's biggest triumph? A case could be made for the field men with their hydrometers, or the potato-curing techniques, or the potato computer, which turned the making of French fries from an art into a science. But we should not forget

Ronald McDonald, the clown who made the McDonald's name irresistible to legions of small children. Kroc understood that taste comprises not merely the food on our plate but also the associations and assumptions and prejudices we bring to the table—that half the battle in making kids happy with their meal was calling what they were eating a Happy Meal. The marketing of healthful fast food will require the same degree of subtlety and sophistication. The nutrition movement keeps looking for a crusader—someone who will bring about better public education and tougher government regulations. But we need much more than that. We need another Ray Kroc.

Analyzing Rhetorical Choices

1. Gladwell's essay fits subtly into the classification mode. How does it do so? What subcategories appear in this essay? Analyze the essay carefully: How does classification enable Gladwell to make his argument?
2. What is Gladwell's tone in the essay, and how does his tone vary? What particular phrases or words help to set the tone?
3. For what purpose does Gladwell use scientific and social-scientific evidence in the essay? Is it effective?

Writing About Issues and Contexts

1. In a country that has seen a number of corporate scandals marking the beginning of the 21st century, what are the ethical issues that this article raises either directly or by implication?
2. Comment on Gladwell's assertion that "We like fries not in spite of the fact that they're unhealthy but because of it." Why do some people find unhealthful foods appealing?
3. Do you agree or disagree with Gladwell's statement, "We need another Ray Kroc"? Why does Gladwell say this?

Randall E. Majors wrote and published widely in a variety of areas, having also coauthored a study guide for college students entitled Will This Be On the Test? *He taught at California State University, Hayward, and was active in gay and lesbian movements. "America's Emerging Gay Culture" was written for* Intercultural Communication, *a volume of essays edited by Larry Samovar and Richard Porter and published in 1991. Majors died of AIDS in 1995.*

Randall E. Majors

America's Emerging Gay Culture

A gay culture, unique in the history of homosexuality, is emerging in America. Gay people from all walks of life are forging new self-identity concepts, discovering new political and social power, and building a revolutionary new life style. As more people "come out," identify themselves as gay, and join with others to work and live as openly gay people, a stronger culture takes shape with each passing year.

There have always been homosexual men and women, but never before has there emerged the notion of a distinct "culture" based on being gay. A useful way to analyze this emerging gay culture is to observe the communication elements by which gay people construct their life styles and social institutions. Lesbians and gay men, hereafter considered together as gay people, are creating a new community in the midst of the American melting pot. They are building social organizations, exercising political power, and solidifying a unique sense of identity—often under repressive and sometimes dangerous conditions. The following essay is an analysis of four major communication elements of the American gay culture: the gay neighborhood, gay social groups, gay symbols, and gay meeting behavior. These communication behaviors will demonstrate the vibrancy and joy that a new culture offers the American vision of individual freedom and opportunity.

The Gay Neighborhood

Most cultural groups find the need to mark out a home turf. American social history has many examples of ethnic and social groups who create their own special communities, whether by withdrawing from the larger culture or by forming specialized groups within it. The utopian communities of the Amish or Shakers are examples of the first, and ghetto neighborhoods in large urban areas are examples of the latter.

This need to create a group territory fulfills several purposes for gay people. First, a gay person's sense of identity is reinforced if there is a special place that is somehow imbued with "gayness." When a neighborhood becomes the home of many gay people, the ground is created for a feeling of belonging and sharing with others. Signs of gayness, whether overt symbols like rainbow flags or more subtle cues such as merely the presence of other gay people on the street, create the feeling that a certain territory is special to the group and hospitable to the group's unique values.

5   How do you know when a neighborhood is gay? As with any generality, the rule of thumb is that "enough gay people in a neighborhood and it becomes a gay neighborhood." Rarely do gay people want to paint the streetlamps lavender, but the presence of many more subtle factors gives a gay character to an area. The most subtle cues are the presence of gay people as they take up residence in a district. Word spreads in the group that a certain area is starting to look attractive and open to gay members. There is often a move to "gentrify" older, more affordable sections of a city and build a new neighborhood out of the leftovers from the rush to the suburbs. Gay businesses, those operated by or catering to gay people, often develop once enough clientele is in the area. Social groups and services emerge that are oriented toward the members of the neighborhood. Eventually, the label of "gay neighborhood" is placed on an area, and the transformation is complete. The Castro area in San Francisco, Greenwich Village in New York, New Town in Chicago, the Westheimer district in Houston, and West Hollywood or Silver Lake in Los Angeles are examples of the many emergent gay neighborhoods in cities across America.

A second need fulfilled by the gay neighborhood is the creation of a meeting ground. People can recognize and meet each other more easily when a higher density of like population is established. It is not easy to grow up gay in America; gay people often feel "different" because of their sexual orientations. The surrounding heterosexual culture often tries to imprint on everyone sexual behaviors and expectations that do not suit gay natures. Because of this pressure, gay people often feel isolated and alienated, and the need for a meeting ground is very important. Merely knowing that there is a specific place where other gay people live and work and play does much to anchor the psychological aspect of gayness in a tangible, physical reality. A gay person's sense of identity is reinforced by knowing that there is a home base, or a safe place where others of a similar persuasion are nearby.

Gay neighborhoods reinforce individual identity by focusing activities and events for members of the group. Celebrations of group unity and pride, demonstrations of group creativity and accomplishment, and services to individual members' needs are more easily developed when they are centralized. Gay neighborhoods are host to all the outward elements of a community—parades, demonstrations, car washes, basketball games, petition signing, street fairs, and garage sales.

A critical purpose for gay neighborhoods is that of physical and psychological safety. Subcultural groups usually experience some degree of persecution and oppression from the larger surrounding culture. For gay people, physical safety is a very real concern—incidences of homophobic assaults or harassment are common in most American cities. By centralizing gay activities, some safeguards can be mounted, as large numbers of gay people living in proximity create a deterrence to violence. This may be informal awareness of the need to take extra precautions and to be on the alert to help other gay people in distress or in the form of actual street patrols or social groups, such as Community United Against Violence in San Francisco. A sense of psychological safety follows from these physical measures. Group consciousness raising on neighborhood safety and training in safety practices create a sense of group cohesion. The security inspired by the group thus creates a psychic comfort that offsets the paranoia that can be engendered by alienation and individual isolation.

Another significant result of gay neighborhoods is the political reality of "clout." In the context of American grassroots democracy, a predominantly gay population in an area can lead to political power. The concerns of gay people are taken more seriously by politicians and elected officials representing an area where voters can be registered and mustered into service during elections. In many areas, openly gay politicians represent gay constituencies directly and voice their concerns in ever-widening forums. The impact of this kind of democracy-in-action is felt on other institutions as well: police departments, social welfare agencies, schools, churches, and businesses. When a group centralizes its energy, members can bring pressure to bear on other cultural institutions, asking for and demanding attention to the unique needs of that group. Since American culture has a strong tradition of cultural diversity, gay neighborhoods are effective agents in the larger cultural acceptance of gay people. The gay rights movement, which attempts to secure housing, employment, and legal protection for gay people, finds its greatest support in the sense of community created by gay neighborhoods.

Gay Social Groups

10   On a smaller level than the neighborhood, specialized groups fulfill the social needs of gay people. The need for affiliation—to make friends, to share recreation, to find life partners, or merely to while away the time—is a strong drive in any group of people. Many gay people suffer from an isolation caused by rejection by other people or by their own fear of being discovered as belonging to an unpopular group. This homophobia leads to difficulty in identifying and meeting other gay people who can help create a sense of dignity and caring. This is particularly true for gay teenagers who have limited opportunities to meet other gay people. Gay social groups serve the important function of helping gay people locate each other so that this affiliation need can be met.

The development of gay social groups depends to a large degree on the number of gay people in an area and the perceived risk factor. In smaller towns and cities, there are often no meeting places, which exacerbates the problem of isolation. In some small towns a single business may be the only publicly known meeting place for gay people within hundreds of miles. In larger cities, however, an elaborate array of bars, clubs, social groups, churches, service agencies, entertainment groups, stores, restaurants, and the like add to the substance of a gay culture.

The gay bar is often the first public gay experience for a gay person, and it serves as a central focus for many people. Beyond the personal need of meeting potential relationship partners, the gay bar also serves the functions of entertainment and social activity. Bars offer a wide range of attractions suited to gay people: movies, holiday celebrations, dancing, costume parties, live entertainment, free meals, boutiques, and meeting places for social groups. Uniquely gay forms of entertainment, such as drag shows and disco dancing, were common in gay bars before spreading into the general culture. Bars often become a very central part of a community's social life by sponsoring athletic teams, charities, community services, and other events as well as serving as meeting places.

The centrality of the bar in gay culture has several drawbacks, however. Young gay people are denied entrance because of age restrictions, and there may be few other social outlets for them. A high rate of alcoholism among urban gay males is prominent. With the spread of Acquired Immune Deficiency Syndrome (AIDS), the use of bars for meeting sexual partners has declined dramatically as gay people turn to developing more permanent relationships.

Affiliation needs remain strong despite these dangers, however, and alternative social institutions arise that meet these needs. In large urban areas, where gay culture is more widely-developed, social groups include athletic organizations that sponsor teams and tournaments; leisure activity clubs in such areas as country-and-western dance, music, yoga, bridge, hiking, and recreation; religious groups such as Dignity (Roman Catholic), Integrity (Episcopal), and the Metropolitan Community Church (MCC); volunteer agencies such as information and crisis hotlines and charitable organizations; and professional and political groups such as the Golden Gate Business Association of San Francisco or the national lobby group, the Gay Rights Task Force. A directory of groups and services is usually published in urban gay newspapers, and their activities are reported on and promoted actively. Taken together, these groups compose a culture that supports and nourishes a gay person's life.

Gay Symbols

15   Gay culture is replete with symbols. These artifacts spring up and constantly evolve as gayness moves from an individual, personal experience into a more complex public phenomenon. All groups express their ideas and values in symbols, and the gay culture, in spite of its relatively brief history, has been quite creative in symbol making.

The most visible category of symbols is in the semantics of gay establishment names. Gay bars, bookstores, restaurants, and social groups want to be recognized and patronized by gay people, but they do not want to incur hostility from the general public. This was particularly true in the past when the threat of social consequences was greater. In earlier days, gay bars, the only major form of gay establishment, went by code words such as "blue" or "other"—the Blue Parrot, the Blue Goose, the Other Bar, and Another Place.

Since the liberalization of culture after the 1960s, semantics have blossomed in gay place names. The general trend is still to identify the place as gay, either through affiliation (Our Place or His 'N' Hers), humor (the White Swallow or Uncle Charley's), high drama (the Elephant Walk or Backstreet), or sexual suggestion (Ripples, Cheeks, or Rocks). Lesbians and gay men differ in this aspect of their cultures.

Lesbian place names often rely upon a more personal or classical referent (Amanda's Place or the Artemis Cafe), while hypermasculine referents are commonly used for gay male meeting places (the Ramrod, Ambush, Manhandlers, the Mine Shaft, the Stud, or Boots). Gay restaurants and nonpornographic bookstores usually reflect more subdued names, drawing upon cleverness or historical associations: Dos Hermanos, Women and Children First, Diana's, the Oscar Wilde Memorial Bookstore, and Walt Whitman Bookstore. More commonly, gay establishments employ general naming trends of location, ownership, or identification of product or service similar to their heterosexual counterparts. The increasing tendency of business to target and cater to gay markets strengthens the growth and diversity of gay culture.

A second set of gay symbols are those that serve as member-recognition factors. In past ages such nonverbal cues were so popular as to become mythical: the arched eyebrow of Regency England, the green carnation of Oscar Wilde's day, and the "green shirt on Thursday" signal of mid-century America. A large repertoire of identifying characteristics has arisen in recent years that serves the functions of recognizing other gay people and focusing on particular interests. In the more sexually promiscuous period of the 1970s, popular identifying symbols were a ring of keys worn on the belt, either left or right depending upon sexual passivity or aggressiveness, and the use of colored handkerchiefs in a rear pocket coded to desired types of sexual activity. Political sentiments are commonly expressed through buttons, such as the "No on 64" campaign against the LaRouche initiative in California in 1986. The pink triangle as a political symbol recalls the persecution and annihilation of gay people in Nazi Germany. The lambda symbol, an ancient Greek referent, conjures up classical images of gay freedom of expression. Stud earrings for men are gay symbols in some places, though such adornment has evolved and is widely used for the expression of general countercultural attitudes. The rainbow and the unicorn, mythical symbols associated with supernatural potency, also are common signals of gay enchantment, fairy magic, and spiritual uniqueness to the more "cosmic" elements of the gay community.

Another set of gay symbols to be aware of are the images of gay people as portrayed in television, film, literature, and advertising. The general heterosexual culture controls these media forms to a large extent, and the representations of gay people in those media take on a straight set of expectations and assumptions. The results are stereotypes that often oversimplify gay people and their values and do not discriminate the subtleties of human variety in gay culture. Since these stereotypes are generally unattractive, they are often the target of protests by gay people. Various authors have addressed the problem of heterosexual bias in the areas of film and literature. As American culture gradually becomes more accepting of and tolerant toward gay people, these media representations become more realistic and sympathetic, but progress in this area is slow.

20   One hopeful development in the creation of positive gay role models has been the rise of an active gay market for literature. Most large cities have bookstores that stock literature supportive of gay culture. A more positive image for gay people is created through gay characters, heroes, and stories that deal with the important issues of family, relationship, and social responsibility. This market is constantly threatened by harsh economic realities, however, and gay literature is not as well developed as it might be.

Advertising probably has done the most to popularize and integrate gay symbols into American culture. Since money making is the goal of advertising, the use of gay symbols has advanced more rapidly in ad media than in the arts. Widely quoted research suggests that gay people, particularly men, have large, disposable incomes, so they become popular target markets for various products: tobacco, body-care products, clothing, alcohol, entertainment, and consumer goods. Typical gay-directed advertising in these product areas includes appeals based upon male bonding, such as are common in tobacco and alcohol sales ads, which are attractive to both straight and gay men since they stimulate the bonding need that is a part of both cultures.

Within gay culture, advertising has made dramatic advances in the past ten years, due to the rise of gay-related businesses and products. Gay advertising appears most obviously in media specifically directed at gay markets, such as gay magazines and newspapers, and in gay neighborhoods. Gay products and services are publicized with many of the same means as are their straight counterparts. Homoerotic art is widely used in clothing and body-care product ads. The male and female body are displayed for their physical and sexual appeal. This eroticizing of the body may be directed at either women or men as a desirable sexual object, and perhaps strikes at a subconscious homosexual potential in all people. Prominent elements of gay advertising are its use of sexuality and the central appeal of hypermasculinization. With the rise of sexual appeals in general advertising through double entendre, sexual punning, subliminal seduction, and erotic art work, it may be that gay advertising is only following suit in its emphasis on sexual appeals. Hugely muscled bodies and perfected masculine beauty adorn most advertising for gay products and services. Ads for greeting cards, billboards for travel service, bars, hotels, restaurants, and clothing stores tingle to the images of Hot 'N' Hunky Hamburgers, Hard On Leather, and the Brothel Hotel or its crosstown rival, the Anxious Arms. Some gay writers criticize this use of advertising as stereotyping and distorting gay people, and certainly, misconceptions about the diversity in gay culture are more common than understanding. Gay people are far more average and normal than the images that appear in public media would suggest.

Gay Meeting Behavior

The final element of communication in the gay culture discussed here is the vast set of behaviors by which gay people recognize and meet one another. In more sexually active days before the concern for AIDS, this type of behavior was commonly called cruising. Currently, promiscuous sexual behavior is far less common than it once was, and cruising has evolved into a more standard meeting behavior that helps identify potential relationship partners.

Gay people meet each other in various contexts: in public situations, in the workplace, in gay meeting places, and in the social contexts of friends and acquaintances. Within each context, a different set of behaviors is employed by which gay people recognize someone else as gay and determine the potential for establishing a relationship. These behaviors include such nonverbal signaling as frequency and length of interaction, posture, proximity, eye contact, eye movement and facial gestures, touch, affect displays, and paralinguistic signals. The constraints of each situation and the personal styles of the communicators create great differences in the effectiveness and ease with which these behaviors are displayed.

25   Cruising serves several purposes besides the recognition of other gay people. Most importantly, cruising is an expression of joy and pride in being gay. Through cruising, gay people communicate their openness and willingness to interact. Being gay is often compared to belonging to a universal—though invisible—fraternity or sorority. Gay people are generally friendly and open to meeting other gay people in social contexts because of the common experience of rejection and isolation they have had growing up. Cruising is the means by which gay people communicate their gayness and bridge the gap between stranger and newfound friend.

Cruising has become an integral part of gay culture because it is such a commonplace behavior. Without this interpersonal skill—and newcomers to gay life often complain of the lack of comfort or ease they have with cruising—a gay person can be at a distinct disadvantage in finding an easy path into the mainstream of gay culture. While cruising has a distinctly sexual overtone, the sexual subtext is often a symbolic charade. Often the goals of cruising are no more than friendship, companionship, or conversation. In this sense, cruising becomes more an art form or an entertainment. Much as the "art of conversation" was the convention of a more genteel cultural age, gay cruising is the commonly accepted vehicle of gay social interaction. The sexual element, however, transmitted by double meaning, clever punning, or blatant nonverbal signals, remains a part of cruising in even the most innocent of circumstances.

In earlier generations, a common stereotype of gay men focused on the use of exaggerated, dramatic, and effeminate body language—the "limp wrist" image. Also included in this negative image of gay people was cross-gender dressing, known as "drag," and a specialized, sexually suggestive argot called "camp." Some gay people assumed these social roles because that was the picture of "what it meant to be gay," but by and large these role behaviors were overthrown by the gay liberation of the 1970s. Gay people became much less locked into these restraining stereotypes and developed a much broader means of social expression. Currently, no stereotypic behavior would adequately describe gay communication style—it is far too diverse and integrated into mainstream American culture. Cruising evolved from these earlier forms of communication, but as a quintessential gay behavior, cruising has replaced the bitchy camp of an earlier generation of gay people.

The unique factor in gay cruising, and the one that distinguishes it from heterosexual cruising, is the level of practice and refinement the process receives. All cultural groups have means of introduction and meeting, recognition, assessment, and negotiation of a new relationship. In gay culture, however, the "courtship ritual" or friendship ritual of cruising is elaborately refined in its many variants and contexts. While straight people may use similar techniques in relationship formation and development, gay people are uniquely self-conscious in the centrality of these signals to the perpetuation of their culture. There is a sense of adventure and discovery in being "sexual outlaws," and cruising is the shared message of commitment to the gay life style.

Conclusion

These four communication elements of gay culture comprise only a small part of what might be called gay culture. Other elements have been more widely discussed elsewhere: literature, the gay press, religion, politics, art, theater, and relationships. Gay culture is a marvelous and dynamic phenomenon, driven and buffeted by the energies of intense feeling and creative effort. Centuries of cultural repression that condemned gay people to disgrace and persecution have been turned upside down in a brief period of history. The results of this turbulence have the potential for either renaissance or cataclysm. The internalized fear and hatred of repression is balanced by the incredible joy and idealism of liberation. Through the celebration of its unique life style, gay culture promises to make a great contribution to the history of sexuality and to the rights of the individual. Whether it will fulfill this promise or succumb to the pressures that any creative attempt must face remains to be seen.

Analyzing Rhetorical Choices

1. Through what modes in addition to classification does Majors make his argument? Are his arguments effective? Explain and defend your position.
2. Majors analyzes, in his words, "four major elements of the American gay culture." What are the elements of each category? What are the subcategories that explicate these main categories? Are they effective? In what ways are they expansive, and in what ways are they limiting?
3. Analyze Majors's discussion about the role of symbols in gay culture. How do these symbols also classify—and perhaps create additional stereotypes as a result?

Writing About Issues and Contexts

1. Majors focuses on the notion of "gay culture" as if to suggest that there is just one. Might it be possible for there to be more than one "gay culture," indeed several "gay cultures"? How so?
2. According to the article, what function is served by the development of a gay neighborhood? What gives a gay neighborhood its distinctiveness?
3. Comment on the ways that Majors discusses images of gays in popular media. Has this evolved or changed since 1991 when this article was published? Compare and/or contrast these differences, based on your own observations and reading.

When Time *magazine started its new "Computers" section in 1982,* **Philip Elmer-DeWitt** *became its first writer. In fact, he was among the few on the staff who was experienced with technology. As the senior editor for technology, Elmer-DeWitt has written on various issues, including genetics, cloning, and pornography in cyberspace. The following essay appeared in* Time *in 1994.*

Philip Elmer-DeWitt

Bards of the Internet

One of the unintended side effects of the invention of the telephone was that writing went out of style. Oh, sure, there were still full-time scribblers—journalists, academics, professional wordsmiths. And the great centers of commerce still found it useful to keep on hand people who could draft a memo, a brief, a press release or a contract. But given a choice between picking up a pen or a phone, most folks took the easy route and gave their fingers—and sometimes their mind—a rest.

Which makes what's happening on the computer networks all the more startling. Every night, when they should be watching television, millions of computer users sit down at their keyboards; dial into CompuServe, Prodigy, America Online or the Internet; and start typing—E-mail, bulletin-board postings, chat messages, rants, diatribes, even short stories and poems. Just when the media of McLuhan were supposed to render obsolete the medium of Shakespeare, the online world is experiencing the greatest boom in letter writing since the eighteenth century.

"It is my overwhelming belief that e-mail and computer conferencing is teaching an entire generation about the flexibility and utility of prose," writes Jon Carroll, a columnist at the San Francisco *Chronicle.* Patrick Nielsen Hayden, an editor at Tor Books, compares electronic bulletin boards with the "scribblers' compacts" of the late eighteenth and early nineteenth centuries, in which members passed letters from hand to hand, adding a little more at each turn. David Sewell, an associate editor at the University of Arizona, likens netwriting to the literary scene Mark Twain discovered in San Francisco in the 1860s, "when people were reinventing journalism by grafting it onto the tall-tale folk tradition." Others hark back to Tom Paine and the Revolutionary War pamphleteers, or even to the Elizabethan era, when, thanks to Gutenberg, a generation of English writers became intoxicated with language.

But such comparisons invite a question: If online writing today represents some sort of renaissance, why is so much of it so awful? For it can be very bad indeed: sloppy, meandering, puerile, ungrammatical, poorly spelled, badly structured and at times virtually content free. "HEY!!!!" reads an all-too-typical message on the Internet, "I THINK METALLICA IZ REEL KOOL DOOD!!!!"

5   One reason, of course, is that E-mail is not like ordinary writing. "You need to think of this as 'written speech,'" says Gerard Van der Leun, literary agent based in Westport, Connecticut, who has emerged as one of the preeminent stylists on the Net. "These things are little more considered than coffeehouse talk and a lot less considered than a letter. They're not to have and hold; they're to fire and forget." Many online postings are composed "live" with the clock ticking, using rudimentary word processors on computer systems that charge by the minute and in some cases will shut down without warning when an hour runs out.

That is not to say that with more time every writer on the Internet would produce sparkling copy. Much of the fiction and poetry is second-rate or worse, which is not surprising given that the barriers to entry are so low. "In the real world," says Mary Anne Mohanraj, a Chicago-based poet, "it takes a hell of a lot of work to get published, which naturally weeds out a lot of the garbage. On the Net, just a few keystrokes sends your writing out to thousands of readers."

But even among the reams of bad poetry, gems are to be found. Mike Godwin, a Washington-based lawyer who posts under the pen name "mnemonic," tells the story of Joe Green, a technical writer at Cray Research who turned a moribund discussion group called rec.arts.poems into a real poetry workshop by mercilessly critiquing the pieces he found there. "Some people got angry and said if he was such a god of poetry, why didn't he publish his poems to the group?" recalls Godwin. "He did, and blew them all away." Green's *Well Met in Minnesota*, a mock-epic account of a face-to-face meeting with a fellow network scribbler, is now revered on the Internet as a classic. It begins, "The truth is that when I met Mart I was dressed as the *Canterbury Tales*. Rather difficult to do as you might suspect, but I wanted to make a certain impression."

The more prosaic technical and political discussion groups, meanwhile, have become so crowded with writers crying for attention that a

Darwinian survival principle has started to prevail. "It's so competitive that you have to work on your style if you want to make any impact," says Jorn Barger, a software designer in Chicago. Good writing on the Net tends to be clear, vigorous, witty and above all brief. "The medium favors the terse," says Crawford Kilian, a writing teacher at Capilano College in Vancouver, British Columbia. "Short paragraphs, bulleted lists, and one-liners are the units of thought here."

Some of the most successful netwriting is produced in computer conferences, where writers compose in a kind of collaborative heat, knocking ideas against one another until they spark. Perhaps the best examples of this are found on the WELL, a Sausalito, California, bulletin board favored by journalists. The caliber of discussion is often so high that several publications—including the *New York Times* and the *Wall Street Journal*—have printed excerpts from the WELL.

10   Curiously, what works on the computer networks isn't necessarily what works on paper. Netwriters freely lace their prose with strange acronyms and "smileys," the little faces constructed with punctuation marks and intended to convey the winks, grins and grimaces of ordinary conversations. Somehow it all flows together quite smoothly. On the other hand, polished prose copied onto bulletin boards from books and magazines often seems long-winded and phony. Unless they adjust to the new medium, professional writers can come across as self-important blowhards in debates with more nimble networkers. Says Brock Meeks, a Washington-based reporter who covers the online culture for *Communications Daily*: "There are a bunch of hacker kids out there who can string a sentence together better than their blue-blooded peers simply because they log on all the time and write, write, write."

There is something inherently democratizing—perhaps even revolutionary—about the technology. Not only has it enfranchised thousands of would-be writers who otherwise might never have taken up the craft, but it has also thrown together classes of people who hadn't had much direct contact before: students, scientists, senior citizens, computer geeks, grassroots (and often blue-collar) bulletin-board enthusiasts and most recently the working press.

"It's easy to make this stuff look foolish and trivial," says Tor Books Nielsen Hayden. "After all, a lot of everyone's daily life is foolish and trivial. I mean, really, smileys? Housewives in Des Moines who log on as VIXEN?"

But it would be a mistake to dismiss the computer-message boards or to underestimate the effect a lifetime of dashing off E-mail will have on a generation of young writers. The computer networks may not be Brook Farm or the Globe Theatre, but they do represent, for millions of people, a living breathing life of letters. One suspects that the Bard himself, confronted with the Internet, might have dived right in and never logged off.

Analyzing Rhetorical Choices

1. Why would Elmer-DeWitt begin an essay about the Internet with the telephone? What larger lesson might he be trying to communicate?
2. How does Elmer-DeWitt classify various writers on the Internet? For what purpose? How are they—or are they not—"bards"?
3. What seems to be Elmer-DeWitt's own attitude about writing on the Internet? Examine his argument closely (is it inductive or deductive?), using examples to demonstrate your points.

Writing About Issues and Contexts

1. What is the downside of the Chicago-based poet's well-intended statement that "On the Net, just a few keystrokes sends your writing out to thousands of readers"? How could Internet writing be both "awful" and yet have created a "renaissance"?
2. Do you agree with Elmer-DeWitt's statement that "There is something inherently democratizing—perhaps even revolutionary—about the technology"? Is the author somewhat dismissive of some who partake in this "democracy"?
3. How has the Internet changed since this essay was published in 1994? What differences does the essay's age make—or not—to some of the arguments Elmer-DeWitt makes?
4. In your view, how have e-mail and other forms of cyberwriting—the abbreviations of instant messaging, for instance—changed the ways people write? Have these hindered, helped, or merely provided different occasions for writing? Use the essay and evidence of your own to demonstrate your points.

Strategies for Writers: Classification

1. Classifying is a natural function of the human mind. However, to classify can also be to stereotype. When is classification positive? When is it negative? How have you classified the people in this class? In this book? In this discussion group? How do you classify your professors? Compare notes with your classmates. Are their classifications as accurate as yours? Are there equally valid—or invalid—ways to type the same thing?

2. Review the essays and questions in this chapter. Which essays seem to use classification most effectively and appropriately? Which, in your view, are less effective? Why?

3. How do you classify the varieties of your educational experience? Compare your categories to those of Zinsser in "College Pressures."

4. Classification is also tied to comparison and contrast and definition. How could Margaret Atwood's essay on pornography also be considered definition? Are there other ways to classify pornography that might depart from Atwood's essay?

5. Judith Viorst created eight categories to describe friends. Each category is distinguished by the level of intimacy of the friendship, and each is clearly defined. The essay focuses on categories and their definitions, with the comparison and contrast of each category implied rather than made explicit. Find a key term or concept and provide various degrees of categories and definitions, developing an essay that echoes the strategies used by Viorst.

Research and Writing Assignments

1. As noted elsewhere in this chapter, to classify is also to define. Philip Elmer-DeWitt classifies, in complex ways, the various permutations of cyberspace and, by implication, the various types of literacy attributed to (or needed by) those participating in Internet-based activities. In addition to the importance of access to computers and the Internet for such participation, extend Elmer-DeWitt's classifications to delineate the types of literacies necessary for full participation in technologically based activities. What assumptions do you make in deciding on the names of your classifications?

2. Gloria Anzaldúa's "How to Tame a Wild Tongue" and Malcolm Gladwell's "The Trouble with Fries" use more subtle forms of classification than do other entries in this chapter. For instance, Anzaldúa's essay might well fit into the chapter on process, if we look merely at its title. Gladwell's "classifying" comes about more by implication than by direct naming of categories. Compare these two apparently disparate essays, looking closely at their differing ways of classifying and the other rhetorical strategies the authors use to make their arguments. How does each author cross the boundaries of rhetorical strategies to create an effective essay?

3. Using your discretion as you research this complex and controversial topic, find appropriate counterarguments to Margaret Atwood's way of classifying and defining pornography. Find at least two other writers who address the topic, looking closely at the assumptions behind their ways of classifying pornography and the ways in which they make their arguments, comparing and contrasting them with Atwood's. How do these writers use classification as effective rhetorical strategies, if they do? Which are more effective? Less effective? Why?

4. How do Judith Viorst and Randall E. Majors classify with different goals and for different purposes? Viorst delineates the varieties within the category of friendship; Majors adds new categories to the ways of classifying gays and lesbians. Using research on techniques other writers might use to "classify" similar topics, examine how Viorst and Majors either expand or limit the effectiveness of classification as a rhetorical strategy for argument.

5. Using William Zinsser's "College Pressures" as your starting point, examine the Web sites of several universities, making sure to include several highly competitive and less competitive institutions. How do these schools classify themselves, their students, and the presumed experience of students on campus? What do these institutions reveal about themselves, directly and perhaps inadvertently? Additionally, how do these relate to the "college pressures" revealed by Zinsser?

7
Process Analysis

Writers choose to compose in the mode of process analysis because they are motivated by the need to explain. Often they possess a specific expertise and are asked to teach what they know to a more general public. Some process essays provide explanations that focus on *how*—how to dress for success, how to get from one place to another, how to hit a curve ball, how to assemble a doll collection. Such essays are, in essence, narratives of instruction intended to teach a lesson or a set of skills. Sometimes, however, writers choose to describe a more subtle process, namely the process of discovery. Writers with this purpose in mind are concerned less about offering a set of directions and more about describing a process of personal development that leads to increased insight and understanding—about specific life goals, social circumstances, the nature of experience.

Both kinds of essays fit in the process analysis mode because both are temporal in nature; that is, they both can be used to describe a process that has a beginning, middle, and end. That means that a process analysis essay tells a story, sometimes quite literally, and often resembles a work of narrative, although its primary purpose is always to explain how to do something or how to achieve a specific objective. Perhaps the best way to describe a process analysis essay is to say that it has a highly applied-use value and wants to teach us a lesson we can follow.

Writing process analysis essays may seem easy at first blush, but it is a challenging mode to do well. For example, you have probably purchased a bicycle, computer desk, or DVD player that came in a box labeled "Assembly Required" and then attempted to follow the enclosed instructional manual. Sometimes the instructions guide you effortlessly through the process; other times they probably frustrated and befuddled you. Usually, the failure can be traced to the writer lacking necessary information, assuming knowledge on the part of the consumer, or omitting key steps and information. Occasionally, the writing is bad—paragraphs lack focus and transition, steps are poorly described, the order of assembly is incorrect, the syntax is snarled. Efficient and clear instructions are not easy to write. More and more companies are employing professional writers to do this work, and these writers must find a way to describe complex processes in precise language so that those with little or no knowledge can follow them.

Examples of process analysis can be found everywhere. A quick Internet search of the best-selling books in America reveals titles like *How to Make Enduring Friendships*, *How to Find the Ideal Spouse*, *How to Succeed in College*, and *How to Make a Killing on Wall Street*. Such titles fill countless pages of publishers' catalogs. Television and radio shows abound informing people how to live a healthy life, how to solve cat and dog behavior problems, how to lose weight, how to shop online. All are examples of process analysis.

Interested in driving from Little Rock, Arkansas, to Austin, Texas, but don't know the route? No problem. Just log onto the Internet, do a quick search, and download a map and directions. The Yahoo! map opposite offers a relatively simple example of process analysis, but even this task requires a comprehensive knowledge of roads and routes along with the ability to compose in a clear and organized fashion.

It is worth noting that this map has certain features that can be found in many process analysis essays. First, it includes illustrations, a helpful feature not always feasible when writing an academic essay. Visual aids, when appropriate, can be a great help to readers and are a useful form of exemplification. Second, the map signals its purpose clearly from the beginning, indicating that it is a Yahoo! map describing how to get from Little Rock to Austin. Third, the directions are clear, explicit, and logically organized, citing specific turning directions, streets, and mileage indicators. Finally, the map includes a cautionary statement about its own veracity, advising users to "do a reality check and make sure the road still exists"—a statement that, surprisingly, is not intended for comic effect. Since even the best-described process analysis can end in failure (accidents happen and cannot always be prevented), it is useful to remain aware of one's fallibility when offering instructions to others.

Process analysis essays come in many styles, tones, and levels of difficulty. Many are direct, informational, and written in a fairly "neutral" tone and style. Middle Tennessee State University offers its stu-

Yahoo! Maps

Maps Home

Maps | **Driving Directions**

Starting from:	❶ Little Rock, AR <u>Save Address</u>	
Arriving at:	❷ Austin, TX <u>Save Address</u>	<u>Get Reverse Directions</u>
Distance: 514.1 miles	**Approximate Travel Time:** 7 hours 54 mins	

🖃 <u>Email Directions</u>   🖨 <u>Printable Version</u>   ☐ <u>Text Only Driving Directions</u>

Full Route — **Destination** - <u>Interactive Map</u>

Directions	Miles	
1. Start on **STATE CAPITOL**	0.1	↑
2. Bear Left on a local road	0.0	↱
3. Turn Right on **MARTIN LUTHER KING JR DR**	0.1	↱
4. Turn Left on **W 7TH ST**	0.4	↰
5. Turn Right on **S CHESTER ST**	0.2	↱
6. Take the **I-630 EAST** ramp	0.2	↗
7. Merge on **I-630 EAST**	1.1	↑
8. Take the **I-30 WEST** exit towards **TEXARKANA**, exit **#139B**	0.3	↗
9. Merge on **I-30 WEST**	1.6	↗
10. Continue on **I-30 WEST/I-440 WEST**	0.4	↑
11. Continue on **I-30 WEST**	303.2	↑
12. Take the **I-635 SOUTH** exit, exit **#56B**	1.0	↑
13. Merge on **I-635 SOUTH**	8.4	↗
14. Continue on **I-20 WEST**	11.9	↑
15. Take the **I-35E SOUTH** exit towards **WACO**, exit **#467B**	0.9	↗
16. Merge on **I-35E SOUTH**	46.7	↗
17. Take the **I-35 SOUTH** exit	0.5	↑
18. Merge on **I-35 SOUTH**	136.3	↱
19. Take the **8TH - 3RD STS** exit, exit **#234B**	0.1	↗
20. Continue on **N I-35**	0.3	↱
21. Turn Right on **E 4TH ST**	0.4	↱
22. Turn Right on **BRAZOS ST**	0.1	↱

Distance: 514.1 miles   **Approximate Travel Time:** 7 hours 54 mins

Yahoo! Travel Deals

Best Fares to Austin - <u>Little Rock from $131.00, More...</u>   **Car Rentals** - <u>Search for a car rental in Austin</u>
Best Hotel Rates - <u>Northpark Executive Suite Hotel from $69.95, More...</u>

When using any driving directions or map, it's a good idea to do a reality check and make sure the road still exists, watch out for construction, and follow all traffic safety precautions. This is only to be used as an aid in planning.

dents a short process analysis on the Wesley Foundation Web site (*http://www.mtsu.edu/~wesleyfo/roommates.html*). The focus is on getting along with your roommate.

Roommate: Friend or Foe?

Living with a roommate can be a great experience.
But it can also be a horror story.

Maybe it's your first time away from home. Most likely, it is the first time you have lived with someone who isn't a family member. While it is possible to get along well from the start with your roommate, not many find it so easy. Often, living with a roommate requires work.

There is no easy formula for living with roommates. Below are some suggestions from those who gone through dorm life:

- When you first move in, try to reach agreement with your roommate about these things: housekeeping; telephone: cost and use; shared expenses; visiting hours; sleeping hours: reconciling the early bird with the night owl; space: closet, study, personal; borrowing: clothes, books, personal property; playing music: type, volume, hours.
- Clear communication from the start. Be aware of what bugs you and let your roommate know.
- Keep communicating. If your roommate does something that irritates you, tell your roomie, not the person across the hall.
- Maintain a sense of humor.
- Do things with your roommate outside of the room. Going to a movie may help remind you that your roommate is human.
- Don't expect people to know how you are feeling—tell them.
- Go into dorm living with a realistic attitude. Resign yourself to the fact that concessions will have to be made.
- Respect your roommate as a person and respect their stuff.
- Don't take all comments personally.
- If things aren't going well, talk to your residence advisor or campus ministry folks.
- Remember, not everyone can get along with everyone else. If the situation gets bad, get out. Check on policies about moving to a different room.
- After all, the above suggestions are easier said than done. Godspeed! Keep the faith.
- Lastly, keep in mind that living with a previously total stranger is an adventure where the outcome is largely up to you. You may find that your roommate is indeed a foe. However, you may make a friend who becomes a lifelong confidant. Above all, learning to get along with a roommate is a valuable education for marriage and family life.

This Web document is practical and obviously intended for students, with its informal word choice, breezy practicality, and upbeat tone. The list of suggestions it enumerates could be reformulated into an informative process analysis essay about roommate relationships or refashioned into a more tongue-in-cheek essay about "surviving a roommate" or "how to persuade a roommate to bunk elsewhere so that you end up with a single room"!

Humor can be an effective device when writing process analysis, as seen in the following Web column by two well-known public radio personalities, Tom and Ray Magliozzi, whose call-in show is featured on many public radio stations. This October 1999 exchange, which can be found at their Web site (*http://cartalk.cars.com/Columns*), is transcribed from one of the many phone calls they receive and answer on the air and is an example of how sound advice can be offered with a humorous tone.

Dear Tom and Ray:

My '97 Honda Civic EX recently developed a new feature: The blue windshield washer solution has been colonized by some pink slime that smells like somebody's unwashed gym clothes. My microbiologist co-worker says that there are some forms of microbial life that can live in alcohol-containing solutions, like wiper fluid. My husband was trying to figure out how to remove the reservoir to clean it out, but it looks like it won't come out unless we take the bumper off first. Is there an easy way to clean out this container?—Elaine

Tom: Sure. With a garden hose.

Ray: You CAN take the whole reservoir out without actually removing the bumper, but you need to remove the inner fender liner, and that's a pain in the butt, too. So the hose is the tool of choice here.

Tom: The windshield-washer reservoir is a closed system. There's the tank, a little pump and a rubber tube that carries the liquid to the windshield. That's it. So you won't harm or contaminate anything else by sticking the garden hose in there.

Ray: Pop off the top, stick the hose in there and let it overflow for 5 or 10 minutes. While you're doing that, use the windshield washer a few times to clean out the rubber tubes, too.

Tom: Then put a little bit of bleach in the water—along with a couple of expired penicillin tablets from your medicine cabinet—and let it sit. A day or two later, give the thing a scrub with one of those long-handled kitchen pot scrubbers, and put the hose in it again.

Ray: And when you're all done, you can siphon out the bulk of the water and fill it back up with soapy blue stuff.

Tom: And if the microbes come back after that, call the Centers for Disease Control and Prevention in Atlanta. Tell them you're willing to donate a reservoir of rare microbes to science, but they'll have to come and swap out your windshield-washer container for you if they want them.

The Magliozzi brothers' transcript illustrates that an explanation of a particular process often includes additional helpful information—in this case, the structure of the washer reservoir. Whenever writing process analysis essays, a useful rule-of-thumb is that you should know much more about your subject than you end up including in the essay. Writers who exhaust all their knowledge almost certainly do not yet possess sufficient knowledge to do the best possible job. The Magliozzi brothers possess so much knowledge about car repair that they generally make accurate diagnoses of problems based on verbal accounts from the cars' owners.

Clearly, process analysis essays offer many opportunities to experiment with tone, format, and structure. They also require very careful and perceptive analyses of purpose and audience. Do you want primarily to offer an explicit description of a process, as does Frederick Douglass in his essay, or do you prefer to offer an account of a process of discovery, as does Fan Shen? Both essays use descriptions of processes to open up significant subjects, including identity, subjectivity, and cultural difference. In terms of audience, do your readers already possess information so that you can write more technically about your subject? Do they have specific needs and interests? Why would they want to read your process analysis? What benefits would they receive?

It is also worth noting that visualization can be very important when writing process analysis. More than most other modes, process analysis asks writers to place themselves within very specific settings, to get situated within the procedures or stages being described. Whether explaining how to get a conk (Malcolm X) or what it is like for a Huaorani Indian to visit a contemporary American city (Joe Kane), process analysis writers need to be able to place themselves within the situations they are describing and write so that readers can visualize them, at times possibly closing their eyes and imagining the contexts in as much detail as possible. Ultimately, the best process analysis essays are those that invite readers to relive experiences in some thoughtful and productive way.

Frederick Douglass (1817?–1883) was born into slavery in Maryland. Although severely beaten for several attempts to escape, he finally succeeded in 1838 and fled to Massachusetts, where he became an agent and spokesman for the Massachusetts Anti-Slavery League. He lectured on slavery in Great Britain, where money was collected for his freedom, whereupon he took the last name of Douglass. Considered the first African American to gain national stature, Douglass edited an abolitionist paper, The North Star, *from 1847 to 1860, and was among those to convince President Abraham Lincoln to issue the Emancipation Proclamation. "Learning to Read and Write" comes from Douglass's autobiography,* The Narrative of the Life of Frederick Douglass, An American Slave *(1845).*

Frederick Douglass

Learning to Read and Write

I lived in Master Hugh's family about seven years. During this time, I succeeded in learning to read and write. In accomplishing this, I was compelled to resort to various stratagems. I had no regular teacher. My mistress, who had kindly commenced to instruct me, had, in compliance with the advice and direction of her husband, not only ceased to instruct, but had set her face against my being instructed by anyone else. It is due, however, to my mistress to say of her, that she did not adopt this course of treatment immediately. She at first lacked the depravity indispensable to shutting me up in mental darkness. It was at least necessary for her to have some training in the exercise of irresponsible power, to make her equal to the task of treating me as though I were a brute.

My mistress was, as I have said, a kind and tender-hearted woman; and in the simplicity of her soul she commenced, when I first went to live with her, to treat me as she supposed one human being ought to treat another. In entering upon the duties of a slaveholder, she did not seem to perceive that I sustained to her the relation of a mere chattel, and that for her to treat me as a human being was not only wrong, but dangerously so. Slavery proved as injurious to her as it did to me. When I went there, she was a pious, warm, and tender-hearted woman. There was no sorrow or suffering for which she had not a tear. She had bread for the hungry, clothes for the naked, and comfort for every mourner that came within her reach. Slavery soon proved its ability to divest her of these heavenly qualities. Under its influence, the tender heart became stone, and the lamb-like disposition gave way to one of tiger-like fierceness. The first step in her downward course was in her ceasing to instruct me. She now commenced to practise her husband's precepts. She finally became even more violent in her opposition than her husband himself. She was not satisfied with simply doing as well as he had commanded; she seemed anxious to do better. Nothing seemed to make her more angry than to see me with a newspaper. She seemed to think that here lay the danger. I have had her rush at me with a face made all up of fury, and snatch from me a newspaper, in a manner that fully revealed her apprehension. She was an apt woman; and a little experience soon demonstrated, to her satisfaction, that education and slavery were incompatible with each other.

From this time I was most narrowly watched. If I was in a separate room any considerable length of time, I was sure to be suspected of having a book, and was at once called to give an account of myself. All this, however, was too late. The first step had been taken. Mistress, in teaching me the alphabet, had given me the *inch*, and no precaution could prevent me from taking the *ell*.

The plan which I adopted, and the one by which I was most successful, was that of making friends of all the little white boys whom I met in the street. As many of these as I could, I converted into teachers. With their kindly aid, obtained at different times and in different places, I finally succeeded in learning to read. When I was sent on errands, I always took my book with me, and by going one part of my errand quickly, I found time to get a lesson before my return. I used also to carry bread with me, enough of which was always in the house, and to which I was always welcome; for I was much better off in this regard than many of the poor white children in our neighborhood. This bread I used to bestow upon the hungry little urchins, who, in return, would give me that more valuable bread of knowledge. I am strongly tempted to give the names of two or three of those little boys, as a testimonial of the gratitude and affection I bear them; but prudence forbids;—not that it would injure me, but it might embarrass them; for it is almost an unpardonable offence to teach slaves to read in this Christian country. It is enough to say of the dear little fellows, that they lived on Philpot Street, very near Durgin and Bailey's ship-yard. I used to talk this matter of slavery over with them. I would sometimes say to them, I wished I could be as free as they would be when they got to be men. "You will be free as soon as you are twenty-one, *but I am a slave for life!* Have not I as good a right to be free as you have?" These words used to trouble them; they would express for me the liveliest sympathy, and console me with the hope that something would occur by which I might be free.

5   I was now about twelve years old, and the thought of being *a slave for life* began to bear heavily upon my heart. Just about this time, I got hold of a book entitled "The Columbian Orator." Every opportunity I got, I used to read this book. Among much of other interesting matter, I found in it a dialogue between a master and his slave. The slave was represented as having run away from his master three times. The dialogue represented the conversation which took place between them, when the slave was retaken the third time. In this dialogue, the whole argument in behalf of slavery was brought forward by the master, all of which was disposed of by the slave. The slave was made to say some very smart as well as impressive things in reply to his master—things which had the desired though unexpected effect; for the conversation resulted in the voluntary emancipation of the slave on the part of the master.

In the same book, I met with one of Sheridan's mighty speeches on and in behalf of Catholic emancipation. These were choice documents to me. I read them over and over again with unabated interest. They gave tongue to interesting thoughts of my own soul, which had frequently flashed through my mind, and died away for want of utterance. The moral which I gained from the dialogue was the power of truth over the conscience of even a slaveholder. What I got from Sheridan was a bold denunciation of slavery, and a powerful vindication of human rights. The reading of these documents enabled me to utter my thoughts, and to meet the arguments brought forward to sustain slavery; but while they relieved me of one difficulty, they brought on another even more painful than the one of which I was relieved. The more I read, the more I was led to abhor and detest my enslavers. I could regard them in no other light than a band of successful robbers, who had left their homes, and gone to Africa, and stolen us from our homes, and in a strange land reduced us to slavery. I loathed them as being the meanest as well as the most wicked of men. As I read and contemplated the subject, behold! that very discontentment which Master Hugh had predicted would follow my learning to read had already come, to torment and sting my soul to unutterable anguish. As I writhed under it, I would at times feel that learning to read had been a curse rather than a blessing. It had given me a view of my wretched condition, without the remedy. It opened my eyes to the horrible pit, but to no ladder upon which to get out. In moments of agony, I envied my fellow-slaves for their stupidity. I have often wished myself a beast. I preferred the condition of the meanest reptile to my own. Any thing, no matter what, to get rid of thinking! It was this everlasting thinking of my condition that tormented me. There was no getting rid of it. It was pressed upon me by every object within sight or hearing, animate or inanimate. The silver trump of freedom had roused my soul to eternal wakefulness. Freedom now appeared, to disappear no more forever. It was heard in every sound, and seen in every thing. It was ever present to torment me with a sense of my wretched condition. I saw nothing without seeing it, I heard nothing without hearing it, and felt nothing without feeling it. It looked from every star, it smiled in every calm, breathed in every wind, and moved in every storm.

I often found myself regretting my own existence, and wishing myself dead; and but for the hope of being free, I have no doubt but that I should have killed myself, or done something for which I should have been killed. While in this state of mind, I was eager to hear anyone speak of slavery. I was a ready listener. Every little while, I could hear something about the abolitionists. It was some time before I found what the word meant. It was always used in such connections as to make it an interesting word to me. If a slave ran away and succeeded in getting clear, or if a slave killed his master, set fire to a barn, or did any thing very wrong in the mind of a slaveholder, it was spoken of as the fruit of *abolition*. Hearing the word in this connection very often, I set about learning what it meant. The dictionary afforded me little or no help. I found it was "the act of abolishing," but then I did not know what was to be abolished. Here I was perplexed. I did not dare to ask any one about its meaning, for I was satisfied that it was something they wanted me to know very little about. After a patient waiting, I got one of our city papers, containing an account of the number of petitions from the north, praying for the abolition of slavery in the District of Columbia, and of the slave trade between the States. From this time I understood the words *abolition* and *abolitionist*, and always drew near when that word was spoken, expecting to hear something of importance to myself and fellow-slaves. The light broke in upon me by degrees. I went one day down on the wharf of Mr. Waters; and seeing two Irishmen unloading a scow of stone, I went, unasked, and helped them. When we had finished, one of them came to me and asked me if I were a slave. I told him I was. He asked, "Are ye a slave for life?" I told him that I was. The good Irishman seemed to be deeply affected by the statement. He said to the other that it was a pity so fine a little fellow as myself should be a slave for life. He said it was a shame to hold me. They both advised me to run away to the north; that I should find friends there, and that I should be free. I pretended not to be interested in what they said, and treated them as if I did not understand them; for I feared they might be treacherous. White men have been known to encourage slaves to escape, and then, to get the reward, catch them and return them to their masters. I was afraid that these seemingly good men might use me so; but I neverthe- less remembered their advice, and from that time I resolved to run away. I looked forward to a time at which it would be safe for me to escape. I was too young to think of doing so immediately; besides, I wished to learn how to write, as I might have occasion to write my own pass. I con- soled myself with the hope that I should one day find a good chance. Meanwhile, I would learn to write.

The idea as to how I might learn to write was suggested to me by being in Durgin and Bailey's ship-yard, and frequently seeing the ship carpenters, after hewing, and getting a piece of timber ready for use, write on the timber the name of that part of the ship for which it was in- tended. When a piece of timber was intended for the larboard side, it would be marked thus—"L." When a piece was for the starboard side, it would be marked thus—"S." A piece for the larboard side forward, would be marked thus—"L. F." When a piece was for starboard side forward, it would be marked thus—"S. F." For larboard aft, it would be marked thus—"L. A." For starboard aft, it would be marked thus— "S. A." I soon learned the names of these letters, and for what they were intended when placed upon a piece of timber in the ship-yard. I immedi- ately commenced copying them, and in a short time was able to make the four letters named. After that, when I met with any boy who I knew could write, I would tell him I could write as well as he. The next word would be, "I don't believe you. Let me see you try it." I would then make the letters which I had been so fortunate as to learn, and ask him to beat that. In this way I got a good many lessons in writing, which it is quite possible I should never have gotten in any other way. During this time, my copy-book was the board fence, brick wall, and pavement; my pen and ink was a lump of chalk. With these, I learned mainly how to write. I then commenced and continued copying the Italics in Webster's Spelling Book, until I could make them all without looking on the book. By this time, my little Master Thomas had gone to school, and learned how to write, and had written over a number of copy-books. These had been brought home, and shown to some of our near neighbors, and then laid aside. My mistress used to go to class meeting at the Wilk Street meetinghouse every Monday afternoon, and leave me to take care of the house. When left thus, I used to spend the time in writing in the spaces left in master Thomas's copy-book, copying what he had written. I continued to do this until I could write a hand very similar to that of Master Thomas. Thus, after a long, tedious effort for years, I finally succeeded in learning how to write.

Analyzing Rhetorical Choices

1. Douglass's essay is written in a style characteristic of a great many works by highly literate authors in the 19th century. How would you describe that style? What makes it easy or challenging to read? How effective is it in terms of the way it represents the ethos of Douglass?

2. Douglass often adopts a strategy known as antithesis, in which he places two terms close together within a sentence or paragraph for the sake of creating a contrast. Select at least four instances of antithesis, and offer your own paraphrase of what he is saying. In a short paragraph, comment on the rhetorical effectiveness of this device.

3. Douglass writes, "I am strongly tempted to give the names of two or three of those little boys, as a testimonial of the gratitude and affections I bear them; but prudence forbids;—not that it would injure me, but it might embarrass them; for it is almost an unpardonable offence to teach slaves to read in this Christian country." Offer a critique of this sentence in terms of its structure and tone.

Writing About Issues and Contexts

1. How is it possible that "Slavery proved as injurious to [his mistress] as it did to [Douglass]? (Consider how this is similar to the observations made by Orwell in "Shooting an Elephant," p. 61) What does this statement tell us about Douglass's view of human nature?

2. How does Douglass support his contention that "education and slavery were incompatible with each other"?

3. Compare Douglass's essay with Kenneth Stampp's, in which Stampp describes the process by which slaves are made "to stand in fear." How might Douglass's statement about education and slavery being incompatible apply to Stampp's essay?

4. It might be said that Douglass manipulates many of the people around him to learn how to read. Is this manipulation positive? Is it justified?

Born in Chicago, **David Mura** *(1952–   ) was educated at Grinnell College, Vermont College, and the University of Minnesota. A performance artist, Mura is also a writer of essays, fiction, and poetry and has published in* The Nation, The American Poetry Review, Crazyhorse, The New Republic, *and* The Missouri Review, *among others. In addition to grants from the National Endowment for the Arts, Mura has won numerous honors, including the Lila Wallace Reader's Digest Writer's Award in 1995. His published works include* After We Lost Our Way *(1989);* Turning Japanese: Memoirs of a Sansei *(1990), which documents his stay in Japan; and* Where the Body Meets Memory: An Odyssey of Race, Sexuality, and Identity *(1996). With African American writer Alexs Pate, he has developed and appeared in a performance piece titled* Secret Colors. *The following essay was originally published in the* New York Times.

David Mura

How America Unsexes the Asian Male

The Japanese-American actor Marc Hayashi once said to me: "Every culture needs its eunuchs. And we're it. Asian-American men are the eunuchs of America." I felt an instant shock of recognition.

To my chagrin, I came close to being one such eunuch on screen in the Coen brothers' movie "Fargo."

The call for the role seemed perfect: a Japanese-American man, in his late 30's, a bit portly, who speaks with a Minnesota accent.

I am a sansei, a third-generation Japanese-American. I've lived in Minnesota for 20 years. Though not portly, I'm not thin. A writer and a performance artist, I had done one small film for PBS.

5   After I passed the first two readings, my wife and I talked about what other parts might follow and even joked about moving to Hollywood. But in the end, the Coens found another Asian-American actor.

But when I saw the much-acclaimed "Fargo," I said to myself, "Thank God I didn't get the part." The character I would have played is Mike Yanagita, a Japanese-American who speaks with a thick Minnesota accent and awkwardly attempts a pass at an old high school friend, Marge Gunderson, a rural police chief who is visibly pregnant.

He then tells of marrying a mutual acquaintance from high school and of her recent death from cancer. A few scenes later, Marge learns that this marriage was fiction: the acquaintance is not only alive, but has also complained to the police that Mike has been harassing her.

The Japanese-American character has no relevance to Marge's investigation. He is there mainly for humor. The humor is based on his derangement and his obvious illusions that Marge or their acquaintance would ever find him attractive.

I recognized this character as only the latest in a long line of Asian and Asian-American male nerds. Often, as in "Fargo," such a character will pant after white women, ridiculous in his desires. In the movies, as in the culture as a whole, Asian-American men seem to have no sexual clout. Or sexual presence.

10   Americans rarely talk about race and sex together. It's still taboo. Yet, I often wonder what people make of me and my wife, who is three-quarters WASP and one-quarter Hungarian Jew. Recently we went shopping with my sister Linda and our children. Several people, all white, mistook Linda for the wife, the mother. Was that because many whites find it difficult to picture an Asian-American man with a white woman?

In fiction, when East meets West, it is almost always a Western man meeting an Asian woman. There is constant reinforcement for the image of the East as feminine and the stereotype of Asian women as exotic, submissive and sensual. From "Madama Butterfly" to "The Karate Kid, Part II" and "Miss Saigon," the white man who falls in love with an Asian woman has been used to proffer the view that racial barriers cannot block the heart's affections.

But such pairings simply place white men at the screen's center and reinforce a hierarchy of power and sexual attractiveness. They play on the stereotype of the East as feminine. And where does that leave Asian men?

A salient feature of the play "M. Butterfly" is that it affirms this feminine view of Asian men. In it, a French diplomat conducts a lengthy love affair with someone he believes is a woman but is actually a Chinese transvestite. The affair proves that Asian manhood is indeed difficult to find, at least for white Westerners. And when the "mistress" strips to a highly buffed and masculine body, it is not just the diplomat who gasps, but the audience as well.

And the stereotypes continue. In the sitcom "All-American Girl," Margaret Cho played a hip Korean-American who dated white boys in defiance of her mother's wishes. The brother was a studious, obsequious geek who dated no one.

15   Asian and Asian-American men are simply not seen as attractive or sexual beings by the mainstream culture. What could be attractive about the horny, thick-glassed, nerdy Asian guy, ridiculous in his desires for white women?

How little things change. As a boy I watched Mickey Rooney as the Japanese buffoon neighbor in "Breakfast at Tiffany's" and knew I never wanted to be associated with this snarling, bucktoothed creature who shouted at Audrey Hepburn, "Miss Gorrightry, Miss Gorrightry," and panted when she offered to let him photograph her; I identified with John Wayne against the Japs; in "Have Gun Will Travel," I was a cowboy like Paladin, not the Chinese messenger who ran into the hotel lobby shouting, "Terragram for Mr. Paradin."

To me as a child, Asian features, Asian accents—these were all undesirable. They weren't part of my image of a real all-American boy.

For a while this seemed to work. My parents, interned during World War II, wanted to distance themselves from their ethnic roots. We lived in an all-white suburb, where I generally felt like one of the crowd. Then came adolescence, and my first boy-girl party. As usual, I was the only Asian-American and person of color in the room. But when we began to play spin the bottle, I felt a new sense of difference from the others. And then the bottle I'd spun pointed to a girl I had a crush on, and she refused to kiss me.

Did that have to do with race? I had no language to express how race factored into the way the others perceived me, nor did they. But if the culture had told me Asian men were nerds or goofy houseboys, the white kids at the party must have received the same message.

20   In college, in the early 1970's, my reaction to the sexual place assigned to me took the form of compulsive sexuality: rampant promiscuity with white women and an obsession with pornography. There was definitely a racial component to it: my desires focused specifically on white women. I thought if I was with a white woman, then I would be as "good" as a white guy.

It took me years to figure out what was going on. It helped to read Frantz Fanon, the great Caribbean author and psychiatrist. In "Black Skin, White Masks," he writes of how the black man who constantly sleeps with white women has the illusion that his feelings of inferiority will somehow be erased by this act.

Gradually, I began to ask questions about how I learned what was sexually attractive and what images the culture gave me of myself.

How, for instance, does race factor in attraction? A popular way around such questions is to say that love sees no color.

I don't believe that. We are taught to see and process race early on. Race may not be the sole determinant in interracial relationships, but it is a factor. When I look at my wife, for example, I'm aware my desires for her cannot be separated from the ways the culture has inculcated me with standards of white beauty.

25 And when I told Alexs Pate, an African-American novelist, about Marc Hayashi's comment about the eunuchization of Asian-American men, he replied, "And black men are the sexual demons."

One is undersexed, the other, oversexed. Everyone knows who possesses a normal, healthy sense of sexuality.

Recently, after a panel discussion on "identity art," an elderly white man came up and complimented me on a performance I'd appeared in with my friend Alexs. Then he asked, "Weren't you in 'Fargo,' too?"

"No," I replied. "That wasn't me."

Analyzing Rhetorical Choices

1. Why do you think Mura opens his essay in this way? Why does he quote Marc Hayashi rather than stating this view himself?
2. How do you respond to the short paragraphs in this essay? Discuss whether or not you find them effective and how they influence the overall stylistic effect.
3. What is suggested by the last two paragraphs of the essay? Is this strategy effective? Why or why not?

Writing About Issues and Contexts

1. Are there examples from your reading or viewing of films that contradict Mura's representation of Asian males? If so, what are they? Do these override Mura's contentions, add another stereotype, or "round out" a view of Asian men?
2. According to Mura, what is the "process" by which stereotypes get created? Are there other ways that we in the United States create these stereotypes? Of whom? With what result?

3. Mura writes that "In fiction, when East meets West, it is almost always a Western man meeting an Asian woman," and "Race may not be the sole determinant in interracial relationships, but it is a factor." How might you support or refute these statements?

4. Do you think Mura would have made a mistake by appearing in that role in *Fargo*? Comment on whether you think Mura's concerns are justified.

An explorer and travel writer, **Joe Kane** *(1963–   ) first traveled to the Amazon region to join an expedition attempting to make the first source-to-sea navigation of the Amazon in 1985. Based on that arduous experience, Kane wrote* Running the Amazon *(1989), a best-seller that has been translated into 13 languages. Kane also ended up in the* Guinness Book of World Records *as the first man to navigate the entire Amazon River. Winner of the Overseas Press Club Award for outstanding environmental reporting, Kane spent two years living with the Huaorani (pronounced "wah-rahn-ee") tribe of Ecuador, investigating the impact that modern civilization and big oil had on their land and life. The book* Savages *(1995) is the result; the following selection is its prologue. Kane describes two processes: one centered on Moi, the other on himself.*

Joe Kane
Prologue to *Savages*

Though Moi hit the streets of Washington, D.C., at the evening rush hour, he walked in the city as he does in the forest—in slow, even strides. He kept his eyes to the ground and his knees bent, and he planted his broad feet deliberately, heel and toe, yet lightly as raindrops. It was the walk of a man accustomed to slippery terrain. I found myself stutter-stepping all the way down Pennsylvania Avenue, but Moi slid through the pedestrian horde like a fish parting water. He stopped only once, to study a squirrel climbing a maple tree: meat.

Moi wore dark khaki pants, a starched white dress shirt, a blue-and-gray striped tie, and brown leather shoes. The shoes were borrowed but the clothes were new, and though he was not entirely comfortable in them, he cut a handsome figure. Only the unusually high set of his cheekbones, the distinctive cut of his thick black hair—straight across his eyes, halfway down his back—and the rack of shoulders that threatened to burst the seams of his shirt hinted at the distance Moi had come: His journey had begun deep in the Ecuadorian Amazon, in the homeland of his people, the Huaorani, a small but fearsome nation of hunter-gatherers who have lived in isolation for so long that they speak a language unrelated to any other on earth. It had taken Moi nearly two weeks to reach Washington. Traveling by foot, canoe, bus, rail, and air, he had crossed centuries.

Tucked into a small handwoven palm-string bag he'd brought from home were his passport, his toothbrush, his bird-feather crown, and a letter addressed to the President of the United States of North America. The letter invited the president to visit the Huaorani. Moi wanted the president to explain to the People, as the Huaorani call themselves, exactly why it was that the United States of North America was trying to destroy them. "The whole world must come and see how the Huaorani live well," the letter said. "We live with the spirit of the jaguar. We do not want to be civilized by your missionaries or killed by your oil companies. Must the jaguar die so that you can have more contamination and television?"

At the White House gate Moi reached into his bag and carefully removed his crown. It was made from owl, eagle, toucan, parrot, and wild turkey feathers, and when he jammed it down on his jet black hair a thousand colors seemed to burst from the plumes. But the gate was closed, and for a long time Moi stood and stared silently through the iron fence.

5   Then he said, "That house looks pretty small. Are you sure the government lives here?"

"The president lives here, with his family."

"Where are the soldiers? Are they underground?"

"Probably. And in back, and inside."

He gripped the fence, as if testing its strength, and his eyes narrowed in calculation: He went into the Huaorani zone, as I'd come to think of it. When he returned he said, "I believe I can climb this fence and reach the front door before the soldiers get me."

10   "It will not work, Moi."

"It will not work if I do not try."

"The soldiers will be on you like a boa on a tree rat."

"I will climb the trees and hide. I will pretend I am hunting monkeys."

But I dissuaded him, at least for the moment, and we walked on. The sidewalks were full. Traffic roared.

15   "There are so many cars," he said. "How long have they been here? A million years?"

"Much less."

"A thousand years?"

"No. Eighty, perhaps."

He was silent then, but after a while he asked, "What will you do in ten more years? In ten years your world will be pure metal. Did your god do this?"

20   Dusk turned to night, and as we approached our hotel Moi stopped beneath a streetlamp. He pointed to the street. "More people,

more cars, more petroleum, more chaos," he said. Then he pointed straight up at the light. "But *there* are the Huaorani, all alone in the middle of the world."

Moi had been brought to Washington by a team of lawyers from the Sierra Club Legal Defense Fund, which, on behalf of the Huaorani, had filed a petition with the Inter-American Commission on Human Rights, an arm of the Organization of American States. Since 1967 American oil development in the Oriente—as the Ecuadorian Amazon is known—had proceeded virtually without regulation. Every day the petroleum industry was dumping millions of gallons of untreated toxic pollutants into a watershed extending over fifty thousand square miles of rain forest, and it had opened the area up to such rapid and uncontrolled colonization that it was on a pace to be almost completely deforested early in the next century. No one was arguing whether oil exploitation had damaged the Oriente—with the possible exception of gold mining in Brazil, it was the worst case of toxic contamination in the entire Amazon. The debate was over the extent of the damage. The Ecuadorian government had estimated the cost of cleaning up the mess made by Texaco and Petroecuador, the state oil company, at $5 billion. Texaco—whose pipeline had dumped into the Oreinte more than one and a half times as much oil as the Exxon *Valdez* spilled off the coast of Alaska—had offered a settlement worth about $12 million. In any case, the consequences had been borne most heavily by the Oriente's 150,000 indigenous people, and the surest measure of what loomed for the Huaorani could be found a hundred miles north of their territory, in the homeland of the Cofan Indians. The Cofans were a small but thriving nation when Texaco opened its first commercial well on their land, in 1972. Twenty years later, their culture was all but gone.

Moi arrived in Washington scant months before oil production was to begin in the Huaorani territory. The SCLDF petition charged that this would be ethnocide—that for the sake of enough oil to meet U.S. energy needs for thirteen days, the Huaorani way of life would be destroyed—and asked the commission to investigate. The commission has no powers of enforcement, but its moral authority is enormous, and an investigation was one of the few avenues left for the Huaorani if they were to have any chance of avoiding annihilation. The lawyers hoped that Moi's testimony would persuade the commission to act.

But the American embassy in Quito had a history of working closely with the petroleum industry, and days before Moi was scheduled to testify, it denied him a visa. The embassy argued that because Moi had no tangible assets tying him to Ecuador, there was a risk that he would disappear inside the United States as an illegal immigrant. It could be argued that, on the contrary, Moi's assets run deeper than just about anyone else's in Ecuador, for the Huaorani hold legal title to a good chunk of the territory they have always occupied. But they hold that title communally, and, the embassy maintained, this arrangement made Moi a landless peasant.

At least it did until the right question bounced onto the right desk at the State Department: Why was a plaintiff in a human-rights case being denied a visa? When I met Moi in Washington, one of the first things he did was produce his brand-new passport and show me the visa. "The embassy changed its mind," he said. "It has invited me to visit your country for five years."

25   As Moi saw it, he was engaged in a war, and the Huaorani were ready to fight that war with spears made from the hardest wood in the forest—"spears that can kill fifteen men without breaking," he said. Though there have probably never been more of the Huaorani than there are today—about 1,300—they have, for as long as anyone knows, roamed a territory the size of Massachusetts and fended off all comers: the Incas; the Spanish conquistadores; the rubber barons; the armies of Ecuador and Peru; modern-day colonists and prospectors; and, always, their land-hungry indigenous neighbors, the Quichua and the Shuar, who together outnumber the Huaorani by more than a hundred to one.

But fighting the Company—as the Huaorani call all interests with rights to the petroleum beneath their land—is something else again. Under Ecuadorian law, the Huaorani have no control over oil production and no share in its revenues. The Company planned to extract more than 200 million barrels of raw crude from Huaorani territory, and in its quest to exploit that oil, it had revealed itself to be an enemy far more powerful than any the Huaorani had ever known: an enemy that, as Moi saw it, killed by destroying the source of all life, the forest itself.

Though it had been almost a year since I'd last seen Moi (we'd spent months traveling together in the Amazon), when he came to my hotel room he greeted me in the Huaorani way, virtually without expression, as if only a few minutes had passed since we last spoke. "Chong," he said—that is how he pronounces "Joe"—and then he handed me his bag and his spears and walked into the room. Our relationship had been defined long ago, without words. In the forest, where I was helpless, he had watched out for me at all times; in the city, I owed him no less.

We stayed at the hotel four nights. Moi discovered televised baseball, *The Washington Post*, and modern warfare. Baseball, a game of spears and rocks, he enjoyed for its technique, but beyond that he found television useless. The *Post* he studied carefully each morning, mainly the airline ads (other than foot and canoe, small planes are the only transportation known inside the Huaorani territory) and the photographs. Of the latter he was most taken by the somewhat violent shots of an uprising in Russia. He asked me to translate the accompanying stories, and he peppered me with questions.

One morning he asked, "The United States and Russia fought a big war, did they not?"

30   "Yes, they did. It lasted many years."

"Which country did they fight it in? Here or there?"

"Neither."

"That is impossible."

"They fought it in other countries."

35   "That makes no sense. That would be like the Huaorani fighting the Shuar in Quichua territory."

"Something like that."

He laughed. "That is a very stupid way to make war."

Moi spent most of the first night working on the statement he would make to the commission. He wrote it out twice in the ten-cent notebook he always carried in his back pocket, and then he read it aloud, practicing his gestures. He would wear his shirt and tie, and over them his jaguar-tooth necklace, his string bag, and the reed tube in which he carried blowgun darts. "In the forest I wear this," he said, touching his necklace, "but your world wants me to wear this," and he tugged on his tie.

He read slowly, with little of the force or charm that came so naturally when he spoke. "Your ideas are good," I said, "but use your own words. Speak as you would without the paper."

40   "You mean speak like the jaguar," he said. The Huaorani consider the jaguar the most powerful force in the forest. (Moi's grandfather was a "jaguar shaman"—a shaman with the ability to transform himself into a jaguar—and, as such, one of the most revered men in the culture.)

Later, exhausted, Moi told me he wanted to clean up and go to bed. For the Huaorani, bathing is communal. In late afternoon people all head down to the river, and they hang out there for what seems forever, soaping up, swimming, gossiping, joking, and flirting. By comparison a hotel shower seemed soulless. Still, Moi disappeared into the bathroom for about an hour. I heard the water go on and off several times. When he finally emerged, he was wearing only his shorts, and his skin was red as a boiled lobster.

"Tomorrow, I would like a new hotel room," he said.

"Why?"

"I would like a room that also has cold water."

45 He dressed himself completely and had me tie his tie. Then, fully clothed, he got into bed. As he does at home, he would wake several times during the night—to eat, to pace our suite, to analyze the new sounds he was hearing.

He pulled the blankets up to his chin. "Chong," he said, "will we win?"

"You will try your best."

"We must win or the Huaorani will disappear forever."

Then he closed his eyes and, as always, fell asleep in seconds.

50 The strange journey that had brought me to Moi and Moi to the United States had begun two and a half years earlier, in March of 1991, when an odd and disturbing letter surfaced at the San Francisco headquarters of the Rainforest Action Network. The letter was tucked into an envelope that bore no postmark. No one was quite sure when it had arrived, or how it had burrowed its way into the stacks of paper crammed into the office of RAN Executive Director Randall Hayes. At first Hayes was not sure what the letter said, either, because it was written in Spanish, a language spoken neither by him nor, according to almost all of what little information was available about them, by the Huaorani, whose elected representatives the letter's authors claimed to be.

I was working at the RAN offices part-time, helping Hayes edit his publications, and he asked if I'd translate the letter and try to find out if it was authentic. It was written on plain white paper and typed on a manual typewriter, and it was addressed, simply, "General Manager, DuPont-Conoco Company, United States of North America." "The company Conoco is discussing the life of the Huaorani in meetings in which the Huaorani are not present," the letter said; on their own land, the Huaorani "are treated as if we were guests." The letter expressed absolute opposition to oil exploitation in Huaorani territory, and it warned that "the Huaorani know the problems of the whole world . . . and we will defend our land." It was signed, in flourishing script, by the officers of something called the Organization of the Huaorani Nation of the Ecuadorian Amazon. A cover note asked Hayes to forward the letter to Edgar S. Woolard, the chairman and

CEO of DuPont—the corporate parent of Conoco, which held oil rights to the Huaorani lands. It advised Hayes to be careful, because "the Company has many spies."

Conoco was scheduled to begin building roads and pipelines in the Huaorani territory within a few months, but the letter had the potential to place the project in serious jeopardy. Though Conoco had already invested $90 million to explore the Huaorani land for oil, and though it predicted eventual revenues of $2 billion, DuPont had to weigh these sums against the cost of being branded as trampling on the rights of, and quite possibly destroying, rain forest natives.

But was the letter for real?

Many environmental and human-rights groups claimed to be working on behalf of the Huaorani, or the land they lived on. Letter-writing campaigns, boycotts, lawsuits, grants, and foundations were being pitched and caught by the likes of CARE, Cultural Survival, The Nature Conservancy, the Natural Resources Defense Council, Wildlife Conservation International, the Sierra Club, the World Wildlife Fund, and a dozen other organizations, including RAN itself. In terms of both cost and reward, the money involved was substantial—tens of millions of dollars—and the infighting bitter. The positions staked out by the groups ran the gamut, from absolute opposition to Conoco to outright support (the argument being, mainly, that oil development of the Huaorani land was inevitable and that Conoco was the best of a number of bad alternatives). When I called around to the various offices, however, no one could convincingly vouch for—or produce evidence against—the letter. In fact, no one knew how to contact the Huaorani. For all the ruckus being raised, all that could be said with certainty about the Huaorani, whoever they might be, was that American oil companies coveted their land, American missionaries their souls, American environmentalists their voice. But no one knew what the Huaorani wanted. No one really knew who the Huaorani were.

55   Hayes and I elected to send the mysterious letter along to Edgar Woolard, and to publish the text in RAN's quarterly newsletter, even though RAN didn't have the time or money to research it as thoroughly as it cried out to be. If it was a fraud, Conoco, or any of the forces that stood to benefit from the Conoco development (including those in the environmental community), would find a way to expose it as such. But if it was authentic—if it was genuinely as desperate and wild and unlikely a shot in the dark as it seemed to be—then it was a

voice that had to be heard. Woolard's decision on whether to allow Conoco to proceed with production development was expected within months.

So stated, our role seemed clear. But for me, at least, it was more complicated than that.

After the letter became public, it was denounced by Conoco and its supporters, who claimed, variously, that the Huaorani were illiterate and could not have written it, or that the Huaorani had written it but had done so under the coercion of "outsiders," or that the Huaorani who wrote it did not really represent all the Huaorani. But, still, no one offered hard proof of these claims, and there was no word either way from Edgar Woolard. The situation troubled me, in many ways. I had spent some time along the Amazon in Peru and Brazil, and, like a lot of people, I wanted to do something to help save the rain forest. And so after a decade as a working journalist, I'd crossed the street and tried to become an activist. But I quickly found environmental activism exhausting and bewildering, a bumper-car ride that veered from crisis to crisis without cease. There never seemed to be enough money, enough time, or enough information to do the work that had to be done. The Huaorani mystery brought it all to a head. If the letter was real, who had written it? And if it *wasn't* real, who had written it?

I decided to quit RAN and go back to South America to look for some answers. The dateline on the Huaorani letter said "Coca." That seemed as good a place as any to start.

Analyzing Rhetorical Choices

1. Why do you think Kane chooses to begin his prologue with the short narrative of Moi in Washington, D.C., and then provide the background information about why he is there? Shouldn't these sections be reversed? Why or why not?

2. What is the significance of the following paragraph:

    > Dusk turned to night, and as we approached our hotel Moi stopped beneath a streetlamp. He pointed to the street. "More people, more cars, more petroleum, more chaos," he said. Then he pointed straight up at the light. "But *there* are the Huaorani, all alone in the middle of the world."

    Why do you think Kane chooses to end a section of the prologue with this passage?

3. Analyze the rhetorical effectiveness of the following passage, paying particular attention to word choice, word patterns, and how Kane positions himself in relation to his subject:

> For all the ruckus being raised, all that could be said with certainty about the Huaorani, whoever they might be, was that American oil companies coveted their land, American missionaries their souls, American environmentalists their voice. But no one knew what the Huaorani wanted. No one really knew who the Huaorani were.

4. Based on your analysis of the prologue, how does Kane encourage you to continue reading? What does he do to motivate you to read the entire book, *Savages*?

Writing About Issues and Contexts

1. Why does Kane describe in detail the contents of Moi's palm-string bag? What do they tell us about Moi and his mission?
2. What is Moi's perspective on the White House, automobile traffic, and his own prowess? What do his comments tell us about his culture and his character?
3. If process analysis can properly be described as a "narrative of instruction," how do you analyze the processes that Moi and Kane experience? What lessons do they learn? What lessons do they impart to the reader?

Kenneth M. Stampp *(1912–   ) was born in Milwaukee, Wisconsin, and is the author of many noted works in history, including* And the War Came *(1950),* The Peculiar Institution: Slavery in the Antebellum South *(1956), and* The Causes of the Civil War *(1991). He is professor emeritus at the University of California at Berkeley, and has taught at Oxford University and the University of Munich. A recipient of many awards including two Guggenheim Fellowships, Stampp earned his Ph.D. from the University of Wisconsin in 1942. This essay comes from* The Peculiar Institution.

Kenneth M. Stampp

To Make Them Stand in Fear

A wise master did not take seriously the belief that Negroes were natural-born slaves. He knew better. He knew that Negroes freshly imported from Africa had to be broken to bondage; that each succeeding generation had to be carefully trained. This was no easy task, for the bondsman rarely submitted willingly. Moreover, he rarely submitted completely. In most cases there was no end to the need for control—at least not until old age reduced the slave to a condition of helplessness.

Masters revealed the qualities they sought to develop in slaves when they singled out certain ones for special commendation. A small Mississippi planter mourned the death of his "faithful and dearly beloved servant" Jack: "Since I have owned him he has been true to me in all respects. He was an obedient trusty servant. . . . I never knew him to steal nor lie and he ever set a moral and industrious example to those around him. . . . I shall ever cherish his memory." A Louisiana sugar planter lost a "very valuable Boy" through an accident: "His life was a very great one. I have always found him willing and obedient and never knew him to fail to do anything he was put to do." These were "ideal" slaves, the models slaveholders had in mind as they trained and governed their workers.

How might this ideal be approached? The first step, advised those who wrote discourses on the management of slaves, was to establish and maintain strict discipline. An Arkansas master suggested the adoption of the "Army Regulations as to the discipline in Forts." "They must obey at all times, and under all circumstances, cheerfully and with alacrity," affirmed a Virginia slaveholder. "It greatly impairs the happiness of a negro, to be allowed to cultivate an insubordinate temper. Unconditional submission is the only footing on which slavery should be placed. It is precisely similar to the attitude of a minor to his parent, or a soldier to his general." A South Carolinian limned a perfect relationship between a slave and his master: "that the slave should know that his master is to govern absolutely, and he is to obey implicitly. That he is never for a moment to exercise either his will or judgment in opposition to a positive order."

The second step was to implant in the bondsmen themselves a consciousness of personal inferiority. They had "to know and keep their places," to "feel the difference between master and slave," to understand that bondage was their natural status. They had to feel that African ancestry tainted them, that their color was a badge of degradation. In the country they were to show respect for even their master's nonslaveholding neighbors; in the towns they were to give way on the streets to the most wretched white man. The line between the races must never be crossed, for familiarity caused slaves to forget their lowly station and to become "impudent."

5   Frederick Douglass explained that a slave might commit the offense of impudence in various ways: "in the tone of an answer; in answering at all; in not answering; in the expression of countenance; in the motion of the head; in the gait, manner and bearing of the slave." Any of these acts, in some subtle way, might indicate the absence of proper subordination. "In a well regulated community," wrote a Texan, "a negro takes off his hat in addressing a white man. . . . Where this is not enforced, we may always look for impudent and rebellious negroes."

The third step in the training of slaves was to awe them with a sense of their master's enormous power. The only principle upon which slavery could be maintained, reported a group of Charlestonians, was the "principle of fear." In his defense of slavery James H. Hammond admitted that this, unfortunately, was true but put the responsibility upon the abolitionists. Antislavery agitation had forced masters to strengthen their authority: "We have to rely more and more on the power of fear. . . . We are determined to continue masters, and to do so we have to draw the reign tighter and tighter day by day to be assured that we hold them in complete check." A North Carolina mistress, after subduing a troublesome domestic, realized that it was essential "to make them stand in fear"!

In this the slaveholders had considerable success. Frederick Douglass believed that most slaves stood "in awe" of white men; few could free themselves altogether from the notion that their masters were "invested with a sort of sacredness." Olmsted saw a small white girl stop a slave on the road and boldly order him to return to his plantation. The slave fearfully obeyed her command. A visitor in Mississippi claimed that a master, armed only with a whip or cane, could throw himself among a score of bondsmen and cause them to "flee with terror." He accomplished this by the "peculiar tone of authority" with which he spoke. "Fear, awe, and obedience . . . are interwoven into the very nature of the slave."

The fourth step was to persuade the bondsmen to take an interest in the master's enterprise and to accept his standards of good conduct. A South Carolina planter explained: "The master should make it his business to show his slaves, that the advancement of his individual interest, is at the same time an advancement of theirs. Once they feel this, it will require but little compulsion to make them act as it becomes them." Though slaveholders induced only a few chattels to respond to this appeal, these few were useful examples for others.

The final step was to impress Negroes with their helplessness, to create in them "a habit of perfect dependence" upon their masters. Many believed it dangerous to train slaves to be skilled artisans in the towns, because they tended to become self-reliant. Some thought it equally dangerous to hire them to factory owners. In the Richmond tobacco factories they were alarmingly independent and "insolvent." A Virginian was dismayed to find that his bondsmen, while working at an iron furnace, "got a habit of roaming about and *taking care of themselves.*" Permitting them to hire their own time produced even worse results. "No higher evidence can be furnished of its baneful effects," wrote a Charlestonian, "than the unwillingness it produces in the slave, to return to the regular life and domestic control of the master."

10 A spirit of independence was less likely to develop among slaves kept on the land, where most of them became accustomed to having their master provide their basic needs, and where they might be taught that they were unfit to look out for themselves. Slaves then directed their energies to the attainment of mere "temporary ease and enjoyment." "Their masters," Olmsted believed, "calculated on it in them—do not wish to cure it—and by constant practice encourage it."

Here, then, was the way to produce the perfect slave: accustom him to rigid discipline, demand from him unconditional submission, impress upon him his innate inferiority, develop in him a paralyzing fear of white men, train him to adopt the master's code of good behavior, and instill in him a sense of complete dependence. This, at least, was the goal.

But the goal was seldom reached. Every master knew that the average slave was only an imperfect copy of the model. He knew that some bondsmen yielded only to superior power—and yielded reluctantly. This complicated his problem of control.

Analyzing Rhetorical Choices

1. How do you interpret the tone of Stampp's opening, "A wise master did not take seriously the belief that Negroes were natural-born slaves. He knew better."

2. Stampp thoroughly describes a process. What is his point in doing so? How does his objective, factual tone reinforce the overall intention?

3. Stampp follows almost an identical format paragraph by paragraph. Describe the format, and comment on the overall rhetorical effectiveness of this kind of structural repetition.

Writing About Issues and Contexts

1. Compare this essay to Frederick Douglass's "Learning to Read and Write." How does the Douglass essay reinforce Stampp's analysis?

2. Why is the psychological control of slaves so significant to the process Stampp enumerates? How is keeping slaves on the plantation equally significant? Why?

3. Is the kind of training that Stampp details a kind of brainwashing? Is it similar to the kind of training that military recruits or political converts experience? Describe the similarities and differences between teaching someone how to be "a slave" and teaching someone how to be a soldier, a patriot, or even an extremely obedient child.

Fan Shen is a translator and writer who lives in the United States. Originally from the People's Republic of China, he taught at Rockland Community College in New York and currently teaches at Rochester Community and Technical College. Shen has translated three books from English to Chinese. He has also written articles for publications in China and the United States.

Fan Shen

The Classroom and the Wider Culture: Identity as a Key to Learning English Composition

One day in June 1975, when I walked into the aircraft factory where I was working as an electrician, I saw many large-letter posters on the walls and many people parading around the workshops shouting slogans like "Down with the word 'I'!" and "Trust in masses and the Party!" I then remembered that a new political campaign called "Against Individualism" was scheduled to begin that day. Ten years later, I got back my first English composition paper at the University of Nebraska-Lincoln. The professor's first comments were: "Why did you always use 'we' instead of 'I'?" and "Your paper would be stronger if you eliminated some sentences in the passive voice." The clashes between my Chinese background and the requirements of English composition had begun. At the center of this mental struggle, which has lasted several years and is still not completely over, is the prolonged, uphill battle to recapture "myself."

In this paper I will try to describe and explore this experience of reconciling my Chinese identity with an English identity dictated by the rules of English composition. I want to show how my cultural background shaped—and shapes—my approaches to my writing in English and how writing in English redefined—and redefines—my *ideological* and *logical* identities. By "ideological identity" I mean the system of values that I acquired (consciously and unconsciously) from my social and cultural background. And by "logical identity" I mean the natural (or Oriental) way I organize and express my thoughts in writing. Both had to be modified or redefined in learning English composition. Becoming aware of the process of redefinition of these different identities is a mode of learning that has helped me in my efforts to write in English, and, I hope, will be of help to teachers of English composition in this country. In presenting my case for this view, I will use examples from both my composition courses and literature courses, for I believe that writing papers for both kinds of courses contributed to the development of my "English identity." Although what I will describe is based on personal experience, many Chinese students whom I talked to said that they had had the same or similar experiences in their initial stages of learning to write in English.

Identity of the Self: Ideological and Cultural

Starting with the first English paper I wrote, I found that learning to compose in English is not an isolated classroom activity, but a social and cultural experience. The rules of English composition encapsulate values that are absent in, or sometimes contradictory to, the values of other societies (in my case, China). Therefore, learning the rules of English composition is, to a certain extent, learning the values of Anglo-American society. In writing classes in the United States I found that I had to reprogram my mind, to redefine some of the basic concepts and values that I had about myself, about society, and about the universe, values that had been imprinted and reinforced in my mind by my cultural background, and that had been part of me all my life.

Rule number one in English composition is: Be yourself. (More than one composition instructor has told me, "Just write what *you* think.") The values behind this rule, it seems to me, are based on the principle of protecting and promoting individuality (and private property) in this country. The instruction was probably crystal clear to students raised on these values, but, as a guideline of composition, it was not very clear or useful to me when I first heard it. First of all, the image or meaning that I attached to the word "I" or "myself" was, as I found out, different from that of my English teacher. In China, "I" is always subordinated to "We"—be it the working class, the Party, the country, or some other collective body. Both political pressure and literary tradition require that "I" be somewhat hidden or buried in writings and speeches; presenting the "self" too obviously would give people the impression of being disrespectful of the Communist Party in political writings and boastful in scholarly writings. The word "I" has often been identified with another "bad" word, "individualism," which has become a synonym for selfishness in China. For a long time the words "self" and "individualism" have had negative connotations in my mind, and the negative force of the words naturally extended to the field of literary studies. As a result, even if I had brilliant ideas, the "I" in my papers always had to show some modesty by not competing with or trying to stand above the names of ancient and modern authoritative figures. Appealing to Mao or other Marxist authorities became the required way (as well as the most "forceful" or "persuasive" way) to prove one's point in written discourse. I remember that in China I had even committed what I can call "reversed plagiarism"— here, I suppose it would be called "forgery"—when I was in middle school: willfully attributing some of my thoughts to "experts" when I needed some arguments but could not find a suitable quotation from a literary or political "giant."

5   Now, in America, I had to learn to accept the words "I" and "self" as something glorious (as Whitman did), or at least something not to be ashamed of or embarrassed about. It was the first and probably biggest step I took into English composition and critical writing. Acting upon my professor's suggestion, I intentionally tried to show my "individuality" and to "glorify" "I" in my papers by using as many "I's" as possible—"I think," "I believe," "I see"—and deliberately cut out quotations from authorities. It was rather painful to hand in such "pompous" (I mean immodest) papers to my instructors. But to an extent it worked. After a while I became more comfortable with only "the shadow of myself." I felt more at ease to put down *my* thoughts without looking over my shoulder to worry about the attitudes of my teachers or the reactions of the Party secretaries, and to speak out as "bluntly" and "immodestly" as my American instructors demanded.

But writing many "I's" was only the beginning of the process of redefining myself. Speaking of redefining myself is, in an important sense, speaking of redefining the word "I." By such a redefinition I mean not only the change in how I envisioned myself, but also the change in how *I* perceived the world. The old "I" used to embody only one set of values, but now it had to embody multiple sets of values. To be truly "myself," which I knew was a key to my success in learning English composition, meant *not to be my Chinese self* at all. That is to say, when I write in English I have to wrestle with and abandon (at least temporarily) the whole system of ideology which previously defined me in myself. I had to forget Marxist doctrines (even though I do not see myself as a Marxist by choice) and the Party lines imprinted in my mind and familiarize myself with a system of capitalist/bourgeois values. I had to put aside an ideology of collectivism and adopt the values of individualism. In composition as well as in literature classes, I had to make a fundamental adjustment: If I used to examine society and literary materials through the microscopes of Marxist dialectical materialism and historical materialism, I now had to learn to look through the microscopes the other way around, i.e., to learn to look at and understand the world from the point of view of "idealism." (I must add here that there are American professors who use a Marxist approach in their teaching.)

The word "idealism," which affects my view of both myself and the universe, is loaded with social connotations, and can serve as a good example of how redefining a key word can be a pivotal part of redefining my ideological identity as a whole.

To me, idealism is the philosophical foundation of the dictum of English composition: "Be yourself." In order to write good English, I knew that I had to be myself, which actually meant not to be my Chinese self. It meant that I had to create an English self and be *that* self. And to be that English self, I felt, I had to understand and accept idealism the way a Westerner does. That is to say, I had to accept the way a Westerner sees himself in relation to the universe and society. On the one hand, I knew a lot about idealism. But on the other hand, I knew nothing about it. I mean I knew a lot about idealism through the propaganda and objections of its opponent, Marxism, but I knew little about it from its own point of view. When I thought of the word "materialism"—which is a major part of Marxism and in China has repeatedly been "shown" to be the absolute truth—there were always positive connotations, and words like "right," "true," etc., flashed in my mind. On the other hand, the word "idealism" always came to me with the dark connotations that surround words like "absurd," "illogical," "wrong," etc. In China "idealism" is depicted as a ferocious and ridiculous enemy of Marxist philosophy. Idealism, as the simplified definition imprinted in my mind had it, is the view that the material world does not exist: that all that exists is the mind and its ideas. It is just the opposite of Marxist dialectical materialism which sees the mind as a product of the material world. It is not too difficult to see that idealism, with its idea that mind is of primary importance, provides a philosophical foundation for the Western emphasis on the value of individual human minds, and hence individual human beings. Therefore, my final acceptance of myself as of primary importance—an importance that overshadowed that of authority figures in English composition—was, I decided, dependent on an acceptance of idealism.

My struggle with idealism came mainly from my efforts to understand and to write about works such as Coleridge's *Biographia Literaria* and Emerson's "Over-Soul." For a long time I was frustrated and puzzled by the idealism expressed by Coleridge and Emerson—given their ideas, such as "I think, therefore I am" (Coleridge obviously borrowed from Descartes) and "the transparent eyeball" (Emerson's view of himself)—because in my mind, drenched as it was in dialectical materialism, there was always a little voice whispering in my ear "You are, therefore you think." I could not see how human consciousness, which is not material, could create apples and trees. My intellectual conscience refused to let me believe that the human mind is the primary world and the material world secondary. Finally, I had to imagine that I was looking at a world with my head upside down. When I imagined that I was in a new body (born with the head upside down) it was easier to forget biases imprinted in my subconsciousness about idealism, the mind, and my former self. Starting from scratch, the new inverted self—which I called my "English Self" and into which I have transformed myself—could understand and *accept* with ease, idealism as "the truth" and "himself" (i.e., my English Self) as the "creator" of the world.

10   Here is how I created my new "'English Self." I played a "game" similar to ones played by mental therapists. First I made a list of (simplified) features about writing associated with my old identity (the Chinese Self), both ideological and logical, and then beside the first list I added a column of features about writing associated with my new identity (the English Self). After that I pictured myself getting out of my old identity, the timid, humble, modest Chinese "I," and creeping into my new identity (often in the form of a new skin or a mask), the confident, assertive, and aggressive English "I." The new "Self" helped me to remember and accept the different rules of Chinese and English composition and the values that underpin these rules. In a sense, creating an English Self is a way of reconciling my old cultural values with the new values required by English writing, without losing the former.

An interesting structural but not material parallel to my experiences in this regard has been well described by Min-zhan Lu in her important article, "From Silence to Words: Writing as Struggle" (*College English 49* [April 1987]: 437–48). Min-zhan Lu talks about struggles between two selves, an open self and a secret self, and between two discourses, a mainstream Marxist discourse and a bourgeois discourse her parents wanted her to learn. But her struggle was different from mine.

Her Chinese self was severely constrained and suppressed by mainstream cultural discourse, but never interfused with it. Her experiences, then, were not representative of those of the majority of the younger generation who, like me, were brought up on only one discourse. I came to English composition as a Chinese person, in the fullest sense of the term, with a Chinese identity already fully formed.

Identity of the Mind: Illogical and Alogical

In learning to write in English, besides wrestling with a different ideological system, I found that I had to wrestle with a logical system very different from the blueprint of logic at the back of my mind. By "logical system" I mean two things: the Chinese way of thinking I used to approach my theme or topic in written discourse, and the Chinese critical/logical way to develop a theme or topic. By English rules, the first is illogical, for it is the opposite of the English way of approaching a topic; the second is alogical (nonlogical), for it mainly uses mental pictures instead of words as a critical vehicle.

The Illogical Pattern

In English composition, an essential rule for the logical organization of a piece of writing is the use of a "topic sentence." In Chinese composition, "from surface to core" is an essential rule, a rule which means that one ought to reach a topic gradually and "systematically" instead of "abruptly."

The concept of a topic sentence, it seems to me, is symbolic of the values of a busy people in an industrialized society, rushing to get things done, hoping to attract and satisfy the busy reader very quickly. Thinking back, I realized that I did not fully understand the virtue of the concept until my life began to rush at the speed of everyone else's in this country. Chinese composition, on the other hand, seems to embody the values of a leisurely paced rural society whose inhabitants have the time to chew and taste a topic slowly. In Chinese composition, an introduction explaining how and why one chooses this topic is not only acceptable, but often regarded as necessary. It arouses the reader's interest in the topic little by little (and this is seen as a virtue of composition) and gives him/her a sense of refinement. The famous Robert B. Kaplan "noodles" contrasting a spiral Oriental thought process with a straight-line Western approach ("Cultural Thought Patterns in Inter-Cultural Education," *Readings on English as a*

Second Language, Ed. Kenneth Croft, 2nd ed., Winthrop, 1980, 403–10) may be too simplistic to capture the preferred pattern of writing in English, but I think they still express some truth about Oriental writing. A Chinese writer often clears the surrounding bushes before attacking the real target. This bush-clearing pattern in Chinese writing goes back two thousand years to Kong Fuzi (Confucius). Before doing anything, Kong says in his *Luen Yu (Analects)*, one first needs to call things by their proper names (expressed by his phrase "Zheng Ming"). In other words, before touching one's main thesis, one should first state the "conditions" of composition: how, why, and when the piece is being composed. All of this will serve as a proper foundation on which to build the "house" of the piece. In the two thousand years after Kong, this principle of composition was gradually formalized (especially through the formal essays required by imperial examinations) and became known as "Ba Gu," or the eight-legged essay. The logic of Chinese composition, exemplified by the eight-legged essay, is like the peeling of an onion: Layer after layer is removed until the reader finally arrives at the central point, the core.

15   *Ba Gu* still influences modern Chinese writing. Carolyn Matalene has an excellent discussion of this logical (or illogical) structure and its influence on her Chinese students' efforts to write in English ("Contrastive Rhetoric: An American Writing Teacher in China," *College English 47* [November 1985]: 789–808). A recent Chinese textbook for composition lists six essential steps (factors) for writing a narrative essay, steps to be taken in this order: time, place, character, event, cause, and consequence (*Yuwen Jichu Zhishi Liushi Jiang* [*Sixty Lessons on the Basics of the Chinese Language*], Ed. Beijing Research Institute of Education, Beijing Publishing House, 1981, 525–609). Most Chinese students (including me) are taught to follow this sequence in composition.

The straightforward approach to composition in English seemed to me, at first, illogical. One could not jump to the topic. One had to walk step by step to reach the topic. In several of my early papers I found that the Chinese approach—the bush-clearing approach—persisted, and I had considerable difficulty writing (and in fact understanding) topic sentences. In what I deemed to be topic sentences, I grudgingly gave out themes. Today, those papers look to me like Chinese papers with forced or false English openings. For example, in a narrative paper on a trip to New York, I wrote the forced/false topic sentence, "A trip to New York in winter is boring." In the next few paragraphs, I talked about the weather, the people who went with me, and so on, before I talked about what I learned from the trip. My real thesis was that one could always learn something even on a boring trip.

The Alogical Pattern

In learning English composition, I found that there was yet another cultural blueprint affecting my logical thinking. I found from my early papers that very often I was unconsciously under the influence of a Chinese critical approach called the creation of "yijing," which is totally non-Western. The direct translation of the word "yijing" is: yi, "mind or consciousness," and jing, "environment." An ancient approach which has existed in China for many centuries and is still the subject of much discussion, yijing is a complicated concept that defies a universal definition. But most critics in China nowadays seem to agree on one point, that yijing is the critical approach that separates Chinese literature and criticism from Western literature and criticism. Roughly speaking, yijing is the process of creating a pictorial environment while reading a piece of literature. Many critics in China believe that yijing is a creative process of inducing oneself, while reading a piece of literature or looking at a piece of art, to create mental pictures, in order to reach a unity of nature, the author, and the reader. Therefore, it is by its very nature both creative and critical. According to the theory, this nonverbal, pictorial process leads directly to a higher ground of beauty and morality. Almost all critics in China agree that yijing is not a process of logical thinking—it is not a process of moving from the premises of an argument to its conclusion, which is the foundation of Western criticism. According to yijing, the process of criticizing a piece of art or literary work has to involve the process of creation on the reader's part. In yijing, verbal thoughts and pictorial thoughts are one. Thinking is conducted largely in pictures and then "transcribed" into words. (Ezra Pound once tried to capture the creative aspect of yijing in poems such as "In a Station of the Metro." He also tried to capture the critical aspect of it in his theory of imagism and vorticism, even though he did not know the term "yijing.") One characteristic of the yijing approach to criticism, therefore, is that it often includes a description of the created mental pictures on the part of the reader/critic and his/her mental attempt to bridge (unite) the literary work, the pictures, with ultimate beauty and peace.

In looking back at my critical papers for various classes, I discovered that I unconsciously used the approach of yijing, especially in some of my earlier papers when I seemed not yet to have been in the grip of Western logical critical approaches. I wrote, for instance, an essay entitled "Wordsworth's Sound and Imagination: The Snowdon Episode." In the major part of the essay I described the pictures that flashed in my mind while I was reading passages in Wordsworth's long poem, *The Prelude*.

> I saw three climbers (myself among them) winding up the mountain in silence "at the dead of night," absorbed in their "private thoughts." The sky was full of blocks of clouds of different colors, freely changing their shapes, like oily pigments disturbed in a bucket of water. All of a sudden, the moonlight broke the darkness "like a flash," lighting up the mountain tops. Under the "naked moon," the band saw a vast sea of mist and vapor, a silent ocean. Then the silence was abruptly broken, and we heard the "roaring of waters, torrents, streams/Innumerable, roaring with one voice" from a "blue chasm," a fracture in the vapor of the sea. It was a joyful revelation of divine truth to the human mind: the bright, "naked" moon sheds the light of "higher reasons" and "spiritual love" upon us; the vast ocean of mist looked like a thin curtain through which we vaguely saw the infinity of nature beyond; and the sounds of roaring waters coming out of the chasm of vapor cast us into the boundless spring of imagination from the depth of the human heart. Evoked by the divine light from above, the human spring of imagination is joined by the natural spring and becomes a sustaining source of energy, feeding "upon infinity" while transcending infinity at the same time. . . .

Here I was describing my own experience more than Wordsworth's. The picture described by the poet is taken over and developed by the reader. The imagination of the author and the imagination of the reader are thus joined together. There was no "because" or "therefore" in the paper. There was little *logic*. And I thought it was (and it is) criticism. This seems to me a typical (but simplified) example of the yijing approach. (Incidentally, the instructor, a kind professor, found the paper interesting, though a bit "strange.")

20   I am not saying that such a pattern of "alogical" thinking is wrong—in fact some English instructors find it interesting and acceptable—but it is very non-Western. Since I was in this country to learn the English language and English literature, I had to abandon Chinese "pictorial logic," and to learn Western "verbal logic."

If I Had to Start Again

The change is profound: Through my understanding of new meanings of words like "individualism," "idealism," and "I," I began to accept the underlying concepts and values of American writing, and by learning to use "topic sentences" I began to accept a new logic. Thus, when I write papers in English, I am able to obey all the general rules of English composition. In doing this I feel that I am writing through, with, and because of a new identity. I welcome the change, for it has added a new dimension to me and to my view of the world. I am not saying that I have entirely lost my Chinese identity. In fact I feel that I will never lose it. Any time I write in Chinese, I resume my old identity, and obey the rules of Chinese composition such as "Make the 'I' modest," and "Beat around the bush before attacking the central topic." It is necessary for me to have such a Chinese identity in order to write authentic Chinese. (I have seen people who, after learning to write in English, use English logic and sentence patterning to write Chinese. They produce very awkward Chinese texts.) But when I write in English, I imagine myself slipping into a new "skin," and I let the "I" behave much more aggressively and knock the topic right on the head. Being conscious of these different identities has helped me to reconcile different systems of values and logic, and has played a pivotal role in my learning to compose in English.

Looking back, I realize that the process of learning to write in English is in fact a process of creating and defining a new identity and balancing it with the old identity. The process of learning English composition would have been easier if I had realized this earlier and consciously sought to compare the two different identities required by the two writing systems from two different cultures. It is fine and perhaps even necessary for American composition teachers to teach about topic sentences, paragraphs, the use of punctuation, documentation, and so on, but can anyone design exercises sensitive to the ideological and logical differences that students like me experience—and design them so they can be introduced at an early stage of an English composition class? As I pointed out earlier, the traditional advice "Just be yourself" is not clear and helpful to students from Korea, China, Vietnam, or India. From "Be yourself" we are likely to hear either "Forget your cultural habit of writing" or "Write as you would write in your own language." But neither of the two is what the instructor meant or what we want to do. It would be helpful if he or she pointed out the different cultural/ideological connotations of the word "I," the connotations that exist in a group-centered culture and an individual-centered culture. To sharpen the contrast, it might be useful to design papers on topics like "The Individual vs. The Group: China vs. America" or "Different 'I's' in Different Cultures."

Carolyn Matalene mentioned in her article (789) an incident concerning American businessmen who presented their Chinese hosts with gifts of cheddar cheese, not knowing that the Chinese generally do not like cheese. Liking cheddar cheese may not be essential to writing English prose, but being truly accustomed to the social norms that stand behind ideas such as the English "I" and the logical pattern of English composition—call it "compositional cheddar cheese"—is essential to writing in English. Matalene does not provide an "elixir" to help her Chinese students like English "compositional cheese," but rather recommends, as do I, that composition teachers not be afraid to give foreign students English "cheese," but to make sure to hand it out slowly, sympathetically, and fully realizing that it tastes very peculiar in the mouths of those used to a very different cuisine.

Analyzing Rhetorical Choices

1. How does Shen create a rhetorical ethos through his writing that speaks with authority and connects with the reader?

2. Shen cites many writers and texts in his effort to describe the process of his becoming literate in English. Do these sources contribute to the persuasiveness of his account? How do you assess their effectiveness?

3. Given what Shen writes about "ideological identity," is this essay composed more from a Chinese or from an American "identity"? Explain your response and what the difference is between the two in terms of rhetorical choices made by the writer. In responding, explain why you think he includes so much about Chinese ways of composing.

Writing About Issues and Contexts

1. Shen believes that "Rule number one in English composition is: Be yourself." Do you believe that this is the case? Why or why not? What assumptions lie behind Shen's statement? Is this a helpful concept for American-born students? Why or why not?

2. What do you think of Shen's view of the topic sentence? How does his discussion explain his cultural perspectives? How might it help you articulate yours?

3. Do you agree that "the process of learning to write in English is in fact a process of creating and defining a new identity and balancing it with the old identity"? Is this as true for native speakers as it is for nonnative speakers of English?

*One of eight children, **Malcolm Little** (1925–1965) was born in Omaha, Nebraska. Driven out of Nebraska by the Ku Klux Klan because of preaching a form of black nationalism, Malcolm's father moved the family to Michigan; there, when Malcolm was six, the Reverend Earl Little was murdered. Malcolm X ultimately ended up in foster homes and, though he did well in school, was discouraged from pursuing his dream of becoming a lawyer. He ended up in prison for burglary, and as an inmate engaged in an intensive self-education program. Greatly influenced by the writings of Elijah Muhammad, founder of the group now known as the Nation of Islam, Malcolm X became a well-known member, an adherent of Islam, and a disciple of its leader. In 1963, he left the group, then known as the Black Muslims, and founded a competing organization. In 1964 he narrated his life story to Alex Haley (author of* Roots*) and that account was published in 1965 as* The Autobiography of Malcolm X, *an excerpt of which follows here. Malcolm X was assassinated in 1965 by three men, reputedly followers of the Black Muslim leader, Elijah Muhammad.*

Malcolm X

My First Conk

Shorty soon decided that my hair was finally long enough to be conked. He had promised to school me in how to beat the barber shops' three- and four-dollar price by making up congolene, and then conking ourselves.

I took the little list of ingredients he had printed out for me, and went to a grocery store, where I got a can of Red Devil lye, two eggs, and two medium-sized white potatoes. Then at a drugstore near the poolroom, I asked for a large jar of vaseline, a large bar of soap, a large-toothed comb and a fine-toothed comb, one of those rubber hoses with a metal spray-head, a rubber apron, and a pair of gloves.

"Going to lay on that first conk?" the drugstore man asked me. I proudly told him, grinning, "Right!"

Shorty paid six dollars a week for a room in his cousin's shabby apartment. His cousin wasn't at home. "It's like the pad's mine, he spends so much time with his woman," Shorty said. "Now, you watch me—"

5   He peeled the potatoes and thin-sliced them into a quart-sized Mason fruit jar, then started stirring them with a wooden spoon as he gradually poured in a little over half the can of lye. "Never use a metal spoon; the lye will turn it black," he told me.

A jelly-like, starchy-looking glop resulted from the lye and potatoes, and Shorty broke in the two eggs, stirring real fast—his own conk
and dark face bent down close. The congolene turned pale-yellowish.
"Feel the jar," Shorty said. I cupped my hand against the outside, and
snatched it away. "Damn right, it's hot, that's the lye," he said. "So
you know it's going to burn when I comb it in—it burns bad. But the
longer you can stand it, the straighter the hair."

He made me sit down, and he tied the string of the new rubber
apron tightly around my neck, and combed up my bush of hair. Then,
from the big vaseline jar, he took a handful and massaged it hard all
through my hair and into the scalp. He also thickly vaselined my neck,
ears and forehead. "When I get to washing out your head, be sure to
tell me anywhere you feel any little stinging," Shorty warned me,
washing his hands, then pulling on the rubber gloves, and tying on his
own rubber apron. "You always got to remember that any congolene
left in burns a sore into your head."

The congolene just felt warm when Shorty started combing it in.
But then my head caught fire.

I gritted my teeth and tried to pull the sides of the kitchen table
together. The comb felt as if it was raking my skin off.

10   My eyes watered, my nose was running. I couldn't stand it any
longer; I bolted to the washbasin. I was cursing Shorty with every
name I could think of when he got the spray going and started soap
lathering my head.

He lathered and spray-rinsed, lathered and spray-rinsed, maybe
ten or twelve times, each time gradually closing the hot-water faucet,
until the rinse was cold, and that helped some.

"You feel any stinging spots?"

"No," I managed to say. My knees were trembling.

"Sit back down, then. I think we got it all out okay."

15   The flame came back as Shorty, with a thick towel, started drying
my head, rubbing hard. *"Easy, man, easy!"* I kept shouting.

"The first time's always worst. You get used to it better before
long. You took it real good, homeboy. You got a good conk."

When Shorty let me stand up and see in the mirror, my hair hung
down in limp, damp strings. My scalp still flamed, but not as badly; I
could bear it. He draped the towel around my shoulders, over my rubber apron, and began again vaselining my hair.

I could feel him combing, straight back, first the big comb, then
the fine-tooth one.

Then, he was using a razor, very delicately, on the back of my
neck. Then, finally, shaping the sideburns.

20   My first view in the mirror blotted out the hurting. I'd seen some pretty conks, but when it's the first time, on your *own* head, the transformation, after the lifetime of kinks, is staggering.

The mirror reflected Shorty behind me. We both were grinning and sweating. And on top of my head was this thick, smooth sheen of shining red hair—real red—as straight as any white man's.

How ridiculous I was! Stupid enough to stand there simply lost in admiration of my hair now looking "white," reflected in the mirror in Shorty's room. I vowed that I'd never again be without a conk, and I never was for many years.

This was my first really big step toward self-degradation: when I endured all of that pain, literally burning my flesh to have it look like a white man's hair. I had joined that multitude of Negro men and women in America who are brainwashed into believing that the black people are "inferior"—and white people "superior"—that they will even violate and mutilate their God-created bodies to try to look "pretty" by white standards.

Look around today, in every small town and big city, from two-bit catfish and soda-pop joints into the "integrated" lobby of the Waldorf-Astoria, and you'll see conks on black men. And you'll see black women wearing these green and pink and purple and red and platinum-blonde wigs. They're all more ridiculous than a slapstick comedy. It makes you wonder if the Negro has completely lost his sense of identity, lost touch with himself.

25   You'll see the conk worn by many, many so-called "upper class" Negroes, and, as much as I hate to say it about them, on all too many Negro entertainers. One of the reasons that I've especially admired some of them, like Lionel Hampton and Sidney Poitier, among others, is that they have kept their natural hair and fought to the top. I admire any Negro man who has never had himself conked, or who has had the sense to get rid of it—as I finally did.

I don't know which kind of self-defacing conk is the greater shame—the one you'll see on the heads of the black so-called "middle class" and "upper class," who ought to know better, or the one you'll see on the heads of the poorest, most downtrodden, ignorant black men. I mean the legal-minimum-wage ghetto-dwelling kind of Negro, as I was when I got my first one. It's generally among these poor fools that you'll see a black kerchief over the man's head, like Aunt Jemima; he's trying to make his conk last longer, between trips to the barbershop. Only for special occasions is this kerchief-protected conk exposed—to show off how "sharp" and "hip" its owner is. The ironic thing is that I have never heard any woman, white or black, express any admiration for a conk. Of course, any white woman with a black man isn't thinking about his hair. But I don't see how on earth a black woman with any race pride could walk down the street with any black man wearing a conk—the emblem of his shame that he is black.

To my own shame, when I say all of this, I'm talking first of all about myself—because you can't show me any Negro who ever conked more faithfully than I did. I'm speaking from personal experience when I say of any black man who conks today, or any white-wigged black woman, that if they gave the brains in their heads just half as much attention as they do their hair, they would be a thousand times better off.

Analyzing Rhetorical Choices

1. Describe the process for getting a conk. In what ways does this process describe another process that has little to do with straightening hair? How can the "simple" process of hair straightening convey this larger meaning?

2. Why do you think Malcolm X informs the reader that "you can't show me any Negro who ever conked more faithfully than I did"? How does this statement influence the reader's perception of Malcolm X in terms of his overall argument about conking?

3. Comment on Malcolm X's use of irony and understatement. What effects do these have on you as a reader?

4. What impression of Malcolm X is conveyed by this excerpt? What aspects of his language and story evoke your sense of the man?

Writing About Issues and Contexts

1. When Malcolm X refers to the conk as a "self-defacing" shame, he evokes a strong history of internalized oppression on the part of African Americans. What does he mean?

2. When he writes of "the black so-called 'middle class' and 'upper class,'" why does Malcolm X use the term *so-called* and put the words *middle class* and *upper class* in quotation marks? Why did Malcolm X view the African American middle and upper classes as "so-called" classes? Explain ways in which this situation may or may not have changed since Malcolm X wrote these words.

3. Malcolm X describes the process of conking, but he does so in the form of a story rather than as a set of instructions. Why do you think he chooses this method of deploying this mode?

4. What implicit statement does Malcolm X make when he writes: "And on top of my head was this thick, smooth sheen of shining red hair—real red—as straight as any white man's"?

Born in England, the daughter of a baron and baroness, **Jessica Mitford**
*(1917–1996) rebelled against her rich and conservative parents, coming
to the United States at the age of 21 and living out the rest of her life in
this country, at first working in sales and as a bartender. She did not begin her writing career until she was 38 years old. Called "Queen of the
Muckrackers" by* Time *magazine, Mitford's notoriety as an investigative
reporter was solidified with the book from which the following excerpt is
taken. Titled* The American Way of Death *(1963), it offered a witty and
brilliant attack on the funeral industry in the United States. The book
horrified its readers—and angered those in the funeral industry. Mitford's
other books include an analysis of prisons,* Kind and Unusual
Punishment *(1974), and a critique of the business of giving birth,* The
American Way of Birth *(1994).*

Jessica Mitford

The American Way
of Death

Embalming is indeed a most extraordinary procedure, and one
must wonder at the docility of Americans who each year pay hundreds
of millions of dollars for its perpetuation, blissfully ignorant of what it
is all about, what is done, how it is done. Not one in ten thousand has
any idea of what actually takes place. Books on the subject are extremely hard to come by. They are not to be found in most libraries or
bookshops.

In an era when huge television audiences watch surgical operations in the comfort of their living rooms, when, thanks to the ani-
mated cartoon, the geography of the digestive system has become
familiar territory even to the nursery school set, in a land where the
satisfaction of curiosity about almost all matters is a national pastime,
the secrecy surrounding embalming can, surely, hardly be attributed
to the inherent gruesomeness of the subject. Custom in this regard has
within this century suffered a complete reversal. In the early days of
American embalming, when it was performed in the home of the deceased, it was almost mandatory for some relative to stay by the embalmer's side and witness the procedure. Today, family members who

might wish to be in attendance would certainly be dissuaded by the funeral director. All others, except apprentices, are excluded by law from the preparation room.

A close look at what does actually take place may explain in large measure the undertaker's intractable reticence concerning a procedure that has become his major *raison d'être*. Is it possible he fears that public information about embalming might lead patrons to wonder if they really want this service? If the funeral men are loath to discuss the subject outside the trade, the reader may, understandably, be equally loath to go on reading at this point. For those who have the stomach for it, let us part the formaldehyde curtain. . . .

The body is first laid out in the undertaker's morgue—or rather, Mr. Jones is reposing in the preparation room—to be readied to bid the world farewell.

5   The preparation room in any of the better funeral establishments has the tiled and sterile look of a surgery, and indeed the embalmer-restorative artist who does his chores there is beginning to adopt the term "dermasurgeon" (appropriately corrupted by some mortician-writers as "demisurgeon") to describe his calling. His equipment, consisting of scalpels, scissors, augers, forceps, clamps, needles, pumps, tubes, bowls, and basin, is crudely imitative of the surgeon's, as is his technique, acquired in a nine- or twelve-month post-high-school course in an embalming school. He is supplied by an advanced chemical industry with a bewildering array of fluids, sprays, pastes, oils, powders, creams, to fix or soften tissue, shrink or distend it as needed, dry it here, restore the moisture there. There are cosmetics, waxes, and paints to fill and cover features, even plaster of Paris to replace entire limbs. There are ingenious aids to prop and stabilize the cadaver: a Vari-Pose Head Rest, the Edwards Arm and Hand Positioner, the Repose Block (to support the shoulders during the embalming), and the Throop Foot Positioner, which resembles an old-fashioned stocks.

Mr. John H. Eckles, president of the Eckles College of Mortuary Science, thus describes the first part of the embalming procedure: "In the hands of a skilled practitioner, this work may be done in a comparatively short time and without mutilating the body other than by slight incision—so slight that it scarcely would cause serious inconvenience if made upon a living person. It is necessary to remove the blood, and doing this not only helps in the disinfecting, but removes the principal cause of disfigurements due to discoloration."

Another textbook discusses the all-important time element: "The earlier this is done, the better, for every hour that elapses between death and embalming will add to the problems and complications encountered. . . ." Just how soon should one get going on the embalming? The author tells us, "On the basis of such scanty information made available to this profession through its rudimentary and haphazard system of technical research, we must conclude that the best results are to be obtained if the subject is embalmed before life is completely extinct—that is, before cellular death has occurred. In the average case, this would mean within an hour after somatic death." For those who feel that there is something a little rudimentary, not to say haphazard, about this advice, a comforting thought is offered by another writer. Speaking of fears entertained in early days of premature burial, he points out, "One of the effects of embalming by chemical injection, however, has been to dispel fears of live burial." How true; once the blood is removed, chances of live burial are indeed remote.

To return to Mr. Jones, the blood is drained out through the veins and replaced by embalming fluid pumped in through the arteries. As noted in *The Principles and Practices of Embalming,* "every operator has a favorite injection and drainage point—a fact which becomes a handicap only if he fails or refuses to forsake his favorites when conditions demand it." Typical favorites are the carotid artery, femoral artery, jugular vein, subclavian vein. There are various choices of embalming fluid. If Flextone is used, it will produce a "mild, flexible rigidity. The skin retains a velvety softness, the tissues are rubbery and pliable. Ideal for women and children." It may be blended with B. and G. Products Company's Lyf-Lyk tint, which is guaranteed to reproduce "nature's own skin texture . . . the velvety appearance of living tissue." Suntone comes in three separate tints: Suntan; Special Cosmetic Tint, a pink shade "especially indicated for young female subjects"; and Regular Cosmetic Tint, moderately pink.

About three to six gallons of a dyed and perfumed solution of formaldehyde, glycerin, borax, phenol, alcohol, and water is soon circulating through Mr. Jones, whose mouth has been sewn together with a "needle directed upward between the upper lip and gum and brought out through the left nostril," with the corners raised slightly "for a more pleasant expression." If he should be buck-toothed, his teeth are cleaned with Bon Ami and coated with colorless nail polish. His eyes, meanwhile, are closed with flesh-tinted eye caps and eye cement.

10   The next step is to have at Mr. Jones with a thing called a trocar. This is a long, hollow needle attached to a tube. It is jabbed into the abdomen, poked around the entrails and chest cavity, the contents of which are pumped out and replaced with "cavity fluid." This done,

and the hole in the abdomen sewn up, Mr. Jones's face is heavily creamed (to protect the skin from burns which may be caused by leakage of the chemicals), and he is covered with a sheet and left unmolested for a while. But not for long—there is more, much more, in store for him. He has been embalmed, but not yet restored, and the best time to start restorative work is eight to ten hours after embalming, when the tissues have become firm and dry.

The object of all this attention to the corpse, it must be remembered, is to make it presentable for viewing in an attitude of healthy repose. "Our customs require the presentation of our dead in the semblance of normality . . . unmarred by the ravages of illness, disease or mutilation," says Mr. J. Sheridan Mayer in his *Restorative Art*. This is rather a large order since few people die in the full bloom of health, unravaged by illness and unmarked by some disfigurement. The funeral industry is equal to the challenge: "In some cases the gruesome appearance of a mutilated or disease-ridden subject may be quite discouraging. The task of restoration may seem impossible and shake the confidence of the embalmer. This is the time for intestinal fortitude and determination. Once the formative work is begun and affected tissues are cleaned or removed, all doubts of success vanish. It is surprising and gratifying to discover the results which may be obtained."

The embalmer, having allowed an appropriate interval to elapse, returns to the attack, but now he brings into play the skill and equipment of sculptor and cosmetician. Is a hand missing? Casting one in plaster of Paris is a simple matter. "For replacement purposes, only a cast of the back of the hand is necessary; this is within the ability of the average operator and is quite adequate." If a lip or two, a nose or an ear should be missing, the embalmer has at hand a variety of restorative waxes with which to model replacements. Pores and skin texture are simulated by stippling with a little brush, and over this cosmetics are laid on. Head off? Decapitation cases are rather routinely handled. Ragged edges are trimmed, and head joined to torso with a series of splints, wires and sutures. It is a good idea to have a little something at the neck—a scarf or high collar—when time for viewing comes. Swollen mouth? Cut out tissue as needed from inside the lips. If too much is removed, the surface contour can easily be restored by padding with cotton. Swollen necks and cheeks are reduced by removing tissue through vertical incisions made down each side of the neck. "When the deceased is casketed, the pillow will hide the suture incisions . . . as an extra precaution against leakage, the suture may be painted with liquid sealer."

The opposite condition is more likely to present itself—that of emaciation. His hypodermic syringe now loaded with massage cream, the embalmer seeks out and fills the hollowed and sunken areas by injection. In this procedure the backs of the hands and fingers and the underchin area should not be neglected.

Positioning the lips is a problem that recurrently challenges the ingenuity of the embalmer. Closed too tightly, they tend to give a stern, even disapproving expression. Ideally, embalmers feel, the lips should give the impression of being ever so slightly parted, the upper lip protruding slightly for a more youthful appearance. This takes some engineering, however, as the lips tend to drift apart. Lip drift can sometimes be remedied by pushing one or two straight pins through the inner margin of the lower lip and then inserting them between the two front upper teeth. If Mr. Jones happens to have no teeth, the pins can just as easily be anchored in his Armstrong Face Former and Denture Replacer. Another method to maintain lip closure is to dislocate the lower jaw, which is then held in its new position by a wire run through holes which have been drilled through the upper jaws at the midline. As the French are fond of saying, *il faut souffrir pour être belle.*[1]

15   If Mr. Jones has died of jaundice, the embalming fluid will very likely turn him green. Does this deter the embalmer? Not if he has intestinal fortitude. Masking pastes and cosmetics are heavily laid on, burial garments and casket interiors are color-correlated with particular care, and Jones is displayed beneath rose-colored lights. Friends will say, "How *well* he looks." Death by carbon monoxide, on the other hand, can be rather a good thing from an embalmer's viewpoint: "One advantage is the fact that this type of discoloration is an exaggerated form of a natural pink coloration." This is nice because the healthy glow is already present and needs but little attention.

The patching and filling completed, Mr. Jones is now shaved, washed, and dressed. Cream-based cosmetic, available in pink, flesh, suntan, brunette, and blonde, is applied to his hands and face, his hair is shampooed and combed (and, in the case of Mrs. Jones, set), his hands manicured. For the horny-handed son of toil special care must be taken; cream should be applied to remove ingrained grime, and the nails cleaned. "If he were not in the habit of having them manicured in life, trimming and shaping is advised for better appearance—never questioned by kin."

---

[1] It is necessary to suffer to be beautiful.

Jones is now ready for casketing (this is the present participle of the verb "to casket"). In this operation his right shoulder should be depressed slightly "to turn the body a bit to the right and soften the appearance of lying flat on the back." Positioning the hands is a matter of importance, and special rubber positioning blocks may be used. The hands should be cupped slightly for a more lifelike, relaxed appearance. Proper placement of the body requires a delicate sense of balance. It should lie as high as possible in the casket, yet not so high that the lid, when lowered, will hit the nose. On the other hand, we are cautioned, placing the body too low "creates the impression that the body is in a box."

Jones is next wheeled into the appointed slumber room where a few last touches may be added—his favorite pipe placed in his hand or, if he was a great reader, a book propped into position. (In the case of little Master Jones a Teddy bear may be clutched.) Here he will hold open house for a few days, visiting hours 10 A.M. to 9 P.M.

Analyzing Rhetorical Choices

1. How well does Mitford illustrate the process of embalming?
2. What is the tone of this excerpt? What aspects of Mitford's language use indicate this? How does it provide counterpoint to the subject of the essay? What is the effect of this contrast?
3. Mitford makes use of many technical terms in her process analysis. How effective are these citations? How do they influence your perception of her authority in terms of describing embalming?
4. Why does Mitford name the corpse? How does this rhetorical decision affect your response to the essay?

Writing About Issues and Contexts

1. How does Mitford's essay implicate the reader—and the consumer—in the practices of embalming? For what purpose?
2. Comment on the ways in which the funeral industry takes advantage of consumers, according to Mitford. What is the effect of "kin" rarely questioning an embalmer's techniques? How does Mitford illustrate that funerals are not for the dead but for those who survive? Why?
3. Is Mitford guilty of insensitivity in writing this essay? Is she demonstrating insufficient regard for both the funeral industry and the grieving survivors? Offer your views in a response that attacks or defends Mitford's account.

Paul Roberts *(1917–1967) was an English professor with a specialization in linguistics. Educated at San Jose State University and the University of California at Berkeley, Roberts taught at San Jose State and Cornell University and directed the Center for American Studies in Rome. His textbooks, which were well known to anyone attending high school or college in the 1950s and 1960s, include* Understanding Grammar *(1954) and his best-known work,* Understanding English *(1958), from which this excerpt is taken.*

Paul Roberts

How to Say Nothing in 500 Words

Nothing About Something

It's Friday afternoon, and you have almost survived another week of classes. You are just looking forward dreamily to the weekend when the English instructor says: "For Monday you will turn in a five-hundred-word composition on college football."

Well, that puts a good big hole in the weekend. You don't have any strong views on college football one way or the other. You get rather excited during the season and go to all the home games and find it rather more fun than not. On the other hand, the class has been reading Robert Hutchins in the anthology and perhaps Shaw's "Eighty-Yard Run," and from the class discussion you have got the idea that the instructor thinks college football is for the birds. You are no fool, you. You can figure out what side to take.

After dinner you get out the portable typewriter that you got for high school graduation. You might as well get it over with and enjoy Saturday and Sunday. Five hundred words is about two double-spaced pages with normal margins. You put in a sheet of paper, think up a title, and you're off:

Why College Football Should Be Abolished

College football should be abolished because it's bad for the school and also bad for the players. The players are so busy practicing that they don't have any time for their studies.

This, you feel, is a mighty good start. The only trouble is that it's only thirty-two words. You still have four hundred and sixty-eight to go, and you've pretty well exhausted the subject. It comes to you that you do your best thinking in the morning, so you put away the type-writer and go to the movies. But the next morning you have to do your washing and some math problems, and in the afternoon you go to the game. The English instructor turns up too, and you wonder if you've taken the right side after all. Saturday night you have a date, and Sunday morning you have to go to church. (You shouldn't let English assignments interfere with your religion.) What with one thing and an-other, it's ten o'clock Sunday night before you get out the typewriter again. You make a pot of coffee and start to fill out your views on col-lege football. Put a little meat on the bones.

Why College Football Should Be Abolished

In my opinion, it seems to me that college football should be abol-ished. The reason why I think this to be true is because I feel that football is bad for the colleges in nearly every respect. As Robert Hutchins says in his article in our anthology in which he discusses college football, it would be better if the colleges had race horses and had races with one another, because then the horses would not have to attend classes. I firmly agree with Mr. Hutchins on this point, and I am sure that many other students would agree too.

One reason why it seems to me that college football is bad is that it has become too commercial. In the olden times when people played football just for the fun of it, maybe college football was all right, but they do not play football just for the fun of it now as they used to in the old days. Nowadays college football is what you might call a big business. Maybe this is not true at all schools, and I don't think it is especially true here at State, but certainly this is the case at most colleges and universities in America nowadays, as Mr. Hutchins points out in his very interesting ar-ticle. Actually the coaches and alumni go around to the high schools and offer the high school stars large salaries to come to their colleges and play football for them. There was one case where a high school star was of-fered a convertible if he would play football for a certain college.

Another reason for abolishing college football is that it is bad for the players. They do not have time to get a college education, because they are so busy playing football. A football player has to practice every afternoon from three to six, and then he is so tired that he can't concentrate on his studies. He just feels like dropping off to sleep after dinner, and then the next day he goes to his classes without having studied and maybe he fails the test.

(Good ripe stuff so far, but you're still a hundred and fifty-one words from home. One more push.)

> Also I think college football is bad for the colleges and the universities because not very many students get to participate in it. Out of a college of ten thousand students only seventy-five or a hundred play football, if that many. Football is what you might call a spectator sport. That means that most people go to watch it but do not play it themselves.

(Four hundred and fifteen. Well, you still have the conclusion, and when you retype it, you can make the margins a little wider.)

> These are the reasons why I agree with Mr. Hutchins that college football should be abolished in American colleges and universities.

5   On Monday you turn it in, moderately hopeful, and on Friday it comes back marked "weak in content" and sporting a big "D."

This essay is exaggerated a little, not much. The English instructor will recognize it as reasonably typical of what an assignment on college football will bring in. He knows that nearly half of the class will contrive in five hundred words to say that college football is too commercial and bad for the players. Most of the other half will inform him that college football builds character and prepares one for life and brings prestige to the school. As he reads paper after paper all saying the same thing in almost the same words, all bloodless, five hundred words dripping out of nothing, he wonders how he allowed himself to get trapped into teaching English when he might have had a happy and interesting life as an electrician or a confidence man.

Well, you may ask, what can you do about it? The subject is one on which you have few convictions and little information. Can you be expected to make a dull subject interesting? As a matter of fact, this is precisely what you are expected to do. This is the writer's essential task. All subjects, except sex, are dull until somebody makes them interesting. The writer's job is to find the argument, the approach, the angle, the wording that will take the reader with him. This is seldom easy, and it is particularly hard in subjects that have been much discussed: College Football, Fraternities, Popular Music, Is Chivalry Dead?, and the like. You will feel that there is nothing you can do with such subjects except repeat the old bromides. But there are some things you can do which will make your papers, if not throbbingly alive, at least less insufferably tedious than they might otherwise be.

Avoid the Obvious Content

Say the assignment is college football. Say that you've decided to be against it. Begin by putting down the arguments that come to your mind: it is too commercial, it takes the students' minds off their studies, it is hard on the players, it makes the university a kind of circus instead of an intellectual center, for most schools it is financially ruinous. Can you think of any more arguments just off hand? All right. Now when you write your paper, *make sure that you don't use any of the material on this list.* If these are the points that leap to your mind, they will leap to everyone else's too, and whether you get a "C" or a "D" may depend on whether the instructor reads your paper early when he is fresh and tolerant or late, when the sentence "In my opinion, college football has become too commercial," inexorably repeated, has brought him to the brink of lunacy.

Be against college football for some reason or reasons of your own. If they are keen and perceptive ones, that's splendid. But even if they are trivial or foolish or indefensible, you are still ahead so long as they are not everybody else's reasons too. Be against it because the colleges don't spend enough money on it to make it worth while, because it is bad for the characters of the spectators, because the players are forced to attend classes, because the football stars hog all the beautiful women, because it competes with baseball and is therefore un-American and possibly Communist inspired. There are lots of more or less unused reasons for being against college football.

10   Sometimes it is a good idea to sum up and dispose of the trite and conventional points before going on to your own. This has the advantage of indicating to the reader that you are going to be neither trite nor conventional. Something like this:

> We are often told that college football should be abolished because it has become too commercial or because it is bad for the players. These arguments are no doubt very cogent, but they don't really go to the heart of the matter.

Then you go to the heart of the matter.

Take the Less Usual Side

One rather simple way of getting interest into your paper is to take the side of the argument that most of the citizens will want to avoid. If the assignment is an essay on dogs, you can, if you choose, explain that dogs are faithful and lovable companions, intelligent, useful as

guardians of the house and protectors of children, indispensable in police work—in short, when all is said and done, man's best friends. Or
you can suggest that those big brown eyes conceal, more often than
not, a vacuity of mind and an inconstancy of purpose; that the dogs
you have known most intimately have been mangy, ill-tempered
brutes, incapable of instruction; and that only your nobility of mind
and fear of arrest prevent you from kicking the flea-ridden animals
when you pass them on the street.

Naturally, personal convictions will sometimes dictate your approach. If the assigned subject is "Is Methodism Rewarding to the
Individual?" and you are a pious Methodist, you have really no choice.
But few assigned subjects, if any, will fall in this category. Most of
them will lie in broad areas of discussion with much to be said on both
sides. They are intellectual exercises and it is legitimate to argue now
one way and now another, as debaters do in similar circumstances.
Always take the side that looks to you hardest, least defensible. It will
almost always turn out to be easier to write interestingly on that side.

This general advice applies where you have a choice of subjects. If
you are to choose among "The Value of Fraternities" and "My
Favorite High School Teacher" and "What I Think About Beetles," by
all means plump for the beetles. By the time the instructor gets to your
paper, he will be up to his ears in tedious tales about the French
teacher at Bloombury High and assertions about how fraternities build
character and prepare one for life. Your views on beetles, whatever
they are, are bound to be a refreshing change.

Don't worry too much about figuring out what the instructor thinks
about the subject so that you can cuddle up with him. Chances are his
views are no stronger than yours. If he does have convictions and you oppose them, his problem is to keep from grading you higher than you deserve in order to show he is not biased. This doesn't mean that you should
always cantankerously dissent from what the instructor says; that gets
tiresome too. And if the subject assigned is "My Pet Peeve," do not begin,
"My pet peeve is the English instructor who assigns papers on 'my pet
peeve.'" This was still funny during the War of 1812, but it has sort of lost
its edge since then. It is in general good manners to avoid personalities.

Slip Out of Abstraction

15   If you will study the essay on college football . . . you will perceive
that one reason for its appalling dullness is that it never gets down to
particulars. It is just a series of not very glittering generalities: "football

is bad for the colleges," "it has become too commercial," "football is a big business," "it is bad for the players," and so on. Such round phrases thudding against the reader's brain are unlikely to convince him, though they may well render him unconscious.

If you want the reader to believe that college football is bad for the players, you have to do more than say so. You have to display the evil. Take your roommate, Alfred Simkins, the second-string center. Picture poor old Alfy coming home from football practice every evening, bruised and aching, agonizingly tired, scarcely able to shovel the mashed potatoes into his mouth. Let us see him staggering up to the room, getting out his econ textbook, peering desperately at it with his good eye, falling asleep and failing the test in the morning. Let us share his unbearable tension as Saturday draws near. Will he fail, be demoted, lose his monthly allowance, be forced to return to the coal mines? And if he succeeds, what will be his reward? Perhaps a slight ripple of applause when the third-string center replaces him, a moment of elation in the locker room if the team wins, of despair if it loses. What will he look back on when he graduates from college? Toil and torn ligaments. And what will be his future? He is not good enough for pro football, and he is too obscure and weak in econ to succeed in stocks and bonds. College football is tearing the heart from Alfy Simkins and, when it finishes with him, will callously toss aside the shattered hulk.

This is no doubt a weak enough argument for the abolition of college football, but it is a sight better than saying, in three or four variations, that college football (in your opinion) is bad for the players.

Look at the work of any professional writer and notice how constantly he is moving from the generality, the abstract statement, to the concrete example, the facts and figures, the illustration. if he is writing on juvenile delinquency, he does not just tell you that juveniles are (it seems to him) delinquent and that (in his opinion) something should be done about it. He shows you juveniles being delinquent, tearing up movie theatres in Buffalo, stabbing high school principals in Dallas, smoking marijuana in Palo Alto. And more than likely he is moving toward some specific remedy, not just a general wringing of the hands.

It is no doubt possible to be *too* concrete, too illustrative or anecdotal, but few inexperienced writers err this way. For most the soundest advice is to be seeking always for the picture, to be always turning general remarks into seeable examples. Don't say, "Sororities teach girls the social graces." Say "Sorority life teaches a girl how to carry on a conversation while pouring tea, without sloshing the tea into the

saucer." Don't say, "I like certain kinds of popular music very much."
Say, "Whenever I hear Gerber Spinklittle play 'Mississippi Man' on the
trombone, my socks creep up my ankles."

Get Rid of Obvious Padding

20   The student toiling away at his weekly English theme is too often
tormented by a figure: five hundred words. How, he asks himself, is he
to achieve this staggering total? Obviously by never using one word
when he can somehow work in ten.

He is therefore seldom content with a plain statement like "Fast
driving is dangerous." This has only four words in it. He takes
thought, and the sentence becomes:

> In my opinion, fast driving is dangerous.

Better, but he can do better still:

> In my opinion, fast driving would seem to be rather dangerous.

If he is really adept, it may come out:

> In my humble opinion, though I do not claim to be an expert on
> this complicated subject, fast driving, in most circumstances, would
> seem to be rather dangerous in many respects, or at least so it would
> seem to me.

Thus four words have been turned into forty, and not an iota of content has been added.

Now this is a way to go about reaching five hundred words, and if
you are content with a "D" grade, it is as good a way as any. But if you
aim higher, you must work differently. Instead of stuffing your sentences with straw, you must try steadily to get rid of the padding, to
make your sentences lean and tough. If you are really working at it,
your first draft will greatly exceed the required total, and then you will
work it down, thus:

> It is thought in some quarters that fraternities do not contribute as
> much as might be expected to campus life.
> Some people think that fraternities contribute little to campus life.

> The average doctor who practices in small towns or in the country
> must toil night and day to heal the sick.
> Most country doctors work long hours.

> When I was a little girl, I suffered from shyness and embarrassment in the presence of others.
>
> I was a shy little girl.

> It is absolutely necessary for the person employed as a marine fireman to give the matter of steam pressure his undivided attention at all times.
>
> The fireman has to keep his eye on the steam gauge.

You may ask how you can arrive at five hundred words at this rate. Simply. You dig up more real content. Instead of taking a couple of obvious points off the surface of the topic and then circling warily around them for six paragraphs, you work in and explore, figure out the details. You illustrate. You say that fast driving is dangerous, and then you prove it. How long does it take to stop a car at forty and at eighty? How far can you see at night? What happens when a tire blows? What happens in a head-on collision at fifty miles an hour? Pretty soon your paper will be full of broken glass and blood and headless torsos, and reaching five hundred words will not really be a problem.

Call a Fool a Fool

Some of the padding in freshman themes is to be blamed not on anxiety about the word minimum but on excessive timidity. The student writes, "In my opinion, the principal of my high school acted in ways that I believe every unbiased person would have to call foolish." This isn't exactly what he means. What he means is, "My high school principal was a fool." If he was a fool, call him a fool. Hedging the thing about with "in-my-opinion's" and "it-seems-to-me's" and "as-I-see-it's" and "at-least-from-my-point-of-view's" gains you nothing. Delete these phrases whenever they creep into your paper.

25   The student's tendency to hedge stems from a modesty that in other circumstances would be commendable. He is, he realizes, young and inexperienced, and he half suspects that he is dopey and fuzzy-minded beyond the average. Probably only too true. But it doesn't help to announce your incompetence six times in every paragraph. Decide what you want to say and say it as vigorously as possible, without apology and in plain words.

Linguistic diffidence can take various forms. One is what we call *euphemism*. This is the tendency to call a spade "a certain garden implement" or women's underwear "unmentionables." It is stronger in some eras than others and in some people than others but it always operates more or less in subjects that are touchy or taboo: death, sex, madness, and so on. Thus we shrink from saying "He died last night" but say instead "passed away," "left us," "joined his Maker," "went to his reward." Or we try to take off the tension with a lighter cliché: "kicked the bucket," "cashed in his chips," "handed in his dinner pail." We have found all sorts of ways to avoid saying *mad* "mentally ill," "touched," "not quite right upstairs," "feeble-minded," "inno-cent," "simple," "off his trolley," "not in his right mind." Even such a now plain word as *insane* began as a euphemism with the meaning "not healthy."

Modern science, particularly psychology, contributes many poly-syllables in which we can wrap our thoughts and blunt their force. To many writers there is no such thing as a bad schoolboy. Schoolboys are maladjusted or unoriented or misunderstood or in need of guidance or lacking in continued success toward satisfactory integration of the per-sonality as a social unit, but they are never bad. Psychology no doubt makes us better men or women, more sympathetic and tolerant, but it doesn't make writing any easier. Had Shakespeare been confronted with psychology, "To be or not to be" might have come out "To con-tinue as a social unit or not to do so. That is the personality problem. Whether 'tis a better sign of integration at the conscious level to dis-play a psychic tolerance toward the maladjustments and repressions induced by one's lack of orientation in one's environment or—" But Hamlet would never have finished the soliloquy.

Writing in the modern world, you cannot altogether avoid modern jargon. Nor, in an effort to get away from euphemism, should you salt your paper with four-letter words. But you can do much if you will mount guard against those roundabout phrases, those echoing polysyl-lables that tend to slip into your writing to rob it of its crispness and force.

Beware of the Pat Expression

Other things being equal, avoid phrases like "other things being equal." Those sentences that come to you whole, or in two or three doughy lumps, are sure to be bad sentences. They are no creation of yours but pieces of common thought floating in the community soup.

30   Pat expressions are hard, often impossible, to avoid, because they come too easily to be noticed and seem too necessary to be dispensed

with. No writer avoids them altogether, but good writers avoid them more often than poor writers.

By "pat expressions" we mean such tags as "to all practical intents and purposes," "the pure and simple truth," "from where I sit," "the time of his life," "to the ends of the earth," "in the twinkling of an eye," "as sure as you're born," "over my dead body," "under cover of darkness," "took the easy way out," "when all is said and done," "told him time and time again," "parted the best of friends," "stand up and be counted," "gave him the best years of her life," "worked her fingers to the bone." Like other clichés, these expressions were once forceful. Now we should use them only when we can't possibly think of anything else.

Some pat expressions stand like a wall between the writer and thought. Such a one is "the American way of life." Many student writers feel that when they have said that something accords with the American way of life or does not they have exhausted the subject. Actually, they have stopped at the highest level of abstraction. The American way of life is the complicated set of bonds between a hundred and eighty million ways. All of us know this when we think about it, but the tag phrase too often keeps us from thinking about it.

So with many another phrase dear to the politician: "this great land of ours," "the man in the street," "our national heritage." These may prove our patriotism or give a clue to our political beliefs, but otherwise they add nothing to the paper except words.

Colorful Words

The writer builds with words, and no builder uses a raw material more slippery and elusive and treacherous. A writer's work is a constant struggle to get the right word in the right place, to find that particular word that will convey his meaning exactly, that will persuade the reader or soothe him or startle or amuse him. He never succeeds altogether—sometimes he feels that he scarcely succeeds at all—but such successes as he has are what make the thing worth doing.

35   There is no book of rules for this game. One progresses through everlasting experiment on the basis of ever-widening experience. There are few useful generalizations that one can make about words as words, but there are perhaps a few.

Some words are what we call "colorful." By this we mean that they are calculated to produce a picture or induce an emotion. They are dressy instead of plain, specific instead of general, loud instead of soft. Thus, in place of "Her heart beat," we may write "Her heart *pounded, throbbed, fluttered, danced.*" Instead of "He sat in his chair," we may say, "He *lounged, sprawled, coiled.*" Instead of "It was hot," we may say, "It was *blistering, sultry, muggy, suffocating, steamy, wilting.*"

However, it should not be supposed that the fancy word is always better. Often it is as well to write "Her heart beat" or "It was hot" if that is all it did or all it was. Ages differ in how they like their prose. The nineteenth century liked it rich and smoky. The twentieth has usually preferred it lean and cool. The twentieth-century writer, like all writers, is forever seeking the exact word, but he is wary of sounding feverish. He tends to pitch it low, to understate it, to throw it away. He knows that if he gets too colorful, the audience is likely to giggle.

See how this strikes you: "As the rich, golden glow of the sunset died away along the eternal western hills, Angela's limpid blue eyes looked softly and trustingly into Montague's flashing brown ones, and her heart pounded like a drum in time with the joyous song surging in her soul." Some people like that sort of thing, but most modern readers would say, "Good grief," and turn on the television.

Colored Words

Some words we would call not so much colorful as colored—that is, loaded with associations, good or bad. All words—except perhaps structure words—have associations of some sort. We have said that the meaning of a word is the sum of the contexts in which it occurs. When we hear a word, we hear with it an echo of all the situations in which we have heard it before.

40   In some words, these echoes are obvious and discussable. The word *mother*, for example, has, for most people, agreeable associations. When you hear *mother* you probably think of home, safety, love, food, and various other pleasant things. If one writes, "She was like a mother to me," he gets an effect which he would not get in "She was like an aunt to me." The advertiser makes use of the associations of *mother* by working it in when he talks about his product. The politician works it in when he talks about himself.

So also with such words as *home, liberty, fireside, contentment, patriot, tenderness, sacrifice, childlike, manly, bluff, limpid.* All of these words are loaded with favorable associations that would be rather hard to indicate in a straightforward definition. There is more than a literal difference between "They sat around the fireside" and

"They sat around the stove." They might have been equally warm and happy around the stove, but *fireside* suggests leisure, grace, quiet tradition, congenial company, and *stove* does not.

Conversely, some words have bad associations. *Mother* suggests pleasant things, but *mother-in-law* does not. Many mothers-in-law are heroically lovable and some mothers drink gin all day and beat their children insensible, but these facts of life are beside the point. The thing is that *mother* sounds good and *mother-in-law* does not.

Or consider the word *intellectual*. This would seem to be a complimentary term, but in point of fact it is not, for it has picked up associations of impracticality and ineffectuality and general dopiness. So also with such words as *liberal, reactionary, Communist, socialist, capitalist, radical, schoolteacher, truck driver, undertaker, operator, salesman, huckster, speculator*. These convey meanings on the literal level, but beyond that—sometimes, in some places—they convey contempt on the part of the speaker.

The question of whether to use loaded words or not depends on what is being written. The scientist, the scholar, try to avoid them; for the poet, the advertising writer, the public speaker, they are standard equipment. But every writer should take care that they do not substitute for thought. If you write, "Anyone who thinks that is nothing but a Socialist (or Communist or capitalist)," you have said nothing except that you don't like people who think that, and such remarks are effective only with the most naïve readers. It is always a bad mistake to think your readers more naïve than they really are.

Colorless Words

45   But probably most student writers come to grief not with words that are colorful or those that are colored but with those that have no color at all. A pet example is *nice*, a word we would find it hard to dispense with in casual conversation but which is no longer capable of adding much to a description. Colorless words are those of such general meaning that in a particular sentence they mean nothing. Slang adjectives, like *cool* ("That's real cool") tend to explode all over the language. They are applied to everything, lose their original force, and quickly die.

Beware also of nouns of very general meaning, like *circumstances, cases, instances, aspects, factors, relationships, attitudes, eventualities*, etc. In most circumstances you will find that those cases of writing which contain too many instances of words like these will in this and other aspects have factors leading to unsatisfactory relationships with the reader resulting in unfavorable attitudes on his part and perhaps other eventualities, like a grade of "D." Notice also what "etc." means. It means "I'd like to make this last longer, but I can't think of any more examples."

Analyzing Rhetorical Choices

1. Roberts actually describes two processes in this essay: one that he thinks will result in a poor essay and one that he thinks will result in a better one. Are both processes described clearly and vividly? Why do you think he chooses to describe both ways of composing an essay?

2. Roberts addresses the reader directly as "you" at the opening of this essay and he reverts to it frequently throughout the remainder. But he also shifts to first-person plural (*we* and *us*) and to third-person singular (*the writer*) and the largely impersonal *one* elsewhere. Describe the effects these various shifts have on you as you read. Why do you think he keeps shifting his perspective?

3. Describe Roberts's tone and illustrate your answer by citing a number of specific word choices and phrasing that he adopts.

Writing About Issues and Contexts

1. What do you think of Roberts's contention that "the difference between a 'C' or a 'D' may depend on who grades the paper"? How does Roberts implicate both students and teachers? Write a short statement, agreeing or disagreeing with Roberts's statement.

2. Students seem to hold certain assumptions about writing, according to Roberts. What are they? Explain whether these assumptions make sense to you.

3. Discuss Roberts's use of *color* in relation to words (colorless, colorful, and so forth). How do they relate to his advice to students?

Strategies for Writers: Process

1. As you have seen in "Learning to Read and Write" and "My First Conk," a process analysis can both describe a material event and signify a larger meaning about social, political, economic, or cultural values. In discussion with your classmates, determine how the process you plan to describe can take on significant meaning beyond the basic process itself. You may find as you do so that you are developing a narrative or the beginning of an implied argument.

2. Try to visualize the process you plan to describe, then describe it in specific visual terms to your classmates. You may consider spatial arrangements just as you would for description. How does description enhance your process? Use the experience of talking to your classmates to help you structure your draft. Once you have the process analysis written, try it out on your colleagues, asking them to help you develop a clear and well-illustrated explanation of the process you have chosen to describe.

3. The readings in this chapter show that process analyses are rarely neutral. For instance, Kenneth Stampp delineates, step-by-step, the process by which someone is able to dehumanize someone else and reinforce the master/slave relationship. Can you write a similarly ironic process description that represents a particular perspective that you believe in?

4. Process analysis often expresses a perspective and a sense of one's relationships with others along with relevant, clear detail. Douglass accomplishes this in "Learning to Read and Write." He also suggests that to keep slaves illiterate was also to define them as subhuman; the process of learning to read becomes a process of creating humanity. How does process interact with definition in this essay, where to define slavery as subhuman is part of the process of maintaining slavery—and where slavery is also dependent on withholding the process of literacy? How do these issues also relate to the Stampp essay? Further, David Mura discusses the implicit processes that stereotype the Asian male. As Mura has talked about the unsexing of the Asian male, what are other implicit and explicit processes that we observe in our interactions with others and in popular culture?

5. As you write your process analysis, clarify your own perspective or evaluation of your subject, as Joe Kane does in his prologue to *Savages*. What do you imply by what you write?

6. Perhaps more than most modes, process analysis requires careful attention to detail and a high degree of accuracy so that the reader can understand the process being described or evaluated. Notice how carefully Paul Roberts and Fan Shen structure their processes and the wealth of exemplification each of them includes. As you write, be sure to include useful detail, and check your accuracy. Errors of fact, typographical errors, and other forms of careless writing erode a reader's confidence in any writer.

Research and Writing Assignments

1. For Douglass, learning how to read was also learning how to be free, how to engage the world as a citizen and not a slave. Explore a similar process of learning how to be literate, either your own or someone else's, and write an essay that describes that process and what it meant. To do the necessary research for this essay, you may want to speak to your family members about your own literacy development, or contact a community literacy center or a public library so that you can research the literacy development of someone else

2. How does a person become enslaved? Certainly both Frederick Douglass and Kenneth Stampp consider various elements of how that process occurs, with Douglass writing from the perspective of the slave and Stampp from the slave owner. Is slavery a condition of mind as much as a condition of body? What are the psychological and physiological changes that must occur for someone to be enslaved? In an essay that draws upon research, analyze the process of enslavement. If you do not wish to write about the enslavement of African Americans, consider other forms of "capturing" and holding people within relationships that erase their individual wills, such as religious cults, spousal abuse, domestic workers who are purchased by wealthy families.

3. Malcolm X, David Mura, and Fan Shen delineate the ways in which minorities often feel they must make compromises to fit into the dominant culture. Compare and contrast the various perspectives in these essays about whether those who do not consider themselves "mainstream" need to compromise individual qualities in order to become "assimilated." As part of your focus, you might want to consider Fan Shen's statement that

"Rule number one in English composition is: Be Yourself." Can those who identify themselves as part of a "minority" remain true to this advice and yet also be part of the mainstream?

4. In his prologue to *Savages*, Joe Kane quotes Moi as saying, "We must win or the Huaroani will disappear forever." Kane's book focuses on the conflict between preservation and development, the rights of native people versus the rights of the government, the old and traditional ways versus the new and modern. Drawing on the selection by Kane and John McPhee's "Encounters with the Archdruid" (p. 220) as well as any additional research you can do, write an essay that describes a specific process of development. You might write about the loss of agricultural or park lands in your immediate neighborhood, the need to build additional power plants, the damming of a river, or the creation of additional landfill space. What choices do we have to make in the process of trying to maintain our values and our lifestyles? Are we indeed in danger of seeing the Huaroani disappear forever? If that is to occur, is it an inevitable cost of maintaining our quality of life?

5. Jessica Mitford writes about embalming as "an extraordinary procedure." In explicit detail, she reveals a process that is hidden to most eyes and that we might not usually think about. Using Mitford as your model, select another process about which one usually does not write, and "unwrap" and reveal it (using, if you wish, Mitford's directness, adroit use of detail, and possibly even her wry sense of humor). Write about a process that you can share with both your teacher and your classmates—one that is uncommon and unusual but something that can be written about in an open forum.

6. Paul Roberts offers us specific advice about how to write an essay. Using Roberts as a departure point, describe your own composing process. Do not feel that you have to agree or disagree with Roberts. Instead, create an ethnographic analysis of your own actions, writing rhythms, false starts, genuine patterns, and ultimate successes. What kinds of activities enable you to write well? What kinds of challenges and crises do you confront when you write? In your essay, include, as Roberts does, as much exemplification as possible so as to help your reader visualize what you do, why you do it, what works, and what doesn't.

8

Comparison and Contrast

Many decisions you make, including those that have brought you to this point as a college student, are based on the similarities and differences you consider. You have most likely pondered the prospects of life with a college degree and the prospects of life without one. You have probably thought about the merits of the school you attend relative to those of other institutions. In addition, you have probably thought about the likenesses and distinctions among majors, schedules, and instructors. You have already seen how the use of *comparison* (likeness) and *contrast* (distinction) is frequently crucial to clarifying issues, making an argument, arriving at a decision, or establishing a framework for discussion.

As with all writing techniques, comparison and contrast should serve the purpose you have set for a particular piece of writing. At times you will be asked explicitly—usually on an exam—to compare and contrast people, practices, and ideas. In such cases, comparison and contrast would be the primary pattern of development, and the similarities and differences you write about would often be related to a clearly defined thesis. If asked to compare and contrast the Kennedy inauguration with the first Clinton inauguration, you could assert that the Clinton inauguration in 1993 was a deliberate attempt to imitate Kennedy's 1961 inauguration. You could then comment on such elements as the political situations, the similar sound bites in each inaugural address, the almost identical length of the speeches, and the participation in each ceremony of a poet from the incoming president's home state.

When you have been assigned the task of writing about how two things are the same or different, the reason for using comparison and contrast will be evident. For example, Jodi Kantor was probably asked to review two boxing memoirs, and "Wham, Bam, Thanks a Bunch!" was the result. In other instances, however, you will need to convey clearly the purpose of the comparison and contrast. Poet and cultural critic Quincy Troupe, for instance, uses comparison and contrast in his memoir *Miles and Me* to account for the cool music and demeanor of legendary trumpeter and East St. Louis native Miles Davis. After writing about the great drum and bugle corps marching bands of St. Louis and East St. Louis, which incorporate German traditions and African American innovations, Troupe continues his description:

> These bands developed a style of playing the bugle, later transferred to the cornet and trumpet, that became known as the St. Louis "running" style. Pioneered by Eddie Randall, Levi Madison, Harold "Shorty" Baker, and Clark Terry (Miles' first real mentor in trumpet style) and perfected by Miles (who, in his youth, had played in several East St. Louis marching bands), it was characterized by musical ideas, chords, and notes strung together in a continuous blowing, dialoging manner, akin to a fast-talking conversationalist. (Trumpeter Lester Bowie, from St. Louis, provides an example of this style today.)
>
> This distinctive St. Louis sound was connected to the great trumpet tradition of New Orleans by the musicians who traveled on the riverboats shuttling up and down the Mississippi. But where New Orleans trumpet players employed a hotter, bigger, brassier style (as exemplified by Buddy Bolden, Freddie Keppard, Louis Armstrong, Al Hirt, Wynton Marsalis, Nicholas Payton, and Terrence Blanchard), the St. Louis style was generally cooler, more subtle and conversational (although it, too, could be hot and brassy at times).
>
> The different styles came out of different cultures. New Orleans is a lively city with a coastal culture heavily influenced by the French, Spanish, Native American, and African peoples. With its Mardi Gras, Congo Square, African ring dance, Voodoo Queen Marie Laveau, African drumming, Cajun fiddling, and Creole cooking, the culture of the Crescent City is thoroughly intermingled like a great big pot of gumbo or jambalaya.
>
> St. Louis, on the other hand, is a city founded by the French but controlled by Germans. And although many other ethnic groups (French, Italians, Jews, Hungarians, Native Americans, and African Americans) have had an impact, the culture is pervasively German. It is more Calvinistic than Catholic, more marching band than Mardi

Gras. It is a culture where a show of emotion is considered uncouth, almost uncivilized. Thus, a much more restrained musical culture developed among St. Louis blacks, one that took a much cooler approach. The one city-wide parade, the Veil Prophet Parade, was for nearly one hundred years a whites-only event. (The parade and ball were finally integrated in the 1970s.) Such parades were sedate, dull affairs. I witnessed many and never saw anyone dance with any saints or speak to any spirits. Blacks had the Annie Malone Parade to get by on, but even this was no joyous, celebratory affair; rather, it was cool and laid back. If New Orleans is gumbo and jambalaya, St. Louis is chitterlings, barbecue, mashed potatoes and gravy. That Miles grew up in this cooler musical milieu is reflected in his approach to music and in the man himself.

While Troupe acknowledges some similarity between the St. Louis sound and the New Orleans trumpet tradition, he highlights the contrast between the two. He thus explains why one culture—St. Louis—could produce a Miles Davis when it did, while another culture—New Orleans—could not. The line of reasoning could be represented as follows: lively mix of French, Spanish, Native American, and African cultures→Catholic→Mardi Gras→emotional, openly celebratory→a culture that can be likened to gumbo or jambalaya→local models, like Louis Armstrong and Al Hirt, who play the "hot, brassy" style→thus no Miles Davis, *but* pervasive German influence in the St. Louis area→Calvinistic→restrained marching bands→African American musical innovation that emphasized coolness→a culture that can be likened to mashed potatoes and gravy→local models, like Eddie Randall and Clark, who play the "running" style→Miles Davis. It is a given that Miles's tremendous individual talent is an essential part of the equation.

Troupe's analysis is richly detailed and contains relevant points of contrast. When writing an essay in the comparison-and-contrast mode, you might find it useful to brainstorm a list of the features that seem relevant to exploring your topic. You could then cluster those features into pairs or groups, eliminating any that do not readily help your case. For instance, people might on average be a little taller, or shorter, in St. Louis than in New Orleans, but that would not have helped Troupe develop his point about the respective trumpet traditions.

Whether you brainstorm and cluster features in advance of writing a first draft or mainly generate comparisons as you develop your essay, you will want to settle on a dominant pattern of presentation. The two patterns are generally referred to as the subject-by-subject and point-by-point methods, respectively, though most writing reflects some mixture of the two. In the subject-by-subject method, you describe all the relevant features of one subject before you describe the features of a second or subsequent subjects. Troupe, for instance, could have finished his description of the St. Louis musical style and culture before mentioning New Orleans. In other words, his organization might have been as follows:

Subject A—The St. Louis Trumpet Style

1. Characteristics of the sound
2. Notable musicians
3. History
4. Development
5. Surrounding culture

Subject B—The New Orleans Trumpet Style

1. Characteristics of the sound
2. Notable musicians
3. History
4. Development
5. Surrounding culture

Because the overall analysis is fairly brief, such a choice may not have affected his readers. However, if Troupe had used a dozen pages to explain one set of phenomena followed by a dozen pages to explain the other group of experiences, then the reading would have taken on a different quality. Because of the limitations of memory, it is virtually impossible for us to keep all the points of comparison and contrast in mind when reading lengthy pieces. Thus, if your goal as a writer is to leave only a general impression of similarity and difference, a subject-by-subject comparison may be the appropriate technique. On the other hand, if your goal is to create sharper images of comparison and contrast, the point-by-point method would better suit your needs. The point-by-point method is closer to what Troupe actually used. Although not entirely precise, his presentation can be represented in the following way:

Point A—The trumpet styles of St. Louis and New Orleans are related, yet different

1. Connected because of musicians' travel along the Mississippi River
2. Different characteristics of the two sounds

3. Notable musicians who exemplify the two sounds

Point B—The styles evolved from different cultures

1. Different ethnic contributions and influences
2. Different secular rituals and dominant religious influences
3. Different degrees of outward expressiveness

Of course, you should experiment with these types of arrangements, as Troupe undoubtedly has, to come up with what you feel works best for a particular piece. In this chapter, the subject-by-subject method is dominant in the pieces by Bruce Catton and R. A. Hudson. The point-by-point technique is illustrated well by Bharati Mukherjee, Jodi Kantor, and Deborah Tannen.

As you develop an essay using comparison and contrast, you will want to use appropriate transitional words or phrases to keep your readers oriented. The longer the piece of writing, the more important is the use of such devices. Words such as *similarly, likewise,* and *however* are often used as markers. Common phrases include "in the same vein," "on the other hand," and various constructions using the word *more* (for example, "more marching band than Mardi Gras").

A special type of comparison worth mentioning is the *analogy.* This is when one thing is explained in terms of another. In an extended analogy, Bart Giamatti, former commissioner of Major League baseball, explains sport in terms of work:

> The basis of sport is work. Running, jumping, lifting, pushing, bending, pulling, planting the legs, and using the back—these exertions are essential to physical labor and to athletic competition. The closeness of a given game to the rituals and effort of work invests the game with dignity; without that proximity to labor, the game would merely be a release from work instead of a refinement of it. The radical difference between work and game, however, occurs when limits or rules are imposed on this labor, patterns which acknowledge that this new work, this sport is not a matter of life and death. Whereas, that work, the work of your back and arms, in field or mill, on ship or in forest, was crucial to your survival, and to the survival of those dependent on you, this work is different; it is delimited, separate, independent, a refinement of reality but distinct. This work is fully as serious and difficult as real work, but this unreal work is not coextensive with life. This work of sport, usually but not always at some predetermined point, will have

an end. It will be over, not to begin again with the sun. This work, unlike that real work, does not sustain life in any immediate and practical way, such as providing food; but this unreal serious work does sustain life in the sense that it makes life bearable. It allows all of us to go back renewed to whatever real work we do, perhaps to go back for a moment redeemed.

For Giamatti, sport is not really *like* work in a way that would bear simple comparison; it is connected to work in an integral way. Sport is not the *opposite* of work; it is a version of it. Through effective comparison and contrast, Giamatti evokes the power of the subject, revealing sport in its complexities, its levels of connection with the larger world.

Bruce Catton (1899–1978) was born in Petoskey, Michigan, and attended Oberlin College. A Navy veteran who served during World War I, he had notable careers in both civil service and journalism. He served on the War Production Board and worked for the departments of Commerce and the Interior. In addition, he was the longtime senior editor of American Heritage. *A Civil War expert, he published several books on the conflict, including* Mr. Lincoln's Army *(1951) and* A Stillness at Appomattox *(1953), which won a Pulitzer Prize and National Book Award. The essay in this chapter was first published in a collection of essays titled* The American Story *(1956).*

Bruce Catton

Grant and Lee: A Study in Contrasts

When Ulysses S. Grant and Robert E. Lee met in the parlor of a modest house at Appomattox Court House, Virginia, on April 9, 1865, to work out the terms for the surrender of Lee's Army of Northern Virginia, a great chapter in American life came to a close, and a great new chapter began.

These men were bringing the Civil War to its virtual finish. To be sure, other armies had yet to surrender, and for a few days the fugitive Confederate government would struggle desperately and vainly, trying to find some way to go on living now that its chief support was gone. But in effect it was all over when Grant and Lee signed the papers. And the little room where they wrote out the terms was the scene of one of the poignant, dramatic contrasts in American history.

They were two strong men, these oddly different generals, and they represented the strengths of two conflicting currents that, through them, had come into final collision.

Back of Robert E. Lee was the notion that the old aristocratic concept might somehow survive and be dominant in American life.

5   Lee was tidewater Virginia, and in his background were family, culture, and tradition . . . the age of chivalry transplanted to a New World which was making its own legends and its own myths. He embodied a way of life that had come down through the age of knighthood and the English country squire. America was a land that was beginning all over again, dedicated to nothing much more complicated

than the rather hazy belief that all men had equal rights and should have an equal chance in the world. In such a land Lee stood for the feeling that it was somehow of advantage to human society to have pronounced inequality in the social structure. There should be a leisure class, backed by ownership of land; in turn, society itself should be keyed to the land as the chief source of wealth and influence. It would bring forth (according to this ideal) a class of men with a strong sense of obligation to the community; men who lived not to gain advantage for themselves, but to meet the solemn obligations which had been laid on them by the very fact that they were privileged. From them the country would get its leadership; to them it could look for the higher values—of thought, of conduct, of personal deportment—to give it strength and virtue.

Lee embodied the noblest elements of this aristocratic ideal. Through him, the landed nobility justified itself. For four years, the Southern states had fought a desperate war to uphold the ideals for which Lee stood. In the end, it almost seemed as if the Confederacy fought for Lee; as if he himself was the Confederacy . . . the best thing that the way of life for which the Confederacy stood could ever have to offer. He had passed into legend before Appomattox. Thousands of tired, underfed, poorly clothed Confederate soldiers, long since past the simple enthusiasm of the early days of the struggle, somehow considered Lee the symbol of everything for which they had been willing to die. But they could not quite put this feeling into words. If the Lost Cause, sanctified by so much heroism and so many deaths, had a living justification, its justification was General Lee.

Grant, the son of a tanner on the Western frontier, was everything Lee was not. He had come up the hard way and embodied nothing in particular except the eternal toughness and sinewy fiber of the men who grew up beyond the mountains. He was one of a body of men who owed reverence and obeisance to no one, who were self-reliant to a fault, who cared hardly anything for the past but who had a sharp eye for the future.

These frontier men were the precise opposites of the tidewater aristocrats. Back of them, in the great surge that had taken people over the Alleghenies and into the opening Western country, there was a deep, implicit dissatisfaction with a past that had settled into grooves. They stood for democracy, not from any reasoned conclusion about the proper ordering of human society, but simply because they had grown up in the middle of democracy and knew how it worked. Their society might have privileges, but they would be privileges each man had won for himself. Forms and patterns meant nothing. No man was born to anything, except perhaps to a chance to show how far he could rise. Life was competition.

Yet along with this feeling had come a deep sense of belonging to a national community. The Westerner who developed a farm, opened a shop, or set up in business as a trader, could hope to prosper only as his own community prospered—and his community ran from the Atlantic to the Pacific and from Canada down to Mexico. If the land was settled, with towns and highways and accessible markets, he could better himself. He saw his fate in terms of the nation's own destiny. As its horizons expanded, so did his. He had, in other words, an acute dollars-and-cents stake in the continued growth and development of his country.

10   And that, perhaps, is where the contrast between Grant and Lee becomes most striking. The Virginia aristocrat, inevitably, saw himself in relation to his own region. He lived in a static society which could endure almost anything except change. Instinctively, his first loyalty would go to the locality in which that society existed. He would fight to the limit of endurance to defend it, because in defending it he was defending everything that gave his own life its deepest meaning.

The Westerner, on the other hand, would fight with an equal tenacity for the broader concept of society. He fought so because everything he lived by was tied to growth, expansion, and a constantly widening horizon. What he lived by would survive or fall with the nation itself. He could not possibly stand by unmoved in the face of an attempt to destroy the Union. He would combat it with everything he had, because he could only see it as an effort to cut the ground out from under his feet.

So Grant and Lee were in complete contrast, representing two diametrically opposed elements in American life. Grant was the modern man emerging; beyond him, ready to come on the stage, was the great age of steel and machinery, of crowded cities and a restless burgeoning vitality. Lee might have ridden down from the old age of chivalry, lance in hand, silken banner fluttering over his head. Each man was the perfect champion of his cause, drawing both his strengths and his weaknesses from the people he led.

Yet it was not all contrast, after all. Different as they were—in background, in personality, in underlying aspiration—these two great soldiers had much in common. Under everything else, they were marvelous fighters. Furthermore, their fighting qualities were really very much alike.

Each man had, to begin with, the great virtue of utter tenacity and fidelity. Grant fought his way down the Mississippi Valley in spite of acute personal discouragement and profound military handicaps. Lee hung on in the trenches at Petersburg after hope itself had died. In each man there was an indomitable quality . . . the born fighter's refusal to give up as long as he can still remain on his feet and lift his two fists.

15   Daring and resourcefulness they had, too; the ability to think faster
and move faster than the enemy. These were the qualities which gave
Lee the dazzling campaigns of Second Manassas and Chancellorsville
and won Vicksburg for Grant.

Lastly, and perhaps greatest of all, there was the ability, at the end, to
turn quickly from war to peace once the fighting was over. Out of the way
these two men behaved at Appomattox came the possibility of a peace of
reconciliation. It was a possibility not wholly realized, in the years to
come, but which did, in the end, help the two sections to become one nation again . . . after a war whose bitterness might have seemed to make
such a reunion wholly impossible. No part of either man's life became him
more than the part he played in this brief meeting in the McLean house at
Appomattox. Their behavior there put all succeeding generations of
Americans in their debt. Two great Americans, Grant and Lee—very different, yet under everything very much alike. Their encounter at
Appomattox was one of the great moments of American history.

Analyzing Rhetorical Choices

1. Catton largely relies on the subject-by-subject technique to con-
    trast and compare Grant and Lee. In which ways do you find this
    pattern of comparison and contrast effective?
2. Catton uses the adjective *great* to describe both an era that was
    ending and one that was beginning. Does *great* seem appropriate
    to you as a description of both eras? Explain your response.
3. Although Catton asserts that Grant and Lee were of different
    backgrounds, aspirations, and personalities, he does not detail how
    their personalities differed. What information about the personali-
    ties of the two generals do you think would have improved the au-
    thor's analysis?

Writing About Issues and Contexts

1. Although slavery is not mentioned in the text, how might your
    knowledge of its existence shape your response to Catton's essay?
2. A significant number of soldiers who became invested in and
    fought for the Confederacy were, in fact, Northerners who had re-
    located. How does this fact affect your response to Catton's por-
    trayal of Lee?
3. In what ways do succeeding generations remain indebted to Grant
    and Lee?

A native of Calcutta, India, **Bharati Mukherjee** *(1940–   ) grew up in India and Europe. She received a bachelor's degree from the University of Calcutta and a master's from the University of Baroda. Mukherjee came to the United States in 1961 to pursue a degree at the University of Iowa and has resided since in the United States or Canada. She currently holds the rank of distinguished professor of English at the University of California at Berkeley. Her books include* The Tiger's Daughter *(1972),* Darkness *(1985),* Jasmine *(1989),* The Holder of the World *(1993),* Leave It to Me *(1997), and* Desirable Daughters *(2002). The following article originally appeared in the* New York Times *in 1996.*

Bharati Mukherjee

Two Ways to Belong in America

This is a tale of two sisters from Calcutta, Mira and Bharati, who have lived in the United States for some 35 years, but who find themselves on different sides in the current debate over the status of immigrants. I am an American citizen and she is not. I am moved that thousands of long-term residents are finally taking the oath of citizenship. She is not.

Mira arrived in Detroit in 1960 to study child psychology and preschool education. I followed her a year later to study creative writing at the University of Iowa. When we left India, we were almost identical in appearance and attitude. We dressed alike, in saris; we expressed identical views on politics, social issues, love, and marriage in the same Calcutta convent-school accent. We would endure our two years in America, secure our degrees, then return to India to marry the grooms of our father's choosing.

Instead, Mira married an Indian student in 1962 who was getting his business administration degree at Wayne State University. They soon acquired the labor certifications necessary for the green card of hassle-free residence and employment.

Mira still lives in Detroit, works in the Southfield, Mich., school system, and has become nationally recognized for her contributions in the fields of pre-school education and parent-teacher relationships. After 36 years as a legal immigrant in this country, she clings passionately to her Indian citizenship and hopes to go home to India when she retires.

5   In Iowa City in 1963, I married a fellow student, an American of Canadian parentage. Because of the accident of his North Dakota birth, I bypassed labor-certification requirements and the race-related "quota" system that favored the applicant's country of origin over his or her merit. I was prepared for (and even welcomed) the emotional strain that came with marrying outside my ethnic community. In 33 years of marriage, we have lived in every part of North America. By choosing a husband who was not my father's selection, I was opting for fluidity, self-invention, blue jeans and T-shirts, and renouncing 3,000 years (at least) of case-observant, "pure culture" marriage in the Mukherjee family. My books have often been read as unapologetic (and in some quarters overenthusiastic) texts for cultural and psychological "mongrelization." It's a word I celebrate.

Mira and I have stayed sisterly close by phone. In our regular Sunday morning conversations, we are unguardedly affectionate. I am her only blood relative on this continent. We expect to see each other through the looming crises of aging and ill health without being asked. Long before Vice President Gore's "Citizenship U.S.A." drive, we'd had our polite arguments over the ethics of retaining an overseas citizenship while expecting the permanent protection and economic benefits that come with living and working in America.

Like well-raised sisters, we never said what was really on our minds, but we probably pitied one another. She, for the lack of structure in my life, the erasure of Indianness, the absence of an unvarying daily core. I, for the narrowness of her perspective, her uninvolvement with the mythic depths or the superficial pop culture of this society. But, now, with the scapegoating of "aliens" (documented or illegal) on the increase, and the targeting of long-term legal immigrants like Mira for new scrutiny and new self-consciousness, she and I find ourselves unable to maintain the same polite discretion. We were always unacknowledged adversaries, and we are now, more than ever, sisters.

"I feel used," Mira raged on the phone the other night. "I feel manipulated and discarded. This is such an unfair way to treat a person who was invited to stay and work here because of her talent. My employer went to the I.N.S. and petitioned for the labor certification. For over 30 years, I've invested my creativity and professional skills into the improvement of *this* country's pre-school system. I've obeyed all the rules, I've paid my taxes, I love my work, I love my students, I love the friends I've made. How dare America now change its rules in midstream? If America wants to make new rules curtailing benefits of legal immigrants, they should apply only to immigrants who arrive after those rules are already in place."

To my ears, it sounded like the description of a long-enduring, comfortable yet loveless marriage, without risk or recklessness. Have we the right to demand, and to expect, that we be loved? (That, to me is the subtext of the arguments by immigration advocates.) My sister is an expatriate, professionally generous and creative, socially courteous and gracious, and that's as far as her Americanization can go. She is here to maintain an identity, not to transform it.

10   I asked her if she would follow the example of others who have decided to become citizens because of the anti-immigration bills in Congress. And here, she surprised me. "If America wants to play the manipulative game, I'll play it, too," she snapped. "I'll become a U.S. citizen for now, then change back to Indian when I'm ready to go home. I feel some kind of irrational attachment to India that I don't to America. Until all this hysteria against legal immigrants, I was totally happy. Having my green card meant I could visit any place in the world I wanted to and then come back to a job that's satisfying and that I do very well."

In one family, from two sisters alike as peas in a pod, there could not be a wider divergence of immigrant experience. America spoke to me—I married it—I embraced the demotion from expatriate aristocrat to immigrant nobody, surrendering those thousands of years of "pure culture," the saris, the delightfully accented English. She retained them all. Which of us is the freak?

Mira's voice, I realize, is the voice not just of the immigrant South Asian community but of an immigrant community of the millions who have stayed rooted in one job, one city, one house, one ancestral culture, one cuisine, for the entirety of their productive years. She speaks for greater numbers than I possibly can. Only the fluency of her English and the anger, rather than fear, born of confidence from her education, differentiate her from the seamstresses, the domestics, the technicians, the shop owners, the millions of hard-working but effectively silenced documented immigrants as well as their less fortunate "illegal" brothers and sisters.

Nearly 20 years ago, when I was living in my husband's ancestral homeland of Canada, I was always well-employed but never allowed to feel part of the local Quebec or larger Canadian society. Then, through a Green Paper that invited a national referendum on the unwanted side effects of "nontraditional" immigration, the Government officially turned against its immigrant communities, particularly those from South Asia.

I felt then the same sense of betrayal that Mira feels now. I will never forget the pain of that sudden turning, and the casual racist outbursts the Green Paper elicited. That sense of betrayal had its desired effect and drove me, and thousands like me, from the country.

15   Mira and I differ, however, in the ways in which we hope to interact with the country that we have chosen to live in. She is happier to live in America as expatriate Indian than as an immigrant American. I need to feel like a part of the community I have adopted (as I tried to feel in Canada as well). I need to put roots down, to vote and make the difference that I can. The price that the immigrant willingly pays, and that the exile avoids, is the trauma of self-transformation.

Analyzing Rhetorical Choices

1.   Concerning her relationship with Mira, Mukherjee writes, "Like well-raised sisters, we never said what really was on our minds. . . ." In your view, how much does this description help to explain their relationship?

2.   Regarding Mira's complaint about proposed immigration rules, Mukherjee suggests that "it sounded like the description of a long-enduring, comfortable yet loveless marriage, without risk or restlessness." Do you agree with her analogy? Is there another way you would describe Mira's position?

Writing About Issues and Contexts

1.   How would you answer the author's question, "which one of us is the freak?"

2.   Do you agree with Mira's position or Bharati's? Is there a middle ground between the two?

3.   How does Mukherjee's last sentence take on added significance after the events of September 11, 2001?

Following a brief stint at Harvard Law School and a year as an aide to Rudolph Giuliani, **Jodi Kantor** *(1976–   ) became an editor at* Slate, *the most popular online magazine with more than two million visitors per month. In March 2003, she was made the Arts & Leisure editor of the* New York Times. *The following is a review of* The Boxer's Heart *by Kate Sekules and* Looking for a Fight *by Lynn Snowden Picket.*

Jodi Kantor

Wham! Bam! Thanks a Bunch!

Two Memoirs by Women Who Took Up Boxing and Became Dangerous

Most memoirs describe their authors' getting bruised in some way, but the new ones by Kate Sekules and Lynn Snowden Picket are satisfyingly literal about it. Both women took up boxing as a hobby, and the books describe how they bled their way from neophytes to confirmed pugilists.

If you were just glancing over their books, Sekules and Picket would look like twins: both edit or write for glossy magazines, trained at Gleason's Gym in Brooklyn and took up boxing in the mid-1990's, when they were in their mid-30's. But their differences begin with their respective attractions to the ring. Sekules, bored with Manhattan's aerobics-industrial complex, is simply looking for a new workout. She enumerates various traumas that might account for her desire to box—a comically wussy athletic education, a lingering case of the body-image blues. But in listing them, she sounds more like an actor searching for a character's motivation than someone truly brimming with fury. Meanwhile, Picket is every bit as angry as the title of her book suggests. She has just suffered through a humiliating divorce—her husband had been cheating—and plans to avenge herself in the ring: "I'm full of rage and I want to beat someone up. I want to know what it is to have physical power over men. I want to inspire fear. I want to matter," she says.

Each alights at Gleason's Gym, the storied training ground of fighters from Jake LaMotta to Larry Holmes, and immediately swoons over its warped mirrors, bloodstained canvases and general air of sweaty antiglamour. At first, there's something laughably Bobo-ish about these well-heeled women—Sekules is an editor at Food & Wine magazine, while Picket bids on art at Sotheby's—venturing to Brooklyn to find their inner grit among the tough-guy habitués of Gleason's. But Sekules is appealingly self-aware about the project: "There is no doubt that part of what I'm falling in love with is the thing my very presence here will help subvert; that is, boxing as it used to seem—an arcane testosterone ghetto, photogenic and romantic, adoringly treated in black-and-white by Scorsese in *Raging Bull* or Bruce Weber in *Broken Noses.*"

Arrivistes they may be, but dilettantes they're not. Before long, Sekules and Picket are each sparring regularly, and they acquire the pur-pled knuckles, blackened eyes and bloody noses to prove it. Sparring—which is part workout, part scrimmage—has its own etiquette, and some of the books' best moments come as Sekules and Picket puzzle over how to hit hard enough to be taken seriously, but not so aggressively as to turn casual challenges into all-out slugfests. This calculation is made even trickier by their sex: the men they face are reluctant to hit a woman, but even more reluctant to be beaten by one.

5   As they work their way toward their first real bouts, the authors provide a steady flow of vivid anecdotes, from Picket's account of how sudden stops in the ring eventually knock a boxer's toenails off, to Sekules's description of how, before her pro debut, the local boxing commissioner demands "visual evidence" that she is really female. Both are graceful sportswriters, but Picket's small, grating tic of relay-ing superfluous details—in particular, what she's wearing—often in-terferes both with her narrative and her desire to be taken seriously. And whereas Picket expresses little contact with or affinity for fellow women fighters, Sekules gives us a sense of women's boxing as a thriv-ing movement. Her comrades include Jill Matthews, a punk rocker and rabbi's daughter; Karyn Kusama, director of the recent film *Girlfight;* and Lucia Rijker, a champion fighter and practicing Buddhist. (But not Lynn Snowden Picket. If the authors' paths crossed, neither men-tions it.)

Sekules also includes a rousing history of female boxing, stretch-ing from the earliest recorded bout in 1722 to Christy Martin's 1996 fight against Deirdre Gogarty on the Mike Tyson-Frank Bruno under-card, which upstaged the men's match, providing a symbolic rebuke to

Tyson, who had just finished serving time for rape. This interest in other women fighters, past and present, provides welcome context for Sekules's own quest and keeps her solipsism quotient in check.

If Sekules and Picket are any example, women boxers still have much to prove. The writers are mistaken for battered women by well-meaning strangers, Picket is propositioned by her trainer and Sekules is sought out by guys looking for sadomasochistic kinks. Sekules makes more of these insults, interspersing her story with frequent asides on gender, sports and violence. But the action in the gym is so much more effectively rendered, and the subtext already so rich and pronounced, that these reflections feel windy and superfluous. "Women are born with a lightning rod, and whether we honor it or not, it is the feminine principle, a subcutaneous awareness of connect-edness," writes the otherwise reliable Sekules.

In the end, Sekules seems to get from boxing what she came for: a stronger body and sense of self, as well as a gymload of new friends. Picket, on the other hand, picks up some nasty habits. For one thing, she can no longer keep her hands to herself. She slugs a hapless guy who accidentally sloshes beer on her at a fight; a teenager who startles her in Central Park; and her boyfriend's brother, after he jokingly lands a sucker punch on her at a party. Worse, she punches a stranger who brings his young son to Gleason's one day and shouts out unin-vited instructions as she spars. Brushing away contrition about hitting him in front of his son, she chortles: "Never tell a woman what to do if she happens to be wearing boxing gloves."

Ironically, when Picket really does need to defend herself, she can't: after her nose is bloodied by an overaggressive sparring partner, Picket drags her slight-bodied, sensitive boyfriend to the gym and threatens to dump him if he doesn't defend her honor by threatening her assailant. Instead of making her feel powerful, boxing eventually makes her paranoid and panicky, even fearful that "someone's out there, waiting to beat me up." Finally, during her first real bout, a rev-elation hits her: "This is like getting into a car accident for sport," she thinks, and a little more than 10 pages later she's quit boxing entirely. Picket finishes her book by solemnly itemizing the brain damage that the sport can inflict. She declares her boxing project "ludicrous and deranged," and claims that had she known then what she does now, she never would have stepped into the ring in the first place.

10   Which would have been a shame. Sekules and Picket may not be-long beside A. J. Liebling and Norman Mailer in the boxing writer hall of fame, but their girl-next-door approaches are still absorbing. These

writers bridge the gap between the fans who find boxing thrilling and the detractors who find it senselessly brutal by showing us how one can become the other. And who has ever watched a boxing match without wondering what it would be like to participate? Reading about Muhammad Ali and the other greats doesn't quite satisfy this urge; while we want to know and understand them, few of us could ever see ourselves in their boots. For those of us, male or female, who will never get in the ring, these books provide an idea of how we might perform there and what it might do to us.

Analyzing Rhetorical Choices

1. Kantor's essay is a combination of the subject-by-subject and point-by-point techniques. Are the lines of argument, the notions of comparisons and contrasts, kept clear enough for you? Support your response.
2. Does Kantor's selection of details or anecdotes create interest on your part in the books she reviews? If so, why?
3. What is your response to such phrases as "testosterone ghetto," "Manhattan's aerobics-industrial complex," and "solipsism quotient"? Whom does she envision as her audience?

Writing About Issues and Contexts

1. How do you feel about what, according to this article, motivates these women to box?
2. Kantor disagrees with Sekules's idea of a feminine principle. Do you agree with Sekules or Kantor? Explain your choice.
3. Assuming that you were only going to pick one of these books to read, which one would you choose? Why do you make that choice?

*Cornel West (1953–   ) is a professor of African American Studies at
Princeton University. A native of Tulsa, Oklahoma, he received his undergraduate degree from Harvard and graduate degrees from Princeton. He
has taught at several universities, including Harvard and Yale. His research interests include African American critical thought, social theory,
modern and postmodern philosophy and literature, and the future of
black youth. One of the nation's most popular lecturers, West's books in-*
clude Beyond Eurocentrism and Multiculturalism *(1993),* Race Matters
(1993), and The Cornel West Reader *(1999). The selection that follows is
from* Jews and Blacks: A Dialogue on Race, Religion, and Culture in
America, *which he coauthored with Michael Lerner in 1995.*

Cornel West
Blacks and Jews

Why are Blacks and Jews in the United States the most unique
and fascinating people in modern times? Why have both groups contributed so disproportionately to the richness and vitality in American
life? Can we honestly imagine what twentieth-century American
democracy would be like without the past and present doings and suf-
ferings of Blacks and Jews? What forms will progressive politics take,
if any, with escalating tensions between these two historically liberal
groups?

When historians look back on the emergence, development, and
decline of American civilization, they obviously will note its distinctive
features—constitutional democracy and precious liberties (with its
class, gender, and especially racial constraints), material prosperity,
technological ingenuity, ethnic and regional diversity, market-driven
yet romantic popular culture, relative lack of historical consciousness,
and an obsession with progress in the future. Yet these historians
would miss much if they failed to acknowledge and examine the two
most extraordinary peoples in U.S. history—people of African descent
and people of Jewish origins and persuasion. Needless to say, all people
are, in some significant sense, extraordinary. But Blacks and Jews
stand out in a glaring manner.

Both Jews and Blacks are a pariah people—a people who had to
make and remake themselves as outsiders on the margins of American

society and culture. Both groups assumed that the status quo was unjust and therefore found strategies to survive and thrive against the odds. Both groups defined themselves as a people deeply shaped by America but never *fully* a part of America. Both groups appealed to biblical texts and relied on communal bonds to sustain themselves—texts that put a premium on justice, mercy, and solidarity with the downtrodden, and bonds shot through with a deep distrust, suspicion, even paranoia, toward the powerful and privileged. Both groups have been hated and despised peoples who find it difficult, if not impossible, to fully overcome group insecurity and anxiety as well as truly be and love themselves as individuals and as a people. Wearing the masks, enduring petty put-downs, and coping with subtle insults remains an everyday challenge for most Blacks and some Jews in America.

Both groups are the most modern of modern people in that they have created new and novel ways of life, innovative and improvisational modes of being in the world. Their entree into modernity as degraded Others—dishonored slaves (Blacks) and devalued non-Christians (Jews)—forced them to hammer out the most un-American yet modern of products—tragicomic dispositions toward reality that put sadness, sorrow, and suffering at the center of their plights and predicaments. This tragicomic character of the Black and Jewish experiences in modernity—coupled with a nagging moral conscience owing to undeniable histories of underdog status and unusual slavery-to-freedom narratives in authoritative texts—haunts both groups.

5   And what Blacks and Jews have done with their intelligence, imagination, and ingenuity is astounding. Twentieth-century America—a century that begins only a generation after the emancipation of penniless, illiterate, enslaved Africans and the massive influx of poor Eastern European Jewish immigrants—is unimaginable without the creative breakthroughs and monumental contributions of Blacks and Jews. At the very highest levels of achievement, we have Louis Armstrong and Aaron Copland, Duke Ellington and Leonard Bernstein, John Coltrane and George Gershwin, Sarah Vaughan and Irving Berlin, Toni Morrison and Saul Bellow, W. E. B. Du Bois and Hannah Arendt, Romare Bearden and Jackson Pollock, August Wilson and Arthur Miller, Paul Robeson and Pete Seeger, Ralph Ellison and Irving Howe, Kathleen Battle and Beverly Sills, Richard Pryor and Lenny Bruce, Willie Mays and Sandy Koufax, Andre Watts and Itzhak Perlman, Jacob Lawrence and Mark Rothko, Babyface (Kenneth Edmonds) and Carole King, Thurgood Marshall and Louis Brandeis, Marvin Gaye and Bob Dylan,

James Baldwin and Norman Mailer, Lorraine Hansberry and Neil Simon, Aretha Franklin and Barbra Streisand, Billy Strayhorn and Stephen Sondheim. This short and incomplete list of towering Black and Jewish figures is neither an act of providence nor a mere accident. Rather it is the result of tremendous talent, discipline, and energy of two ostracized groups who disproportionately shape the cultural life of this country.

Furthermore, Jewish power and influence—though rarely wielded in a monolithic manner—in the garment industry, show business, medical and legal professions, journalism, and the academy—has had a major impact on the shaping of American life. We are reminded of the fundamental centrality of learning in Jewish life when we realize that as of 1989, of fifty American Nobel Laureates in the medical sciences—such as biochemistry and physiology—seventeen were Jews.

This latter point—the matter of relative Jewish zeal in business and education—is a delicate one. It does not mean that Jews are innately smarter than others or that they are involved in some secret conspiracy to control the banks and newspapers, as implied by the anti-Semitic remarks of General George Brown, Chairman of the Joint Chiefs of Staff, in a lecture at Duke University in 1974. Instead these realities reflect the dominant Jewish ways of gaining access to resources, status, and power against anti-Semitic exclusions in other spheres and over three thousand years of autonomous institution-building based on self-help and self-development around literary and mathematical skills.

African-Americans also have a rich history of business enterprise and scientific achievements—yet the entrepreneurial ethic has been set back by racist attacks (nearly two-thirds of those lynched at the turn of the century were businessmen), and exclusion from significant access to capital and credit, weak communal bonds to sustain business efforts, underfunded Black schools and colleges that downplay independent business efforts, and vicious stereotypes that undercut motivation to study math and natural sciences.

In fact, the fundamental differences between Blacks and Jews in America have been the vast impact of slavery and Jim Crow on limiting the Black quest for self-confidence in literary and scientific matters, and the containment of most Black folk in rural and agrarian areas until World War II, where access to literacy was difficult. In stark contrast, American Jews have always been primarily an urban people trying to find safe niches in industrial (and anti-Semitic) America, who fall back on strong and long traditions of independent institution-building. In this regard, the experiences of Blacks and Jews have been qualitatively different in a deeply racist and more mildly anti-Semitic America.

10   Yet, ironically, Jews and Blacks have been linked in a kind of symbiotic relation with each other. Whether they are allies or antagonists, they are locked into an inescapable embrace principally owing to their dominant status of degraded Others, given the racist and Christian character of the American past and present. First, because anti-Black and anti-Jewish waves are an omnipresent threat in this country. Second, because their support of progressive politics cast them as potential threats to the status quo in their critical and dissenting roles. And third, because both groups not only have a profound fascination with each other but also because they have much at stake in their own collective identities as a pariah and "chosen" people—be it in covenant with a God that "chooses" to side with the underdog or against a nation that "chooses" to treat them unequally or unkindly.

When Michael Lerner—from whom I've learned so much and come to love so dearly—and I began our dialogue, we knew we had to build upon the rich legacies of Martin Luther King, Jr., and Abraham Joshua Heschel. We had to cast our exchange in such a way that we highlighted moral ideals and existential realities bigger and better than both Black and Jewish interests. We had to examine what it means to be human as Jews and Blacks and how this relates to keeping alive the best of a precious yet precarious experiment in democracy. We also had to examine the ways in which we could revitalize progressive politics in the light of prophetic traditions in the Black and Jewish heritages. This is why our Black-Jewish dialogue—much like relevant, Black-Brown, Jewish-Asian or Black-Red dialogue—is but an instance of the human struggle for freedom and democracy. And any such struggle is predicated on the democratic faith that we everyday people can critically examine our individual and collective pasts, honestly confront our difficult present, and imaginatively project an all-embracing moral vision for the future. Our courageous foremothers and forefathers as well as our innocent children and grandchildren deserve nothing less.

Analyzing Rhetorical Choices

1. West opens his essay with a series of questions. What is the effect of this strategy? Would the impact be different if he had opened with statements instead? For example, what if he had written,

"Blacks and Jews in the United States are the most unique and fascinating people in modern times"?
2. What does the phrase "progressive politics" mean to you as used in the first paragraph? Why do you think West uses this phrase?
3. Like Catton, West develops part of his argument without citing sources. Is his argument nonetheless logical or credible in your opinion? Defend your point of view.

Writing About Issues and Contexts

1. In the first sentence of the second paragraph, West suggests that the decline of American civilization is a given. In the last paragraph, he writes of "keeping alive the best of a precious yet precarious experiment in democracy." What is your response to these remarks?
2. What important dialogues would you add to the list given by West in the final paragraph? Why?

R. A. Hudson (1939–   ) is a professor of linguistics at University College London. An advocate of teaching more language awareness in schools, Richard Hudson is a founding member of the Committee for Linguistics in Education. His scholarly publications include Word Meaning *(1995) and* English Grammar *(1998). The excerpt in this chapter is from his 1980 text,* Sociolinguistics.

R. A. Hudson
Language Worlds

An Imaginary World

What, then, is there to say about language in relation to society? It may be helpful to start by trying to imagine a society (and a language) about which there is very *little* to say. The little world described below is completely imaginary, and most sociolinguists—perhaps all of them—would agree that it is highly unlikely that any such world either does or even could exist, given what we know about both language and society.

In our imaginary world there is a society which is clearly defined by some natural boundary, impassable in either direction. The purpose of postulating this boundary is to guarantee, on the one hand, that no members of other communities join this one, bringing their own languages with them, and, on the other, that members of this community never leave it and take their language to another, thereby complicating the perfect coincidence between language and community.

Everybody in this society has exactly the same language—they know the same constructions and the same words, with the same pronunciation and the same range of meanings for every single word in the language. (Any deviation from such an exact identity raises the possibility of statements such as "Person A knows pronunciation M, but Person B knows pronunciation N, for the same word," which would be a statement about language in relation to society.) An obvious problem is that very young members of the society, just learning to talk, must necessarily be different from everybody else. We might get round this problem by saying that child language is the domain of a branch of psychology rather than sociology, and that psychology can provide general principles of language acquisition which will allow us to predict every respect in which the language of children in this society deviated from the language of the adults. If psychology were able to provide the necessary principles, then there would be a good deal to say about language in relation to individual development, but nothing about language in relation to society. Needless to say, no psychologist would dream of claiming that this was possible, even in principle.

A consequence of the complete absence of any differences between members of this community is that language change is thereby ruled out, since such change normally involves a difference between the oldest and youngest generations, so that when the former all die only the forms used by the latter survive. Since change seems to affect every language so far studied, this makes the language of our imaginary community unique. The only way to allow for change in a totally homogeneous community is to assume that every change affects every member of the community absolutely and simultaneously: one day, nobody has the new form, the next day, everybody has it. (It is very hard to see any mechanism which could explain such change, short of community-wide telepathy!)

5   Another characteristic of the community we are considering is that *circumstances* have no influence on what people say, either with respect to its content or its form. There are no "formal" and "informal" situations, requiring different kinds of vocabulary (such as *receive* versus *get*) or different pronunciations for words (like *not* versus *-n't*). Nor are there any "discussions" and "arguments," or "requests" and "demands," each requiring not only particular forms but also particular meanings. (For instance, in an argument you *attack* the other person's position, but in a discussion you *consider* it.) Nor are there any differences between the beginnings, middles and ends of conversations, such as would require greetings and farewells. None of these differences due to circumstances exist because if they did they would require statements about society—in particular, about social interaction. Indeed, if we discount any influence of the social context, it is doubtful if speech is possible at all, since spoken messages are generally geared specifically to the needs of the audience.

Finally, we must assume that there is no connection between the culture of the postulated community and the meanings which its language (especially its vocabulary) allows it to express. The language must therefore contain no words such as *cricket* or *priest*, whose meanings could be stated only with reference to a partial description of the culture. To assume otherwise would be to allow rich and interesting statements about language in relation to society, since culture is one of the most important characteristics of society. Exactly what kinds of concepts the members of this community *would* be able to express is not clear—possibly they would only be able to assert logical truths such as "If p and q, then p," since any other kinds of word are likely to involve some reference to the community's culture.

All in all, our blue-print for a community is an uncompromising one. All the restrictions imposed on it were necessary in order to guarantee that there should be nothing to say about its language in relation to society, beyond the simple statement "Such-and-such community speak language X." However, it will be noticed that this statement is precisely the kind which is generally made by linguists (or laymen) about a language, and exhausts what they feel obliged to say about the language in relation to society. The purpose of this section has been to show that the only kind of community (or language) for which such a statement could be remotely adequate is a fictitious one.

A Real but Exotic World

We now turn to a real world, in which there is a great deal to be said about language in relation to society. It is the very exotic world of the north-west Amazon, described by A.P. Sorensen (1971) and J. Jackson (1974).

Geographically, the area in question is half in Brazil and half in Colombia, coinciding more or less with the area in which a language called Tukano can be relied on as a *lingua franca* (i.e., a trade language widely spoken as a non-native language). It is a large area, but sparsely inhabited; around 10,000 people in an area the size of England. Most of the people are indigenous Indians, divided into over twenty tribes, which are in turn grouped in five "phratries" (groups of related tribes). There are two crucial facts to be remembered about this community. First, each tribe speaks a different language—sufficiently different to be mutually incomprehensible and, in some cases, genetically unrelated (i.e., not descended from a common "parent" language). Indeed, the *only* criterion by which tribes can be distinguished from each other is by their language. The second fact is that the five phratries (and thus all twenty-odd tribes) are exogamous (i.e., a man must not marry a woman from the same phratry or tribe). Putting these two facts together, it is easy to see the main linguistic consequence: a man's wife *must* speak a different language from him.

10   We now add a third fact: marriage is patrilocal (the husband and wife live where the husband was brought up), and there is a rule that

the wife should not only live where the husband was brought up, but should also use his language in speaking to their children (a custom that might be called "patrilingual marriage"). The linguistic consequence of this rule is that a child's mother does not teach her own language to the child, but rather a language which she speaks only as a foreigner—as though everyone in Britain learned their English from a foreign au-pair girl. One can thus hardly call the children's first language their "mother-tongue" except by a stretch of the imagination. The reports of this community do not mention any widespread disruption in language learning or general "deterioration" of the languages concerned, so we can assume that a language can be transmitted efficiently and accurately even under these apparently adverse circumstances, through the influence of the father, the rest of the father's relatives and the older children. It is perhaps worth pointing out that the wife goes to live in a "long-house" in which the husband's brothers and parents also live, so there is no shortage of contacts with native speakers of the father's language.

What is there to say about language in relation to such a society? First, there is the question of relating languages as wholes to speakers, assuming for simplicity that it is possible to talk usefully about "languages as wholes." For any given language X, it will first be necessary to define who are its native speakers, but since this means referring to some tribe, and tribes are in fact defined solely with reference to language, there is clearly a problem. The solution is either to list all the long-houses belonging to the tribe concerned, or to specify the geographical area (or areas) where the tribe lives. (Most tribes do in fact have their own territory, which does not overlap with that of other tribes.) However, it will have to be borne in mind that about a quarter of the native speakers of language X will be made up of the married women who are dispersed among the other tribes, and similarly about a quarter of the people living in the area designated as "language X territory" will be *non*-native speakers of X, being wives from other tribes. Indeed, any given long-house is likely to contain native speakers of a variety of languages, on the assumption that brothers need not be attracted to girls of the same "other" tribe. In addition to the native speakers of language X, there will be people who speak it as non-natives, with every degree of fluency from almost native-speaker to minimal. Thus anyone wishing to write a grammar for language X will need to say precisely for whom the grammar is claimed to be true—just for the native speakers left at home in the tribal area, or for all native speakers including those dispersed among the other tribes, or for all speakers, native or non-native, in the tribal area.

Secondly, there is the question of discourse: how is speech used in social interaction? There are questions which arise out of the number of languages available: for instance, how do people get by when they travel around within the area, as they very often do? Are they expected to use the language of the long-house which they are visiting? Apparently not—the choice of language is based solely on the convenience of the people concerned (except for the rule requiring wives to use their husbands' language when speaking to their children). If the visitor does not know the long-house language, but someone there knows his, they will use the visitor's when speaking to him. What about language itself as a subject of conversation? Here too practical needs are put first, namely the need to know as many languages as possible in order to make it easier both to travel and (for young people) to find a partner. It is quite normal to talk about a language, learning its vocabulary and phrases from it, and this continues into old age; yet people generally do not know how many languages they can speak, and do not think of language learning as a way of gaining prestige. Perhaps this is what we might expect in a society where everyone can be expected to speak *at least* (i) his father's language, (ii) his mother's language (which she will certainly have taught her children with a view to their seeking partners among her tribe) and (iii) the lingua franca, Tukano (which may also be the language of his father or his mother). However, in addition to the aspects of discourse which are directly related to multilingualism, there are many other things to be said about the relations between speech and the social circumstances in this complex Amazonian society. For instance, there is a rule that if you are listening to someone whom you respect, you should repeat after him, word-for-word, everything he says, at least for the first few minutes of his talking.

Thirdly, there is the question of the relation of language to culture, on which we have little information in the reports on the north-west Amazon referred to above, but on which we can make some safe guesses. For instance, it would be surprising if any of the languages concerned lacked a word for "long-house" or "tribe," and we might reasonably expect a word for "phratry" (though such higher-level concepts often lack names). Similarly, we may predict that most concepts relevant to the culture will have words in each language to express them, and that most words in each language will express cultural concepts, definable only in terms of the culture concerned.

In the world of the north-west Amazon there is probably nothing that a linguist could satisfactorily say about any language without at the same time making some fairly complicated statement about it in relation to society. In particular, he could not say *which* language he was describing by referring to some pre-defined community who use it (in the way in which he might feel entitled to talk about, say, "British English" or "Birmingham English"). The main source of this complexity is the rule of "linguistic exogamy," which might not be expected to be very widespread in the world. However, the other source is the amount of individual bilingualism (or, more accurately, multilingualism), which makes it hard to decide who is a speaker of a given language and who is not. This characteristic, of wide-spread multilingualism, is anything but exceptional in the world as a whole, as an armchair sociolinguist can easily deduce from the fact that there are some four or five thousand languages in the world, but only about 140 nation states. At least some states must therefore contain a very large number of languages, and probably most contain a fair number, with an average between 30 and 35. In view of the need for communication with neighbouring communities and government agencies, it is fair to assume that many members of most communities are multilingual. It is worthwhile bearing this conclusion in mind in reading the next section, since it shows that the monolingual communities familiar to many of us may in fact be highly exceptional and even "exotic" from a global perspective.

A Real and Familiar World

15   Readers are now invited to consider the world in which they themselves grew up. It is unlikely that any reader has had a background quite as linguistically exciting as the one described above, but most of us will certainly find that there is more to be said about our own sociolinguistic worlds than might be expected and much of it is surprisingly interesting.

In order to focus their thinking, readers may find it helpful to imagine themselves, reasonably fluent in Tukano, sitting in a long-house in the north-west Amazon, telling the residents about their language, in the way that travelling Indians in the area are presumably asked to do if they reach a long-house unfamiliar with their language. The kind of information they would be expected to provide would cover both very general and very specific matters. Who else speaks the language? Where do the speakers live? Do they speak any other languages? What do they say when they first meet a stranger? What is the word meaning "phratry"? What are the meals eaten at different times of day called? Are there any special ways of talking to young children? How do you count? Is there any way of showing that you're quoting what somebody else has told you? How do you show that the thing you're referring to is already known to the addressee? Are there different ways of pronouncing any of the words according to where you come from? In answering every one of these questions, something will not only have been said about the language but also about one aspect or another of the society that uses it; and such questions could be multiplied by the inquisitive long-house residents until a complete description of the strangers' language has been provided.

The point of this exercise is to make readers aware of how much there is to say about their own language in relation to society.

Analyzing Rhetorical Choices

1. Hudson's main point is that to study language most fully, you must consider the overall society in which any language variety is spoken. Do the examples he chooses to make his case form a strong argument or not? Support your response.

2. For a lengthy piece of comparison-and-contrast writing, we would generally recommend a point-by-point rather than subject-by-subject approach. Yet Hudson seems to use the latter method to good effect. What accounts for his apparent success?

Writing About Issues and Contexts

1. Hudson mentions the custom of repeating someone's words as a show of respect. Can you think of "peculiar" rules in any of the languages you speak that are similar to this?

2. Relative to your native language, how would you answer some of the questions in Hudson's penultimate paragraph?

A widely published essayist born in San Francisco, **Richard Rodriguez**
*(1944–   ) is an editor at Pacific News Service and a contributing editor
at* Harper's Magazine, U.S. News & World Report, *and the* Los Angeles
Times. *In 1997, he received the Peabody Award for his broadcast work.
Rodriguez grew up in Sacramento, California, and is a graduate of
Stanford and Columbia. His books include* Hunger of Memory: The
Education of Richard Rodriguez *(1982),* Days of Obligation: An
Argument with My Mexican Father *(1993), and* Brown: The Last
Discovery of America *(2002). "Aria" is from* Hunger of Memory.

Richard Rodriguez

Aria

Supporters of bilingual education imply today that students like
me miss a great deal by not being taught in their family's language.
What they seem not to recognize is that, as a socially disadvantaged
child, I considered Spanish to be a private language. What I needed to
learn in school was that I had the right—and the obligation—to speak
the public language of *los gringos.* The odd truth is that my first-grade
classmates could have become bilingual, in the conventional sense of
that word, more easily than I. Had they been taught (as upper-middle-
class children are often taught early) a second language like Spanish
or French, they could have regarded it simply as that: another public
language. In my case such bilingualism could not have been so quickly
achieved. What I did not believe was that I could speak a single public
language.

Without question, it would have pleased me to hear my teachers
address me in Spanish when I entered the classroom. I would have felt
much less afraid. I would have trusted them and responded with ease.
But I would have delayed—for how long postponed?—having to learn
the language of public society. I would have evaded—and for how long
could I have afforded to delay?—learning the great lesson of school,
that I had a public identity.

Fortunately, my teachers were unsentimental about their responsibility. What they understood was that I needed to speak a public language. So their voices would search me out, asking me questions. Each
time I'd hear them, I'd look up in surprise to see a nun's face frowning

at me. I'd mumble, not really meaning to answer. The nun would persist, "Richard, stand up. Don't look at the floor. Speak up. Speak to the entire class, not just to me!" But I couldn't believe that the English language was mine to use. (In part, I did not want to believe it.) I continued to mumble. I resisted the teacher's demands. (Did I somehow suspect that once I learned public language my pleasing family life would be changed?) Silent, waiting for the bell to sound, I remained dazed, diffident, afraid.

Because I wrongly imagined that English was intrinsically a public language and Spanish an intrinsically private one, I easily noted the difference between classroom language and the language of home. At school, words were directed to a general audience of listeners. ("Boys and girls.") Words were meaningfully ordered. And the point was not self-expression alone but to make oneself understood by many others. The teacher quizzed: "Boys and girls, why do we use that word in this sentence? Could we think of a better word to use there? Would the sentence change its meaning if the words were differently arranged? And wasn't there a better way of saying much the same thing?" (I couldn't say. I wouldn't try to say.)

5   Three months. Five. Half a year passed. Unsmiling, ever watchful, my teachers noted my silence. They began to connect my behavior with the difficult progress my older sister and brother were making. Until one Saturday morning three nuns arrived at the house to talk to our parents. Stiffly, they sat on the blue living room sofa. From the doorway of another room, spying the visitors, I noted the incongruity—the clash of two worlds, the faces and voices of school intruding upon the familiar setting of home. I overheard one voice gently wondering, "Do your children speak only Spanish at home, Mrs. Rodriguez?" While another voice added, "That Richard especially seems so timid and shy."

That Rich-heard!

With great tact the visitors continued, "Is it possible for you and your husband to encourage your children to practice their English when they are home?" Of course, my parents complied. What would they not do for their children's well-being? And how could they have questioned the Church's authority which those women represented? In an instant, they agreed to give up the language (the sounds) that had revealed and accentuated our family's closeness. The moment after the visitors left, the change was observed. "*Ahora,* speak to us *en inglés,*" my father and mother united to tell us.

At first, it seemed a kind of game. After dinner each night, the family gathered to practice "our" English. (It was still then *inglés*, a language foreign to us, so we felt drawn as strangers to it.) Laughing, we would try to define words we could not pronounce. We played with strange English sounds, often over-anglicizing our pronunciations. And we filled the smiling gaps of our sentences with familiar Spanish sounds. But that was cheating, somebody shouted. Everyone laughed. In school, meanwhile, like my brother and sister, I was required to attend a daily tutoring session. I needed a full year of special attention. I also needed my teachers to keep my attention from straying in class by calling out, *Rich-heard*—their English voices slowly prying loose my ties to my other name, its three notes, *Ri-car-do*. Most of all I needed to hear my mother and father speak to me in a moment of seriousness in broken—suddenly heartbreaking—English. This scene was inevitable: One Saturday morning I entered the kitchen where my parents were talking in Spanish. I did not realize that they were talking in Spanish however until, at the moment they saw me, I heard their voices change to speak English. Those *gringo* sounds they uttered startled me. Pushed me away. In that moment of trivial misunderstanding and profound insight, I felt my throat twisted by unsounded grief. I turned quickly and left the room. But I had no place to escape to with Spanish. (The spell was broken.) My brother and sisters were speaking English in another part of the house.

Again and again in the days following, increasingly angry, I was obliged to hear my mother and father: "Speak to us *en inglés*." (*Speak.*) Only then did I determine to learn classroom English. Weeks after, it happened: One day in school I raised my hand to volunteer an answer. I spoke out in a loud voice. And I did not think it remarkable when the entire class understood. That day, I moved very far from the disadvantaged child I had been only days earlier. The belief, the calming assurance that I belonged in public, had at last taken hold.

10   Shortly after, I stopped hearing the high and loud sounds of *los gringos*. A more and more confident speaker of English, I didn't trouble to listen to *how* strangers sounded, speaking to me. And there simply were too many English-speaking people in my day for me to hear American accents anymore. Conversations quickened. Listening to persons who sounded eccentrically pitched voices, I usually noted their sounds for an initial few seconds before I concentrated on *what* they were saying. Conversations became content-full. Transparent. Hearing someone's *tone* of voice—angry or questioning or sarcastic or happy or

sad—I didn't distinguish it from the words it expressed. Sound and word were thus tightly wedded. At the end of a day, I was often bemused, always relieved, to realize how "silent," though crowded with words, my day in public had been. (This public silence measured and quickened the change in my life.)

At last, seven years old, I came to believe what had been technically true since my birth: I was an American citizen.

But the special feeling of closeness at home was diminished by then. Gone was the desperate, urgent, intense feeling of being at home; rare was the experience of feeling myself individualized by family intimates. We remained a loving family, but one greatly changed. No longer so close; no longer bound tight by the pleasing and troubling knowledge of our public separateness. Neither my older brother nor sister rushed home after school anymore. Nor did I. When I arrived home there would often be neighborhood kids in the house. Or the house would be empty of sounds.

Following the dramatic Americanization of their children, even my parents grew more publicly confident. Especially my mother. She learned the names of all the people on our block. And she decided we needed to have a telephone installed in the house. My father continued to use the word *gringo*. But it was no longer charged with the old bitterness or distrust. (Stripped of any emotional content, the word simply became a name for those Americans not of Hispanic descent.) Hearing him, sometimes, I wasn't sure if he was pronouncing the Spanish word *gringo* or saying gringo in English.

Matching the silence I started hearing in public was a new quiet at home. The family's quiet was partly due to the fact that, as we children learned more and more English, we shared fewer and fewer words with our parents. Sentences needed to be spoken slowly when a child addressed his mother or father. (Often the parent wouldn't understand.) The child would need to repeat himself. (Still the parent misunderstood.) The young voice, frustrated, would end up saying, "Never mind"—the subject was closed. Dinners would be noisy with the clinking of knives and forks against dishes. My mother would smile softly between her remarks; my father at the other end of the table would chew and chew at his food, while he stared over the heads of his children.

15   My *mother!* My *father!* After English became my primary language, I no longer knew what words to use in addressing my parents. The old Spanish words (those tender accents of sound) I had used earlier—*mamá* and *papá*—I couldn't use anymore. They would have

been too painful reminders of how much had changed in my life. On the other hand, the words I heard neighborhood kids call *their* parents seemed equally unsatisfactory. *Mother* and *Father; Ma, Papa, Pa, Dad, Pop* (how I hated the all-American sound of that last word especially)—all these terms I felt were unsuitable, not really terms of address for *my* parents. As a result, I never used them at home. Whenever I'd speak to my parents, I would try to get their attention with eye contact alone. In public conversations, I'd refer to "my parents" or "my mother and father."

My mother and father, for their part, responded differently, as their children spoke to them less. She grew restless, seemed troubled and anxious at the scarcity of words exchanged in the house. It was she who would question me about my day when I came home from school. She smiled at small talk. She pried at the edges of my sentences to get me to say something more. (What?) She'd join conversations she overheard, but her intrusions often stopped her children's talking. By contrast, my father seemed reconciled to the new quiet. Though his English improved somewhat, he retired into silence. At dinner he spoke very little. One night his children and even his wife helplessly giggled at his garbled English pronunciation of the Catholic Grace before Meals. Thereafter he made his wife recite the prayer at the start of each meal, even on formal occasions, when there were guests in the house. Hers became the public voice of the family. On official business, it was she, not my father, one would usually hear on the phone or in stores, talking to strangers. His children grew so accustomed to his silence that, years later, they would speak routinely to his shyness. (My mother would often try to explain: Both his parents died when he was eight. He was raised by an uncle who treated him like little more than a menial servant. He was never encouraged to speak. He grew up alone. A man of few words.) But my father was not shy, I realized, when I'd watch him speaking Spanish with relatives. Using Spanish, he was quickly effusive. Especially when talking with other men, his voice would spark, flicker, flare alive with sounds. In Spanish, he expressed ideas and feelings he rarely revealed in English. With firm Spanish sounds, he conveyed a confidence and authority English would never allow him.

The silence at home, however, was finally more than a literal silence. Fewer words passed between parent and child, but more profound was the silence that resulted from my inattention to sounds. At about the time I no longer bothered to listen with care to the sounds of English in public, I grew careless about listening to the sounds family members made when they spoke. Most of the time I heard someone speaking at home and didn't distinguish his sounds from the words people uttered in public. I didn't even pay much attention to my parents' accented and ungrammatical speech. At least not at home. Only when I was with them in public would I grow alert to their accents. Though, even then, their sounds caused me less and less concern. For I was increasingly confident of my own public identity.

I would have been happier about my public success had I not sometimes recalled what it had been like earlier, when my family had conveyed its intimacy through a set of conveniently private sounds. Sometimes in public, hearing a stranger, I'd hark back to my past. A Mexican farmworker approached me downtown to ask directions to somewhere. "*¿Hijito . . . ?*" he said. And his voice summoned deep longing. Another time, standing beside my mother in the visiting room of a Carmelite convent, before the dense screen which rendered the nuns shadowy figures, I heard several Spanish-speaking nuns—their busy, singsong overlapping voices—assure us that yes, yes, we were re-membered, all our family was remembered in their prayers. (Their voices echoed faraway family sounds.) Another day, a dark-faced old woman—her hand light on my shoulder—steadied herself against me as she boarded a bus. She murmured something I couldn't quite com-prehend. Her Spanish voice came near, like the face of a never-before-seen relative in the instant before I was kissed. Her voice, like so many of the Spanish voices I'd hear in public, recalled the golden age of my youth. Hearing Spanish then, I continued to be a careful, if sad, lis-tener to sounds. Hearing a Spanish-speaking family walking behind me, I turned to look. I smiled for an instant, before my glance found the Hispanic-looking faces of strangers in the crowd going by.

Today I hear bilingual educators say that children lose a degree of "in-dividuality" by becoming assimilated into public society. (Bilingual schooling was popularized in the seventies, that decade when middle-class ethnics began to resist the process of assimilation—the American melting pot.) But the bilingualists simplistically scorn the value and necessity of as-similation. They do not seem to realize that there are *two* ways a person is individualized. So they do not realize that while one suffers a diminished sense of *private* individuality by becoming assimilated into public society, such assimilation makes possible the achievement of *public* individuality.

20   The bilingualists insist that a student should be reminded of his difference from others in mass society, his heritage. But they equate mere separateness with individuality. The fact is that only in private—

with intimates—is separateness from the crowd a prerequisite for individuality. (An intimate draws me apart, tells me that I am unique, unlike all others.) In public, by contrast, full individuality is achieved, paradoxically, by those who are able to consider themselves members of the crowd. Thus it happened for me: Only when I was able to think of myself as an American, no longer an alien in *gringo* society, could I seek the rights and opportunities necessary for full public individuality. The social and political advantages I enjoy as a man result from the day that I came to believe that my name, indeed, is *Rich-heard Road-ree-guess*. It is true that my public society today is often impersonal. (My public society is usually mass society.) Yet despite the anonymity of the crowd and despite the fact that the individuality I achieve in public is often tenuous—because it depends on my being one in a crowd—I celebrate the day I acquired my new name. Those middle-class ethnics who scorn assimilation seem to me filled with decadent self-pity, obsessed by the burden of public life. Dangerously, they romanticize public separateness and they trivialize the dilemma of the socially disadvantaged.

My awkward childhood does not prove the necessity of bilingual education. My story discloses instead an essential myth of childhood—inevitable pain. If I rehearse here the changes in my private life after my Americanization, it is finally to emphasize the public gain. The loss implies the gain: The house I returned to each afternoon was quiet. Intimate sounds no longer rushed to the door to greet me. There were other noises inside. The telephone rang. Neighborhood kids ran past the door of the bedroom where I was reading my schoolbooks—covered with shopping-bag paper. Once I learned public language, it would never again be easy for me to hear intimate family voices. More and more of my day was spent hearing words. But that may only be a way of saying that the day I raised my hand in class and spoke loudly to an entire roomful of faces, my childhood started to end.

Analyzing Rhetorical Choices

1. As arguments against bilingual education programs, how effective are the personal anecdotes Rodriguez offers?
2. Rodriguez asserts that supporters of bilingual education are engaging in "decadent self-pity." However, he does not much develop this assertion. What, in your view, would illustrate his point more fully or count as sufficient evidence?

Writing About Issues and Contexts

1. Rodriguez believes that some cultural loss is an inevitable part of learning. Concerning his education, he reflects that "Fortunately, my teachers were unsentimental about their responsibility." How similar is your position to his? Elaborate.
2. In a similar vein, would you trade in the name Ricardo for Richard? Why or why not?

*Born in Fort Defiance, Arizona, poet, essayist, and playwright **Laura Tohe** (1952–   ) is a Diné (Navajo). She was raised on a reservation and later earned a bachelor's degree from the University of New Mexico, as well as master's and doctoral degrees from the University of Nebraska. She is currently an associate professor of English at Arizona State University at Tempe. Her books include a poetry collection,* Making Friends with Water *(1986), and a poetry and prose memoir,* No Parole Today *(1999), from which the following selection is taken.*

Laura Tohe
Our Tongues Slapped into Silence

In first grade I was five years old, the youngest and smallest in my class, always the one in front at group picture time. The principal put me in first grade because I spoke both Diné and English. Because of that, I skipped Beginner class.

All my classmates were Diné and most of them spoke only the language of our ancestors. During this time, the government's policy meant to assimilate us into the white way of life. We had no choice in the matter; we had to comply. The taking of our language was a priority.

Dick and Jane Subdue the Diné

See Father.
See Mother.
See Dick run.
See Jane and Sally laugh.
   oh, oh, oh
See Spot jump.
   oh, oh, oh
See Eugene speak Diné
See Juanita answer him
   oh, oh, oh
See teacher frown.
   uh oh, uh oh

In first grade our first introduction to Indian School was Miss Rolands, a black woman from Texas, who treated us the way her people had been treated by white people. Later I learned how difficult it was for black teachers to find jobs in their communities, so they took jobs with the Bureau of Indian Affairs in New Mexico and Arizona in the 1950s and 60s.

5   Miss Rolands found it difficult to adjust to living in a mostly Diné community, connected to the outside world by only a dirt road that was sometimes impassable in the winter.

> *See Eugene with red hands, shape of ruler.*
> *oh, oh, oh*
> *See Eugene cry.*
> *oh, oh, oh*
> *See Juanita stand in corner, see tears fall down face.*
>
> *oh, oh, oh*

In first grade we received the first of our Dick and Jane books that introduced us to the white man's world through Father, Mother, Dick, Jane, Puff and Spot. These and other characters said and did what we thought all white people did: drive cars to the farm, drain maple juice from trees, and say oh, oh, oh a lot.

> *Oh see us draw pictures*
> *of brown horses under blue clouds.*
> *We color eyes black, hair black.*
> *We draw ears and leave out mouth.*
>
> *Oh see, see, see, see.*

Miss Rolands, an alien in our world, stood us in the corner of the classroom or outside in the hallway to feel shame for the crime of speaking Diné. Other times our hands were imprinted with red slaps from the ruler. In later classes we headed straight for the rear of classrooms, never asked questions, and never raised our hand. Utter one word of Diné and the government made sure our tongues were drowned in the murky waters of assimilation.

Analyzing Rhetorical Choices

1.   Tohe mixes actual and imagined lines from a reading text. In what ways is this a worthwhile rhetorical device in your estimation?

2. How do you interpret the phrase "the murky waters of assimilation"? Why are those waters considered murky?

Writing About Issues and Contexts

1. In what ways do you find Tohe's argument about education either more or less convincing than that of Rodriguez?
2. The author announces, "the taking of our language was a priority." Why do language issues become central in discussions of assimilation?
3. Tohe recalls that Miss Rolands, an African American, "treated us the way her people had been treated by white people." What are all the things you think she means by this statement?

Born in Brooklyn to Irish immigrant parents, **Frank McCourt** *(1930–)
and his brothers were taken back to Ireland by his parents when he was
four years old. He grew up in Limerick, Ireland, and returned to the
United States in 1949. Although he never attended high school, he convinced an admissions officer to allow him to enroll at New York
University. He subsequently taught in high schools and colleges for 30
years. His 1996 memoir,* Angela's Ashes, *won the 1997 Pulitzer Prize for
biography. In 1999, he published a sequel,* 'Tis: A Memoir, *from which
the following selection is drawn.*

Frank McCourt
From 'Tis: A Memoir

Teaching nine hours a week at New York Technical College in
Brooklyn was easier than twenty-five hours a week at McKee
Vocational and Technical High School. Classes were smaller, students
older, and there were none of the problems a high school teacher has to
deal with, the lavatory pass, the moaning over assignments, the mass
of paperwork created by bureaucrats who have nothing to do but create new forms. I could supplement my reduced salary by teaching at
Washington Irving Evening High School or substituting at Seward
Park High School and Stuyvesant High School.

The chairman of the English Department at the community college asked me if I'd like to teach a class of paraprofessionals. I said yes
though I had no notion of what a paraprofessional was.

That first class I found out. Here were thirty-six women, African-
American with a sprinkling of Hispanics, ranging in age from early
twenties to late fifties, teacher aides in elementary schools and in college now with government help. They'd get two-year associate degrees
and, perhaps, continue their education so that someday they might become fully qualified teachers.

That night there was little time for teaching. After I had asked the
women to write a short autobiographical essay for the next class they
gathered up their books and filed out, apprehensive, still unsure of
themselves, of each other, of me. I had the whitest skin in the room.

5   When we met again the mood was the same except for one woman
who sat with her head on the desk, sobbing. I asked what was the matter. She raised her head, tears on her cheeks.

I lost my books.

Oh, well, I said, you'll get another set of books. Just go to the English Department and tell them what happened.

You mean I won't get throwed out of college?

No, you won't be throwed, thrown out of college.

10   I felt like patting her head but I didn't know how to pat the head of a middle-aged woman who has lost her books. She smiled, we all smiled. Now we could begin. I asked for their compositions and told them I'd read some aloud though I wouldn't use their real names.

The essays were stiff, self-conscious. As I read I wrote some of the more common misspelled words on the chalkboard, suggested changes in structure, pointed out grammatical errors. It was all dry and tedious till I suggested the ladies write simply and clearly. For their next assignment they could write on anything they liked. They looked surprised. Anything? But we don't have anything to write about. We don't have no adventures.

They had nothing to write about, nothing but the tensions of their lives, summer riots erupting around them, assassinations, husbands who so often disappeared, children destroyed by drugs, their own daily grind of housework, jobs, school, raising children.

They loved the strange ways of words. During a discussion on juvenile delinquency Mrs. Williams sang out, No kid o' mine gonna be no yoot.

Yoot?

15   Yeah, you know. Yoot. She held up a newspaper where the headline howled, Youth Slays Mom.

Oh, I said, and Mrs. Williams went on, These yoots, y'know, runnin' around slayin' people. Killin' 'em, too. Any kid o' mine come home actin' like a yoot an' out he go on his you-know-what.

The youngest woman in the class, Nicole, turned the tables on me. She sat in the back in a corner and never spoke till I asked the class if they'd like to write about their mothers. Then she raised her hand. How about your mother, Mr. McCourt?

Questions came like bullets. Is she alive? How many children did she have? Where's your father? Did she have all those children with one man? Where is she living? Who's she living with? She's living alone? Your mother's living alone and she has four sons? How come?

They frowned. They disapproved. Poor lady with four sons shouldn't be living alone. People should take care of their mothers but what do men know? You can never tell a man what it's like to be a mother and if it wasn't for the mothers America would fall apart.

20   In April Martin Luther King was killed and classes were suspended for a week. When we met again I wanted to beg forgiveness for my race. Instead I asked for the essays I had already assigned. Mrs. Williams was indignant. Look, Mr. McCourt, when they tryin' to burn your house down you ain't sittin' around writin' no cawm-po-zishuns.

In June Bobby Kennedy was killed. My thirty-six ladies wondered what was happening to the world but they agreed you have to carry on, that education was the only road to sanity. When they talked about their children their faces brightened and I became irrelevant to their talk. I sat on my desk while they told each other that now they were in college themselves they stood over their kids to make sure the homework was done.

On the last night of classes in June there was a final examination. I watched those dark heads bent over papers, the mothers of two hundred and twelve children, and I knew, that no matter what they wrote or didn't write on those papers, no one would fail.

They finished. The last paper had been handed in but no one was leaving. I asked if they had another class here. Mrs. Williams stood and coughed. Ah, Mr. McCourt, I must say, I mean we must say, it was a wonderful thing to come to college and learn so much about English and everything and we got you this little something hopin' you'll like it an' all.

She sat down, sobbing, and I thought, This class begins and ends in tears.

25   The gift was passed up, a bottle of shaving lotion in a fancy red and black box. When I sniffed it I was nearly knocked over but I sniffed again with gusto and told the ladies I'd keep the bottle forever in memory of them, this class, their yoots.

Instead of going home after that class I took the subway to West Ninety-sixth Street in Manhattan and called my mother from a street telephone.

Would you like to have a snack?

I don't know. Where are you?

I'm a few blocks away.

30   Why?

I just happened to be in the neighborhood.

Visiting Malachy?

No. Visiting you.

Me? Why should you be visiting me?

35   For Christ's sake, you're my mother and all I wanted to do was invite you out for a snack. What would you like to eat?

She sounded doubtful. Well, I love them jumbo shrimps they have in the Chinese restaurants.

All right. We'll have jumbo shrimps.

But I don't know if I'm able for them this minute. I think I'd prefer to go to the Greeks for a salad.

All right. I'll see you there.

40 She came into the restaurant gasping for breath and when I kissed her cheek I could taste the salt of her sweat. She said she'd have to sit a minute before she could even think of food, that if she hadn't given up the cigarettes she'd be dead now.

She ordered the feta salad and when I asked her if she liked it she said she loved it, she could live on it.

Do you like that cheese?

What cheese?

The goat cheese.

45 What goat cheese?

The white stuff. The feta. That's goat cheese.

'Tis not.

'Tis.

Well, if I knew that was goat cheese I'd never touch it because I was attacked by a goat once out the country in Limerick and I'd never eat a thing that attacked me.

50 It's a good thing, I told her, you were never attacked by a jumbo shrimp.

Analyzing Rhetorical Choices

1. What are all the elements compared or contrasted in McCourt's essay? Which are more important than others? Why?

2. Unlike most texts, McCourt's piece does not include quotation marks around words we would take to be direct quotes. Why do you think he employs this method? Does it have any particular effect on you as a reader?

3. How realistic do you find the "yoot" episode and Mrs. Williams's comments? Explain.

Writing About Issues and Contexts

1. Have you discovered that your high school and college experiences differ as McCourt describes? Is there now no moaning over assignments?

2. Concerning his students, McCourt offers that "They had nothing to write about, nothing but the tensions of their lives, summer riots

erupting around them, assassinations, husbands who so often disappeared, children destroyed by drugs, their own daily grind of housework, job, school, raising children." What other assumptions might you make about their lives? In your eyes, would his description accurately reflect many lives today compared to 1968? Support your response.

3. Why does McCourt visit his mother when he does?

***Deborah Tannen** (1945–   ) is a university professor and a professor of linguistics at Georgetown University. Born in Brooklyn, New York, she be- came partially deaf as the result of a childhood illness. Her subsequent interest in nonverbal communication led to formal study in linguistics. She earned a Ph.D. at the University of California at Berkeley. Her nu- merous books include* That's Not What I Meant!: How Conversational Style Makes or Breaks Your Relations with Others *(1986);* You Just Don't Understand: Women and Men in Conversation *(1990), which stayed on the* New York Times *best-seller list for almost four years;* The Argument Culture *(1999); and* I Only Say This Because I Love You: How the Way We Talk Can Make or Break Family Relationships Throughout Our Lives *(2001). The following adaptatation from* You Just Don't Understand *was published in the* Washington Post.

Deborah   Tannen

Sex, Lies, and Conversation

I was addressing a small gathering in a suburban Virginia living room—a women's group that had invited men to join them. Throughout the evening, one man had been particularly talkative, fre- quently offering ideas and anecdotes, while his wife sat silently beside him on the couch. Toward the end of the evening, I commented that women frequently complain that their husbands don't talk to them. This man quickly concurred. He gestured toward his wife and said, "She's the talker in our family." The room burst into laughter; the man looked puzzled and hurt. "It's true," he explained. "When I come home from work I have nothing to say. If she didn't keep the conversa- tion going, we'd spend the whole evening in silence."

This episode crystallizes the irony that although American men tend to talk more than women in public situations, they often talk less at home. And this pattern is wreaking havoc with marriage.

The pattern was observed by political scientist Andrew Hacker in the late '70s. Sociologist Catherine Kohler Riessman reports in her new book *Divorce Talk* that most of the women she interviewed—but only a few of the men—gave lack of communication as the reason for their divorces. Given the current divorce rate of nearly 50 percent, that amounts to millions of cases in the United States every year—a virtual epidemic of failed conversation.

In my own research, complaints from women about their husbands most often focused not on tangible inequities such as having given up the chance for a career to accompany a husband to his, or doing far more than their share of daily life-support work like cleaning, cooking, social arrangements and errands. Instead, they focused on communication: "He doesn't listen to me," "He doesn't talk to me." I found, as Hacker observed years before, that most wives want their husbands to be, first and foremost, conversational partners, but few husbands share this expectation of their wives.

5   In short, the image that best represents the current crisis is the stereotypical cartoon scene of a man sitting at the breakfast table with a newspaper held up in front of his face, while a woman glares at the back of it, wanting to talk.

Linguistic Battle of the Sexes

How can women and men have such different impressions of communication in marriage? Why the widespread imbalance in their interests and expectations?

In the April [1990] issue of *American Psychologist,* Stanford University's Eleanor Maccoby reports the results of her own and others' research showing that children's development is most influenced by the social structure of peer interactions. Boys and girls tend to play with children of their own gender, and their sex-separate groups have different organizational structures and interactive norms.

I believe these systematic differences in childhood socialization make talk between women and men like cross-cultural communication, heir to all the attraction and pitfalls of that enticing but difficult enterprise. My research on men's and women's conversations uncovered patterns similar to those described for children's groups.

For women, as for girls, intimacy is the fabric of relationships, and talk is the thread from which it is woven. Little girls create and maintain friendships by exchanging secrets; similarly, women regard conversation as the cornerstone of friendship. So a woman expects her husband to be a new and improved version of a best friend. What is important is not the individual subjects that are discussed but the sense of closeness, of a life shared, that emerges when people tell their thoughts, feelings, and impressions.

10   Bonds between boys can be as intense as girls', but they are based less on talking, more on doing things together. Since they don't assume talk is the cement that binds a relationship, men don't know what kind of talk women want, and they don't miss it when it isn't there.

Boys' groups are larger, more inclusive, and more hierarchical, so boys must struggle to avoid the subordinate position in the group. This may play a role in women's complaints that men don't listen to them. Some men really don't like to listen, because being the listener makes them feel one down, like a child listening to adults or an employee to a boss.

But often when women tell men, "You aren't listening," and the men protest, "I am," the men are right. The impression of not listening results from misalignment in the mechanics of conversation. The misalignment begins as soon as a man and a woman take physical positions. This became clear when I studied videotapes made by psychologist Paul Dorval of children and adults talking to their same-sex best friends. I found that at every age, the girls and women faced each other directly, their eyes anchored on each other's faces. At every age, the boys and men sat at angles to each other and looked elsewhere in the room, periodically glancing at each other. They were obviously attuned to each other, often mirroring each other's movements. But the tendency of men to face away can give women the impression they aren't listening even when they are. A young woman in college was frustrated: Whenever she told her boyfriend she wanted to talk to him, he would lie down on the floor, close his eyes, and put his arm over his face. This signaled to her, "He's taking a nap." But he insisted he was listening extra hard. Normally, he looks around the room, so he is easily distracted. Lying down and covering his eyes helped him concentrate on what she was saying.

Analogous to the physical alignment that women and men take in conversation is their topical alignment. The girls in my study tended to talk at length about one topic, but the boys tended to jump from topic to topic. The second-grade girls exchanged stories about people they knew. The second-grade boys teased, told jokes, noticed things in the room and talked about finding games to play. The sixth-grade girls talked about problems with a mutual friend. The sixth-grade boys talked about fifty-five different topics, none of which extended over more than a few turns.

Listening to Body Language

Switching topics is another habit that gives women the impression men aren't listening, especially if they switch to a topic about themselves. But the evidence of the tenth-grade boys in my study indicates otherwise. The tenth-grade boys sprawled across their chairs with bodies parallel and eyes straight ahead, rarely looking at each other. They looked as if they were riding in a car, staring out the windshield. But they were talking about their feelings. One boy was upset because a girl had told him he had a drinking problem, and the other was feeling alienated from all his friends.

15   Now, when a girl told a friend about a problem, the friend responded by asking probing questions and expressing agreement and understanding. But the boys dismissed each other's problems. Todd assured Richard that his drinking was "no big problem" because "sometimes you're funny when you're off your butt." And when Todd said he felt left out, Richard responded, "Why should you? You know more people than me."

Women perceive such responses as belittling and unsupportive. But the boys seemed satisfied with them. Whereas women reassure each other by implying, "You shouldn't feel bad because I've had similar experiences," men do so by implying, "You shouldn't feel bad because your problems aren't so bad."

There are even simpler reasons for women's impression that men don't listen. Linguist Lynette Hirschman found that women make more listener-noise, such as "mhm," "uhuh," and "yeah," to show "I'm with you." Men, she found, more often give silent attention. Women who expect a stream of listener-noise interpret silent attention as no attention at all.

Women's conversational habits are as frustrating to men as men's are to women. Men who expect silent attention interpret a stream of listener-noise as overreaction or impatience. Also, when women talk to each other in a close, comfortable setting, they often overlap, finish each other's sentences and anticipate what the other is about to say. This practice, which I call "participatory listenership," is often perceived by men as interruption, intrusion, and lack of attention.

A parallel difference caused a man to complain about his wife, "She just wants to talk about her own point of view. If I show her another view, she gets mad at me." When most women talk to each other, they assume a conversationalist's job is to express agreement and support. But many men see their conversational duty as pointing out the other side of an argument. This is heard as disloyalty by women, and refusal to offer the requisite support. It is not that women don't want to see other points of view, but that they prefer them phrased as suggestions and inquiries rather than as direct challenges.

20   In his book *Fighting for Life*, Walter Ong points out that men use "agonistic," or warlike, oppositional formats to do almost anything; thus discussion becomes debate, and conversation becomes a competitive sport. In contrast, women see conversation as a ritual means of establishing rapport. If Jane tells a problem and June says she has a similar one, they walk away feeling closer to each other. But this attempt at establishing rapport can backfire when used with men. Men take too literally women's ritual "troubles talk," just as women mistake men's ritual challenges for real attack.

The Sounds of Silence

These differences begin to clarify why women and men have such different expectations about communication in marriage. For women, talk creates intimacy. Marriage is an orgy of closeness: you can tell your feelings and thoughts, and still be loved. Their greatest fear is being pushed away. But men live in a hierarchical world, where talk maintains independence and status. They are on guard to protect themselves from being put down and pushed around.

This explains the paradox of the talkative man who said of his silent wife, "She's the talker." In the public setting of a guest lecture, he felt challenged to show his intelligence and display his understanding of the lecture. But at home, where he has nothing to prove and no one to defend against, he is free to remain silent. For his wife, being home means she is free from the worry that something she says might offend someone, or spark disagreement, or appear to be showing off; at home she is free to talk.

The communication problems that endanger marriage can't be fixed by mechanical engineering. They require a new conceptual framework about the role of talk in human relationships. Many of the psychological explanations that have become second nature may not be helpful, because they tend to blame either women (for not being assertive enough) or men (for not being in touch with their feelings). A sociolinguistic approach by which male-female conversation is seen as cross-cultural communication allows us to understand the problem and forge solutions without blaming either party.

Once the problem is understood, improvement comes naturally, as it did to the young woman and her boyfriend who seemed to go to sleep when she wanted to talk. Previously, she had accused him of not listening, and he had refused to change his behavior, since that would be admitting fault. But then she learned about and explained to him the differences in women's and men's habitual ways of aligning themselves in conversation. The next time she told him she wanted to talk, he began, as usual, by lying down and covering his eyes. When the familiar negative reaction bubbled up, she reassured herself that he really was listening. But then he sat up and looked at her. Thrilled, she asked why. He said, "You like me to look at you when we talk, so I'll try to do it." Once he saw their differences as cross-cultural rather than right and wrong, he independently altered his behavior.

25   Women who feel abandoned and deprived when their husbands won't listen to or report daily news may be happy to discover their husbands trying to adapt once they understand the place of small talk in women's relationships. But if their husbands don't adapt, the women may still be comforted that for men, this is not a failure of intimacy. Accepting the difference, the wives may look to their friends or family for that kind of talk. And husbands who can't provide it shouldn't feel their wives have made unreasonable demands. Some couples will still decide to divorce, but at least their decisions will be based on realistic expectations.

In these times of resurgent ethnic conflicts, the world desperately needs cross-cultural understanding. Like charity, successful cross-cultural communication should begin at home.

Analyzing Rhetorical Choices

1. Along with R. A. Hudson, Tannen perhaps adopts the most objective and academic tone of the writers in this chapter, referring to several formal studies to develop her argument. Is her means of arguing effective? Why or why not? For example, how does she make appropriate use of psychologist Paul Dorval's tapes of same-sex conversations to draw conclusions about intersex conversations?

2. Unlike Hudson, Tannen opts for point-by-point development, proceeding, for example, through a series of gender contrasts with respect to "physical alignment," "switching topics," "staying on topic," "listener-noise," and "participatory listenership." Comment on whether this is an effective choice. Would you prefer to read about all the traits of one sex first and then about all the traits of the other? Explain your preference.

3. In making reference to males and females, Tannen sometimes lists females first (women and men) and at other times lists males first (boys and girls). What is the effect on you, if any, of these choices?

Writing About Issues and Contexts

1. How do you apply Tannen's theories to your own environment and relationships? Do you think an understanding of her arguments will help you in some of the conversations in which you participate? Support your viewpoint.

2. What is your level of optimism about the prospects of cross-cultural understanding in general, the kind that Tannen, in her closing paragraph, says the world desperately needs?

Strategies for Writers:
Comparison and Contrast

1. Many essays in this chapter have argued, instructed, or conveyed memoir by using comparison and contrast. Jodi Kantor, Bharati Mukherjee, and Richard Rodriguez, for example, narrate their personal experiences as they make arguments about the subjects with which they are concerned. R. A. Hudson and Deborah Tannen use comparison and contrast in presentations that are scholarly. Develop a similar kind of comparison-and-contrast essay.

2. Plan a narrative or essay in which comparison and contrast would serve your purposes and be of interest to your envisioned audience. As you write, list as many relevant points of comparison and contrast as you can generate. You will probably want to decide whether you will use a dominant development pattern of subject by subject or point by point. In general, the longer your intended piece of writing, the more likely it is that you will want to use the point-by-point technique. Cornel West uses this approach admirably. Even when he expands on the point he makes about African American and Jewish contributions, he lists the 44 names he cites in Black-Jewish pairs according to their areas of achievement. For example, he writes, "Marvin Gaye and Bob Dylan, James Baldwin and Norman Mailer, Lorraine Hansberry and Neil Simon." (He does not write Marvin Gaye, James Baldwin, and Lorraine Hansberry; Bob Dylan, Norman Mailer, and Neil Simon.)

3. Decide whether your tone will be formal or informal. Do you need to sound more like Bruce Catton or Frank McCourt? In addition, consider whether you would be most effective speaking in first, second, or third person. Will you feature dialogue? Will the dialogue accurately represent the language varieties you are attempting to portray?

4. Compose your draft and share it with friends, classmates, and your instructor. Note what they consider to be strengths and weaknesses of your text and consider their comments carefully as you revise. As always, revisit questions of tone, language choice, and selection of details.

5. Consider some of the other rhetorical devices used by the authors in this chapter. For example, note the rhythm and parallelism to highlight differences that Mukherjee uses in her open-

ing paragraph: "I am an American citizen and she is not. I am moved that thousands of long-term residents are finally taking the oath of citizenship. She is not." You might cite other works, even including parody in the manner of Tohe.

6. You can practice comparison-and-contrast methods by giving yourself assignments like the one that Jodi Kantor had as a reviewer for the *New York Times*. Compare and contrast two books or articles related to any of your courses.

Research and Writing Assignments

1. In the manner of Bruce Catton, compare and contrast two historical figures that interest you. Consult print and electronic sources to obtain ample information on your subjects, and integrate the relevant sources with your own observations, citing your sources carefully. Be sure to consider family background, regional origins, personality traits, personal philosophies, and significant actions.

2. Bharati Mukherjee argues that immigrants in the United States may attempt total assimilation or try to hold on completely to their native cultures. Identify and describe additional viewpoints that immigrants might hold and other methods they might use to conduct their lives. Compare and contrast your ideas with those of Mukherjee and those she attributes to her sister.

3. In "Wham! Bam! Thanks a Bunch!" Jodi Kantor considers two boxing memoirs by women. Compare and contrast Kantor's remarks and those of the authors to the arguments about boxing made by Norman Mailer (see "Boxing as a Metaphor for Life" in Chapter 9 and Norman Cousins (see "Who Killed Benny Paret?" in Chapter 10).

4. Name two ethnic or cultural groups other than African Americans and Jews that have made stellar contributions to the development of the United States. List at least 10 achievers from each group, and try to form intergroup pairs as Cornel West does in his essay. Also compare and contrast the groups as a whole and share your overall perspective on their achievements.

5. Revisit and answer the questions that R. A. Hudson poses toward the end of "Language Worlds." Share your responses with a classmate who has also answered these questions; then write

an essay in which you analyze, compare, and contrast the two sets of answers. Include reflection about how this assignment informs your view of how language operates.

6. Richard Rodriguez, Laura Tohe, and Frank McCourt make arguments either explicitly or implicitly about the best way to teach language in school. Their opinions are part of a larger conversation about policy issues such as bilingual education or the proposed English Language Amendment. Consult material on these issues, and write an essay expressing your own views. In the process, compare and contrast the suggestions or practices of Rodriguez, Tohe, and McCourt to one another and to your own ideas.

7. In "Sex, Lies, and Conversation," Deborah Tannen suggests that talk between men and women is like cross-cultural communication. Observe people at home, in your neighborhood, at work, or on campus to see if the characteristics concerning male and female verbal behavior that Tannen describes are evident. Write an essay detailing the differences, if any, that you notice.

9
Cause and Effect

One of the most basic intellectual impulses is to link cause with effect, effect with cause: This fundamental intellectual operation helps us solve problems and understand actions. It rains, and the next day flowers bloom on the front lawn. A cold front blows in off the lake, and six inches of snow fall. Most of us perceive these activities as linked, even if the linkage is not always explicit. The rain may not be the direct cause of the blooming; the cold front may not be the direct cause of the snow. But the appearance of a cause/effect relationship is there, and we make the connection. Much of the time we are correct, but just because one event follows another is insufficient grounds to assume that one is the *cause* of the other. This is one of the major lessons that Brent Staples drives home in "A Black Man Ponders His Ability to Alter Space."

Even when a situation seems obvious, it is not always easy to link cause with effect. A friend might have had an auto accident that caused her minor injury, a clear case of cause and effect. Yes, the accident (cause) produced the injury (effect), but the more compelling question is what caused the accident? Bad weather? A defective auto part? Driver inattention or inexperience? Cell phone usage? A distracting passenger? The other driver? Alcohol consumption? Darkness? An unavoidable twist of fate? Making a clear connection between causes and effects is not always easy. Often it takes extensive research or scientific investigation to find the relationship, and even then that answer may be hypothetical or represent a best-guess scenario.

Perhaps the most complicated—and yet worthwhile—aspect of tracing a cause/effect relationship is determining the true or ultimate cause(s) of an effect. The current international debate about global warming points to a variety of possible causes—such as the inevitable natural cycles of weather, increased carbon dioxide in the atmosphere produced primarily by the internal combustion engine, and the loss of forested lands and especially rain forest terrain. Which causes are primary? How can we validate some potential causes and eliminate others, especially when the stakes are so high for industrialized nations like the United States? Scientific analysis is extremely helpful, but science alone has so far not proven persuasive.

Those on the environmental side of the debate have a clear view of the cause of global warming and how best to prevent it. Here, for example, is a brief analysis by EcoBridge, a Web site devoted to "the environmental education of the public."

Causes of Global Warming

Transport Sector—Choice of Vehicles
Twenty percent (20%) of U.S carbon dioxide emissions comes from the burning of gasoline in internal-combustion engines of cars and light trucks (minivans, sport utility vehicles, pick-up trucks, and jeeps). (20) Vehicles with poor gas mileage contribute the most to global warming. For example, according to the E.P.A.'s 2000 Fuel Economy Guide, a new Dodge Durango sport utility vehicle (with a 5.9 liter engine) that gets 12 miles per gallon in the city will emit an estimated 800 pounds of carbon dioxide over a distance of 500 city miles. In other words for each gallon of gas a vehicle consumes, 19.6 pounds of carbon dioxide are emitted into the air. (21) A new Honda Insight that gets 61 miles to the gallon will only emit about 161 pounds of carbon dioxide over the same distance of 500 city miles. Sport utility vehicles were built for rough terrain, off road driving in mountains and deserts. When they are used for city driving, they are so much overkill to the environment. If one has to have a large vehicle for their family, station wagons are an intelligent choice for city driving, especially since their price is about half that of a sport utility. Inasmuch as SUVs have a narrow wheel base in respect to their higher silhouette, they are four times as likely as cars to roll over in an accident. (33)

About another 10% of U.S. carbon dioxide emissions comes from trucks used mostly for commercial purposes. (20)

The gas mileage of 2000 model vehicles averaged 28.1 miles per gallon, the worst fuel economy since 1980. The main reason for the decline in gas mileage was the popularity of the SUV, garnering about 50% of car sales in 2000. If car manufacturers were to increase their fleets' average gas mileage about 3 miles per gallon, this country could save a million barrels of oil every day, while U.S. drivers would save $25 billion in fuel costs annually.

Senator Joseph Lieberman says, "If we can get 3 miles more per gallon from our cars, we'll save 1 million barrels of oil a day, which is exactly what the (Arctic National Wildlife) Refuge at its best in Alaska would produce." (81)

Transport Sector—City Gridlock

Cities are tolerating gridlock. In 1996 according to an annual study by traffic engineers (as reported in the *San Francisco Chronicle* December 10, 1996) from Texas A & M University, it was found that drivers in Los Angeles and New York City alone wasted 600 million gallons of gas annually while just sitting in traffic. The 600 million gallons of gas translates to about 7.5 million tons of carbon dioxide in just those two cities.

Electricity Generation

We burn coal and oil to power much of our electrical output. About 36% of U.S. carbon dioxide emissions stem from the burning of these fossil fuels. (7)

Deforestation

This planet is losing its forests; 34 million acres each year through burning and cutting. We are losing millions of acres of rainforests each year, the equivalent in area to the size of Italy. (22) The destroying of tropical forests alone is throwing hundreds of millions of tons of carbon dioxide into the atmosphere each year. We are also losing temperate forests. The temperate forests of the world account for an absorption rate of 2 billion tons of carbon annually. (3) In the temperate forests of Siberia alone, the earth is losing 10 million acres per year.

Methane

Levels of atmospheric methane, a powerful greenhouse gas, have risen 145% in the last 100 years. (18) Methane is derived from sources such as rice paddies, bovine flatulence, bacteria in bogs and fossil fuel production.

References

(3) Keeling, Ralph, Stephen Piper, Martin Heimann. "Global and hemispheric carbon dioxide sinks deduced from changes in atmospheric oxygen concentration" *Nature*, Vol. 381 May 16, 1996.

(7) Marland, Gregg and Angela Pippin. "United States Emissions of Carbon Dioxide to the Earth's Atmosphere by Economic Activity." Oak Ridge National Laboratory. 1990.

(18) World Wildlife Fund (WWF): "Explaining climate change/a WWF overview of the new science."

(20) Climate Action Network report. "What's New About Global Warming."

(21) Marland, Gregg. Carbon Dioxide Information Analysis Center, Oak Ridge National Laboratory, Oak Ridge, TN.

(22) Rainforest Action Network. Press Release, October 16, 1996.

(33) Taken from an article in the *San Francisco Chronicle*, December 12, 1997 originating in the *New York Times* by Keith Bradsher.

(81) During the vice-presidential debates, Joseph Lieberman mentioned this interesting statistic. October 5, 2000.

From EcoBridge's point of view, the cause/effect relationship is clear. Greenhouse gases, especially the carbon dioxide emitted in passenger vehicle exhaust, are destroying our environment. To support this contention, EcoBridge cites a variety of sources to support their cause/effect analysis, although many of them are predisposed to agree with their perspective—always a danger when analyzing a complex subject.

Is there agreement with EcoBridge concerning the causes of the problem? No, at least not according to the Heritage Foundation. Writing at the time that the United States was considering whether to sign the international Kyoto Protocol on Global Warming (the United States declined to sign), the authors of the following excerpt, Angela Antonelli, Brett D. Schaefer, and Alex Annett, find that insufficient evidence exists to link global warming with human fossil fuel consumption or other such causes.

The Road to Kyoto: How the Global Climate Treaty Fosters Economic Impoverishment and Endangers U.S. Security

. . . there is still no consensus in the scientific community either on the causes of global warming or on the extent to which it may threaten future generations. For example:

- A 1992 Gallup poll found that only 17 percent of the members of the Meteorological Society and the American Geophysical Society think global warming in the 20th century has been the result of greenhouse gas emissions, principally carbon dioxide from burning fossil fuels.[5]
- Only 13 percent of climate scientists polled in a 1992 Greenpeace survey believe that runaway global warming will occur as a consequence of continuing current patterns of energy use.[6]

- Scientists in a May 1997 article in *Science* estimated that it will be a decade or longer before they will know whether human activity is, in fact, causing climate changes.[7]

Despite such admissions from the scientific community, environmentalists continue to espouse the need to cut back on man-made emissions of greenhouse gases like carbon dioxide or face deadly consequences later. Do it, they exhort, or the atmosphere will warm to the point where melting ice caps cause devastating floods and drought-induced crop failures trigger global famine. Do it, they admonish, so that future generations will not be forced to live in a world permanently damaged by environmental recklessness and an obsession with economic growth at the expense of all else. Do it, they promise, because the costs are minimal and the benefits incalculable.

But Americans and Congress should be responding: Is it really this simple? Is the science behind the global warming phenomenon this precise? Will the economic costs really be minimal? Will countries be judged equally and fairly in the quest for "safer" skies? Who will write the new regulations? The Kyoto Protocol to the UNFCCC to be considered in December will impose economically devastating, legally binding limits on U.S. citizens and businesses. Considering the far-reaching consequences of the treaty, the facts about climate change, greenhouse gases, and international emissions regulations must be brought to light.

References

[5] H. Sterling Burnett, "Myths of Global Warming," National Center for Policy Analysis *Brief Analysis* No. 230, May 23, 1997, p. 1.

[6] Ibid.

[7] Richard A. Kerr, "Greenhouse Forecasting Still Cloudy," *Science*, Vol. 276 (May 16, 1997), p. 1042; also available on the Internet at http://www.umi.com/pqdwe...Deli=1+Mtd=2+ReqType=309.

According to this point of view, science still disagrees about the causes of global warming. Although written just a few years ago, it is worth noting that the authors cite as evidence polls taken at least five years earlier, throwing their argument somewhat into doubt. Both EcoBridge and the Heritage Foundation offer thoughtful analyses that must be evaluated according to their logic, the credibility of their sources, and the degree to which causes and effects are shown to be integrally related.

The disagreement about the causes and effects of global warming illustrates that such relationships are often complex, and it is usually the complex ones that reward the writer. Part of the problem derives from leaping to false conclusions based on misperception, contiguity, or accidental association. Science—even good and thorough scientific experimentation—can produce contradictory results. Some events occur after others, but are not necessarily caused by them. Consider superstitious practices: Does walking underneath a ladder or breaking a mirror really cause you bad luck? Sometimes effects are produced because we believe they will occur, even if they are not directly linked to the cause—an effect known as self-fulfilling prophecy.

The entire mystery story genre, for example, is predicated on the assumption that what looks like the obvious cause is wrong: The butler didn't do it, as Perry Mason repeatedly discovered. The role of the writer producing a cause/effect essay is similar to that of a crime investigator, except that in most cases, there is not just one cause or effect but many. Discovering and evaluating the complex relationships between a range of causes and effects is one of the significant challenges and satisfactions of writing in this mode.

To analyze such relationships, the writer must consider a broad spectrum of possibilities, questions, and concerns. If writing about global warming, for example, a writer might want to investigate the current scientific evidence between fossil fuel consumption and higher temperatures. Or changes over time in temperature in a specific geographic area. Or a specific element (such as water temperature glacial melt). Or the specific conclusions of a range of experienced researchers. Or the writer might choose to blend personal experience, if meaningful and appropriate, with the formal analysis of others, as Sharon Begley does in "The Stereotype Trap."

Whenever possible, it is useful to explore a subject from a scientific, historical, or otherwise factual basis. This kind of essay only makes sense to write (and read), however, if the subject is unfamiliar to the reader or sufficiently unknown, compelling, useful, or complex; it is then worth the effort to both write and read about it. Newspapers and magazines are filled with these kinds of essays: the effect of color on mood, the causes of inflation, the likely causes of Alzheimer's and how best to prevent it. We can see this approach in Atul Gawande's essay, "Cold Comfort," which sets out to explain the cause of the common cold and how best to prevent it, primarily by citing 70 years of scientific and cultural history. Part of the fascination of reading this essay is that Gawande playfully cites a wide range of research scientists while remaining aware that the common cold continues to confound them—and us.

Remember, writing a cause/effect essay should teach both you and your audience something that you did not know, something you hadn't realized or thought through clearly. When completed, it should have a strong logical line running through it so your reader can distinguish causes from effects and is persuaded that you, the writer, understand the subject. Writing this kind of essay provides an opportunity to find answers that resolve questions, thereby introducing more clarity into our lives. To write a cause/effect essay is to find the ligaments in the bones, the logical order that links multiple and complex events. To understand causes and effects is to gain some measure of control in the world.

Atul Gawande (1966–   ) is a practicing surgeon in a Boston hospital that he would prefer to leave anonymous so he is not deluged with phone calls. Gawande received his MD from Harvard Medical School and an MPH degree from the Harvard School of Public Health. A staff writer for The New Yorker, *Gawande is the author of* Complications: A Surgeon's Notes on an Imperfect Science *(2002). He lives in Newton, Massachusetts, with his wife and three children.*

Atul Gawande
Cold Comfort

There is, when you look into it, not a lot that makes sense about the common cold. For one thing, there is the name. As cold experts have pointed out, in almost all Indo-European languages one of the words or phrases for the malady plays on the word for low temperature. In Italian, the common cold is *raffreddore*, from *freddo*, meaning cold. In Hindi, the word *sardi* denotes both being made cold and a cold itself. The notion that a chill puts you at risk of catching a cold is ancient and nearly universal. Yet science has found no evidence for it. One of the first studies on the matter was led by Sir Christopher Andrewes, of the Common Cold Research Unit, in Salisbury, England, a half century ago. He and his team took a group of volunteers—half of whom had been kept warm and comfortable and half of whom had been made to take a bath, stand dripping wet without a towel in a drafty corridor for half an hour, and finally get dressed but wear wet socks for several hours—and inoculated them with cold virus up their noses. Despite a measurable drop in body temperature and considerable misery, the chilled group didn't get any more colds than the warm group. (It was work like this that earned Andrewes his knighthood.) Follow-up experiments have since demonstrated that being chilled has no effect on either the likelihood of catching a cold or the severity of a cold once you've caught it. Indeed, colds are common at every latitude and longitude in the world—in the Sahara, in Greenland, in Delhi, in Ulaanbaatar.

All the same, colds are curiously seasonal. No matter what the temperature or how subtle the change in weather, in most parts of the world the cold season begins with a peak in early fall, drones on through winter, and peaks again in mid-spring. In summer, whether it's

July in Vladivostok or January in Canberra, colds almost disappear. All of this raises a basic question: How do you catch a cold, anyway?

As the Canadian cold historian J. Barnard Gilmore points out in his 1998 book "In Cold Pursuit," some of the most provocative reports on the subject have come from small, isolated communities—island villages, nuclear submarines, rural trading posts. Among these is a 1931 field study of Longyear City, an Arctic coal-mining settlement on the island of Spitsbergen, midway between the Norwegian mainland and the North Pole. For seven to nine months of the year, the town's five hundred residents were iced in, and during that time colds were almost nonexistent. Legend had it, however, that the arrival in port of the first ship of summer invariably brought with it a full-blown cold epidemic. J. Harlan Paul, a physician, and H. L. Freese, a microbiologist, decided to go to Longyear City to investigate.

The two scientists arrived in September, 1930, and spent eleven months on Spitsbergen. They found, as expected, that colds died out soon after the last boat of the year departed. The long winter that followed was quiet. Then, in May, the ice began to melt and break up. And on May 23rd, at 9 P.M., the first steamer of the 1931 season arrived in port with mail and fifty new workers for the mine. The researchers made sure they boarded the steamer while it was still out in the fjord and before anyone had disembarked. They examined each of the passengers carefully. None had any signs of a cold. A new worker was evidently in an early stage of infection; within a few hours of leaving the ship he developed symptoms of a cold.

5　　Less than forty-eight hours later, three townspeople developed new colds. One was a storekeeper, another an outdoor worker, and the third a miner. Paul and Freese retraced everyone's steps. They found that only the first two victims had come into close contact with any of the new arrivals. More puzzlingly, they reported, "We were unable to trace any direct contact between the man with a 'cold' who had arrived on the first boat and these three men."

Nevertheless, from that point the illness spread swiftly. Within a week, eighty-four people had come down with colds. One week later, about a hundred more caught the bug. By the end of the first month, three-quarters of the winter residents had been afflicted. Yet the researchers also discovered that there was a small but apparently hardy group of people who, despite frequent exposure, never developed the cold. A virus had travelled through town, Paul and Freese concluded, but they could not explain how.

American adults suffer an average of between two and four colds a year, and children six to eight. Although even scientists sometimes talk of "the cold virus," there is no one virus that causes colds. Since the nineteen-fifties, five families of viruses have been known to cause colds, including the coronaviruses, the parainfluenza viruses, and the adenoviruses. The most common and familiar of these is the rhinovirus family, which accounts for around forty per cent of colds and itself breaks down into at least a hundred genetically distinct viruses. The cause of approximately a third of all colds remains unknown.

Once any of these viruses get to the lining of your nose and start an infection, the miseries are pretty much the same. Symptoms usually begin from between eight and twenty-four hours after infection (though some viruses may incubate for as long as five days). On the first day of illness, you typically notice that your throat is sore or scratchy. On the second and third days, the membranes of your nose and sinuses thicken to the point of obstruction. A thin, clear secretion (made up primarily of mucoid proteins and water, but also of sloughed cells and large concentrations of virus) flows freely from the nasal lining. Inflammatory molecules in the fluid irritate the edges of your nostrils, turning them raw and red. As the cold persists, the secretions become dense and gluey. Then, after four or five days, the passages begin to open up again. For about a third of cold sufferers, a cough—caused by persistent inflammation in the upper airway—becomes the longest-lasting and most annoying problem. As a rule, cold symptoms usually go away in about a week, though for about a quarter of victims it may take two.

Antibodies from previous exposure can protect you from a particular cold-virus strain, but repeat infections are not at all uncommon. And, with so many different strains of virus circulating, you are usually an open target. Under ordinary conditions, introduction of a single rhinovirus case into the home will lead within a few days to infection in one-quarter to three-quarters of the other household members. It need not be just one virus, either. A study of Seattle families found as many as four viruses infecting a family at once.

10   Figuring out precisely how cold viruses pass between people has been particularly vexing. Researchers at the time of the First World War were able to demonstrate what now seems obvious: you can induce a cold by taking a concentrate from the nasal secretions of someone who has an active cold and placing it directly into either the nose or the eyes of a healthy person. (The virus placed in the eye runs down into the nose via the tear ducts.) Curiously, although the technique has

been perfected over the decades, even direct inoculation with purified virus doesn't uniformly succeed. A few people—under ten per cent—do not get infected, despite having no antibody to the virus. Furthermore, according to nasal specimens and antibody tests, about one out of four people will develop an active viral infection yet have no symptoms of a cold—the so-called silent cold. Biopsy studies have now shown that cold viruses generally infect only a tiny portion of the nose and do very little damage by themselves. Rather, it's the inflammatory response—the attack on the virus by white blood cells and antibodies—that causes the miserable swelling and secretions. For whatever reason, there are people who, at least some of the time, manage to rid themselves of an infection without mounting this response. They can be floridly infected, shed large amounts of virus, and pass the bug on to other people, but continue to feel fine themselves.

In the nineteen-forties, high-speed flash photographs demonstrated that an ordinary sneeze expels particles like a 12-gauge spraying bird shot—sending out droplets by the thousand from the mouth and nose at velocities approaching a hundred miles an hour. A British study published in *The Lancet* showed that a culture plate placed three feet from a sneezing subject would collect more than nineteen thousand bacterial colonies. Droplets could float for minutes, and smaller particles a few microns in diameter could hover in the air for days. The conclusion that colds were transmitted by air was taken as more or less self-evident. Proving it was another matter.

In the summer of 1950, Sir Christopher Andrewes conducted a series of experiments re-creating the isolation of Spitsbergen. He assembled a dozen volunteers and deposited them in group of houses provided by the Duke of Sutherland, on the otherwise uninhabited island of Eilean nan Ron, off the northern coast of Scotland. After the volunteers were sequestered for ten weeks, six strangers who had recently been infected with purified rhinovirus were inserted into the group. The entrance of these "invaders" was carefully scripted. First, they spent three hours in an empty room in one of the houses, making sure they were "liberal in the way they disseminated nasal discharge," as Sir Christopher later wrote. Half an hour after they left, four of the island dwellers, designated Party A in his report, were brought in to occupy the contaminated room. The invaders then entered a second room. Here Party B was present but was separated from them by a blanket that had been stretched across the room, with space above and below to allow air to pass freely. The two groups shared the room for several hours. Testing demonstrated that fine droplets from the infected group had indeed travelled throughout the room. Finally, the invaders went to a separate house, where they lived and ate with another group, Party C, for three days, providing maximum exposure. The subjects were then closely monitored for colds over the next few days. To everyone's surprise, no one in any of the parties developed a cold. Later studies attempting to demonstrate the transmission of virus through the air were hardly more successful.

In 1984, researchers at the University of Wisconsin at Madison reported the results of their own odd series of experiments. In the first set, volunteers were infected with rhinovirus, and when they were at the peak of their colds and shedding large quantities of virus they were seated at a table in a tiny, unventilated room, three feet from healthy subjects. The researchers had everyone talk, sneeze, and, weirdly, sing during the next few hours. The result? Nine subjects were exposed; none came down with colds.

The researchers went on to conduct what became their best-known experiment. This time, they had their infected volunteers kiss the healthy test subjects, assuming that this would transmit the virus easily. Each subject was kissed on the mouth for a minimum of one minute. (Beyond this, the precise mechanics were not specified. "The donors and recipients were instructed to use the kissing technique most natural for them," the researchers reported.) The cold sufferers kissed sixteen subjects in all. The results was just one confirmed case of rhinovirus infection.

15   When they were sent home to their families, however, the experimentally inoculated people spread their colds easily and widely. The conclusion scientists drew was that a sneeze or a cough or a kiss might theoretically be capable of transmitting a cold, but it did so only rarely, and a brief exposure seemed unlikely to succeed. Some other mechanism was presumed to be more important, and this was how attention shifted to nose-wiping.

In a rather suggestive experiment, Sir Christopher's research team set up on a person's nose an apparatus with a thin tube that trickled out a clear fluid at the same rate a cold would. This fluid, however, contained an invisible fluorescent dye. With the device in place, the volunteer spent a few hours socializing with a group of people in a room—eating, chatting, playing cards. At the end, the experimenters turned out the lights and used an ultraviolet lamp to illuminate the dye. To their horror, the dye had gone everywhere—all over the person's face and hands, onto his food, onto the playing cards, onto other people's hands, and even around *their* noses. As an American observational study of an audience at a medical conference later found, in ordinary circumstances one in three adults picks his nose every hour. People rub their eyes even more frequently.

The hands had to be the culprit, and a team of scientists at the University of Virginia—Jack Gwaltney, Owen Hendley, and Richard Wenzel—provided the first persuasive evidence of this. In 1973, the team reported in the *New England Journal of Medicine* a set of studies which established a convincing chain of causation. The researchers examined ten subjects who had active colds and readily found that four had virus on their hands. When drops of extracts from their mucus were permitted to dry on nylon, wool, silk, Formica, stainless steel, wood, and other surfaces, live virus could still be recovered three hours later. This was true of virus placed on skin, too. (The virus survived well on most nonporous surfaces but hardly at all on facial tissue or cotton handkerchiefs.) If volunteers touched the contaminated surfaces—including other people's hands—the virus was picked up at least sixty per cent of the time. In another test, volunteers were asked to touch a contaminated plastic surface with a finger and immediately either rub their eyes or put their fingers up their noses. Four out of the eleven became infected. In a follow-up study, healthy volunteers were told to rub their eyes and probe their noses after holding coffee cups that had been handled by cold sufferers who had just wiped their own noses. Fifty per cent developed colds.

And so, it was concluded, contact with your hands is how a cold virus gets passed around. It need not involve direct contact with people who have a cold. Hence the familiar advice that the best way to avoid a cold is to wash your hands frequently and not touch people with colds, especially children. That's hard to put into practice, though. When Jack Gwaltney—who has now done close to forty years of research on the common cold and is recognized as the world's foremost expert on it—is asked what he does to reduce his exposure in the cold season, he says it's pretty much hopeless. "I tried to be careful about washing my hands when my grandchildren were little, especially when they had those two ropes of mucus coming down," he recalls. "But you were still going to pick them up and hug them, and they were still going to go around touching everything. There's no avoiding it."

When he feels himself coming down with a cold, Gwaltney takes ibuprofen and an antihistamine for the next week. These won't stop a cold, but they are among the few interventions reliably proven to alleviate symptoms. The ibuprofen reduces coughing and the antihistamine reduces obstruction and runniness—although you have to take an older antihistamine, like chlorpheniramine (Chlor-Trimeton) or clemastine (Tavist), the kind that you buy over the counter and that makes you drowsy. The new ones, like Allegra and Claritin, are too narrow in their effects to work for colds. Petrolatum-based ointments are thought to protect the nostrils against the inflammatory drizzle if they're used when symptoms begin, but there are no reliable studies to prove it. What about zinc? The only consistent effect that well-designed trials have reported is that it tastes bad. Antibiotics? No benefit. Vitamin C? It won't prevent colds, according to dozens of studies, but at high doses it may reduce symptoms modestly (though not as much as an antihistamine). Echinacea? Inadequately tested. How about drinking lots of fluids, as doctors always tell you to do? There's no basis for it. As one cold researcher put it, "I'm not sure it even makes sense."

20   Some drugs in the research pipeline have been gathering attention of late. A new group, known as capsid-binding agents, are designed to attach to rhinoviruses and, among other things, stop them from fastening to the cells of your nasal membranes. One of these compounds recently made headlines when two randomized trials with more than two thousand patients showed that it could reduce both the severity and the duration of a rhinovirus cold. Another new group of drugs to emerge, the 3C protease inhibitors, are designed to block replication of rhinoviruses once they've penetrated your nasal cells. There have been promising preliminary results in clinical trials of one such agent, which has now been given the unpronounceable name ruprintrivir. (Manufacturers like to give drugs unpronounceable generic names because then the only thing you'll remember is whatever brand name they eventually choose.) So far, the measurable effect of each of these drugs has been modest—perhaps reducing the duration of a weeklong cold by a day or two. Even if they come to market, they will work only for a subset of cold viruses and will have to be obtained through a doctor and started no later than the first day of a cold. They're also bound to be expensive. It seems likely that a cure for the common cold will remain elusive.

We may have better luck stopping colds from spreading in the first place. At a recent scientific conference, Ronald Turner, formerly of the Medical University of South Carolina, announced the results of testing antiseptic skin cleansers that contained pyroglutamic acid or salicylic acid. Unlike most soaps, these cleansers not only killed cold viruses on people's hands immediately but continued to do so for hours afterward. Despite having their hands intentionally contaminated with rhinovirus and being made to probe their nostrils and rub their eyes, volunteers who had earlier washed with solutions containing one of the compounds developed fewer colds than those who used a control solution. As it turns out, pyroglutamic acid is a common ingredient in ordinary skin moisturizers, and salicylic acid is used in over-the-counter acne treatments. An effective antiviral lotion may already be on the shelves.

Will these cleansers stop viruses in the real world, though? One would think so, given all the studies about hand-spread colds. Yet there always seems to be at least one study that doesn't quite square with whatever tidy theories the scientists concoct. When it comes to colds, that study is the Wisconsin poker experiment, conducted almost twenty years ago. The cold researchers at the University of Wisconsin surmised that if the main route by which colds were spread was from hand to hand (or object to hand) and then from hand to nose or eyes, preventing people from touching their noses and eyes should stop virtually all colds. So they devised a simple but clever experiment. They took healthy volunteers and volunteers who had laboratory-induced colds and put them in a room to play a marathon session of poker from eight in the morning until eleven at night. Half of the healthy subjects were allowed to play cards normally, and the other half were restrained by devices that were designed to prevent them from touching any part of their own heads or faces as they played. Some of them wore a three-foot-wide clear plastic collar; others wore an orthopedic brace that kept their arms from bending more than forty degrees. The devices were removed only for meals and trips to the bathroom. At those times, the subjects' hands were disinfected and gloved the way a surgeon's hands would be for an operation. (Assistants were provided in the event that nose-scratching was needed.) Subjects were closely monitored for the subsequent development of colds.

The results still confound cold experts. More than half of the restrained volunteers developed colds afterward—just as many as among the unrestrained volunteers. Tests confirmed that in all cases they had caught the same virus that the sick volunteers were carrying. The scientists could not say how.

There is something almost beautifully crafty about the common cold. It knows us better then we know ourselves—living and travelling and multiplying by means of an unnoticed touch, a quick, involuntary wipe of an eye, or perhaps some tic we have not yet recognized. As every textbook that addresses the subject is forced at some point to say, "Other factors may be involved." Nonetheless, there are a few things that can be said with certainty: May will come, colds will subside, and no one will know why.

Analyzing Rhetorical Choices

1. Gawande writes an extremely factual account of the common cold, but he also occasionally indulges in wry, tongue-in-cheek expressions and ironic statements. Locate at least three such statements and discuss how they affect your response to the essay.
2. Find several instances of technical terms in the essay. How does Gawande's use of technical information affect you as a reader? Why do you think he uses terms that most laypeople would not know?
3. How does Gawande organize his essay? How would you describe the logic of his presentation?

Writing About Issues and Contexts

1. Why is writing about the common cold significant?
2. What causes a cold? How are colds transmitted? What do we know—and not know—about this common yet mysterious illness?
3. Given what Gawande reports, what is the difference between a hypothesis and a proof? Do all hypotheses require proof? What does the relationship between hypothesis and proof tell us about the relationship between cause and effect?

*The eldest of nine children, **Brent Staples** (1951–) grew up in Chester, Pennsylvania, a small town just outside Philadelphia. Staples attended a special college-prep program at Philadelphia Military College and Penn Morton College to hone his academic skills and went on to earn his undergraduate degree from Widener University and his master's and doctoral degrees in psychology from the University of Chicago. Staples is a member of the* New York Times *editorial board and has published a variety of articles and essays along with his best-selling memoir,* Parallel Time: Growing Up in Black and White *(1994). "A Black Man Ponders His Ability to Alter Public Space" recounts Staples's experience as a tall black man walking in the city, an experience that resonates with current concerns about racial stereotypes and profiling.*

Brent Staples

A Black Man Ponders His Ability to Alter Public Space

My first victim was a woman—white, well dressed, probably in her early twenties. I came upon her late one evening on a deserted street in Hyde Park, a relatively affluent neighborhood in an otherwise mean, impoverished section of Chicago. As I swung onto the avenue behind her, there seemed to be a discreet, uninflammatory distance between us. Not so. She cast back a worried glance. To her, the youngish black man—a broad six feet two inches with a beard and billowing hair, both hands shoved into the pockets of a bulky military jacket—seemed menacingly close. After a few more quick glimpses, she picked up her pace and was soon running in earnest. Within seconds she disappeared into a cross street.

That was more than a decade ago. I was twenty-two years old, a graduate student newly arrived at the University of Chicago. It was in the echo of that terrified woman's footfalls that I first began to know the unwieldy inheritance I'd come into—the ability to alter public space in ugly ways. It was clear that she thought herself the quarry of a mugger, a rapist, or worse. Suffering a bout of insomnia, however, I was stalking sleep, not defenseless wayfarers. As a softy who is scarcely able to take a knife to a raw chicken—let alone hold it to a person's throat—I was surprised, embarrassed, and dismayed all at once. Her flight made me feel like an accomplice in tyranny. It also made it clear that I was indistinguishable from the muggers who occasionally seeped into the area from the surrounding ghetto. That first encounter, and those that followed, signified that a vast, unnerving gulf lay between nighttime pedestrians—particularly women—and me. And I soon gathered that being perceived as dangerous is a hazard in itself. I only needed to turn a corner into a dicey situation, or crowd some frightened, armed person in a foyer somewhere, or make an errant move after being pulled over by a policeman. Where fear and weapons meet—and they often do in urban America—there is always the possibility of death.

In that first year, my first away from my hometown, I was to become thoroughly familiar with the language of fear. At dark, shadowy intersections in Chicago, I could cross in front of a car stopped at a traffic light and elicit the *thunk, thunk, thunk, thunk* of the driver—black, white, male, or female—hammering down the door locks. On less traveled streets after dark, I grew accustomed to but never comfortable with people who crossed to the other side of the street rather than pass me. Then there were the standard unpleasantries with policemen, doormen, bouncers, cab drivers, and others whose business it is to screen out troublesome individuals *before* there is any nastiness.

I moved to New York nearly two years ago and I have remained an avid night walker. In central Manhattan, the near-constant crowd cover minimizes tense one-on-one street encounters. Elsewhere—visiting friends in SoHo, where sidewalks are narrow and tightly spaced buildings shut out the sky—things can get very taut indeed.

5   Black men have a firm place in New York mugging literature. Norman Podhoretz in his famed (or infamous) 1963 essay, "My Negro Problem—And Ours," recalls growing up in terror of black males; they "were tougher than we were, more ruthless," he writes—and as an adult on the Upper West Side of Manhattan, he continues, he cannot constrain his nervousness when he meets black men on certain streets. Similarly, a decade later, the essayist and novelist Edward Hoagland extols a New York where once "Negro bitterness bore down mainly on other Negroes." Where some see mere panhandlers, Hoagland sees "a mugger who is clearly screwing up his nerve to do more than just *ask* for money." But Hoagland has "the New Yorker's quick-hunch posture for broken-field maneuvering," and the bad guy swerves away.

I often witness that "hunch posture," from women after dark on the warrenlike streets of Brooklyn where I live. They seem to set their faces on neutral and, with their purse straps strung across their chests bandolier style, they forge ahead as though bracing themselves against being tackled. I understand, of course, that the danger they perceive is not a hallucination. Women are particularly vulnerable to street violence, and young black males are drastically overrepresented among the perpetrators of that violence. Yet these truths are no solace against the kind of alienation that comes of being ever the suspect, against being set apart, a fearsome entity with whom pedestrians avoid making eye contact.

It is not altogether clear to me how I reached the ripe old age of twenty-two without being conscious of the lethality nighttime pedestrians attributed to me. Perhaps it was because in Chester, Pennsylvania, the small, angry industrial town where I came of age in the 1960s, I was scarcely noticeable against a backdrop of gang warfare, street knifings, and murders. I grew up one of the good boys, had perhaps a half-dozen fist fights. In retrospect, my shyness of combat has clear sources.

Many things go into the making of a young thug. One of those things is the consummation of the male romance with the power to intimidate. An infant discovers that random flailings send the baby bottle flying out of the crib and crashing to the floor. Delighted, the joyful babe repeats those motions again and again, seeking to duplicate the feat. Just so, I recall the points at which some of my boyhood friends were finally seduced by the perception of themselves as tough guys. When a mark cowered and surrendered his money without resistance, myth and reality merged—and paid off. It is, after all, only manly to embrace the power to frighten and intimidate. We, as men, are not supposed to give an inch of our lane on the highway; we are to seize the fighter's edge in work and in play and even in love; we are to be valiant in the face of hostile forces.

Unfortunately, poor and powerless young men seem to take all this nonsense literally. As a boy, I saw countless tough guys locked away; I have since buried several, too. They were babies, really—a teenage cousin, a brother of twenty-two, a childhood friend in his mid-twenties—all gone down in episodes of bravado played out in the streets. I came to doubt the virtues of intimidation early on. I chose, perhaps even unconsciously, to remain a shadow—timid, but a survivor.

10   The fearsomeness mistakenly attributed to me in public places often has a perilous flavor. The most frightening of these confusions occurred in the late 1970s and early 1980s when I worked as a journalist in Chicago. One day, rushing into the office of a magazine I was

writing for with a deadline story in hand, I was mistaken for a burglar. The office manager called security and, with an ad hoc posse, pursued me through the labyrinthine halls, nearly to my editor's door. I had no way of proving who I was. I could only move briskly toward the company of someone who knew me.

Another time I was on assignment for a local paper and killing time before an interview. I entered a jewelry store on the city's affluent Near North Side. The proprietor excused herself and returned with an enormous red Doberman pinscher straining at the end of a leash. She stood, the dog extended toward me, silent to my questions, her eyes bulging nearly out of her head. I took a cursory look around, nodded, and bade her good night. Relatively speaking, however, I never fared as badly as another black male journalist. He went to nearby Waukegan, Illinois, a couple of summers ago to work on a story about a murderer who was born there. Mistaking the reporter for the killer, police hauled him from his car at gunpoint and but for his press credentials would probably have tried to book him. Such episodes are not uncommon. Black men trade tales like this all the time.

In "My Negro Problem—And Ours," Podhoretz writes that the hatred he feels for blacks makes itself known to him through a variety of avenues—one being his discomfort with that "special brand of paranoid touchiness" to which he says blacks are prone. No doubt he is speaking here of black men. In time, I learned to smother the rage I felt at so often being taken for a criminal. Not to do so would surely have led to madness—via that special "paranoid touchiness" that so annoyed Podhoretz at the time he wrote the essay.

I began to take precautions to make myself less threatening. I move about with care, particularly late in the evening. I give a wide berth to nervous people on subway platforms during the wee hours, particularly when I have exchanged business clothes for jeans. If I happen to be entering a building behind some people who appear skittish, I may walk by, letting them clear the lobby before I return, so as not to seem to be following them. I have been calm and extremely congenial on those rare occasions when I've been pulled over by the police.

And on late-evening constitutionals along streets less traveled by, I employ what has proved to be an excellent tension-reducing measure: I whistle melodies from Beethoven and Vivaldi and the more popular classical composers. Even steely New Yorkers hunching toward nighttime destinations seem to relax, and occasionally they even join in the tune. Virtually everybody seems to sense that a mugger wouldn't be warbling bright, sunny selections from Vivaldi's *Four Seasons*. It is my equivalent of the cowbell that hikers wear when they know they are in bear country.

Analyzing Rhetorical Choices

1. Why do you think Staples chooses to open his essay with the sentence, "My first victim was a woman—white, well dressed, probably in her early twenties."?

2. Staples begins a central section of his essay with the sentence: "Many things go into the making of a young thug." How appropriate is the word *thug*? Analyze the next two paragraphs in terms of Staples's reasoning, cause-and-effect connections, word choice, and rhetorical effectiveness. Explain whether or not he makes his argument persuasively.

3. Throughout his essay, Staples depicts himself as the fearsome force and others ("black, white, male, or female") as his victims. Yet the metaphor he evokes at the end reverses this scenario. Is Staples contradicting himself? Why do you think he makes this rhetorical move?

Writing About Issues and Contexts

1. Is the fear felt by Staples's "first victim" justified? Is Staples's anger at being thought of as a criminal justified? Explain your responses, and offer an analysis that attempts to reconcile these two points of view.

2. Staples writes, "Where fear and weapons meet—and they often do in urban America—there is always the possibility of death." Why does Staples include this statement in his essay? Does he really have to worry about being killed? Do his "victims"? Offer your own analysis of the relationships between fear, weapons, and death.

3. Offer your own analysis of Staples's solutions to his problems. Are his solutions reasonable and sensible? Can you suggest other possibilities? Is he side-stepping the problem?

Born in Englewood, New Jersey, **Sharon Begley** *(1956–   ) graduated from Yale in 1977 with a degree in combined sciences, with an emphasis in physics. She began her professional writing career as a science researcher at* Newsweek *in 1977, rose to senior editor for science, and was hired in 2002 by the* Wall Street Journal *to launch a featured science column. Coauthor of* The Mind and the Brain *(2002), Begley wrote many major pieces for* Newsweek, *including "Science Finds God," "Are We All a Little Crazy?" "Your Child's Brain," and "Beyond Prozac." She has received numerous awards for her work, including a Clarion Award from the Association for Women in Communications for "excellence in clear, concise communication" and a 1993 Aviation/Space Writers Association Premier Award. "The Stereotype Trap" first appeared in* Newsweek *in November 2000.*

Sharon Begley

The Stereotype Trap

The students had no idea of the real purpose of the study they had volunteered for—it is, after all, standard operating procedure in psychology to keep subjects in the dark on that little point. (If volunteers know they're being studied for, say, whether they will help a blind child cross a busy street, it tends to skew their behavior.) So when 40 black and 40 white Princeton undergraduates volunteered to play mini-golf, the psychologists dissembled a bit. This is a test of "natural ability," Jeff Stone and his colleagues informed some of the kids. This is a test of "the ability to think strategically," they told others. Then the students—nongolfers all—played the course, one at a time. Among those told the test measured natural ability, black students scored, on average, more than four strokes better than whites. In the group told the test gauged strategic savvy, the white kids scored four strokes better, the researchers reported last year. "When people are reminded of a negative stereotype about themselves—'white men can't jump' or 'black men can't think'—it can adversely affect performance," says Stone, now at the University of Arizona.

Another group of students, 46 Asian-American female undergrads at Harvard, thought they were taking a tough, 12-question math test. Before one group attacked the advanced algebra, they answered written questions emphasizing ethnicity ("How many generations of your family have lived in America?"). Another group's questionnaire subtly reminded them of their gender ("Do you live on a co-ed or single-sex dorm floor?"). Women who took the math test after being reminded of their Asian heritage—and thus, it seems, the stereotype that Asians excel at math—scored highest, getting 54 percent right. The women whose questionnaire implicitly reminded them of the stereotype that, for girls, "math is hard," as Barbie infamously said, scored lowest, answering 43 percent correctly.

The power of stereotypes, scientists had long figured, lay in their ability to change the behavior of the person holding the stereotype. If you think women are ninnies ruled by hormonal swings, you don't name them CEO; if you think gays are pedophiles, you don't tap them to lead your Boy Scout troop. But five years ago Stanford University psychologist Claude Steele showed something else: it is the *targets* of a stereotype whose behavior is most powerfully affected by it. A stereotype that pervades the culture the way "ditzy blondes" and "forgetful seniors" do makes people painfully aware of how society views them— so painfully aware, in fact, that knowledge of the stereotype can affect how well they do on intellectual and other tasks. Now, with half a decade of additional research under their belts, psychologists are discovering the power of stereotypes not only over blacks, but over women, members of ethnic minorities and the elderly, too. And the research is shedding light on such enduring mysteries as why black kids, even those from middle-class families and good schools, often score lower than white kids on standardized tests.

In their seminal 1995 study, Steele and Joshua Aronson, now at New York University, focused on how the threat posed by stereotypes affects African-Americans. They reasoned that whenever black students take on an intellectual task, like an SAT, they face the prospect of confirming widely held suspicions about their brainpower. This threat, the psychologists suspected, might interfere with performance. To test this hunch, Steele and Aronson gave 44 Stanford undergrads questions from the verbal part of the tough Graduate Record Exam. One group was asked, right before the test, to indicate their year in school, age, major and other information. The other group answered all that, as well as one final question: what is your race? The results were sobering. "Just listing their race undermined the black students' performance," says Steele, making them score significantly worse than blacks who did not note their race, and significantly worse than all whites. But the performance of black Stanfordites who were not explicitly reminded of their race equaled that of whites, found the scientists.

5   You do not even have to believe a negative stereotype to be hurt by it, psychologists find. As long as you care about the ability you're being tested on, such as golfing or math, and are familiar with the stereotype ("girls can't do higher math"), it can sink you. What seems to happen is that as soon as you reach a tough par 3 or a difficult trig problem, the possibility of confirming, and being personally reduced to, a painful stereotype causes enough distress to impair performance. "If you are a white male and you find yourself having difficulty, you may begin to worry about failing the test," says psychologist Paul Davies of Stanford in an upcoming paper. But "if you are a black male . . . you begin to worry . . . about failing your race by confirming a negative stereotype." It's a sort of "oh God, they really are right about people like me" reaction.

       You don't outgrow it, either. Becca Levy of Yale showed over-60 volunteers subliminal messages (through words flashed quickly on a monitor) and then tested them on memory. Seniors who saw words like "Alzheimer's," "senile" and "old" always scored worse than seniors who saw words like "wise" and "sage"—in some tests, 64 percent better. Does it matter? In a follow-up, Levy used the same subliminal priming. But this time she asked the volunteers whether they would accept life-prolonging medical intervention. Those seniors primed with positive stereotypes usually said yes; those reminded of senility and frailty said no. "What's so frightening," says Levy, "is that the stereotype, at least in the short run, overwhelms long-held beliefs."

       Stereotypes seem to most affect the best and the brightest. Only if you're black and care about academics, or female and care about math, will you also care if society thinks you're bad at those things. A girl whose sense of self-worth is tied up in her poetry, for instance, is less likely to freeze up when her facility with calculus is belittled. To test the effect of the "bimbo" stereotype, scientists at the University of Waterloo in Ontario showed men and women undergrads TV commercials with and without gender stereotypes. (In one, a student says her primary goal in college is to meet "cute guys.") Then the students, who all said they were good at math and that it mattered to them, took a standardized test. Women who saw the commercials with female stereotypes not only did worse on the math problems than did women who saw gender-neutral commercials, as well as worse than men: they actively avoided math problems in favor of verbal ones. But the effect of stereotypes didn't end there. Women who saw stereotyped ads expressed less interest in math-based careers like financial analysis and physics afterward, and more interest in math-free fields like writing.

"Exposure to stereotypic commercials persuades women to withdraw" from fields like math and science where they are the targets of stereotypes, Davies says. Of course, if the stereotype is positive, it can induce you to persist in something you're supposed to be good at even if you're not. Steele admits sheepishly that he keeps playing sports (even though he's no Tiger Woods) because, as a black man, he's told by society that he's a natural.

The power of stereotypes may explain the persistent gap between black and white kids on standardized tests even when the black kids come from middle and upper socioeconomic classes. Tellingly, that gap widens with age. Little kids have comparable scores on standardized tests, but by sixth grade, black kids lag by two full grade levels in many districts. It is around sixth grade, Steele points out, that "race becomes a big factor in the social organization of school"—and hence a more powerful reminder of which group you belong to.

Can the pernicious effects of stereotypes be vanquished? If no one reminds you of a negative stereotype, your performance doesn't suffer. It can actually improve if instead you think of a positive stereotype—Steele recommends bellowing something like "You are Stanford students!" but clearly that has limited applicability. Deception helps, too: if women are told that a difficult math test reveals no gender differences, finds Stephen Spencer of Waterloo, they perform as well as men. Otherwise, women score much lower. While such manipulations may weaken the brutal power of stereotypes, at the end of the day they remain manipulations. But until stereotypes fade away, that may be the best we can hope for.

Analyzing Rhetorical Choices

1. Begley begins this report by summarizing two independent scientific studies, each of which is focused on the consequences of stereotypes on behavior, athletic behavior in the one case and academic behavior in the other. Why is this an effective way to begin?

2. Begley uses some descriptive words and phrases and at times adopts something of a breezy tone. Some examples include, "If you think women are ninnies ruled by hormonal swings," "the 'bimbo' stereotype," "ditzy blondes," "the best and the brightest," "freeze up," and so on. What effects do these kinds of zippy, and at times commonplace, phrases have on the report—on its tone, seriousness, readability, and overall effectiveness?

3. Speaking of word choice, in the third paragraph, Begley uses the phrase "with half a decade of additional research under their

belts." She could have written instead, "with five years of additional research under their belts." Why do you think she chooses the former and not the latter? Examine the essay for other usage choices that similarly reinforce the kind of tone and perspective that Begley wants to impart to the reader.

4. That this piece was written for *Newsweek,* a popular news magazine with a national audience, obviously affected how and why it was written. What ways do you think its being written for *Newsweek* shaped it in terms of style, length, complexity, and structure?

Writing About Issues and Contexts

1. To what groups does the title "The Stereotype Trap" refer? Who gets stereotyped? Who gets trapped? Why? How?

2. Begley reports that "You do not even have to believe a negative stereotype to be hurt by it." How is that possible? What accounts for the power of negative stereotyping? And why is it that negative stereotypes seem to affect "the best and the brightest"?

3. Why are the effects of negative stereotyping important? What long-term direct and indirect influence do they have on those groups (Asians, blacks, women, short people, whomever) that are a frequent target of negative stereotyping?

4. Begley does not provide much analysis of positive stereotyping. Can you provide some examples that you have either witnessed or indulged in? If positive stereotypes have a positive effect on performance, does this mean that stereotyping is not necessarily a bad thing? How should we respond to this issue of stereotyping in society?

A graduate of the University of California at Berkeley, **Eric Hansen**
*(1948–   ) has spent much of his life traveling and writing. In 1975, he
spent a year living in villages along the border of Nepal and Tibet, and in
1982 he traveled extensively in the Borneo rain forest and lived with a
small group of nomadic hunters and gatherers known as Penan. As he recounts in an interview, "At the time, these people had never seen tinned
food, a telephone, or the ocean, and they had little knowledge of life beyond the forest." Hansen is the author of several books, including*
Stranger in the Forest *(1988), from which this selection is taken, and*
Orchid Fever *(2000). Hansen had hoped that orchid cultivation would
allow the Penan to continue to live in the Borneo rain forest, after their
hunting grounds were largely destroyed through cultivation, but that
proved impossible. He continues to be interested in the rural and traditional people of Asia and the Asian rim, including the nomadic goat
herders of Mongolia and the wool traders of Western Tibet, Nepal, and
Northern India.*

Eric   Hansen

The Bali Saleng

"The people are afraid," Pa Biah warned me. "Don't travel by
yourself; it is not safe. The people know you have come to the valley.
They may hurt you if they see you alone in the jungle."

The red glow from Pa Biah's cheroot gradually faded, and as he
coaxed the fire back to life with his foot, we sipped hot bitter tea from
chipped enamel mugs. Ibu Iting, his wife, sat nearby. She was making
thread by pulling strands of cotton from the edge of an old piece of
fabric. While holding the ends of two strands in her left hand, she
twisted them together by rubbing them between her right hand and
thigh. She threaded her needle and continued to listen to our conversation as she patched a well-worn pair of trousers.

"Last year," Pa Biah continued, *"bali saleng* was described as a
brown-skinned man with long black hair and pointed teeth. He wore a
powder blue, short-sleeved, military-type shirt with matching shorts.
He had a special set of spring-powered shoes that enabled him to jump
four meters in the air and ten meters away in a single bound. He could
spring through the air to cover long distances quickly and capture
people by surprise. After tying up his victim with strips of rattan, he

would take the blood from the wrist or the foot with a small knife and rubber pump. The corpse would then be hoisted with vines up into the jungle canopy so that searchers could not find it."

Listening attentively, I tried to imagine a police department's composite sketch of such an individual. The image of *bali saleng* was still too farfetched for me to take seriously.

5   "A *bali saleng* cannot be killed by man," Pa Biah continued. "Bullets bounce off him, spears cannot pierce his body, and when he gets old he will take on a young man without family and train him."

Pa Biah went on to tell me that the year before a pregnant woman was reported to have been killed by a *bali saleng* near the village of Long Ampung. Pregnant women are considered prime targets because they contain the blood of two people.

That night the people of Long Nawang locked themselves into their family quarters and did not open their doors until daybreak.

I listened to Pa Biah's stories with interest, but I failed to recognize my own imminent danger. I was placing too much confidence in my knowledge of the language and too little importance on the power of fear. Instead of accepting the people's beliefs as something real and adjusting my behavior accordingly, I was relying on a false sense of security. With nearly eighteen hundred jungle miles behind me, I had become careless.

The next morning I got up and left at dawn—alone. I didn't get far. Four hours up the valley, as I followed the Kayan River southeast from Long Nawang, I was attacked in the village of Long Uro. The first thing I heard was the frantic pounding of children's feet along hardwood planks of the longhouse porch. There were a few startled cries from the women then the sound of men's voices. It all happened very quickly. It took me a moment to realize that I was the cause of the commotion.

10   A group of about two dozen men, some armed with spears, came down to the trail where I was standing. After some excited questioning and gesturing (not all of which I understood), I felt their hands on me. I was stripped of my pack and forced to the ground. I didn't resist. I sat in the dirt with my back to a drainage ditch as the men formed a tight semicircle in front of me. For the next two hours they fired accusations at me in Indonesian. I was repeatedly questioned and cross-examined. My mind became alert, and I was careful not to show my fear. They wanted to know why I was by myself, why I didn't have a cooking pot, what I was doing in the Kayan River valley, and how I had come over the mountains from Sarawak. My answers didn't sound

very convincing, and I soon realized how vulnerable I was. The experience of facing so many frightened people was intimidating. My belongings were ransacked: shotgun shells, diaries, salt, clothing, and half-finished letters to friends littered the ground. I was repeatedly asked about the contents of my pack. After two men had gone through everything, I realized that they had been looking for spring-powered shoes, the small blood knife, and the rubber pump.

Over and over they repeated two questions: "Why do you walk by yourself?" and "Why aren't you afraid of *bali saleng?*"

The fact is that no one in Borneo walks by himself in the jungle. It is too easy to fall down or to get lost or sick. Every year people disappear in the rain forest without a trace. Solo travel isn't done except by the spirits. It was difficult to explain to these villagers why I had no fear. By now hours had passed, and I felt my energy fading. These frightened, angry people, with their excited sing-song manner of speaking, were exhausting me. Here in a village of practicing animists was a middle-class Westerner arguing about evil spirits in their jungle. By consistently basing my answers on logic and reasoning, I was only making the situation worse. I would have merely increased their suspicions if I had claimed not to believe in spirits. How could I possibly be convincing? I asked myself. It became irrelevant and unimportant to me whether they understood who I really was. By this time I wanted only one thing: to be able to leave the village safely. I realized that I had to accept their fear and deal with it on their terms. It was absurd for me to try to convince them that one of their greatest fears was unfounded. A solution came to me unexpectedly.

The Kenyah, as do all the inland people, have a tradition of amulets, charms, and spell-breakers. The collective term for these items is *jeemat.* A *jeemat* can be made from a wide assortment of materials; the most common are seedpods, bones, wood shavings, crushed insects, beeswax, cowrie shells, and odd-shaped black pebbles known as hook stones. A *jeemat* can be made by man or found, but the most powerful ones (the hook stones) are given by a spirit or ghost. Directions for their use are revealed during a dream. It is very bad luck to lose or give away a charm that has come from the spirits. *Jeemats* are usually worn around the neck or wrist and are an important part of one's personal adornment. They are visible proof of one's faith in the power of the spirit world.

With this in mind, I remembered I was wearing a small, stuffed fabric banana pin that a friend had given me before I started my trip. The pin was about three inches long and had a bright yellow, polka-dot peel. The banana was removable. It could be dangled at the end of a short safety string. Until that moment in Long Uro, I had used the pin only to amuse people.

15   "This," I said, gesturing to the pin, "is my *jeemat*. It protects me from *bali saleng*." It caught them off guard; it also aroused their interest. One of the men came forward to touch the banana, but I cautioned him not to. He stopped three feet away from me.

"It has very strong *obat*," I said. *Obat* has many definitions: magic, power, or medicine. "Be careful, this charm was made especially for me by a spirit. That is why I'm not afraid to walk alone in the jungle." The mood of the interrogation changed as interest shifted to my banana pin.

"Where did it come from?" "What is it made of?" "Do you have more?" "How much would one cost?" they wanted to know.

I did not concoct my banana-pin story because I thought my tormentors were simple-minded or childish. Quite the opposite. The Kenyah have a highly developed relationship with the spirit world. I couldn't think of any other story they might believe. From generations of experience, they know how to coexist with both good and bad spirits. Firmly rooted in the twentieth century, I certainly didn't have anything to teach them. I was the outsider, the ignorant one. I had great respect for all the inland people. With their unique forms of architecture, social organization, and sophisticated farming techniques, they have established themselves in an incredibly difficult environment. The decision to present the banana pin as a powerful charm not only helped save me in this situation, but also forced me to reconsider how I was responding to the people. I stopped being the observer and began to accept their supernatural world, and my journey was never the same. In that single moment I grew much closer to my experiences.

The tension eased after I had revealed the power of the banana-pin charm. A few obstinate older men insisted on going over the fine points of my story, but the rest seemed to think I was probably harmless. I was flushed with relief. The blood and adrenaline pounded through my body and made my fingertips and toes ache. I felt light-headed and blessed to have survived this incident unharmed.

20   I was free to go, but it was too late to continue up the valley to my original destination—Long Sungai Barang. I had to spend the night in Long Uro. Dozens of eyes stared at me through knotholes and cracks in the rough wooden walls as I ate a miserable and lonely dinner. I was served half-rotten fish pounded in a mortar, bones and all. Having finished my meal, I strung my mosquito net in a filthy corner, unrolled my mat, and escaped into an exhausted sleep.

During the night there must have been more discussion because in the morning, just after I left the village, I came upon a young man standing at the side of the pathway. He was barefoot, well muscled, and dressed in blue shorts. He wore white gloves and held a large unsheathed parang at his side. He didn't respond to my greeting as I approached, but as I passed he fell into step a few feet behind me. I continued on for a short while then decided it would be better to confront him. I turned to speak, but he had vanished into the undergrowth. I knew that he could be no more than fifty feet from where I stood, but I couldn't see him. For months this jungle had seemed so benign and giving. How quickly it had become frightening. It was clear to me that at any moment I might be ambushed and killed.

Farther up the valley I passed abandoned farm huts and stopped briefly in the village of Lidung Payau to ask directions to the village of Long Sungai Barang. On the far side of Lidung Payau, I saw what I soon realized was a cage fashioned out of logs six inches in diameter. The structure was raised off the ground and had a slat floor that let excrement out and the flies in. The cage measured six feet by five feet by four feet and had a shingled roof. It was "home" not to an animal, but to a man. There were no doors or windows. I later learned that the inhabitant, barely visible between the gaps in the horizontal logs, had lived in the cage for more than two years. I don't know what his crime was. The cloud of furiously buzzing blackflies must have driven him mad. I looked upon this wretched man as a fellow sufferer, but when I tried to speak with him, he moved to the far side of his cage, and I could sense his fear of my presence.

I no longer had my sense of security and self-confidence. I lost track of time. As my anxiety mounted, a few hundred yards began to seem like miles. My thinking became erratic and unsound. There was no turning back, and for the first time since leaving Long Sungai Anai three days earlier, I began to panic. I sensed that I was being watched. Soaked in perspiration, I paused frequently to look over my shoulder and listen for the sound of human voices or of jungle knives slashing through the undergrowth. I scanned the surrounding walls of impenetrable green and brown foliage, but I could detect nothing. There were only the normal sounds of the jungle: the wind, the flutter of leaves, dripping water, and rubbing branches. I could see black hornbills perched nearby, so I called to them. I wanted to hear something friendly and reassuring, but their calls came back to me sounding like strangled pleas.

I hurried on to Long Sungai Barang, hoping that word of the incident in Long Uro hadn't preceded me. I wanted a fresh start. I now realized the full extent of my naiveté, my incredible stupidity. I was completely alone and vulnerable. I didn't know what else to do except to keep walking and to try to relax. I stopped frequently, considered going back, couldn't decide, then continued on. Whenever I sat down to rest and clear my mind, a new wave of anxiety would engulf me.

25   I knew that Long Sungai Barang was the last village in the upper Kayan River valley. If the people there weren't friendly, I would be trapped. Four hundred miles of primary rain forest separated me from the most accessible coast.

It was late afternoon by the time I entered the longhouse at Sungai Barang. I was disoriented and confused, and my legs were bleeding freely from leeches and barbed vines. I was led to the headman's room. While he was being summoned, I was surrounded by about a dozen Kenyah men. I could feel the deep, painful grooves that the straps of the rattan pack had cut into my shoulders. My shirt was pasted to my back from the heat of the day. The men seemed relaxed and curious, but I felt they looked right through me and sensed my uncertainty.

We talked about the approaching rice harvest for perhaps ten minutes; then to my left I heard the familiar creak and slam of a sapling-powered hardwood door. In midsentence I looked up, expecting to see the headman, but there before me stood a young, white-skinned woman with golden hair. She was dressed in a flowered sarong and a blouse. She was barefoot, pretty, and smiling. I was completely unnerved. It just wasn't possible for her to be there. I became incredulous and even more confused. Finally I just smiled back and felt my pent-up fears and anxieties begin to dissolve.

The first thing I noticed as she stood there was the fragrance of her skin. It wasn't the scent of soap or perfume; it was the scent of another culture, another world, a fresh, wonderful smell that made me question my attraction to smoky jungle campfires and eating wild animals. We spoke Indonesian. There was no urgency to our voices. In Kenyah fashion we began with trivial matters in order to mask the real intent of our conversation, and gradually we led up to the important questions. More people came into the room. They sat quietly, watched, and listened. Eventually the temptation to speak our own language was overwhelming. The woman smiled again and in perfect English said, "I'm Cynthia. I live next door. The headman won't be back until late tonight. Would you like to come over to my place for a visit?"

Analyzing Rhetorical Choices

1. In what ways is it effective to open with the direct statement of Pa Biah? Why does Hansen mention that he "tried to imagine a police department's composite sketch of such an individual"? What is the point of introducing this notion of a Western police department here?

2. How do Hansen's language choices reinforce his sense of fear and anxiety?

3. Explain what Hansen means by writing that the "young, white-skinned woman with the golden hair" has a skin fragrance that was "the scent of another culture, another world, a fresh, wonderful smell that made me question my attraction to smoky jungle campfires and eating wild animals." What has happened here, both in terms of the narrative and the style? What are the causes and effects of this sudden change?

Writing About Issues and Contexts

1. Is Hansen right to make light of the *bali saleng*? What, if anything, should Hansen be afraid of?

2. What is the root cause of the villagers' fear? What underlies their belief system? Is their belief system more or less primitive than Hansen's?

3. Hansen writes, "For months this jungle had seemed so benign and giving. How quickly it had become frightening." What accounts for this sudden, dramatic shift?

4. Reconsider Orwell's "Shooting an Elephant" (Chapter 2) in light of Hansen's essay. How does each reveal the potential for conflict when different cultures meet?

Louise Erdrich (1954–   ) is perhaps best known for her novel Love
Medicine *(1984) as well as other works that focus on the experience
of Native Americans:* The Beet Queen *(1986),* Tracks *(1988), and*
The Bingo Palace *(1994). In contrast, her novel* The Master Butchers
Singing Club *(2003) focuses on the immigrant-German-father side
of her family. Part Chippewa Indian, Erdrich was raised in North
Dakota where her parents worked at the Bureau of Indian Affairs
boarding school, which she attended. She received a bachelor's
degree from Dartmouth in 1976 and a master's in creative writing
from Johns Hopkins in 1979. Her fiction has appeared in many
magazines and reviews; "Sister Godzilla" appeared first in* The
Atlantic Monthly.

Louise Erdrich

Sister Godzilla

The door banged shut, and then the children were alone with their
sixth-grade teacher. It was the first day of school, in the fall of 1963.
The habits of Franciscan nuns still shrouded all but their faces, so
each of the new nun's features was emphasized, read forty times over
in astonishment. Outlined in a stiff white frame of starched linen,
Sister's eyes, nose, and mouth leaped out, a mask from a dream, a
great rawboned jackal's muzzle.

"Oh, Christ," Toddy Crieder said, just loud enough for Dot to
hear.

Dot Adare, a troublemaker, knew Toddy was in love with her and
usually ignored him, but the nun's extreme ugliness was irresistible.

"Godzilla," she whispered.

5   The teacher's name was Sister Mary Anita Groff. She was young,
in her twenties or thirties, and so swift of movement, for all her hulk-
ing size, that walking from the back of the room to the front, she surprised her students, made them picture an athlete's legs and muscles
concealed in the flow of black wool. When she swept the air in a gesture meant to include them all in her opening remarks, her hands fixed
their gazes. They were the opposite of her face. Her hands were beautiful, as white as milk glass, the fingers straight and tapered. They
were the hands in the hallway print of Mary underneath the cross.
They were the hands of the Apostles, cast in plastic and lit at night on
the tops of television sets. Praying hands.

Ballplayer's hands. She surprised them further by walking onto the graveled yard at recess, her neckpiece cutting hard into the flesh beneath her heavy jaw. When, with a matter-of-fact grace, she pulled from the sleeve of her gown a mitt of dark mustard-colored leather and raised it, a thrown softball dropped in. Her skill was obvious. Good players rarely stretch or change their expressions. They simply tip their hands toward the ball like magnets, and there it is. As a pitcher, Mary Anita was a swirl of wool, as graceful as the windblown cape of Zorro, an emotional figure that stirred Dot so thoroughly that as she pounded home plate—a rubber dish mat—and beat the air twice in practice swings, choked up on the handle, tried to concentrate, Dot knew she would have no choice but to slam a home run.

She did not. In fact, she whiffed, in three strikes, never ticking the ball or fouling. Purely disgusted with herself, she sat on the edge of the bike rack and watched as Sister gave a few balls away and pitched easy hits to the rest of the team. It was as if the two had sensed from the beginning what was to come. Or, then again, perhaps Mary Anita's information came from Dot's former teachers, living in the red-brick convent across the road. Hard to handle. A smart-off. Watch out when you turn your back. They were right. After recess, her pride burned, Dot sat at her desk and drew a dinosaur draped in a nun's robe, its mouth open in a roar. The teeth, long and jagged, grayish-white, held her attention. She worked so hard on the picture that she barely noticed as the room hushed around her. She felt the presence, though, the shadow of attention that dropped over her as Mary Anita stood watching. As a mark of her arrogance, Dot kept drawing.

She shaded in the last tooth and leaned back to frown at her work. The page was plucked into the air before she could pretend to cover it. No one made a sound. Dot's heart beat with excitement.

"You will remain after school," the nun pronounced.

10   The last half hour passed. The others filed out the door. And then the desk in front of Dot filled suddenly. There was the paper, the carefully rendered dinosaur caught in mid-roar. Dot stared at it furiously, her mind a blur of anticipation. She was not afraid.

"Look at me," Mary Anita said.

Dot found that she didn't want to, that she couldn't. Then her throat filled. Her face was on fire. Her lids hung across her eyeballs like lead shades. She traced the initials carved into her desktop.

"Look at me," Mary Anita said to her again, and Dot's gaze was drawn upward, upward on a string, until she met the eyes of her teacher, deep brown, electrically sad. Their very stillness shook Dot.

"I'm sorry," she said.

15   When those two unprecedented words dropped from her lips, Dot knew, beyond reason and past bearing, that something terrible had occurred. She felt dizzy. The blood rushed to her head so fast that her ears ached, yet the tips of her fingers fell asleep. Her eyelids prickled and her nose wept, but at the same time her mouth went dry. Her body was a thing of extremes, contradicting itself.

"When I was young," Sister Mary Anita said, "as young as you are, I felt a great deal of pain when I was teased about my looks. I've long since accepted my . . . deformity. A prognathic jaw runs in our family, and I share it with an uncle. But I must admit, the occasional insult, or a drawing such as yours, still hurts."

Dot began to mumble and then stopped, desperate. Sister Mary Anita waited, and then handed her her own handkerchief.

"I'm sorry," Dot said again. She wiped her nose. The square of white material was cool and fresh. "Can I go now?"

"Of course not," Mary Anita said.

20   Dot was confounded. The magical two words, an apology, had dropped from her lips. Yet more was expected. What?

"I want you to understand something," the nun said. "I've told you how I feel. And I expect that you will never hurt me again."

The nun waited, and waited, until their eyes met. Then Dot's mouth fell wide. Her eyes spilled over. She knew that the strange feelings that had come upon her were the same feelings that Mary Anita had felt. Dot had never felt another person's feelings, never in her life.

"I won't do anything to hurt you," she blubbered passionately. "I'll kill myself first."

"I'm sure that will not be necessary," Sister Mary Anita said.

25   Dot tried to rescue her pride then, by turning away very quickly. Without permission, she ran out the schoolroom door, down the steps, and on into the street, where at last the magnetic force of the encounter weakened, and suddenly she could breathe. Even that was different, though. As she walked, she began to realize that her body was still fighting itself. Her lungs filled with air like two bags, but every time they did so, a place underneath them squeezed so painfully that the truth suddenly came clear.

"I love her now," she blurted out. She stopped on a crack, stepping on it, sickened. "Oh, God, I am *in love*."

Toddy Crieder was a hollow-chested, envious boy whose reputation had never recovered from the time he was sent home for eating tree bark. In the third grade he had put two crayons up his nose, pretend tusks. The pink one got stuck, and Toddy had to visit the clinic. This year, already, his stomach had been pumped in the emergency room. Dot despised him, but that only seemed to fuel his adoration of her.

Coming into the schoolyard the second day, a bright, cool morning, Toddy ran up to Dot, his thin legs knocking.

30   "Yeah," he cried. "Godzilla! Not bad, Adare."

He wheeled off, the laces of his tennis shoes dragging. Dot looked after him and felt the buzz inside her head begin. How she wanted to stuff that name back into her mouth, or at least Toddy's mouth.

"I hope you trip and murder yourself!" Dot screamed.

But Toddy did not trip. For all of his clumsiness, he managed to stay upright, and as Dot stood rooted in the center of the walk, she saw him whiz from clump to clump of children, laughing and gesturing, filling the air with small and derisive sounds. Sister Mary Anita swept out the door, a wooden-handled brass bell in her hand, and when she shook it up and down, the children, who played together in twos and threes, swung toward her and narrowed or widened their eyes and turned eagerly to one another. Some began to laugh. It seemed to Dot that all of them did, in fact, and that the sound, jerked from their lips, was large, uncanny, totally and horribly delicious.

"Godzilla, Godzilla," they called under their breath. "Sister Godzilla."

Before them on the steps, the nun continued to smile into their faces. She did not hear them—yet. But Dot knew she would. Over the bell her eyes were brilliantly dark and alive. Her horrid jagged teeth showed in a smile when she saw Dot, and Dot ran to her, thrusting a hand into her lunch bag and grabbing the cookies that her mother had made from whatever she could find around the house—raisins, con-

35   gealed Malt-O-Meal, the whites of eggs.

"Here!" Dot shoved a sweet, lumpy cookie into the nun's hand. It fell apart, distracting Sister as the children pushed past.

The students seemed to forget the name off and on all week. Some days they would move on to new triumphs or disasters—other teachers occupied them, or some small event occurred in the classroom. But then Toddy Crieder would lope and careen among them at recess, would pump his arms and pretend to roar behind Sister Mary Anita's back as she stepped up to the plate. As she swung and connected with the ball and gathered herself to run, her veil lifting, the muscles in her shoulders like the curved hump of a raptor's wings, Toddy would move along behind her, rolling his legs the way Godzilla did in the movie. In her excitement, dashing base to base, her feet long and limber in black laced shoes, Mary Anita did not notice. But Dot looked on, the taste of a penny caught in her throat.

"Snakes live in holes. Snakes are reptiles. These are Science Facts." Dot read aloud to the class from her Discovery science book. "Snakes are not wet. Some snakes lay eggs. Some have live young."

"Very good," Sister said. "Can you name other reptiles?"

Dot's tongue fused to the back of her throat.

40   "No," she croaked.

"Anyone else?" Sister asked.

Toddy Crieder raised his hand. Sister recognized him.

"How about Godzilla?"

Gasps. Small noises of excitement. Mouths agape. Admiration for Toddy's nerve rippled through the rows of children like a wind across a field. Sister Mary Anita's great jaw opened, opened, and then snapped shut. Her shoulders shook. No one knew what to do at first. Then she laughed. It was a high-pitched, almost birdlike sound, a thin laugh like the highest notes on the piano. The children all hesitated, and then they laughed with her, even Toddy Crieder. Eyes darting from one child to the next, to Dot, Toddy laughed.

45   Dot's eyes crossed with urgency. When Sister Mary Anita turned to new work, Dot crooked her arm beside her like a piston and leaned across Toddy's desk.

"I'm going to give you one right in the breadbasket," she said.

With a precise boxer's jab she knocked the wind out of Toddy, left him gasping, and turned to the front, face clear, as Sister began to speak.

Furious sunlight. Black cloth. Dot sat on the iron trapeze, the bar pushing a sore line into the backs of her legs. As she swung, she watched Sister Mary Anita. The wind was harsh, and the nun wore a pair of wonderful gloves, black, the fingers cut off of them so that her hands could better grip the bat. The ball arced toward her sinuously and dropped. Her bat caught it with a thick, clean sound, and off it soared. Mary Anita's habit swirled open behind her. The cold bit her cheeks red. She swung to third, glanced, panting, over her shoulder, and then sped home. She touched down lightly and bounded off.

Dot's arms felt heavy, weak, and she dropped from the trapeze and went to lean against the brick wall of the school building. Her heart thumped in her ears. She saw what she would do when she grew up: declare her vocation, enter the convent. She and Sister Mary Anita would live in the nuns' house together, side by side. They would eat, work, eat, cook. To relax, Sister Mary Anita would hit pop flies and Dot would catch them.

50   Someday, one day, Dot and Mary Anita would be walking, their hands in their sleeves, long habits flowing behind.

"Dear Sister," Dot would say, "remember that old nickname you had the year you taught the sixth grade?"

"Why, no," Sister Mary Anita would say, smiling at her. "Why, no."

And Dot would know that she had protected her, kept her from harm.

It got worse. Dot wrote some letters, tore them up. Her hand shook when Sister passed her in the aisle, and her eyes closed, automatically, as she breathed in the air that closed behind the nun. Soap—a harsh soap. Faint carbolic mothballs. That's what she smelled like. Dizzying. Dot's fists clenched. She pressed her knuckles to her eyes and very loudly excused herself. She went to the girls' bathroom and stood in a stall. Her life was terrible. The thing was, she didn't want to be a nun.

55   "I don't want to!" she whispered, desperate, to the whitewashed tin walls that shuddered if a girl bumped them. "There must be another way."

She would have to persuade Mary Anita to forsake her vows, to come and live with Dot and her mother in the house just past the edge of town. How would she start, how would she persuade her teacher?

Someone was standing outside the stall. Dot opened the door a bit and stared into the great craggy face.

"Are you feeling all right? Do you need to go home?" Sister Mary Anita was concerned.

Fire shot through Dot's limbs. The girls' bathroom, a place of secrets, of frosted glass, its light mute and yet brilliant, paralyzed her. But she gathered herself. Here was her chance, as if God had given it to her.

60   "Please," Dot said, "let's run away together!"

Sister paused. "Are you having troubles at home?"

"No," Dot said.

Sister's milk-white hand came through the doorway and covered Dot's forehead. Dot's anxious thoughts throbbed against the lean palm. Staring into the eyes of the nun, Dot gripped the small metal knob on the inside of the door and pushed. Then she felt herself falling forward, slowly turning like a leaf in the wind, upheld and buoyant in the peaceful roar. It was as though she would never reach Sister's arms, but when she did, she came back with a jolt.

"You *are* ill," Sister said. "Come to the office, and we'll call your mother."

65   As Dot had known it would, perhaps from that moment in the girls' bathroom, the day came. The day of her reckoning.

Outside, in the morning schoolyard, after mass and before first bell, everyone crowded around Toddy Crieder. In his arms he held a wind-up tin Godzilla, a big toy, almost knee-high, a green-and-gold replica painted with a fierce eye for detail. The scales were perfect overlapping crescents, and the eyes were large and manic, pitch-black, oddly human. Toddy had pinned a sort of cloak on the thing, a black scarf. Dot's arms thrust through the packed shoulders, but the bell rang, and Toddy stowed the toy under his coat. His eyes picked Dot from the rest.

"I had to send for this!" he cried. The punch hadn't turned him against Dot, only hardened his resolve to please her. He vanished through the heavy wine-red doors of the school. Dot stared at the ground. The world went stark, the colors harsh in her eyes. The small brown pebbles of the playground leaped off the tarred and sealed earth. She took a step. The stones seemed to crack and whistle under her feet.

"Last bell!" Sister Mary Anita called. "You'll be late!"

Morning prayer. The pledge. Toddy drew out the suspense of his audience, enjoying the glances and whispers. The toy was in his desk. Every so often he lifted the lid and then looked around to see how many children were watching him duck inside to make adjustments. By the time Sister started the daily reading lesson, the tension in the room was so acute that not even Toddy could bear it any longer.

70   The room was large, high-ceilinged, floored with slats of polished wood. Round lights hung on thick chains, and the great rectangular windows let through enormous sheaves of radiance. This large class had been in the room for more than two years. Dot had spent most of every day in the room. She knew its creaks, the muted clunk of desks rocking out of floor bolts, the mad thumping in the radiators like the sound of a thousand imprisoned elves, and so she heard and immediately registered the click and grind of Toddy's windup key. Sister Mary

Anita did not. The teacher turned to the chalkboard, her book open on the desk, and began to write instructions for the children to copy.

She was absorbed, calling out the instructions as she wrote. Her arm swept up and down, it seemed to Dot, in a frighteningly innocent joy. She was inventing a lesson, some way of doing things, not a word of which was being taken in. All eyes were on the third row, where Toddy Crieder sat. All eyes were on his hand as he wound the toy up to its limit and bent over and set it on the floor. Then the eyes were on the toy itself, as Toddy lifted his hand away and the thing moved forward on its own.

The scarf it wore did not hamper the beast's progress, the regular thrash of its legs. The tiny claw hands beat forward like pistons and the thick metal tail whipped from side to side as the toy moved down the center of the aisle toward the front of the room, toward Sister Mary Anita, who stood, back turned, immersed in her work at the board.

Dot had gotten herself placed in the first row, to be closer to her teacher, and so she saw the creature up close just before it headed into the polished open space of floor at the front of the room. Its powerful jaws thrust from the black scarf; its great teeth were frozen, exhibited in a terrible smile. Its painted eyes had an eager and purposeful look.

Its movement faltered as it neared Mary Anita. The children caught their breath, but the thing inched forward, made slow and fascinating progress, directly toward the hem of her garment. She did not seem to notice. She continued to talk, to write, circling numbers and emphasizing certain words with careful underlines. And as she did so, as the moment neared, Dot's brain finally rang. She jumped as though it were the last bell of the day. She vaulted from her desk. Two steps took her across that gleaming space of wood at the front of the room. But just as she bent down to scoop the toy to her chest, a neat black boot slashed, inches from her nose. Sister Mary Anita had whirled, the chalk fixed in her hand. Daintily, casually, she had lifted her habit and kicked the toy dinosaur into the air. The thing ascended, pedaling its clawed feet, the scarf blown back like a sprung umbrella. The trajectory was straight and true. The toy knocked headfirst into the ceiling and came back down in pieces. The children ducked beneath the rain of scattered tin. Only Dot and Mary Anita stood poised, unmoving, focused on the moment between them.

75   Dot could look nowhere but at her teacher. But when she lifted her eyes this time, Sister Mary Anita was not looking at her. She had

turned her face away, the rough cheek blotched as if it had borne a slap, the gaze hooded and set low. Sister walked to the window, her back again to Dot, to the class, and as the laughter started, uncomfortable and groaning at first, then shriller, fuller, becoming its own animal, Dot felt an unrecoverable tenderness boil up in her. Inwardly she begged the nun to turn and stop the noise. But Sister did not. She let it wash across them both without mercy. Dot lost sight of her unspeakable profile as Mary Anita looked out into the yard. Bathed in brilliant light, the nun's face went as blank as a sheet of paper, as the sky, as featureless as all things that enter heaven.

Analyzing Rhetorical Choices

1. Erdrich begins with an opening that has considerable shock value when she writes that "Sister's eyes, nose, and mouth leaped out, a mask from a dream, a great rawboned jackal's muzzle." How does this description set the tone for what follows?

2. Erdrich describes Toddy Crieder as "a hollow-chested, envious boy." What does the phrase "hollow-chested" imply about Crieder, especially in relation to his emotions?

3. Erdrich sometimes uses short phrases that function as sentences: "Praying hands." "Ballplayer's hands." "Gasps." "Small noises of excitement." "Mouths agape." "Furious sunlight." "Black cloth." What rhetorical effect do these sentences have? Why do you think Erdrich uses them so frequently?

4. Explain the significance, to you, of the last sentence of this story: "Bathed in brilliant light, the nun's face went as blank as a sheet of paper, as the sky, as featureless as all things that enter heaven."

Writing About Issues and Contexts

1. Why is it significant that Mary Anita Groff is a nun?

2. How would you describe this love that an 11- or 12-year-old girl has for a grown woman, one who is so physically grotesque?

3. What is the significance of Sister Mary Anita's hands? Why does Erdrich dwell on them to so great an extent?

4. At the heart of this story is the complex emotional dynamic among three key individuals: Dot, Sister Mary Anita Groff, and Toddy

Crieder. How would you describe both the causes and the effects that lie at the heart of this story?

5. The other children play the role of spectators, but they are not impartial or sympathetic toward Sister Mary Anita. What perspective does Erdrich offer concerning the children? Are they innocent? What is their relationship to their teacher, to Toddy Crieder, and to the event that climaxes the story?

*Born in New Jersey, **Norman Mailer** (1923–   ) grew up in Brooklyn, ex-
celling in the sciences in high school and majoring in engineering at
Harvard, where he earned a bachelor's degree in 1943. His first novel,
The Naked and the Dead (1948), made Mailer an overnight sensation
with its dramatic, gritty depictions of men in wartime. Since then, Mailer
has published many novels, essays, articles, and works of nonfiction, including Advertisements for Myself (1959), The Executioner's Song
(1979), and his Pulitzer Prize–winning account of America during the
Vietnam war, Armies of the Night (1968). The essay presented here is
characteristic of Mailer's often torrential style and is an excerpt from his
long essay, "Ten Thousand Words a Minute," which analyzes the sport of
boxing, with a particular focus on two bouts: one between Emile Griffith
and Benny Kid Paret and the other between Floyd Patterson and Sonny
Liston. For those not entirely up on their boxing history, Floyd Patterson
was an extremely popular fighter in the 1950s, while Sonny Liston was
the opponent whom Muhammad Ali defeated to gain the World
Heavyweight Championship in 1964.*

Norman Mailer
Boxing as a Metaphor for Life

On the afternoon of the night Emile Griffith and Benny Paret were
to fight a third time for the welterweight championship, there was
murder in both camps. "I hate that kind of guy," Paret had said earlier
to Pete Hamill about Griffith. "A fighter's got to look and talk and act
like a man." One of the Broadway gossip columnists had run an item
about Griffith a few days before. His girl friend saw it and said to
Griffith, "Emile, I didn't know about you being that way." So Griffith
hit her. So he said. Now at the weigh-in that morning, Paret had insulted Griffith irrevocably, touching him on the buttocks, while making a few more remarks about his manhood. They almost had their
fight on the scales.

The accusation of homosexuality arouses a major passion in many
men; they spend their lives resisting it with a biological force. There is
a kind of man who spends every night of his life getting drunk in a
bar, he rants, he brawls, he ends in a small rumble on the street;

women say, "For God's sakes, he's homosexual. Why doesn't he just turn queer and get his suffering over with." Yet men protect him. It is because he is choosing not to become homosexual. It was put best by Sartre who said that a homosexual is a man who practices homosexuality. A man who does not, is not homosexual—he is entitled to the dignity of his choice. He is entitled to the fact that he chose not to become homosexual, and is paying presumably his price.

The rage in Emile Griffith was extreme. I was at the fight that night, I had never seen a fight like it. It was scheduled for fifteen rounds, but they fought without stopping from the bell which began the round to the bell which ended it, and then they fought after the bell, sometimes for as much as fifteen seconds before the referee could force them apart.

Paret was a Cuban, a proud club fighter who had become welterweight champion because of his unusual ability to take a punch. His style of fighting was to take three punches to the head in order to give back two. At the end of ten rounds, he would still be bouncing, his opponent would have a headache. But in the last two years, over the fifteen-round fights, he had started to take some bad maulings.

5   This fight had its turns. Griffith won most of the early rounds, but Paret knocked Griffith down in the sixth. Griffith had trouble getting up, but made it, came alive and was dominating Paret again before the round was over. Then Paret began to wilt. In the middle of the eighth round, after a clubbing punch had turned his back to Griffith, Paret walked three disgusted steps away, showing his hindquarters. For a champion, he took much too long to turn back around. It was the first hint of weakness Paret had ever shown, and it must have inspired a particular shame, because he fought the rest of the fight as if he were seeking to demonstrate that he could take more punishment than any man alive. In the twelfth, Griffith caught him. Paret got trapped in a corner. Trying to duck away, his left arm and his head became tangled on the wrong side of the top rope. Griffith was in like a cat ready to rip the life out of a huge boxed rat. He hit him eighteen right hands in a row, an act which took perhaps three or four seconds, Griffith making a pent-up whimpering sound all the while he attacked, the right hand whipping like a piston rod which has broken through the crankcase, or like a baseball bat demolishing a pumpkin. I was sitting in the second row of that corner—they were not ten feet away from me, and like everybody else, I was hypnotized. I had never seen one man hit another so hard and so many times. Over the referee's face came a look of woe as if some spasm had passed its way through him, and then he

leaped on Griffith to pull him away. It was the act of a brave man. Griffith was uncontrollable. His trainer leaped into the ring, his manager, his cut man, there were four people holding Griffith, but he was on an orgy, he had left the Garden, he was back on a hoodlum's street. If he had been able to break loose from his handlers and the referee, he would have jumped Paret to the floor and whaled on him there.

And Paret? Paret died on his feet. As he took those eighteen punches something happened to everyone who was in psychic range of the event. Some part of his death reached out to us. One felt it hover in the air. He was still standing in the ropes, trapped as he had been before, he gave some little half-smile of regret, as if he were saying, "I didn't know I was going to die just yet," and then, his head leaning back but still erect, his death came to breathe about him. He began to pass away. As he passed, so his limbs descended beneath him, and he sank slowly to the floor. He went down more slowly than any fighter had ever gone down, he went down like a large ship which turns on end and slides second by second into its grave. As he went down, the sound of Griffith's punches echoed in the mind like a heavy ax in the distance chopping into a wet log.

Paret lay on the ground, quivering gently, a small froth on his mouth. The house doctor jumped into the ring. He knelt. He pried Paret's eyelid open. He looked at the eyeball staring out. He let the lid snap shut. He reached into his satchel, took out a needle, jabbed Paret with a stimulant. Paret's back rose in a high arch. He writhed in real agony. They were calling him back from death. One wanted to cry out, "Leave the man alone. Let him die." But they saved Paret long enough to take him to a hospital where he lingered for days. He was in coma. He never came out of it. If he lived, he would have been a vegetable. His brain was smashed. But they held him in life for a week, they fed him chemicals, and made exploratory operations into his skull, and fed details of his condition to The Goat. And The Goat kicked clods of mud all over the place, and spoke harshly of prohibiting boxing. There was shock in the land. Children had seen the fight on television. There were editorials, gloomy forecasts that the Game was dead. The managers and the prizefighters got together. Gently, in thick, depressed hypocrisies, they tried to defend their sport. They did not find it easy to explain that they shared an unstated view of life which was religious.

It was of course not that religion which is called Judeo-Christian. It was an older religion, a more primitive one—a religion of blood, a murderous and sensitive religion which mocks the effort of the understanding to approach it, and scores the lungs of men like D. H.

Lawrence, and burns the brain of men like Ernest Hemingway when they explore out into the mystery, searching to discover some part of the secret. It is the view of life which looks upon death as a condition which is more alive than life or unspeakably more deadening. As such it is not a very attractive notion to the Establishment. But then the Establishment has nothing very much of even the Judeo-Christian tradition. It has a respect for legal and administrative aspects of justice, and it is devoted to the idea of compassion for the poor. But the Establishment has no idea of death, no tolerance for Heaven or Hell, no comprehension of bloodshed. It sees no logic in pain. To the Establishment these notions are a detritus from the past.

Like a patient submerged beneath the plastic cover of an oxygen tent, boxing lives on beneath the cool, bored eyes of the doctors in the Establishment. It would not take too much to finish boxing off. Shut down the oxygen, which is to say, turn that switch in the mass media which still gives sanction to organized pugilism, and the fight game would be dead.

10   But the patient is permitted to linger for fear the private detectives of the Establishment, the psychiatrists and psychoanalysts, might not be able to neutralize the problem of gang violence. Not so well as the Game. Of course, the moment some piece of diseased turnip capable of being synthesized cheaply might prove to have the property of tranquilizing a violent young man for a year, the Establishment would wipe out boxing. Every time a punk was arrested, the police would prescribe a pill, and violence would walk the street sheathed and numb. Of course the Mob would lose revenue, but then the Mob is also part of the Establishment, it, and the labor unions and the colleges and the newspapers and the corporations are all part of the Establishment. The Establishment is never simple. It needs the Mob to grease the chassis on its chariot. Therefore, the Mob would be placated. In a society with strong central government, it is not so difficult to turn up a new source of revenue. What is more difficult is to enter the plea that violence may be an indispensable element of life. This is not the place to have the argument: it is enough to say that if the liberal Establishment is right in its unstated credo that death is a void, and man leads out his life suspended momentarily above that void, why then there is no argument at all. Whatever shortens life is monstrous. We have not the right to shorten life, since life is the only possession of the psyche, and in death we have only nothingness. What then can there be said in defense of sports-car racing, war, or six-ounce gloves?

But if we go from life into a death which is larger than our life has been, or into a death which is small, if death comes to nothing for one man because he swallowed his death in his life, and if for another death is alive with dimension, then the certitudes of the Establishment lose power. A drug which offers peace to a pain may dull the nerve which could have taught the mind how to carry that pain into the death which comes on the next day or on the decades that follow. A tranquilizer gives coma to an anxiety which may later smell of the dungeon, beneath the ground. If we are born into life as some living line of intent from an eternity which may have tortured us or nurtured us in death, then we may be obliged to go back to death with more courage and art than we left it. Or face the dim end of going back with less.

That is the existential venture, the unstated religious view of boxers trying to beat each other into unconsciousness or, ultimately, into death. It is the culture of the killer who sickens the air about him if he does not find some half-human way to kill a little in order not to deaden all. It is a defense against the plague, against that plague which comes from violence converted into the nausea of all that nonviolence which is void of peace. Paret's death was with horror, but not all the horror was in the beating, much was in the way his death was cheated. Which is to say that his death was twice a nightmare. I knew that something in boxing was spoiled forever for me, that there would be a fear in watching a fight now which was like the fear one felt for any *novillero* when he was having an unhappy day, the bull was dangerous, and the crowd was ugly. You knew he could get hurt. There is fascination in seeing that the first time, but it is not as enjoyable as one expects. It is like watching a novelist who has written a decent book get run over by a car.

Something in boxing was spoiled. But not the principle, not the right for one man to try to knock another out in the ring. That was perhaps not a civilized activity, but it belonged to the tradition of the humanist, it was a human activity, it showed a part of what man was like, it belonged to his ability to create art and artful movement on the edge of death or pain or danger or attack, and it had much to say about the subtleties of human style. For there are boxers whose bodies move like a fine brain, and there are others who pound the opposition down with the force of a trade-union leader, there are fools and wits and patient craftsmen among boxers, wild men full of a sense of outrage, and steady oppressive peasants, clever spoilers, dogged infantrymen who walk forward all night, hypnotists (like Liston), dancers, lovers, mothers giving a scolding, horsemen high on their legs. There is knowledge to be found about our nature, and the nature of animals, of big cats, lions, tigers, gorillas, bears, walruses (Archie Moore), birds, elephants, jackals, bulls. No, I was not down on boxing, but I loved it with freedom no longer. It was more like somebody in your family was fighting now. And the feeling one had for a big fight was no longer clear of terror in its excitement. There was awe in the suspense.

But then there is nothing else very much like being at a Heavyweight Championship fight. It is to some degree the way a Hollywood premiere once ought to have been; it's a big party with high action—there is the same rich flush of jewelry, bourbon, bare shoulders, cha-cha, silk, the promise that a life or two will be changed by tonight; it is even a bit like a political convention; it is much more like an event none of us will ever see—conceive of sitting in a classic arena waiting for a limited war with real bullets to begin between a platoon of Marines and two mounted squads of Russian Cossacks—you'd have the sensation of what a Heavyweight Championship can promise. A great heavyweight fight could take place in the center of a circus.

15   Ideally, it should take place in New York. Because Broadway turns out and Hollywood flies in with Las Vegas on the hip, and many of the wings and dovecotes and banlieues of what even a couple of years ago was called Café Society is there, and International Set (always seeing their first fight), and Big Business, and every good-looking call girl in New York, and some not so good-looking, and all the figures from the history pages of prizefighting in America, as well as ghosts there are some to claim—the ghost of Benny Leonard, the ghost of Harry Greb. Plus all the models, loose celebrities, socialites of high and lower rank, hierarchies from the racetrack, politicians, judges, and—one might offer a prayer if one really cared—one sociologist of wit and distinction ought to be there to capture for America the true status of its conflicting aristocracies: does Igor Cassini rate with Mickey Rooney or does Roger Blough get a row in front of Elizabeth Taylor? Is Frank Sinatra honored before Mrs. Woodward? Does Zsa Zsa Gabor come in ahead of Mayor Wagner? The First Sociologists of America are those professionals who sell the hot seats for a big fight in New York.

In Chicago, there was little of this. If there are nine circles to Hell, there were nine clouds over this fight. D'Amato was not licensed to manage in New York. Small matter. Patterson once again would fight in New York without him. But Liston was not cleared to fight by the State Boxing Commission—the shadow of the Establishment lay against him. So the fight was transferred to Chicago which promptly took fire. If Patterson-Liston was not clean enough for New York, it was not cool enough for Chicago. The local newspapers gave the kind of publicity one tastes in cold canned food. The stories on training were buried. Interest was greater outside the city than within. Yet little of Broadway arrived and less of Hollywood. You cannot get producers and movie stars to travel a distance to watch two Negroes fight. A bitch lives to see a white man fight a black man. She's not prejudiced—depending on the merits, she'll root for either, but a Negro against a Negro wets no juice.

And then there was poor weather. The day before the fight was misty, chilly. It rained on and off, and cleared inconclusively on Tuesday, which was cold. Fight night was cold enough to wear a topcoat. Comiskey Park was far from filled. It could hold fifty thousand for a big fight; it ended with less than twenty in paid admissions. Twenty-six thousand people showed. Proportions were poor. Because of theatre television, Patterson would make more money on this fight than any fighter had ever made, and there was much local interest in cities all over America. Parties were got up to go to the theatre, see it on television. The press coverage was larger than average, larger let us say than any of the three Johansson fights or the Marciano-Walcott fights. It was the biggest fight in ten years, it was conceivably the biggest fight since Louis fought Schmeling the second time, and yet nobody in the city where it was fought seemed to care. Radio, with its roaring inside hysteria, had lost to television, that grey eminence which now instructed Americans in the long calm of Ecclesiastes: vanity of vanities, all events are vanity.

So for a celebrity hunter, ringside was nothing formidable at this fight. The good people of Chicago turned out modestly. The very good people—which is to say, the very rich—turned out for ringside, and had a chance to cross the outfield grass, luminous green in the half-light of the baseball towers, and walk to their seats under the great folded wings of the grandstand. Ever since the Romans built the Colosseum, arenas take on a prehistoric breath at night—one could be a black ant walking inside the circle a pterodactyl must have made with its wing as it slept. Or is it hills like dark elephants of which we speak?

I had a seat in the working press five rows from the ring. An empty seat away was Jimmy Baldwin. There had been a chill between us in the last year. Not a feud, but bad feeling. We had been glad, however, to see each other in Chicago. Tacitly, settling no differences, not talking about it, we had thought to be friendly. But the unsettled differences were still there. Two nights ago, at a party, we had had a small fight. We each insulted the other's good intentions and turned away. Now we sat with a hundred-pound cake of ice on the empty seat between us. After ten minutes, I got up and went for a walk around the ring.

20   The Press section occupied the first six rows. Back of us was an aisle which made a larger square around the square of the ring. On the other side of this aisle was the first row of ringside seats. This was as close as you could come to the fight if you had entered by buying a ticket. So I took a sampling of the house as I walked around the square. If this had been New York, you would expect to find twelve movie stars in the front row. But this was Chicago. Behind us were a muster of local Irish politicians, big men physically in the mold of Jimmy Braddock, not unhappy tonight with their good seats.

The front row to my right and the front row across the ring from me was given over in part to the Mob. They were the most intricate faces one would find this side of Carpaccio or Bellini, chins with hooks and chisels, nostrils which seemed to screw the air up into the head, thin-lipped mouths like thin-nosed pliers, eyes which behind their dark glasses scrutinized your interior until they could find the tool in you which would work for them, and then would flip away like the turning of a card. Yes, those two rows of seats made up a right angle of *don capos* and a few very special Catholic priests, thin, ascetic, medieval in appearance, as well as a number of field officers dressed in black like subalterns, but older, leaner, with more guilds at their command. They were well-seated. They filled close to every seat around the corner.

It proved to be Patterson's corner.

That was art. They did not have to do much more. Sitting there, they could devote their study to Patterson. He would see them when he came back to his corner, his seconds would be obliged to look at them each time a new round began and they climbed down the steps from the corner. The back of the cornermen's necks would be open to detailed inspection, the calves of Patterson's leg, as he sat resting on the stool, would be a ready target for mental arrows. Like Lilliputians they could shoot thousands of pins into Gulliver.

I completed the tour. The last row, Liston's corner, was routine: musclemen, mobsters, business-sporting, a random sample. Turning the angle I came back to my seat, and sat watching a preliminary, shivering a little in the cold. It was much too cold for a fight. The sensitivity to magic I had felt earlier in the evening would not come back. There was just a dull sense of apprehension. Everything was wrong.

25   The preliminaries ended. Visiting fighters were called up from the crowd to take a bow. Archie Moore drew a large hand: he was wearing a black-silk cape with a white lining and he twirled the cape with éclat. It said: "Go away, all solemn sorcerers, the magic man is here."

Patterson and Liston arrived within a minute of each other. The visiting fighters who were gathered in the ring said hello to each man, shook their gloves, and went back to their seats.

The Star-Spangled Banner was played. Liston stood in his corner with his handlers, the referee stood in the middle of the ring, and Cus D'Amato stood alone, eight feet away from Patterson and his seconds. Since D'Amato was across from me, I could see his face clearly. It was as pale as his white sweater. His face was lifted to the sky, his eyes were closed. While the anthem played, D'Amato held his hand to his heart as if he were in anguish. I had the impression he was praying with fear.

The anthem ended, the fighters took their instructions from the referee, and stripped their robes. Their bodies made a contrast. Liston, only an inch taller than Patterson, weighed 214 pounds to Patterson's 189. But the difference was not just in weight. Liston had a sleek body, fully muscled, but round. It was the body of a strong man, but the muscles looked to have been shaped by pleasure as much as by work. He was obviously a man who had had some very good times.

Whereas Patterson still had poverty in his muscles. He was certainly not weak, there was whipcord in the way he was put together, but it was still the dry, dedicated body of an athlete, a track man, a disciplinarian: it spoke little of leisure and much of the gym. There was a lack eating at it, some misery.

30   The bell rang.

Liston looked scared.

Patterson looked grim.

They came together with no vast impact, trying for small gains. Each was moving with large respect for the other. Liston had the unhappy sweaty look in his eye of the loudest-talking champion on a city block—he has finally gotten into a fight with one of the Juniors, and he knows this Junior can fight. If he loses he's got much to lose. So Liston was trying to make Junior keep distance.

Patterson was not doing much. He threw a fast left hook which missed, then he circled a bit, fighting from a crouch. He lunged in once very low, trying to get under Liston's long jab and work to the stomach, but his timing was not acute and he drew back quickly. There had been no inspiration, no life, and a hint of clumsiness. But it had been intellectually sound. It caused no harm. Then he tried again, feinting a left hook, and slipping Liston's left jab, but as he came in close, Liston grabbed him with both arms, and they bulled back and forth until the referee separated them. Now, they each had an unhappy look on their faces as if they were big men who had gotten into an altercation in a bar, and didn't like the physical activity of fighting. Each of them looked like it would take three or four rounds to warm up.

35   All this had used a minute. Liston seemed to have gained the confidence that he was stronger, and he began crowding Patterson to the rope, throwing a good many punches, not left hooks, not left jabs, not uppercuts or straight rights, just thick, slow, clubbing punches. None of them landed on Patterson's body or head, they all banged on his arms, and occasionally Patterson would bang Liston back on the arm. It is a way of fighting. A strong slow fighter will sometimes keep hitting the other man on the shoulder or the biceps until his arms go dead. If the opponent is in condition, it is a long procedure. I was surprised at how slow Liston's punches were. From ringside, they looked easy to block. He had a way of setting himself and going "ahem" before he threw the punch. It is, of course, one thing to block punches from your seat at ringside, and another to block them in a ring, but when a fighter is punching with real speed and snap, you can't block the punches from where you sit. Even from thirty feet away, you are fooled.

All that was fooling me now was Patterson. He seemed sluggish. He was not getting hit with Liston's punches, but he was not hitting back, he seemed to miss one small opportunity after another. He was fighting like a college heavyweight who has gone in to work with a professional and is getting disheartened at the physical load of such sparring. He had the expression on his face of somebody pushing a Cadillac which has run out of gas.

Then occurred what may have been the most extraordinary moment ever seen in a championship fight. It was very spooky. Patterson, abruptly, without having been hurt in any visible way, stood up suddenly out of his crouch, his back a foot from the ropes, and seemed to look half up into the sky as if he had seen something there or had been struck by something from there, by some transcendent bolt, and then he staggered like a man caught in machine-gun fire, and his legs went, and he fell back into the ropes. His left glove became tangled in the top rope, almost as Paret's arm had been tangled, and that murmur of death, that visitation which had passed into Madison Square Garden on the moment Paret began to die, seemed a breath from appearing now, Patterson looked at Liston with one lost look, as if somehow he had been expecting this to happen ever since the night it happened to Paret; it was the look of a man saying, "Don't kill me," and then Liston hit him two or three ill-timed punches, banging a sloppy stake into the ground, and Patterson went down. And he was out. He was not faking. He had started to pass out at the moment he stood straight on his feet and was struck by that psychic bolt which had come from wherever it had come.

Patterson rolled over, he started to make an attempt to get to his feet, and Baldwin and I were each shouting, "Get up, get up!" But one's voice had no force in it, one's will had no life.

Patterson got up somewhere between a quarter and a half second too late. You could see the critical instant pass in the referee's body, and Patterson was still getting his glove off the ground. The fight was over: 2:06 of the First. It must have been the worst fight either fighter had ever had.

40   Liston looked like he couldn't believe what had happened. He was blank for two or three long seconds, and then he gave a whoop. It was an artificial, tentative whoop, but it seemed to encourage him because he gave another which sounded somewhat better, and then he began to whoop and whoop and laugh and shout because his handlers had come into the ring and were hugging him and telling him he was the greatest fighter that ever lived. And Patterson, covered quickly with his bathrobe, still stunned, turned and buried his head in Cus D'Amato's shoulder.

From the stands behind us came one vast wave of silence. Here and there sounded cheers or applause, but you could hear each individual voice or pair of hands clapping into the silence.

"What happened?" said Baldwin.

What did happen? Everybody was to ask that question later. But in private.

The descriptions of the fight fed next morning to The Goat showed no uncertainty. They spoke of critical uppercuts and powerful left hooks and pulverizing rights. Liston talked of dominating Patterson with left hands, Patterson's people said it was a big right which did the job, some reporters called the punches crunching, others said they were menacing, brutal, demolishing. One did not read a description of the fight which was not authoritative. The only contradiction, a most minor contradiction, is that with one exception, a wire-service photograph used everywhere of a right hand by Liston which has apparently just left Patterson's chin, there were no pictures—and a point was made of looking at a good many—which show Liston putting a winning glove into Patterson's stomach, solar plexus, temple, nose, or jaw. In fact there is not a single picture of Liston's glove striking Patterson at all. It is not highly probable the photographers missed every decent punch. Fight photographers are capable of splitting the strictest part of a second in order to get the instant of impact. The fine possibility is that there was no impact. There was instead an imprecise beating, that is a beating which was not convincing if the men were anywhere near to equal in strength. Something had happened to Patterson, however. He fought as if he were down with jaundice. It was not that he did not do his best; he always did his determined best; he did just that against Liston. It is just that his best this night was off the spectrum of his normal condition. Something had struck at him. From inside himself or from without, in that instant he straightened from his crouch and stared at the sky, he had the surprise of a man struck by treachery.

45   Now I am forced to give a most improper testimony, because I felt as if I were a small part of that treachery and one despairs of trying to explain how that could be so.

A man turns to boxing because he discovers it is the best experience of his life. If he is a good fighter, his life in the center of the ring is more intense than it can be anywhere else, his mind is more exceptional than at any other time, his body has become a live part of his brain. Some men are geniuses when they are drunk; a good fighter feels a bit of genius when he is having a good fight. This illumination comes not only from the discipline he has put on his body or the concentration of his mind to getting ready for his half hour in the open, but no, it comes as well from his choice to occupy the stage on an adventure whose end is unknown. For the length of his fight, he ceases to be a man and becomes a Being, which is to say he is no longer finite in the usual sense, he is no longer a creature of a given size and dress with a name and some habits which are predictable. Liston-in-the-ring was not just Sonny Liston; much more he was the nucleus of that force at Comiskey Park (and indeed from everywhere in the world from which such desire could reach) which wished him to win or hated

him with an impotence that created force, to wit, hated him less than
it feared him, and so betrayed its hate since the telepathic logic of the
unconscious makes us give our strength to those we think to hate but
favor despite ourselves. Just so, Patterson-in-the-ring was not Floyd
Patterson sparring in his gym, but was instead a vehicle of all the will
and all the particular love which truly wished him to win, as well as a
target of all the hatred which was not impotent but determined to
strike him down.

When these universes collided, the impact if not clear was total.
The world quivered in some rarefied accounting of subtle psychic
seismographs, and the stocks of certain ideal archetypes shifted their
status in our country's brain. Sex had proved superior to Love still
one more time, the Hustler had taken another pool game from the
Infantryman, the Syndicate rolled out the Liberal, the Magician
hyped the Artist, and, since there were more than a few who insisted
on seeing them simply as God and the Devil (whichever much or little
of either they might be), then the Devil had shown that the Lord was
dramatically weak.

The Goat would demand that this fight be reported in a veritable
factology of detail. America could not listen to questions. The professional witnesses to the collision, the pipers of cancer gulch, were
obliged to testify to a barrage of detailed punches, and the fighters re-
examining their own history in such a mirror of prose would be forced
to remake the event in their mind. Yet so long as one kept one's memory, the event was unclear. The result had been turned by betrayal.
And it was by one's own person that the guilt was felt. I had been there
with half a body from half a night of sleep for too many nights, and
half a brain from too many bouts of drinking drinks I did not want
that much, and dim in concentration because I was brooding about the
loss of a friendship which it was a cruel and stupid waste to lose. And
Baldwin too had been brooding. We had sat there like beasts of burden, empty of psychic force to offer our fighter.

Now, too late, in the bout's sudden wake, like angels whose wings
are wet, we buried our quarrel; this time it might stay buried for a
while. "My Lord," said Jimmy, "I lost seven hundred and fifty dollars
tonight."

50   Well, we laughed. I had lost no more than a paltry twenty-eight.

Later, I went back to the dressing room. But Patterson's door was
locked. Over a hundred reporters were jammed into Liston's room, so
many that one could not see the new champion, one could only hear
his voice. He was resounding very much like Clark Gable now, late

Gable with the pit of his mannerism—that somewhat complacent jam of much too much love for the self. Liston had the movie star's way of making the remark which cuts, then balming it with salve. "Did you take your ugly pills?" says the actor to the leading lady, and gives his smile at her flush. "Why honey, dear child, I'm only kidding." So Liston said, "This one time he hurt me was when he got up to a knee at nine. I was afraid he would come all the way up." Which was class. It whipped. A minute later, some banana oil was uncorked. "Yessir," said Liston at large, "Floyd is a heck of a man."

I left that dressing room and tried to get into Patterson's, but the door was still locked. Ingemar Johansson was standing nearby. They were interviewing him over a pay telephone for a radio program. Johansson had a bewildered combative look as if someone had struck him on the back of the head with a loaded jack. He had knocked Patterson down for seven times in one round, there had been wild lightning and "toonder," but he had not been able to keep Patterson down. Now Liston had taken Floyd out with a punch or two or three no witness would agree upon.

"Do you think you can beat Liston," was the interviewer's question.

"I don't know," said Johansson.

55   "Do you think you have a chance?"

Johansson looked sad and Swedish. "One always has a chance," he said. "I would make my fight and fight it, that's all."

One never did get into Patterson's dressing room. After a while I left and walked around the empty ringside seats. It was cold now. Some of the events of the last few days were coming back to me in the cold air of Comiskey Park. They were not agreeable to contemplate. I had done a few unattractive things. I did not want to count them.

Analyzing Rhetorical Choices

1. What techniques does Mailer use to describe the viciousness of the Griffith/Paret bout?

2. Mailer revels in a stream-of-consciousness, torrential outpouring of words and ideas, many of which lead to one another through loose association. Analyze the effects of some specific instances of Mailer's penchant for merging various ideas, concepts, and allusions:

    a. "So the fight was transferred to Chicago which promptly took fire."

    b. "Radio, with its roaring inside hysteria, had lost to television, that grey eminence which now instructed Americans in the long calm of Ecclesiastes: vanity of vanities, all events are vanity."

3. Mailer tends to use personifications in this essay. The Goat personifies the news media and the public craving for gossip, information, and analysis; the Establishment refers to all those with money and power who in some way support the boxing world; the Mob is . . . well, the Mob. Write a short analysis of Mailer's tendency to use personification, evaluating whether you think this rhetorical strategy is a successful one.

4. One of the challenging aspects of this essay is its allusions. Select five allusions to people or ideas that are unfamiliar to you, research them, and come into class with a paragraph or two about each. How do these allusions enrich Mailer's essay, once you know to what (or whom) he is referring?

Writing About Issues and Contexts

1. According to Mailer, why do men fight? What is it that they want to prove or disprove?

2. What effect does the death of Paret have on Mailer, and by extension, on all fans of boxing?

3. According to popular perception, Patterson was a refined, classy, gentlemanly fighter, while Liston was a brutal street thug. Given these views, what effect does Patterson's defeat have on most viewers of the fight? What does Mailer mean in the last paragraph when he states that "the stocks of certain ideal archetypes shifted their status in our country's brain"?

4. Given what Mailer writes here, should boxing be outlawed? Offer an argument, based on Mailer's analysis in this essay. You will likely want to refer to Norman Cousins's essay (Chapter 10), which also focuses on the Griffith/Paret fight.

Born in Pittsburgh, Pennsylvania, **Michael Davitt Bell** (1941–1997)
earned a bachelor's degree from Yale University and a Ph.D. from
Harvard, where he specialized in American literature. Beginning in 1981,
he served as J. Leland Miller Professor of American History, Literature,
and Eloquence at Williams College. Most of his scholarly work is in 19th
century American fiction. His books include Hawthorne and the Historical
Romance of New England (1971), The Development of American
Romance: The Sacrifice of Relation (1980), and The Problem of
American Realism: Studies in the Cultural History of a Literary Idea
(1993). He died in 1997, shortly after the following essay was published
in The Atlantic Monthly.

Michael Davitt Bell

Magic Time: Observations of a Cancer Casualty

For four years I've been battling (as they always say) cancer, and
now I've lost. I'm told I have the proverbial six months to live—which
I might, with luck and additional chemotherapy, be able to stretch to a
year. The sarcoma that appeared in my right thigh in the summer of
1992, that first metastasized in my lung in 1994 and cost me a kidney
a year later, has now spread all through my lungs. Beyond doubt I'm
dying. Nothing unusual here, of course—except that I find I not only
am reconciled to my fate but also have achieved a strange kind of happiness that's new in my experience.

In 1979 I had another cancer, a melanoma that was removed in a
simple outpatient procedure and did not recur. But by the end of my
first year of treatment for the sarcoma, with chemotherapy, radiation,
surgery to remove the original tumor, more chemotherapy, I had descended into a depression so severe that all sense of self was gone, all
desire, except for a persistent, repetitive series of affect-free fantasies
of specific and detailed ways I might kill myself.

I doubt that I can account fully for the level of happiness, even eu-
phoria, I've now reached, three years later and in the face of much
worse news. But some of it comes, I'm sure, from the fact that since the
cancer's appearance in my lung in the summer of 1994 revealed that
the original treatment hadn't eliminated the disease, and thus the sta-

tistical odds of my surviving were close to nil, I have determined to be open and honest with other people about my disease and my prognosis. I think this has also allowed me to be open and honest with myself.

My relationships with friends and family—above all with my two daughters, now in their twenties, whose mother and I divorced when they were small—have thus taken on an emotional openness and intensity almost inconceivable for someone who, like me, grew up in an upper-middle-class WASP family in the Midwest, a family in which the word "love" was never spoken or heard except, perhaps, to express admiration for an object or article of clothing ("I just *love* the way that sweater looks on you!"). So I find I'm not overcome with remorse or anger, or with terror of the fate awaiting me; instead I'm cherishing each moment, each mundane experience I have left. This is, for me, a magic time.

5   My own experience may be quite different from the experience of others in similar circumstances, or of those who love and care for them. But the general point here, a lesson I can share, is that for me over the past four years, after the traumas of treatment and of confronting my own death, the experience of dying of cancer may have been fundamentally about etiquette, about how one deals socially with people who don't have cancer and don't, for excellent reasons, really want to talk about it. Doctors, famously, need to keep professionally distant from their dying patients, and some even see such patients as a reproach, a token of failure. Friends and family don't want to seem intrusive or insensitive, and we are inevitably an unwelcome reminder of their own mortality. Nor are we who are about to die innocent of evasions and avoidance. I'd even guess that the popularity of cancer support groups stems from the chance not only to talk about common fears and experiences but also to be in a setting where this particular problem of etiquette, of figuring out how to talk to people who don't have cancer, who aren't dying, is for the moment suspended. Between the living and the dying a kind of wall seems to persist, a barrier of fear, shame, and perhaps most of all embarrassment.

I remember reading, back in the 1970s, a sociological study of paranoid behavior. Instead of analyzing the supposed paranoids for clinical symptoms, the researchers interviewed them *and* the people with whom they were routinely in contact: family, friends, fellow workers. What became evident was that when the supposed paranoids entered a room, these others actually did feel embarrassed and change the subject; they *had* been talking about the supposed paranoids behind their backs. So it is, perhaps, with the problem of etiquette for the dying.

Nevertheless, the wall can be breached; lines of communication can be kept open. As I say, I believe that my determination to keep breaching the wall accounts for my success in achieving acceptance and happiness in the face of my impending death. And this determination has extended even to strangers. People I've never met before— people I run into in stores, or at roadside rest stops where I'm walking my dog—ask what happened to the leg that was permanently stiffened by the removal of the original tumor. I don't put them off with "surgery" or "I hurt it." Briefly, I tell them what happened—describing the tumor, the surgery, sometimes even mentioning my current prognosis—and they're interested, concerned. Mindless pleasantry is transformed into actual conversation.

"Thanks for asking," I say to them, and I mean it.

"Hey," they reply. "Good luck!"

10   Worse things could happen.

To speak of manners in the context of cancer and dying may seem jarring, even insincere, but it shouldn't. For as the great novelists of manners, the Jane Austens and the Henry Jameses, all knew, the etiquette of communication and miscommunication, the comedy of understanding and misunderstanding, is not only deeply fascinating and entertaining but also profoundly significant. These novelists knew that once the misunderstandings have been cleared up, just before the ending, the possibility of love and of true communication has come to exist. And much more love, more interesting love, is possible than if no difficulties and misunderstandings had occurred in the first place. After all, you can't have the satisfying resolution of the ending if you don't start with conflict and crisis.

We who are about to die have relationships with our doctors, of course, and here, too, the etiquette of communication, what one might call bedside manners, raises interesting problems and complications.

My oncologist read an earlier version of this essay, and we discussed it over lunch. Although he liked it for the most part, he had one suggestion. "Don't you think," he said, "you should say more about your doctors?"

All right. With one exception my doctors have been wonderful. Again and again they've saved my life, or at least prolonged it, and I've been lucky to have prescribed for me the latest, least invasive procedures. Drastic as the treatment of my sarcoma seemed, it could have been much worse. Ten years ago the recommended procedure would have been to remove my leg at the hip.

15   Why, then, had I said so little about my doctors? What my oncologist may not have understood is how small a part doctors play in our *experience* of having cancer. We wait in hallways or antechambers for our appointments, often for a long time, and when at last we see our doctors, the consultations are understandably brief. In the hospital, where doctors govern everything we do, our direct experience of them is even more marginal: we're patients twenty-four hours a day, and our doctors' appearances on their rounds seem a matter of nanoseconds, something we might miss entirely if we were to blink. What's weirdest of all in this experience is the stark contrast between our doctors' pervasive power and their absence. Perhaps this is like the believer's experience of the deity.

Early in my treatment for sarcoma, in 1993, PBS broadcast Bill Moyers's series *Healing and the Mind*—programs about alternative, holistic methods for treating life-threatening diseases. Moyers avoided, I thought, one of the less agreeable implications of holistic approaches to illness: if you can help yourself get better by developing a more positive attitude, then it's your fault if you're not getting better, or are in fact dying.

Healing and the Mind did touch on another standard implication of the mind-body approach. At the heart of this approach is a familiar indictment of American medicine: that our doctors are educated to treat diseases rather than people, taught to deal with us impersonally, as carriers of symptoms, rather than holistically, as suffering individuals. This complaint is in some measure justified, to be sure. But as early as during my first hospital stay for chemotherapy I realized that this may be exactly what we want our doctors to do. We have far more at stake than they do in keeping everything but the clinical, technical details at bay. In such circumstances we may *want* to think of ourselves as sets of symptoms, as meat that's being fixed, rather than as people whose very souls are being sucked into our sickness. And then, while our doctors are doing their best to cure us, we blame them for our own denial.

Speaking of doctors, I finally decided recently that I should read the best seller by Sherwin B. Nuland, M.D., How We Die. Am I wrong, or has American taste in best sellers been getting weirder? How We Die: the ultimate self-help book—the last one you'll ever need! I've long fantasized that one might make the charts with a book called *Health Tips for the Dead*—or, even better, *More Health Tips for the Dead.*

I'm imagining myself here as a standup comic, or maybe a stand-up-while-I-can-still-stand (or while-you-can-still-stand-me) comic. I can't see if you're really out there—it's so dark, and I've got these stage lights in my eyes, and my jokes are getting no response, not a sound, not even the clink of ice in a glass, an idle cough or two.

20   "Hey!" I want to shout into the darkness, the silence. "Hey! Help me out! I'm *dying* up here!"

I know I'm being flippant. What's more important, I know why. We who are about to die (or at least this has been true in my case) sometimes focus on our relations with others in order to deny the most difficult and terrifying aspect of what I might call terminal etiquette: keeping open our lines of love and communication with ourselves. This is what I lost utterly during my terrible first year of treatment; I lost touch with who I was, with all sense of desire or purpose, and thus lost, as well, all sense of my connection to others, even my daughters.

From November through early February of that year I lived alone in an apartment in Boston, where I had had to move for treatment. I underwent two rounds of chemotherapy, in November and December, and then six weeks of radiation, beginning immediately after Christmas. I remember that late in January my younger daughter, who was then still in college, came up to stay for a week on her break between semesters. One night, as we played gin rummy before going to bed, I tried desperately to hide from her the shaking in my hand that left me barely able to hold my cards. I was that scared of the empty and meaningless hours looming in my future, of the sleepless night awaiting me, of the fact that I had no idea whatever of how I would spend the coming day. And this happened every night, with or without visitors. During the days I was numb, seeing everything as if from a great distance. I had lost the ability to cry. Although I had bought a portable stereo to console me in my exile, I had pretty much stopped listening to music. I tried, but I simply couldn't remember my life before the beginning of all this horror, what it had been like to be the person I had been. And I couldn't imagine ever returning to that life once my treatment was completed; I would never again be that person, or any person; nor would I be able to rediscover the emotional basis of my love for my friends or my daughters.

Once my definitive death sentence was upon me, I determined that this would not happen to me again, that I would not lose my ability to love and communicate with myself, and with it my ability to love others. For within ourselves is the highest wall, with its grim towers and parapets. On the near side stands the self that still functions in the sunny world of the mundane, the self so little different from you, my reader. On the far side lurks and slouches the unbearable, almost gothic knowledge of what is soon to happen: the awful pain, the progressive loss of personal autonomy and control of bodily function, and then (what will, of course, happen in time to all of us) the absolute and irrevocable annihilation of our very selves. In this process I will lose myself for sure, at the end; but I must not do so in the way I did during that terrible first year of treatment.

The popular name of this wall is Denial, and even to think of breaching it, of peering over at the dark and tangled wilderness on the other side, teeming with creatures of unspeakable disproportion, seems almost more than anyone should have to bear. Nevertheless, and often to the horror of my friends, I chose to read Nuland's book, to read the chapters devoted to exactly how one dies of cancer. If I was to love myself, to accept myself sufficiently to maintain my open love for those most dear to me, I just had to know.

25   Nuland describes, in considerable detail, the physical processes of dying from the most common forms of disease and trauma. He wants to dispel, he writes, the "scenarios" we compose about death—notably "the longed-for ideal of 'death with dignity.'" A story he tells at the outset identifies both his main purpose and his principal target audience—people whose loved ones are dying. The story is about a woman he had almost certainly cured of breast cancer, whose mother had then died of the same disease. The daughter had been horrified by the process. "Dr. Nuland," she had protested in despair, "there was no dignity in my mother's death!" Nuland reports that he offered her comfort by telling her, from his own expert perspective, that this was not unusual, that he had not often seen much dignity in the process by which we die.

Nuland's purpose seems clear enough. People about to go through the death of a loved one will be cured of their despair, much as all those mothers who turned to Dr. Spock in the 1950s were cured of their potential guilt: by being assured that what terrifies them is perfectly "normal." (Nuland's other great fifties touch—recalling to me my admiration as a teenager for James Dean in *Rebel Without a Cause*—is his extended description of cancer cells as "the juvenile delinquents of cellular society," as a "mob of maladjusted adolescents raging against the society from which it sprang." Could I start *identifying* with this disease?)

Fine, I thought, as I read Nuland's story of the woman horrified by her mother's hideous death; she's reassured. But what's in this story for his other potential audience: people who are themselves about to die, like me? Are we supposed to feel better about the agony we antici- pate—the loss of independence and bodily function, the onset of disin- tegration and pain? Are we supposed to feel better about all of this be- cause it's *normal*?

And why all the detail? "When we are familiar with the patterns of the illness that afflicts us," Nuland answers, "we disarm our imag- inings." So I read about the details of cancer, and how it finally kills you, as I sat on the deck of my country house on a radiant afternoon in early summer, with my yellow Labrador retriever lying at my side.

"Unrestrained and patternless growth," I read,

> enables a cancer to force its way into nearby vital structures to engulf them, prevent their functioning, and choke off their vitality. By this means, and by destroying the organs from whose stem cells they are made, the masses of cancer cells kill the gradually sickening person after feasting on the nutrients that were to have sustained him.

30 My dog shifted herself out of the sunlight and back into the slowly moving shadow cast by the deck umbrella, and I read about how tu- mors expand so rapidly that they exhaust the available blood supply. "The result," Nuland explains,

> is that a portion of an enlarging tumor may die, literally of malnutri- tion and oxygen lack. It is for this reason that cancers tend to ulcerate and bleed, sometimes producing thick, slimy deposits of necrotic tis- sue (from the Greek *nekrosis*, meaning "becoming dead") within their centers or at the periphery. . . . This is precisely why the ancients re- ferred to *karkinoma* as the "stinking death."

A hummingbird hovered above the bright-red feeder I had filled with sugar solution, and then darted for the woods across my lawn. The air was almost completely still. "Pneumonia and abscesses," I read,

> along with urinary and other infections, are frequently the immediate causes of death of cancer patients, and sepsis is their common termi- nal event. The profound weakness of severe cachexia [nutritional de-

pletion] does not permit effective coughing and respiration, increasing the chances of pneumonia and inhalation of vomitus. The final hours are sometimes accompanied by those deep, gurgling respirations that are one of the forms of the death rattle.

Whew! I guess my response should have been *What a relief!* As if my undisarmed imaginings could ever have come up with anything *this* bad. "Stinking death" indeed! I thought of Lauren Bacall's account, in the autobiography she published years ago, of what Bogart smelled like as he neared death, with so much of the tissue in his body already dead and rotting. I thought of the young widow who told me, shortly after the melanoma had been removed from my back, that by the time her husband had finally died from the spread of *his* melanoma, he'd lost half his body weight—and something like 80 percent of what remained had been cancer or necrotic tissue.

But Nuland is right, of course: it's essential to know just what to expect—or at least this has turned out to be true for me. And he's right, too, about the most urgent reason for this. "Real control," he observes, "requires one's own knowledge about the ways of sickness and death."

I'm not convinced that we can reach such knowledge without direct experience, but for me, at all events, it has seemed crucial to stay in touch with some concrete, if imaginary, pre-vision of my near and inevitable future. And for me the key word is "control." I want the story of my dying, however painful and disgusting it may be, to be *my* story, *my* "scenario," at least as much as possible. After all, it's the only story I have left.

Analyzing Rhetorical Choices

1. How does Bell stimulate the reader's interest in the opening two paragraphs?
2. Critique Bell's account of his response to Sherwin Nuland's book. He states that he is being flippant, but is that flippancy effective here? Why or why not?
3. At one point, Bell writes, "We who are about to die have relationships with our doctors." Why do you think he chooses this phrasing and places it so prominently in the essay? To what historical image or scene is he rhetorically linking himself?

4. When Bell writes, "My dog shifted herself out of the sunlight and back into the slowly moving shadow cast by the deck umbrella, and I read about how tumors expand so rapidly that they exhaust the available blood supply," is he simply stating facts or foreshadowing his own fate? Explain your viewpoint.

Writing About Issues and Contexts

1. What has allowed Bell to be open and honest with himself about cancer and human mortality?
2. What is Bell saying here about the kind of etiquette that surrounds someone who is dying of cancer? Why is this particular form of etiquette difficult for him? How is this problem reinforced by his anecdote about the sociological study of paranoid behavior?
3. What has Bell's losing struggle with cancer taught him? What lesson(s) does he want to teach us?
4. How do you read Bell's final paragraph? What does he mean by stating that he wants "the story of my dying, however painful and disgusting it may be, to be *my* story, *my* 'scenario'"?

Born in Boston to a father who was a physicist and mother who was an artist, **Sebastian Junger** *(1962–   ) has as primary literary influences major nonfiction writers Barry Lopez, Joan Didion, Peter Matthiessen, Norman Maclean, and Michael Herr.* The Perfect Storm *(1997), Junger's first book, was an improbable best-seller, given its highly detailed and technical focus on storms, swordfishing, and the history of Gloucester fishermen. The book was made into a feature film. Junger's second book,* Fire, *was published in 2001. This selection is from* The Perfect Storm.

Sebastian Junger
The Zero-Moment Point

Behold a pale horse, and his name who sat on him was Death, and Hell followed with him.

—Revelation 6:8

In the 1950s and 1960s, the U.S. Government decided to detonate a series of nuclear devices in the Pacific Ocean. The thinking was that deep water would absorb the shock wave and minimize the effect on the environment, while still allowing scientists to gauge the strength of the explosions. But an oceanographer named William Van Dorn, associated with the Scripps Institute in La Jolla, California, warned then that a nuclear explosion in the wrong place "could convert the entire continental shelf into a surf zone."

Concerned, the Navy ran a series of wave tank tests to see what kind of stresses their fleet could take. (They'd already lost three destroyers to a typhoon in 1944. Before going down the ships had radioed that they were rolling through arcs of 140 degrees. They downflooded through their stacks and sank.) The Navy subjected model destroyers and aircraft carriers to various kinds of waves and found that a single nonbreaking wave—no matter how big it was—was incapable of sinking a ship. A single *breaking* wave, though, would flip a ship end over end if it was higher than the ship was long. Typically, the ship would climb the wave at an angle of forty-five degrees, fail to gain the top, and then slide back down the face. Her stern would bury itself into the trough, and the crest of the wave would catch her bow and flip her over. This is called pitch-poling; Ernie Hazard was pitchpoled on Georges Bank. It's one of the few motions that can end ship-to-shore communication instantly.

Another is a succession of waves that simply drives the boat under—"founders," as mariners say. The dictionary defines founder as "to cave in, sink, fail utterly, collapse." On a steel boat the windows implode, the hatches fail, and the boat starts to downflood. The crew is prevented from escaping by the sheer force of the water pouring into the cabin—it's like walking into the blast of a firehose. In that sense, pitch-poling is better than foundering because an overturned boat traps air in the hold and can stay afloat for an hour or more. That might allow members of the crew to swim out a doorway and climb into a life raft. The rafts are designed to inflate automatically and release from the boat when she goes down. In theory the EPIRB floats free as well, and begins signalling to shore. All the crew has to do is stay alive.

By the late hours of October 28th the sea state is easily high enough to either pitch-pole the *Andrea Gail* or drive her under. And if she loses power—a clogged fuel filter, a fouled prop—she could slew to the side and roll. The same rule applies to capsizing as to pitch-poling: the wave must be higher than the boat is wide. The *Andrea Gail* is twenty feet across her beam. But even if the boat doesn't get hit by a nonnegotiable wave, the rising sea state allows Billy less and less leeway to maneuver. If he maintains enough speed to steer, he beats the boat to pieces; if he slows down, he loses rudder control. This is the end result of two days of narrowing options; now the only choice left is whether to go upsea or down, and the only outcome is whether they sink or float. There's not much in between.

5   If the conditions don't subside, the most Billy can realistically hope for is to survive until dawn. Then at least they'll have a chance of being rescued—now it's unthinkable. "In violent storms there is so much water in the air, and so much air in the water, that it becomes impossible to tell where the atmosphere stops and the sea begins," writes Van Dorn. "That may literally make it impossible to distinguish up from down." In such conditions a helicopter pilot could never pluck six people off the deck of a boat. So, for the next eight hours, the crew of the *Andrea Gail* must keep the pumps and engine running and just hope they don't encounter any rogue waves. Seventy-footers are roaming around the sea state like surly giants and there's not much Billy can do but take them head-on and try to get over the top before they break. If his floodlights are out he wouldn't even have that option—he'd just feel a drop into the trough, a lurch, and the boat starting up a slope way too steep to survive.

"Seventy foot seas—I'd be puttin' on my diapers at that point," says Charlie Reed. "I'd be quite nervous. That's higher than the highest point on the *Andrea Gail*. I once came home from the Grand Banks in thirty-five-foot seas. It was a scary fuckin' thought— straight up, straight down, for six days. My guess is that Billy turned side-to and rolled. You come off one of those seas cocked, the next one comes at a different angle, it pushes the boat around and then you roll. If the boat flips over—even with everything dogged down— water's gonna get in. The boat's upside-down, the plywood's buckling, that's the end."

When Ernie Hazard went over on Georges Bank in 1982, the motion wasn't a violent one so much as a huge, slow somersault that laid the boat over on her back. Hazard remembers one wave spinning them around and another lifting them end over end. It wasn't like rolling a car at high speeds, it was more like rolling a house. Hazard was thirty-three at the time; three years earlier he'd answered a newspaper ad and got a job on the *Fair Wind*, a lobster boat out of Newport, Rhode Island. The storm hit on their last trip of the year, late November. The crew were all good friends; they celebrated the end of their season at a steakhouse and then left for Georges Bank late the next morning. The winds were light and the forecast called for several more days of fair weather. By dawn it was blowing a hundred:

> We were driving the boat well. You point the boat into the sea and try to hold your own until it blows out—stay there, take your pounding. You balance the boat, flood the tanks, try to save what you have on deck. There was the typical howling of wind in the wires and there was a lot of foam because of the wind, yellow foam, spindrift. We'd lose power on the waves because they were more foam than water, the propeller just couldn't bite.
>
> It happened quick. We were close to the edge of the continental shelf and the seas were getting large, starting to break. Cresting. I remember looking out the pilothouse and this monster wave came and broke over the bow and forced us backwards. There was nothing to hold us there and we must have dug the stern in and then spun around. Now we're in a full following sea. We never went more than one more wave when we buried our bow in the trough and flipped over. There was the wave breaking and then a sensation of the boat turning, and the next thing I knew we were upside-down. Floating inside the boat.
>
> I happened to surface in a small air pocket and I didn't know if I was upside-down or standing on the walls or what. I made a dive into the pilothouse and I could see some light—it could have been a win-

dow or a porthole, I don't know—and when I got back up into the wheelhouse there was no more air. It was all gone. I was thinking, "This is it. Just take a mouthful of water and it's over." It was very matter-of-fact. I was at a fork in the road and there was work to do—swim or die. It didn't scare me, I didn't think about my family or anything. It was more businesslike. People think you always have to go for life, but you don't. You can quit.

For reasons that he still doesn't understand, Hazard didn't quit. He made a guess and swam. The entire port side of the cabin was welded steel and he knew if he picked that direction, he was finished. He felt himself slide through a narrow opening—the door? a window?—and suddenly he was back in the world. The boat was hull-up, sliding away fast, and the life raft was convulsing at the end of its tether. It was his only hope; he wriggled out of his clothes and started to swim.

Whether the *Andrea Gail* rolls, pitch-poles, or gets driven down, she winds up, one way or another, in a position from which she cannot recover. Among marine architects this is known as the zero-moment point—the point of no return. The transition from crisis to catastrophe is fast, probably under a minute, or someone would've tripped the EPIRB. (In fact the EPIRB doesn't even signal when it hits the water, which means it has somehow malfunctioned. In the vast majority of cases, the Coast Guard knows when men are dying offshore.) There's no time to put on survival suits or grab a life vest; the boat's moving through the most extreme motion of her life and there isn't even time to shout. The refrigerator comes out of the wall and crashes across the galley. Dirty dishes cascade out of the sink. The TV, the washing machine, the VCR tapes, the men, all go flying. And, seconds later, the water moves in.

10   When a boat floods, the first thing that happens is that her electrical system shorts out. The lights go off, and for a few moments the only illumination is the frenetic blue of sparks arcing down into the water. It's said that people in extreme situations perceive things in distorted, almost surreal ways, and when the wires start to crackle and burn, perhaps one of the crew thinks of fireworks—of the last Fourth of July, walking around Gloucester with his girlfriend and watching colors blossom over the inner harbor. There'd be tourists shuffling down Rogers Street and fishermen hooting from bars and the smell of gunpowder and fried clams drifting through town. He'd have his whole life ahead of him, that July evening; he'd have every choice in the world.

And he wound up swordfishing. He wound up, by one route or another, on this trip, in this storm, with this boat filling up with water and one or two minutes left to live. There's no going back now, no rescue helicopter that could possibly save him. All that's left is to hope it's over fast.

When the water first hits the trapped men, it's cold but not paralyzing, around fifty-two degrees. A man can survive up to four hours in that temperature if something holds him up. If the boat rolls or flips over, the men in the wheelhouse are the first to drown. Their experience is exactly like Hazard's except that they don't make it out of the wheelhouse to a life raft; they inhale and that's it. After that the water rises up the companionway, flooding the galley and berths, and then starts up the inverted engine room hatch. It may well be pouring in the aft door and the fish hatch, too, if either failed during the sinking. If the boat is hull-up and there are men in the engine room, they are the last to die. They're in absolute darkness, under a landslide of tools and gear, the water rising up the companionway and the roar of the waves probably very muted through the hull. If the water takes long enough, they might attempt to escape on a lungful of air—down the companionway, along the hall, through the aft door and out from under the boat—but they don't make it. It's too far, they die trying. Or the water comes up so hard and fast that they can't even think. They're up to their waists and then their chests and then their chins and then there's no air at all. Just what's in their lungs, a minute's worth or so.

The instinct not to breathe underwater is so strong that it overcomes the agony of running out of air. No matter how desperate the drowning person is, he doesn't inhale until he's on the verge of losing consciousness. At that point there's so much carbon dioxide in the blood, and so little oxygen, that chemical sensors in the brain trigger an involuntary breath whether he's underwater or not. That is called the "break point"; laboratory experiments have shown the break point to come after eighty-seven seconds. It's a sort of neurological optimism, as if the body were saying, *Holding our breath is killing us, and breathing in might not kill us, so we might as well breathe in.* If the person hyperventilates first—as free divers do, and as a frantic person might—the break point comes as late as 140 seconds. Hyperventilation initially flushes carbon dioxide out of the system, so it takes that much longer to climb back up to critical levels.

Until the break point, a drowning person is said to be undergoing "voluntary apnea," choosing not to breathe. Lack of oxygen to the brain causes a sensation of darkness closing in from all sides, as in a camera aperture stopping down. The panic of a drowning person is mixed with an odd incredulity that this is actually happening. Having never done it before, the body—and the mind—do not know how to die gracefully. The process is filled with desperation and awkwardness. "So *this* is drowning," a drowning person might think. "So *this* is how my life finally ends."

15   Along with the disbelief is an overwhelming sense of being wrenched from life at the most banal, inopportune moment imaginable. "I can't die, I have tickets to next week's game," is not an impossible thought for someone who is drowning. The drowning person may even feel embarrassed, as if he's squandered a great fortune. He has an image of people shaking their heads over his dying so senselessly. The drowning person may feel as if it's the last, greatest act of stupidity in his life.

These thoughts, shriek through the mind during the minute or so that it takes a panicked person to run out of air. When the first involuntary breath occurs most people are still conscious, which is unfortunate, because the only thing more unpleasant than running out of air is breathing in water. At that point the person goes from voluntary to involuntary apnea, and the drowning begins in earnest. A spasmodic breath drags water into the mouth and windpipe, and then one of two things happen. In about ten percent of people, water—anything—touching the vocal cords triggers an immediate contraction in the muscles around the larynx. In effect, the central nervous system judges something in the voice box to be more of a threat than low oxygen levels in the blood, and acts accordingly. This is called a laryngospasm. It's so powerful that it overcomes the breathing reflex and eventually suffocates the person. A person with laryngospasm drowns without any water in his lungs.

In the other ninety percent of people, water floods the lungs and ends any waning transfer of oxygen to the blood. The clock is running down now; half-conscious and enfeebled by oxygen depletion, the person is in no position to fight his way back up to the surface. The very process of drowning makes it harder and harder not to drown, an exponential disaster curve similar to that of a sinking boat.

Occasionally someone makes it back from this dark world, though, and it's from these people that we know what drowning feels like. In 1892 a Scottish doctor named James Lowson was on a steamship bound for Colombo, Sri Lanka, when they ran into a typhoon and went down in the dead of night. Most of the 150 people on board sank with the ship, but Lowson managed to fight his way out of the hold and over the side. The ship sank out from under his feet, dragging him down, and the last thing he remembers is losing consciousness underwater. A few minutes later the buoyancy of his life vest shot him to the surface, though, and he washed up on an island and lived to write about his experiences in the *Edinburgh Medical Journal*. He attributed the clarity of his recollection to the "preternatural calm" of people facing death. It's as close as one is going to get to the last moments of the *Andrea Gail:*

> All afternoon the hammering of the big seas on the doomed vessel went on, whilst night came only to add darkness to our other horrors. Shortly before ten o'clock three tremendous seas found their way down the stokehole, putting out the fires, and our situation was desperate. The end came shortly before midnight, when there was a heavy crash on the reef, and the vessel was lying at the bottom of the Straits of Formosa in under a minute.
>
> With scarcely time to think I pulled down the life-belts and, throwing two to my companions, tied the third on myself and bolted for the companionway. There was no time to spare for studying humanity at this juncture, but I can never forget the apparent want of initiative in all I passed. All the passengers seemed paralyzed—even my companions, some of them able military men. The stewards of the ship, uttering cries of despair and last farewells, blocked the entrance to the deck, and it was only by sheer force I was able to squeeze past them. Getting out on deck, a perfect mountain of water seemed to come from overhead, as well as from below, and dashed me against the bridge companionway. The ship was going down rapidly, and I was pulled down with her, struggling to extricate myself.
>
> I got clear under water and immediately struck out to reach the surface, only to go farther down. This exertion was a serious waste of breath, and after ten or fifteen seconds the effort of inspiration could no longer be restrained. It seemed as if I was in a vice which was gradually being screwed up tight until it felt as if the sternum and spinal column must break. Many years ago my old teacher used to describe how painless and easy a death by drowning was—"like falling about in a green field in early summer"—and this flashed across my brain at the time. The "gulping" efforts became less frequent, and the pressure seemed unbearable, but gradually the pain seemed to ease up. I appeared to be in a pleasant dream, although I had enough will power to think of friends at home and the sight of the Grampians, familiar to me as a boy, that was brought into my view. Before losing consciousness the chest pain had completely disappeared and the sensation was actually pleasant.
>
> When consciousness returned, I found myself at the surface, and managed to get a dozen good inspirations. Land was about four hun-

dred yards distant, and I used a bale of silk and then a long wooden plank to assist me to shore. On landing, and getting behind a sheltering rock, no effort was required to produce copious emesis. After the excitement, sound sleep set in, and this sleep lasted three hours, when a profuse diarrhea came on, evidently brought on by the sea water ingested. Until morning broke all my muscles were in a constant tremor which could not be controlled. (Several weeks later) I was sleeping in a comfortable bed and, late in the evening, a nightmare led to my having a severe struggle with the bedroom furniture, finally taking a "header" out of the bed and coming to grief on the floor.

Lowson guesses that laryngospasm prevented water from entering his lungs when he was unconscious. The crew of the *Andrea Gail* either have laryngospasms or completely inundated lungs. They are suspended, open-eyed and unconscious, in the flooded enclosures of the boat. The darkness is absolute and the boat may already be on her way to the bottom. At this point only a massive amount of oxygen could save these men. They have suffered, at most, a minute or two. Their bodies, having imposed increasingly drastic measures to keep functioning, have finally started to shut down. Water in the lungs washes away a substance called surfactant, which enables the alveoli to leach oxygen out of the air. The alveoli themselves, grape-like clusters of membrane on the lung wall, collapse because blood cannot get through the pulmonary artery. The artery has constricted in an effort to shunt blood to areas of the lungs where there is more oxygen. Unfortunately, those don't exist. The heart labors under critically low levels of oxygen and starts to beat erratically—"like a bag full of worms," as one doctor says. This is called ventricular fibrillation. The more irregularly the heart beats, the less blood it moves and the faster life functions decline. Children—who have proportionally stronger hearts than adults—can maintain a heartbeat for up to five minutes without air. Adults die faster. The heart beats less and less effectively until, after several minutes, there's no movement at all. Only the brain is alive.

20   The central nervous system does not know what has happened to the body; all it knows is that not enough oxygen is getting to the brain. Orders are still being issued—*Breathe! Pump! Circulate!*— that the body cannot obey. If the person were defibrillated at that moment, he might possibly survive. He could be given cardiopulmonary resuscitation, put on a respirator, and coaxed back to life. Still, the body is doing everything it can to delay the inevitable. When cold water touches the face, an impulse travels along the trigeminal and vagus nerves to the central nervous system and lowers the metabolic rate. The pulse slows down and the blood pools where it's needed most, in the heart and skull. It's a sort of temporary hibernation that drastically reduces

the body's need for oxygen. Nurses will splash ice water on the face of a person with a racing heart to trigger the same reaction.

The diving reflex, as this is called, is compounded by the general effect of cold temperature on tissue—it preserves it. All chemical reactions, and metabolic processes, become honey-slow, and the brain can get by on less than half the oxygen it normally requires. There are cases of people spending forty or fifty minutes under lake ice and surviving. The colder the water, the stronger the diving reflex, the slower the metabolic processes, and the longer the survival time. The crew of the *Andrea Gail* do not find themselves in particularly cold water, though; it may add five or ten minutes to their lives. And there is no one around to save them anyway. The electrical activity in their brain gets weaker and weaker until, after fifteen or twenty minutes, it ceases altogether.

The body could be likened to a crew that resorts to increasingly desperate measures to keep their vessel afloat. Eventually the last wire has shorted out, the last bit of decking has settled under the water. Tyne, Pierre, Sullivan, Moran, Murphy, and Shatford are dead.

Analyzing Rhetorical Choices

1. How do Junger's technical details contribute to the overall effectiveness of his account, particularly his account of the act of drowning?
2. Junger refers to the captain, Billy Tyne, by just his first name, Billy. How does this familiarity affect the reader?
3. Analyze the various stylistic and rhetorical devices that Junger employs in the three paragraphs beginning with, "When a boat floods, the first thing that happens is that her electrical system shorts out." How would you describe his language, his use of transitions, his formality or informality, his choice of verbs and descriptive words and phrases?

Writing About Issues and Contexts

1. Cite at least three cause-and-effect relationships described by Junger. How does he use the cause-and-effect relationship to create momentum in the reader to keep turning pages?
2. How does Junger make us experience what Billy Tyne and the crew are experiencing aboard the *Andrea Gail*, considering that he was not there and cannot know for sure what happened to the ship?
3. In what ways does Junger compare what happens to the crew to what happens to their ship? Why do you think he does that?

Strategies for Writers: Cause and Effect

1. The mode of cause and effect, more than most ways of organizing your essays, is closely tied to logic. Think of several mishaps that have occurred to you or that you've seen on television. With your classmates, discuss the causes and the ultimate effects of these mini-disasters. Then think of other effects and trace their causes, particularly in relation to people featured in the media. Some possibilities: Jackie Mason, Michael Jackson, Tonya Harding, Gary Hart, Ingrid Bergman. How did these figures become the object of public scorn? How, if at all, did they alter that public perception?

2. Cause-and-effect relationships also connect very directly to argument. Fallacious reasoning has its root in poorly conceived cause and effect. Rigorous thinking directly connects an effect with its real cause, not simply something that is associated with the effect. Many superstitions, for example, have their foundations in false cause-and-effect relations. Eric Hansen's discussion of superstition, for example, draws on this apparent relation between a consequence and its supposed cause. How does his account compare with Sharon Begley's in "The Stereotype Trap"? What other misuses of cause-and-effect have you noticed? Consider the self-fulfilling prophecy: An effect can actually be created, even if you or someone else has merely invented the cause. ("I am female; therefore, I am not good at math," or "She's Asian American; therefore she must be good at math.")

3. Debate with your classmates whether poor writing is a result of not knowing grammar or whether using a particular language variety is evidence of poor writing ability or lack of intelligence. Why are some varieties of language more acceptable than others? Consider engaging in library research on this controversial topic. How do we use or misuse cause-and-effect to reinforce our stereotypes of various people and groups in terms of their language use?

4. Compare and contrast the cause-and-effect arguments in the articles written by Norman Cousins (Chapter 10) and Norman Mailer (this chapter). Can you look beyond the immediate causes of the fighter's death? To what effect? Which one of these essays has the most compelling argument? Does it involve clear cause-and-effect? Explain.

5. The cause-and-effect relationships in Louise Erdrich's story, "Sister Godzilla," are far more ambiguous than one would usually expect. What is the cause-and-effect relationship between the nun's grotesque appearance and the various effects this has on her students? One of the fascinating things about cause-and-effect relationships is the way in which we are often left to speculate, rather than having the relationship spelled out in formulaic fashion. What other essays in this section evoke this sense of ambiguity? Why? What might be another subject that allows you to engage in this type of rich analysis?

6. Both Atul Gawande and Sebastian Junger draw on highly scientific frameworks to explore their subjects. In what ways does their reliance upon empirical research influence the way they develop and present their subjects? How effective are these two presentations? What kinds of readers do they anticipate by writing the way they do?

Research and Writing Assignments

1. Atul Gawande uses his medical school background and understanding of the scientific method to analyze the causes of the common cold. He posits a hypothesis, examines the scientific experiment that is set up to test that hypothesis, and then reports the results. What is particularly striking, however, is that this scientific method fails to solve the two basic questions that concern Gawande—namely, what causes a cold and how best to prevent one. In an essay, examine the strengths and weaknesses of the scientific method, especially when it comes to health issues. During the past 30 or so years, the medical establishment has issued recommendations and advisories concerning eggs, butter, margarine, fen-fen, hormone supplements, preservatives, and herbal remedies, among others. Choose a specific subject, research what the scientific establishment has reported, and write an essay that weighs the strengths and weaknesses of their methods and conclusions. What can we learn from scientific analysis? What are the lengths and limits of this kind of inquiry?

2. "A Black Man Ponders His Ability to Alter Public Space," "The Stereotype Trap," and "Sister Godzilla" explore the consequences of stereotypes and superficial judgments based on

physical characteristics, both those we apply to others and those we (sometimes unconsciously) apply to ourselves. In an essay that draws on both personal history and library research, offer your views on the power, both negative and positive, of stereotyping and how we might best disrupt the negative cause-and-effect relationship negative stereotyping creates. How do we distinguish between positive and negative stereotyping? (Is there such a thing as positive stereotyping?) Can we have one without the other? How do we overcome negative stereotypes? How can we get beyond superficial impressions rooted in mis-understanding? If stereotyping is impossible to eliminate, how do we control it within our personal and professional lives? There are enough questions and issues here to form the subject of a book, so focus your essay on a particular kind of stereotyp-ing or a specific incident. You might want to reread related se-lections by Toni Cade Bambara, Countee Cullen, and Henry Louis Gates, Jr. (Chapter 5); Frederick Douglass (Chapter 7); and Cornel West (Chapter 8).

3. Eric Hansen's account of traveling in the Borneo countryside explores two competing ways of understanding cause and ef-fect: a Western way that honors scientific logic and a more na-tive way that honors a religious, mythic, and spiritual logic. We are often tempted to call the latter superstition. In an essay that draws on library research, explore the subject of superstition by examining one such practice among native people in America, Africa, Europe, or Asia. You might want to focus on forms of behavior that center on certain major rites of passage: birth, adolescence, marriage, or death. What forms of logic prevail? How does this particular practice make sense within this cul-ture? What insights does it provide in terms of some of our own "superstitious" practices?

4. Should boxing be outlawed? Does boxing represent an impor-tant aspect of the sporting tradition? Now that women are box-ing professionally, does the sport offer a more humane sense of competition than that described by Norman Mailer (and repre-sented elsewhere in this book by Elizabeth Alexander, Jodi Kantor, and Norman Cousins)? Offer your perspective in an es-say that takes these three selections into account. Researching the history and tradition of boxing should be part of the work you do in writing your essay.

5. Michael Davitt Bell writes, "Beyond doubt I'm dying. Nothing unusual here, of course—except that I find I not only am reconciled to my fate but also have achieved a strange kind of happiness that's new in my experience." Using this statement as a departure point, write an essay addressed to the general public that considers how we can best make sense of the inevitability of death. Certainly, many religions are concerned with death (and a possible afterlife), but in your essay, be aware that many readers (including religious ones) do not share this view. How do you think all of us can make sense of death and integrate this thinking into our lives in useful and productive ways, as Bell apparently did?

6. The selections by Norman Mailer, Michael Davitt Bell, and Sebastian Junger all focus (at least in part) on death. So do several other essays in this book, such as those by E. B. White (Chapter 3) and Jessica Mitford (Chapter 7). Junger's writing in particular is almost a blow-by-blow description of the last moments in a capsized ship, with specific attention on what likely happened to the *Andrea Gail* as she foundered and sank with the loss of all men on board. Why does the subject of death fascinate most readers? Why is it such a constant in stories, essays, poems, drama? Write an essay that draws on Junger's piece and other essays in this book to analyze why so many authors write about a subject whose meaning must elude us.

10
Argument

The Importance of Argument

It might be said that the world moves forward primarily through two modes: narration and argument, the modes that open and close this book. Narration can act as a powerful mode for change: Through the telling of stories, people often attempt to change each other's ideas, views, and values—think of the Bible and other religious and mythic accounts, novels and illustrative stories, films and television. From inspirational biographies of people like Gandhi or the seven astronauts who died aboard the shuttle *Columbia*, to the wringing confessions we hear in the popular media such as on *Oprah* and *Dr. Phil*, to the imaginative tales we enjoy in *Harry Potter* and *Lord of the Rings*—the narratives we hear change us, sometimes profoundly.

At least as important as narration, however, is argument, that other life-changing mode. Unlike narration, which appeals strongly to the imagination, argument appeals to the logical part of our minds, for it depends upon the presentation of proof, evidence, and clear reasoning in order to push us toward a specific conclusion, often while showing the inadequacies of another perspective. While narration depends on character, conflict, motion, and setting to move us forward, argument depends on logic, empirical evidence, abstract thinking, and formal analysis. Although argument can be expressed in a variety of modes, including narration, the kinds of arguments highlighted in this section are generally founded on rhetorical principles that are *presentational* and *expositional* in character. These are the kinds of arguments we hear when, for example, Colin Powell made a presentation to the United Nations General Assembly arguing that Saddam Hussein possessed weapons of mass destruction, was concealing them, represented a threat to his neighbors and the world, and therefore must be removed from power, either by the UN, an international coalition, or by the United States acting largely alone. They are also the kinds of arguments we hear when lawyers present their cases to the Supreme Court about gun control, abortion rights, or capital punishment; when legislators advocate for specific forms of legislation centered on tax reform or universal health coverage; when salespeople in an appliance store try to persuade customers to buy the latest model of television or a snappy new personal digital assistant.

Argument is thus a vitally important mode, one with universal value in our culture. To argue well is to find ways to persuade others to change their minds and actions; thus argument and persuasion are closely bound up with each other. Persuasion is the means by which skilled writers and speakers make their arguments effective by choosing the best examples, excellent wording and phrasing, and the most artful and sophisticated ways to present their evidence. Rather than create artificial distinctions between *argument* and *persuasion*, we'll consider argument to include that famous dictum, "all the available means of persuasion." A good argument draws upon all those persuasive elements that have been discussed and illustrated throughout this book. Further, we will restrict this discussion to arguments that have an ethical basis, thus excluding propaganda, diatribes, and physical intimidation from our discussion. No doubt rants and threats alter behavior, but they have little to do with the kinds of careful, considered reasoning that is most prized in academic settings.

Even when the subject is focused in this way, it is perhaps not surprising that argument is often viewed negatively by many people. "Don't give me an argument about that," one friend might say to another. "She's got a lot of ideas but is way too argumentative," someone might say about an acquaintance. "Every time we get together, all he does is argue with me," another complains. Few of us look forward to getting into an argument, and most of us would rather not spend time with someone who is argumentative. That said, our intention in this section of *Rhetorical Choices* is to rehabilitate the term *argument*, especially in the context of academic writing. Writing a good argument essay is considered by many teachers and students to be the most challenging assignment of all because it is the most complex and abstract in terms of form and structure. In many academic disciplines, learning how to engage in constructive argument is the litmus test for accomplishment: It is the chief way one demonstrates mastery of a subject. Offering a hypothesis and developing forms of proof in a science class on genetic engineering or advocating for the universality of individual civil liberties in a political science class are both forms of advanced argumentation. English, philosophy, history, sociology, and many other disciplines require students to develop a specific perspective and develop the means to support it through careful research and analysis. This chapter introduction itself offers a series of brief arguments *about* argument, thus reinforcing how ubiquitous it is to our thinking and being in the world.

"It's the Economy Stupid"

The best way to illustrate how argument works is to analyze it in operation. Printed below are two short opinion essays on the economy, specifically on tax cut legislation. Although focused on the Bush tax cut proposals put before Congress in 2003, they have a timeless quality: Economists, politicians, and everyday Americans are continuously debating the role of the federal government, local/state/federal autonomy, how best to fuel the nation's economy, whether federal tax dollars should be increased or decreased, whether tax dollars should be allocated to the poor in order to improve their lives and fund social programs, or whether tax dollars should be allocated to wealthier Americans in order to fuel investment and individual savings. Here are two perspectives that offer contrasting arguments on these timeless and complex concerns.

Tax Cuts Alone Cannot Shrink Government
Without reform, government spending threatens to eliminate the economic benefits of last year's tax cut.
by Wayne T. Brough, Ph.D.

The U.S. Treasury recently announced that the government is running a deficit of <u>$66.5 billion</u> for the first seven months of the fiscal year. Increased government spending coupled with a downturn in revenues has pushed the federal government back into deficit spending. Despite this dramatic swing in fiscal balances, the federal budget continues to flounder in Congress, with the Senate unwilling or unable to even establish parameters to limit federal spending. Indeed, the congressional urge to spend is threatening to eliminate the economic benefits of lower taxes.

With time running short, Senate Majority Leader Tom Daschle (D-SD) has yet to bring a budget resolution to the floor. The resolution is an important step in the budgetary process, because it provides overall guidelines for spending. Without the resolution, there are fewer constraints on the appropriations process and more room for mischief when bills come to the floor. Some have suggested the House and Senate adopt "deeming resolutions" or extend the expiring budget caps to constrain appropriators, but with the Senate unwilling to adopt a budget resolution, it is not evident that the alternatives would fare any better.

While Republicans attribute the deficit's return to the war on terrorism and Democrats blame it on President Bush's tax cut, the simple fact remains that Congress lacks the fiscal discipline to live within its means. The growth of government is well chronicled. The recent $190 billion farm bill dropped all pretense of attempting a more market-based approach to agriculture. In addition, Congress is moving forward with a supplemental spending bill of almost $30 billion, along with a budget that includes $768 billion in discretionary spending.

Government spending not only means a greater burden for American taxpayers, it also has an impact on the economy's performance. A <u>study</u> by Professors Richard K. Vedder and Lowell E. Galloway demonstrates that throughout the 20th century, as the size of government grew, the economy suffered. Conversely, the greatest economic growth occurred as the role of government in the economy receded. The study also suggests that it is not surprising that surpluses have turned to deficits. Since World War II, increased federal spending has quickly dissipated any surpluses.

True to form, Congress continues to spend at a pace that diverts resources from productive uses in the private sector to redistributive uses by the government. Discretionary spending has increased significantly, much of it not related to defense. At the same time, Congress has repeatedly failed to address ailing entitlement programs that are a significant strain on the fiscal budget. This budget year, Social Security, Medicare, and Medicaid have been the largest drain on federal revenues and should warrant serious federal oversight. Each of these programs is staving off failure; outdated policies, changing demographics, and simple waste, fraud, and abuse are chronic problems. Without much-needed reform, these entitlement programs will continue to increase pressure on the federal budget.

President Bush ran on a platform of lower taxes, and Congress passed the legislation enacting those tax cuts. Voting for the tax cut meant more than a tax rebate for constituents; it was an important vote about the size and scope of government. The American people opted for a smaller government. Unfortunately, Congress has yet to deliver. It is important to remember that tax cuts alone cannot boost the economy—government spending must follow suit. If the government does not alter its behavior, resources will continue to flow from the private sector to government coffers.

When Congress continues spending in the wake of a tax cut, the bill eventually comes due, and the federal government will need to have the wherewithal to pay. The government has three options, none of which is conducive to economic growth. The first option is to print money. However, as the 1970s demonstrated, inflation can have a debilitating effect on economic growth. The second option is to borrow. The federal government can seek to raise money in the financial markets, which, again, has adverse effects on economic growth. While deficits may not directly translate into higher interest rates, many government programs have marginal, or even negative, rates of return, so excessive government spending will result in lower economic growth than if resources were left in the more productive private sector. Finally, a Congress determined to spend can simply abandon tax cuts, which many in Congress appear willing to do; opting instead to generate more revenues to satisfy profligate policies.

Sadly, Congress has done little to heed the call for a more limited government. The Senate used procedural rules to block a permanent reduction in taxes, leaving all of the Bush tax cuts to expire after ten years. The Death Tax, which is costly to administer and a poor source of revenue, is up for repeal, but the Senate leadership is playing games to minimize the chances of actually eliminating the tax. And Congress continues to spend in the face of burgeoning deficits. For many in Congress, it seems to be business as usual, which suggests that further reforms may be necessary to secure the benefits of tax cuts. Institutional reforms that make it more difficult to raise taxes or increase spending levels may be an important element of efforts to limit the size and scope of government. In the past, Congress has successfully avoided balanced budget amendments, supermajorities for tax increases and other restraints on congressional behavior. But in the face of renewed government expansion and rising deficits, it may be time to revisit ways to impose fiscal discipline on Congress.

Trickle Down Again
by Matthew Rothschild

George W. Bush's stimulus program is a stimulus for the country club set.

This year, according to the Citizens for Tax Justice, the top 1% of Americans—those making $374,000 or more—stand to gain $30,000 each, while the lowest 20% will get only a $6 tax cut. Go buy yourself a cheeseburger and a beer on George!

Looking at it another way, the top 5% will get 47% of the benefits, while the bottom 60% will get only 8% of the benefits.

What's more, eliminating the dividend tax is permanent, while other tax breaks in the plan are temporary.

Aside from being grossly skewed toward his golfing buddies, Bush's plan is not a smart way to jump-start the economy.

First of all, it is back-loaded. Robert Greenstein, executive director of the Center on Budget and Policy Priorities, notes, "It would cost $674 billion through 2013 but would put out only $102 billion in the first year, the period when the stimulus is needed."

And secondly, it is geared precisely to the population that is least likely to spend the money right away. The wealthy traditionally save more than the poor and the middle class, who have pressing needs that they are waiting to meet but can't afford.

A tax cut to the poor and middle class would be spent on vital things in a hurry, thus injecting money into the economy and spurring growth. But just fattening a wealthy person's bank balance would not do much for the economy.

There are obvious things that would help: exempting the first $10,000 or $20,000 of payroll taxes, or giving states more money to make up for the deficits they face, as the Democrats proposed. (Instead, Bush's abolition of the dividend tax will hurt states because they won't collect their own share of dividend taxes, and tax-free state bonds will no longer be as attractive to investors who would now invest in stocks giving tax-free dividends.)

Bush did propose a few things that might help, like upping the child care credit, extending unemployment benefits, and offering re-training grants to up to 1.2 million workers.

And Bush is right to be worried about the lagging economy, and to be willing to go deeper into deficit to try to dig us out. The Republicans make strange Keynesians, but that doesn't mean they're wrong here. The U.S. deficit as a percentage of GDP has been falling, so the United States is not about to go bankrupt. And the economy needs an injection of spending to ward off a recession and a crisis of overcapacity leading to deflation.

Deficits are not the serious problem they are made out to be. But Republicans have been playing games with this issue forever. When the budget used to be in a deficit, they moaned and groaned and said there was no room for any spending on urgent social programs. Now, when the budget is again in deficit, they say they can give away $674 billion in taxes and run up an Iraq war bill that may be anywhere from $50 billion to $200 billion. (There is always money for war, corporations, and the rich, it seems, and never for health care, housing, or the elimination of hunger and poverty.)

Democrats are right to call Republicans hypocrites here, but they shouldn't be advocating less spending. They should be advocating spending that is fairer and more productive.

For Bush's part, I can't imagine why he would want to propose such a lopsided tax program.

I guess he just couldn't resist sending early Valentines presents to all his friends.

Each of these authors writes with passion, has a clear focus or central idea that he wants to develop, and possesses knowledge about his subject. Brough and Rothschild are not writing in opposition to each other, although if put on a panel they might well disagree about how best to allocate taxes and the role of the federal government. Let's examine each essay more closely and then ask a series of questions that would help us determine the strengths and weaknesses offered by each of these arguments.

Brief Summary, Wayne T. Brough, "Tax Cuts Alone Cannot Shrink Government": Brough believes tax cuts are generally beneficial because, he contends, the smaller the size of the government, the stronger the economy. He states that "as the size of government grew, the economy suffered. Conversely, the greatest economic growth occurred as the role of government in the economy receded." He further states that the American people support this view (they supported Bush's tax cut proposal in 2000), and once we cut taxes, the only way to improve the economy is for Congress to curb spending.

Brief Summary, Matthew Rothschild, "Trickle Down Again": Rothschild believes that the Bush tax cut proposal for 2003 is unfair and unjust. He makes that point in his first sentence: "George W. Bush's stimulus program is a stimulus for the country club set." He does not address the issue of government spending or the size of the federal government. Rather, his focus is on the scope and nature of the tax cut, which in his view puts money into the wrong hands: "A tax cut to the poor and middle class would be spent on vital things in a hurry, thus injecting money into the economy and spurring growth. But just fattening a wealthy person's bank balance would not do much for the economy." To end the recession, spur the economy, and serve specific social interests, Rothschild wants the tax cuts to go to the poor and to improve health care, housing, and hunger relief for low- and middle-income families.

Analyzing Arguments

How effective are Wayne Brough and Matthew Rothschild in making their respective arguments? We'll examine various strategies of each, although the following discussion is not intended to be exhaustive. We invite you to engage in a further discussion about the various rhetorical strategies that they employ—and how effective they are in persuading you of their different positions.

State Thesis Early

Brough puts his thesis into the title and subtitle of his essay. The argument is explicit: government must reform itself by shrinking (its size and its spending) in order to solidify the benefits of the 2001 tax cuts (and any future tax cuts enabled by federal legislation). Rothschild implies his argument in his title (tax cuts that go primarily to the rich are known as "trickle down" proposals because the financial benefits slowly trickle down to the middle and working class). His first sentence states his thesis and the rest of the essay expands on that idea.

Establish Your Authority

Rothschild is a regular columnist for *The Progressive*, the periodical that published this review. His credentials are well known to his readers, who follow his columns regularly in that magazine. Like any author who writes a column for a newspaper or magazine, he establishes trust in his readers by speaking with authority and knowledge over time. Brough writes for an organization known as the Citzens for a Sound Economy, who sponsor his column. He also puts the abbreviation "Ph.D." after his name, to signal his academic credential.

Cite Facts and Statistics

Brough's essay, which was written for the Internet, embeds a URL link (underscored) to support his assertion about the $66.5 trillion deficit. He discusses specific details of the budget and the Congress: the $190 billion farm bill, Congress's supplemental spending bill, overall congressional spending, Daschle's and Bush's actions. Rothschild's essay, which was written for a specific printed magazine, cites specific statistics (and the sources for those statistics) along with specific budget details.

Cite Knowledgeable/Trustworthy Authorities

Rothschild cites reputable sounding people and organizations: Citizens for Tax Justice and Robert Greenstein, the director of the Center on Budget and Policy Priorities. Brough cites the study by

Professors Vedder and Galloway (note that they also presumably have doctorates, as he does) and includes a URL link to that study.

Create a Persuasive Rhetorical Persona

Brough creates a formal persona: he is "Wayne T. Brough, Ph.D." and his choice of language has few individualistic elements in terms of word choice, phrasing, tone, or style. His paragraphs tend to be about 80–170 words long, suggesting that he concentrates on his subject in some depth. Rothschild, on the other hand, uses highly individualistic words and phrases, his tone is colloquial, and his personal views about his subject get expressed immediately. His paragraphs are very short, often just one sentence, suggesting that he sees no need to develop his subjects in great detail, perhaps because he thinks his audience already generally agrees with him.

End with a Strong Statement That Reflects the Major Argument

Rothschild closes with a cheeky one-sentence paragraph that returns us to his opening statement about a stimulus program for the "country club set." Brough's final sentence reminds us of his thesis, namely that it may now be necessary to "impose fiscal discipline on Congress." Both essays close with statements that evoke their opening statements and major arguments.

We could focus on many more strategies for writing successful argument essays, but we hope the preceding discussion provides a starting point. By including two very different perspectives written in very different styles to quite different audiences, we hope to indicate that argument is a supple mode that is open to a variety of approaches. More than almost any other mode, however, an argument essay must be written with a keen awareness of audience. After all, the entire thrust of an argument is to persuade, to change someone's values and views. Your argument will be particularly effective if you take into account the potential assumptions, perspectives, and objections of your audience. In their different ways, both Brough and Rothschild do this effectively. This does not mean that a writer distorts or subverts his or her point of view, but it does mean a writer must find ways to state that point of view so that it gets carefully considered by readers.

In this chapter we see how another accomplished writer expresses her awareness of audience in "It's a Jungle Out There." Camille Paglia begins with a specific thesis (or proposition), stating it dramatically and boldly:

> Rape is an outrage that cannot be tolerated in civilized society. Yet feminism, which has waged a crusade for rape to be taken more seriously, has put young women in danger by hiding the truth about sex from them.

She then supports her thesis by discussing date rape, the nature of young men, and the politically interested nature of feminism, using a variety of sources to support her position. This is the same pattern we see in the Brough and Rothschild essays—and in many other argument essays.

Because the mode of argument depends substantially on forms of evidence and logic, it can be undermined by false thinking. Certain kinds of false thinking occur so often that they have been categorized into fallacies. We list some of the more prominent ones here so that you can guard against them.

- **The false binary:** assuming that a subject must be analyzed in terms of two opposing notions (black or white, yes or no). "If the Congress raises federal income taxes, the result will be either economic inflation or economic depression."
- **Argumentum ad hominem:** directing criticism toward the character or personality of the individual making the argument rather than the argument itself. Ad hominem fallacies are often intended to be insulting since they damage someone's character. "Wayne Brough argues for Congress to impose limits on its own spending because he is insensitive and possesses not a whit of sympathy for the working poor."
- **Non sequitur:** making a statement that does not follow logically from the statements (premises) that precede it. Non sequitur (which means "does not follow" in Latin) is a form of disjointed logic. "If we raise taxes, we could resolve some of the racial tensions in this country."
- **Begging the question:** assuming that the statement to be proven is already true or factual. Begging the question sidesteps logical analysis because, incorrectly, the speaker/writer makes an assumption that what is being proven is already true. "The nation's economy matters to all politicians—and to all Americans—because it is so important."
- **False analogy:** making a false claim that one idea or object is like another. Analogies can be powerful, but false analogies distort the

claim an author is making. "The economy is like a balloon: if it over-inflates, it will pop!"

- **Hasty generalization:** offering a sweeping conclusion or making a major assertion without first assessing all the evidence. "No Congressperson has ever voted to cut subsidies to voters in his or her own district."
- **Post hoc, ergo propter hoc:** assuming a false cause/effect relationship just because one event follows another. The phrase comes from Latin and means "after this, therefore on account of this" and describes the logical fallacy that just because B follows A, B was caused by A. "The last time federal spending was reduced, American productivity decreased by 14%."
- **Weak, poor, or inadequate authority:** citing authorities who either have little factual knowledge or lack authority to support the thesis being developed. "My roommate said the Republican tax proposal would help college students" or "Lots of people agree that the Democratic tax plan would improve our prosperity."

It is difficult to guard against these fallacies, but one of the best protections is to remain aware of the kind of thinking that you are doing.

Most logical thinking falls into one of two broad categories: inductive or deductive. *Inductive thinking* examines the particulars, looking for similarities that allow the writer to move from the specific to the general (without, of course, drawing hasty generalizations). *Deductive thinking* moves from the general to the specific, with an emphasis on how a general set of principles or a general idea will lead to a specific result. Curtis Chang offers an excellent example of inductive thinking in this chapter, since he forms his essay on specific facts, assertions, and research. Camille Paglia mostly uses deductive thinking in her essay, since she makes assertions and then elaborates on them and offers specific examples.

Whether you use inductive or deductive reasoning, it is important to remain aware that the mode of argument demands that you analyze your assumptions, formulate your thesis carefully, find persuasive forms of proof, take stock of your audience, and create a persuasive rhetoric that fuses style with form with clear thinking. No wonder so many students and teachers find argument to be the most challenging mode of all.

A prolific writer noted for his politically conservative viewpoint, **William F. Buckley, Jr.** *(1925–   ), is equally known for an acerbic wit tempered with charm. Buckley has written more than 20 works on politics and government, along with several novels and books on sailing. His first book,* God and Man at Yale, *was published in 1951, after Buckley graduated from that institution. The founding editor of* The National Review, *a politically conservative magazine, Buckley was awarded the Presidential Medal of Freedom in 1991. From 1966 to 1999, Buckley hosted* Firing Line, *a weekly program televised throughout the United States.*

William F. Buckley, Jr.

Why Don't We Complain?

It was the very last coach and the only empty seat on the entire train, so there was no turning back. The problem was to breathe. Outside, the temperature was below freezing. Inside the railroad car the temperature must have been about 85 degrees. I took off my overcoat, and a few minutes later my jacket, and noticed that the car was flecked with the white shirts of the passengers. I soon found my hand moving to loosen my tie. From one end of the car to the other, as we rattled through Westchester County, we sweated; but we did not moan.

I watched the train conductor appear at the head of the car. "Tickets, all tickets, please!" In a more virile age, I thought, the passengers would seize the conductor and strap him down on a seat over the radiator to share the fate of his patrons. He shuffled down the aisle, picking up tickets, punching commutation cards. *No one addressed a word to him.* He approached my seat, and I drew a deep breath of resolution. "Conductor," I began with a considerable edge to my voice. . . . Instantly the doleful eyes of my seatmate turned tiredly from his newspaper to fix me with a resentful stare: What question could be so important as to justify my sibilant intrusion into his stupor? I was shaken by those eyes. I am incapable of making a discreet fuss, so I mumbled a question about what time we were due in Stamford (I didn't even ask whether it would be before or after dehydration could be expected to set in), got my reply, and went back to my newspaper and to wiping my brow.

The conductor had nonchalantly walked down the gauntlet of eighty sweating American freemen, and not one of them had asked him to explain why the passengers in that car had been consigned to suffer. There is nothing to be done when the temperature *outdoors* is 85 degrees, and indoors the air conditioner has broken down; obviously when that happens there is nothing to do, except perhaps curse the day that one was born. But when the temperature outdoors is below freezing, it takes a positive act of will on somebody's part to set the temperature *indoors* at 85. Somewhere a valve was turned too far, a furnace overstocked, a thermostat maladjusted: something that could easily be remedied by turning off the heat and allowing the great outdoors to come indoors. All this is so obvious. What is not obvious is what has happened to the American people.

It isn't just the commuters, whom we have come to visualize as a supine breed who have got on to the trick of suspending their sensory faculties twice a day while they submit to the creeping dissolution of the railroad industry. It isn't just they who have given up trying to rectify irrational vexations. It is the American people everywhere.

5   A few weeks ago at a large movie theater I turned to my wife and said, "The picture is out of focus." "Be quiet," she answered. I obeyed. But a few minutes later I raised the point again, with mounting impatience. "It will be all right in a minute," she said apprehensively. (She would rather lose her eyesight than be around when I make one of my infrequent scenes.) I waited. It was *just* out of focus—not glaringly out, but out. My vision is 20-20, and I assume that is the vision, adjusted, for most people in the movie house. So, after hectoring my wife throughout the first reel, I finally prevailed upon her to admit that it *was* off, and very annoying. We then settled down, coming to rest on the presumption that: a) someone connected with the management of the theater must soon notice the blur and make the correction; or b) that someone seated near the rear of the house would make the complaint in behalf of those of us up front; or c) that—any minute now—the entire house would explode into catcalls and foot stamping, calling dramatic attention to the irksome distortion.

What happened was nothing. The movie ended, as it had begun, *just* out of focus, and as we trooped out, we stretched our faces in a variety of contortions to accustom the eye to the shock of normal focus.

I think it is safe to say that everybody suffered on that occasion. And I think it is safe to assume that everyone was expecting someone else to take the initiative in going back to speak to the manager. And it is probably true even that if we had supposed the movie would run right through the blurred image, someone surely would have summoned up the purposive indignation to get up out of his seat and file his complaint.

But notice that no one did. And the reason no one did is because we are all increasingly anxious in America to be unobtrusive, we are reluctant to make our voices heard, hesitant about claiming our rights; we are afraid that our cause is unjust, or that if it is not unjust, that it is ambiguous; or if not even that, that it is too trivial to justify the horrors of a confrontation with Authority; we will sit in an oven or endure a racking headache before undertaking a head-on, I'm-here-to-tell-you complaint. That tendency to passive compliance, to a heedless endurance, is something to keep one's eyes on—in sharp focus.

I myself can occasionally summon the courage to complain, but I cannot, as I have intimated, complain softly. My own instinct is so strong to let the thing ride, to forget about it—to expect that someone will take the matter up, when the grievance is collective, in my behalf—that it is only when the provocation is at a very special key, whose vibrations touch simultaneously a complexus of nerves, allergies, and passions, that I catch fire and find the reserves of courage and assertiveness to speak up. When that happens, I get quite carried away. My blood gets hot, my brow wet, I become unbearably and unconscionably sarcastic and bellicose; I am girded for a total showdown.

10   Why should that be? Why could not I (or anyone else) on that railroad coach have said simply to the conductor, "Sir"—I take that back: that sounds sarcastic—"Conductor, would you be good enough to turn down the heat? I am extremely hot. In fact, I tend to get hot every time the temperature reaches 85 degr—." Strike that last sentence. Just end it with the simple statement that you are extremely hot, and let the conductor infer the cause.

Every New Year's Eve I resolve to do something about the Milquetoast in me and vow to speak up, calmly, for my rights, and for the betterment of our society, on every appropriate occasion. Entering last New Year's Eve I was fortified in my resolve because that morning at breakfast I had had to ask the waitress three times for a glass of milk. She finally brought it—after I had finished my eggs, which is when I don't want it anymore. I did not have the manliness to order her to take the milk back, but settled instead for a cowardly sulk, and ostentatiously refused to drink the milk—though I later paid for it—rather than state plainly to the hostess, as I should have, why I had not drunk it, and would not pay for it.

So by the time the New Year ushered out the Old, riding in on my morning's indignation and stimulated by the gastric juices of resolution that flow so faithfully on New Year's Eve, I rendered my vow. Henceforward I would conquer my shyness, my despicable disposition to supineness. I would speak out like a man against the unnecessary annoyances of our time.

Forty-eight hours later, I was standing in line at the ski repair store in Pico Peak, Vermont. All I needed, to get on with my skiing, was the loan, for one minute, of a small screwdriver, to tighten a loose binding. Behind the counter in the workshop were two men. One was industriously engaged in servicing the complicated requirements of a young lady at the head of the line, and obviously he would be tied up for quite a while. The other—"Jiggs," his workmate called him—was a middle-aged man, who sat in a chair puffing a pipe, exchanging small talk with his working partner. My pulse began its telltale acceleration. The minutes ticked on. I stared at the idle shopkeeper, hoping to shame him into action, but he was impervious to my telepathic reproof and continued his small talk with his friend, brazenly insensitive to the nervous demands of six good men who were raring to ski.

Suddenly my New Year's Eve resolution struck me. It was now or never. I broke from my place in line and marched to the counter. I was going to control myself. I dug my nails into my palms. My effort was only partially successful.

15   "If you are not too busy," I said icily, "would you mind handing me a screwdriver?"

Work stopped and everyone turned his eyes on me, and I experienced that mortification I always feel when I am the center of centripetal shafts of curiosity, resentment, perplexity.

But the worst was yet to come. "I am sorry, sir," said Jiggs deferentially, moving the pipe from his mouth. "I am not supposed to move. I have just had a heart attack." That was the signal for a great whirring noise that descended from heaven. We looked, stricken, out the window, and it appeared as though a cyclone had suddenly focused on the snowy courtyard between the shop and the ski lift. Suddenly a gigantic army helicopter materialized, and hovered down to a landing. Two men jumped out of the plane carrying a stretcher, tore into the ski shop, and lifted the shopkeeper onto the stretcher. Jiggs bade his companion good-bye and was whisked out the door, into the plane, up to the heavens, down—we learned—to a nearby army hospital. I looked up manfully—into a score of man-eating eyes. I put the experience down as a reversal.

As I write this, on an airplane, I have run out of paper and need to reach into my briefcase under my legs for more. I cannot do this until my empty lunch tray is removed from my lap. I arrested the stewardess as she passed empty-handed down the aisle on the way to the kitchen to fetch the lunch trays for the passengers up forward who haven't been served yet. "Would you please take my tray?" "Just a *moment*, sir!" she said, and marched on sternly. Shall I tell her that since she is headed for the kitchen *anyway*, it could not delay the feeding of the other passengers by more than two seconds necessary to stash away my empty tray? Or remind her that not fifteen minutes ago she spoke unctuously into the loudspeaker the words undoubtedly devised by the airline's highly paid public relations counselor: "If there is anything I or Miss French can do for you to make your trip more enjoyable, *please* let us—" I have run out of paper.

I think the observable reluctance of the majority of Americans to assert themselves in minor matters is related to our increased sense of helplessness in an age of technology and centralized political and economic power. For generations, Americans who were too hot, or too cold, got up and did something about it. Now we call the plumber, or the electrician, or the furnace man. The habit of looking after our own needs obviously had something to do with the assertiveness that characterized the American family familiar to readers of American literature. With the technification of life goes our direct responsibility for our material environment, and we are conditioned to adopt a position of helplessness not only as regards the broken air conditioner, but as regards the overheated train. It takes an expert to fix the former, but not the latter; yet these distinctions, as we withdraw into helplessness, tend to fade away.

20   Our notorious political apathy is a related phenomenon. Every year, whether the Republican or the Democratic Party is in office, more and more power drains away from the individual to feed vast reservoirs in far-off places; and we have less and less say about the shape of events which shape our future. From this alienation of personal power comes the sense of resignation with which we accept the political dispensations of a powerful government whose hold upon us continues to increase.

An editor of a national weekly news magazine told me a few years ago that as few as a dozen letters of protest against an editorial stance of his magazine was enough to convene a plenipotentiary meeting of the board of editors to review policy. "So few people complain, or make their voices heard," he explained to me, "that we assume a dozen letters represent the inarticulated views of thousands of readers." In the past ten years, he said, the volume of mail has noticeably decreased, even though the circulation of his magazine has risen.

When our voices are finally mute, when we have finally suppressed the natural instinct to complain, whether the vexation is trivial or grave, we shall have become automatons, incapable of feeling. When Premier Khrushchev first came to this country late in 1959 he was primed, we are informed, to experience the bitter resentment of the American people against his tyranny, against his persecutions, against the movement which is responsible for the great number of American deaths in Korea, for billions in taxes every year, and for life everlasting on the brink of disaster; but Khrushchev was pleasantly surprised, and reported back to the Russian people that he had been met with overwhelming cordiality (read: apathy), except, to be sure, for "a few fascists who followed me around with their wretched posters, and should be horsewhipped."

I may be crazy, but I say there would have been lots more posters in a society where train temperatures in the dead of winter are not allowed to climb to 85 degrees without complaint.

Analyzing Rhetorical Choices

1. How would you describe Buckley's tone in this essay? Is he irritable, peevish, outraged, calm, thoughtfully reflective? In a short paragraph, describe the tone and cite a few specific phrases to support your view.

2. Buckley is trying to make a point about being more assertive. Yet once he resolves to complain or make his desires explicit, he recounts to the reader the humiliation he suffers in the Jiggs episode. Why do you think he does that? What does the episode tell us about Buckley? Does it make his argument more or less persuasive? Why?

3. Look closely at Buckley's use of language—for instance, when he writes, "whether the vexation is trivial or grave, we shall have become automatons, incapable of feeling." What do his choices say about his assumptions regarding audience? What kind of persona does he create with his word choices?

4. How does Buckley end this essay? Why do you think he reminds us once again of the train episode?

Writing About Issues and Contexts

1. How would you describe Buckley's method of arguing? Does he appeal to emotion? To reason? What means does he use to try to persuade us of his central argument about the necessity of starting to complain?

2. When Buckley says to Jiggs, "If you're not too busy, would you mind handing me a screwdriver?" is he overstepping his bounds? Is he rude and insensitive? How would you defend or critique his actions?

3. Comment on Buckley's statement that "The reluctance of . . . Americans to assert themselves in minor matters is related to our increased sense of helplessness in an age of technology." Write a short paragraph agreeing or disagreeing with this perspective.

4. Offer your own analysis concerning America's "notorious political apathy." Do you agree with Buckley that Americans are apathetic? Why or why not?

A writer of both fiction and nonfiction, **Joy Williams** *(1944–   ) is a graduate of the University of Iowa Writers' Workshop. She has written four novels, including* State of Grace, *which was nominated for the National Book
Award,* The Changeling, Breaking and Entering, *and* The Quick and the
Dead, *which was nominated for a Pulitzer. She has also published numerous stories, essays, and articles. Williams has been described as a writer
with fierce passions who has a deep interest in conservation issues. Both
the passion and the love for wildlife are evinced in the following selection.*

Joy Williams
The Killing Game

Death and suffering are a big part of hunting. A big part. Not that
you'd ever know it by hearing hunters talk. They tend to downplay the
killing part. To kill is to put to death, extinguish, nullify, cancel, destroy. But from the hunter's point of view, it's just a tiny part of the experience. *The kill is the least important part of the hunt,* they often
say, or, *Killing involves only a split second of the innumerable hours
we spend surrounded by and observing nature . . .* For the animal, of
course, the killing part is of considerably more importance. José
Ortega y Gasset, in *Meditations on Hunting,* wrote, *Death is a sign of
reality in hunting. One does not hunt in order to kill; on the contrary,
one kills in order to have hunted.* This is the sort of intellectual blather
that the "thinking" hunter holds dear. The conservation editor of *Field
& Stream,* George Reiger, recently paraphrased this sentiment by saying, *We kill to hunt, and not the other way around,* thereby making it
truly fatuous. A hunter in West Virginia, one Mr. Bill Neal, blazed
through this philosophical fog by explaining why he blows the toes off
tree raccoons so that they will fall down and be torn apart by his dogs.
That's the best part of it. It's not any fun just shooting them.

Instead of monitoring animals—many animals in managed areas
are tagged, tattooed, and wear radio transmitters—wildlife managers
should start hanging telemetry gear around hunters' necks to study
their attitudes and listen to their conversations. It would be grisly listening, but it would tune out for good the *suffering as sacrament* and
spiritual experience blather that some hunting apologists employ. *The
unease with which the good hunter inflicts death is an unease not
merely with his conscience but with affirming his animality in the*

midst of his struggles toward humanity and clarity, Holmes Rolston III
drones on in his book *Environmental Ethics.*

There is a formula to this in literature—someone the protagonist
loves has just died, so he goes out and kills an animal. This makes him
feel better. But it's kind of a sad feeling-better. He gets to relate to
Death and Nature in this way. Somewhat. But not really. Death is still
a mystery. Well, it's hard to explain. It's sort of a semireligious thing
. . . Killing and affirming, affirming and killing, it's just the cross the
"good" hunter must bear. The bad hunter just has to deal with postkill
letdown.

Many are the hunter's specious arguments. Less semireligious but
a long-standing favorite with them is the vegetarian approach: you eat
meat, don't you? If you say no, they feel they've got you—you're just a
vegetarian attempting to impose your weird views on others. If you say
yes, they accuse you of being hypocritical, of allowing your genial
A&P butcher to stand between you and reality. The fact is, the chief
attraction of hunting is the pursuit and murder of animals—the meat-
eating aspect of it is trivial. If the hunter chooses to be *ethical* about it,
he might cook his kill, but the meat of most animals is discarded.
Dead bear can even be dangerous! A bear's heavy hide must be
skinned at once to prevent meat spoilage. With effort, a hunter can
make okay chili, *something to keep in mind,* a sports rag says, *if you
take two skinny spring bears.*

5   As for subsistence hunting, please . . . Granted that there might be
one "good" hunter out there who conducts the kill as spiritual exercise
and two others who are atavistic enough to want to supplement their
Chicken McNuggets with venison, most hunters hunt for the hell of it.

For hunters, hunting is fun. Recreation is play. Hunting is recreation. Hunters kill for play, for entertainment. They kill for the thrill of
it, to make an animal "theirs." (The Gandhian doctrine of nonposses-
sion has never been a big hit with hunters.) The animal becomes the
property of the hunter by its death. Alive, the beast belongs only to itself. This is unacceptable to the hunter. *He's yours . . . He's mine . . . I
decided to . . . I decided not to . . . I debated shooting it, then I decided
to let it live . . .* Hunters like beautiful creatures. A "beautiful" deer, elk,
bear, cougar, bighorn sheep. A "beautiful" goose or mallard. Of course,
they don't stay "beautiful" for long, particularly the birds. Many birds
become rags in the air, shredded, blown to bits. *Keep shooting till they
drop!* Hunters get a thrill out of seeing a plummeting bird, out of seeing
it crumple and fall. *The big pheasant folded in classic fashion.* They get
a kick out of "collecting" new species. *Why not add a unique harlequin*

duck to your collection? Swan hunting is satisfying. *I let loose a three-inch Magnum. The large bird only flinched with my first shot and began to gain altitude. I frantically ejected the round, chambered another, and dropped the swan with my second shot. After retrieving the bird I was amazed by its size. The swan's six-foot wingspan, huge body, and long neck made it an impressive trophy.* Hunters like big animals, trophy animals. A "trophy" usually means that the hunter doesn't deign to eat it. Maybe he skins it or mounts it. Maybe he takes a picture. *We took pictures, we took pictures.* Maybe he just looks at it for a while. The disposition of the "experience" is up to the hunter. He's entitled to do whatever he wishes with the damn thing. It's dead.

Hunters like categories they can tailor to their needs. There are the "good" animals—deer, elk, bear, moose—which are allowed to exist for the hunter's pleasure. Then there are the "bad" animals, the vermin, varmints, and "nuisance" animals, the rabbits and raccoons and coyotes and beavers and badgers, which are disencouraged to exist. The hunter can have fun killing them, but the pleasure is diminished because the animals aren't "magnificent."

Then there are the predators. These can be killed any time, because, hunters argue, they're predators, for godssakes.

Many people in South Dakota want to exterminate the red fox because it preys upon some of the ducks and pheasant they want to hunt and kill each year. They found that after they killed the wolves and coyotes, they had more foxes than they wanted. The ring-necked pheasant is South Dakota's state bird. No matter that it was imported from Asia specifically to be "harvested" for sport, it's South Dakota's state bird and they're proud of it. A group called Pheasants Unlimited gave some tips on how to hunt foxes. *Place a small amount of larvicide* [a grain fumigant] *on a rag and chuck it down the hole . . . The first pup generally comes out in fifteen minutes . . . Use a .22 to dispatch him . . . Remove each pup shot from the hole. Following gassing, set traps for the old fox who will return later in the evening . . .* Poisoning, shooting, trapping—they make up a sort of sportsman's triathlon.

10   In the hunting magazines, hunters freely admit the pleasure of killing to one another. *Undeniable pleasure radiated from her smile. The excitement of shooting the bear had Barb talking a mile a minute.* But in public, most hunters are becoming a little wary about raving on as to how much fun it is to kill things. Hunters have a tendency to call large animals by cute names—"bruins" and "muleys," "berry-fed blackies" and "handsome cusses" and "big guys," thereby implying a

balanced jolly game of mutual satisfaction between the hunter and the hunted—*Bam, bam, bam, I get to shoot you and you get to be dead.* More often, though, when dealing with the nonhunting public, a drier, businesslike tone is employed. Animals become a "resource" that must be "utilized." Hunting becomes "a legitimate use of the resource." Animals become a product like wool or lumber or a crop like fruit or corn that must be "collected" or "taken" or "harvested." Hunters love to use the word *legitimate.* (Oddly, Tolstoy referred to hunting as "evil legitimized.") *A legitimate use, a legitimate form of recreation, a legitimate escape, a legitimate pursuit.* It's a word they trust will slam the door on discourse. Hunters are increasingly relying upon their spokesmen and supporters, state and federal game managers and wildlife officials, to employ the drone of a solemn bureaucratic language and toss around a lot of questionable statistics to assure the nonhunting public (93 percent!) that there's nothing to worry about. The pogrom is under control. The mass murder and manipulation of wild animals is just another business. Hunters are a tiny minority, and it's crucial to them that the millions of people who don't hunt not be awakened from their long sleep and become antihunting. Nonhunters are okay. Dweeby, probably, but okay. A hunter *can respect the rights* of a nonhunter. It's the "antis" he despises, those *misguided, emotional, not-in-possession-of-the-facts, uninformed zealots who don't understand nature . . . Those dime-store ecologists cloaked in ignorance and spurred by emotion . . . Those doggy-woggy types, who under the guise of being environmentalists and conservationists are working to deprive him of his precious right to kill.* (Sometimes it's just a *right;* sometimes it's a *God-given* right.) Antis can be scorned, but nonhunters must be pacified, and this is where the number crunching of wildlife biologists and the scripts of *professional resource managers* come in. Leave it to the professionals. They know what numbers are the good numbers. Utah determined that there were six hundred sandhill cranes in the state, so permits were issued to shoot one hundred of them. Don't want to have too many sandhill cranes. California wildlife officials reported "sufficient numbers" of mountain lions to "justify" renewed hunting, even though it doesn't take a rocket scientist to know the animal is extremely rare. (It's always a dark day for hunters when an animal is adjudged *rare.* How can its numbers be "controlled" through hunting if it scarcely exists?) A recent citizens' referendum prohibits the hunting of the mountain lion in perpetuity—not that the lions aren't killed anyway, in California and all over the West, hundreds of them annually by the government as part of the scandalous Animal Damage

Control Program. Oh, to be the lucky hunter who gets to be an official government hunter and can legitimately kill animals his buddies aren't supposed to! Montana officials, led by K. L. Cool, that state's wildlife director, have definite ideas on the number of buffalo they feel can be tolerated. Zero is the number. Yellowstone National Park is the only place in America where bison exist, having been annihilated everywhere else. In the winter of 1988, nearly six hundred buffalo wandered out of the north boundary of the park and into Montana, where they were immediately shot at point-blank range by lottery-winning hunters. It was easy. And it was obvious from a video taken on one of the blow-away-the-bison days that the hunters had a heck of a good time. The buffalo, Cool says, threaten ranchers' livelihoods by doing damage to property—by which he means, I guess, that they eat the grass. Montana wants zero buffalo; it also wants zero wolves.

Large predators—including grizzlies, cougars, and wolves—are often the most "beautiful," the smartest and wildest animals of all. The gray wolf is both a supreme predator and an endangered species, and since the Supreme Court recently affirmed that ranchers have no constitutional right to kill endangered predators—apparently some God-given rights are not constitutional ones—this makes the wolf a more or less lucky dog. But not for long. A small population of gray wolves has recently established itself in northwestern Montana, primarily in Glacier National Park, and there is a plan, long a dream of conservationists, to "reintroduce" the wolf to Yellowstone. But to please ranchers and hunters, part of the plan would involve immediately removing the wolf from the endangered-species list. Beyond the park's boundaries, he could be hunted as a "game animal" or exterminated as a "pest." (Hunters kill to hunt, remember, except when they're hunting to kill.) The area of Yellowstone where the wolf would be restored is the same mountain and high-plateau country that is abandoned in winter by most animals, including the aforementioned luckless bison. Part of the plan, too, is compensation to ranchers if any of their far-ranging livestock is killed by a wolf. It's a real industry out there, apparently, killing and controlling and getting compensated for losing something under the Big Sky.

Wolves gotta eat—a fact that disturbs hunters. Jack Atcheson, an outfitter in Butte, said, *Some wolves are fine if there is control. But there never will be control. The wolf-control plan provided by the Fish and Wildlife Service speaks only of protecting domestic livestock. There is no plan to protect wildlife . . . There are no surplus deer or elk in Montana . . . Their numbers are carefully managed. With uncontrolled wolf populations, a lot of people will have to give up hunting just to feed wolves. Will you give up your elk permit for a wolf?*

It won't be long before hunters start demanding compensation for animals they aren't able to shoot.

Hunters believe that wild animals exist only to satisfy their wish to kill them. And it's so easy to kill them! The weaponry available is staggering, and the equipment and gear limitless. *The demand for big boomers has never been greater than right now,* Outdoor Life *crows, and the makers of rifles and cartridges are responding to the craze with a variety of light artillery that is virtually unprecedented in the history of sporting arms . . .* Hunters use grossly overpowered shotguns and rifles and compound bows. They rely on four-wheel-drive vehicles and three-wheel ATVs and airplanes . . . *He was interesting, the only moving, living creature on that limitless white expanse. I slipped a cartridge into the barrel of my rifle and threw the safety off . . .* They use snowmobiles to run down elk, and dogs to run down and tree cougars. It's easy to shoot an animal out of a tree. It's virtually impossible to miss a moose, a conspicuous and placid animal of steady habits . . . *I took a deep breath and pulled the trigger. The bull dropped. I looked at my watch: 8:22. The big guy was early. Mike started whooping and hollering and I joined him. I never realized how big a moose was until this one was on the ground. We took pictures . . .* Hunters shoot animals when they're resting . . . *Mike selected a deer, settled down to a steady rest, and fired. The buck was his when he squeezed the trigger. John decided to take the other buck, which had jumped up to its feet. The deer hadn't seen us and was confused by the shot echoing about in the valley. John took careful aim, fired, and took the buck. The hunt was over . . .* And they shoot them when they're eating . . . *The bruin ambled up the stream, checking gravel bars and backwaters for fish. Finally he plopped down on the bank to eat. Quickly, I tiptoed into range . . .* They use decoys and calls . . . *The six point gave me a cold-eyed glare from ninety steps away. I hit him with a 130-grain Sierra boattail handload. The bull went down hard. Our hunt was over . . .* They use sex lures . . . *The big buck raised its nose in the air, curled back its lips, and tested the scent of the doe's urine. I held my breath, fought back the shivers, and jerked off a shot. The 180-grain spire-point bullet caught the buck high on the back behind the shoulder and put it down. It didn't get up . . .* They use walkie-talkies, binoculars, scopes . . . *With my 308 Browning BLR, I steadied the 9X cross hairs on the front of the bear's massive shoulders and squeezed. The bear cartwheeled backward for fifty yards . . . The second Federal Premium 165-grain bullet found its mark. Another shot anchored the bear for good . . .* They bait deer with corn. They spread popcorn on golf courses for Canada geese and they douse meat baits with fry grease and honey for bears . . . *Make the baiting site redolent of inner-city doughnut shops.* They use blinds and tree stands and mobile stands. They go out in groups, in gangs, and employ "pushes" and "drives." So many methods are effective. So few rules apply. It's fun! . . . *We kept on repelling the swarms of birds as they came in looking for shelter from that big ocean wind, emptying our shell belts . . .* A species can, in the vernacular, be *pressured by hunting* (which means that killing them has decimated them), but that just increases the fun, the *challenge.* There is practically no criticism of conduct within the ranks . . . *It's mostly a matter of opinion and how hunters have been brought up to hunt . . .* Although a recent editorial in *Ducks Unlimited* magazine did venture to primly suggest that one should *not fall victim to greed-induced stress through piggish competition with others.*

15   But hunters are piggy. They just can't seem to help it. They're overequipped . . . insatiable, malevolent, and vain. They maim and mutilate and despoil. And for the most part, they're inept. Grossly inept.

Camouflaged toilet paper is a must for the modern hunter, along with his Bronco and his beer. Too many hunters taking a dump in the woods with their roll of Charmin beside them were mistaken for white-tailed deer and shot. Hunters get excited. They'll shoot anything—the pallid ass of another sportsman or even themselves. A Long Island man died last year when his shotgun went off as he clubbed a wounded deer with the butt. Hunters get mad. They get restless and want to fire! They want to use those assault rifles and see foamy blood on the ferns. Wounded animals can travel for miles in fear and pain before they collapse. Countless gut-shot deer—*if you hear a sudden, squashy thump, the animal has probably been hit in the abdomen*—are "lost" each year. "Poorly placed shots" are frequent, and injured animals are seldom tracked, because most hunters never learned how to track. The majority of hunters will shoot at anything with four legs during deer season and anything with wings during duck season. Hunters try to nail running animals and distant birds. They become so overeager, *so aroused*, that they misidentify and misjudge, spraying their "game" with shots but failing to bring it down.

The fact is, hunters' lack of skill is a big, big problem. And nowhere is the problem worse than in the new glamour recreation, bow hunting. These guys are elitists. They doll themselves up in camouflage, paint their faces black, and climb up into tree stands from which they attempt the penetration of deer, elk, and turkeys with modern, multiblade, broadhead arrows shot from sophisticated, easy-to-draw compound bows. This "primitive" way of hunting appeals to many, and even the nonhunter may feel that it's a "fairer" method, requiring more strength and skill, but bow hunting is the cruelest, most wanton form of wildlife disposal of all. Studies conducted by state fish and wildlife departments repeatedly show that bow hunters wound and fail to retrieve as many animals as they kill. An animal that flees, wounded by an arrow, will most assuredly die of the wound, but it will be days before he does. Even with a "good" hit, the time elapsed between the strike and death is exceedingly long. *The rule of thumb has long been that we should wait thirty to forty-five minutes on heart and lung hits, an hour or more on a suspected liver hit, eight to twelve hours on paunch hits, and that we should follow immediately on hindquarter and other muscle-only hits, to keep the wound open and bleeding,* is the advice in the magazine *Fins and Feathers.* What the hunter does as he hangs around waiting for his animal to finish with its terrified running and dying hasn't been studied—maybe he puts on more makeup, maybe he has a highball.

• • •

"Quality" hunting is as rare as the Florida panther. What you've got is a bunch of guys driving over the plains, up the mountains, and through the woods with their stupid tag that cost them a couple of bucks and immense coolers full of beer and body parts. There's a price tag on the right to destroy living creatures for play, but it's not much. *A big-game hunting license is the greatest deal going since the Homestead Act,* Ted Kerasote writes in *Sports Afield. In many states residents can hunt big game for more than a month for about $20.* It's cheaper than taking the little woman out to lunch. It's cheap all right, and it's because killing animals is considered *recreation* and is underwritten by state and federal funds. In Florida, state moneys are routinely spent on "youth hunts," in which kids are guided to shoot deer from stands in wildlife-management areas. The organizers of these events say that these staged hunts *help youth to understand man's role in the ecosystem.* (Drop a doe and take your place in the ecological community, son . . .)

Hunters claim (they don't actually believe it but they've learned to say it) that they're doing nonhunters a favor, for if they didn't *use* wild animals, wild animals would be useless. They believe that they're just *helping Mother Nature control populations (you wouldn't want those deer to die of starvation, would you?).* They claim that their tiny fees provide *all* Americans with wild lands and animals. (People who don't hunt get to enjoy animals all year round while hunters get to enjoy them only during hunting season . . .) Ducks Unlimited feels that it, in particular, is a selfless provider and environmental champion. Although members spend most of their money lobbying for hunters and raising ducks in pens to release later over shooting fields, they do save some wetlands, mostly by persuading farmers not to fill them in. *See that little pothole there the ducks like? Well, I'm gonna plant more soybeans there if you don't pay me not to* . . . Hunters claim many nonsensical things, but the most nonsensical of all is that they *pay their own way.* They do not pay their own way. They *do* pay into a perverse wildlife-management system that manipulates "stocks" and "herds" and "flocks" for hunters' killing pleasure, but these fees in no way cover the cost of highly questionable ecological practices. For some spare change . . . *the greatest deal going* . . . hunters can hunt on public lands— national parks, state forests—preserves for hunters!—which the non-hunting and antihunting public pay for. (Access to private lands is becoming increasingly difficult for them, as experience has taught people that hunters are obnoxious.) Hunters kill on millions of acres of land all over America that are maintained with general taxpayer revenue, but the most shocking, really twisted subsidization takes place on national wildlife refuges. Nowhere is the arrogance and insidiousness of this small, aggressive minority more clearly demonstrated. Nowhere is the murder of animals, the manipulation of language, and the distortion of public intent more flagrant. The public perceives national wildlife refuges as safe havens, as sanctuaries for animals. And why wouldn't they? The word *refuge* of course *means* shelter from danger and distress. But the dweeby nonhunting public—they tend to be so literal. The word has been reinterpreted by management over time and now hunters are invited into more than half of the country's more than 440 wildlife "sanctuaries" each year to bang them up and kill more than half a million animals. This is called *wildlife-oriented recreation.* Hunters think of this as being no less than their due, claiming that refuge lands were purchased with duck stamps (. . . *our duck stamps paid for it . . . our duck stamps paid for it . . .*). Hunters equate those stupid stamps with the mystic, multiplying power of the Lord's loaves and fishes, but of 90 million acres in the Wildlife Refuge System, only 3 million were bought with hunting-stamp revenue. Most wildlife "restoration" programs in the states are translated into clearing land to increase deer habitats (so that too many deer will require hunting . . . you wouldn't want them to die of starvation, would you?) and trapping animals for restocking and study (so hunters can shoot more of them). Fish and game agencies hustle hunting—instead of conserving wildlife, they're killing it. It's time for them to get in the business of protecting and preserving wildlife and creating balanced ecological systems instead of pimping for hunters who want their deer/duck/pheasant/turkey—animals stocked to be shot.

20   Hunters' self-serving arguments and lies are becoming more preposterous as nonhunters awake from their long, albeit troubled, sleep. Sport hunting is immoral; it should be made illegal. Hunters are persecutors of nature who should be prosecuted. They wield a disruptive power out of all proportion to their numbers, and pandering to their interests—the special interests of a group that just wants to kill things—is mad. It's preposterous that every year less than 7 percent of the population turns the skies into shooting galleries and the woods and fields into abattoirs. It's time to stop actively supporting and passively allowing hunting, and time to stigmatize it. It's time to stop being conned and cowed by hunters, time to stop pampering and coddling them, time to get them off the government's duck-and-deer dole, time to stop thinking of wild animals as "resources" and "game," and start thinking of them as sentient beings that deserve our wonder and respect, time to stop allowing hunting to be creditable by calling it "sport" and "recreation." Hunters make wildlife *dead, dead, dead*. It's time to wake up to this indisputable fact. As for the hunters, it's long past check-out time.

Analyzing Rhetorical Choices

1. How do you explain the use of italics in this essay? What, exactly, do they represent, and how effective are they in helping Williams support her argument?

2. Discuss Williams's tone in this essay. What kinds of tonal shifts do you detect and on what basis do you think she makes them?

3. Where does Williams make her argument explicit? Evaluate the effectiveness of the argument in terms of its placement. In what ways, if any, would the essay's effectiveness be altered if the argument were placed somewhere else?

4. Why do you think Williams published this essay in *Esquire* magazine, a publication noted predominately for its male readers?

Writing About Issues and Contexts

1. Evaluate at least three of the statements by hunters that appear in this essay in terms of their logic and persuasiveness. How do you evaluate Williams's perspective and analyses of these prohunting statements?

2. What parallels does Williams draw between wild animal predators and hunters?

3. What is Williams's primary purpose in the long paragraph beginning, "Hunters believe that wild animals exist only to satisfy their wish to kill them." Analyze the effectiveness of this paragraph in terms of how she critiques the hunters' perspective, and discuss in what ways it sets up the short paragraph that follows.

4. In what ways is this essay an effective argument against hunting? In what ways is it less successful? Another way of thinking about this is to ask whether this essay has altered your perspective about hunting? Whatever your answer, explain it by making reference to specific sections of this essay that you find either effective or ineffective.

Born in Kansas City and with degrees from the University of Missouri and Yale, **Paul Shepard** *(1925–1996) became one of the founders of the American ecology movement. His teachings and writings have influenced many, including the well-known nature writers Barry Lopez and Peter Matthiessen. For the last 20 years of his life, he held the position of Avery Professor of Natural Philosophy and Human Ecology at Pitzer College and the Claremont Graduate School. His published works include* The Tender Carnivore and the Sacred Game *(1973) and* Man in the Landscape *(1967, 1991). The selection that follows is an excerpt from the latter book and explores the complex relation between human beings and nature, with a special focus on the volatile subject of hunting. It is worth noting that Shepard loved the outdoors, was an avid birder, and was a hunter and fisherman as well.*

Paul Shepard

Hunting and Human Values

Killing animals for the meat industry or for scientific research can be rationalized to the satisfaction of all but a few, but hunting for sport is frequently regarded as morally indefensible. Some of my acquaintances class hunting with war and murder. They are humane and humanist, with broad literary knowledge, articulate and very keen, as it were, in the slaughter of the advocates of hunting. In a debate in *The Saturday Review*, for instance, Joseph Wood Krutch carved up his hunter opponent and served him to the readers, steaming in his own juices.

Hunting has been defended by the fiction that sporting activity in the field somehow prepared a young man for a higher plane of conduct in human affairs. But whatever validity this idea had became obsolete with the end of aristocratic social structure. It has been held that the hunt promotes character, self-reliance, and initiative—an untenable Theodore Roosevelt belief. The development of leadership does not depend on killing. Assertions are sometimes made about instinctive needs and vague primitive satisfactions and psychological benefits, but the sharpest opponents of hunting appear simply not to have forgiven Darwin and Freud to begin with. To suggest that hunting has psychic or evolutionary values only infuriates. Others claim that the hunter is really attempting to escape the roar and friction of civilization, to squeeze out of society's trammels for a few hours of recuperation. The outraged response is, of course, that hunting with a camera is equally rewarding and more uplifting. According to the Faulkner and Hemingway interpretation, hunting is a manipulation of symbols for proving one's virility or otherwise coping with the erosion of the human personality and the decadence of civilization.

Opposition to hunting for sport has its accusing finger on the act of killing. Determinism gives no out. We cannot plead that we are bipedal carnivorous mammals and damned to kill. We must discover what it means to search for an equilibrium between the polarities of nature and God. We find that to share in life is to participate in a traffic of energy and materials, the ultimate origin of which is a mystery, but which has its immediate source in the bodies of plants and other animals. As a society, we may be in danger of losing sight of this fact, kept vividly before us in hunting.

The condemnation of killing wild animals assumes that death is the worst of natural events, that order in nature is epitomized by living objects rather than the complex flow patterns of which objects are temporary formations. The implication is that carnivorous predation as a whole is evil. The anti-hunters face a paradox of their own making. Dr. Schweitzer, who did not believe in hunting for sport, sprinkled his jungle writings with accounts of righteous killing of predators. Europeans and Americans in the same *Zeitgeist* have always destroyed predators, the big cats, eagles, wolves, bears, and pests such as rodents, insects, and birds.

5   Joseph Wood Krutch condemns the hunter for killing, claiming that the distinction between life and death is one of the most absolute boundaries which we know. But this is not so. Life has atomic as well as planetary dimensions. The most satisfactory definitions and descriptions of life are in physical and chemical terms of events and processes which, occurring in a certain harmony, produce what we call life. The organic and the inorganic are mingled inextricably in the living body.

The traditional insistence upon the overwhelmingly tragic and unequivocal nature of death ignores the adaptive role of early death in most animal populations. It presumes that the landscape is a collection of *things*. In this view the dissolution of body and personality are always tragic and disruptive, and do not contribute to the perfection of an intelligible world. But death, as transformation in a larger system, is an essential aspect of elegant patterns which are orderly as well as beautiful: without death growth could not occur, energy could not flow beyond plants, nutrient substances would be trapped forever. Without death the pond, the forest, the prairie, the city could not exist. The extremely complicated structure of living communities has yet to be fully explored, but constitutes a field pattern. Plants and animals participate in them without question in an attitude of acceptance which in human terms would be called faith.

The unfortunate social and economic misapplication of Darwin's theory in the late nineteenth century can still be seen in reluctance to accept evolution as a significant factor in man's highest as well as his more primitive activities. Evolutionary theory also had the curious effect on some people of making nature seem more chaotic instead of less. Evolution is unrelated to the fate of individuals. We have projected our notions of ethics and our terror of death into our perception of all life. Animals die before they have lived out their potential life span; that is characteristic of the natural world and essential to our understanding of it.

A moral criterion is sometimes offered for killing limited to the necessity for food and defense. This logically opposes the sportsman and approves of the slaughterhouse. Under primitive conditions killing meant something quite different than it does in the modern slaughterhouse or by the broadscale application of chemical pesticides. The events of daily life in a hunting society are permeated with universal significance immediate to every individual. No activity of life is regarded as "merely" physical, but always related to a whole, partly unseen. We cannot now adopt animistic superstition nor regain that kind of consciousness, but we admire the poignant sense of the interpenetration of man and nature which primitive life ritualizes and we may seek its results. Primitive ways are nearly gone but we acknowledge that such reverence for life is more reverent and is better ecology than a fanatic emphasis on fear of death and the attempt at godship by judging all instances and causes of death among animals. To our repugnance for soil (dirt), parasitism (disease), and decay (slime) we add predation. We condemn it as though it were murder, and extend "justice" into biotic realms where it is meaningless, incorporating democracy with its protection of the "weak" and containment of the "strong." Man dominates some parts of nature, but there is no process known by which this vindicates extending his social ethics, his democracy, or any other ideological or moral system into the adaptations of populations or the interrelations of species.

Does the hunter not interfere in natural patterns and upset nature's balance? Yes and no. Man is not a demigod operating above and outside nature. But nature is in him as well as he in it. Nature's balance is always slightly upset.

10   Individuals are important. The taking of a life, so evanescent in a cosmic scheme, is nonetheless profoundly moving to us as individuals. Killing an animal probably obliterates an awareness somewhat similar to our own consciousness. As sympathetic and vulnerable humans, we are confronted with mystery by the death of any creature. This is why the tension over killing is so incisive and urgent. Our sympathy for a fellow creature is felt intensely at the crucial moment of death. Yet that emotion fulfills a cultural and personal necessity for evidence of our connection to large-scale processes in a moment of profound intensity. If the death is so experienced our response may be regarded as a form of behavior which unites men with nature rather than alienating them.

Mental well-being is defined by a model of cultural behavior. Culture is an interface between man and his environment. Collective dreams and myths, apprehended symbolically, change slowly with the healthy functioning of society and the psychic security of its members. There is in literary and pictorial arts an iconography of hunting. With its artistic heritage, hunting is much more than a wanton vestige of barbarism. It is intimately associated with social order and with love. "Venery" is an archaic term meaning both sexual pursuit and hunting game—the foundation of love. The origins of human compassion belong to the hunters of old.

Hunting may be an inherent behavior, but it is not *only* an instinct. It is a framework of organization which acknowledges an extra-human context. Killing is not justified simply as indigenous or venerable. But it is a historical part of the activity of a people. It has a place in the total fabric of what they have become, a mode of their relationship to nature. For perhaps 95 percent of their history men and "near-men" have been hunters. Primitive peoples ritualize hunting except where hunting societies and the technological world have collided, where cultural deterioration has reduced customary inhibition to wanton killing.

Probably the richest collection of the ceremonies of propitiation of wild spirits by hunters is Sir James G. Frazer's *The Golden Bough*. If anthropologically obsolete, Frazer's perspective and genius for collecting remain nonetheless monumental. To judge from *The Golden Bough*, hunting has been universally bound by ceremonial preparation and epilogue. When British Columbian Lillooet Indians dispose of the bones of their kill in a certain way, saying, "See! I treated you respect-fully. Nothing shall defile you! May I be successful in hunting and trapping!" they are not only seeking to perpetuate their food supply. They do more than solicit success and spiritual acquiescence. Their ceremony makes less distinction between subject and object than we assume in the orthodox sense of magic. Even Frazer's view of ritual as coercive and petitionary was perhaps too restrictive. The ceremony is also an affirmation and participation, not only manipulative but at-tuning, assimilative, and confrontative. Imitative magic is prototech-nological and prescientific, but that part emphasizing "we-hood" and the participating in a larger whole are religious.

Both magic and religion in primitive ritual reveal fundamental components of the hunter's attitude. The organized ceremony simulta-neously serves a magic and a religious purpose, and ecological and social functions as well. The ceremony is aimed at maintaining equi-librium in the total situation. The whole of life, corporeal and spiri-tual, is affected. The prey, or parts of it, are killed ritually and eaten sacramentally. By following the prescribed style the hunters sacrifice the prey in evocation of events too profound for conscious understand-ing. By its own self-imposed limitations the ritual hunt renounces fur-ther killing in favor of a larger context of interrelationship. If the preliminary solicitation is effective and the traditional procedure is fol-lowed, the hunt is successful. Unlike farmers who must labor in the fields and who earn by their sweat a grudging security within nature, the primitive hunter gets "something for nothing." The kill is a gift. Its bestowal depends on the conduct of the hunters. Without this gift the hunter will die. As Malinowski says, "food is the main link between man and his surroundings" and "by receiving it he feels the forces of destiny and providence." Of all foods meat is the gift *par excellence* because shortage of protein, not shortage of food *per se*, is the essence of starvation. The elusiveness of the quarry explicitly symbolizes the continuing dependence of human life on powers beyond human con-trol. Hunting provides the logical nucleus for the evolution of com-munal life with its celebrations of a biosocial participation mystique and the sharing of the kill.

15   What do the hunt and kill actually do for the hunter? They con-firm his continuity with the dynamic life of animal populations, his role in the complicated cycles of elements, his sharing in the sweep of evolution, and his place in the patterns of the flow of energy and in the web of his own society.

It may at first seem irrelevant to seek present values for us in the strongly schematized hunting behavior of primitive man. But "our deepest experience, needs, and aspirations are the same, as surely as the crucial biological and psychic transitions occur in the life of every human being and force culture to take account of them in aesthetic forms," says Richard V. Chase. Many anthropologists report that there is widespread belief in the immortality of the spirits of all living things, a point of view which we may be too barbaric to share. Frazer wrote, about the time Schweitzer was conceiving of "Reverence for Life," "If I am right in thus interpreting the thought of primitive man, the savage view of the nature of life singularly resembles the modern scientific doctrine of the conservation of energy." The idea of organic interrelationship which ecologists explore may spring not from inductive science at all, but from a rather fundamental human attitude toward the landscape. In these terms, the hunt is a singular expression of our identity with natural processes and is carried on with veneration appropriate to the mystery of those events.

This concept transcends particular economic situations. Men in all sorts of societies—primitive, pastoral, agricultural, and technical—continue to hunt fervently. The hunt has ceased to be the main source of food, but remains the ritual symbol of a larger transaction. The prey represents all that is received, whether from a host of animal gods, an arbitrary god, or from the law of probability.

It is sometimes said that hunters are cruel, insensitive, and barbaric. In fact, however, the hunter may experience life and death deeply. In a poem called "Castles and Distances" Richard Wilbur writes:

> *Oh, it is hunters alone*
> *Regret the beastly pain, it is they who love the foe*
> *That quarries out their force, and every arrow*
> *Is feathered soft with wishes to atone;*
>   *Even the surest sword in sorrow*
>   *Bleeds for its spoiling blow.*

>   *Sometimes, as one can see*
> *Carved at Amboise in a high relief, on the lintel stone*
> *Of the castle chapel, hunters have strangely come*
> *To a mild close of the chase, bending the knee*
>   *Instead of the bow, struck sweetly dumb*
>   *To see from the brow bone*

> *Of the hounded stag a cross*
> *Grown, and the eyes clear with grace. . . .*

In urban and technological situations hunting continues to put us in close touch with nature, to provoke the study of natural history, and to nourish the idea of conservation. Even royalty is subject to the uncertainty of the gift. From the Middle Ages we have numerous examples of the values of the hunt. Its forms coincided with social structure in complex royal households and its practice stimulated first-hand observation at a time when hearsay and past authority were the main sources of information. The unique work of Frederick II in thirteenth-century ornithology is an example, an advance in the understanding of birds gathered during hunting trips afield. A more recent example is the work of the late Aldo Leopold. A hunter and a forester, his career was a living documentation of the slow sensitizing of a man to his environment through the medium of gun and dog. In postulating a "split rail value" for hunting, Leopold observed that hunting is a reenactment of a historically important activity when contact with the natural environment and the virtues of this contact were less obscured by modern urban life.

Civilization extends the means of food and energy distribution and of storage against lean years. The ultimate origin of food in the soil is no longer apparent to the average person, as even agriculture is a closed industrial process. In this engineered and insulated atmosphere the natural world has become a peripheral relic, a strange, sometimes entertaining, sometimes frightening curiosity. What has become of *the gift?* It has receded from view except for those who seek it. They may be found in the open country trying their luck. By various arbitrary limitations, both behavioral and mechanical, the hunter curbs his technological advantage. This peculiar assemblage of legal, ethical, and physical restraints constitutes sportsmanship, a contemporary ritual. The hunt is arbitrarily limited. The hunter brings to focus his whole physical and spiritual attention on the moment of the kill. He expects to eat the quarry, even though economically it is dietetically irrelevant. Yet he will cook and eat it in a mood of thoughtful celebration known only to hunters.

20   It follows that hunting is not just an excuse to get out of doors. Killing and eating the prey are the most important things that hunters do. The successful hunt is a solemn and yet glad event. It places man for a moment in vital rapport with a universe from which civilization tends to separate him by its fostering of an illusion of superiority and independence. The natural environment will always be mysterious,

evoking an awe to be shared among all men who take the trouble to see it. If modern sportsmanship is a shallow substitute for the complex mythology or unifying ceremony of other cultures, we must acknowledge that only a part of the society hunts, that ritual forms of this technological era are still young and poorly defined, and that we are part of an age which may be said to be living on the accumulated capital—cultural and biological—of a million years of hardship, death, effort, and invention. Given a hard-earned margin magnified by machines, human society may behave irresponsibly for a time and forget the ties that bind it to the world.

Regardless of the technological advance, man remains part of and dependent upon nature. The necessity of signifying and recognizing this relationship remains, though it may not seem so. The hunter is our agent of awareness. He is not only an observer but a participant and receiver. He knows that man is a member of a natural community and that the processes of nature will never become so well understood or controlled that faith will cease to be important.

Analyzing Rhetorical Choices

1. Discuss Shepard's opening sentence, "Killing animals for the meat industry or for scientific research can be rationalized to the satisfaction of all but a few, but hunting for sport is frequently regarded as morally indefensible." What assumptions lie behind this statement? In what ways is this an effective opening to this essay?
2. Analyze the tone that Shepard adopts. How would you describe it, and how do Shepard's diction and sentence structure reinforce it?
3. Why do you think Shepard includes the lines from Richard Wilbur's poem, "Castles and Distances," and why is it placed at this point in the essay? Discuss its effectiveness in helping Shepard reinforce his argument.
4. What does Shepard mean by calling the natural world "a gift" and hunting "a ritual"? How do these word choices affect your response to Shepard's perspective?

Writing About Issues and Contexts

1. What rationalizations for hunting does Shepard offer? Analyze their persuasiveness in terms of logic and ethical justification.
2. Outline the structure of Shepard's argument. How does he build his case for the place of hunting within contemporary human society?

3. Shepard writes that "The hunt has ceased to be the main source of food, but remains the ritual symbol of a larger transaction." What does he mean by the phrase "larger transaction"? Who—or what—are involved in this transaction, and what exactly is being exchanged?

4. Offer your views concerning whether "The hunter is our agent of awareness" by analyzing two or three key arguments that Shepard makes concerning the human and the natural.

Born in Union City, New Jersey, **Norman Cousins** *(1915–1990) was a graduate of the Teacher's College of Columbia University. A writer for the* New York Evening Post *and* Current History *magazine, he joined the* Saturday Review *in 1940. He became editor of the* Review *in 1942 and served until 1978. Cousins lectured widely on world events and wrote a number of books that supported the power of positive thinking to combat illness, as in* Anatomy of an Illness, *published in 1979. He served as an adjunct professor of psychiatry at the UCLA medical school.*

Norman Cousins

Who Killed Benny Paret?

Sometime about 1935 or 1936 I had an interview with Mike Jacobs, the prizefight promoter. I was a fledgling reporter at that time; my beat was education but during the vacation season I found myself on varied assignments, all the way from ship news to sports reporting. In this way I found myself sitting opposite the most powerful figure in the boxing world.

There was nothing spectacular in Mr. Jacobs' manner or appearance; but when he spoke about prize fights, he was no longer a bland little man but a colossus who sounded the way Napoleon must have sounded when he reviewed a battle. You knew you were listening to Number One. His saying something made it true.

We discussed what to him was the only important element in successful promoting—how to please the crowd. So far as he was concerned, there was no mystery to it. You put killers in the ring and the people filled your arena. You hire boxing artists—men who are adroit at feinting, parrying, weaving, jabbing, and dancing, but who don't pack dynamite in their fists—and you wind up counting your empty seats. So you searched for the killers and sluggers and maulers— fellows who could hit with the force of a baseball bat.

I asked Mr. Jacobs if he was speaking literally when he said people came out to see the killer.

5   "They don't come out to see a tea party," he said evenly. "They come out to see the knockout. They come out to see a man hurt. If they think anything else, they're kidding themselves."

Recently, a young man by the name of Benny Paret was killed in the ring. The killing was seen by millions; it was on television. In the twelfth round, he was hit hard in the head several times, went down, was counted out, and never came out of the coma.

The Paret fight produced a flurry of investigations. Governor Rockefeller was shocked by what happened and appointed a committee to assess the responsibility. The New York State Boxing Commission decided to find out what was wrong. The District Attorney's office expressed its concern. One question that was solemnly studied in all three probes concerned the action of the referee. Did he act in time to stop the fight? Another question had to do with the role of the examining doctors who certified the physical fitness of the fighters before the bout. Still another question involved Mr. Paret's manager; did he rush his boy into the fight without adequate time to recuperate from the previous one?

In short, the investigators looked into every possible cause except the real one. Benny Paret was killed because the human fist delivers enough impact, when directed against the head, to produce a massive hemorrhage in the brain. The human brain is the most delicate and complex mechanism in all creation. It has a lacework of millions of highly fragile nerve connections. Nature attempts to protect this exquisitely intricate machinery by encasing it in a hard shell. Fortunately, the shell is thick enough to withstand a great deal of pounding. Nature, however, can protect man against everything except man himself. Not every blow to the head will kill a man—but there is always the risk of concussion and damage to the brain. A prizefighter may be able to survive even repeated brain concussions and go on fighting, but the damage to his brain may be permanent.

In any event, it is futile to investigate the referee's role and seek to determine whether he should have intervened to stop the fight earlier. That is not where the primary responsibility lies. The primary responsibility lies with the people who pay to see a man hurt. The referee who stops a fight too soon from the crowd's viewpoint can expect to be booed. The crowd wants the knockout; it wants to see a man stretched out on the canvas. This is the supreme moment in boxing. It is nonsense to talk about prizefighting as a test of boxing skills. No crowd was ever brought to its feet screaming and cheering at the sight of two men beautifully dodging and weaving out of each other's jabs. The time the crowd comes alive is when a man is hit hard over the heart or the head, when his mouthpiece flies out, when the blood squirts out of his nose or eyes, when he wobbles under the attack and his pursuer continues to smash at him with pole-ax impact.

10   Don't blame it on the referee. Don't even blame it on the fight managers. Put the blame where it belongs—on the prevailing mores that regard prizefighting as a perfectly proper enterprise and vehicle of entertainment. No one doubts that many people enjoy prizefighting and will miss it if it should be thrown out. And that is precisely the point.

Analyzing Rhetorical Choices

1. How does Cousins attempt to persuade? Is he successful? Why does Cousins begin with his interview with Mike Jacobs? Why is it significant that Jacobs is a fight promoter?

2. Cousins uses a number of strategies throughout his argument, including direct quotation, a switch to second person in the third paragraph, and an explicit description of boxing's brutal effects in paragraph nine, among others. Analyze the effectiveness of such strategies in persuading you that Cousins is right.

3. Does Cousins appear to be targeting a particular audience for this essay? What evidence from the text might indicate this?

Writing About Issues and Contexts

1. What does this article say about human nature? What evidence supports your contention? Do you agree that "the only important element in successful promoting" is "how to please the crowd"? Why or why not?

2. Explain the reaction of the New York State Boxing Commission, the district attorney, the governor of New York, and others to the death of Benny Paret. Do you think their responses were sincere? Cynical? Troubled?

3. Who does bear responsibility for the death of Benny Paret? Explain your answer by referring to Cousins (and, if you wish, Norman Mailer's essay in Chapter 9).

Born in Atlanta and a graduate of Morehouse College, Crozer Theological Seminary, and Boston University (where he earned his Ph.D.), **Dr. Martin Luther King, Jr.** *(1929–1968), is possibly the most admired civil rights leader of his or any other time. He achieved national prominence in 1955 as a result of his personal courage and oratorical skills as he led the boycott against segregated buses in Montgomery, Alabama. In 1957, King and other southern black ministers founded the Southern Christian Leadership Conference, through which King emphasized the goal of black voting rights. He published his first book in 1958,* Stride Toward Freedom: The Montgomery Story. *Known particularly for his advocacy of nonviolent strategies to bring about change, King's renown grew as he became* Time *magazine's Man of the Year in 1964, and in the same year, the recipient of the Nobel Peace Prize. King wrote "Letter from Birmingham Jail" in response to "A Call for Unity," a letter written by eight Birmingham clergymen and published in a local newspaper. King was assassinated in April 1968.*

Martin Luther King, Jr.

Letter from Birmingham Jail

My Dear Fellow Clergymen:

While confined here in the Birmingham city jail, I came across your recent statement calling my present activities "unwise and untimely." Seldom do I pause to answer criticism of my work and ideas. If I sought to answer all of the criticisms that cross my desk, my secretaries would have little time for anything other than such correspondence in the course of the day, and I would have no time for constructive work. But since I feel that you are men of genuine good will and that your criticisms are sincerely set forth, I want to try to answer your statement in what I hope will be patient and reasonable terms.

I think I should indicate why I am here in Birmingham, since you have been influenced by the view which argues against "outsiders coming in." I have the honor of serving as president of the Southern Christian Leadership Conference, an organization operating in every southern state, with headquarters in Atlanta, Georgia. We have some eighty-five affiliated organizations across the South, and one of them is the Alabama Christian Movement for Human Rights. Frequently we share staff, educational, and financial resources with our affiliates. Several months ago the affiliate here in Birmingham asked us to be on call to engage in a nonviolent direct-action program if such were deemed necessary. We readily consented, and when the hour came, we lived up to our promise. So I, along with several members of my staff, am here because I was invited here. I am here because I have organizational ties here.

But more basically, I am in Birmingham because injustice is here. Just as the prophets of the eighth century B.C. left their villages and carried their "thus saith the Lord" far beyond the boundaries of their home towns, and just as the Apostle Paul left his village of Tarsus and carried the gospel of Jesus Christ to the far corners of the Greco-Roman world, so am I compelled to carry the gospel of freedom beyond my own home town. Like Paul, I must constantly respond to the Macedonian call for aid.

Moreover, I am cognizant of the interrelatedness of all communities and states. I cannot sit idly by in Atlanta and not be concerned about what happens in Birmingham. Injustice anywhere is a threat to justice everywhere. We are caught in an inescapable network of mutuality, tied in a single garment of destiny. Whatever affects one directly, affects all indirectly. Never again can we afford to live with the narrow, provincial "outside agitator" idea. Anyone who lives inside the United States can never be considered an outsider anywhere within its bounds.

5   You deplore the demonstrations taking place in Birmingham. But your statement, I am sorry to say, fails to express a similar concern for the conditions that brought about the demonstrations. I am sure that none of you would want to rest content with the superficial kind of social analysis that deals merely with effects and does not grapple with underlying causes. It is unfortunate that demonstrations are taking place in Birmingham, but it is even more unfortunate that the city's white power structure left the Negro community with no alternative.

In any nonviolent campaign there are four basic steps: collection of the facts to determine whether injustices exist; negotiation; self-purification; and direct action. We have gone through all these steps in Birmingham. There can be no gainsaying the fact that racial injustice engulfs this community. Birmingham is probably the most thoroughly segregated city in the United States. Its ugly record of brutality is widely known. Negroes have experienced grossly unjust treatment in the courts. There have been more unsolved bombings of Negro homes and churches in Birmingham than in any other city in the nation. These are the hard, brutal facts of the case. On the basis of these conditions, Negro leaders sought to negotiate with the city fathers. But the latter consistently refused to engage in good-faith negotiation.

Then, last September, came the opportunity to talk with leaders of Birmingham's economic community. In the course of the negotiations, certain promises were made by the merchants—for example, to remove the stores' humiliating racial signs. On the basis of these promises, the Reverend Fred Shuttlesworth and the leaders of the Alabama Christian Movement for Human Rights agreed to a moratorium on all demonstrations. As the weeks and months went by, we realized that we were the victims of a broken promise. A few signs, briefly removed, returned; the others remained.

As in so many past experiences, our hopes had been blasted, and the shadow of deep disappointment settled upon us. We had no alternative except to prepare for direct action, whereby we would present our very bodies as a means of laying our case before the conscience of the local and national community. Mindful of the difficulties involved, we decided to undertake a process of self-purification. We began a series of workshops on nonviolence, and we repeatedly asked ourselves: "Are you able to accept blows without retaliating?" "Are you able to endure the ordeal of jail?" We decided to schedule our direct-action program for the Easter season, realizing that except for Christmas, this is the main shopping period of the year. Knowing that a strong economic-withdrawal program would be the by-product of direct action, we felt that this would be the best time to bring pressure to bear on the merchants for the needed change.

Then it occurred to us that Birmingham's mayoral election was coming up in March, and we speedily decided to postpone action until after election day. When we discovered that the Commissioner of Public Safety, Eugene "Bull" Connor, had piled up enough votes to be in the run-off, we decided again to postpone action until the day after the run-off so that the demonstrations could not be used to cloud the issues. Like many others, we wanted to see Mr. Connor defeated, and to this end we endured postponement after postponement. Having aided in this community need, we felt that our direct-action program could be delayed no longer.

10   You may well ask, "Why direct action? Why sit-ins, marches, and so forth? Isn't negotiation a better path?" You are quite right in calling for negotiation. Indeed, this is the very purpose of direct action. Nonviolent direct action seeks to create such a crisis and foster such a

tension that a community which has constantly refused to negotiate is forced to confront the issue. It seeks so to dramatize the issue that it can no longer be ignored. My citing the creation of tension as part of the work of the nonviolent-resister may sound rather shocking. But I must confess that I am not afraid of the word "tension." I have earnestly opposed violent tension, but there is a type of constructive, nonviolent tension which is necessary for growth. Just as Socrates felt that it was necessary to create a tension in the mind so that individuals could rise from the bondage of myths and half-truths to the unfettered realm of creative analysis and objective appraisal, so must we see the need for nonviolent gadflies to create the kind of tension in society that will help men rise from the dark depths of prejudice and racism to the majestic heights of understanding and brotherhood.

The purpose of our direct-action program is to create a situation so crisis-packed that it will inevitably open the door to negotiation. I therefore concur with you in your call for negotiation. Too long has our beloved Southland been bogged down in a tragic effort to live in monologue rather than dialogue.

One of the basic points in your statement is that the action that I and my associates have taken in Birmingham is untimely. Some have asked: "Why didn't you give the new city administration time to act?" The only answer that I can give to this query is that the new Birmingham administration must be prodded about as much as the outgoing one, before it will act. We are sadly mistaken if we feel that the election of Albert Boutwell as mayor will bring the millennium to Birmingham. While Mr. Boutwell is a much more gentle person than Mr. Connor, they are both segregationists, dedicated to maintenance of the status quo. I have hoped that Mr. Boutwell will be reasonable enough to see the futility of massive resistance to desegregation. But he will not see this without pressure from devotees of civil rights. My friends, I must say to you that we have not made a single gain in civil rights without determined legal and nonviolent pressure. Lamentably, it is an historical fact that privileged groups seldom give up their privileges voluntarily. Individuals may see the moral light and voluntarily give up their unjust posture; but, as Reinhold Niebuhr has reminded us, groups tend to be more immoral than individuals.

We know through painful experience that freedom is never voluntarily given by the oppressor; it must be demanded by the oppressed. Frankly, I have yet to engage in a direct-action campaign that was "well timed" in the view of those who have not suffered unduly from the disease of segregation. For years now I have heard the word

"Wait!" It rings in the ear of every Negro with piercing familiarity. This "Wait" has almost always meant "Never." We must come to see, with one of our distinguished jurists, that "justice too long delayed is justice denied."

We have waited for more than 340 years for our constitutional and God-given rights. The nations of Asia and Africa are moving with jet-like speed toward gaining political independence, but we still creep at horse-and-buggy pace toward gaining a cup of coffee at a lunch counter. Perhaps it is easy for those who have never felt the stinging darts of segregation to say, "Wait." But when you have seen vicious mobs lynch your mothers and fathers at will and drown your sisters and brothers at whim; when you have seen hate-filled policemen curse, kick, and even kill your black brothers and sisters; when you see the vast majority of your twenty million Negro brothers smothering in an airtight cage of poverty in the midst of an affluent society; when you suddenly find your tongue twisted and your speech stammering as you seek to explain to your six-year-old daughter why she can't go to the public amusement park that has just been advertised on television, and see tears welling up in her eyes when she is told that Funtown is closed to colored children, and see ominous clouds of inferiority beginning to form in her little mental sky, and see her beginning to distort her personality by developing an unconscious bitterness toward white people; when you have to concoct an answer for a five-year-old son who is asking "Daddy, why do white people treat colored people so mean?"; when you take a cross-country drive and find it necessary to sleep night after night in the uncomfortable corners of your automobile because no motel will accept you; when you are humiliated day in and day out by nagging signs reading "white" and "colored"; when your first name becomes "nigger," your middle name becomes "boy" (however old you are) and your last name becomes "John," and your wife and mother are never given the respected title "Mrs."; when you are harried by day and haunted by night by the fact that you are a Negro, living constantly at tiptoe stance, never quite knowing what to expect next, and are plagued with inner fears and outer resentments; when you are forever fighting a degenerating sense of "nobodiness"— then you will understand why we find it difficult to wait. There comes a time when the cup of endurance runs over, and men are no longer willing to be plunged into the abyss of despair. I hope, sirs, you can understand our legitimate and unavoidable impatience.

15   You express a great deal of anxiety over our willingness to break laws. This is certainly a legitimate concern. Since we so diligently urge

people to obey the Supreme Court's decision of 1954 outlawing segregation in the public schools, at first glance it may seem rather paradoxical for us consciously to break laws. One may well ask: "How can you advocate breaking some laws and obeying others?" The answer lies in the fact that there are two types of laws: just and unjust. I would be the first to advocate obeying just laws. One has not only a legal but a moral responsibility to obey just laws. Conversely, one has a moral responsibility to disobey unjust laws. I would agree with St. Augustine that "an unjust law is no law at all."

Now, what is the difference between the two? How does one determine whether a law is just or unjust? A just law is a man-made code that squares with the moral law or the law of God. An unjust law is a code that is out of harmony with the moral law. To put it in the terms of St. Thomas Aquinas: An unjust law is a human law that is not rooted in eternal law and natural law. Any law that uplifts human personality is just. Any law that degrades human personality is unjust. All segregation statutes are unjust because segregation distorts the soul and damages the personality. It gives the segregator a false sense of superiority and the segregated a false sense of inferiority. Segregation, to use the terminology of the Jewish philosopher Martin Buber, substitutes "I-it" relationship for an "I-thou" relationship and ends up relegating persons to the status of things. Hence segregation is not only politically, economically, and sociologically unsound, it is morally wrong and sinful. Paul Tillich has said that sin is separation. Is not segregation an existential expression of man's tragic separation, his awful estrangement, his terrible sinfulness? Thus it is that I can urge men to obey the 1954 decision of the Supreme Court, for it is morally right; and I can urge them to disobey segregation ordinances, for they are morally wrong.

Let us consider a more concrete example of just and unjust laws. An unjust law is a code that a numerical or power majority group compels a minority group to obey but does not make binding on itself. This is *difference* made legal. By the same token, a just law is a code that a majority compels a minority to follow and that it is willing to follow itself. This is *sameness* made legal.

Let me give another explanation. A law is unjust if it is inflicted on a minority that, as a result of being denied the right to vote, had no part in enacting or devising the law. Who can say that the legislature of Alabama which set up that state's segregation laws was democratically elected? Throughout Alabama all sorts of devious methods are used to prevent Negroes from becoming registered voters, and there are some counties in which, even though Negroes constitute a majority of the population, not a single Negro is registered. Can any law enacted under such circumstances be considered democratically structured?

Sometimes a law is just on its face and unjust in its application. For instance, I have been arrested on a charge of parading without a permit. Now, there is nothing wrong in having an ordinance which requires a permit for a parade. But such an ordinance becomes unjust when it is used to maintain segregation and to deny citizens the First-Amendment privilege of peaceful assembly and protest.

20   I hope you are able to see the distinction I am trying to point out. In no sense do I advocate evading or defying the law, as would the rabid segregationist. That would lead to anarchy. One who breaks an unjust law must do so openly, lovingly, and with a willingness to accept the penalty. I submit that an individual who breaks a law that conscience tells him is unjust, and who willingly accepts the penalty of imprisonment in order to arouse the conscience of the community over its injustice, is in reality expressing the highest respect for law.

Of course, there is nothing new about this kind of civil disobedience. It was evidenced sublimely in the refusal of Shadrach, Meshach, and Abednego to obey the laws of Nebuchadnezzar, on the ground that a higher moral law was at stake. It was practiced superbly by the early Christians, who were willing to face hungry lions and the excruciating pain of chopping blocks rather than submit to certain unjust laws of the Roman Empire. To a degree, academic freedom is a reality today because Socrates practiced civil disobedience. In our own nation, the Boston Tea Party represented a massive act of civil disobedience.

We should never forget that everything Adolf Hitler did in Germany was "legal" and everything the Hungarian freedom fighters did in Hungary was "illegal." It was "illegal" to aid and comfort a Jew in Hitler's Germany. Even so, I am sure that, had I lived in Germany at the time, I would have aided and comforted my Jewish brothers. If today I lived in a Communist country where certain principles dear to the Christian faith are suppressed, I would openly advocate disobeying that country's anti-religious laws.

I must make two honest confessions to you, my Christian and Jewish brothers. First, I must confess that over the past few years I have been gravely disappointed with the white moderate. I have almost reached the regrettable conclusion that the Negro's great stumbling block in the stride toward freedom is not the White Citizen's Counciler or the Ku Klux Klanner, but the white moderate, who is more devoted to "order" than to justice; who prefers a negative peace which is the absence of tension to a positive peace which is the presence of justice; who constantly says, "I agree with you in the goal you seek, but I cannot agree with your methods of direct action"; who paternalistically believes he can set the timetable for another man's freedom; who lives by a mythical concept of time and who constantly advises the Negro to wait for a "more convenient season." Shallow understanding from people of good will is more frustrating than absolute misunderstanding from people of ill will. Lukewarm acceptance is much more bewildering than outright rejection.

I had hoped that the white moderate would understand that law and order exist for the purpose of establishing justice and that when they fail in this purpose they become the dangerously structured dams that block the flow of social progress. I had hoped that the white moderate would understand that the present tension in the South is a necessary phase of the transition from an obnoxious negative peace, in which the Negro passively accepted his unjust plight, to a substantive and positive peace, in which all men will respect the dignity and worth of human personality. Actually, we who engage in nonviolent direct action are not the creators of tension. We merely bring to the surface the hidden tension that is already alive. We bring it out in the open, where it can be seen and dealt with. Like a boil that can never be cured so long as it is covered up but must be opened with all its ugliness to the natural medicines of air and light, injustice must be exposed, with all the tension its exposure creates, to the light of human conscience and the air of national opinion, before it can be cured.

25   In your statement you assert that our actions, even though peaceful, must be condemned because they precipitate violence. But is this a logical assertion? Isn't this like condemning a robbed man because his possession of money precipitated the evil act of robbery? Isn't this like condemning Socrates because his unswerving commitment to truth and his philosophical inquiries precipitated the act by the misguided populace in which they made him drink hemlock? Isn't this like condemning Jesus because his unique God-consciousness and never-ceasing devotion to God's will precipitated the evil act of crucifixion? We must come to see that, as the federal courts have consistently affirmed, it is wrong to urge an individual to cease his efforts to gain his basic constitutional rights because the quest may precipitate violence. Society must protect the robbed and punish the robber.

I had also hoped that the white moderate would reject the myth concerning time in relation to the struggle for freedom. I have just received a letter from a white brother in Texas. He writes: "All

Christians know that the colored people will receive equal rights eventually, but it is possible that you are in too great a religious hurry. It has taken Christianity almost two thousand years to accomplish what it has. The teachings of Christ take time to come to earth." Such an attitude stems from a tragic misconception of time, from the strangely irrational notion that there is something in the very flow of time that will inevitably cure all ills. Actually, time itself is neutral; it can be used either destructively or constructively. More and more I feel that the people of ill will have used time much more effectively than have the people of good will. We will have to repent in this generation not merely for the hateful words and actions of the bad people, but for the appalling silence of the good people. Human progress never rolls in on wheels of inevitability; it comes through the tireless efforts of men willing to be co-workers with God, and without this hard work, time itself becomes an ally of the forces of social stagnation. We must use time creatively, in the knowledge that the time is always ripe to do right. Now is the time to make real the promise of democracy and transform our pending national elegy into a creative psalm of brotherhood. Now is the time to lift our national policy from the quicksand of racial injustice to the solid rock of human dignity.

You speak of our activity in Birmingham as extreme. At first I was rather disappointed that fellow clergymen would see my nonviolent efforts as those of an extremist. I began thinking about the fact that I stand in the middle of two opposing forces in the Negro community. One is a force of complacency, made up in part of Negroes who, as a result of long years of oppression, are so drained of self-respect and a sense of "somebodiness" that they have adjusted to segregation; and in part of a few middle-class Negroes who, because of a degree of academic and economic security and because in some ways they profit by segregation, have become insensitive to the problems of the masses. The other force is one of bitterness and hatred, and it comes perilously close to advocating violence. It is expressed in the various black nationalist groups that are springing up across the nation, the largest and best-known being Elijah Muhammad's Muslim movement. Nourished by the Negro's frustration over the continued existence of racial discrimination, this movement is made up of people who have lost faith in America, who have absolutely repudiated Christianity, and who have concluded that the white man is an incorrigible "devil."

I have tried to stand between these two forces, saying that we need emulate neither the "do-nothingism" of the complacent nor the hatred and despair of the black nationalist. For there is the more excellent way of love and nonviolent protest. I am grateful to God that, through the influence of the Negro church, the way of nonviolence became an integral part of our struggle.

If this philosophy had not emerged, by now many streets of the South would, I am convinced, be flowing with blood. And I am further convinced that if our white brothers dismiss as "rabblerousers" and "outside agitators" those of us who employ nonviolent direct action, and if they refuse to support our nonviolent efforts, millions of Negroes will, out of frustration and despair, seek solace and security in Black-nationalist ideologies—a development that would inevitably lead to a frightening racial nightmare.

30   Oppressed people cannot remain oppressed forever. The yearning for freedom eventually manifests itself, and that is what has happened to the American Negro. Something within has reminded him of his birthright of freedom, and something without has reminded him that it can be gained. Consciously or unconsciously, he has been caught up by the *Zeitgeist*, and with his black brothers of Africa and his brown and yellow brothers of Asia, South America, and the Caribbean, the United States Negro is moving with a sense of great urgency toward the promised land of racial justice. If one recognizes this vital urge that has engulfed the Negro community, one should readily understand why public demonstrations are taking place. The Negro has many pent-up resentments and latent frustrations, and he must release them. So let him march; let him make prayer pilgrimages to the city hall; let him go on freedom rides—and try to understand why he must do so. If his repressed emotions are not released in nonviolent ways, they will seek expression through violence; this is not a threat but a fact of history. So I have not said to my people, "Get rid of your discontent." Rather, I have tried to say that this normal and healthy discontent can be channeled into the creative outlet of nonviolent direct action. And now this approach is being termed extremist.

But though I was initially disappointed at being categorized as an extremist, as I continued to think about the matter I gradually gained a measure of satisfaction from the label. Was not Jesus an extremist for love: "Love your enemies, bless them that curse you, do good to them that hate you, and pray for them which despitefully use you, and persecute you." Was not Amos an extremist for justice: "Let justice roll down like waters and righteousness like an everflowing stream." Was not Paul an extremist for the Christian gospel: "I bear in my body the marks of the Lord Jesus." Was not Martin Luther an extremist: "Here I stand; I cannot do otherwise, so help me God." And John Bunyan: "I will stay in jail to the end of my days before I make a butchery of my conscience." And Abraham Lincoln: "This nation cannot survive half slave and half free." And Thomas Jefferson: "We hold these truths to be self-evident, that all men are created equal. . . ." So the question is not whether we will be extremists, but what kind of extremists we will be. Will we be extremists for hate or for love? Will we be extremists for the preservation of injustice or for the extension of justice? In that dramatic scene on Calvary's hill three men were crucified. We must never forget that all three were crucified for the same crime—the crime of extremism. Two were extremists for immorality, and thus fell below their environment. The other, Jesus Christ, was an extremist for love, truth, and goodness, and thereby rose above his environment. Perhaps the South, the nation, and the world are in dire need of creative extremists.

I had hoped that the white moderate would see this need. Perhaps I was too optimistic; perhaps I expected too much. I suppose I should have realized that few members of the oppressor race can understand the deep groans and passionate yearnings of the oppressed race, and still fewer have the vision to see that injustice must be rooted out by strong, persistent, and determined action. I am thankful, however, that some of our white brothers in the South have grasped the meaning of this social revolution and committed themselves to it. They are still all too few in quantity, but they are big in quality. Some—such as Ralph McGill, Lillian Smith, Harry Golden, James McBridge Dabbs, Anne Braden, and Sarah Patton Boyle—have written about our struggle in eloquent and prophetic terms. Others have marched with us down nameless streets of the South. They have languished in filthy, roach-infested jails, suffering the abuse and brutality of policemen who view them as "dirty nigger-lovers." Unlike so many of their moderate brothers and sisters, they have recognized the urgency of the moment and sensed the need for powerful "action" antidotes to combat the disease of segregation.

Let me take note of my other major disappointment. I have been so greatly disappointed with the white church and its leadership. Of course, there are some notable exceptions. I am not unmindful of the fact that each of you has taken some significant stands on this issue. I commend you, Reverend Stallings, for your Christian stand on this past Sunday, in welcoming Negroes to your worship service on a non-segregated basis. I commend the Catholic leaders of this state for integrating Spring Hill College several years ago.

But despite these notable exceptions, I must honestly reiterate that I have been disappointed with the church. I do not say this as one of those negative critics who can always find something wrong with the church. I say this as a minister of the gospel, who loves the church; who was nurtured in its bosom; who has been sustained by its spiritual blessings and who will remain true to it as long as the cord of life shall lengthen.

35   When I was suddenly catapulted into the leadership of the bus protest in Montgomery, Alabama, a few years ago, I felt we would be supported by the white church. I felt that the white ministers, priests, and rabbis of the South would be among our strongest allies. Instead, some have been outright opponents, refusing to understand the freedom movement and misrepresenting its leaders; all too many others have been more cautious than courageous and have remained silent behind the anesthetizing security of stained glass windows.

In spite of my shattered dreams, I came to Birmingham with the hope that the white religious leadership of this community would see the justice of our cause and, with deep moral concern, would serve as the channel through which our just grievances could reach the power structure. I had hoped that each of you would understand. But again I have been disappointed.

I have heard numerous southern religious leaders admonish their worshipers to comply with a desegregation decision because it is the law, but I have longed to hear white ministers declare: "Follow this decree because integration is morally right and the Negro is your brother." In the midst of blatant injustices inflicted upon the Negro, I have watched white churchmen stand on the sideline and mouth pious irrelevancies and sanctimonious trivialities. In the midst of a mighty struggle to rid our nation of racial and economic injustice I have heard many ministers say: "Those are social issues, with which the gospel has no real concern." And I have watched many churches commit themselves to a completely otherworldly religion which makes a strange, un-Biblical distinction between body and soul, between the sacred and the secular.

I have traveled the length and breadth of Alabama, Mississippi, and all the other southern states. On sweltering summer days and crisp autumn mornings I have looked at the South's beautiful churches with their lofty spires pointing heavenward. I have beheld the impressive outlines of her massive religious-education buildings. Over and over I have found myself asking: "What kind of people worship here? Who is their God? Where were their voices when the lips of Governor Barnett dripped with words of interposition and nullification? Where were they when Governor Wallace gave a clarion call for defiance and hatred? Where were their voices of support when bruised and weary Negro men and women decided to rise from the dark dungeons of complacency to the bright hills of creative protest?"

Yes, these questions are still in my mind. In deep disappointment I have wept over the laxity of the church. But be assured that my tears have been tears of love. There can be no deep disappointment where there is not deep love. Yes, I love the church. How could I do otherwise? I am in the rather unique position of being the son, the grandson, and the great-grandson of preachers. Yes, I see the church as the body of Christ. But, oh! How we have blemished and scarred that body through social neglect and through fear of being nonconformists.

40   There was a time when the church was very powerful—in the time when the early Christians rejoiced at being deemed worthy to suffer for what they believed. In those days the church was not merely a thermometer that recorded the ideas and principles of popular opinion; it was a thermostat that transformed the mores of society. Whenever the early Christians entered a town, the people in power became disturbed and immediately sought to convict the Christians for being "disturbers of the peace" and "outside agitators." But the Christians pressed on, in the conviction that they were "a colony of heaven," called to obey God rather than man. Small in number, they were big in commitment. They were too God-intoxicated to be "astronomically intimidated." By their effort and example they brought an end to such ancient evils as infanticide and gladiatorial contests.

Things are different now. So often the contemporary church is a weak, ineffectual voice with an uncertain sound. So often it is an archdefender of the status quo. Far from being disturbed by the presence of the church, the power structure of the average community is consoled by the church's silent—and often even vocal—sanction of things as they are.

But the judgment of God is upon the church as never before. If today's church does not recapture the sacrificial spirit of the early church, it will lose its authenticity, forfeit the loyalty of millions, and be dismissed as an irrelevant social club with no meaning for the twentieth century. Every day I meet young people whose disappointment with the church has turned into outright disgust.

Perhaps I have once again been too optimistic. Is organized religion too inextricably bound to the status quo to save our nation and the world? Perhaps I must turn my faith to the inner spiritual church, the church within the church, as the true *ekklesia* and the hope of the world. But again I am thankful to God that some noble souls from the ranks of organized religion have broken loose from the paralyzing chains of conformity and joined us as active partners in the struggle for freedom. They have left their secure congregations and walked the streets of Albany, Georgia, with us. They have gone down the highways of the South on tortuous rides for freedom. Yes, they have gone to jail with us. Some have been dismissed from their churches, have lost the support of their bishops and fellow ministers. But they have acted in the faith that right defeated is stronger than evil triumphant. Their witness has been the spiritual salt that has preserved the true meaning of the gospel in these troubled times. They have carved a tunnel of hope through the dark mountain of disappointment.

I hope the church as a whole will meet the challenge of this decisive hour. But even if the church does not come to the aid of justice, I have no despair about the future. I have no fear about the outcome of our struggle in Birmingham, even if our motives are at present misunderstood. We will reach the goal of freedom in Birmingham and all over the nation, because the goal of America is freedom. Abused and scorned though we may be, our destiny is tied up with America's destiny. Before the pilgrims landed at Plymouth, we were here. Before the pen of Jefferson etched the majestic words of the Declaration of Independence across the pages of history, we were here. For more than two centuries our forebears labored in this country without wages; they made cotton king; they built the homes of their masters while suffering gross injustice and shameful humiliation—and yet out of a bottomless vitality they continued to thrive and develop. If the inexpressible cruelties of slavery could not stop us, the opposition we now face will surely fail. We will win our freedom because the sacred heritage of our nation and the eternal will of God are embodied in our echoing demands.

45   Before closing I feel impelled to mention one other point in your statement that has troubled me profoundly. You warmly commended the Birmingham police force for keeping "order" and "preventing violence." I doubt that you would have so warmly commended the police force if you have seen its dogs sinking their teeth into unarmed, nonviolent Negroes. I doubt that you would so quickly commend the policemen if you were to observe their ugly and inhumane treatment of Negroes here in the city jail; if you were to watch them push and curse old Negro women and young Negro girls; if you were to see them slap and kick old Negro men and young boys; if you were to observe them, as they did on two occasions, refuse to give us food because we wanted to sing our grace together. I cannot join you in your praise of the Birmingham police department.

It is true that the police have exercised a degree of discipline in handling the demonstrators. In this sense they have conducted themselves rather "nonviolently" in public. But for what purpose? To preserve the evil system of segregation. Over the past few years I have consistently preached that nonviolence demands that the means we use must be as pure as the ends we seek. I have tried to make clear that it is wrong to use immoral means to attain moral ends. But now I must affirm that it is just as wrong, or perhaps even more so, to use moral means to preserve immoral ends. Perhaps Mr. Connor and his policemen have been rather nonviolent in public, as was Chief Pritchett in Albany, Georgia, but they have used the moral means of nonviolence to maintain the immoral end of racial injustice. T. S. Eliot has said, "The last temptation is the greatest treason: To do the right deed for the wrong reason."

I wish you had commended the Negro sit-inners and demonstrators of Birmingham for their sublime courage, their willingness to suffer, and their amazing discipline in the midst of great provocation. One day the South will recognize its real heroes. They will be the James Merediths, with the noble sense of purpose that enables them to face jeering and hostile mobs, and with the agonizing loneliness that characterizes the life of the pioneer. They will be old, oppressed, battered Negro women, symbolized in a seventy-two-year-old woman in Montgomery, Alabama, who rose up with a sense of dignity and with her people decided not to ride segregated buses, and who responded with ungrammatical profundity to one who inquired about her weariness: "My feets is tired, but my soul is at rest." They will be the young high school and college students, the young ministers of the gospel and a host of their elders, courageously and nonviolently sitting in at lunch counters and willingly going to jail for conscience' sake. One day the South will know that when these disinherited children of God sat down at lunch counters, they were in reality standing up for what is best in the American dream and for the most sacred values in our Judaeo-Christian heritage, thereby bringing our nation back to those great wells of democracy which were dug deep by the founding fathers in their formulation of the Constitution and the Declaration of Independence.

Never before have I written so long a letter. I'm afraid it is much too long to take your precious time. I can assure you that it would have been much shorter if I had been writing from a comfortable desk, but what else can one do when he is alone in a narrow jail cell, other than write long letters, think long thoughts, and pray long prayers?

If I have said anything in this letter that overstates the truth and indicates an unreasonable impatience, I beg you to forgive me. If I have said anything that understates the truth and indicates my having a patience that allows me to settle for anything less than brotherhood, I beg God to forgive me.

50   I hope this letter finds you strong in the faith. I also hope that circumstances will soon make it possible for me to meet each of you, not as an integrationist or a civil-rights leader but as a fellow clergyman and a Christian brother. Let us all hope that the dark clouds of racial prejudice will soon pass away and the deep fog of misunderstanding will be lifted from our fear-drenched communities, and in some not too distant tomorrow the radiant stars of love and brotherhood will shine over our great nation with all their scintillating beauty.

Yours for the cause of Peace and Brotherhood,

MARTIN LUTHER KING, JR.

Analyzing Rhetorical Choices

1. Why would King have chosen the form of a letter for this response rather than asking for a column in the newspaper that had published the "A Call for Unity"? What effect does this have? What might this indicate about King's purpose?

2. Toward the middle of the essay, King writes, "I must make two honest confessions to you . . ." Why does he wait so long to directly address the clergy to whom he writes this letter? What is the effect of this strategy? What aspects of the letter would have changed had King written this first? How?

3. Look carefully at King's choice of words. For instance, what situation does he evoke when he says that in the South, people "live in monologue rather than dialogue"? Why would King say that we must break unjust laws "openly" and "lovingly"? How do choices such as these fit with King's overall strategy for the letter?

4. King makes various religious and other contextual references in the letter. Why? To what effect? What assumptions, then, does King seem to be making about his readers?

Writing About Issues and Contexts

1. Explore the various definitions of *civil disobedience* and the extent to which King's letter exemplifies them. Does King justify his argument that civil disobedience in some cases is justified?

2. What is the difference between a legal responsibility and a moral responsibility?

3. King states, "Oppressed people cannot remain oppressed forever." Assess this statement in terms of your historical knowledge of oppressed people. As part of your response, define the term *oppressed people.*

One of America's most distinguished architectural critics, **Paul Goldberger** *(1950–   ) graduated from Yale University in 1972. Goldberger was architecture critic and cultural news editor at the* New York Times *for twenty-five years before becoming chief architecture critic for* The New Yorker *in 1997. A Pulitzer Prize winner in 1984, Goldberger's published works include* The City Observed *(1979) and* The Skyscraper *(1983). His forthcoming book on the redevelopment of the World Trade Center site will be published by Random House in 2003. "Building Plans" represents a subtle form of argument at a time when the practical implications of tragedy bring other implications to the fore. It appeared in a special issue of* The New Yorker *devoted entirely to the September 11 attacks and published on September 26, 2001.*

Paul Goldberger

Building Plans: What the World Trade Center Meant

There have been skyscrapers in New York for more than a century, and we are accustomed to seeing the bigger, stronger buildings crowd out the smaller, weaker ones. Height is our most potent architectural currency. The Metropolitan Life campanile reigned once, then the Woolworth Building and, briefly, the Chrysler Building, then the Empire State Building and the World Trade Center towers, those two vertical lines that anchored the composition of the skyline for twenty-five years. The towers were not beautiful buildings. They were gargantuan and banal, blandness blown up to a gigantic size. But size was the point, and the people who stood in line to visit the hundred-and-seventh-floor observation deck or eat at Windows on the World and buy little souvenir snow globes with the towers inside understood this, just as real-estate developers did, and as the terrorists who rammed their planes into the towers last week did.

With the invention of the passenger elevator in the mid-nineteenth century and the steel frame two decades later, an intimate connection was forged between the tallest tower in the city and the biggest corporation, the richest bank, or whatever financial entity wanted to be seen as running the place. Before there were skyscrapers, the horizon in most cities was dominated by church steeples. (In New York, the tallest thing was Richard Upjohn's Trinity Church, built in 1846.) The earliest skyscrapers wrested control of the skyline from God and gave it to Mammon, where it has pretty much remained. In 1913, a fawning minister called the Woolworth Building the "cathedral of commerce," in celebration of the triumph of corporate power that Cass Gilbert's lyrical Gothic skyscraper represented. It is a pretty straight line from the Woolworth Building to the World Trade Center. The architectural dressing changed, but the basic idea of building as high as you could to express power became a convention in almost every city, first in this country and then, by the nineteen-eighties, around the world.

The urge to make buildings higher and higher has been fading for the last few years, for purely practical reasons. Constructing towers of a hundred stories or more isn't much of a challenge technologically today, but it is not particularly economical, either. It never was. The space on the lower floors that is given up to make room for elevator shafts to the upper floors cuts into rentable space. The World Trade Center was a dinosaur in this sense, although the economics of the place got a lot better over time, and just two months ago the Port Authority concluded a deal to lease the towers for $3.2 billion to the developer Larry Silverstein, who then hired David Childs, of Skidmore, Owings & Merrill, to upgrade the complex. Childs has designed several new towers in New York, including the A.O.L. Time Warner Center that is going up at Columbus Circle. Silverstein hoped to fix up the Trade Center's image and turn it into a kind of downtown Rockefeller Center.

The very tallest buildings have usually been put up by people more interested in attention-getting value than in immediate financial return. That was the motivation of Governor Nelson Rockefeller and the Port Authority in the nineteen-sixties, when the World Trade Center was conceived, and it is the motivation for the entrepreneurs who have built or plan to build tall buildings in cities like Shanghai, Hong Kong, and Kuala Lumpur, where the Petronas Towers, the tallest skyscrapers in the world at the moment, were built in 1998. The destruction of the World Trade Center may well put an end to this kind of thing. "I think many of our clients would not want to build such a visible symbol, that they will want to build not so iconic and not so tall, the way the wealthy in Mexico started driving around in Volkswagens instead of Jaguars," David Childs said a few days ago.

5   The Trade Center was structurally innovative. Earlier skyscrapers were supported by complex frames of steel or concrete columns and

beams. Their exteriors were a "curtain wall" of metal, glass, or masonry hung from the frame, and their interiors were broken up by the grid of columns and beams. The Trade Center was more like a vast tube. Its exterior walls were a kind of steel mesh that supported most of the building's structural weight, freeing the interior floors from the usual maze of columns. The architects, Minoru Yamasaki and Emery Roth & Sons, and the engineer, Leslie Robertson, did not invent this tubular system. It was used earlier by Fazlur Khan and Myron Goldsmith, of Skidmore, Owings & Merrill, for an apartment house in Chicago finished in 1965. But the use of it at the Trade Center towers, which at the time of their construction were the tallest buildings in the world, represented an enormous advance. It was part of a tendency toward lightness in the design of almost everything—from cars and telephones to buildings.

Lighter does not mean weaker, of course. The relative lightness of the twin towers compared with, say, the Empire State Building, which has a steel frame and limestone cladding, does not appear to have been a factor in their collapse. Nothing about the design of the buildings seems to be intrinsically at fault. The towers withstood the assaults. They did not fall over, and their tops did not slice off. It was the explosions of the jet fuel that did the buildings in, not the impact of the jetliners themselves, and the buildings did not collapse until some time after the crashes—well over an hour for one tower, just under an hour for the other. Steel softens and melts under tremendous heat—it is, after all, created by the heat of the forge—and it was only a matter of time before the extraordinary heat of the fire would take its toll. The Trade Center was "amazingly robust," said Bill Baker, an engineer at the Skidmore firm who has designed the structural systems for several new skyscrapers. "It took a large commercial jet and the explosion, and it still stood, which is a lot to ask of any building." Fireproofing, Baker explained, "is really just a matter of buying time, and the building did buy time. There was basically an hour and forty minutes, and while a lot of people didn't make it out, a lot of people did."

The structural system of a skyscraper is designed to support the mass of the building itself—so that it does not collapse of its own weight—and to protect it from natural forces such as earthquakes and wind. Wind affects every skyscraper. The taller a building is, the greater the forces of wind pummelling it. Engineers have become so good at handling this that buildings don't fall down and they don't usually sway noticeably, either. But there isn't any building, except maybe the Pyramids, that could withstand the consequences of an enormous jetliner smashing into it with a full load of fuel. "You can't design for that, just like you can't design for the epicenter of an earthquake," David Childs said. William Pedersen, of Kohn Pedersen Fox, the architect of the new financial center planned for Shanghai, which would be slightly taller than the towers in Kuala Lumpur, says that when his firm was designing that building, there were no discussions of planes fully loaded with fuel flying into it. "If there is a physical way to protect a building from this, which I doubt, it would be prohibitive in cost, and the natural light would disappear."

Architecture doesn't usually work symbolically until it has been around for a while. The Woolworth Building went up less than a decade after the Wright Brothers took their first flight at Kitty Hawk. It still stands, just a few blocks to the east of the site of the World Trade Center, and it looked tiny in the televised shots of lower Manhattan last week, a delicate, dignified artifact.

Many of our greatest urban symbols achieve their meaning by connecting monumentality with the business of everyday life. Unlike cities such as Washington, D.C., New York has few pure monuments, with no purpose other than to inspire. There is the Statue of Liberty, but almost every other symbol of New York combines architectural ambition with the prosaic. People drive and walk across the Brooklyn Bridge every day. They ride their bicycles in Central Park, they board trains at Grand Central, and they go to work in Rockefeller Center or the Empire State Building. The Eiffel Tower is vastly more beautiful than the Trade Center was—so, for that matter, is the Empire State Building—but it is not part of life in Paris in quite the same way that the skyscrapers are part of life in New York. When the Eiffel Tower was built, a gaggle of artists and writers protested that it had nothing to do with Paris. No one could make that point about our skyscrapers. They were part of the city's essence from the day they went up.

10   We count on our urban symbols to be present. They are not supposed to evaporate. When buildings go away, they go almost as slowly as they came, piece by piece. The architect Cesar Pelli estimates that if the World Trade Center had been demolished conventionally it would have taken two years to dismantle. Pelli, who designed the World Financial Center, four squat towers next to the Trade Center, said to me that he thought of his buildings as "a set of foothills beside the mountain, and now the mountain is gone." It was an enormous familiar presence. As the years passed, it seemed to take on the quality of a huge piece of minimalist sculpture, and its dullness was almost a

virtue. Now that the Trade Center has become a martyr to terrorism, I suspect that architectural criticism of it will cease altogether. It has become a noble monument of a lost past. It is no more possible to know what will replace it as a symbol than it is to know what, if anything, will be built someday where the towers stood. But when the biggest thing in a city that prizes bigness becomes the most fragile thing, and the void has more weight than the solid, the rules of city-building change.

Analyzing Rhetorical Choices

1. How does Goldberger use expert testimony to reinforce and support his argument? Evaluate the effectiveness of this strategy.

2. Analyze and comment on Goldberger's use of examples—particularly as they relate to architectural history and the Twin Towers themselves. What purposes do these details serve?

3. Comment on Goldberger's rather matter-of-fact tone and largely straightforward declarative sentences. Does this style diminish or enhance the implications of his essay? What effects does his tone have on this subject?

Writing About Issues and Contexts

1. How does Goldberger communicate the larger and symbolic value of the World Trade Center? For what purpose?

2. Comment on Goldberger's statement that the Trade Center "seemed to take on the quality of a huge piece of minimalist sculpture, and its dullness was almost a virtue," contrasted with its having "become a martyr to terrorism." How does this essay move beyond the architectural details it provides?

3. Goldberger writes, "We count on our urban symbols to be present. They are not supposed to evaporate." What might be the implications of this statement—that is, beyond architecture?

*Although very much a political feminist, **Camille Paglia** (1947–   ) inspires controversy with her outspoken challenges and critiques of feminism. Born in upstate New York and educated at the State University of New York at Binghamton and Yale, Paglia has published several books, including* Sexual Personae: Art and Decadence from Nefertiti to Emily Dickinson *(1990), her best-selling scholarly work;* Sex, Art, and American Culture *(1992), from which the following essay is taken;* Vamps and Tramps *(1994); and a book analyzing Alfred Hitchcock's* The Birds *(1998). "It's a Jungle Out There" appeared first in* Newsday, *a Long Island, New York, newspaper.*

Camille Paglia

It's a Jungle Out There

Rape is an outrage that cannot be tolerated in civilized society. Yet feminism, which has waged a crusade for rape to be taken more seriously, has put young women in danger by hiding the truth about sex from them.

In dramatizing the pervasiveness of rape, feminists have told young women that before they have sex with a man, they must give consent as explicit as a legal contract's. In this way, young women have been convinced that they have been the victims of rape. On elite campuses in the Northeast and on the West Coast, they have held consciousness-raising sessions, petitioned administrations, demanded inquests. At Brown University, outraged, panicky "victims" have scrawled the names of alleged attackers on the walls of women's rest rooms. What marital rape was to the '70s, "date rape" is to the '90s.

The incidence and seriousness of rape do not require this kind of exaggeration. Real acquaintance rape is nothing new. It has been a horrible problem for women for all of recorded history. Once fathers and brothers protected women from rape. Once the penalty for rape was death. I come from a fierce Italian tradition where, not so long ago in the motherland, a rapist would end up knifed, castrated, and hung out to dry.

But the old clans and small rural communities have broken down. In our cities, on our campuses far from home, young women are vulnerable and defenseless. Feminism has not prepared them for this. Feminism keeps saying the sexes are the same. It keeps telling women they can do anything, go anywhere, say anything, wear anything. No, they can't. Women will always be in sexual danger.

5   One of my male students recently slept overnight with a friend in a passageway of the Great Pyramid in Egypt. He described the moon and sand, the ancient silence and eerie echoes. I will never experience that. I am a woman. I am not stupid enough to believe I could ever be safe there. There is a world of solitary adventure I will never have. Women have always known these somber truths. But feminism, with its pie-in-the-sky fantasies about the perfect world, keeps young women from seeing life as it is.

We must remedy social injustice whenever we can. But there are some things we cannot change. There are sexual differences that are based in biology. Academic feminism is lost in a fog of social constructionism. It believes we are totally the product of our environment. This idea was invented by Rousseau. He was wrong. Emboldened by dumb French language theory, academic feminists repeat the same hollow slogans over and over to each other. Their view of sex is naive and prudish. Leaving sex to the feminists is like letting your dog vacation at the taxidermist's.

The sexes are at war. Men must struggle for identity against the overwhelming power of their mothers. Women have menstruation to tell them they are women. Men must do or risk something to be men. Men become masculine only when other men say they are. Having sex with a woman is one way a boy becomes a man.

College men are at their hormonal peak. They have just left their mothers and are questing for their male identity. In groups, they are dangerous. A woman going to a fraternity party is walking into Testosterone Flats, full of prickly cacti and blazing guns. If she goes, she should be armed with resolute alertness. She should arrive with girlfriends and leave with them. A girl who lets herself get dead drunk at a fraternity party is a fool. A girl who goes upstairs alone with a brother at a fraternity party is an idiot. Feminists call this "blaming the victim." I call it common sense.

For a decade, feminists have drilled their disciples to say, "Rape is a crime of violence but not of sex." This sugar-coated Shirley Temple nonsense has exposed young women to disaster. Misled by feminism, they do not expect rape from the nice boys from good homes who sit next to them in class.

10   Aggression and eroticism are deeply intertwined. Hunt, pursuit, and capture are biologically programmed into male sexuality. Generation after generation, men must be educated, refined, and ethically persuaded away from their tendency toward anarchy and

brutishness. Society is not the enemy, as feminism ignorantly claims. Society is woman's protection against rape. Feminism, with its solemn Carry Nation repressiveness, does not see what is for men the eroticism or fun element in rape, especially the wild, infectious delirium of gang rape. Women who do not understand rape cannot defend themselves against it.

The date-rape controversy shows feminism hitting the wall of its own broken promises. The women of my '60s generation were the first respectable girls in history to swear like sailors, get drunk, stay out all night—in short, to act like men. We sought total sexual freedom and equality. But as time passed, we woke up to cold reality. The old double standard protected women. When anything goes, it's women who lose.

Today's young women don't know what they want. They see that feminism has not brought sexual happiness. The theatrics of public rage over date rape are their way of restoring the old sexual rules that were shattered by my generation. Because nothing about the sexes has really changed. The comic film *Where the Boys Are* (1960), the ultimate expression of '50s man-chasing, still speaks directly to our time. It shows smart, lively women skillfully anticipating and fending off the dozens of strategies with which horny men try to get them into bed. The agonizing date-rape subplot and climax are brilliantly done. The victim, Yvette Mimieux, makes mistake after mistake, obvious to the other girls. She allows herself to be lured away from her girlfriends and into isolation with boys whose character and intentions she misreads. *Where the Boys Are* tells the truth. It shows courtship as a dangerous game in which the signals are not verbal but subliminal.

Neither militant feminism, which is obsessed with politically correct language, nor academic feminism, which believes that knowledge and experience are "constituted by" language, can understand preverbal or non-verbal communication. Feminism, focusing on sexual politics, cannot see that sex exists in and through the body. Sexual desire and arousal cannot be fully translated into verbal terms. This is why men and women misunderstand each other.

Trying to remake the future, feminism cut itself off from sexual history. It discarded and suppressed the sexual myths of literature, art, and religion. Those myths show us the turbulence, the mysteries and passions of sex. In mythology we see men's sexual anxiety, their fear of women's dominance. Much sexual violence is rooted in men's sense of psychological weakness toward women. It takes many men to deal with one woman. Woman's voracity is a persistent motif. Clara Bow, it was rumored, took on the USC football team on weekends. Marilyn Monroe, singing "Diamonds Are a Girl's Best Friend," rules a conga line of men in tuxes. Half-clad Cher, in the video for "If I Could Turn Back Time," deranges a battleship of screaming sailors and straddles a pink-lit cannon. Feminism, coveting social power, is blind to woman's cosmic sexual power.

15   To understand rape, you must study the past. There never was and never will be sexual harmony. Every woman must take personal responsibility for her sexuality, which is nature's red flame. She must be prudent and cautious about where she goes and with whom. When she makes a mistake, she must accept the consequences and, through self-criticism, resolve never to make that mistake again. Running to Mommy and Daddy or the campus grievance committee is unworthy of strong women. Posting lists of guilty men in the toilet is cowardly, infantile stuff.

The Italian philosophy of life espouses high-energy confrontation. A male student makes a vulgar remark about your breasts? Don't slink off to whimper and simper with the campus shrinking violets. Deal with it. On the spot. Say, "Shut up, you jerk! And crawl back to the barnyard where you belong!" In general, women who project this take-charge attitude toward life get harassed less often. I see too many dopey, immature, self-pitying women walking around like melting sticks of butter. It's the Yvette Mimieux syndrome: Make me happy. And listen to me weep when I'm not.

The date-rape debate is already smothering in propaganda churned out by the expensive Northeastern colleges and universities, with their overconcentration of boring, uptight academic feminists and spoiled, affluent students. Beware of the deep manipulativeness of rich students who were neglected by their parents. They love to turn the campus into hysterical psychodramas of sexual transgression, followed by assertions of parental authority and concern. And don't look for sexual enlightenment from academe, which spews out mountains of books but never looks at life directly.

As a fan of football and rock music, I see in the simple, swaggering masculinity of the jock and in the noisy posturing of the heavy-metal guitarist certain fundamental, unchanging truths about sex. Masculinity is aggressive, unstable, combustible. It is also the most creative cultural force in history. Women must reorient themselves toward the elemental powers of sex, which can strengthen or destroy.

The only solution to date rape is female self-awareness and self-control. A woman's number one line of defense is herself. When a real rape occurs, she should report it to the police. Complaining to college committees because the courts "take too long" is ridiculous. College administrations are not a branch of the judiciary. They are not equipped or trained for legal inquiry. Colleges must alert incoming students to the problems and dangers of adulthood. Then colleges must stand back and get out of the sex game.

Analyzing Rhetorical Choices

1. How would you describe Paglia's "voice"? Cite several passages in which you clearly identify this voice, and describe how it affects you as a reader.
2. How effective are Paglia's ways of backing up her central argument, which intertwines a critique of feminism with outrage against rape? Which strategies are more effective than others? Are her arguments complete? Reductive? Effective, despite any shortcomings?
3. Paglia's argument is both forthright and humorous. How so? How might she infuriate some and enlighten or educate others?

Writing About Issues and Contexts

1. If you are not familiar with them, look up Paglia's various references. What is the usefulness of her references to popular culture and historical and literary figures? How do they add to or detract from her argument?
2. Is Paglia correct that academic feminists are emboldened by "dumb French language theory"? That feminists have "drilled their disciples to say, 'Rape is a crime of violence, but not of sex'"? What research would you need to do to determine the validity of these statements?
3. What is your response to Paglia's description of college men? How much of her argument depends on the accuracy of this depiction?

Lani Guinier (1949–   ) has written extensively on issues related to civil rights. Her work led President Bill Clinton to nominate her in 1993 for the post of assistant attorney general for civil rights. Conservative politicians attacked her ideas, and, in the eyes of many, misinterpreted her legal writing, leading to Clinton's withdrawal of her nomination. Since then, Guinier has published two books, including The Tyranny of the Majority: Fundamental Fairness in Representative Democracy *(1994), from which this excerpt is taken. The book outlines Guinier's proposals for ensuring fairness in voting and governing processes, a stance inspired in part by the work of John Stuart Mill. In 1998, she published* Lift Every Voice: Turning a Civil Rights Setback into a New Vision of Social Justice, *in which she discusses her unsuccessful nomination. Guinier is considered by many to be a "scholar and activist of unparalleled stature in the field of civil rights."*

Lani Guinier

The Tyranny of the Majority

I have always wanted to be a civil rights lawyer. This lifelong ambition is based on a deep-seated commitment to democratic fair play—to playing by the rules as long as the rules are fair. When the rules seem unfair, I have worked to change them, not subvert them. When I was eight years old, I was a Brownie. I was especially proud of my uniform, which represented a commitment to good citizenship and good deeds. But one day, when my Brownie group staged a hatmaking contest, I realized that uniforms are only as honorable as the people who wear them. The contest was rigged. The winner was assisted by her milliner mother, who actually made the winning entry in full view of all the participants. At the time, I was too young to be able to change the rules, but I was old enough to resign, which I promptly did.

To me, fair play means that the rules encourage everyone to play. They should reward those who win, but they must be acceptable to those who lose. The central theme of my academic writing is that not all rules lead to elemental fair play. Some even commonplace rules work against it.

The professional milliner competing with amateur Brownies stands as an example of rules that are patently rigged or patently subverted. Yet, sometimes, even when rules are perfectly fair in form, they serve in practice to exclude particular groups from meaningful participation. When they do not encourage everyone to play, or when, over the long haul, they do not make the losers feel as good about the outcomes as the winners, they can seem as unfair as the milliner who makes the winning hat for her daughter.

Sometimes, too, we construct rules that force us to be divided into winners and losers when we might have otherwise joined together. This idea was cogently expressed by my son, Nikolas, when he was four years old, far exceeding the thoughtfulness of his mother when she was an eight-year-old Brownie. While I was writing one of my law journal articles, Nikolas and I had a conversation about voting prompted by a *Sesame Street Magazine* exercise. The magazine pictured six children: four children had raised their hands because they wanted to play tag; two had their hands down because they wanted to play hide-and-seek. The magazine asked its readers to count the number of children whose hands were raised and then decide what game the children would play.

5   Nikolas quite realistically replied, "They will play both. First they will play tag. Then they will play hide-and-seek." Despite the magazine's "rules," he was right. To children, it is natural to take turns. The winner may get to play first or more often, but even the "loser" gets something. His was a positive-sum solution that many adult rule-makers ignore.

The traditional answer to the magazine's problem would have been a zero-sum solution: "The children—all the children—will play tag, and only tag." As a zero-sum solution, everything is seen in terms of "I win; you lose." The conventional answer relies on winner-take-all majority rule, in which the tag players, as the majority, win the right to decide for all the children what game to play. The hide-and-seek preference becomes irrelevant. The numerically more powerful majority choice simply subsumes minority preferences.

In the conventional case, the majority that rules gains all the power and the minority that loses gets none. For example, two years ago Brother Rice High School in Chicago held two senior proms. It was not planned that way. The prom committee at Brother Rice, a boys' Catholic high school, expected just one prom when it hired a disc jockey, picked a rock band, and selected music for the prom by consulting student preferences. Each senior was asked to list his three favorite songs, and the band would play the songs that appeared most frequently on the lists.

Seems attractively democratic. But Brother Rice is predominantly white, and the prom committee was all white. That's how they got two proms. The black seniors at Brother Rice felt so shut out by the "democratic process" that they organized their own prom. As one black student put it: "For every vote we had, there were eight votes for what they wanted. . . . [W]ith us being in the minority we're always outvoted. It's as if we don't count."

Some embittered white seniors saw things differently. They complained that the black students should have gone along with the majority: "The majority makes a decision. That's the way it works."

10   In a way, both groups were right. From the white students' perspective, this was ordinary decisionmaking. To the black students, majority rule sent the message: "we don't count" is the "way it works" for minorities. In a racially divided society, majority rule may be perceived as majority tyranny.

That is a large claim, and I do not rest my case for it solely on the actions of the prom committee in one Chicago high school. To expand the range of the argument, I first consider the ideal of majority rule itself, particularly as reflected in the writings of James Madison and other founding members of our Republic. These early democrats explored the relationship between majority rule and democracy. James Madison warned, "If a majority be united by a common interest, the rights of the minority will be insecure." The tyranny of the majority, according to Madison, requires safeguards to protect "one part of the society against the injustice of the other part."

For Madison, majority tyranny represented the great danger to our early constitutional democracy. Although the American revolution was fought against the tyranny of the British monarch, it soon became clear that there was another tyranny to be avoided. The accumulations of all powers in the same hands, Madison warned, "whether of one, a few, or many, and whether hereditary, self-appointed, or elective, may justly be pronounced the very definition of tyranny."

As another columnist suggested in papers published in Philadelphia, "We have been so long habituated to a jealousy of tyranny from monarchy and aristocracy, that we have yet to learn the dangers of it from democracy." Despotism had to be opposed "whether it came from Kings, Lords or the people."

The debate about majority tyranny reflected Madison's concern that the majority may not represent the whole. In a homogeneous society, the interest of the majority would likely be that of the minority also. But in a heterogeneous community, the majority may not represent all competing interests. The majority is likely to be self-interested and ignorant or indifferent to the concerns of the minority. In such case, Madison observed, the assumption that the majority represents the minority is "altogether fictitious."

15   Yet even a self-interested majority can govern fairly if it cooperates with the minority. One reason for such cooperation is that the self-interested majority values the principle of reciprocity. The self-interested majority worries that the minority may attract defectors from the majority and become the next governing majority. The Golden Rule principle of reciprocity functions to check the tendency of a self-interested majority to act tyrannically.

So the argument for the majority principle connects it with the value of reciprocity: You cooperate when you lose in part because members of the current majority will cooperate when they lose. The conventional case for the fairness of majority rule is that it is not really the rule of a fixed group—The Majority—on all issues; instead it is the rule of shifting majorities, as the losers at one time or on one issue join with others and become part of the governing coalition at another time or on another issue. The result will be a fair system of mutually beneficial cooperation. I call a majority that rules but does not dominate a Madisonian Majority.

The problem of majority tyranny arises, however, when the self-interested majority does not need to worry about defections. When the majority is fixed and permanent, there are no checks on its ability to be overbearing. A majority that does not worry about defectors is a majority with total power.

In such a case, Madison's concern about majority tyranny arises. In a heterogeneous community, any faction with total power might subject "the minority to the caprice and arbitrary decisions of the majority, who instead of consulting the interest of the whole community collectively, attend sometimes to partial and local advantages."

"What remedy can be found in a republican Government, where the majority must ultimately decide," argued Madison, but to ensure "that no one common interest or passion will be likely to unite a majority of the whole number in an unjust pursuit." The answer was to disaggregate the majority to ensure checks and balances or fluid, rotating interests. The minority needed protection against an overbearing majority, so that "a common sentiment is less likely to be felt, and the requisite concert less likely to be formed, by a majority of the whole."

20   Political struggles would not be simply a contest between rulers and people; the political struggles would be among the people themselves. The work of government was not to transcend different interests but to reconcile them. In an ideal democracy, the people would rule, but the minorities would also be protected against the power of majorities. Again, where the rules of decisionmaking protect the minority, the Madisonian Majority rules without dominating.

But if a group is unfairly treated, for example, when it forms a racial minority, *and* if the problems of unfairness are not cured by conventional assumptions about majority rule, then what is to be done? The answer is that we may need an *alternative* to winner-take-all majoritarianism. In this book, a collection of my law review articles, I describe the alternative, which, with Nikolas's help, I now call the "principle of taking turns." In a racially divided society, this principle does better than simple majority rule if it accommodates the values of self-government, fairness, deliberation, compromise, and consensus that lie at the heart of the democratic ideal.

In my legal writing, I follow the caveat of James Madison and other early American democrats. I explore decisionmaking rules that might work in a multi-racial society to ensure that majority rule does not become majority tyranny. I pursue voting systems that might disaggregate The Majority so that it does not exercise power unfairly or tyrannically. I aspire to a more cooperative political style of decisionmaking to enable all of the students at Brother Rice to feel comfortable attending the same prom. In looking to create Madisonian Majorities, I pursue a positive-sum, taking-turns solution.

Structuring decisionmaking to allow the minority "a turn" may be necessary to restore the reciprocity ideal when a fixed majority refuses to cooperate with the minority. If the fixed majority loses its incentive to follow the Golden Rule principle of shifting majorities, the minority never gets to take a turn. Giving the minority a turn does not mean the minority gets to rule; what it does mean is that the minority gets to influence decisionmaking and the majority rules more legitimately.

Instead of automatically rewarding the preferences of the monolithic majority, a taking-turns approach anticipates that the majority rules, but is not overbearing. Because those with 51 percent of the votes are not assured 100 percent of the power, the majority cooperates with, or at least does not tyrannize, the minority.

25   The sports analogy of "I win; you lose" competition within a political hierarchy makes sense when only one team can win; Nikolas's intuition that it is often possible to take turns suggests an alternative approach. Take family decisionmaking, for example. It utilizes a taking-turns approach. When parents sit around the kitchen table deciding on a vacation destination or activities for a rainy day, often they do not simply rely on a show of hands, especially if that means that the older children always prevail or if affinity groups among the children (those who prefer movies to video games, or those who prefer baseball to playing cards) never get to play their activity of choice. Instead of allowing the majority simply to rule, the parents may propose that everyone takes turns, going to the movies one night and playing video games the next. Or as Nikolas proposes, they might do both on a given night.

    Taking turns attempts to build consensus while recognizing political or social differences, and it encourages everyone to play. The taking-turns approach gives those with the most support more turns, but it also legitimates the outcome from each individual's perspective, including those whose views are shared only by a minority.

    In the end, I do not believe that democracy should encourage rule by the powerful—even a powerful majority. Instead, the idea of democracy promises a fair discussion among self-defined equals about how to achieve our common aspirations. To redeem that promise, we need to put the idea of taking turns and disaggregating the majority at the center of our conception of representation. Particularly as we move into the twenty-first century as a more highly diversified citizenry, it is essential that we consider the ways in which voting and representational systems succeed or fail at encouraging Madisonian Majorities.

    To use Nikolas's terminology, "it is no fair" if a fixed, tyrannical majority excludes or alienates the minority. It is no fair if a fixed, tyrannical majority monopolizes all the power all the time. It is no fair if we engage in the periodic ritual of elections, but only the permanent majority gets to choose who is elected. Where we have tyranny by The Majority, we do not have genuine democracy.

Analyzing Rhetorical Choices

1. Why does Guinier choose to begin her essay as she does, with a personal story? What effect does this have?
2. Why does Guinier alternate other personal stories with her theoretical argument? For what purpose? In what ways is the anecdote

about her son Nikolas effective or ineffective as a means of conveying her argument?

3. In what ways can you guess, by her prose style and method of arguing, that Guinier has a legal background?

Writing About Issues and Contexts

1. What is Guinier saying about the ways in which "we construct rules that force us to be divided into winners and losers when we might have joined together"?

2. After describing the episode at Brother Rice High School, Guinier writes, "In a way, both groups were right." How is this possible?

3. What is Guinier's "positive-sum, taking turns" approach? How does it tie together the personal stories and legal sources she uses in delineating her argument? To what effect?

Born in Taiwan in 1968 and raised in Chicago, **Curtis Chang** *(1968–   ) was educated at Harvard University, where he graduated in 1990 with a bachelor's degree in government. At Harvard, Chang founded the Minority Student Alliance and wrote essays for the* Harvard Political Review, *also winning the Michael C. Rockefeller Fellowship for Travel Abroad. In addition to being a teaching fellow at Harvard, he directed the InterVarsity Christian Fellowship campus ministry in Boston. His book,* Taking Every Thought Captive: A Postmodern Correspondence with Augustine and Aquinas, *was published in 2000. Chang now serves as Expansion Ministries Pastor of a congregation in San Jose, California. "Streets of Gold" was written when Chang was a first-year student at Harvard. In addition to its strong stand, Chang's essay is also a model of accountability in its research and documentation.*

Curtis Chang

Streets of Gold: The Myth of the Model Minority

Over one hundred years ago, an American myth misled many of my ancestors. Seeking cheap labor, railroad companies convinced numerous Chinese that American streets were paved with gold. Today, the media portray Asian-Americans as finally mining those golden streets. Major publications like *Time, Newsweek, U.S. News & World Report, Fortune, The New Republic,* the *Wall Street Journal,* and the *New York Times Magazine* have all recently published congratulatory "Model Minority" headline stories with such titles as:

America's Super Minority
An American Success Story
A "Model Minority"
Why They Succeed
The Ultimate Assimilation
The Triumph of Asian-Americans.

But the Model Minority is another "Streets of Gold" tale. It distorts Asian-Americans' true status and ignores our racial handicaps. And the Model Minority's ideology is even worse than its mythology. It attempts to justify the existing system of racial inequality by blaming the victims rather than the system itself.

The Model Minority myth introduces us as an ethnic minority that is finally "making it in America," as stated in *Time* (Doerner 42). The media consistently define "making it" as achieving material wealth, wealth that flows from our successes in the workplace and the school-room. This economic achievement allegedly proves a minority can, as *Fortune* says, "lay claim to the American dream" (Ramirez 149).

Trying to show how "Asian-Americans present a picture of afflu-ence and economic success," as the *New York Times Magazine* puts it (Oxnam 72), nine out of ten of the major Model Minority stories of the last four years relied heavily on one statistic: the family median in-come. The median Asian-American family income, according to the U.S. Census Survey of Income and Education data, is $22,713 com-pared to $20,800 for white Americans. Armed with that figure, na-tional magazines such as *Newsweek* have trumpeted our "remarkable, ever-mounting achievements" (Kasindorf et al. 51).

5   Such assertions demonstrate the truth of the aphorism "Statistics are like a bikini. What they reveal is suggestive, but what they conceal is vital." The family median income statistic conceals the fact that Asian-American families generally (1) have more children and live-in relatives and thus have more mouths to feed; (2) are often forced by necessity to have everyone in the family work, averaging *more* than two family income earners (whites only have 1.6) (Cabezas 402); and (3) live disproportionately in high cost of living areas (i.e., New York, Chicago, Los Angeles, and Honolulu) which artificially inflate income figures. Dr. Robert S. Mariano, professor of economics at the University of Pennsylvania, has calculated that

> when such appropriate adjustments and comparisons are made, a dif-ferent and rather disturbing picture emerges, showing indeed a clearly disadvantaged group. . . . Filipino and Chinese men *are no better off than black men with regard to median incomes.* (55)[1]

Along with other racial minorities, Asian-Americans are still scraping for the crumbs of the economic pie.

------

[1]The picture becomes even more disturbing when one realizes the higher in-come figures do not necessarily equal higher quality of life. For instance, in New York Chinatown, more than 1 out of 5 work more than 57 hours per week, almost 1 out of 10 elderly must labor more than 55 hours per week (Nishi 503).

Throughout their distortion of our status, the media propagate two crucial assumptions. First, they lump all Asian-Americans into one monolithic, homogeneous, yellow-skinned mass. Such a view ignores the existence of an incredibly disadvantaged Asian-American underclass. Asians work in low-income and low-status jobs two to three times more than whites (Cabezas 438). Recent Vietnamese refugees in California are living like the Appalachian poor. While going to his Manhattan office, multimillionaire architect I. M. Pei's car passes Chinese restaurants and laundries where 72% of all New York Chinese men still work (U.S. Bureau of the Census qtd. in Cabezas 443).

But the media make an even more dangerous assumption. They suggest that (alleged) material success is the same thing as basic racial equality. Citing that venerable family median income figure, magazines claim Asian-Americans are "obviously nondisadvantaged folks," as stated in *Fortune* (Seligman 64). Yet a 1979 United States Equal Employment Opportunity Commission study on Asian-Americans discovered widespread anti-Asian hiring and promotion practices. Asian-Americans "in the professional, technical, and managerial occupations" often face "modern racism—the subtle, sophisticated, systemic patterns and practices . . . which function to effect and to obscure the discriminatory outcomes" (Nishi 398). One myth simply does not prove another: Neither our "astonishing economic prosperity" (Ramirez 152) nor a racially equal America exist.

An emphasis on material success also pervades the media's stress on Asian-Americans' educational status at "the top of the class" ("Asian Americans" 4). Our "march into the ranks of the educational elite," as *U.S. News & World Report* puts it (McBee et al. 41), is significant, according to *Fortune*, because "all that education is paying off spectacularly" (Ramirez 149). Once again, the same fallacious assumptions plague this "whiz kids" image of Asian-Americans.

The media again ignore the fact that class division accounts for much of the publicized success. Until 1976, the U.S. Immigration Department only admitted Asian immigrants that were termed "skilled" workers. "Skilled" generally meant college educated, usually in the sciences since poor English would not be a handicap. The result was that the vast majority of pre-1976 Asian immigrants came from already well-educated, upper-class backgrounds—the classic "brain drain" syndrome (Hirschman and Wong 507-10).

10   The post-1976 immigrants, however, come generally from the lower, less educated classes (Kim 24). A study by Professor Elizabeth Ahn Toupin of Tufts University matched similar Asian and non-Asian

students *along class lines* and found that Asian-Americans "did not perform at a superior academic level to non-Asian students. Asian-Americans were more likely to be placed on academic probation than their white counterparts. . . . Twice as many Asian-American students withdrew from the university" (12).

Thus, it is doubtful whether the perceived widespread educational success will continue as the Asian-American population eventually balances out along class lines. When 16.2% of all Chinese have less than four years of schooling (*four times* the percentage of whites) (Azores 73), it seems many future Asian-Americans will worry more about being able to read a newspaper rather than a Harvard acceptance letter.

Most important, the media assume once again that achieving a certain level of material or educational success means achieving real equality. People easily forget that to begin with, Asians invest heavily in education since other means of upward mobility are barred to them by race. Until recently, for instance, Asian-Americans were barred from unions and traditional lines of credit (Yun 23-24).[2] Other "white" avenues to success, such as the "old-boy network," are still closed to Asian-Americans.

When *Time* claims "as a result of their academic achievement Asians are climbing the economic ladder with remarkable speed," it glosses over an inescapable fact: There is a white ladder and then there is a yellow one. Almost all of the academic studies on the *actual returns Asians receive* from their education point to prevalent discrimination. A striking example of this was found in a City University of New York research project which constructed résumés with equivalent educational backgrounds. Applications were then sent to employers, one group under an Asian name and a similar group under a Caucasian name. Whites received interviews five times more than Asians (Nishi 399). The media never headline even more shocking data that can be easily found in the U.S. Census. For instance, Chinese and Filipino males only earned respectively 74% and 52% as much as their *equally educated* white counterparts. Asian females fared even worse. Their salaries were only 44% to 54% as large as equivalent white males' paychecks (Cabezas 391). Blacks suffer from this same statistical disparity. We Asian-Americans are indeed a Model Minority—a perfect model of racial discrimination in America.

Yet this media myth encourages neglect of our pressing needs. "Clearly, many Asian-Americans and Pacific peoples are invisible to

---

[2]For further analysis on the role racism plays in Asian-Americans' stress on education and certain technical and scientific fields, see Suzuki (44).

the governmental agencies," reported the California State Advisory Committee to the U.S. Commission on Civil Rights. "Discrimination against Asian-Americans and Pacific peoples is as much the result of omission as commission" (qtd. in Chun 7). In 1979, while the president praised Asian-Americans' "successful integration into American society," his administration revoked Asian-Americans' eligibility for minority small business loans, devastating thousands of struggling, newly arrived small businessmen. Hosts of other minority issues, ranging from reparations for the Japanese-American internment to the ominous rise of anti-Asian violence, are widely ignored by the general public.

15   The media, in fact, insist to the general populace that we are not a true racial minority. In an attack on affirmative action, the *Boston Globe* pointed out that universities, like many people, "obviously feel that Asian-Americans, especially those of Chinese and Japanese descent, are brilliant, privileged, and wrongly classified as minorities" ("Affirmative Non-actions" 10). Harvard Dean Henry Rosovsky remarked in the same article that "It does not seem to me that as a group, they are disadvantaged. . . . Asian-Americans appear to be in an odd category among other protected minorities."

The image that we Asians aren't like "other minorities" is fundamental to the Model Minority ideology. Any elementary-school student knows that the teacher designates one student the model, the "teacher's pet," in order to set an example for others to follow. One only sets up a "model minority" in order to communicate to the other "students," the blacks and Hispanics, "Why can't you be like that?" The media, in fact, almost admit to "grading" minorities as they headline Model Minority stories "Asian-Americans: Are They Making the Grade?" (McBee et al.). And Asians have earned the highest grade by fulfilling one important assignment: identifying with the white majority, with its values and wishes.

Unlike blacks, for instance, we Asian-Americans have not vigorously asserted our ethnic identity (a.k.a. Black Power). And the American public has historically demanded assimilation over racial pluralism.[3] Over the years, *Newsweek* has published titles from

---

[3]A full discussion of racial pluralism versus assimilation is impossible here. But suffice it to say that pluralism accepts ethnic cultures as equally different; assimilation asks for a "melting" into the majority. An example of the assimilation philosophy is the massive "Americanization" programs of the late 1880s, which successfully erased Eastern European immigrants' customs in favor of Anglo-Saxon ones.

"Success Story: Outwhiting the Whites" to "The Ultimate Assimilation," which lauded the increasing number of Asian-white marriages as evidence of Asian-Americans' "acceptance into American society" (Kantrowitz et al. 80).

Even more significant is the public's approval of how we have succeeded in the "American tradition" (Ramirez 164). Unlike the blacks and Hispanics, we "Puritan-like" Asians (Oxnam 72) disdain governmental assistance. A *New Republic* piece, "The Triumph of Asian-Americans," similarly applauded how "Asian-Americans pose no problems at all" (Bell 30). The media consistently compare the crime-ridden image of other minorities with the picture of law-abiding Asian parents whose "well-behaved kids" hit books and not the streets ("Asian Americans" 4).

Some insist there is nothing terrible about whites conjuring up our "tremendous" success, divining from it model American traits, then preaching, "Why can't you blacks and Hispanics be like that?" After all, one might argue, aren't those traits desirable?

20   Such a view, as mentioned, neglects Asian-Americans' true and pressing needs. Moreover, this view completely misses the Model Minority image's fundamental ideology, an ideology meant to falsely grant American absolution from its racial barriers.

David O. Sears and Donald R. Kinder, two social scientists, have recently published significant empirical studies on the underpinnings of American racial attitudes. They consistently discovered that Americans' stress on "values, such as 'individualism and self-reliance, the work ethic, obedience, and discipline' . . . can be invoked, however perversely, to feed racist appetites" (qtd. in Kennedy 88). In other words, the Model Minority image lets Americans' consciences rest easy. they can think: "It's not our fault those blacks and Hispanics can't make it. They're just too lazy. After all, look at the Asians."[4] Consequently, American society never confronts the systemic racial and economic factors underlying such inequality. The victims instead bear the blame.

---

[4]This phenomenon of blaming the victim for racial inequality is as old as America itself. For instance, southerners once eased their consciences over slavery by labeling blacks as animals lacking humanity. Today, America does it by labeling them as inferior people lacking "desirable" traits. For an excellent further analysis of this ideology, actually widespread among American intellectuals, see *Iron Cages: Race and Culture in 19th-Century America* by Ronald T. Takaki.

This ideology behind the Model Minority image is best seen when we examine one of the first Model Minority stories, which suddenly appeared in the mid-1960s. It is important to note that the period was marked by newfound, strident black demands for equality and power.

> At a time when it is being proposed that hundreds of billions be spent to uplift Negroes and other minorities, the nation's 300,000 Chinese-Americans are moving ahead on their own—with no help from anyone else. . . . Few Chinese-Americans are getting welfare handouts—or even want them. . . . They don't sit around moaning. ("Success Story of One Minority Group" 73)

The same article then concludes that the Chinese-American history and accomplishment "would shock those now complaining about the hardships endured by today's Negroes."

Not surprisingly, the dunce-capped blacks and Hispanics resent us apple-polishing, "well-behaved" teacher's pets. Black comedian Richard Pryor performs a revealing routine in which new Asian immigrants learn from whites their first English word: "Nigger." And Asian-Americans themselves succumb to the Model Minority's deceptive mythology and racist ideology.[5] "I made it without help," one often hears among Asian circles; "why can't they?" In a 1986 nationwide poll, only 27% of Asian-American students rated "racial understanding" as "essential." The figure plunged 9% in the last year alone (a year marked by a torrent of Model Minority stories) (Hune). We "whitewashed" Asians have simply lost our identity as a fellow, disadvantaged minority.

But we don't even need to look beyond the Model Minority stories themselves to realize that whites see us as "whiter" than blacks—but not quite white enough. For instance, citing that familiar median family income figure, *Fortune* magazine of 17 May 1982 complained that the Asian-American community is in fact "getting *more* than its share of the pie" (Seligman 64). For decades, when white Americans were

---

[5]America has a long history of playing off one minority against the other. During the early 1900s, for instance, mining companies in the west often hired Asians solely as scabs against striking black miners. Black versus Asian hostility and violence usually followed. This pattern was repeated in numerous industries. In a larger historical sense, almost every immigrant group has assimilated, to some degree, the culture of antiblack racism.

leading the nation in every single economic measure, editorials arguing that whites were getting more than *their* share of the pie were rather rare.

25   No matter how "well-behaved" we are, Asian-Americans are still excluded from the real pie, the "positions of institutional power and political power" (Kuo 289). Professor Harry Kitano of UCLA has written extensively on the plight of Asian-Americans as the "middle-man minority," a minority supposedly satisfied materially but forever racially barred from a true, *significant* role in society. Empirical studies indicate that Asian-Americans "have been channeled into lower-echelon white-collar jobs having little or no decision making authority" (Suzuki 38). For example, in *Fortune*'s 1,000 largest companies, Asian-American nameplates rest on a mere half of one percent of all officers' and directors' desks (a statistical disparity worsened by the fact that most of the Asians founded their companies) (Ramirez 152). While the education of the upper-class Asians may save them from the bread lines, their race still keeps them from the boardroom.

Our docile acceptance of such exclusion is actually one of our "model" traits. When Asian-Americans in San Francisco showed their first hint of political activism and protested Asian exclusion from city boards, the *Washington Monthly* warned in a long Asian-American article, "Watch out, here comes another group to pander to" ("The Wrong Way" 21). *The New Republic* praised Asian-American political movements because

> Unlike blacks or Hispanics, Asian-American politicians have the luxury of not having to devote the bulk of their time to an "Asian-American agenda," and thus escape becoming prisoners of such an agenda. . . . The most important thing for Asian-Americans . . . is simply "being part of the process." (Bell 31)

This is strikingly reminiscent of another of the first Model Minority stories:

> As the Black and Brown communities push for changes in the present system, the Oriental is set forth as an example to be followed—a minority group that has achieved success through adaptation rather than confrontation. (*Gidra* qtd. in Chun 7)

But it is precisely this "present system," this system of subtle, persistent racism that we all must confront, not adapt to. For example, we Asians gained our right to vote from the 1964 Civil Rights Act that blacks marched, bled, died, and, in the words of that original Model

Minority story, "sat around moaning for." Unless we assert our true identity as a minority and challenge racial misconceptions and inequalities, we will be nothing more than techno-coolies—collecting our wages but silently enduring basic political and economic inequality.

This country perpetuated a myth once. Today, no one can afford to dreamily chase after that gold in the streets, oblivious to the genuine treasure of racial equality. When racism persists, can one really call any minority a "model"?

Works Cited

"Affirmative Non-actions." Op-ed. *Boston Globe* 14 Jan. 1985: 10.

"Asian Americans, The Drive to Excel." *Newsweek on Campus* April 1984: 4-13.

Asian American Studies: Contemporary Issues. Proc. from East Coast Asian American Scholars Conf. 1986.

Azores, Fortunata M. "Census Methodology and the Development of Social Indicators for Asian and Pacific Americans." United States Commission on Civil Rights 70-79.

Bell, David A. "The Triumph of Asian-Americans." *New Republic* 15 & 22 July 1985: 24-31.

Cabezas, Armado. "Employment Issues of Asian Americans." United States Commission on Civil Rights.

Chun, Ki-Taek. "The Myth of Asian American Success and Its Educational Ramifications." *IRCD Bulletin* Winter/Spring 1980.

Doerner, William R. "To America with Skills." *Time* 8 July 1985: 42-44.

Dutta, Manoranjan. "Asian/Pacific American Employment Profile: Myth and Reality—Issues and Answers." United States Commission on Civil Rights 445-89.

Hirschman, Charles, and Morrison G. Wong. "Trends in Socioeconomic Achievement Among Immigrants and Native-Born Asian-Americans, 1960–1976." *Sociological Quarterly* 22.4 (1981): 495-513.

Hune, Shirley. Keynote address. East Coast Asian Student Union Conference. Boston University. 14 Feb. 1987.

Kahng, Anthony. "Employment Issues." United States Commission on Civil Rights 1980.

Kantrowitz, Barbara, et al. "The Ultimate Assimilation." *Newsweek* 24 Nov. 1986: 80.

Kasindorf, Martin, et al. "Asian-Americans: A 'Model Minority.'" *Newsweek* 6 Dec. 1982: 39-51.

Kennedy, David M. "The Making of a Classic. Gunnar Myrdal and Black-White Relations: The Use and Abuse of *An American Dilemma.*" *Atlantic* May 1987: 86-89.

Kiang, Peter. Personal interview. 1 May 1987.

Kim, Illsoo. "Class Division Among Asian Immigrants: Its Implications for Social Welfare Policy." *Asian American Studies* 24-25.

Kuo, Wen H. "On the Study of Asian-Americans: Its Current State and Agenda." *Sociological Quarterly* 20.2 (1979): 279-90.

Mariano, Robert S. "Census Issues." United States Commission on Civil Rights 54-59.

McBee, Susanna, et al. "Asian-Americans: Are They Making the Grade?" *U.S. News & World Report* 2 Apr. 1984: 41-47.

Nishi, Setsuko Matsunaga. "Asian American Employment Issues: Myths and Realities." United States Commission on Civil Rights 397-99, 495-507.

Oxnam, Robert B. "Why Asians Succeed Here." *New York Times Magazine* 30 Nov. 1986: 72+.

Ramirez, Anthony. "America's Super Minority." *Fortune* 24 Nov. 1986: 148-49.

Seligman, Daniel. "Keeping Up: Working Smarter." *Fortune* 17 May 1982: 64.

"Success Story of One Minority Group in the U.S." *U.S. News & World Report* 26 Dec. 1966: 73-76.

"Success Story: Outwhiting the Whites." *Newsweek* 21 June 1971: 24-25.

Sung, Betty Lee. *A Survey of Chinese American Manpower and Employment.* New York: Praeger, 1976.

Suzuki, Bob H. "Education and the Socialization of Asian Americans: A Revisionist Analysis of the 'Model Minority' Thesis." *Amerasia Journal* 4.2 (1977): 23-51.

Toupin, Elizabeth Ahn. "A Model University for a Model Minority." *Asian American Studies* 10-12.

United States Commission on Civil Rights. *Civil Rights Issues of Asian and Pacific Americans: Myths and Realities.* 1980.

"The Wrong Way to Court Ethnics." *Washington Monthly* May 1986: 21-26.

Yun, Grace. "Notes from Discussions on Asian American Education." *Asian American Studies* 20-24.

Analyzing Rhetorical Choices

1. How does Chang's use of language—and the connotations of his language—reinforce the content of the essay? For instance, consider terms like *old boy network*, *techno-coolies*, and others.
2. How does Chang attempt to anticipate his audience's objections? Is this strategy effective? Why or why not?
3. What is Chang's point of view regarding his argument? Does he side with anyone in particular? What effect does this have?
4. In making his argument, analyze which aspects are based on emotion and which on logic. What are the effects of Chang's choices?

Writing About Issues and Contexts

1. Research the possible ways of defining *ideology*. What, exactly, do you think Chang means by the "Model Minority's ideology"?
2. In what ways does Chang think Asians are like blacks and other minorities? In what ways are they different?
3. Chang critiques the way many Americans respond to the social and economic problems of minorities in America. Is he right? Offer your own analysis as to whether "American society" blames the victims.

Strategies for Writers: Argument

1. As you determine what you will argue, you may want to reread some of the essays in this chapter—as well as those elsewhere in this book. For instance, Paul Goldberger's argument is a subtle, implicit one; Martin Luther King, Jr.'s, more explicit. As with the other modes presented in this book, it is also important to consider your audience. Would a more implicit or explicit argument work best?

2. Will you argue inductively or deductively? William F. Buckley, for instance, argues inductively, using specific instances to make a broader argument. Joy Williams also primarily uses an inductive form of argument, citing specific passages from magazines and articles and then critiquing them. Paul Shepard and Martin Luther King, Jr., on the other hand, work deductively, establishing principles and positions and then arguing from them. Some essays blend both forms of argument, at times moving from the particular to the general, and at other times from the general back to the particular. Which method will work best for your subject and your individual style?

3. Will you employ the Rogerian techniques mentioned in the introductory section of this chapter? Martin Luther King, Jr., and Paul Shepard might be said to argue in a Rogerian fashion, encouraging readers to appreciate viewpoints that might counter their own. Both assume friendship and goodwill on the part of their readers, even those who might potentially object. This strategy emerges from their own ethical relationship to their audiences, their view that argument is not about pounding an opponent into submission but rather engaging in meaningful dialogue and mutual consideration. (Contrast this approach to the perspectives taken by Joy Williams, Curtis Chang, and Camille Paglia, for example.) Will a Rogerian approach work best for your essay?

4. How will you select your evidence? A good argument depends on specific examples—as you can see in Paul Goldberger's essay on architecture and in Curtis Chang's essay on the "model minority." An audience of your peers will have a different set of expectations than, say, an audience of business persons or college professors. What evidence will be most useful to you? Will you use library sources, the Internet, personal interviews, statistical data, or other forms of research to help you demonstrate your knowledge and authority?

5. Debate the various facets of your argument with your classmates. Check the logic of your arguments against the fallacies outlined at the start of this chapter. Have you unknowingly fallen victim to fallacious reasoning? Once you have checked for fallacies, the next step is to determine if your classmates find your arguments effective and your evidence useful in proving your argument. In classroom discussions, try to develop an ear for good argument. Do you notice logic operating differently in different cultural contexts? Are you or your classmates responding to arguments on the basis of logic, emotion, friendship, identification?

6. What really persuades you to someone else's position? Do you see patterns in the ways you and your classmates respond to certain issues and questions? Does the way someone uses language affect the ways you respond to that argument or whether you take it seriously? (Recall the letter to the editor written by the teacher with an unconventional command of English described in Chapter 1.) Is Curtis Chang more able to write about the issues that concern him because he is Asian? Is Camille Paglia able to write about rape more effectively because she is a woman? Discuss these arguments—and the issues that surround arguments—in conversation and as you exchange drafts.

7. It is worth remembering that many writers begin the writing process because they have a particular argument or perspective that they believe in. Then they read, engage in research, talk to colleagues, and often find that their views change, that what they believed before no longer holds true for them. As you move through the research and writing process, is this same phenomenon happening to you? Have you modified or even reversed your arguments as you have researched and written? Do you need to revise substantially so that your essay reflects your more considered perspective?

Research and Writing Assignments

1. In "Letter from Birmingham Jail," Martin Luther King, Jr. offers a passionate defense of civil disobedience, stating that "I would be the first to advocate obeying just laws. Conversely, one has a moral responsibility to disobey unjust laws." Likewise, William F. Buckley's "Why Don't We Complain?" and Camille Paglia's "It's a Jungle Out There" also rely to some extent on a common assumption that individuals need to take

charge of their own lives and assume responsibility for their own actions. In an essay that cites one or more of these essays closely, develop an argument about civil obedience, and the relationship between law, morality, and religion. To make this essay manageable, focus on a specific issue or concern that brings these contending forces into focus, and then engage in library research on a topic such as civil rights conflicts in 1960s America, antiwar protests during a time of national conflict (Vietnam, Iraq), violating anticensorship laws, the history of women's suffrage, or conscientious objectors to war during the 1940s. How can we best decide when laws are just and when they are unjust? Who gets to decide such questions? How do we best take responsibility for our own actions?

2. Lani Guinier critiques one of the major principles of democracy, the tenet that the majority rules. "Where we have tyranny by The Majority," Guinier writes, "we do not have genuine democracy." In an essay that makes consistent use of Guinier's essay, write a proposal for how decision making in American public life can be structured so that decisions are made most fairly. If you decide to adopt Guinier's proposal of "taking turns," explain how that would work in practical terms. If you decide that the majority should rule, offer an explanation that takes into account the views of minority groups in this country. You might want to read some of the work of James Madison and Alexis de Tocqueville, both of whom have made important contributions to our thinking about democratic forms of government.

3. Dialogue is often difficult between two individuals with opposing perspectives, yet true, meaningful dialogue should always be a goal for those engaging in argument. Create such a dialogue between two individuals meeting at a coffee shop or some other calm setting, one who agrees with Joy Williams that hunting is cruel and should be banned and the other who agrees with Paul Shepard that hunting is an elementary part of nature and the wilderness experience. Although these two individuals hold very different views, create a dialogue that allows them genuinely to speak and to listen. Your dialogue may or may not offer a resolution to this ongoing debate about hunting, but it should draw on the works of both Williams and Shepard—and it should not result in fist-pounding, red-faced pontificating.

4. Each of the essays in this section to some extent challenges or critiques a dominant public perception. For instance, Curtis Chang openly challenges the notion of the Asian American as

the "Model Minority" (similar to what Emily Tsao does in her essay in Chapter 5). Chang does this by developing a central argument about what the phrase "Model Minority" means and then citing a great deal of research to challenge that notion and to reaffirm his view that this is a myth and that Asian Americans, like other minorities, must "assert our true identity as a minority and challenge racial misconceptions and inequalities." Write a follow-up essay to Chang's in which you engage in research that challenges another misconception or inequality—one related to race, gender, class, family, or academic life—that has a personal meaning for you. You might want to begin by thinking about a group around whom stereotypical views have formed (freshmen, blacks, women, men, bratty brothers, absent fathers), then search for sociological studies that illuminate your subject, and finally write an essay that argues for a reconception of that stereotype based on your research.

5. In his essay, Paul Goldberger writes about buildings as iconographic symbols. Choose a building on your own campus or in your own neighborhood and analyze it in terms of how its design, function, and meaning relate to one another. How do the aesthetics of the building reinforce or counteract its intended use? How do you interpret the various design features of the building: its windows, its entryways, its towers, its use of internal and external space? In what ways, if any, can the building be seen as a tool, an art object, an expression of educational or economic philosophy, a symbol or cultural expression, like the World Trade Center? In your essay, be sure to include frequent mention of specific design features, and be sure to tie those features to an overall structure that assesses its meaning and value.

6. In their essays, Norman Cousins, Joy Williams, and Paul Shepard are all concerned with violence. Since both boxing and hunting are forms of recreation and sport, the question arises: When, if ever, do such entertainments cross the line and become inappropriate or even immoral and destructive to society? In an essay that carefully analyzes the arguments made by Cousins, Williams, and Shepard, offer your perspective about this controversy. Should boxing or hunting be outlawed? Should dogfighting or deer hunting (or violent video games) be banned? In your essay, develop some specific criteria that you think can be applied to help in thinking about this issue.

Credits

Ackerman, Diane. "The Omnivore's Picnic" and "The Bloom of a Taste Bud" from *A Natural History of the Senses* by Diane Ackerman, copyright © 1990 by Diane Ackerman. Used by permission of Random House, Inc.

Alexander, Elizabeth. "Narrative: Ali" Copyright © 2001. Reprinted from *Antebellum Dream Book* with the permission of Graywolf Press, Saint Paul, Minnesota.

Alexie, Sherman. "Father Coming Home" by Sherman Alexie. Reprinted from *The Business of Fancydancing* © 1992 by Sherman Alexie, by permission of Hanging Loose Press.

Alvarez, Julia. From *How the Garcia Girls Lost Their Accents*. Copyright © 1991 by Julia Alvarez. Published by Plume an imprint of Dutton Signet, a division of Penguin USA and originally in hardcover by Algonquin Books of Chapel Hill. Reprinted by permission of Susan Bergholz Literary Services, New York. All rights reserved.

Antonelli, Angela, Brett D. Schaefer, and Alex Annett. From "The Road to Kyoto: How the Global Climate Treaty Fosters Economic Impoverishment and Endangers U.S. Security" by Angela Antonelli, Brett D. Schaefer, and Alex Annett, from the Heritage Foundation, (http://www.heritage.org), October 6, 1997. Reprinted by permission of The Heritage Foundation.

Anzaldúa, Gloria. Excerpt from "How to Tame a Wild Tongue" from - *Borderlands/La Frontera: The New Mestiza* by Gloria Anzaldúa. Copyright © 1987, 1999 by Gloria Anzaldúa. Reprinted by permission of Aunt Lute Books.

Atwood, Margaret. "Pornography" by Margaret Atwood, © 1983, first appeared in *Chatelaine Magazine*. Reprinted by permission of the author.

Bambara, Toni Cade. "The Lesson," copyright © 1972 by Toni Cade Bambara, from *Gorilla, My Love* by Toni Cade Bambara. Used by permission of Random House, Inc.

Begley, Sharon. "The Stereotype Trap" by Sharon Begley. From *Newsweek*, November 6, 2000 © 2000 Newsweek, Inc. All rights reserved. Reprinted by permission.

Dillard, Annie. Pages 45–49 from *An American Childhood*. Copyright © 1987 by Annie Dillard. Reprinted by permission of HarperCollins Publishers Inc.

Douglass, Frederick. "Learning to Read and Write" from *The Narrative of the Life of Frederick Douglass, an American Slave*, by Frederick Douglass. 1845.

Ehrenreich, Barbara. "What I've Learned From Men" by Barbara Ehrenreich from *Ms. Magazine*, August 1985. Reprinted by permission of *Ms. Magazine*, © 1985.

Ehrlich, Gretel. "About Men," from *The Solace of Open Spaces* by Gretel Ehrlich, copyright © 1985 by Gretel Ehrlich. Used by permission of Viking Penguin, a division of Penguin Putnam Inc.

Elmer-DeWitt, Philip. "Bards of the Internet" by Philip Elmer-DeWitt. Copyright © 1994 TIME Inc. Reprinted by permission.

Erdrich, Louise. "Sister Godzilla" by Louise Erdrich. Copyright © 2001 by Louise Erdrich. Originally published in *The Atlantic Monthly*. Reprinted with permission of The Wylie Agency, Inc.

Gates, Henry Louis, Jr. "Delusions of Grandeur" by Henry Louis Gates, Jr. Copyright © 1991 by Henry Louis Gates, Jr.. Originally published in *Sports Illustrated*. Reprinted by permission of the author.

Gawande, Atul. "Cold Comfort" by Atul Gawande, from the March 11, 2002 issue of *The New Yorker*. Copyright © 2002 by Atul Gawande. Reprinted by permission of the author.

Gladwell, Malcolm. "The Trouble With Fries" by Malcolm Gladwell, from the March 5, 2001 issue of *The New Yorker*. Copyright © 2001 by Malcolm Gladwell. Reprinted by permission of the author.

Goldberger, Paul. "Building Plans" by Paul Goldberger, from the September 24, 2001 issue of *The New Yorker*. Copyright © 2001 by Paul Goldberger. Reprinted by permission of the author.

Guinier, Lani. Reprinted with the permission of The Free Press, a Division of Simon & Schuster Adult Publishing Group, from *The Tyranny of the Majority: Fundamental Fairness in Representative Democracy* by Lani Guinier. Copyright © 1994 by Lani Guinier.

Hansen, Eric. From *Stranger in the Forest* by Eric Hansen. Copyright © 1988 by Eric Hansen. Reprinted by permission of Frederick Hill Bonnie Nadell Associates.

Hofer, Mark, and Matthew J. Hofer. "The True Meaning of Patriotism" by Mark Hofer II and Matthew J. Hofer, from *Carolina Review*, (http://www.unc.edu/cr), March 2002, and *Broadside Magazine*, (http://www.thebroadside.org), May 2002. Reprinted by permission of the authors.

Hudson, Richard A. Excerpted from *Sociolinguistics* by Richard A. Hudson. Copyright © 1996 by Richard A. Hudson. Reprinted with the permission of Cambridge University Press.

Wang, Amy. "The Same Difference" by Amy Wang, from *Philadelphia Inquirer Sunday Magazine*, 1993. Reprinted by permission of The Philadelphia Inquirer.

West, Cornel. "Introduction" by Cornel West, from *Blacks and Jews* by Michael Lerner and Cornel West, copyright © 1995 by Michael Lerner and Cornel West. Used by permission of Grosset & Dunlap, Inc., a division of Penguin Putnam Inc.

White, E.B. "Once More to the Lake" from *One Man's Meat*, text copyright © 1941 by E. B. White. Copyright renewed. Reprinted by permission of Tilbury House, Publishers, Gardiner, Maine.

Wiesel, Eli. "How Can We Understand Their Hatred?" by Eli Wiesel, from the April 7, 2002 issue of *Parade Magazine*. Reprinted with permission of *Parade*, Copyright © 2002, and from the author.

Wilbur, Richard. "Castles and Distances" from *Ceremony and Other Poems* by Richard Wilbur, copyright © 1950 and renewed 1978 by Richard Wilbur. Reprinted by permission of Harcourt, Inc.

Williams, Joy. "The Killing Game" by Joy Williams. Copyright © 1990 by Joy Williams. First appeared in *Esquire*. Reprinted by permission of International Creative Management, Inc.

Wright, Richard. Chapter XIII from *Black Boy*. Copyright 1937, 1942, 1944, 1945 by Richard Wright. Copyright renewed 1973 by Ellen Wright. Reprinted by permission of HarperCollins Publishers Inc.

Yahoo! Maps Screen Shot created using data and technology developed by Navigation Technologies Corporation. Reprinted by permission of Navigation Technologies Corporation.

Zinsser, William. "College Pressures" by William Zinsser. Copyright © 1979 by William K. Zinsser. Reprinted by permission of the author.

Index

Additional Titles of Interest

Albee, Edward, *Three Tall Women*

Alger, Horatio, *Ragged Dick and Struggling Upward*

Allison, Dorothy, *Bastard out of Carolina*

Alvarez, Julia, *How the Garcia Girls Lost Their Accent*

Augustine, St., *The Confessions of St. Augustine*

Austen, Jane, *Persuasion*

Austen, Jane, *Pride and Prejudice*

Austen, Jane, *Sense and Sensibility*

Azuela, Mariano, *The Underdogs*

Behn, Aphra, *Oroonoko, The Rover, and Other Works*

Bellamy, Edward, *Looking Backward*

Bellow, Saul, *The Adventures of Augie March*

Bloom, Harold, *Shakespeare: The Invention of the Human*

Borowski, Tadeusz, *This Way for the Gas, Ladies and Gentleman*

Bowring, Richard, *The Diary of Lady Murasaki*

Boyle, T. C., *The Tortilla Curtain*

Brontë, Charlotte, *Emma*

Brontë, Charlotte, *Jane Eyre*

Brontë, Charlotte, *Villette*

Brontë, Emily, *Wuthering Heights*

Cather, Willa, *My Ántonia*

Cather, Willa, *O Pioneers!*

Cervantes, Miguel de, *Don Quixote*

Chaucer, Geoffrey, *Canterbury Tales*

Chopin, Kate, *The Awakening*

Christie, Agatha, *Death on the Nile*

Conde, Maryse, *Segu*

Conrad, Joseph, *Nostromo*

Dante, Alighieri, *The Divine Comedy, Volume 1: Inferno*

Defoe, Daniel, *Robinson Crusoe*

Delillo, Don, *White Noise*

Dickens, Charles, *Great Expectations*

Dickens, Charles, *Hard Times*

Dos Passos, John, *Three Soldiers*

Douglass, Frederick, *Narrative of the Life of Frederick Douglass*

Du Bois, W. E. B., *The Souls of Black Folk*

Golding, William, *Lord of the Flies*

Gore, Al, *Earth in the Balance; Ecology in the Human Spirit*

Grahame, Kenneth, *The Wind in the Willows*

Guthrie, Woody, *Bound for Glory*

Hansberry, Lorraine, *A Raisin in the Sun*

Hardy, Thomas, *Jude the Obscure*

Hawthorne, Nathaniel, *The Scarlet Letter*

Homer, *The Iliad*

Homer, *The Odyssey*

Hulme, Keri, *The Bone People*

Hunter, Gordon, *Immigrant Voices, 24 Voices of Becoming American*

Hwang, David Henry, *M. Butterfly*

Jacobs, Harriet, *Incidents in the Life of a Slave Girl*

Jen, Gish, *Typical American*

Karr, Mary, *The Liars Club*

Kempe, Margery, *The Book of Margery Kempe*

Kerouac, Jack, *On the Road*

Kesey, Ken, *One Flew Over the Cuckoo's Nest*

King, Jr., Martin Luther, *Why We Can't Wait*

King, Stephen, *Misery*

Franklin, Benjamin, *The Autobiography and Other Writings*

Lavin, Mary, *In a Café: Selected Stories*

Lewis, Sinclair, *Babbitt*

MacArthur, Brian, *The Penguin Book of 20th Century Speeches*

Machiavelli, *The Prince*

Markandaya, Kamala, *Nectar in a Sieve*

Marx, Karl, *The Communist Manifesto*

McBride, James, *The Color of Water*

McGinniss, Joe, *The Selling of the President*

Miller, Arthur, *The Crucible*

Miller, Arthur, *Death of a Salesman*

Morrison, Toni, *Beloved*

Morrison, Toni, *The Bluest Eye*

Morrison, Toni, *Sula*

Naylor, Gloria, *The Women of Brewster Place*

O'Brien, Tim, *The Things They Carried*

Orwell, George, *1984*

Plato, *The Republic*

Plato, *The Last Days of Socrates*

Postman, Neil, *Amusing Ourselves to Death*

Raybon, Patricia, *My First White Friend*

Rose, Mike, *Lives on the Boundary*

Rose, Mike, *Possible Lives*

Rushdie, Salman, *Midnight's Children*

Sanders, M.K., *The Epic of Gilgamesh*

Shakespeare, William, *Four Great Comedies*

Shakespeare, William, *Four Great Tragedies*

Shakespeare, William, *Four Histories*

Shakespeare, William, *Hamlet*

Shakespeare, William, *King Lear*

Shakespeare, William, *Macbeth*

Shakespeare, William, *The Merchant of Venice*

Shakespeare, William, *Othello*

Shakespeare, William, *The Taming of the Shrew*

Shakespeare, William, *Twelfth Night*

Shelley, Mary, *Frankenstein*

Silko, Leslie Marmon, *Ceremony*

Sinclair, Upton, *The Jungle*

Slocum, Joshua, *Sailing Alone Around the World*

Solzhenitsyn, Aleksandr, *One Day in the Life of Ivan Denisovich*

Sophocles, *Three Theban Plays*

Spence, Jonathan D., *The Death of Woman Wang*

Steinbeck, John, *The Grapes of Wrath*

Steinbeck, John, *Of Mice and Men*

Steinbeck, John, *The Pearl*

Stevenson, Robert Louis, *The Strange Case of Dr. Jekyll and Mr. Hyde*

Stowe, Harriet Beecher, *Uncle Tom's Cabin*

Swift, Jonathan, *Gulliver's Travels*

Thoreau, Henry David, *Walden, or Life in the Woods, and On the Duty of Civil Disobedience*

Truth, Sojourner, *The Narrative of Sojourner Truth*

Twain, Mark, *The Adventures of Huckleberry Finn*